A Social History of Scottish Dance

A Social History
of Scottish Dance

ANE CELESTIAL RECREATIOUN

George S. Emmerson

McGill–Queen's University Press
Montreal and London 1972

Designed by Kari Nordby

Printed in Canada

This work has been published with the help of a grant from the Humanities Research Council of Canada, using funds provided by the Canada Council.

To Kate

It was ane celestial recreatioun to behald ther lycht lopene, gal-mouding, stendling bakuart and forduart, dansand base dansis, pavans, galzardis, turdions, braulis and branglis, buffons, with mony uthir lycht dancis, the quhilk ar ouer prolixt to be rehersit.

Complaynt of Scotland

Contents

Introduction 1

Chapter one
Beginnings of European and British Dance 7

Diodorus and Tacitus – Greek Pyrrhic – the Romans – traces of Pyrrhic in Scotland – occasions of dance in primitive society – church and dance – play and festival – medieval festivals – Robin Hood – the Morris – sword dances – Mummers' Play – church as centre of village activities – Abbot of Unreason – bringing in the May – Peeblis to the Play – Christ's Kirk – suppression of revels

Chapter two
Dance in Medieval and Renaissance Scotland 27

Highlander and Lowlander – ritualistic dances – the Morris – hilt-and-point sword dance – Perth Glovers' dance – Sword Dance of Papa Stour – ballad and carol – Rinnce Fada – ring dance – Branle – beginnings of Renaissance court dances – references to dance in Scottish countryside – Branle d'Écosse – Galliard

Chapter three
At the Renaissance Scottish Court 47

Festive dancing at court – minstrels – nuptials of James IV – at the court of Henry VIII – of a dance in the Quenis chalmer – ties with France – Mary Queen of Scots – John Knox – Mary's dancing contrasted with that of Elizabeth

Chapter four
The Scottish Court in England 57

Court of James VI in Scotland and England – dancing at the Tudor court – Puritan commentators – Galliard dancing – Elizabethan dancing – introduction of the Country Dance at court – Playford and The Dancing Master *– civil war period – dancing during the Commonwealth – times of Charles II*

Chapter five
The Seventeenth Century and Scottish Dance 67

Religious troubles – Covenanters – presbytery and episcopacy – burgh and rural conditions – rule of the Kirk – attitude of reformers to the keeping of the Sabbath – restraint on secular activity during "time of sermon" – antagonism to Yule and "superfluous banqueting" – occasions of dance in the countryside – penny weddings, wakes, and baptisms – harvest celebrations – the Kirk and "promiscuous dancing" – occasions for national rejoicing – the Restoration – European-inspired civility among the northeast gentry – dance a part of polite education – Duke of York at Holyrood – burgh dancing masters – Covenanters and dance and music

Chapter six   The Century of Scotland's Most Various Life   83

Scotland's "most energetic, peculiar and most various life" – vitality of Edinburgh society – resemblance to France – pride and poverty – the public assembly – Horn Order – West Bow Assembly – Edinburgh Assembly – directresses – the belles – end of first phase – New Assembly – rival assemblies – Dunn's and Fortune's "Rooms" – oyster parties – Hunters' ball – Capillaire Club – changes in dancing fashion – private parties – conduct of the assembly – visitors' observations – customs – Miss Nicky Murray – George Square Assembly – spread of the public assembly – Duchess of Gordon – West Highlands – the dancing masters – Davie Strange – Edinburgh dancing masters – Signora Violante and Alexander Carlyle – Francis Peacock – dancing school balls – Almack's – conduct of London assemblies – country dancing at London assemblies – Scotch Reel in the English assembly – birth-night balls – Caledonian balls

Chapter seven   Scottish Dancing on the Eighteenth-Century Stage   125

Alexander Carlyle meets Violette on way to London – Scots in London – theatres – dance interludes – America – the denouement

Chapter eight   Dancing in the Countryside   131

Penny wedding – wedding reels – Babbity Bowster – The Bumpkin – The White Cockade finishing dance of South Uist – kissing in the dance – wedding parties – fun at the fair – account from Ayrshire – "penny reels" – harvest home – itinerant dancing master – rockings – in the Highlands – conditions of life – a ceilidh – a dance in the farmhouse kitchen – the laird's ball – social dances

Chapter nine   Dawn of a New Age   145

Passing of the Minuet – introduction of the Quadrille – triumph of the Quadrille, Polka, and Waltz – the Schottische – popularity of the Foursome Reel and Reel of Tulloch – decline of reels and country dancing

Chapter ten   Scottish Dance Tradition   149

French contacts – reeling – earliest record of use of word "reel" – Country Dance – Highland Reel – female dancing – male dancing – high dances – hornpipe stepping among Scots countryfolk – tradition in Cape Breton – stage dance – Hill MS – Ewen MacLachlan's dances – balletic influence

Chapter eleven   The Scotch Reel   165

Reel of four – threesome – medley – technique and execution – printed sources – Peacock – travelling steps – footwear – setting steps – arm and finger positions – "hooch" – the Strathspey – first record of word in allusion to dance – alternative to reel – Strathspey Minuet – Cummings of Strathspey – native land of Highland dancing – other reels in the tradition – "four-handed" and "eight-handed" Reels – Cape

Breton style – Reel of Tulloch – Hullachan – Ninesome, Sixsome, and Eightsome Reels – Shetland and Orkney reels

Chapter twelve   The Familiar High Dances 181

Highland Fling – Seann Triubhas – Gille Callum – broadsword exercise – Dirk Dance – Gille Callum finishing dance – mention of Scottish "Sword Dance" at Drury Lane – broadsword dances

Chapter thirteen   The Jig 193

Derivation of jig – Scottish Jig – Scottish Measure – Old Scots Jig – Auld Glenae – Wooing of the Maiden – Rinnce Fada – Irish Jig – rhythms – jig and Galliard – Pepys and jig

Chapter fourteen   The Hornpipe 205

Characteristics of "Jacky Tar" hornpipe – triple-time original – "double" and "single" hornpipes – Scottish Measure – Nancy Dawson – enthusiasm for entr'acte dances in the eighteenth century – jig and hornpipe as taught by Johnny McGill in 1750 – step dancing in the English and Irish alehouses – stepping in Nova Scotia and New England – John Durang – hornpipe "in the character of a sailor" – Fishar and Aldridge – The Wapping Landlady – Durang and Francis in Philadelphia – Sailors' Hornpipe – hornpipes aboard ship – earliest notices of hornpipes – English hornpipes – origin of term hornpipe

Chapter fifteen   Folk Dances and Reels of the Highlands and Isles 223

Boswell in Skye – nineteenth-century puritanism – recording of surviving memory of folk dances of the Isles and Highland emigrants – weaving and pantomimic dances – West Highland social reels – Shetland and Orkney Reels – cudgel dance – ritualistic remnants and affinities with Ireland, Isle of Man – Norse influence

Chapter sixteen   Dramatic Folk Jigs of the Highlands and Isles 231

Cailleach an Dudain and other folk jigs – death and resurrection theme – dance of death – dramatic play as an intrinsic part of Hebridean social life

Chapter seventeen   From Highlands to Lowlands — The Highland Games 241

Falkirk Tryst – first bagpipe competition – Edinburgh "exhibition of martial music" – dancing introduced – Strathspey twosome – Reel of Tulloch – Gille Callum – Highland Fling – Dirk Dance – other dances suggested – Strathfillan Games – Braemar – Northern Meeting – Brig o' Tilt – other old gatherings – Luss – Cowal – distinguished dancers – competitive female dancing – competition dancing dress – Highland vogue

Chapter eighteen   Taste and Style in Scottish Social Dancing 255

Topham's observations – Scots' love of movement – Lockhart in Glasgow – Hall in Strathspey – Elizabeth Grant in Strathspey – Jaffray in

Aberdeenshire – the poets' view – footwear – the itinerant dancing master's program – enjoyment of technique

Chapter nineteen   The Country Dance   265

The Country Dance in Elizabethan times – contrapassi – Chiarenzana – "Court" Country Dances – longwise formation and progression – Playford and The Dancing Master – vogue in Europe – contredanse – Rameau – antics – time of Charles I – kissing in the dance – Walsh and other publishers – increasing use of Scottish tunes – Thomas Wilson and the English Country Dance

Chapter twenty   The Scottish Country Dance   273

English Country Dance fashion – contrapassi at the Renaissance Scottish court – English longwise dance – early Scottish MS collections of Country Dances – restorations by RSCDS – contents of Drummond Castle MS, Holmain MS, Menzies MS, Bodleian MS – Walsh's Caledonian Country Dances – other sources of Scottish Country Dances – Robert Bremner – John Bowie – Bremner's collection of Reels or Country Dances – Scottish contribution to the Country Dance – teaching of itinerant dancing masters – Robert Burns and Loch Erichtside – active centres in the nineteenth century – field researches of J. F. and T. M. Flett – new strains of dances in the Country Dance style – Country Dance in nineteenth-century Scotland – David Anderson – principal printed sources – practice of dancing masters

Chapter twenty-one   Technique of the Country Dance   285

English comments in the seventeenth century – Cecil Sharp's interpretation of Playford – Minuet and Rigadon interpolations – Feuillet's contributions – Rameau's criticism – Dukes on English dancing – Wilson on technique – pas de basque – Scottish Reel tastes – English corruptions in the Regency period – Wilson on Strathspey steps – Border step – influence of Waltz – task of RSCDS – dance of assembly room versus dance of countryside – technique adopted by RSCDS – "treepling" – evolution of figures

Chapter twenty-two   Apotheosis of the Scottish Country Dance   297

Decline of the Scottish Country Dance – founding of the Scottish Country Dance Society – plan of restoration – advantage for Scottish children – work of the RSCDS – favourite dances of the sixties – modern trends – contemporary practice at Scottish Country Dance balls

Appendix A   The Sword Dance of Papa Stour   303

Appendix B   Highland Reel Steps by Francis Peacock   310

Appendix C   Directors and Directresses of the Edinburgh Assembly   312

Appendix D   Charter of the Northern Meeting   315

Bibliography   319

General Index   335

Index of Names   340

Index of Dances   346

Index of Tunes and Lyrics   351

Illustrations

FIGURES

1 Illustrations of sword play to music   8
2 Dancers traced from an engraved bone plate   15
3 Engravings of English grotesqueries   16
4 Figures showing foot positions in the Branlé d'Écosse   41
5 The Highland Reel   171
6 Dancer in the character of Jack Tar   214
7 Program of the Luss Highland Games, 1893   248
8 Program of the Luss Highland Games, 1908   249
9 Facsimile of a page from Playford's *The Dancing Master*   269

PLATES

between pages 174 and 175

1 Dancing figures from an Anglo-Saxon manuscript
2 Morris dancers from an ornament engraved by Israhel Van Meckenem
3 Festival costume of the Perth Glovers
4 Characters of the May Games
5 Engraving by J. Brooks, showing May Day celebrations
6 French peasants of the fifteenth century dancing a *carole*
7 Engravings of dancing and tumbling
8 The Sword Dance of Papa Stour, drawing by Diny Bentley
9 *The Kermess of St. George*, painting attributed to Peter Breughel
10 Engraving of painting, *Village Festival*, by F. Goodall
11 *A Highland Wedding*, painting by De Witt
12 Old Edinburgh Assembly Rooms in the West Bow
13 The Assembly Rooms, George Street, Edinburgh
14 Badge of office worn by the lady directresses of the Edinburgh Assembly
15 Susanna, Countess of Eglintoun
16 A Country Dance in an English Assembly Room, by Thomas Rowlandson
17 Engraving of a theatrical Highland dancer
18 *Grown Gentlemen Taught to Dance*, by John Collet, engraved for Robert Sayer
19 *A Dancing Lesson at Hopetoun House*
20 *The Penny Wedding*, painting by David Allan
21 Sketch showing Highland dancing at Crathes Castle, Deeside
22 Sketch showing a Highland family returning from a fair after a dance
23 *Linlithgow Marriage*, painting by David Allan
24 *The Allemande Dance*, painting by C. Brandoin

25 Frontispiece from Wilson's *Ballroom Guide*
26 Description of the Gille Callum, Fling, and Reels
27 *Gille Callum*, painting by R. R. McIan
28 *Sir John Halkett, Bart. and Family*, painting by David Allan
29 A sailor and a wench jigging in a tavern
30 A jig at an Irish wedding, an engraving after Wrightson
31 John Durang dancing a hornpipe, drawing by Diny Bentley
32 Nancy Dawson
33 Bobby Watson performing the Sailors' Hornpipe
34 Highland sports at Burnbank, 1884
35 The Reel of Tulloch, danced at Braemar, 1966
36 The Gille Callum, danced at Highland games in Ontario, 1962
37 Flora Macdonald's Fancy, danced at St. Ann's, Nova Scotia, 1963
38 Bobby Watson
39 A new dance fan for 1797

Acknowledgements

To Christopher Grieve, who, as Hugh Macdiarmid, inspired a generation of Scots to new purpose in the pursuit of their traditions in the arts and in letters, I am happy at last to acknowledge a debt of gratitude. I have pleasure also in acknowledging my appreciation of Professor H. Estall of Queen's University, whose scholarly perception and generous influence have significantly contributed to the realization of this book. To Professor Charles Dunn of Harvard University, Dr. Henry Farmer of the University of Glasgow, and Professor Ross Woodman of the University of Western Ontario, I express thanks for valuable encouragement and guidance at a crucial early stage of the work.

It is too easy to take for granted the vision and high purpose of the founders and subscribers of the various nineteenth-century historical, antiquarian, and literary societies and clubs. Without their publications, works of this kind would be immeasurably more difficult to accomplish. I wish also to pay a special tribute to the memory of J. Davis Barnett, engineer and bibliophile, to whose antiquarian zeal I am deeply indebted for the convenience of so many useful references in the collection he endowed to my university.

For access to the above material, I thank the libraries of the University of Western Ontario, University of Glasgow, Harvard University, University of Guelph, University of Toronto, and University of California, Berkeley. I also thank the Mitchell Library, Glasgow, the Scottish National Library, the British Museum, the New York Public Library, and the Toronto Public Library.

In the study of the execution of Highland Dance, I owe much to my gifted mentors, Janet T. MacLachlan and Bobby Watson. For typing the manuscript and its many revisions with such cheerful industry, I thank Marion Burke; and for valuable supporting assistance, Meredith Rogers, Helen Haller, Elizabeth Milliken, Janet Stein, Helen Orr, and Mark and Rosslyn Emmerson. Many of the illustrations were prepared with the generous help of Charles Grant, and proofreading and indexing were greatly facilitated by the hospitable assistance of Tobar Dhu, Tighnabruaich.

I am happy to acknowledge with thanks the material contribution of Matilda Jane Emmerson (Brenneman), and the patience and devotion of my dear wife, to whom I have much satisfaction in dedicating the completed book.

Introduction

This book is primarily concerned with the character and place of Scottish dance in Scottish life from earliest times to the present. It is a synthesis of the cultural and social history of Scotland with dance as its centre. Scotland is treated, not in isolation, but as an integral part of the British Isles and as an ethnical part of Europe. No student of the peoples of the British Isles can overlook their remarkable cultural unity — the evidence of a large body of lore and traditional art that is shared — nor fail to observe their equally remarkable cultural diversity.

Dance draws energy from something deep in the human spirit or psyche and shares the mystical powers of all the arts, music, poetry, and sculpture in particular. It is a vehicle of ecstasy, liberating the body from the mind, the body's mass from gravity, and inspiring with ritualistic power. It has developed in innumerable forms through its genetic mutations and, as one moves out from a centre in the Middle East — north, south, east, and west — the style of dance (and its music) changes as the colours of the rainbow change from the centre to the edges. The colours are definite, but the gradations are not sudden, nor are adjacent colours unrelated; yet at one extreme we have violet, and at the other, red. The dancers of the East place great emphasis on the expressiveness of hands and fingers and body gesture, whereas the peoples of the British Isles on the extreme Atlantic fringe place almost corresponding attention on the feet, with the body being practically inert.

In some societies, the sense of rhythm is highly developed. It is reported of an East African people that they dance with decreasing vigour as the tempo of the rhythm increases, and that certain North American Indians and Eskimos dance to a rhythm differing from that of the accompanying drum, 9/8 to 8/8. In these cases, writes Kurt Sachs, the spectator feels the rightness of the accompaniment blending "into a higher spiritual unity." In the dancing of Europe, however, the rhythms are clear, and the dancing is in obvious coincidence with them.

We must notice, too, the relationship between dance and drama. In primitive dance, there is no precise boundary between the dancer and the actor. Pantomime, especially mimicry of animals and birds and the activities of everyday life, warlike and domestic, is implicit in it. The dancers of ancient Egypt, Greece, and Rome were partial to mime, and even the cultivated social dances of the western Renaissance courts, making much of the precisely defined formal movements which came to form the basis of the technique of what we call ballet, frequently involved mimetic features.

Folk dances with mimetic features have survived into recent times in the Hebrides and in Ireland. In European social dance, such features have moved in and out of fashion over the centuries, but the overall trend has evidently been from the dramatic to pure movement. Pure movement was the supreme characteristic of the Minuet, which was introduced around 1660 and was perhaps the greatest of the courtly social dances. It is also that of the Scottish Highland Reel.

The ancient unity of dance and drama is unsuspectingly acknowledged by those who seek dramatic meaning in the better known Scottish dances. The Fling, they say, was danced by a warrior on a targe, the shakes of the leg representing the casting off of evil spirits. The Reel, they say, is a warrior's dance of exultation after victory. Yet, as we know them, these dances are as undramatic as a Celtic scroll design; they form a class apart from the usual run of folk dances, highly cultured and disciplined.

The Gille Callum, for instance, whatever its Pyrrhic beginnings, is now a chaste exercise of intricate footwork, tracing simple patterns over crossed swords. Precision has replaced savagery, restraint has replaced fury. It may be that this is a Celtic taste, like Celtic art itself. There is more than a suggestion of pantomime, however, in the well-known Seann Triubhas, although it is now shorn of its drama. There is a measure of loss in this, but it is consistent with the taste for pure design that strongly persists in surviving traditional dancing in Scotland.

We must notice, too, that there is folk dance and "art" dance, just as there is folk music and "art" music, and that in the course of time the one has acted as a creative force upon the other.

The book begins with a brief consideration of the racial and cultural emergence of Scotland. Then it discusses the beginnings of European dance as they are known to us, and the effect of Christianity leading to modifications and adaptations of pagan practices to conform to the new religion. A strange and exciting mixture of elements influencing dance comes into view in the Middle Ages, a period which swells into the tide of the Renaissance of which Scotland had only time to feel a stirring.

Two obvious streams of development are followed: the dancing of the people and the dancing of the court. It is convenient and suitable in the discussion of the latter to begin with the courts of the Stewart kings in Scotland and follow them through Mary Queen of Scots to her son, James VI. Mary commands a special place in our study on account of her well-known accomplishments as a dancer and musician and her reputed influence in Scotland. The courts of the later Tudors in England, and particularly that of Elizabeth, are of vital importance to us, not only because they flourished in a glorious period for the arts, and not least the art of the dance, but also because the Scottish court was combined with the court of Elizabeth in 1603. Henceforth the English and Scottish courts were one, and we follow this united stream until it spills out from the court to include the British middle classes as a whole in the eighteenth century, by which time the dances of court and those of the village or clachan drying green had touched and merged at certain important points.

Seventeenth-century Scotland, bereft of a resident sovereign and overtaken by the Reformation, presents a few fascinating mysteries: What really was the attitude of the Kirk to music and dancing? Were dance and music indeed suppressed and forced underground as so many historians would have us believe? Were attitudes the same throughout the whole country? Obviously, to attempt to answer these questions, it is necessary to have some idea of the meaning and extent of the troubles in Scotland at this time, a period of great disturbance and economic distress. This is the justification of what may otherwise be judged an irrelevant digression.

The eighteenth century explodes upon us, the high noon of our subject. All is light! What a pleasure it is to dwell upon it. The select, public dance assemblies full of romantic charm and beauty, the intellectual torrent, artistic efflorescence, and practical genius of the age, obscuring the destruction of the ancient culture which embraced all that is worthwhile and unique in the arts in Scotland — the culture of the Celt. The rustic life of the Lowlands and Highlands in the eighteenth century links us with the popular customs and joys of two centuries before, and sweeps us into modern times and to the end of our tale.

In conclusion I have treated such specific topics as Scottish dance style, Highland Games dancing, folk reels, the high dances, jig and hornpipe, and country dancing, in respective chapters. The music I have had to leave, with much regret, to another book.

Who are the Scots? It is important, in the discussion of the history of Scottish dance, to study their origin and the ethnic influences of early times which affected the Scottish peoples.

The mists which clung to the resplendent forests of ancient Caledonia were more penetrable than the mists of time which obscure our witness of the people who hunted, fished, sang, and danced among them, in the glens, by the rivers, and by the sandy shores. Our hopes rise as we see Pytheas setting sail from Massilia in the fourth century B.C. to reconnoitre the Pretanic Isles, familiar to the Phoenician traders of his time. He landed here and there, sailed within sight of Norway, saw the seas covered with ice, and heard of the "sleeping place of the sun." Had he, in the style of David Livingstone in Africa two thousand years later, explored the Pretanic Isles, he would have found them to be populated mainly by people whom we now call Celts. He very probably would also have found remnants of the pre-Celtic inhabitants and would have been able to tell us whether or not the Picts of Scotland and Ireland were of these people, or Celts, or were of the other great European cultural group, the Germans. There has been no shortage of historians in the past two hundred years ready to assert each, or all, of these explanations of the Picts. The most comprehensive modern treatment of this topic is that edited by F.T. Wainwright, *The Problem of the Picts* (1955).

The great Celtic migrations from their homes in central Europe to France, Spain, the Danube Basin, the Mediterranean, and the British Isles, began some time between 1000 and 600 B.C. They shouldered out the previous inhabitants of these parts, absorbed them, or lived alongside them. One tribe of Celts superimposed itself on another, and thus the Goidels and the Britons in their several components and at long intervals, found a home in the great isles off the coast of Northern Europe. Then the Romans came and went and certain Germanic tribes, the Anglo-Saxons, the Danes, and the Norsemen, moved out ca. 700–900 from their settlements in Jutland, Denmark, and Norway to found new colonies in southeastern and northern Britain, the Hebrides, and Ireland. Thus the part of the British Isles we now call Scotland came to be inhabited by significant communities representative of the two principal ethnical divisions of Western Europe — the Celts and the Germans. These, in turn, comprised four kingdoms: that of the Gaels, Dalriada, embracing Argyll ("The slopes of the Gael") and much of the Hebrides; that of the Picts, called Caledonia by the Romans, embracing the rest of mainland Scotland north of Antonine's Wall; that of the Britons, Strathclyde, stretching from the Clyde to Wales; and that of the Anglo-Saxons, Northumbria, extending from the Forth to the Humber. Place-names within the Pictish territory are Gaelic and British (that is, Welsh) and also, in the north, Scandinavian. Traces of any pre-Celtic language are not identifiable, since that language is unknown, and there is at least a strong argument to support the possibility of local

Germanic settlements preceding the introduction of the Anglo-Saxons on parts of the east coast north of the Firth of Forth.

By the year 1000, we find all united under a Gaelic dynasty, and when modern Scotland took her first step into the civilization of the Middle Ages in the reign of Malcolm III (1058–93), son of an Anglian mother, and, on his father's side, descendant of the royal houses of the Gaels (or Scots), Picts and Britons, these several constituent elements were integrated. Until the thirteenth century, the Norse held dominion over the western island fringe and parts of the northern mainland, as well as Orkney and Shetland. Thus we have the explanation of Sutherland in the extreme north of Scotland — south, that is, of the Norse possessions. In the southwest there was an enclave of Gaelic-Norse (Galloway) separated by the Solway Firth from the British-Norse territory of Cumberland, and graduating into the British region of the middle marches of the Border to the Anglian region of the east.

It was into this amalgamation of peoples that the Anglo-Norman aristocracy was introduced during a period of about a century beginning with Malcolm. Here was a Norman conquest nearly as complete but less violent than had occurred in England. Perhaps the process was too gradual to provoke resistance, but Walter of Coventry uttered the complaint that the kings (ca. 1212) "professed themselves to be rather Frenchmen, both in race and in manners, language and culture; and after reducing the Scots to servitude, they admit only Frenchmen to their friendship and service."[1]

The interlopers — Normans, French, Flemings, and Angles — unlike the Gaels, had a taste for the mercantile and craft activities of town life, and therefore developed burghs strategically placed at estuaries and natural harbours within easy reach of the centres of commerce on the continent.[2]

The language of the major part of Scotland was now Gaelic, and it should be remembered that Gaelic was a familiar tongue in southern Ayrshire almost to the time of Robert Burns and was the working language north of the Clyde estuary as recently as the nineteenth century. It is a curious fact that the Germanic dialect which prevailed on the east coast, at court, and in the centres of commerce, came to be called Scots, certainly by the sixteenth century, while the Gaels, descendants of the original Scots tribes, eschewed the word "Scot" both for themselves and for their language.

The language of a people may not be related to their race, but it is related to their cultural identity. It is shaped over generations to express the lore, slant of thought, humour, and imagination of that people. It is replete with the associations of their sayings and special words and it is influenced by their history and environment. Thus the languages of Scotland — Gaelic, Scots, and Norn, spoken in the Shetland Islands, and courtly French — are cultural signposts which transcend the startling mixture of peoples. They point to affinity with other parts of the British Isles — Lowland Scotland with England; the Highlands and Western Islands with Ireland; and Ireland and Scotland with Wales, and all in varying degrees touch on the cultural heritage of the adjacent coasts of Europe. The Celts, indeed, were torchbearers in the ancient

---

[1] *Walter of Coventry*, vol. 2, p. 206, cited in Alan Orr Anderson, ed., *Scottish Annals from English Chroniclers, A.D. 500–1286* (London, 1908), fn. 6, p. 330.

[2] Malcolm IV specified that certain rents payable to the Church of the Holy Trinity of St. Andrews were due "as well from Scots as from French as well from Flemings as from English, living within or without the burgh."

world, and although regarded by the Romans and Greeks as barbarians, they were acknowledged by them to be barbarians of "a superior kind."[3] The lamp of learning was kept alight by the monks of the Celtic church in their retreats in Ireland and the Hebrides when Europe was eclipsed in the Dark Ages; and when we consider the lore, music, and dance of the British Isles, it is their peculiar artistic genius which pervades the varied texture.

[3] Henri Hubert, *The Rise of the Celts*, p. 13.

1/Beginnings of European and British Dance

Diodorus and Tacitus – Greek Pyrrhic –
the Romans – traces of Pyrrhic in Scotland
– occasions of dance in primitive society –
church and dance – play and festival –
medieval festivals – Robin Hood – the
Morris – sword dances – Mummers' Play –
church as centre of village activities –
Abbot of Unreason – bringing in the May
– Peeblis to the Play – Christ's Kirk –
suppression of revels

The early Roman chroniclers and military explorers passed comments on many aspects of the countries and peoples they encountered in the train of their legions, but one searches in vain for the slightest allusion to social customs involving music and dance. There is much of living conditions, climate, geography, military tactics, weaponry, and even religion, but with the exception of a remark by Diodorus referring to the Lusitani in France, and another by Tacitus to the Germans, there is nothing at all concerning music and dance. They leave us with little indication that the Caledonians did anything but fight, and certainly there appears to have been small opportunity to acquire any other impression.

The Lusitani, a Celtic people, gave their name to a region in France. Diodorus records that they had a recreational dance which he describes as being light and airy and requiring great dexterity and nimbleness of legs and thighs.[1]

Tacitus's reference to the Germans may be found in his *Agricola Germania* (A.D. 100). In this, he comments on what he describes as their "only form of public show" which, he continues, "is the same wherever they foregather." Naked youths, trained to the sport, dance among swords and spears that are levelled at them. Practice begets skill, and skill grace, but they were not professionals, nor were they paid. However adventurous the play, their only reward was the pleasure they gave the spectators.

This description has often been related to the ritualistic sword dances which were a familiar feature of the culture of northern Europe as recently as the seventeenth century. But the weapon dance was a very different affair; its object was the development of military skills, and ritual had no part in it. It is customary to refer to a dance of this kind as a Pyrrhic dance, after a kind of rhythmical weapon drill which formed

---

[1] Quoted in James Logan, *The Scottish Gael*, p. 438.

part of the military education of the Spartans of ancient Greece. This, we are told, was derived from an earlier Greek weapon dance, the Kouretes, which did have religious connotations, and was performed by young men just come to maturity.[2] The conflict in this dance is symbolic of summer against winter, day against night, life against death, so that it does bear some affinity to the symbolism of the European ritualistic sword dance. The name "Pyrrhic," it appears, is derived from Pyrrhos, the son of Achilles.

The Romans, who fell heir to many features of the culture of the Greeks, also performed Pyrrhic dances. Apuleius (ca. 160 A.D.) has left us a description of one, although the performers were young boys and girls: "In order due they moved through graceful figures, now sweeping round in full circle, now linked in slanting line, now massed in squares or breaking away from the throng in separate groups."[3] Similar formations can be seen at military tattoos today, although they are not classed as dances.

The German Pyrrhic dance described by Tacitus is typical of the kind of weapon play which is commonly encountered in primitive societies of hunters and warriors. It seems certain that the Caledonians, who would fall into this class, would be no exception. Certainly there are many traces of weapon dances in Highland lore, although the dances themselves have disappeared, with the possible exception of whatever remnant is represented by the familiar Gille Callum or Sword Dance, and broadsword dance, known today. Cudgel dances — or cudgel play — were known in many parts of the British Isles into the nineteenth century, and an old Skye dancing song, *Bualidh mi u an sa chean* (I will break your head) gives some hint of this. A Dirk Dance was still performed in the Highlands in the nineteenth century and in the Isle of Man to a more recent date. Weapon play to music was familiar to the Greeks and

1 Illustration of sword play to music from a thirteenth-century Anglo-Saxon manuscript. Reproduced from Strutt, *Sports and Pastimes.*

[2] Lincoln Kirstein, *The Book of the Dance*, p. 31.
[3] Ibid., p. 32.

is depicted in the illuminations of some Anglo-Saxon manuscripts from the ninth and thirteenth centuries.[4]

Although recorded history has so little to tell us of music and dance among the early Celtic and Germanic tribes, it is possible to study the dancing habits of the primitive societies existing into our own times, and from their common characteristics draw certain conclusions which seem to be valid for all peoples in an early stage of civilization. As far as the function of, and occasions for, dance are concerned, there is a striking consistency. The occasions for dance are associated with the important events of tribal life, war, hunting, planting, and harvesting, and with the religious or ceremonial recognition of the seasons. Winter represented the time of death, a season of sterility; spring, the awakening to renewed life, a season of fertility; and Midsummer, the season of harvest and fruitfulness. The gods of each or all had to be propitiated, and the magic rites faithfully rehearsed. Dancing played a conspicuous part in these.

Christianity replaced the pagan cults of Europe, and although traces of ancient practices remained in the ceremonies of the new religion, dancing as a part of ritual was eliminated. There have been exceptions, but these are rare. Certainly, the Old Testament Jews sang and danced to the glory of God, as many biblical passages testify, and although dance did not feature in Hebrew worship after Moses, there are no strictures on dancing in the Bible. The early Christian church regarded dancing with considerable suspicion, on account of its association with pagan ritual, and absolutely abhorred the professional dancer or mime, not only because of his lascivious and licentious dances, but because of his historical associations with the excesses of the Romans. Even the Romans, however, despite their addiction to dance entertainment, regarded the professional dancer as a menial. In this they were at one with the Egyptians of many centuries before and with the Greeks. The Greeks, however, developed dancing as a chaste art, and the writings of many of their philosophers, such as Lucian, Plato, Aristotle, and Plutarch, bear testimony to their belief in its beneficial influence on the health of body and mind. It was left to the Romans to cast odium on the art, and their great philosopher, Cicero, declared, "For no man, one may almost say, ever dances when sober, unless perhaps he be a madman; nor in solitude, nor in a moderate and sober party; dancing is the last companion of prolonged feasting, of luxurious situation, and of many refinements." This comment was to be alluded to by John Knox at a historical moment many centuries later.

The anathema of the church did not eliminate the professional entertainer, but he was harried and scolded by ecclesiastics over many centuries. Nevertheless, the players, dancers, ballad singers, acrobats, jugglers, and storytellers survived, as nomads, to become the *ioculatores* of Charlemagne, the *jongleurs* of France, and the janglers of Lowland Scotland or the minstrels.

When Augustine, an emissary of Pope Gregory, arrived in Kent in 597 to convert the Jutes, he made great efforts to suppress their idolatry and other vestiges of their warrior religion, but without much success. Gregory then propounded a policy of absorption. Do not destroy their holy places, he now declared, but "let them become temples of the true God. So the people will have no need to change their places of

---

[4] Reproduced in Joseph Strutt, *Sports and Pastimes of the English People*, pl. 18, p. 295; and in Harrison and Rimmer, pl. 32, *European Musical Instruments* (New York: W. W. Norton, 1964).

concourse, and where of old they were wont to sacrifice cattle to demons, thither let them continue to resort on the day of the saint to whom the church is dedicated, and slay their beasts no longer as a sacrifice, but for a social meal in honour of him whom they now worship."[5] The idols were replaced with relics, and the temples purified with holy water. Thus worship of a new deity was superimposed on the old cults, and some of the ancient religious practices were perpetuated in new guise, although the dancing, the playing, and the masquerading associated with them were manifestations of something with which the more devout ecclesiastics never really came to terms. This evidence should serve as a necessary corrective to those who assume that the Protestant Reformers were the only killjoys.

The people of Europe were deeply attached to their ancient customs, heedless of any pagan significance. After all, these provided their greatest sources of pleasure in a life which was forbidding enough. By medieval times, when the citizenry of Europe come more clearly into view, we see them living hard and playing hard, ever eager to steal whatever freedom they could from the toils of a precarious life. The holy days became holidays. As of old, the holy temple — now the village church — remained the focal point of all festival activity, often to the perplexity of the more devout clergy.

Thomas Aquinas sounded a more tolerant note when, with reference to St. Augustine's censorious view of dancing, he observed that in the latter's time (354-430), Christian people were much mingled with heathen people, and that dances, except where they led to fleshly transgressions and to idleness "and to other vices, as it is right likely they do now in our days," were lawful even on holy days![6] Some, however, just could not abide the gaiety, such as Cardinal Jacques de Vitry, who wrote in 1210: "When a man wishes not to lose his cow, he binds a bell to her neck, that he may hear the sound and be sure that she's still there. Even as the cow that leadeth the rest hath a bell to her neck, so may the woman who leadeth the dance be said to have the devil's bell on hers. For the devil hearing the sound is easy in mind and saith 'I have not lost my cow; she is safely mine.' "[7]

The early ecclesiastics could not fail to observe with disquiet that the processional and ring dances, with flowers and garlands, which welcomed the May over the centuries in many a European and British village were identical in function to the Roman ritual dance of spring, the Florilia.

Indeed, in some European languages the word for dance extends to embrace the ideas of sacrifice or festival. In French it is *danse*; Swiss and Dutch *dans*; Danish *dands*; Spanish and Italian *danza*; German *tanz*; and Gaelic *dannsadh*. These terms derive from the ancient high German *danson* meaning "to stretch" or "to drag." It is perhaps significant also that the other words used in Gaelic with reference to dance — *rinceadh* (ring) and *ruidhleadh* (reel) — are not Celtic but Germanic. This seems to indicate that dancing in Europe, at least in its sense of play and festivity, is of Germanic origin. We cannot go any further than that. Social and ritualistic dancing with no drama may have existed, although in primitive societies dance is always essentially a

---

[5] The Venerable Bede, *Ecclesiastical History of the English Nation*, vol. I, p. 130.

[6] George Gordon Coulton, *Five Centuries of Religion*, Cambridge Studies in Medieval Life and Thought (Cambridge, 1923–50), vol. I, appendix 23.

[7] Cardinal Jacques de Vitry, *Exempla*, ed. Crane (1878), p. 131. Cited in George Gordon Coulton, *Medieval Panorama*, p. 97.

part of drama. We have no hint that Celtic religious ceremonial involved dancing of any kind. Yet from what we know of Celtic culture today, there must have been much music and dancing in everyday life. Can we be so sure, however, when we recall how much mixing there was of Germanic and Celtic elements, even in Ireland, by the early Middle Ages, that what we now assume to be Celtic or Germanic is purely so?

In the study of early British dance practices there is no more fruitful source than the amusements of the medieval holy days, to which, therefore, we now turn.

THE MEDIEVAL FESTIVALS

The popular festivals which come to us from pre-Christian times and which appear with clearest definition in the Middle Ages were originally associated with the important dates of the herdsman's or husbandman's year. Tacitus tells us that when the Romans first came into contact with the Germans, the latter knew only three seasons: winter, spring, and summer. In the primitive reckoning, winter preceded summer, so that the first important event of the year was the beginning of winter. Next was the coming of summer, indicating the renewal of life and a preoccupation with the ideas of fertility. Then came the fulfilment of summer — the harvest. These three basic annual occasions were observed with mystic rites and ceremonial nearly as old as man himself. The relative importance of the festivals varied according to the agricultural practices of the people involved. For herdsmen, the onset of winter was the time for thinning out their herds and hence provided an obvious opportunity for a feast. For tillers of the soil, the corresponding occasion was harvest time.

The two great cultural divisions of northern Europe, the Celtic and Germanic, observed the same festivals: Samhain, the beginning of winter feast; Beltane, the beginning of summer feast; and Lugnasad, the harvest feast.[8] These are discernible to the present day. The simple scheme of three annual festivals has become complicated through the centuries on account of the changes of the calendar imposed by the Romans and by the Christian church. Then the church superimposed its own festivals and, from this a great proliferation of feast days resulted, varying from place to place, but still based upon the three annual festivals. The winter feast, Samhain or Yule, was spread over the winter half of the year from what the church calls All Souls' Day to Twelfth Night. The beginning of summer feast took place on Palm Sunday, Easter, and, most importantly, on May Day and during Whitsuntide. A later variety of this feast was observed on Midsummer Day and Lammastide and as the harvest feast on Michaelmas.[9] Although the festival rites vary in detail from place to place in Europe, they have much in common.

As J. F. Campbell said, in comparing seven or eight versions of the same folktale found in as many European languages, they "consist of a bare tree of branching incidents common to all, and so elaborate that no minds could possibly have invented the whole seven or eight times over, without some common model, and yet no one of these is the model, for the tree is defective in all, and its foliage has something peculiar

---

[8] There are various spellings of the Celtic festival names: *Samain, Beltine, Beltane, Beltain, Lunasdal,* etc.

[9] E. K. Chambers, *The Medieval Stage*, vol. I, p. 114.

to each country in which it grows. They are specimens of the same plant, but their common stock is nowhere to be found."[10]

In the coming of summer or May festival, there are unmistakable indications that at some very early period of European history, human sacrifice was involved to propitiate the gods of fertility. This later became an animal sacrifice, and finally a symbolic sacrifice. In Celtic practices, fire plays an important part, and there are suggestions of sun worship. Folk etymologists have favoured the derivation of the Celtic name of the occasion, Beltein, from Baal, the Hebrew sun god, and *tein*, fire. Thus Beltein is equivalent to Baal-fire. But the fact that there is no Celtic god called *Bel* derogates from an otherwise attractive suggestion. Perhaps, more plausibly, it derives from *bel*, meaning "mouth" or "opening," giving the interpretation of the "beginning" fire!

It is surely no more than practical for a people to use the sun to suggest the points of the compass as the Celts do; but the direction of the sun's daily movement relative to the earth, namely, turning with the right hand to the centre, was to the primitive mind of mystic significance. The Gaelic name given to moving sunwise is *deasil*. Thus in beginning an important task it was believed propitious first to turn deasil — the boat setting out on a voyage, the traveller on a journey — and we notice an old woman calling up good luck for the doctor on his way to a patient by marching deasil round him.[11] It is no accident, therefore, that the ritual dance around the festival bonfire or round the maypole moved deasil. It was also propitious to put the best foot foremost, namely, the right foot. Thus the ritual dance moved deasil and was begun on the right foot. The opposite direction, left hand to centre, was the wrong, the unlucky direction. The Celtic name for this is *cartuaitheail*, the Germanic, *withershins*. Hence witches danced their rounds withershins, and medieval ecclesiastics proceeded *contra solis* on woeful occasions.

In the British Isles, May Day or Beltane, and Yule stand out as the most important festival occasions, and insofar as their ceremonial involved dance in a very fundamental way, they are of special interest. Casting our eyes northward, first of all, and going back a century or more, we see people gathering on Beltane Day at certain time-honoured locations on hill or moorland to enact the ancient rites. An excellent description of these was written into the *First Statistical Account of Scotland* (vol. 11, 1794) by the minister of Callander, Perthshire:

The people of the district have two customs, which are fast wearing out, not only here but all over the Highlands, and therefore ought to be taken notice of while they remain. Upon the first day of May, which is called Baltan or Bal-tein day, all the boys in the township or hamlet meet in the moors. They cut a table in the green sod, of a round figure, by casting a trench in the ground of such circumference as to hold the whole company. They kindle a fire, and dress a repast of egg and milk of the consistence of a custard. They knead a cake of oatmeal, which is toasted at the embers against a stone. After the custard is eaten up, they divide the cake into so many portions, as similar as possible to one another in size and shape, as there are persons in the company. They dab one of these portions all over with charcoal until it be perfectly black. They put all the bits of the cake into a bonnet. Every one, blindfold, draws out a portion. He who holds the bonnet is entitled to the last bit. Who ever draws the black bit is the devoted person who is to be sacrificed to Baal, whose favour they

---

[10] John F. Campbell, *Popular Tales of the West Highlands*, vol. 4, p. 277.
[11] Ibid., p. 287.

mean to implore, in rendering the year productive of the sustenance of man and beast. There is little doubt of these inhuman sacrifices having been once offered in this country as well as in the East, although they now omit the act of sacrificing, and only compel the devoted person to leap three times through the flames; with which the ceremonies of this festival are closed. [P. 620]

The participants in some places marched round the fire three times deasil before eating, and sometimes rowan twigs were carried or worn. The protective act of passing through fire was found in many other popular customs once actively observed in the British Isles and elsewhere. Cattle were driven through the fire or the embers or smoke, and people leapt through the fire to gain protection.

There have been instances of Beltane being celebrated at Midsummer,[12] particularly in Ireland, and whether the Halloween bonfire, once so common in Scotland, was just a later version of Beltane as a Midsummer feast, or part of a separate festival, such as the ones held at harvest or beginning of winter, is a matter for the folklorist.[13]

On the meadows of England and the haughs of Lowland Scotland, the same festivals take on a different dress. "Bringing in the May" is not a matter of ritual fire; there are more flowers, more games, and more play. Summer is in the air, the sun has returned, the elusive cuckoo sings from the woods. Dew appears in the mornings with the low mist on the meadows by the rivers and in the shallows. On the kiss of dawn, young women go forth to cull the sacred pagan pearls from the morning buds and wash themselves more beautiful. "My wife away down with Jane and W. Hewer to Woolwich," writes Pepys from the seventeenth century, "in order to a little ayre, and to lie there tonight, and so to gather May-dew tomorrow morning, which Mrs. Turner hath taught her is the only thing in the world to wash her face with." It was the day on which holy wells were visited, and Robert Fergusson writes from eighteenthcentury Edinburgh:

> On May-Day, in a fairy ring,
> We've seen them round St. Anton's spring,
> Frae grass the caller dew drops wring
>   To weet their een,
> And water clear as crystal spring,
>   To synd them clean.

In many parts of England particularly, young men and girls and the older ones too would spend the whole night in the country, among the woods and groves in merrymaking, or, in other places, set out at dawn, usually accompanied by horns or fiddles and drums. There they would break off branches and twigs of trees, green birch, sycamore, and flowering hawthorn, and bedeck themselves with these. Sprigs or branches, especially of hawthorn, one of the earliest shrubs to blossom, were placed over the doors of the houses. In Scotland the rowan served a similar purpose, the branches being twined and placed over the byre door and on the bindings of the cattle —

---

12 John Jamieson, *Dictionary of the Scottish Language*.

13 County of Aberdeen: "The Midsummer Even fire, a relic of Druidism, was kindled in some parts of this country; the Hallow Even fire, another relic of Druidism, was kindled in Buchan." [John Sinclair, ed., *The Statistical Account of Scotland* 21, no. 145, 1795.]

"rowan-tree and red threed put the witches tae their speed." An elixir to increase the milk yield of cows was made by constructing a rope from the hair that grows on the tails of Highland cattle; after it was drawn through the dewy grass on a May morning, it was hung above the byre.

These activities, however, were only the beginning ones in a day of festivities which, though similar in kind, differed in detail from place to place and from century to century. In medieval times it was the occasion, among the aristocracy, for "diverse warlike shewes" with archery and the like; the English royal and noble families participated, and, as Chaucer explains, "forth goth al the Court, both most and last, to fetch the flouris fresh, and braunch, and blome." The minstrels performed, the villagers danced, often around and in the churchyard and even in the church itself. Later the Morris dance appeared along with its dancers, both professional and amateur. Then, in the fourteenth century, certain dramatic personages entered the scene: first, Robin Hood; then Robin Hood with Little John, Friar Tuck, the Frere, the Fool and others.[14] They were soon associated with the Morris dance, and the ancient anthropomorphic symbol of the man dressed as a woman for Maid Marion. It is suggested that the introduction of Maid Marion to the Robin Hood play was derived from the contemporary French pastorals of Robin and Marion, of which Robert Henryson's fifteenth-century humorous Scots poem "Robin and Makyn" reminds us. Robin Hood became the subject of numerous ballads, romances, comedies, and folk plays, which minstrels carried from place to place, and we are told that in Scotland there was no other subject of romance in minstrelsy which had such a hold on the common folk.[15]

Another class of ritualistic dance, which is sometimes confused with the Morris dance, is the hilt-and-point sword dance. This belongs primarily to the Yule festival and was once familiar in all the European countries, particularly those of the Nordic people, and, in medieval times, was often associated with the initiation rites of certain craft guilds. In this class of dance, the participants are linked together in a circle by their swords held hilt and point, and dance through a series of evolutions to the drum or fiddle, forming various patterns with the swords and often ending with the swords in a locked formation about the neck of one of the dancers. This is the "devoted" person, the counterpart to the person who passes through the Beltane fire. In many versions he is represented as slain and is afterwards brought to life again.

Associated with the Morris dance and the sword dance are guisers and grotesques. These grotesques vary in detail from place to place, but they are fundamentally of two kinds: those whose characters wear the skin or tail of some animal and those whose characters masquerade in the dress of the opposite sex, particularly men dressed as women, called the "besse" and often given the name of Maid Marion. A hobby horse also appears, and its rider is usually supposed to impersonate St. George. Morris dancers blackened their faces and very often sword dancers did likewise. These practices are of significance to the scholar of pre-Christian religions and the origin of folk plays; for instance, the man clad in a beast skin is "the worshipper putting himself by personal contact under the influence and protection of the sacrificed God."[16] The

---

[14] The first recorded mention of Robin Hood occurs in Langland's *Piers Ploughman*, ca. 1377.

[15] Hector Boece, *The Chronicles of Scotland*, bk. 13, fol. 102; and Walter Bower (ca. 1437), *Scotichronicon*, ed., Hearne, vol. 3, p. 774.

[16] Chambers, *The Medieval Stage*, vol. 1, p. 258.

2 Dancers traced from an engraved bone plate in the National Museum, Dublin, from Munster and probably early seventeenth century. Fynes Moryson, an English traveller of the seventeenth century, reported that the Irish "delight much in dancing, using no arts of slow measure of lofty Galliards but only Country Dances of which they have some pleasant to behold, as Balrudery, and the Whip of Dunboyne, and they dance about a fire commonly in the midst of a room holding withes in their hands, and by certain strains drawing one another into the fire; and also the matachine dance, with naked swords, which they make to meet in divers comely postures." It is suggested that the dancers in the engraving are performing a sword dance, but it is much more obvious that they are linked with withes in the manner described by Moryson, and familiar in the original Rinnce Fada. Reproduced from the *Journal of the Royal Society of Antiquarians*, vol. 3, 1933.

practice extended from the West Highlands to Italy, although its meaning was certainly lost by the Middle Ages. Kirk session and burgh records in Scotland after the Reformation contain numerous notices of men being censured for dressing as women and vice versa on festival days.

Then we encounter a type of play which introduces a fool, a hobby horse, a hero or heroes, a doctor, the ubiquitous man in woman's clothing, the blackfaced man, and other characters varying with locality. This play is known to scholars as the Mummers' Play or, in Scotland, the Guisers' Play. If it were not that the play blends with the other elements of the medieval festival games and is closely related to the sword dance, it would not concern us here but, this being so, it warrants our attention.

The central incident of the play is a fight in which one or more champions are slain or hurt and whom the doctor, always boasting of untrammelled skill, restores to life. The doctor is a comic character, and the play often has a humorous slant. It opens with a prologue in which the characters are introduced in turn; then follows the fight and the doctor's intervention. In England, the hero is usually St. George, sometimes along with the other six champions of Christendom. In Scotland, Galatian, Golossian, or Galgacus takes the place of St. George. Galgacus was the renowned leader of the Caledonians in their battle with Agricola A.D. 84. In a version known in Peebles,[17]

[17] Robert Chambers, *Popular Rhymes of Scotland*, p. 169. The earliest attempts to examine these strange but tenacious creatures and customs belong to the nineteenth century: Strutt, *Sports and Pastimes of the English People* (1801); Douce, *Illustrations of Shakespeare* (1838); Burton, *Rushbearing* (1891); culminating in the works of Chambers, *The Medieval Stage* (1903); and J. G. Frazer, *The Golden Bough* (1923).

3 Engravings of English grotesqueries, thirteenth and fourteenth centuries, from manuscript no. 264, Bodleian Library, written and illuminated in the reign of Edward III. Reproduced from Strutt, *Sports and Pastimes*.

Galatian fights the Black Knight. (In others it is Sir William Wallace or the farmers' son.) Another notable character in the Mummers' Play is the fool who appears under such names as Beelzebub, Old Squire, and in a Scottish version known to me, as Johnny Funny.

The style of the play can be gleaned from the following examples:

> *The Champion:* The game, sir! the game sir!
> It is not in your power!
> I'll cut you up in inches
> In less than half an hour
> My head is made of iron,
> My body is made of steel,
> Likewise my feet and knuckle-bones,
> I challenge you the field;
> My body is like a rock, sir,
> My head is like a stone,
> And I shall be Goloshen
> When you are dead and gone.

> *Then to revive the victim, the doctor speaks up:*

> Here comes in old Doctor Brown,
> The best old Doctor in the Town
> "What makes you so good, sir?"
> "Why, my travels."
> "Where have you been?"
> "From hickerty-pickerty hedgehog, three times round the West Indies and back to Old Scotland."
> "Can you cure dead men?"
> "Yes sir, I have a little bottle of inky-pinky in my pocket. So rise up, Jack, and sing."

The Mummers' Play had a wide distribution throughout England and Scotland. It was a feature of the guising at Yule or Hogmanay,[18] and later, as Santa Claus began to dominate that festival, at Halloween. Sir Walter Scott always entertained the Goloshens (named after the hero in the Mummers' Play) at Abbotsford on Christmas Eve. There are few Scots today to whom the word Goloshen would convey anything, but there are still one or two localities in which the Halloween guisers address the householder with the echo of ancientry against the moon: "It's the Goloshens. Please for wir Halloween."[19]

It is possible that the Morris dance, the sword dance, and the Mummers' or Guisers' play are all parts of the same ancient ritual. The alternative view is that they were originally separate activities which merged together in the course of time, drawing further inspiration from the minstrel and troubadour romances, as in the introduction of Robin Hood. The hint of a forgotten pagan note of sacrifice is unmistakable, and also that the person selected for sacrifice was usually one of importance — it is likely

[18] "The Dying Guizard," *The Scotsman* (December 31, 1902), p. 8.
[19] A. L. Taylor, "Galatians, Goloshen and the Inkerman Pace-Eggers," *Saltire Review*, vol. 5, no. 16 (1958), pp. 42–46.

that the selection of a May king or queen, or summer king, or harvest lord is derived from this practice. At Yule, a similar position was occupied by the Master of the Revels who acted as a master of ceremonies, organizing and devising the entertainment. Features and personages of the May Games and the Yule revels are to be found in all the festivals.

The celebration of the "May" in many regions of England was far more elaborate than surviving records suggest was the case in Scotland. There was simply that difference of climate, verdure, and population. In Scotland, the larger celebrations were limited to the east-coast Lowland towns and regions on the Borders. Beltane ritual prevailed elsewhere.

The pagan connotations disturbed the more puritanical churchmen, and the sexual immorality which seemed to cling to what was, after all, a mass incantation to fertility, was vehemently denounced by the Elizabethan Puritans in England. Yet, in the process, they often gave us most vivid word pictures of the festivities, one of which is this description:

Firste, all the wilde heades of the parishe, conventyng together, chuse them a graund capitaine (of mischeef), whom they innoble with the title of my Lord of Misserule, and hym they crown with great solemnitie, and adopt for their kyng. This kyng annoynted, chuseth for the twentie, fourtie, three score, or a hundred lustie guttes like to hymself to waite uppon his lordely maiestie, and to guerde his noble persone. Then every one of these his menne, he investeth with his liveries of greene, yellowe, or some other light wanton colour. And as though that were not (baudie) gaudy enough, I should saie, they bedecke themselves with scarffes, ribons, and laces, hanged all over with golde rynges, precious stones, and other jewelles; this doen, they tye about either legge twentie or fourtie belles, with riche handekercheefes in their handes, and somtymes laied a crosse over their shoulders and neckes, borrowed for the moste parte of their pretie mopsies and loovyng bessies, for bussyng them in the darcke. Thus all things sette in order, then have they their hobbie horses, dragons, and other antiques, together with their baudie pipers and thunderyng drommers, to strike up the devilles daunce withall; then marche these heathen companie towardes the churche and churche-yarde, their pipers pipyng, their drommers thonderyng, their stumppes dauncyng, their belles iynglyng, their handkercheefes swyngyng about their heades like madmen, their hobbie horses and other monsters skirmishyng amongest the throng: and in this sorte they goe to the churche (though the minister bee at praier or preachyng), dauncyng and swyngyng their handkercheefes over their heades, in the churche, like devilles incarnate, with suche a confused noise, that no man can heare his owne voice. Then the foolishe people they looke, they stare, they laugh, they fleere, and mount upon formes and pewes, to see these goodly pageuntes, solemnized in this sort. Then after this aboute the churche they goe againe and againe, and so forth into the churche-yarde, where they have commonly their sommer haules, their bowers, arbours, and banquettyng houses set up, wherein they feaste, banquet, and daunce all that daie, and (peradventure) all that night too. And thus these terrestrial furies spend the Sabbaoth daie!

... anoother sorte of fantasticall fooles bring to these helhoundes (the Lord of Misserule and his complices) some bread, some good ale, some newe cheese ... some one thing, some an other: but if they knewe that as often as they bring any to the maintenaance of these execrable pastymes, they offer sacrifice to the Devil and Sathanas, they would repent and withdrawe their handes, which God graunt they maie.[20]

20 Philip Stubbes, *The Anatomie of Abuses*, rpt. London, 1836, p. 169.

The Church was the centre of village activities. It served not only as the "house of God," but also as a storehouse, courthouse, and even as a prison. The churchyard served as a marketplace, and was used for fairs, sports, and as a dancing green for the boys and girls of the village, who danced in and out of the headstones. If we may appropriate the words of Sir Thomas Overbury, they thought not "the bones of the dead anything bruised, or the worse for it, though the country lasses dance in the churchyard after evensong, Rocke Munday, and the wake in summer, shrovings, the wakefull ketches on Christmas Eve, the hoky, or seed cake."[21]

Bishops throughout the Middle Ages denounced the use of the churchyard for secular pursuits, but to little avail. In this respect the burghs of Scotland differed little from their European counterparts. A thirteenth-century statute of the Diocese of Aberdeen decrees that neither "choree" nor "turpes et inhonesti ludi" be permitted in church or churchyard.[22] *Choree* is a word from the Greek, indicating song and dance combined, which gives us a hint of the nature of the dancing. Similar statutes were issued by the Synod of St. Andrews in the fourteenth century,[23] and even as late as January 4, 1600, the Elgin Kirk Session Records state that "it is appointit, statute, and ordanitt fra this forth that all sic personis as beis found dansing, guysing and singing carrellis through the toune or in the Chanonrie Kirk and other publict places the time callit the halie dayis ... to be put in the joiggis." The records also show that many people continued to offend, and under the date January 7, 1623, there are the following interesting entries: "Dansers — comperit James Tailyour for playing on ane trumpt to ane number of lasses quha war dansing to his playing" and "Gwysseris — James Bonyman, Alex Petrie, John Petrie, Robert Dunbar, Archd. Law. Theas past in ane sword dance in Paul Dunbar his closs and in the kirkyard with maskis and wissoris on their faces. Penaltie of ilk gwysser 40s." Here is a tantalizing mention of a sword dance performed by five masked men and danced in the churchyard.

The earliest definite Scottish reference to the May Game was discovered by Anne J. Mill in the minutes of the Faculty of Arts at St. Andrews (1432)[24] in which the "old" practice of the "Magistrae and Scholars" bringing in May or summer (in disguise on horseback bearing the insignia of kings and emperors) is condemned as useless and dangerous. Festival ridings are mentioned and are still known elsewhere in Scotland, and this was a feature of some Scottish celebrations.

In Edinburgh, as late as the middle of the sixteenth century, and we can consider this representative of similar proceedings in other Scottish towns, the local authorities and people assembled on the approach of festival time to choose the lords of the May Game — Robin Hood, Little John, Lord of Disobedience or the Abbot of Unreason — to "make sports and Jocosites" for them. If the selected actors refused to accept the office of honour, it was regarded as a contravention of the king's letters and, as in Aberdeen, was punishable by the loss of burghal privileges.[25] In Edinburgh, though,

21 Thomas Overbury, "Character of a Franklin," *Miscellaneous Works in Verse and Prose*, ed. E. F. Rimbault (London, 1856), p. 150.

22 A. J. Mill, *Medieval Plays in Scotland*, p. 9.

23 Ibid.

24 Ibid., p. 29.

25 "and quha sover refuisis to accept the said office [lords of Bonaccord] in tyme cuming, beand eleckit thairto be the toun, to tyne his fredome, privelege, takis, and profit he hes or ma haf of the toun, and never to be admittit frathinfurtht to office, honour nor dingnete." [Aberdeen Burgh Records, April 14, 1552.]

a fine could excuse them. The appointments of the lords of the May Game were made
in April or May and, in some cases certainly, were of one year's duration. The duties
included the superintendence for religious plays, the devising of dancing and revels,
and the organization of shows for royalty. They also acted as masters of artillery, and
conducted ridings on the Sundays in May and on holy days. Some of their duties are
well illustrated in the following extract from the Aberdeen Burgh Records, April 14,
1552, which for the sake of ease of reading is quoted with modified spelling:

The said day, the council, all in one voice, havand respect and consideration that the lords
of Bonaccord in times bygane has made ower-many great, sumptuous, and superfluous
banquetting during the time of their reign, and specially in May, whilk was thocht neither
profitable nor godly, and did hurt to sundry young men that were elekit in the said office,
because the last elekit did aye pretend to surmount their predecessors in their riotous and
sumptuous banquetting, and the principal cause and good institution thereof, whilk was in
holding of the gude town in glaidness and blythness, with dances, farces, plays, and games,
in times convenient, negleckit and abusit; and therefore ordaines that in time cummin all
sic sumptuous banquetting be laid down totally except three sober and honest, viz. upon the
saint's day [St. Nicholas], the first Sunday of May and ... Tuesday after Pasche day, and
no honest man to pass to onie of these banquets except on the said three days only."

The festival day was always a Sunday, and people assembled in their best attire and in
military array and marched in blyth procession to some neighbouring field where
preparations had been made for their amusement. Historians pounce on the record
that in 1503 James IV was entertained by Robin Hood at Perth,[26] but this was not a
unique event, and Morris dancing and ritual sword dancing were well known in
medieval Scotland, certainly in the principal east-coast towns and in court festivities.
William Dunbar, the great poet of James IV's time, writes in "Aganis the Solistaris in
Court":

>Some sing, some dance, some tell stories
>Some late at even brings in the Morris ...

and another, Gavin Douglas, in his translation of the *Aeneid* (bk. 13), comments:

>Their hasty fare, their revelling, and deray,
>Their morisis, and sic ryot quhil nere day.

The Lord High Treasurer's Accounts contain numerous expenses for ribbons, "taf-
feteis," "claiths," and bells for festive dancing at this period, and when Mary Queen
of Scots was married to the Dauphin in 1558, there was a "Triumphe and Play" presented in Edinburgh which included dancers adorned with bells "put upon thair
bodyis and leggs" and on "all the parts of thair bodyis thyis." Thirty-one dozen bells
were purchased for this purpose, and the dancers donned their attire in the house of
one of the burgesses.[27]

[26] Lord High Treasurer's Accounts, ii, p. 377.
[27] City of Edinburgh Old Accounts, vol. 1, pp. 269-73. Quoted in Mill, *Medieval Plays in Scotland*,
p. 185.

The court records are our most fruitful source of allusions to the amusements of the aristocracy; for the amusements of the people we have to wait until the Kirk sessions and burghs began to eradicate "superstitious practices" after the Reformation. Looking to the poets, however, we catch an occasional glimpse of peasant recreation prior to that time. Gavin Douglas, in the prologue to book 12 of his translation of the *Aeneid* writes:

> In grassy groves wanderand by spring wells,
> Of blomyt branchis and flowris quhite and rede
> Plettand thar lusty chaiplettis for thar heid;
> Sum sang ring sangis, dansis ledis, and roundis,
> With voices schill, quhill all the dale resounds;
> Whereso they walk into their cavaling
> For amorus lays doith all the rochis ring.

This picture of a May morning is no different from that which we create from English sources. However, let us consult the poem *Peblis to the Play*, supposed to have been written by either King James I or James V. (Incidentally, it would have saved much heat if these monarchs had positively acknowledged their works. Nevertheless, we are safe in dating the circumstances of the poem in the late fifteenth century.)

> At Beltane, when ilk body bownis
> To Peblis to the play,
> To hear the singing and the soundis,
> The solace, sooth to say;
> Be firth and forest furth they found;
> They graithit them full gay;
> God wot that wald they do, that stound,
> For it was their feast day,
> They said,
> Of Peblis to the play.

> All the wenches of the west
> Were up or the cock crew;
> For reiling there micht na man rest,
> For garray and for glew.
> Ane said, "My curches are not prest!"
> Than answerit Meg full blue,
> "To get ane hude, I hold it best!"
> "Be goddis soul that is true"
> Quod she,
> Of Peblis to the play.

And so at Peebles, a notable Border town, the May is brought in as Beltane. From these two first verses we learn that the preparations are the same as for May Day and that "for revelling might no man rest, for preparation and for glee." The remaining verses of the poem create a vigorous picture; it appears there was a market, and

> With, 'hey and how rumblelow'
> The young folk were full bauld.
> The bagpipes blew, and they out-threw
> Out of the towns untauld.
> Lord, sic ane shout was them amang,
> When they were ower the wald...

Then a young man, his hat adorned with birch, with a bow and arrow, says,

> "Merrie maidens, think not lang;
> The weather is fair and smolt.
> He cleikit up ane hie rough sang,
> 'Thair fure ane man to the holt.' "

This last line is one of the earliest mentions of a popular song by name. The maidens and youths meet and go "to the towns end" in jovial array and call at a tavern where they intend to eat and dance, but they are disturbed by a fight over payment, and a near riot develops as they spill out onto the road. A slapstick episode concerning a cadger on the market street intervenes, and seven of the tavern offenders are placed in the stocks. Then Will Swane comes out, sweating, "a meikle millar man":

> "Gif I sall dance have done, lat see,
> Blow up the bagpipe than!
> The schamous dance I maun begin;
> I trow it sall not pane."

He makes heavy weather of it, and the commotion attracts others from the town who apparently join in.

> Then all the wenches te-he they played.

The day was hot, and as the dancers tired, so did the piper who asks for three ha' pennies for half a day's piping.

> "And gif ye will give me richt nocht,
> The meickle de'il gang wi you!"

The dancing done, they take their leave, and Wat Atkin woos fair Alice.

> He whissilit and he pipit boith,
> To mak her blyth that meeting:
> "My honey hairt, how sayis the song
> There sall be mirth at our meeting yit!"

There is no hint here of Morris or sword dancing, guisers, or plays — except in the mention of the young man with bow and arrow. There is much dancing to the bagpipe, but the dances are not described, although we shall presently consult evidence of what these might have been.

The poem *Christ's Kirk on the Green*[28] gives another description of a festival day:

> Was never in Scotland heard nor seen
> Such dancing nor deray,
> Neither at Falkland on the green,
> Or Peeblis at the play.
> As was (of wooers as I ween)
> At Christ's Kirk on a day.

This is the description, in the words of the poet, of a dancing and deray of wooers — and others. It includes some careless archery and cudgelling.

These poems do not tell us a great deal about the festival activities in Scotland, but it is interesting that at Peebles, a Border town, Beltein (Beltane) was the name of the May festival, and that the celebrations did not conform to the pattern set by the east coast and English burghs.

The records of court, burgh, and church reveal that at least in Aberdeen and Edinburgh, and also in Perth, St. Andrews, Elgin, and surrounding parishes, the May Games, as distinct from the fire ceremonials of Beltane, were enjoyed, especially in the fifteenth and sixteenth centuries. It is possible that the explanation of this lies in the early English settlement of tradesmen and merchants in the towns, which was encouraged by the Scottish kings to such an extent that toward the close of the twelfth century the population of the towns and burghs of Scotland is described by an English chronicler as being almost exclusively English.[29]

It is difficult to separate the sword dancers, or buffins, from the Morris dancers in Scotland; both wore ribbons and bells, as in the notable case of the Glovers at Perth, and appear in both May and Yule celebrations. In the Scottish Lord High Treasurer's Accounts there is a payment, for instance, on *May 25, 1505*, "to gysaris dansit in the Kinges chamir," whereas another "to Monsur Lamotis servitouris that dansit ane other morris to the King and Queen" is dated *December 16, 1512*. A typical example, given in the Aberdeen Kirk Session Records, showing that the distinction between the sword dancers and the Morris dancers was not observed occurs in the case of the five men who were summoned at Aberdeen in December, 1605 for going through the town masked and dancing with bells at Yule.

There were two forces at work against the folk plays in the sixteenth century, one civil and the other ecclesiastical. From the civil point of view, revels and disguisings provided a cloak for treasonable activities. Assemblies of the people were feared in that time of insecure thrones and religious unrest. Great changes were in the air, and abuses in church and civil life had brought about a crisis in the affairs of Europe as well as in the affairs of the village. The festivals now began to be regarded as licentious; whether or not they had degenerated is difficult to say, but their abuses now became noticeable. This was also a factor from the ecclesiastical point of view, and although the church had always to make some compromise with the relics of paganism, compromise was now shunned by the Reformers.

The first direct blow to the festivals in Scotland occurred in 1555 when Parliament

---

[28] The most probable location of Christ's Kirk was at Leslie, near the royal palace at Falkland.
[29] William of Newburgh, cited by W. C. Dickinson, *Scotland from the Earliest Times to 1603*, p. 113.

decreed that no one "be chosen Robin Hood, or Little John, Abbot of Unreason, Queens of May or otherwise, neither in Burgh nor to landwart in ony time to come."[30] [Spelling modernized.] Another clause prohibited "any wimmen or others aboot simmer trees singing who make perturbation to the Queen's lieges in the passage through burghs and other landward touns."

The implementation of this act was probably not immediate, otherwise it is difficult to understand how John Kelo, the bellman of Aberdeen, could be accused along with Alexander Burnat, the drummer, ("swesch"), on May 4, 1562, of passing through the streets ("rewis") of the town "with the hand bell, by oppin voce, to convene the haill communitie, or sa mony thairof as wald convene, to pass to the wood to bring in symmer upoun the first Sonday of Maii."[31] The provost and bailies had been informed that the "said John" had done this on behalf of the craftsmen to test the power of the "superioris of the Toun" to stop them. But John Kelo must have been brought to heel, for three years later, May 14 and 18, 1565, several citizens were disenfranchised for disobeying the proclamations made by "John Kelo, bellman" forbidding any persons "to mak ony conventione, with taburne plaing, or pype, or fedill, or have anseinges, to convene the quenis legis, in chusing of Robin Huid, Littill Johnne, Abbot of Ressoune, Queyne of Maii, or sicklyk contraveyne the statutis of parliament, or mak ony tumult, scism, or conventione."[32] Then in 1566, in a reply to a letter from the churches of Geneva, Berne, and other reformed churches, the Scottish Superintendents stated that they were in complete agreement with the constitutional policy regarding the suppression of feast days, "albeit in the keeping of some Festival days, our Church assented not, for only the Sabbath day was kept in Scotland."[33]

The Church may declare against holy days, but it took much petitioning to persuade the monarch to translate this into an act of Parliament. In 1575, the General Assembly of the Church drew up an article to be presented to the regent for the abolition of all holy days except the Sabbath and for the punishment of those who kept Yule and other festivals by ceremonies, banqueting, playing, fasting, "and sic uther vanities." Further petitions were made in 1577 and 1578 which were rewarded in 1581 by an act of Parliament forbidding pilgrimages to wells, chapels, and crosses and the observance of any festival days "and such other monuments of idolatry — as making bonfires, singing of carols in and about the churches at certain seasons of the year and the observance of other superstitious rites to the dishonour of God and the contempt of true religion."[34]

That these customs died very hard is evident from these several acts and from a review of the examples of offences given in this chapter.

The civil authorities did not always acquiesce in the wishes of the more puritanical faction of the ministers, as illustrated by their passionate reaction to the enforced postponement of the Sunday pageants arranged in honour of the queen of James VI in 1590.[35]

[30] *Acts Parl. Scot.*, vol. 2.

[31] J. Stuart, *Extracts from the Council*, vol. 1 (1398–1570), Spalding Club Register of Aberdeen, 1844.

[32] Ibid.

[33] John Knox, *History of the Reformation in Scotland*, ed. W. C. Dickinson, vol. 2, p. 190. Henry VIII severely curtailed the holy days in England, ca. 1536.

[34] *Booke of the Universall Kirk*, ed. Alexander Peterkin (Edinburgh, 1839), pp. 280, 462, 535–36; and *Acts Parl. Scot.*, vol. 3, p. 212.

[35] *Papers Relative to the Marriage of James VI*, Bannatyne Club, Edinburgh, 1828.

There were many violent changes in the way of life of the people during the Reformation, but the love of dancing and sport and of the May Games was too strong for immediate elimination, especially when no suitable diversions were forthcoming as due recreation in a harsh life. Thus, in spite of all the laws, as late as 1625 six men were summoned before the Lanark Presbytery for "fetching hame a maypole and dancing about the same upon Pasche Sunday."[36] This dancing was done to a piper.

Another late example, but this time dissociated with church censure, also comes from Lanark. James Somerville of Drum recalls that when he attended school at the village of Dalserf in 1608, it was customary "to solemnize the first Sunday of May with dancing about a May-pole, firing of pieces, and all manner of revelling then in use."[37] He tells us, too, how he was so anxious to "appear with the bravest" that he travelled to the nearby town of Hamilton before daybreak to purchase "ribbons of divers colours, a new hat and gloves" and gunpowder. The maypole, incidentally, was erected in the churchyard.

The guisings, pipings, and drinkings at Yule and Hogmanay have not yet ceased, and most old customs persisted to some extent until the nineteenth century. The official English church position was confined to the abolition of games in the churchyard.[38] Nevertheless, the preachings and invectives of the Puritans and Divines played havoc with the May Games in Elizabeth's time, although she herself enjoyed the games. King James VI in his *Book of Sports* restored the loss of some festivities and proclaimed that after divine service his good people should not be "disturbed, letted, or discouraged from any lawful recreation; such as dancing, either men or women; archery for men, leaping, vaulting, nor from having of May Games, Whitsun Ales, and Morris Dances." Still prohibited, however, were bear- and bull-baiting and interludes. This warrant was repeated by Charles I in 1633. However, the tide was turned under Cromwell, and the Long Parliament enacted the destruction of all maypoles in 1644. That the reaction to these prohibitions was not always favourable is shown by the following poem:

> These teach that dancing is a Jezebel;
> And Barley-Break the ready way to Hell;
> The Morice idols, Whitsun Ales can be
> But prophane reliques of a jubilee;
> There is a zeal t'expresse how much they do
> The organs hate, have silenced bagpipes too;
> And harmless May-poles all are rail'd upon,
> As if they were the tow'rs of Babylon.
>
> [Thomas Randolph, *Poems*, 1646]

The restoration of the monarchy ushered in a period of reaction, and the games and customs of May and Whitsun were tolerated once more; but fashions were changing.

In addition to the festivals associated with the church calendar — based, as we have observed, on pre-Christian festivals marking the seasons — there was a host of days

---

[36] Lanark Presbytery Records, p. 20.

[37] "The Memorie of the Somervilles," quoted in Robert Chambers, *Domestic Annals of Scotland*, 2nd ed., vol. 1, p. 492.

[38] "Archbishop Grindal's Visitation Articles, 1576," in Chambers, *The Medieval Stage*, vol. 1, p. 181, n. 1.

honoured by towns and craft guilds on the anniversaries associated with their patron saints. Over three hundred such saints' days have been accounted for in Scotland, about forty of them dedicated to the Virgin Mary.[39] It was customary on these occasions to carry an effigy of the patron saint in procession through the town and to take the opportunity to hold a fair, established by royal charter.

At Perth, where there appears to have been a confluence of the Celtic and Germanic cultural streams, the inhabitants observed Corpus Christi, the second Sunday after Whitsunday, when a "play" was performed. The tutelary patron of the Perth Bakers, St. Obert, was also honoured with a "play" on December 10, on which occasion there was disguising, dancing, piping, beating of drums, and carrying of torches. One of the principals was clad in what was called the Devil's coat [Robin Hood?] and another rode a fantastically decorated horse with a man's shoes over its hooves; but the colourful custom fell before the opposition in 1588.[40] On the first day of May, Beltane was long celebrated at the Dragon Hole of Kinnoull Hill, and the sword dance of the Perth Glovers (a craft guild of glove-makers) was the last survivor of its kind on the Scottish mainland.

Even after the passing of the edicts of church and state against the activities associated with the old festivals, the sword dance of the Perth Glovers or Skinners enjoyed such a place in the pageantry of the burgh that it is no surprise to read an ordinance from the town council, on the occasion of the visit of King James VI in 1617, directing "the skynneris to provyde for ane sword dance," and also, interestingly enough, ordering the "baxteris" (bakers) to prepare "the egiptiane dance" (gypsy dance) and the "maister schole ye bairnes gud dance."[41] Sixteen years later, among various preparations for the visit of King Charles I on the occasion of his coronation at Scone, there is recorded instructions to William Duncan, deacon of the Skinners, "to caus exerceis yair men in danceing of ye sword dance."[42] This appears to have been the last time that the ancient rite was performed in Perth.

[39] Michael Barrett, "Ancient Scottish Fairs," *American Catholic Quarterly Review*, vol. 36 (January – October), 1911.

[40] *Spottiswoode Miscellany*, vol. 2, p. 313.

[41] MS Register of Acts of Council, June 23, 1617, quoted in Mill, *Medieval Plays in Scotland*, p. 268.

[42] Ibid., May 20, 1633.

2 / Dance in Medieval and Renaissance Scotland

*Highlander and Lowlander – ritualistic
dances – the Morris – hilt-and-point sword
dance – Perth Glovers' dance – Sword
Dance of Papa Stour – ballad and carol –
Rinnce Fada – ring dance – Branle – beginnings of Renaissance court dances –
references to dance in Scottish countryside –
Branle d'Écosse – Galliard*

Central to the pageant of medieval life, as we have seen, was the church. Christianity and paganism, peculiarly blended, formed the framework on which people cast a mantle of escape from poverty, oppression, disease, and violence on each feast day. The professional entertainers, minstrels, or strolling players amused the lord in his castle and the burgess or villager on the green. The halt, the maimed, and the blind sang ballads, scraped rebecs, blew pipes, and begged piteously between visits to the monasteries and abbeys where charity found a home even when chastity did not.

The nations of the British Isles now emerged. The people of Scotland bled with Wallace and found victory with Bruce, and the field of Bannockburn became a symbol, cherished through many later defeats.

The great bulk of Scotland's population, which at that time was not much more than four hundred thousand, was concentrated in the Lowlands and by the North Sea, particularly along the shores of the Moray Firth and the estuaries of valleys of the larger rivers.[1] According to the standards of the day, Scotland was a rich country.[2] Her east-coast ports and villages were recognizable extensions of those of the Flemings and Dutch; their wynds, gables, and windows were of the same structure as those encountered on the opposite coasts of the North Sea. When we look at a Breughel painting of medieval life in the Low Countries, we can imagine ourselves observing the rural and burghal society of the Scottish Lowlands and eastern fringe. There was the same curling in winter, golf and football, dancing and boisterous games.

[1] T. M. Cooper, "Population of Medieval Scotland," *Scottish Historical Review* 26, no. 101 (April 1947), pp. 1–9.
[2] Ibid., p. 4.

Against this growing civil community with its burghs, villages, and cultivated valleys brooded a backdrop of mountains, lochs, and glens, inhabited by the descendants of the Caledonian tribes of old, who spoke the ancient tongue and lived still in the ancient ways. Some of these, John Major (ca. 1500) tells us had "a wealth of cattle, sheep, and horses"[3] which made them more amenable to the rule of law, while others were wholly absorbed with hunting, fishing, and feuding. Their hardiness was legend; innured to cold and wet, eschewing the comforts of civil life when travelling in other countries, they became noted for endurance, courage, and agility.[4]

The Highlander, enjoying an illustrious heritage of music, poetry, and romance, and a rich tradition of working in metal — his brooches and scroll designs are highly prized today — considered his culture superior to that of the Lowlander. The Highlander was a mountaineer, with the freedom of a mountaineer. His scholars were the successors of those who held the lamp of learning in the Dark Ages of Europe. The sea, the loch, and the mountainside were his, and by these he lived; if his plaid was his sole covering, it was because in these times and in such regions he and his freedom could not otherwise survive.

In the burghs and "landwart" areas, the "householding Scots," as Major described them, toiled from dawn to dusk, in the field and in the craftsmen's booths, with Sunday and holy days affording a welcomed interruption. None more welcome, one may suppose, than the ancient pagan festivals of May Day or Beltane, and Yule. Conspicuous in these festivals, as we have noted, were the Morris and the hilt-and-point sword dances, manifestations of forgotten rites.

RITUALISTIC DANCES OF THE BRITISH ISLES

The term "Morris" is frequently applied indiscriminately to the Morris properly so called, to the hilt-and-point sword dance, and to the guisers associated with them. All are manifestations of primitive ritual which, in the course of time, have developed their own peculiar local forms or variants. The Morris dancers are male and are often adorned with ribbons, garlands, and bells. Their movements contrive to jingle the bells in time to music played by a fiddle or tabor and pipe. Mirrors or reflectors and bells on the person of the dancers, as in the case of the Perth Glovers, emphasize the prophylactic magic running through the mystic rites. In some localities in England, where the Morris and sword dance traditions have been astonishingly well preserved, the dancers perform with sticks, employing movements of combat; in other localities, handkerchiefs are used much in the manner of the swords of the sword dances. Indeed, the linking of dancers by cloths or sticks or the like is a practice reaching back into antiquity. Villages or burghs had their own Morris men or sword dancers specially chosen and trained, and these formed a holy circle or society of performers. They blackened their faces or wore masks, and although the blackened faces can readily be assumed to arise from the supposed Moorish origin of the Morris dance, they acually derive from a practice long predating the impression of the Moors on European consciousness. The ritualistic dancer had good reason to disguise himself. As Violet

---

[3] John Major, *History of Greater Britain*, trans. and ed. A. Constable (Edinburgh, 1892), p. 49.
[4] George Buchanan, *History of Scotland* (Edinburgh, 1821), p. 41.

Alford explained, "the disguise was a rigorous necessity for those who once had to perform terrible deeds in reality, and who continue to perform them in mime."[5]

Nevertheless, in France, Italy, Spain, and other European countries, the word "Morris" is applied to ritualistic dances of the same character as those called Morris in England. The term in French is *Mauresque*; in Italian, *Morisco*; and in Spanish, *Morisca*. The first trace of the Morris grotesqueries in England is their appearance in a pictorial representation on a silver chalice dated 1458; from this date there are increasing references to them in both Scotland and England.

The gradual expulsion of the Moors from Spain was a great event in the life of the early Middle Ages in Europe. What once had threatened to engulf the whole continent was only just stemmed, then ultimately turned back. Christian Europe had been saved and it is no great wonder that the theme of Christian versus Moor should have loomed so large in popular imagination, and hence found its way conspicuously into masques, pageants, and ceremonial processions. During the period of turmoil in Spain, English soldiers were occupying southwest France on the borders of Spain, and came and went from that province from 1152 to 1451. This territory had fallen to the English crown through the marriage of Eleanor of Aquitaine to Henry II. Thus English soldiers could have seen something of the Moriscas in Spain and carried the essence of what they saw to England. Perhaps too, the Crusades had something to do with it. In any case, the theme appears to have been superimposed upon the remnants of primitive rites surviving from the dim past along with their folk characters: the hobby horses, wild mules, and dragons.

One theory states that the Morris dances are derived from the hilt-and-point sword dance, the swords having given way to sticks and the sticks to handkerchiefs in the course of time. Another suggests that they originated in the ancient lustrative processions of which the more recent May Day processional dances are a remnant.[6] It is possible that the processionals are Romano-British or Celtic in origin, for the most primitive surviving processionals are found in Celtic parts of the country — Cornwall, North Wales and Ireland (see reference to Rinnce Fada, p. 32). The Morris, then it is suggested, is what the Saxons made of the earlier processionals.

There is every likelihood that the "stick" dances are of the Pyrrhic variety, as they involve movements which are not encountered in the hilt-and-point dances. It is a striking fact, too, that stick dances are known in Ireland where no tradition of hilt-and-point sword dances has been traced.

In the British Isles, on various grounds, but mainly on grounds of geographical distribution, the hilt-and-point sword dance is associated with Scandinavian influence and the Morris with Saxon influence. It is indisputable that the distribution density of the sword dance is greatest in the Danish part of England. There are two main types of swords, the long sword and the rapper sword. The rapper swords are restricted to Northumbria and long swords to Mercia.[7] The rapper is a thin-bladed knife such as is used by those who scraped skins for use as hides. Hence the rappers were used by

---

[5] Violet Alford, "Morris and Morisca," *Journal of the English Folk Dance and Song Society*, vol. 2 (1935), pp. 41–48. Hereafter cited as *JEFDSS*.

[6] Ibid.

[7] Joseph Needham, "The Geographical Distribution of English Ceremonial Dance Traditions," *JEFDSS*, vol. 3, no. 1 (1936), pp. 1–45.

the Perth Glovers who preserved their sword dance well into the seventeenth century. It is one of the two dances of the kind of which there are descriptions in Scotland. The other is still performed in the Norse province of Shetland — the Sword Dance of Papa Stour.

The dancing dress of the Perth Glovers has been preserved and was first described in a note in Sir Walter Scott's "The Fair Maid of Perth":

This curious vestment is made of fawn coloured silk, in the form of a tunic, with trappings of green and red satin. There accompany it two hundred and fifty-two small circular bells, formed into twenty-one sets of twelve bells each, upon pieces of leather, made to fasten to various parts of the body. What is most remarkable about these bells, is the perfect intonation of each set, and the regular musical intervals between the tone of each. The twelve bells on each piece of leather are of various sizes, yet all combining to form one perfect intonation in concord with the leading note in each set. These concords are maintained not only in each set, but also in the intervals between the various pieces. The performer could thus produce, if not a tune, at least a pleasing and musical chime according as he regulated with skill the movements of his body.

Douglas Kennedy, a noted folklorist, writes:

The head dress consists of hanging ribbons, each ribbon ending in a bell-like object which is actually some form of nut. The costume is very full-cut and evidently was intended to hold padding. The bells in addition to being hung on the shins as in the English Morris, and on the elbows and wrists, are also disposed thickly around the waist.... The hanging ribbons conform to the masks worn by the Austrian "Tresterers" and our English mummers; the padded clothes indicate the scapegoat character of so many of these secret dance societies. In the case of the Perth Glovers we know that it was a custom for the dancers to have glass broken over them. This padded effect, combined with the bells hung around their waists, reminds one inevitably of the Mardi Gras dancers of Belgium and, in fact, of all the ringing dancers marked down by Dr. Wolfram in his pursuit of men's secret societies.[8]

Kennedy opined that a comparison of the photograph of the Perth Glovers' costume with those in Richard Wolfram's book *Deutsche Volkstänze* clearly identifies the Perth Glover as one of the many varieties of medicine men that still survive in different parts of Europe.

As far as is known, the Perth Glovers' dance was last performed before King Charles I on his visit to Perth in 1633. A contemporary account informs us that in this dance there were thirteen dancers clad alike "with greine cappis silver strings and red ribbens whyte shoes and bellis about thair leggis scheiring raperis in their handis and all other abulyement."[9] The dance was intricate. Five dancers each carried a dancer on his shoulders, while the three others danced through the legs and round about, a dance formation and pattern which does not appear to correspond to any of the sword dance figures recorded by Meyer and Müllenhoff in their classic works.[10] The castle formation formed by the dancers mounting each other's shoulders is unique.

[8] Letter to the director, *JEFDSS*, vol. 3, no. 2 (1937), pp. 153–54.
[9] MS Records of the Incorporation of Glovers, Perth, quoted in A. J. Mill, *Medieval Plays in Scotland*, pp. 11 and 271.
[10] E. H. Meyer, *Germanische Mythologie*, 1891; and Von K. Müllenhoff, *Ueber den Scheventtanz*, 1871.

It seems very probable that it was the Perth sword dancers who participated in the celebrations arranged for the reception of Anne of Denmark at Edinburgh in 1589. The Edinburgh Town Treasurer's Accounts itemize the "expenses debursit upon the sword dance and hieland danses," including twelve pair of white shoes, twelve hats of flowers, "belles furneisit to the sword dansaris," payment "to their minstrel" and to "the maister of the sang scole to interteney [entertaining?] his hieland danseris," as well as seventeen "stand of hie land menis claiths."[11]

Men from Perth would certainly be distinguished as Highlanders at that period, for Gaelic was used predominantly in that country until the nineteenth century. Although the celebrations have been recorded in some detail in *Papers Relative to the Marriage of James VI*, no eyewitness accounts of the dancing have been left us, which is a great pity, for in the heading of the accounts surely is our earliest direct allusion to "Highland" dance.

There are many references to Morris and sword dancers (sometimes called buffons) in the records and literature of sixteenth-century Scotland, but other than to the dance of the Perth Glovers, there are practically none in the following century; only the Sword Dance of Papa Stour survived, a dance which is still performed in Papa Stour. We are fortunate in having descriptions of it as it was presented in the early nineteenth century. One of these is by Samuel Hibbert who visited Scotland in 1817 and 1819,[12] another is by Sir Walter Scott contained in his diary for 1814 and in notes to "The Pirate"; and a third description is given by James Wilson who had the dance performed for him on August 30, 1841.[13] These versions have already been compared for us by Alfred Johnston,[14] and his work is freely drawn upon in compiling the elements of the dance in Appendix 1. Dr. R. Cowie, writing in his book *Shetland* in 1879, tells us that "until within the last twenty years the Sword Dance continued to be performed during the winter evenings in Papa Stour" (p. 187).

The noteworthy peculiarity of this drama is the introduction of the seven champions of Christendom, essentially the same as in the Saint George Play, a common form of the folk play in England. This may be a more recent accretion of the play. E. K. Chambers asserts there could have been no seven champions either in the sword dance or Mummers' Play prior to Richard Johnson's *Famous History of the Seven Champions of Christendom* published in 1596, in which the scattered legends of the national heroes were brought together.[15]

RING AND PROCESSIONAL DANCES

The Morris and sword dances were not social dances. As we have noted, they were performed by a select band or mystical brotherhood of the village or burgh or craft guild. The social dances at this period in Europe were communal, comprising rounds or ring dances and human-chain processionals; but even these were associated with

[11] Edinburgh Treasurer's Accounts, 1581–96, quoted in A. J. Mill, *Medieval Plays in Scotland*, p. 200.
[12] Samuel Hibbert, *A Description of the Shetland Islands*, pp. 554–60.
[13] James Wilson, *A Voyage Round the Coasts of Scotland and the Isles*, vol. 2, pp. 355–66.
[14] Alfred W. Johnston, ed., "The Sword Dance, Papa Stour, Shetland," in *Old lore miscellany of Orkney, Shetland, Caithness and Sutherland*.
[15] E. K. Chambers, *The Medieval Stage*, vol. 1, p. 221.

pagan ritual in their festive function. They were executed to vocal music, reinforced
by tabor and pipe as opportunity afforded. The ring was formed round some object,
originally some object of veneration such as a sacred tree or image or one of the
numerous holy wells, and as far as we can gather, the custom was for the ring to
remain stationary, as the leader chanted the narrative line of the ballad, and then to
dance round while responding in unison with the chorus:

> Ane king's dochter said tae anither
> *Brume blumes bonnie and grows sae fair*
> We'll gae ride like sister and brither
> *An' we'll ne'er gae doun tae the brume nae mair*[16]

A dance song of this character was often referred to as a carol, and the activity was
alluded to by the term *choree* in the thirteenth-century statute from Aberdeen.

The chain processional would obviously be more boisterous and more likely to
appeal to the wilder males of the parish; in contrast, the carol was the favourite recreational dance of the ladies. The long chain of skipping revellers writhed through
various involutions and evolutions, sometimes no doubt, as in the celebrated Furry
Dance of Cornwall, trekking through the houses themselves, in one door — or window
— and out another, then in and out the gravestones of the churchyard. The Farandole
of Italy and France was a dance of this form. The dancers skipped in a long snaking
line, then, following the leader, walked rhythmically through such figures as a spiral
or "threading the needle."[17]

There is little trace left of processional dances of this kind in Scotland, but the Irish
Rinnce Fada is of the form, as is evident from the earliest description of this dance, in
James Bonwick's *Who are the Irish?*, as it was performed for James VII on his visit
to Ireland in the seventeenth century. "Three dancers abreast are linked together by
white cloths or handkerchiefs held in the hands, and are followed by a line of dancers
in couples, each couple linked by a cloth in the same way. They first move forward a
few paces in procession, to slow music, then the music changes to a brisk tempo and
the couples pass with a quick step under the arches formed by the leaders, wheel round
in semi-circles to form a variety of figures performed with occasional entrechats and
finally unite in the original formation" (p. 82). It is impressive to compare with this
description the figures of dancers linked by cloths on some ancient Egyptian vases.

Also in Ireland, the Rinnce Teampuill (Temple Round), a form of ring dance, is
still to be encountered danced round the Beltane fire in the present century, the very
name revealing its pre-Christian origin and purpose. The ring dance is probably the
most ancient communal dance form, and there are reminders of this in such records
as that at Errol, February 8, 1594-95, in which two men and four women confess "their
going about in rings and carrelling upon the day callit Youll day." Likewise a group
of people accused of witchcraft in Aberdeen in 1596 were alleged to have danced
"about the mercat and fish cross ane lang space of tym" at Halloween, "under the
conduct and gyding of the dewill" playing before them "on his kynd of instruments."
Among them were one Thomas and another who were "foremost and led the ring,

---

[16] After Francis J. Child, *English and Scottish Popular Ballads*, no. 16E, stanza 1.
[17] Cf. Melusine Wood, *Some Historical Dances*.

and dang Kathren Mitchell, who spoilt [their] dans, and ran nocht sa fast about as the rest."[18]

Traces of these practices remain in the singing games of children, although ring dances were once the ornament of baronial hall and ducal garden as well as the jovial revel of churchyard and village green. Sometimes they might begin with a poet, who asks, "Who is yon knight who leads the dance and louder than all the song he chants?" There are many allusions to these facts in medieval poetry and romance, of which the following lines from Danish ballads are representative:

> Gay goes the dance in Valdemar's Ha'
> The Queen is dancin' foremost of a'
> The Queen and her lassies are dancin' there;
> And Tove is dancin' wi wind-tossed hair.
>> [Alexander Gray, *Historical Ballads of Denmark*]

and

> Gay went the dance in the kirkyard there;
> There danced the knights with sword-blades bare,
> There danced maidens with hair unbound;
> It was the King's daughter sang the Round.
>> [Axel Olrik, *A Book of Danish Ballads*]

The ballad refrains or choruses were often standard phrases, such as "Hay downe, downe, derrie downe," which, it has been suggested, is a later version of "Hai down, ir derrie danno," Welsh for "Come let us hasten to the oaken grove." Other phrases were "Hey trolly lolly," or "Heve alowe rumbelow," a nautical refrain suggesting "Yo heave ho."[19]

Contemporary events were often the subject of popular dance songs in Scotland, as, for instance, after Bannockburn, the following was sung in "daunces in the carols of the maidens and mynstrelles of Scotland, to the reprofe and disdayne of Englyshemen":

> Maydens of Englande, sore maye ye morne,
> For your lemmans ye have lost at Bannockysborne,
> *With heve alowe.*
> What! weneth the King of Englonde
> So soone to have wonne Scotlande?
> *With rumbylowe.*
>> [Robert Fabyan, *Chronicle*, 1516][20]

In France, a particular class of ronde, the Branle, formed the basis from which European Renaissance court dance developed. In this, the dancers performed a series of steps to left and right, producing a progressive movement to the left (deasil) by

---

[18] Gavin Turreff, *Antiquarian Gleanings from Aberdeenshire Records*, p. 54.
[19] Edward Jones, *Musical and Poetical Relics of the Welsh Bards*, p. 128.
[20] See *The New Chronicles of England and France*, ed. H. Ellis (London, 1811).

adjusting the length of the steps or by replacing a step to the right by a turn or entrechat or miming caper. There were five basic Branles, Branle Simple, Branle Double,
Branle Gai, Branle de Bourgogne, and Branle du Haut Barrois, from which, according
to Arbeau, the celebrated writer of *Orchesographie*, a dance textbook in the late
sixteenth century, all other Branles were derived. These were the dances of the peasantry which, like the Farandole in Italy, were adapted to the growing formality of the
life of the aristocracy. Patronage of learning and art and the cultivation of many
refinements, which increasingly distinguished the lives of the feudal overlords from
those of their subjects, influenced dance no less than music and poetry. The age of
chivalry gave impetus to a trend toward dances for couples, dances which increasingly
drew upon instrumental rather than vocal accompaniment, although they largely
adhered to the processional and ring formation of their progenitors. The first of the
dancing masters now aspired to the high social status which dancing masters were to
enjoy in the royal courts of Europe for over three centuries thereafter. Notable among
these, in fifteenth-century Florence, were Domenico di Piacenza and his pupil
Gugliemo Ebreo, who fashioned new dances and dance principles in response to the
taste and sensibility of the Renaissance mind. These involved the execution of pre-
scribed evolutions, what we would call figures, and movements of defined elegance to
match the long trailing gowns and tall headdresses of the ladies, relieved by the
sprightly *piva* and pantomimic *balli* or *balleti*. The latter employed groups of varying
numbers of dancers. In one typical example, the *sobria*, a single lady danced flirtatiously
with four men who tried to steal her from her partner.[21]

The piva and the saltarello were categories of the characteristic dance of the fifteenth
century, the Basse Dance. They used the same music adapted to their differing measures and tempi. The Basse Dance proper consisted of measures of $2 \times 3/2$. Some
scholars interpreted the word *basse* as "low," referring to the terre à terre character
of the steps,[22] while Michiel Toulouse, in the early sixteenth century, writes that it
was so named because it was executed in a more rustic style, "without bearing oneself
as graciously as one might."[23]

In Italy, the dancers originally moved in file, as suggested by the Farandole, while
in France they moved in couples, and Domenico composed a number of Basse Dances
in which three or four dancers moved in figures of eight and the like.

The French Basse Dance embraced three movements, the last of which, the Tordion,
comprising four springs and a cadence, formed the basis for the Galliard of the sixteenth century. The most stately of the Basse Dance forms, however, was the Pavane,
taking its name from *Pavo*, Spanish for peacock. There were Italian, French, and
Spanish versions of this most dignified of dances, and its music became the great
favourite of luters even in far off Scotland. Arbeau wrote in *Orchesographie*:

A nobleman can dance the *Pavane* with cape and sword, and you others dressed in your long
gowns, walking decorously with a studied gravity, and the damsel with chaste demeanour
and eyes cast down, sometimes glancing at the onlookers with a virginal modesty . . . it is

[21] Wood, *Some Historical Dances*; and Otto Gombosi, "About Dance and Dance Music in the Late
Middle Ages," *Musical Quarterly* 27, no. 3 (July 1941.)

[22] G. Desrat, *Dictionnaire de la Danse* (Paris, 1895), p. 49.

[23] Michiel Toulouse, *Sur l'art et instruction de bien dancer*.

used by kings, princes, and great lords, to display themselves on some day of solemn festival with their fine mantles and robes of ceremony; and then the queens and princesses and the great ladies accompany them with the long trains of their dresses let down and trailing behind them, or sometimes carried by damsels. And these Pavanes, played by hautboys and sackbuts, are called the *Grand Bal*, and last until those who dance have circled two or three times round the room, if they do not prefer to dance by advances and retreats. These Pavanes are also used in a masquerade when there is a procession of triumphal chariots of gods and goddesses, emperors or kings resplendent with majesty.

This would be the dance which opened the ball after the wedding of Mary Queen of Scots to the Dauphin in 1558. Queen Mary, her long train borne by a gentleman, moved onto the floor with her partner, the Princess Elizabeth, followed by the Queen of France and the other princesses and duchesses, two and two.[24]

A very different processional, a couples' dance, emerged from Germany in the fourteenth century. This was the Trotto, called the Allemande in France and Britain, and alluded to in Scotland around 1540 as the Almain Haye listed in the *Complaynt of Scotland* (1540). The step was a kind of one – two – three – hop, the hop with the knee raised and toe pointed straight down,[25] near hands joined and held high. In an eighteenth-century form of the dance, there was a movement in which the lady whirled under the man's arm, reminding us of the Schottische and the Gay Gordons. This is the movement which gives its name to the Allemande figure of the Country Dance.

DANCE IN THE SCOTTISH COUNTRYSIDE

By the fifteenth century there were in Scotland many popular social dances which bore the titles of the tunes to which they were performed. Some of these were rounds, and others were no doubt based on the figure of the haye or reel. Others again were Basse Dances from the court, and there is at least one reference in the fifteenth-century Lowland Scots poem *Colkelbie's Sow* to an Italian figure dance of the class described as *contrapassi* by the later Italian dancing masters, Caroso[26] and Negri,[27] and which is of the same style as the longwise Country Dance developed in the British Isles. This particular reference is to Rusty Bully, which is doubtless the same as that described by Toulouse in *Sur l'art et instruction de bien danser* as Roti bolli ioieulx (Roast, boiled happy). Another dance, Orliance, mentioned in the same passage of *Colkelbie* is surely a Basse Dance to the tune given as "Orlyans" (Orleans) by Toulouse.

The complete passage in *Colkelbie* runs as follows:

> Some trottit *Tras* and *Trenas*
> Some balterit *the Bass*
> Some *Perdony* some *Trolly lolly*
> Some *Cock craw thou whill day*
> *Taysbank* and *Terway*

24 *Discours du Grande et Magnifique Triomphe*, Rouen, 1558.
25 Wood, *Some Historical Dances*, p. 16.
26 Fabritio Caroso, *Il Ballarino*.
27 Carlo Negri, *Nuove invenzione di balli*.

> Some *Lincolne* some *Lindsay*
> Some *Joly Lemman daws it not day*
> Some bekkit some bingit
> Some crakkit some cringit,
> Some movit *most mak revell*
> Some Maister Pier de Couzate
> And other some in consate
> At leisure drest to dance
> Some *Ourfute* some *Orliance*
> Some *Rusty bully with a bek*
> And *Every note in others neck*[28]

It describes the revels of a company of herdsmen who set out in search of a lost sow. The style of the dancing is apparently appropriate: "Some bekkit [bowed], some bingit [preened or lunged], some crakkit [cracked], some cringit [cringed]," although others "in conceit at leisure dressed to dance, some *Ourfute* some *Orliance*, some *Rusty bully.* . . ." Some dancers, too, interestingly enough, dressed themselves in the habits of other lands — Cypress, Bohemia, Portugal, Navarre, Spain, Italy, Germany (*Almane*), Naples, Arragon, Ethiopia, Africa, Carthage — and danced the appropriate dances: "With all the dansis of Asia," the "Islands in Ocean," the "farmland of France," in Holland, Flanders, *Friezland*, the German provinces, and Scandinavia. These allusions cover practically the whole range of dancing in the known world of the time. Included also in the list, and presumably therefore distinctive, are Ireland and Argyle!

Of the actual dances named in this passage in *Colkelbie*, Trolly Lolly was apparently a ring or processional carol ("some dance lang trolly lolly" writes Alexander Scott, ca. 1568), and Cock Craw, Taysbank, and Joly Lemman are known as songs. Two dances mentioned but not included in this passage are The sun shene in the south, performed by one named Doby Drymouth, and a carol or ring dance named My deir darling. Another, Perry Pull, suggests a pas seul known in Ireland as Pedro Pill and described by James Bonwick as oriental, Morisque perhaps, for bells adorned the person of the dancer. Indeed, the two swineherds who led the dancing on this boisterous occasion were adorned with bells ("Full of bells fulfull").

The words "Tras" and "Trenass" in "Some trottit *Tras* and *Trenass*" probably refer to steps, tras being a root meaning "across." Thus in Gaelic there are the words *leumtrasd* (cross springs), *aiseug-trasd* (cross passes) and so on.

In the two other Lowland Scottish poems from about the same period, *Peblis to the Play* and *Christ's Kirk*, there are some further allusions to dancing. In the former, one dance is mentioned by name:

> If I shall dance, have done, let see,
> Blow up the bagpipe then.
> The *schamons* dance I must begin. . .
> > [Maitland Folio MS]

All trace of a "salmon's dance" has been lost in Scotland, although one called the Salmon Leap survives in Isle of Man and is doubtless of the same character, a miming dance.

---

[28] Bannatyne MS, 1568, vol. 1, ed. W. Tod Ritchie.

In *Christ's Kirk,* two verses are particularly significant:

> Tom Lutar was their minstrel meet,
> O Lord, as he could lanss,   [leap]
> He played so schill, and sang so sweet,
> While Towsy took a transs;
> Auld Lyghtfute there he did forleit   [forsake]
> And counterfeited France,
> He used himself as man discreet,
> And up took morrice dance
> > Full loud,
> At Christ's Kirk on the green, that day.

> Then Stephen came stepping in with stends   [strides]
> No rink might him arrest,
> Splayfoot he bobbit up with bends,
> For Maud he made request:
> He lap whill, he lay on his lends   [leapt, loins]
> But rising he was priest
> While that he hostit at both the ends,
> For honour of the feast,
> > That day,
> At Christ's Kirk on the green, that day.
> > > [Bannatyne and Maitland MSS]

Again there is a piper, as may be inferred from "play so schill" although, of course, this phrase may possibly refer to the bellows pipes of the Lowlands. The sense here seems to be that Tom Lutar performed the music of an "old" dance called Lightfoot, which he forsook for some imitation of French dancing, or dance music, conducting himself as befitted the latter, that is, discreetly. Then Stephen strode in and bobbed or danced either in a splay-footed manner or performed a dance called Splayfoot, which name calls to mind "Lang plat fuit of gariau" mentioned later in the *Complaynt of Scotland* which we shall discuss presently. William Dauney tells us in *Ancient Scottish Melodies* that in his day (early nineteenth century), dances called Platfute and Backfute were still known in some parts of the country. In Sir David Lindsay's poem *Complaynt of the Papingo*, which belongs to the same period as the more famous *Complaynt of Scotland*, there are the lines, "To learn her language artificial / To play *platfute* and quhissel *fute before*," the latter, of course being "Fute before gossip," a tune which comes to our attention in other quotations.

Apparently in Splayfoot, Flatfoot (that is, Platfute), Backfoot, Lightfoot mentioned above, and in Overfoot (Ourfute) mentioned in *Colkelbie*, we are dealing with a species of dance, or more probably, particular steps which we might, if we saw them today, describe as pas de ba', back step, balance, shuffles, etcetera. Then Stephen leapt (lap), the poet says, "whill he lay on his loins" (or his length). One does hesitate at this point to ponder whether whill is indeed transcribed here for "while," which would make the phrase describe a dance performed in a squatting or hunkered position. Old Saxon drawings illustrate such a performance, and survivals of it were known at least as late as the eighteenth century. Logan wrote in *The Scottish Gael*:

"There was a dance called Rungmor, of which little is now known; from the only description I could get of it, the dancer appeared in some manner to touch the ground with his thighs, without losing his balance" (p. 439).

There is evidence of a Frog Dance in Isle of Man, which would seem to be of this class, and a popular example in the Lowlands of Scotland was known as the Cutty-Hunker Dance, described by an Elgin correspondent in 1871 as a "burlesque on dancing." It was, the correspondent continues, "performed by two dancers, sometimes a woman crouching down to an almost sitting posture, leaning the body forward and grasping her knees tight with both arms, and then leaping from side to side all round the room in the most grotesque fashion imagineable [sic]."[29]

Indeed, Allan Ramsay, in his supplement to *Christ's Kirk* (ca. 1721) has one of his characters dance Cuttymun and Treeladle with the bride. The tune of this name can be found in the Gow collection. It has a rhythm not unlike that of the well-known Gille Callum and was played at a brisk tempo. "May he dance cutty-mun / Wi' his neb to the sun" writes James Hogg in "The Blue and the Yellow" as a euphemism for swinging from a gallows. This tune was known in Shetland as "Cutty," and Patrick Shuldham-Shaw writes that the only thing he could learn about the dance of that name was that it was performed "entirely in a sitting-on-the-heels position."[30] The similarity to the Duck Dance of the West Highlands is obvious.

While we are noting these early references to dancing in Scotland, it is appropriate to turn to that anonymous work to which I have alluded so often already, published in 1548 and entitled *The Complaynt of Scotland*. This book discusses the condition of the country and records the many current practices and customs. The passage of most interest first gives a list of songs which other sources[31] enable us to identify as both folk songs and art songs. The author then continues:

Thir shepherds and their wives sang many other melodious songs, the whilk I have nocht in memory. Then after this sweet celestial harmony, they began to dance in ane ring. Every auld shepherd led his wife be the hand, and every young shepherd led her whom he lovit best. There were eight shepherds, and ilk ane o them had ane sundry instrument to play to the lave. The first had ane drone bagpipe, the next had ane pipe made of ane bledder and of ane reed, the third playit on ane trump, the feyrd on ane corn pipe, the fyft playit on ane pipe made of ane gait horn, the sext playit on ane recorder, the sevent playit on ane fiddle, and the last playit on ane whistle. King Amphion that playit sa sweet on his harp when he keepit his sheep, nor yet Appollo the God of Sapiens, that keepit King Admetus' sheep, with his sweet minstrelsy, none of thir twa playit mair curiously nor did thir eight shepherds; nor yet all the shepherds that Virgil maks mention ... nor Orpheus ... nor Pan ... nor Mercurius ... I beheld nevir ane mair delectable recreatioun. For first they began with twa beks and with a kiss. Euripedes, Iuuenal, Perseus, Horace, nor nane o the satiric poets, whilk movit their bodies as they had been dansand when they pronoucit their tragedies, none of them keepit more geometrical measure nor thir shepherds did in their dancing. ... It was ane celestial recreatioun to behold their licht lopene [leaping], gambolding [gamboling], stendling [striding], backward and forward, dancing Basse Dances, Pavans, Galliards, Turdions, Braulis and Branles, Buffons, with many other licht dances, the whilk are ower prolix to be rehearsit. Yet nochtheless I sal rhearse so many as my ingyne can put in memory.

[29] *Notes and Queries*, 4th series, vol. 3 (1869), p. 356.
[30] Patrick Shuldham-Shaw, "Folk Music and Dance in Shetland," *JEFDSS*, vol. 5 (1946–48), p. 76.
[31] Bannatyne and Maitland MSS, "Gude and Godlie Ballates."

All Christian Men's Dance

The North of Scotland

Hunt's Up

The Comout Entry

Lang Plat Fut of Gariau

Robin Hood

Thom of Lyn

Freris Al

Ennymes

The Lock of Slene

The Gossips Dance

Leaves Green

Makky

The Speyde

The Flail

The Lambs Wind [lammes vynde]

Soutra

Come Kyttil me Nakit Wantonly

Shake leg fute before Gossip

Rank at the Root

Baglap and all

John Armstrang's Dance

The Alman Haye

The Bace of Voragon [Basse of Arragone]

Dangeir

The Beye

The Deid Dance

The Dance of Kilrynne

The Vod and the Val

Shake a Trot

The author makes it very clear that his dancers are extremely proficient. After two bows and curtsies and a kiss, the proceedings open with the men leading their ladies into the ring formation of the dance. A distinction is made between "Braulis" and "Branles," although the terms refer to the same type of dance. It is possible that the "brawl" was a British form of the Branle. The "Buffons" of course, as we have seen, was another name for the sword dance (and dancers), although Arbeau describes a specific dance of this name in *Orchesographie* and possibly this was the form of the dance referred to here.

Although dances were popularly danced to songs of which the tunes were dance measures, nothing is said in the *Complaynt* of dancing to song. We are clearly told that the dances were executed to accompaniment of each of eight instruments in turn. We can be sure that the court dances were accompanied by the recorder and possibly the fiddle, the tabor is not mentioned, and we assume that the remaining dances employed the remaining instruments in addition to the fiddle. We know from later references that the trump, or Jew's harp, was often used for dancing in Scotland, and Martin Martin found it the sole instrument in St. Kilda in the early eighteenth century, which, he wrote significantly, "disposes them to dance mightily."[32]

Of the *licht* dances named, we can identify several as of the pantomimic variety (like the Salmon's Dance already mentioned). Such are The Speyde (Spade) and The Flail which survived in the Hebrides until recent times, and probably also The Gossips Dance and The Deid Dance (Dance of Death) customarily danced at lyke-wakes in one form or another all over Europe.

Others are known as ballads: Robin Hood, Thom of Lyn (Tamlane), and John Armstrang. The latter was a celebrated Border reiver, and the ballad deals with his execution by King James V. In all likelihood these were carols, and we are reminded of Gascoigne's remarks on the derivation of ballad from *ballare*: "And in deed those kinds of rimes serve beste for daunces or light matters."[33]

Foot before Gossip has already come to our attention and may well be the same as

[32] Martin Martin, *Description of the Western Islands of Scotland* (London, 1703).

[33] George Gascoigne, *Certain Notes of Instruction*, 1575. From English Reprints, ed. Edward Arber, London, 1869, p. 38.

Cummer go ye before, a ring dance which a concourse of witches were alleged to have performed at North Berwick in 1590.[34] The Almain Haye is a variant of the Allemande, and The Bace of Voragon is obviously The Basse of Arragone.

It is striking that in their lists of the titles of songs and dances, *Colkelbie's Sow* and the *Complaynt* in no single instance duplicate each other. It is clear, too, that both works are of the nature of allegories. We are not expected to believe that Scottish shepherds actually sang art songs and performed court dances. Interestingly enough, there is no mention of the words "jig" or "hornpipe," although Alexander Scott writing before 1568 mentions the jig in one of his lyrics:

> Sum luvis new cum to toun
> With jigs to mak them joly;
> Sum luvis dance up and doun
> To meiss thair melancoly;
> Sum luvis lang trollie lolly.[35]

We have to turn to England to find the word "hornpipe" used of dance at this period:

> A homely cuntry hornepipe we will daunce
> A sheapheards pretty Gigg to make him sport
> and sing A madringall or roundelay ...[36]

The word "reel" is used in *Colkelbie* in the sense of revelling, and Gavin Douglas half a century or more later uses it in the phrase:

> ither through ither reeland
> tracing mony gaites ...[37]

in which it is apparently used of an interweaving movement akin to one of its uses today, and for which the word "haye" is most often used in English works. Thus Sir John Davies in *Orchestra*, a metrical history of dance, describes dance's beginnings:

> [Love] taught them rounds and winding heys to tread
> And about trees to cast themselves in rings ...

The chain figure, or haye or reel, must have been involved in many early rounds. Other rounds, Davies states, were of the Branle type:

> ... doth demonstrate plain
> The motions seven that are in nature found:
> Upward and downward, forth and back again,
> To this side and to that, and turning round,
> Whereof a thousand brawls he doth compound,
> Which he doth teach unto the multitude,
> And ever with a turn they must conclude.

[34] Robert Chambers, *Domestic Annals of Scotland*, 2nd ed., vol. 1, p. 214.
[35] Bannatyne MS, "Ballat maid to the Derisioun and Scorne of Wantoun Wemen."
[36] Robert Chester, "A Merrimt of Christmas," in Salusbury and Chester, *Poems*, pp. 19–20.
[37] Gavin Douglas, Virgil's *Aeneid* 13.

In this way various localities would produce a favourite round. This is particularly evident in France where there were such rounds as the Branles de Champagne, Branles d'Avignon, and the Branle de Poitou. By the early years of the sixteenth century, the basic Branles were regarded as somewhat vulgar by the aristocracy; but the French court acquired a sense of fun as that century progressed, particularly in the reign of Henry II (1547 – 59), the father-in-law of Mary Queen of Scots, and the Branles were restored to favour as a form worthy of development. Many were devised for masquerades, and these, involving miming and buffoonery in imitation of their subjects — hermits, animals, washerwomen, etcetera — passed into the repertoire. Whether the miming Branles were immodest or bold or even obscene as some historians suggest, must depend upon the mores of the society passing judgement. The dance, The Purpose, which Knox describes as being enjoyed by Queen Mary at Holyrood was probably such a Branle.[38] The eighteenth-century Cotillion exhibited some of this spirit of levity, and it belonged to that strain of French tradition which served as a foil to the studied gravity of French dance at its most exalted.

The dancing masters grouped certain Branles, such as those of various provinces, into suites, and one of these suites, the Branles d'Écosse, is of obvious interest to us. How much is invented or improvised on some characteristic step or movement of the district concerned is a matter which may trouble us; but Arbeau states quite unambiguously that the Branles named after regions were drawn from these regions. Thus we are persuaded to accept that the Branles d'Écosse were drawn from Scotland. They were, according to Arbeau, in fashion in France in the 1560s, and he described two of them in detail.

The characteristic step of the Branle d'Écosse is almost identical to the Strathspey setting step used in Scottish country dancing today: step left on the flat of the foot, making a light stamp; close with the right foot to the left heel, rising on the toes; step left on the ball of the foot, without stamping; hop on the left while crossing the right foot (well pointed) over the left knee. This step is described as the double, and also

Pied croisé droit   Pied croisé gauche

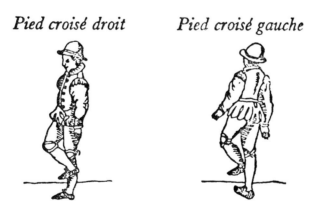

4 Figures showing foot positions in the Branle d'Écosse, from Arbeau, *Orchesographie*.

---

[38] John Knox, *History of the Reformation of Scotland*, ed. W. C. Dickinson, vol. 2, p. 68.

may be performed beginning right. The single step is simply a step sideways on the ball of the foot followed by a hop on the supporting foot as the free foot is crossed in front of the supporting knee.

Using D for double, and S for single, L for left, and R for right, we can write Arbeau's description of the two Branles thus:

1.   A   B   C
      ‾‾LD, RD‾‾   ‾‾LS, RS, LD‾‾   ‾‾RD, LS, RS‾‾

2.   A   B   C   D
    ‾‾LD, RS, LS‾‾   ‾‾RD‾‾   ‾‾LD, RS‾‾   ‾‾pied en l'air R, pied en l'air L‾‾

                       D
    ‾‾pied en l'air R, assemble – entrechat‾‾

Tune 1. 12 bars, 4/4

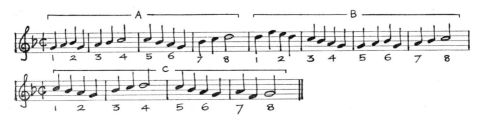

Tune 2. 11 bars, 4/4

There is nothing Scottish about these tunes except for a hint of Rant in the first two phrases of the first (cf. the Hebridean song "Mairi's Wedding"). Mabel Dolmetsch, however, suggests in *Dances of England and France*, that the Branle de Poitou of the Stralloch manuscript fits the Branle d'Écosse exactly. She points out that the Stralloch tune is in common time, whereas the tune for Branle de Poitou should be in triple time: this leads to the suspicion that the Stralloch tune is that associated with what was called the Branle d'Écosse in France. Whatever the facts, there is not much evidence of a characteristic Branle in Scotland, unless it came under the name of round, which is very likely. One suspects that the Branle d'Écosse is a French creation based upon a step or steps used in some Scottish rounds.

Brantôme is said to have recorded that the introduction of many Scottish dances to the French court was due to the young Henri d'Angoulême,[39] son of Henry II of France by Lady Fleming, Mary's aunt and first governess in France. A recent biographer of Mary also refers to Henri's "famous agility in later life at Scottish dances at the French court."[40] But these statements presume too much. All Brantôme says is that

[39] James C. Dick, *The Songs of Robert Burns*, p. xxxviii.
[40] Antonia Fraser, *Mary Queen of Scots* (New York: Delacorte Press, 1969), p. 53.

BRANLE D'ÉCOSSE

when M. le Grand-Prieur (whose office, Michel tells us, was then held by Henri d'Angoulême)[41] toured Scotland and visited the queen of England, he partnered her in a dance. And, adds Brantôme, "he danced well and with much grace, all sorts of dances,

41 Francisque Michel, *Les Écossais en France les Français en Ecosse*, vol. 2 (London, 1862), p. 2.

and he always brought something novel to the court when he returned from a journey."[42] Michel thought this gave us good reason to attribute to Henri the importation to France of the Scottish dances (that is, the Branlés d'Écosse) which Tabouret (Arbeau) indicates as being introduced to France about the middle of the sixteenth century.[43] This is very different from what we would assume from the statements that Henri d'Angoulême introduced Scottish dances to France and was accomplished in their performance.

If, as has also been alleged, Henri accompanied Brantôme on Mary's return to Scotland in 1561, it would have been as a page, for Henri was then only about eleven years of age, having been born around the year 1550, as we may deduce from the recall of Lady Fleming by Mary's mother in 1551. Certainly, Henri's childhood is obscure, but Catherine de' Medici refers to him in a letter in 1565 as "the little Bastard."[44] It is apparent that he was raised in France and remained there all his life, becoming a Grand-Prieur and distinguishing himself as a governor of Provence. He was not called Duke, but simply the bastard of Angoulême or Henri d'Angoulême. He died at Aix in 1586. However, in addition to Henri's influence, there were many ways in which Scottish dances could have been introduced to France.

The taste of the fifteenth-century court for noble simplicity, for Domenico's *aerosa dolcezza di movimenti*, gave way to more exuberant tastes as the sixteenth century progressed. The gay Galliard came into its own, followed by one of its most boisterous derivatives, the Volta; also the Coranto, and several lesser favourites such as the Canaries, the Cascarde, and the Nizzarda were danced.

The Galliard was a sprightly dance in triple or compound-triple time, a virtuoso dance in which the partners set to each other with a range of steps. They changed places (counterpassed) and moved from one part of the room to another between settings. Arbeau described part of the movement of the Galliard: "She danced up to the other end of the room, where her partner, dancing all the time, went to seek her to make some other passages in front of her. And continuing these goings and comings, the dance made new passages to exhibit his skill until the musicians stopped playing."

A Galliard passage or setting took six beats, a step to each of the first five beats, the last being held for a beat. The passages of five steps were called cinq pas and were begun on one foot and then repeated beginning with the other, just as in the Scottish and Irish step dances:

FRONT CROSSES

Bar	Beat	
1	1	Spring left, cross right in front
	2	Spring right, cross left in front
	3	Spring left, cross right

---

[42] ". . . car il dançoit des mieux et de la meilleure grace, et de toutes sortes de dances, et en pourtoit toujours quelque nouvelle à la Court quand il venoit d'un voyage." [Brantôme, *Ouvres Complètes*, tome 3, discourse 66, new ed. (Paris, 1823), p. 158.]

[43] "Nous voilà donc bien autorisé à lui attribuer l'importation des danses écossaises que Tabouret signale chez nous. . . ." [Michel, *Les Écossais en France*, p. 3.]

[44] *Dictionnaire de Biographie Française*, Paris, 1936, article on Henri, chevalier d'Angoulême.

2	4	Spring right, cross left
	5)	(Spring left and point right in front)
	6)	Hold position

Repeat spring right

TOE-AND-HEEL

Bar	Beat	
1	1	Spring right with left toe touching ground in front of the right
	2	Hop right with left heel on ground, toe pointed up
	3	Spring left, with right toe touching ground in front of left
2	4	Hop left with right heel on ground, toe pointed up
	5)	(Leap and fifth position left)
	6)	Hold position

Repeat springing left

A considerable number of cinq pas could be developed; in addition to the ones described, there were the high and low kick, the backward kick (ruade), the sideways kick (ru de vache), and various caprioles and entrechats. The variations were considerable, and the display of virtuosity by some of the accomplished dancers was often startling. We shall have occasion to allude to this virtuosity again when we look at the dancing of the Elizabethans.

Thus in the course of the sixteenth century, the court dance moved from "grave and solemn measures" and "proportion true" to that which was satirized by a character in Brome's *The City Wit* (1653): "Ha! Tricks of twenty: Your Traverses, Slidings, Falling back, Jumps, Closings, Openings, Shorts, Turns, Pacings, Gracings — as for — Corantoes, Lavoltoes, Jigs, Measures, Pavins, Brawls, Galliards, or Canaries" (act 4, scene 1).

Out of this enthusiasm for dance grew an immense store of beautiful music and verses to its measures, as Webbe testified: "Neither is there anie tune or stroke which may be sung or plaide on instruments, which hath not some poetical ditties framed according to the numbers thereof, some to Rogero, some to Trenchmore, to downe right Squire, to Galliardes, to Pavins, to Jigs, to Brawls, to all manner of tunes which everie fiddler knowes better than myselfe."[45]

The affinity of the Galliard with the Scottish Highland Reel is obvious. Both employ a wide range of virtuoso passages, and in both, the partners dance to and for each other rather than with each other, in the spirit of this passage from Burton's *Anatomy of Melancholy*: "Let them take their pleasures, young men and maids, flowering in their age, fair and lovely to behold, well attired, of comely carriage, dancing a Greek Galliarde, and, as their dance requires, keep their time, now turning, now tracing, now apart, now together, now a curtsey, then a caper, etc.; it is a pleasant sight." The Italian dancing master Arena[46] in 1536 likened the Galliard to a cockfight, and

---

[45] Webbe, *Discourse on English Poetry*. See Gregory Smith, ed., *Elizabethan Critical Essays*, vol. 1, p. 272.

[46] Antonius de Arena, *Ad Suos Compagnones, qui sunt de persona friantes; Bassas Dansas and Branlos praticantes* . . . , 1536.

although the ladies were expected to perform modestly, the spectators often incited the girls to greater efforts.[47]

The court dances of these early years derived from folk dances, springing from the refining hands of the court dancing masters. In addition to those dances already mentioned, there were some which enjoyed their greatest favour in the following century. Of these should be mentioned the Gavotte (derived from the Branle Double), the Passepied, Rigaudon, Chaconne, Saraband, Bourée, and Passecaille.

At this period, Scotland did not have a dancing court. The contrast with that of Elizabeth, which, by environment and spirit, pursued dance and music with all its energy, is dramatic. Had Mary been allowed a longer and more settled reign, there would have been a different story. Perhaps, like Elizabeth, she may have found a place for the native dances to the native tunes, although Mary would have had to become much more Scottish to make this feasible. Elizabeth, after all, was English through and through. Then, too, there was the upheaval in men's minds engendered by the Reformation which struck Scotland with peculiar force and drew upon energies which might otherwise have been employed upon the arts. Nevertheless, there was a time when the spirit of the Renaissance touched Scotland, and the common people never ceased to dance and sing when they could.

[47] Simeone Zuccola da Cologna, *La Pazzia del Ballo* (The Madness of Dancing), 1549.

3/At the Renaissance
Scottish Court

Festive dancing at the court – minstrels –
nuptials of James IV – at the court of
Henry VIII – of a dance in the Quenis
chalmer – ties with France – Mary Queen
of Scots – John Knox – Mary's dancing
contrasted with that of Elizabeth

The amusements of the Scottish court can most easily be traced in the Accounts of the Lord High Treasurer. They contain many references to payments to "menstralis, taubroneris, fithelaris, lutaris, harparis, clarscharis, piparis, schawmeris, trumpetis, gysaris and meidinnes that daunsit and tale tellares," and are particularly detailed in the reign of James IV (1488–1513), a reign on which it gives most Scots peculiar pleasure to dwell.

The accounts contain such items as "to Guillian taubroner, for making of ane dans the tyme of the Princis birth," and in January 15, 1507, to "Colin Campbell . . . in recompensation of ane dans maid be him." Both Colin Campbell and Guillian the tabroner are mentioned several times in the accounts in connection with the royal entertainments, Colin Campbell in the earlier part of the reign and Guillian in the latter. At Yule, Colin Campbell and his mummers "brocht in the Morris dauns" (for example, in 1503-4), and Guillian received payment for "ane dans to the King and Queen and for necessaris thereto" and "for ane fars play to King and Queen in Abbey."

The court of James IV has been selected as the most informative for our purpose. There is little information on social dancing to be gleaned from the records of his predecessors; nor is there much to add from the reign of his son. His granddaughter, Mary, is worthy of space to herself in this particular, however, and we shall turn to her shortly.

James IV was an ornament of his time, drawing around him musicians, poets, scholars, and scientists, and succeeding to a greater extent than most of his family in controlling the powerful families of his kingdom. Wherever he passed, and he travelled a great deal, he had a ready ear and eye for the local performers who were called to entertain his company, such as the maidens "that dansit" at his wedding to Margaret Tudor, Henry VIII's sister, and the Abbot of Unreason that "dansit to the King be the Kingis command."

The court celebrated the "Kingis Yole" at Holyrood from early December until Twelfth Night. Each day began with Mass, and festivities followed. Jugglers, acrobats, and guisers entertained the company, until the monotony of revelry was broken by eating and drinking to excess.

Then, with relief no doubt, the company departed to Falkland, "under the Lomond Law," with days of hunting and hawking in the romantic tapestry of the royal forest, its swans, harts, hinds, and wild bear, springing to life at the sound of the horn, and evenings of banqueting, playing cards, or resting to the sound of the lute and the voice of a favourite singer. Then as spring passed to summer, they moved to "Lithgow whose palyce of plesance might be ane pattern in Portugale and France" and where

> The misty vapouris springand up full sweet,
> Maist comfortable to glad all mannis spreit,
> There to thir birdis singis in the shawis
> As minstrelis playis, "The joly day now dawis."[1]

There was Patrick Johnson and his "playaris of Lythgow" and, at Corpus Christi or May, the usual Abbot of Unreason and "gysaris that dansit." Then perhaps a dance in the "Queenis Chamir." Fastern's E'en, Shrove Tuesday, Pasche, and May Day — all were religiously observed. There are many references in the accounts to "gysaris" dancing and to the Morris dances performed by them, but there are no specific references to sword dances at court, nor are we given any hint of the nature of the dances performed by the maidens at Dingwall, Forres, and other places. The Morris dancers were male, but nowhere in the accounts is there a reference to male dancers performing any other kind of dance.

Much has been made of the presence of French, Italian, and English minstrels at court, but a study of the accounts showed that payments to them occurred mostly at times when some diplomatic or other embassy had visited the court. For instance, at the marriage of James IV in 1503, gratuities to eight English minstrels and to "Italian menstrales" are recorded. In 1507, the accounts mention "John Francis five French Menstrales," and occasionally there is notice of a Scots instrumentalist being sent abroad to study his instrument. In 1473, John Browne, Luter, was sent "oure sey to lere his craft," to Bruges, in fact, as is indicated in an item providing for his clothing expenses in the next year. The occasional French or English or Italian minstrel was retained at the Scots court, but there are no grounds for greater assumptions, although when James V died in 1542, five of the fifteen court minstrels were Italian.

For some idea of the social dancing of the court at this time, we look hopefully to the account of the nuptials of James IV, an account of great charm written by one of the queen's party.

Prior to the wedding, the princess rested at Haddington. The king arrived, and after many formalities and civilities, he spoke with the princess. Then, the reporter says:

After some words rehearsed betwixt them, the minstrels began to play a basse dance, the which was danced by the Queen and the Countess of Surrey.

---

[1] Sir David Lindsay, *Testament and Complaynt of our Soverane Lordis Papyngo* (1530), in *The Works of Sir David Lindsay*, vol. 1, 1931, p. 75.

After this done, they played a Rownde, the which was danced by the Lorde Gray leading the Queen, accompanied of many Lords, ladies and Gentlewomen. After was brought wine and bread to the King, the which took the bread, and thereof served the said Queen. Likewise the cups of which he first served her. And after all, the company present drank also.

Incontinent the King began before her to play of the Clavicordes, and after of the lute, which pleased her very much, and she had great pleasure to hear him.

Upon the said clavichord Sir Edward Stannely played a ballade, and sang therewith, which the King commended richt much. And incontinent he called a gentleman of his that could sing well, and made them sing together, the which accorded very well.

Afterward the said Sir Edward Stannely and two of his servants sang a ballade or two, whereof the King gave him good thank.

After all these things fulfilled, the King took licence of the Queen, and kissed her, and also of all his noble company, and went to his horse, on whom he did leap without putting the foot within the stirrup. And the said horse was a right fair courser, and incontinent the King spurred, follow who might. He was arrayed of a jacket of black velvet bordered of the self, and the lists of the said border were of crimson velvet, furred with white.

Subsequent meetings followed a similar pattern, graced by many courtesies. The description continues:

The bord set and served. They washed their hands in humble reverences, and after, set them down together.... After the supper they washed again, with the reverences.... Lasting the said dinner they blew trumpets, minstrels and sakbuts [and after dinner] the minstrels of the chammer began to play, and then danced the Queen and the Countess of Surrey, the Viscountess Lille and the daughter of the house.[2]

Then came the entry to Edinburgh and the marriage ceremony in the Chapel Royal. There was a great tournament, and "triumphe and bancat" at Holyrood which lasted three days. Between every service of the banquet, "thair was ane phairs or ane play." The king's minstrels were gaily dressed in "red and yellow taffeti doublets and yellow and black hose." "Schir Johne Ramsay" was in charge of the preparations for the ball, but the description does not name the dances performed, although it does say the king danced some Basse Dances with the queen and that "after dinner a young man, an Italian, played before the king on a corde very well."[3] That is, he performed on a tight rope.

There were apparently no pageants, which is a pity, because the courtly pageants often provided occasion for the performance of some dance, either court dance or folk dance, and, of course, provided an opportunity for some observer to allude to the dances performed. It certainly illuminates our conjectures regarding the character of English dance, for instance, when the chronicler of Prince Arthur's wedding celebrations at the court of Henry VII, in the year previous to the Scottish royal wedding which we have been discussing, writes of ladies and sailors and "mountaineers" dancing in "a grand set of twenty-four ... with goodly roundels and divers figures."[4]

[2] The quotations here are from John Leland, *Collectanea*, vol. 4, pp. 275–300.

[3] It is tempting to interpret this remark as referring to playing on a monochord, but the phraseology was used of a rope dancer at this period, the rope being called a cord.

[4] Harleian MS 69, quoted in Agnes and Elizabeth Strickland, *Lives of the Queens of England* (1840–48), vol. 2 (New York, 1852), p. 106.

This was followed by some more decorous dancing of the character reported from the wedding of James IV. In the words of the chronicler: "Then came down the Lord Prince [Arthur] and the Lady Cicile [his aunt] and daunced two baas-daunces, and departed up again: and then the Lady Princess and one of her ladies in apparrell after the Spanish guize dauncing other two baas-daunces: third and last came the Duke of York [Henry VIII to be] and the Lady Margaret [future Queen of Scots] his sister ... and sodainly cast off his gowne and daunced in his jacket in so goodly and pleasant a manner that it was to the King and Queen right great and singular pleasure."[5]

It is of passing interest to note that Lady Cicile, the English queen's sister, mentioned in the foregoing, was evidently a great patron of the dance, for some allemande tunes, such as "Cycylya Almaine" and "Cycylya Almaine Blacke," were named after her.

The taste for pageantry led the way for the introduction of the Italian masque. Henry VIII began this new fashion in England at the Christmas festivities of 1512, and it was to survive as a favourite form of court entertainment in England for over a century thereafter. Conditions in Scotland do not seem to have been suitable for a similar development, although the holding of outdoor pageantries associated with coronations, royal progresses, welcomes, and marriages, was a common practice. Mary Queen of Scots did attempt to promote masques at court, but she had little opportunity to do this very often.

The Scottish court in the days of Mary's Jacobean ancestors exuded something of a family atmosphere, an atmosphere which enabled Will Dunbar, the great poet of James IV's time, to poke fun at a dance in the "Quenis chalmer."

OF A DANCE IN THE QUENIS CHALMER

Schir John Sinclair begowthe to dance,
For he was new cum owt of France;
For ony thing that he do mycht,
The ane futt zeid ay onrycht,   [went unright]
    And to the tother wald not gree.
Quoth ane, "Tak wp the quenis knycht:"
    A mirrear dance mycht na man see.

    . . . .

Then cam in Dunbar the Mackar;
On all the flwre thair was nane frackar,   [floor, fresher]
And thair he daunset the dirrye dantoun;
He hoppet lyk a pillie wantoun,
    For luff of Mwsgraeffe, men tellis me;
He trippet, quhill he tint his pantoun: [lost his "pants"]
    A mirrear dance mycht na man se

Than cam in Maestriss Mysgraeffe;
Scho mycht hef lernit all the laeffe;   [lave = the rest]
Quhen I saw hir sa trimlye dance,
Hir guid conwoy and countenance,

[5] Ibid.

> Than for hir saek, I wissitt to be
> The grytast erle, or duik, in France:
> A mirrear dance mycht na man see.
>
> Than cam in Dame Dountebour:
> God waitt gif that scho louket sour!
> Scho maid sic morgeownis with hir hippis.
> For lauchter nain mycht hald their lippis;
>   Quhen scho was danceand byseelye,
> Ane blast of wind soun fra hir slippis:
> A mirrear dance mycht na man see.
>
> . . . .

Notice the association of France with dance even at this date (ca. 1500). The character of this poem can hardly be called courtly. It has all the trappings of a coarse satire passed round for the private amusement of the "club." The poet himself enters it dancing the "dirrye dantoun," whatever that may be. Is this another way of saying derry-down, the common dance refrain? The term "dirrydan" is used by Dunbar in another poem "Ane Brash of Wowing" in which it emerges with a clearer, if dubious, meaning. The relevant verse, in simplified spelling, is as follows:

> He gave til her ane apple rube;
> Gramercy! quod she, my sweet cowhuby.
> Syne the two til ane play began,
> Whilk that they call the dirrydan;
>   Whill baith their boughs did meet in ane.
> Fow wo! quod she, where will ye man?
>   Fow leis me that graceless gane.

The basic character of dancing at the Scottish court in the time of James IV, then, was French with some rounds of possibly native origin, much the same as that at the English court. There are no allusions in the records or chronicles to the *licht* dances being performed at court. At least two of the Scots kings of the late Middle Ages, James I who ruled from 1427 to 1437, and James V, from 1513 to 1542, left a reputation for interest in the music of their native countryside and are serious contenders for the authorship of these boisterous vernacular poems, *Peblis to the Play* and *Christ's Kirk on the Green*, considered in the previous chapter, as well as "The Jolly Beggars" (not to be confused with Burns's poem), and "The Gaberlunzie Man." This being so, and in view of the mixture of basse dances and native *licht* dances in the recreations of *Colkelbie* and the *Complaynt*, it should be expected that the people at court knew and performed the country reels. They were not exactly appropriate for an aspiring aristocracy modelling its manners on those of France; but there were clearly times, even at court, when levity was the rule.

James IV found it more difficult to resist the French queen's challenge to his sense of chivalry, to ride, for her sake, "three feet on English ground," than to resist the force of opinion against the venture within his own council. He fell, as a consequence, with the flower of Scottish manhood at Flodden. What a pity he had not reigned in peace for another twenty years, for then the spirit of the Renaissance would have been more strongly felt in Scotland, and her Golden Age, which promised so much, might have borne the fruit it deserved. As it was, there was much disruption, complicated by the growth of the Reformation and the destructive sorties and plottings of Henry VIII. These were not conditions which could permit the growth of a stable and cultured society.

The ties with France grew stronger, not a little aided by James V's marriage to Mary of Guise, the daughter of a very powerful French house, and the betrothal of the infant Queen Mary to the Dauphin.

In danger of falling into the hands of Henry VIII, Mary was carried off to France when she was scarcely six years of age, and did not return to her native land until thirteen years later, by which time the Reformation in Scotland had almost been effected. These times in Scotland were not conducive to the celestial recreation of the dance, or to many refinements.

But Mary steps from a brutal, sometimes sordid, page of history with such regal grace, charm, generosity, and humanity that it gives substance to the suggestion that everything of elegance and refinement to be found in Scottish life thereafter is some-how attributable to her. This is particularly so of the dance. One frequently encounters the statement that the French influence in Scottish dance is due to her; that somehow the Scottish Country Dance, as it has been restored by the Royal Scottish Country Dance Society, is a harking back to the original form that Mary, it is presumed, brought to Scotland from France. Indeed, as though not even beautiful music could spring from the stony cultural soil of Scotland, it was bruited about in the eighteenth century that Rizzio, Mary's Italian secretary, was the composer of some of the best of Scotland's traditional songs, nay, even the creator of Scottish song!

All of these romantic extravagances have little foundation. The Scottish court en-joyed close ties with France long before the days of Mary Queen of Scots, and it was not unique in drawing heavily upon the social fashions and dances of the French court. This practice was true of all the aristocratic centres of Europe at this time. We have seen, too, that the courts of some of the Italian principalities produced a style of dance which found similar favour alongside that of France and indeed influenced that of France. It was Catherine de' Medici, Mary's mother-in-law, who brought many Italian dance fashions, including the masque, from Florence to the court of France, and therefore she is sometimes named as the founder of ballet. Spain, too, contributed its share of influence on European court dance.

There is no doubt that somehow these influences came to bear on the folk dance of the Scottish Highlands, producing a uniquely cultivated class of traditional dance which today we call Highland Dance. This is not the only class of folk dance found in Scotland; it is simply the most sophisticated expression in dance of the artistic spirit of Scottish Gaelic culture, just as pibroch is in music.

If we seek cultural affinities, perhaps it is the Celtic strain which is the most per-sistent common factor relating France and Scotland, for there seems to be a closer *cultural* affinity between the Scottish Gaels and the French than between either and the English. We shall have occasion to consider possible avenues of French influence on the folk dance culture of the Highlands at a later stage.

Wherever the classical art of dance was manifest, from the sixteenth century on, there was to be found French or Italian influence, and latterly only French. In this respect, then, it can be said with assurance that those aspects of Scottish dance, its deportment and elaboration of technique, which derive from the Renaissance court dance (as does ballet), exhibit the influence of France. They do not establish that the dances themselves belong to France.

The young Queen of Scots carried her considerable talents and personal charm with modesty and comeliness, secure in her privileged position and in the affections of her mother's family. One of her uncles was the Cardinal of Lorraine and another the king's favourite marshal. This very fact carried its penalties, for the attitudes toward Mary of some personages, such as Queen Catherine, were tinctured by their aversion to the influence of Mary's powerful relatives. Her future must have appeared aureate indeed when on April 24, 1558, the day of her wedding to the Dauphin dawned on the spires of Paris, with the thin light of an April morning spreading over the city and the multitude stirring from slumber to throng the environs of the cathedral church of Notre Dame. The enormity of fortune's caprices with her is overwhelming.

Nothing in Mary's experience of royal pageantry could have exceeded in splendour the festivities in the grand hall of the palace upon the occasion of her wedding. Her few attempts to produce a masque or pageant at court after her return to Scotland must have seemed the most pathetic shadow of what she had known in France. What memories to haunt her among the grey shadows of the Palace of the *Haly Rude*!

Although the program has not been recorded, we know from the practice of the time that the formal dances at the wedding would be the Pavane, then the Tordion, followed by the Galliard and some Branles. The nobility, the beauty for eye and ear, and the rich and ravishing ornament can best be imagined. Within two years Mary was to be queen of France, then a widow with no option but to sail for her own throne, where the chill breeze of the North Sea swept through the noisesome closes of the Canongait and stern hills of heather took the place of serried vines.

She sought solace with her lute and virginals in the peace of her chambers in the company of her musical attendants, one of whom was the unfortunate Rizzio. What more natural than that she should on occasion seek the "joyousity," as she expressed it, of the music and dance which she had so long enjoyed as an essential part of her young life.

John Knox, however, was anything but confident of the security of the reformed religion, and viewed with devout concern the fate of the Reformers in France, among whose most active persecutors were Mary's powerful uncles. Mary's contacts and tastes left little place for John Knox, and he feared and hence resented his exclusion from her councils. The royal favour made it more profitable, he complained, "to have been brought up with fiddlers and dancers, and to have been exercised in flinging upon a floor, and in the rest that thereof follows, than to have been nourished in the company of the godly, and exercised in virtue."[6] He petulantly dismissed Mary's courtiers as "scoupars [skippers], dancers, and dalliers with dames."

Matters came to a head when Knox in a sermon given on December 13, 1562, "inveighed sore against the Queen's dancing" and was summoned to answer for it before the queen the next day. He explained that his main complaint was that she regarded "fiddlers and flatterers" of greater account than he, and of dancing, he added,

---

[6] John Knox, *History of the Reformation in Scotland*, ed. W. C. Dickinson, vol. 2, p. 102.

"Madam, albeit in scriptures I found no praise of it, and in profane writers it is termed the gesture rather of those that are mad and in frenzy than of sober men; yet do I not utterly damn it, provided that two vices be avoided: the former, that the principal vocation of those that use that exercise be not neglected for the pleasure of dancing; Secondly, that they dance not, as the Philistines their fathers, for the pleasure that they take in the displeasure of God's people."[7]

The occasion which provoked this incident was a ball on the return of the queen from a visit to the north, possibly in celebration of her twentieth birthday or as a prelude to the customary Yule festivities. In any case, she had just recovered from influenza contracted at the end of her jaunt and probably thought the occasion opportune for a ball. Knox was too oppressed by the vicissitudes of his great cause to regard high spirits at the palace as anything but sardonic levity.

Some rumours of successes of Mary's uncles in suppressing the Huguenots in France had apparently reached Knox when he made his historic sermon. Froude, the historian, has misled many writers by stating that news of the massacre of Vassy had then just arrived; but that event took place a full nine months before Knox's outburst, and contrary to Knox's remarks, there was as yet no "triumph" for Mary's "friends."[8] "Maister Knox," Mary had remarked to the English ambassador, "is so hard unto us that we have laid aside much of our dancing."

If, of an evening, Mary enjoyed music and a few dances, she was doing no more than did her father and grandfather before her. Did she dance the reels or *licht* dances of the Scottish countryside? Perhaps she did at some time or other, but we have no word of it. When she was a girl in France, she sometimes dressed as a Highlander. "When arrayed *à la sovage*, as I have seen her," writes Brantôme in *Vies des Femmes Illustres*, "in the outlandish garb of the wild people of her own realm, her mortal form assumed in that heavy and barbarous dress the semblance of a perfect goddess." Indeed, the French king and queen thought this dress, no doubt the belted plaid and *triubhas*, more becoming to her than any of her rich robes of state. But there is no hint of her performing the appropriate dances.

Even the accounts of her celebrated hunting trip to Athole and the forest of Lude in 1564 say nothing of dancing of any kind; yet surely, with such a concourse of Highlanders feasting round bonfires after the chase, there must have been much music and dancing in the ancient manner. Were there no dances and music in the halls of the laird? There is traditional support for there being a performance of music for the *clarsach*, for Mary on that occasion gifted a clarsach to Beatrix Garden of Banchory, which later came into the possession of Robertson of Lude and ultimately of the Museum of Antiquities, Edinburgh, where it may now be seen. Then on some of her progresses, there is mention of "balling and dancing," as Knox expressed it; but at Athole, nothing.

Of course, nowhere are we told anything of what was danced, and typical references, such as, "after dinner they dance awhile" and "after the marriage followeth cheer and dancing," do not mention specific dances. Only John Knox finds occasion to name a dance: "Amongst the minions of the Court, there was one named Monsieur Chattelett,

---

[7] Ibid., p. 45.
[8] Ibid., p. 43, fn.

a Frenchman, that at that time passed all others in credit with the Queen. In dancing of the Purpose (so term they that dance, in which man and woman talk secretly — wise men would judge such fashions more like to the brothel than to the comeliness of honest women) in this dance the Queen chose Chattelett and Chattelett took the Queen."[9] The indications are that this was a miming Branle of the new fashion. It may be supposed that if there was one such Branle, there were others.

Historians have not been knowledgeable in the subject, and one encounters remarks on Mary's dancing Quadrilles, Cotillions, and Minuets, all dances which were unknown in her time. Mrs. Jamieson in her *Female Sovereigns* wrote on undeclared authority that, "In dancing, Mary was only excelled in the Spanish Minuet by Anne d'Este, the graceful Duchess of Guise, her aunt by marriage; but no lady of the court could excel her in the lively movements of the Galliarde." Possibly "Spanish Minuet" is written in error for the Spanish Pavane which was indeed a favourite of Mary's time.

We know from various sources that Conaeus was not exaggerating when he wrote: "She danced excellently to music on account of her wonderful agility of body, but yet gracefully and becomingly, for by quiet and gentle motion of her limbs she could express any harmony of the strings."[10]

There is further testimony from Sir James Melville in his celebrated account of his embassy to Queen Elizabeth at Windsor in 1564 in his *Memoirs of His Own Life*. Elizabeth was not a little curious about Mary; she wished to know which of them he thought had the better colour of hair and which he thought the "fairest." "They were baith," he was at last pressed to answer, "baith the fairest ladies of their courts, and that the Queen of England was white, but our queen was very luesome [lovely]." Who, then, was the taller? "The Queen of Scots," Sir James replied. "Too tall," said Elizabeth, who thought herself exactly the right height. "Did she play music well?" "Raisonable for a Queen," he replied. Then, who danced the better? "The Queen of Scots," he told her, "dancit not so high and disposedly as she did" (pp. 123–26). Elizabeth danced in a more spirited and sprightly manner, which was the Italian style she had been taught. Mary's dancing was more elegant, more French. It would be difficult to say which of the queens loved music and dance the more, but there is no doubt that Mary was the more sensitive artist. Not for her the bear- and bull-baiting which diverted Elizabeth, nor the massacre of the Huguenots which diverted Catherine de' Medici.

"Sche was sa effable," wrote Sir James Melville in 1564, "sa gratious and discreet that she wan gret estymation, and the hartis of many, baith in England and Scotland, and myn amang the rest, so that I thocht her mair worthy to be servit for little proffet than any uther prence in Europe for gret commodite."

Such has been the impress of Mary's personality that it is difficult to realize that she actively ruled Scotland for barely six years. By the same token, it is easy to understand how, in an artistic sense, she seems to bloom as a rose among thistles, tempting us to attribute all French elegancies of dance and courtliness in sixteenth-century Scotland to her example. Somehow one wishes this were so, it seems a desirable ingredient of her romantic legend. Mary, too, was not as Scottish as Elizabeth was English. Her attachment to the native airs and dances of her people was not as strong as Elizabeth's.

"In my end is my beginning," she said, with no thought of its many meanings.

[9] Ibid., p. 68.
[10] Cf. David Hay Fleming, *Mary Queen of Scots* (London, 1897).

4/The Scottish Court
in England

*Court of James VI in Scotland and
England – dancing at the Tudor court –
Puritan commentators – Galliard
dancing – Elizabethan dancing – intro-
duction of the Country Dance at court –
Playford and* The Dancing Master *– civil
war period – dancing during the
Commonwealth – times of Charles II*

James VI, Mary's son, inherited none of the physical grace of his Stewart ancestors. Awkward, nervous, and superstitious, with weak legs and a tongue too large for his mouth, he was unprepossessing in the extreme. In compensation, he was a precocious scholar and he held his throne longer than all but one or two of Britain's monarchs. His bent was intellectual, as distinct from artistic, and thus, taking all things into consideration, it is no surprise that from a dancing and musical point of view the dying days of the Scottish court are of little significance. Scotland's "Golden Age" had melted away in the heat of battle and dispute, and the century of her "most energetic, peculiar, and most various life" was yet to come. Yet, whatever else Scotland lacked at this eventful time, she still provided many continental universities with masters and scholars, of whom the most fantastic was the "Admirable" Creighton (or Crichton) born in Perth. In Sir Thomas Urquhart's inimitable phrase, he displayed the "ever to be admired" ideal of the Renaissance gallant, "minding his hawking, hunting, tilting, vaulting, riding of well-managed horses, tossing of the pike, handling of the musket, flourishing of colours, dancing, fencing, swimming, jumping, throwing of the bar, playing at the tennis, baloon or long-catch, . . . singing, playing of the lute . . . masking, balling, revelling." And, we may add, Creighton also participated in public disputation with men of learning at the Sorbonne. He had a thorough knowledge of twelve languages, with the apparent exception of Gaelic, a fact which is puzzling until we remember that Urquhart would not consider it a foreign language This versatility, however, could, with justification, be regarded as the Scot's peculiar characteristic or taste. The Scotsman's stage was Europe. England offered no attraction or welcome for him yet.

How the young King James would have envied Creighton! There is a tinge of pathos in an item in the Accounts of the Lord High Treasurer for December, 1580, at which date James was fourteen years of age, recording a gratuity to "Williame Hud-soun, his hienes balladine, as for his extraordinaire panis taiken in teitcheing of his grace to dance." In contradistinction to James's mother, there is little talk of his dancing. Nevertheless, there is note of a payment in the accounts of the following year (1581–82) to Thomas Hutsoun, another of the same family of English violars who attended at James's court,[1] "for furneissing of necessari apparrell an wappinnis to a mask dans as is requisite," and in the same accounts, an item to the repair of "windois in the dansing chalmer."

In 1589, James took to wife the young Princess Anne of Denmark, who, during her later sojourn in London, showed herself to be markedly partial to masques. It seems unlikely that she did not indulge some of this taste during her thirteen years in Scot-land. Her nuptial welcome to Edinburgh in 1590 constituted the last of the elaborate welcomes in Scotland. The cost to the city was embarrassing, but James observed for history that "a King with a new merit wife didna come hame every day!" Of special interest to us are the twelve dancers in this pageant who wore white shoes (cf. the Perth Glovers, p. 26) and hats of flowers, and performed a sword dance. A "hielan" dance also is mentioned, although somewhat ambiguously, and this is the first recorded mention of highland dancing (cf. p. 31).[2]

The great storms of the winter of 1589 which had detained first the princess and then the king himself — after he had braved these storms to "fetch her hame" — gave rise to serious suspicion of the activity of witches (and probably also to the beautiful ballad, "Sir Patrick Spens"). The centre of this activity seems to have been Preston-pans. It was alleged that the devil himself addressed a concourse of sorcerers at North Berwick Kirk, prior to which, at "about eleven hours at even they dancit alangs the Kirk-yard." The witches took hands and danced a reel to Geilie Duncan's trump, singing in one voice "Cummer go Ye."[3]

This report provides us with one of our earliest uses of the word "reel" with refer-ence to dance and is therefore a matter to which we will have occasion to return. Apart from these few points, the reign of James VI, prior to his assumption of the British crown, is by no means fruitful to our purpose. The Scottish court moved to London on the death of Elizabeth and inherited thereby the rich theatrical and dance tradition which the Tudors had nourished.

Robert Copland's set of instructions for the dancing of basse dances "after the man-ner of France," was published in Henry VIII's reign in 1521; it formed an appendix to a book on French grammar for young gentlemen. Ten years later, we are told that the favourite dances were "Basse dances, Bargenettes, Pavions, Turgions, and Roundes."[4] The Bargenette has been identified from musical evidence to have been a carol in Branle form; the Turgion was the Tordion, of course. The Galliard is omit-ted but is mentioned by the same writer some three years later.[5]

There is a painting extant showing Henry dancing the Allemande (Almain) out-doors at Windsor.[6] It seems probable that this was the order of a rustic dance. (The

---

1 There were four: Thomas, William, Robert, and James.
2 *Papers Relative to the Marriage of James VI* (Edinburgh, 1828); and Edinburgh Burgh Records.
3 Robert Chambers, *Domestic Annals of Scotland*, 2nd ed., vol. 1, p. 214.
4 Sir Thomas Elyot, *Boke named the Governour*, bk. 1.
5 Elyot, *The Castel of Helth.*
6 Reproduced in Melusine Wood, *Some Historical Dances.*

term "rustic" is used here to avoid confusion with the term "country.") We have seen the Almain Haye mentioned in Scotland, and it may not be mere coincidence that Almains appear in company with English dances of the countryside in some late sixteenth-century manuscripts.

England had moved steadily toward prosperity and renown, despite the intrigues, petty treasons, and the anomalous coexistence of cruelty and artistic genius: the land of music — Tallis, Byrd, Dowland, and Morley, and of literature — Spenser, Marlowe, Shakespeare, and Bacon.

Dancing was a daily pastime at Elizabeth's court, and de Maisse reported in 1598 in his journal that "in her youth she [Elizabeth] danced very well and composed measures and music and had played them herself and danced them. She takes such pleasure in it that when her maids dance she follows the cadence with her hand and foot. She rebukes them if they do not dance to her liking and without a doubt she is mistress of the art having learnt in the Italian manner to dance high."

In this very same year, another visitor, Hetzner, wrote: "They [the English] excel in dancing and music, for they are active and lively, though of a thicker make than the French."[7] This passion for dancing extended down to the meanest yeoman. It was as though the fabulous tarantula had infected the nation. It may not have been something new, but the protests of the growing sects of Puritans and moralists throw it into prominence. John Northbrooke complained that "it would grieve chaste ears to hear what newe kinds of dances and newe devised gestures the people have devised, and daylye doe devise" and how of "grave women it is a worlde to see nay, a hell to see, howe they will swing, leape, and turn when the pypers and crowders begin to play." He deplored "our hoppings, and leapings, and interminglings men with women" as a sad declension from the religious dancing of the ancients, for, he said, David did not dance "leaping and turning of his bodie with playerlyke movings and gestures" (or perhaps he did!).[8] Northbrooke certainly painted a vivid picture of a boisterous style of dancing—was this what Arbeau had complained of?

Another Puritan could not understand why parents should have their daughters taught to dance, an activity which he associated with "bawdy houses" and which made "Christians worse than pagans." He particularly deplored the new dancing with its "shaking, unclean handling, kissing, bragging, groping" and "a very kind of lechery — foul and rude." It seemed to him that women danced chiefly for the pleasure of kissing — he does not mention the men — and he disliked the common practice of promiscuous kissing, recalling a time when kissing was restricted to kinsfolk!"[9]

Certainly, as we have already noted, the trend over the century was from grace to dexterity. The dances now in fashion were, above all, the Galliard and the Volta, then the Coranto, "Measure," Brawl, Pavane, and Canary. Shakespeare refers to them all, and Morley has much to write about their music. The Galliard became more of an acrobatic display than a dance, especially on the part of the males. It always had been, as Thomas Elyot said, "very vehement exercise," but the Italian taste for virtuoso dancing as exemplified by the "Venetian gentlemen" who "capered so wonderfully" and

[7] Hetzner (1598), quoted in William B. Rye, *England as Seen by Foreigners.*

[8] John Northbrooke, *A treatise against dicing, dancing, plays, and interludes. With other idle pastimes.* First ed. 1577. Ed. J. P. Collier, Shakespeare Society Reprints (London, 1843), pp. 176, 150, and 151.

[9] Lu Emily Pearson, *Elizabethans at Home*, p. 251.

"appeared to have wings on their feet" at a dance in Queen Catherine Parr's apartments in 1543 was now supreme.

It was no longer possible to get by with the basic five steps (*cinquépace*), as Barnaby Riche plaintively remarked in *His Farewell to Militairie Profession*: "Our galliardes are so curious, that they are not for my daunsying, for thei are so full of trickes and tournes, that he whiche hath no more but the plain cinquepace, is no better accoumpted of then a verie bongler; and for my part thei might assone teach me to make a capricornus, as a capre in the right kinde that it should bee."

All this, of course, demanded assiduous practice and took the place of other sport in the interests of young men. Marston satirized the obsession for dance in the person of a gallant named Curio.

> Who ever heard spruce skipping Curio
> Ere prate of ought but of the whirle on toe,
> The turne about ground, Robrus sprauling kicks,
> Fabius caper, Harries tossing tricks?
> Did ever any eare ere heare him speake
> Unlesse his tongue of crosse-points did entreat?
> His teeth doe caper whilst he eates his meat,
> His heeles doe caper whilst he takes his seate;
> His very soule, his intellectuall
> Is nothing but a mincing capreall.
> He dreames of toe-turnes; each gallant he doth meete
> He fronts him with a traverse in the streete.
> Praise but Orchestra, and the skipping art,
> You shall commaund him, faith you have his hart
> Even capring in your fist.
>
> [John Marston, *The Scourge of Villanie*, satire xi]

If anything, of course, the Volta with its "vault" of the women, propelled by the gentlemen's knees and accompanied no doubt by tympanic effects and wild cries and clutches for the petticoats, was more open to censure. It was not the kind of thing Victoria would have relished, but Elizabeth was no "Victorian," as those who had heard her hearty oaths or had been spat upon could testify.

There were apparently real dangers in Elizabethan dancing if we believe Philip Stubbes, who writes in the *Anatomie of Abuses*: "Some have broke their legs with skipping, leaping, turning and vawting." Nor were the risks peculiar to the English scene, for we are told that Lewis, the Archbishop of Magdeburg, "in treading his lavolas and corantos with his mistresse . . . in trying the horsetrick broke his necke."[10]

This exuberance was characteristic of Elizabethan England and of a people who were "vastly fond of great noises that fell the ear, such as the firing of cannon, drums, and the ringing of bells," and who enjoyed brutal entertainment such as bear- and bull-baiting. An English captain was asked by a foreigner if any of his family had been hanged and quartered; when he replied, "Not that I know of," another Englishman whispered, "Don't be surprised, for he is not a gentleman."[11]

---

[10] Thomas Lodge, *Wits Miserie*, 1596.
[11] Litolfi, quoted in William B. Rye, *England as Seen by Foreigners*, p. 110.

London was by now an important mercantile city, although it largely comprised a network of dirty lanes bestrewn with garbage and filth and darkened by overhanging houses. The growing class of merchants and city gentry created a demand for the public dancing schools which now begin to be mentioned. One of the marvels of London, it was said, was the performance of a Galliard dancer in a dancing school: "At our entring hee was beginning a trick as I remember of sixteens and seventeens, I do not very wel remember but wunderfully hee leaped, flung and took on."[12] This was a dance to fit the times.

The identification of Elizabeth with her people, her national consciousness, and her love of music and dancing must have made her very susceptible to the effect of such occasions as that held at Warwick Castle, in 1572, where, we are told, "it pleased her to have the country people, resorting to see her, daunce in the court of the Castell, her Majestie beholding them out of her chamber window; which thing, as it plesid well the country people, so it seemed her Majesty was much delighted, and made very myrry."[13] A similar event is recorded some years later in 1591 at Cowdray during another of Elizabeth's progresses, and doubtless it was no longer a unique event: "In the evening the country people presented themselves to hir Majestie in a pleasant daunce with taber and pipe; and the Lord Montagu and his Lady among them, to the great pleasure of all the beholders, and the gentle applause of hir Majestie."[14]

Some years later, in 1602, we discover the Earl of Shrewsbury writing in a letter, "We are frolic here in Court; much dancing in the privy chamber of Country dances before the Queen's Majesty who is exceedingly pleased therewith: Irish tunes are at this time most pleasing."[15] [Spelling modernized.] The Country Dance had arrived at court, just as the Branles and other dances of the French countryside had arrived at the French court. Clearly the English Country Dances were in the tradition of the *licht* dances of the *Complaynt*, a form of dance uniquely identifiable with the British countryside, with many local variants and versions.

The acceptance of the native country dance as following the court dance in the highest society was a characteristic development of the days of Queen Bess. It was fashionable to dance "high and disposedly" and the "romps" of the countryside were congenial to the temper of the time.

In 1603, after the death of Queen Elizabeth, the English and Scottish courts were one, and the Scottish king fell heir to the practices of his illustrious predecessor. There were great balls in the long galleries, and Country Dances were now firmly entrenched as the closing dances after an evening of "grave measures," Corantos, and Galliards. The comic jigs or song and dance interludes which, to please the queen, Ben Jonson introduced in place of the formal court dances that had formed an essential part of court masques, became characteristic of the masque. Grotesqueries and antics were introduced, and on the occasion of Princess Elizabeth's marriage at Shrovetide in 1614, the lawyers at the Inns of Court produced a masque in which a variety of rural characters were featured, dancing after the country fashion to appropriate music. This

---

[12] *Newes from the North*, 1585, by "T. F."
[13] John Nichols, *The Progresses and Public Processions of Queen Elizabeth*, vol. 1, p. 319.
[14] Ibid., vol. 3, p. 95.
[15] Letter to the Earl of Worcester from the Earl of Shrewsbury, quoted in ibid., vol. 3, p. 40.

masque so pleased His Majesty that he called for an encore.[16] One wishes he had re-corded his observations on this event to let us know in what respects this dancing was novel to him, and if he had seen the like in Scotland.

The introduction of folk dance to entertainment was no new thing in London. It had been a feature of the Elizabethan stage. Gosson wrote in 1582: "For the eye beside the beauties of the houses, and the stage, he (the Devil) sendeth in gearish apparell masks, vauting, tumbling, dauncing of gigges, galiardes, morisies, hobbihorses . . . nothing forgot, that might serve to set out the matter. . . ."[17] Ben Jonson continued this tradition in his masques. It is interesting to note that, in a masque at the wedding of Lord Somerset in 1613, a group of Irishmen danced what was termed "a fading," a dance frequently noticed by Elizabethan dramatists, presumably the Rinnce Fada.

The Gentlemen of the Inns of Court, however, claim our attention on account of their inspiring their bookseller, John Playford, to collect and publish the figures and tunes of 105 Country Dances. This historic book was initially entitled *The English Dancing Master*, a title presumably suggested in contradistinction to a popular charac-ter in a play of the time who was called the "French dancing master." The title was reduced simply to *The Dancing Master* in the second and all further editions.

Incidentally, the lawyers of the Inns of Court made a point of dancing and holding revels on important occasions as well as at Christmas and Easter, a practice which they long thought very necessary as "much conducing to making of gentlemen more fit for their books at other times," as Playford remarks in his introduction.

The year of the publication of *The English Dancing Master* (1651) is surprising because it is the year of the Royalist defeat and the inauguration of Cromwell's puri-tanical rule. An inauspicious time, as Playford apparently recognized ("knowing these times and the Nature of it do not agree") but unavoidable, he said, on account of the impending publication of rival books!

The interesting fact is that in spite of the temper of the times, the collection was apparently in danger of competition and was of sufficient interest to warrant its run-ning to two more editions during the Commonwealth (1652 and 1657). It was ulti-mately to run to eighteen editions produced at intervals until 1725. There were also deletions and additions to the contents throughout the years, and the publication of upwards of a thousand dances and tunes.

John Playford was succeeded by his son Henry in 1684, and the latter by John Young in 1706. Through the editions of *The Dancing Master*, one can trace the changes of fashion and style in the dances over the years, and the first three editions especially provide the earliest printed source of numerous popular airs, Scottish and Irish as well as English.

Charles I and his queen enjoyed dancing, but his reign was marred by a bitter struggle which turned people's minds to great issues and causes. Ten years of this preoccupation darkened the colours of daily life, and the tide of puritanism which had ebbed and flowed since the days of Henry VIII now surged to a flood which over-whelmed some good along with the bad. Nevertheless, it is remarkable that private or domestic dancing was not proscibed, nor were masques, nor music at state functions

---

[16] John Nichols, ed., *The Progresses of King James I* (London, 1828), vol. 2, p. 597.
[17] Stephen Gosson, *Playes Confuted in Five Actions*, 1582.

or in the great houses. It was still possible for English squires to brighten long winter nights with entertainment and dancing with their household, thus perpetuating the traditions of their forefathers, in comparative isolation. Perhaps, as has been suggested,[18] the dances in Playford named after famous houses — Nonesuch, Greenwich, Hudson, and Holmby — were peculiar to these households, a kind of *specialité de la maison*. It seems reasonable. How much of this life was disrupted by the Civil War is difficult to say; but we know that Cromwell danced on occasion, and that an elaborate masque was performed at the weddings of his daughters in 1657 in which the bride and bridegroom and Cromwell himself took part.[19] But theatrical dancing or what was called superstitious, lewd, or lascivious dancing — that which attended the May Games, or the Yule revels — was severely censured.

With the return of the monarchy, something of Elizabethan heartiness was restored and much more besides. John Evelyn writes in his diary that Charles II "brought in a more polite way of living, which passed to luxury and intolerable expense." The French and Italian court dances retained their place of honour at the opening of balls, but the country dances were enjoyed with even greater zeal, and indeed, by the end of the century, had practically displaced all rivals. The Galliard became so subdued that it lost its character and died out. The Coranto also was refined until it became too exacting for all but the most elegant dancers, requiring much dignity and control to carry it off — "very noble it was, and great pleasure to see." This last remark was made by Pepys on the occasion of a ball held by the Duke of York in the time of Charles II: "By and by comes the King and Queen, the Duke and Duchess, and all the great ones; and after seating themselves, the King takes out the Duchess of York, and the Duke, the Duchess of Buckingham; the Duke of Monmouth, my lady Castlemaine; and so other lords other ladies; and they danced the Bransle. After that, the King led a lady a single Coranto; and then the rest of the Lords, one after another, other ladies; very noble it was, and great pleasure to see. Then to country dances; the King leading the first, which he called for; which was, says he *Cuckolds all awry*, the old dance of England. The manner was, when the King dances, all the ladies in the room, and the Queen herself, stand up and indeed he dances rarely, and much better than the Duke of York."

Pepys himself took lessons, although he had difficulty in shedding his puritanical suspicion of dancing. On January 6, 1668, he recorded in his diary that he threw a party for some of his friends after a visit to the theatre: "And so, with much pleasure we went into the house, and there fell to dancing, having extraordinary musick, two viollins, and a base viollin, and Theorbo [lute] four hands, the Duke of Buckingham's musick, the best in towne, lent me by Greeling, and there we set in to dancing. By and by to my house, to a very good supper, and mighty merry, and good musick playings; and after supper to dancing and singing till about twelve at night; and then we had a good sack posset for them, and an excellent cake cost me near 20 s., of our Jane's

---

[18] Margaret Dean-Smith and E. J. Nicol, "The Dancing Master," *JEFDSS*, vol. 4, no. 4 (1943), no. 5 (1944), and no. 6 (1945).

[19] At the wedding of Frances Cromwell, one of the daughters, "They had forty-eight violins, fifty trumpets, and much mirth with frolics, besides mixt dancing (a thing here-to-fore accounted profane) till five of the clock yesterday morning." [Letter from William Dugdale to John Langley, Fifth Report of the Historical Manuscript Commission, p. 157.]

making, which was cut into twenty pieces, there being by this time so many of our company, by the coming in of young Goodyear, and some others of our neighbours, young men that could dance, hearing of our dancing; . . . And so to dancing again, and singing with extraordinary great pleasure, till about twelve in the morning, and then broke up" (*Diary*, January 6, 1668).

Such was the spirit of the times. Dancing masters in the metropolis enjoyed new prosperity; and not only at court but also at various houses in the city there was frequent dancing. Pepys recorded in November 11, 1661, a visit to a dancing school in Fleet Street where he saw "a company of pretty girls dance, but I do not in myself like to have young girls exposed to much vanity." This last remark is characteristic of Pepys's early reaction to new trends. It appears that the sexes were not mixed at the dancing schools, and Count Megallotti, the secretary of the Grand Duke Cosmo who visited London in 1669, wrote that "Dancing is a very common and favourite amusement of the ladies in this country; every evening there are entertainments at different places in the city, at which many ladies and citizens' wives are present, they going to them alone, as they do to the rooms of the dancing master's, at which there are frequently upwards of forty or fifty ladies."[20] He also tells us that the duke had an opportunity of seeing several dances performed in the English style, and that each was "exceedingly well regulated, and executed in the smartest and genteelest manner by very young ladies, whose beauty and gracefulness were shown off to perfection by this exercise."

Whether the same accolade was deserved by the men is doubtful; but there is no doubt that the king and his favourite illegitimate son, the Duke of Monmouth, were among the best in the country, as, according to Courtin, the French ambassador, they were the only expert male dancers at the British court.[21] Of the ladies, Courtin wrote that there were only three who could be considered as good as the best dancers in France: Princess Mary (the Duke of York's elder daughter), the Countess of Derby, and the Duchess of Richmond ("La Belle Stuart," whose confident beauty and chastity perplexed that English court of mistresses) — this despite the almost continuous practice! The same writer tells of a supper presented by the Duchess of Portsmouth at which French dances were danced in the gallery until eleven o'clock when supper was served at two big tables, one for the ladies and the other for the men, after which the company returned to the gallery to dance country dances until three of the morning.

By the time of the events described by Courtin, Playford's *Dancing Master* had run to five editions. It is interesting that in the third edition (1665) "Tunes of the most usual French Dances," mainly corantos, were included for the first and only time, these being arranged for the "treble violin," as were all tunes published in Playford. This instrument, of course, was what we now call the violin, but it only began to supersede the viol at the Restoration, because it was "more airee and brisk." An engraving in the third edition showed how the violin was strung.

The renewed interest in music and dancing must have made the Playfords very

[20] Quoted in William Connor Sydney, *Social Life in England from the Restoration to the Revolution* (London, 1892), pp. 408–9.

[21] Correspondence Angleterre 120, Courtin to Louis XIV, November 26 and December 17, 1676, Archives of the French Foreign Office. Quoted in C. H. Hartmann, *La Belle Stuart*, p. 225.

busy men, for they published other collections of "New theatre Tunes, Ayres, Corants, Sarabands, Jiggs and Hornpipes; and late New French Dances."[22] This was the taste of the period, however, to the exclusion of more serious forms.

Nevertheless, it was during Charles II's reign that the Marquis de Flamarens introduced the Minuet to England, "which he danced with a considerable measure of success."[23] This dance was developed, it is believed, from the Branle de Poitou, by Beauchamps who, along with Pecour, was court dancing master to Louis XIV. Its name is derived from the "minute" steps which first characterized the dance, and the earliest music for it was written by Lully. The Minuet gradually displaced the Courante and became the great dance of the eighteenth century. Other dances which emanated from that source and which are often seen referred to as the new French dances are mainly the Rigadon, Louvre, Bourée, Brittagne, and Passepied, essentially based on folk dances of the French provinces.

Much of this was the work of the Académie Royale de Danse, founded by Louis XIV in 1661, which formalized the technique of dance as never before. Indeed, it was only now that the basic five positions were defined.

Charles II came under this influence while he was resident in the French court for a time, and in this and other ways he was well prepared for his role as the Merry Monarch. It must have moved him to many a chuckle to recall his subscribing to the Covenant of the Scottish Presbyterians and their promotion of his kingship. Indeed, during his reign the struggle of the Scottish Covenanters against the king's bishops and liturgy was, like smouldering embers from past fire, fanned into a flame to litter the Lowland hills with the graves of martyrs and memorials to deep religious passion. No greater contrast to the levity of Charles's court can be imagined.

The end of Charles's ostentatious court came suddenly, as we learn from Evelyn's diary: "I can never forget the inexpressible luxury and profaneness, gaming and all dissoluteness, and as it were total forgetfulness of God (it being Sunday evening) which this day and night I was witness of; the king sitting and toying with his concubines, Portsmouth, Cleveland and Mazarin, etc., a French boy singing love songs in that glorious gallery, while about twenty of the great courtiers and other dissolute persons were at banquet round a large table, a bank of at least 2,000 pounds in gold before them; upon which two gentlemen who were with me made reflections with astonishment. Six days after, was all in the dust."

---

[22] John Playford, *Apollo's Banquet*, 1st ed., 1663.
[23] Comte de Gramont, *Memoirs*, p. 232.

5/The Seventeenth Century and Scottish Dance

Religious troubles – Covenanters – presbytery and episcopacy – burgh and rural conditions – rule of the Kirk – attitude of reformers to the keeping of the Sabbath – restraint on secular activity during "time of sermon" – antagonism to Yule and "superfluous banqueting" – occasions of dance in the countryside – penny weddings, wakes, and baptisms – harvest celebrations – the Kirk and "promiscuous dancing" –..occasions for

national rejoicing – the Restoration – European-inspired civility among the northeast gentry – dance a part of polite education – Duke of York at Holyrood – burgh dancing masters – Covenanters and dance and music

The ancient roots of the royal house of Scotland were transplanted with James into the rich loam of Hampton Court, Windsor, and Whitehall, leaving the ancestral towers yearning for the Stewart glory which never quite came to pass. The removal of the Scottish court meant the removal of the social and artistic centre, whose patronage in those days was essential to the fostering of the formal arts of music, literature, and painting. The loss was compounded by the lack of economic resources of the kind that made England relatively prosperous and by the national unrest occasioned by the monarch's attack on the Presbyterian system of church organization and worship.

This last issue was one which preoccupied the Scottish people through the greater part of the seventeenth century. Three kings in turn tried to impose episcopacy on the Scottish Church and to establish the Anglican service and liturgy. The "divine right" of presbytery came into head-on collision with the "divine right" of kings. The image of Jenny Geddes throwing her stool at the bishop in St. Giles' Church on July, 1637 was to remain a symbol of resistance for many generations of Scottish Presbyterians. A covenant was drawn up, binding its signatories to the defence of the "true" religion, and was carried into every parish; it became the subject of imperious earnestness and fervour.

The army of the Covenanters found common purpose with Cromwell in the war against Charles I; but when the king was disposed of, the issues dividing the two allies led to further conflict and to the English occupation of Scotland during the period of the Commonwealth.

The Restoration inaugurated the period of Merry England, but alas, rejoicing in Scotland was stilled by the speedy return to old issues which seriously impeded social and economic progress, until they were resolved by the Glorious Revolution in 1688 and by the succession of William and Mary in 1689. The new and less disruptive issue, Jacobitism, was thereby introduced.

Toleration was not a characteristic of the times. To those Scots dedicated to the "divine right" of presbytery, the issues at stake were fundamental. The incessant preaching and disputation, aggravated by the severity of authority, inflamed the imagination and exposed the thinly covered superstition inherited by all classes of people from the dark ages of the past. Superimposed on this were extreme economic hardships and the usual outbreaks of pestilence and famine, all variously interpreted as "judgements." It is not remarkable that the appearance of a comet or the occurrence of an earth tremor should lead to superstitious speculation; one can encounter this kind of speculation in Europe even today. But the emotional conditions in Lowland Scotland during the period of the troubles of the Kirk were such that the slightest deviation from normal in the simplest of occurrences, such as the breaking of a shoe-lace, could be regarded as a portent.

To attend a conventicle was to risk death, yet hundreds of the ordinary people of the Lowlands did so. The enormity of the risk increased the feelings of exultation and devotion in the fresh hill-top air and created a memory which impressed itself indelibly on the attitude and convictions of most Lowland Scots for many generations to come.

So heavy has been the impress of these issues on the face and mind of Scotland, that one overlooks the fact that the physical impact of the "troubles" was almost completely isolated to the southwest of the country, the old diocese of Glasgow. Add to this some parts of the Border country, the Lothians, and Fife and the limits of the most uncompromising covenanting region are established. Aberdeenshire and the northeast in general, indeed from the Tay upwards, were not averse to episcopacy. Some families, headed by the Huntly-Gordons in the north and the Douglases and Maxwells in the south, even retained a Catholic profession; but no family not protected by an influential baron could be Catholic and survive, and not even the baron was immune to harassment.

While most of the Highlands were at least nominally Episcopalian or Presbyterian, there were areas in which Catholicism persisted. Today "the Catholic part of the Highlands runs from Banffshire through Inverness-shire, down the Great Glen, out to the west coast in Knoydart and Moydart, across the small isles of Eigg and Canna to South Uist and Barra."[1]

The important burghs in the seventeenth century were Edinburgh and Aberdeen. Next came Dundee, followed by Perth, Stirling, and Glasgow. The town houses were of stone with timber facings and forestairs, and after some disastrous fires, slate roofs were enforced. In Aberdeen and Glasgow, many gardens and orchards were attached to these houses. Edinburgh was a picturesque composition of precipitous outside stairs, startling abutments, gables, and chimneys, clustered before the rock and girt by the city wall. Its skyscrapers (some were fourteen stories high by 1689) presented unique problems of sanitation that took some time to solve. But in no European town were people fastidious about such matters at this time. John Ray, the English naturalist, described in his *Itinerary* "the ordinary Country Houses" as "pitiful cots built of stone, and covered with Turfs having in them but one room, many of them no chimneys, and windows very small holes, and not glazed."

[1] Frank Frazer Darling, ed., *West Highland Survey.*

Since communications were difficult, the roads being impassable to wheeled traffic and only "tolerably good for horses" as one English traveller recorded, one can readily understand the preservation of local characteristics and customs throughout the land.

The essential personal garment was the plaid, usually of tartan. Women wore this draped over their heads and tucked up by the arms to prevent its trailing on the ground. Strangely, this fashion came to be disliked by the burgh authorities as an "uncivil form of behaviour," but they did not manage to suppress it. The plaid was a most convenient garment for even the most genteel ladies venturing on a hurried errand and was more serviceable than an overcoat for the men. Its familiar use continued well into the nineteenth century, as did the wearing of the blue bonnet.

Never was the Kirk's rule to be so absolute as it was at this time. It had an eye and an ear for the doings of the meanest mortal within its parishes, and while it continued to assume a somewhat tyrannous posture until the late eighteenth century, by carrying much of the weight of local government and education and by concerning itself directly with the civil actions of the people, it never asserted itself so forcefully as it did in the seventeenth century. Long sermons, which made great demands on the congregation, were given two or three days a week, at least in the burghs, as were morning and evening prayers, and the head of each family was expected to conduct daily worship within his household. Every effort was made to enforce church attendance, and some of the obvious measures were to prohibit all possible counterattractions and to demand an explanation for nonattendance, tasks which proved to be difficult and unending.

Life was earthy in Scotland, and the Kirk was considered almost a domestic place. Toddlers were likely to wander about and make much noise, and the "barking and perturbation" of dogs, "ane thing that is not comelie to be seen in the house of God," often interrupted the services.[2] Kirk beadles were instructed to carry sticks "not onlie for waking those that sleips in the kirk but also to walk to and from, from corner to corner . . . for removing of bairns and boys out of the kirks, who troubles the samyn by making of din in tyme of divyne service."[3]

There is no doubt that conditions of life in Scotland put a premium on physical hardihood, and it is not surprising that in such circumstances excessive comfort or extravagance might be regarded as a snare of the devil. It was, however, asceticism rather than puritanism which came naturally to the Scots. If one compares the ideas and the legislation of the Puritan regime in England with those of the Scottish Presbyterians, one cannot but notice that the preoccupations of the Kirk were different. Certainly, some Puritan goals were shared, particularly with respect to sexual morality; but even in the matter of enforcing the Sabbath, the Scots were on the whole much less persistent outside the "time of sermon." Of overwhelming importance to the Kirk was the firm establishment of its autonomy and its doctrines, and the elimination of the customs and practices associated with the Church of Rome. Thus, as in England, instrumental music was banned from worship, as were the celebrations of Christmas, or bringing in the May. "Superfluous banqueting," particularly at weddings, offended the ascetic predilections of the Kirk, and efforts were made to restrict this. But seldom do we find an edict prohibiting song or dance *per se*, and this fact is of primary

[2] Records of the Kirk Session and Presbytery of Aberdeen, ca. 1656.
[3] Glasgow Town Council Minutes, 1662, p. 190.

interest to us. Why, if this is so, do so many writers tacitly assume that the recreational arts of dance and song were suppressed and driven underground during the seventeenth century? The assumption arises from a misinterpretation of measures which were taken to enforce church attendance (as was the practice in England) and to eradicate what the Roman Church had regarded as pagan practices and what the Reformers regarded as also papistical practices.

The records testify to the difficulty of achieving these ends. The Yule festivities survived all attacks, and the attitude of the population in general was expressed by the Aberdeen servant girl who was punished in 1652 for saying that when the Reverend Andrew Cant spoke against Yule "he spak like an auld fuil." In this same burgh, a number of women were charged in 1656 for "playing, dansin, and singin off fylthe carrolles on Yeull day, at evin, and on Sonday, at evin, thairefter" and some others were accused of dancing in men's clothing "under silence of nycht, in houss and throcht the toun. . . ."[4]

One of the objections to the Puritan Sunday in England was that it led to "filthy tipplings and drunkenness,"[5] and it comes as a surprise to notice in Scotland the occasional delinquent discovered in an alehouse or tavern "in time of sermon" on a Sunday. Apparently the alehouse conducted business on Sundays. One is surprised, too, that in view of the temper of the times there could have been any occasion for the following ordinance written in the Kirkcaldy Burgh Records: "That na personis passtyme or dans, or reill with dansing and pyping thru the town on Sunday, the tyme of preching or prayers, under the paine of double unlaw; and that nane be fund on the street at sick passtymes after ten hours at evin under the same paine."

The subject of recreation in seventeenth-century Scotland deserves our closer attention. One of the best pictures of rural celebrations is presented by Robert Sempill of Beltrees, Renfrewshire (1595–1668), in "The Elegy of Habbie Simpson Piper of Kilbarchan." This poem, incidentally, is the earliest in that stanza which is uniquely suited to the Scots idiom and was a favourite of Robert Fergusson and Robert Burns:

HABBIE SIMPSON

KILBARCHAN now may say alas!
For she hath lost her game and grace,
Both *Trixie* and *The Maiden Trace*;
  But what remead?
For no man can supply his place
  Hab Simson's dead.

Now who shall play *The Day it Daws*,
Or *Hunts up when the Cock he craws*?
Or who can for our kirk-town cause
  Stand us in stead?
On bagpipes now nobody blaws
  Sin' Habbie's dead.

Or who will cause our shearers shear?
Wha will bend up the brags o'weir,
Bring in the bells, or good play-meir
  In time of need?
Hab Simson could, what needs you speir,
  But now he's dead.

So kindly to his neighbours neist
At Beltane and Saint Barchan's feast
He blew, and then held up his breast,
  As he were weid;
But now we need not him arrest,
  For Habbie's dead.

---

[4] Records of the Kirk Session of Aberdeen (1652), quoted in Gavin Turreff, *Antiquarian Gleanings from Aberdeenshire Records*, p. 176.

[5] James VI, *The Book of Sports*, 1617.

At fairs he play'd before the spear-men,
All gaily graithèd in their gear, man:
Steel bonnets, jacks, and swords so clear
    then
Like only bead:
Now wha will play before such weir-men
    Sin' Habbie's dead?

At clerk-plays, when he wont to come,
His pipe played trimly to the drum;
Like bykes of bees he gart it bum,
    And tun'd his reed:
Now all our pipers may sing dumb,
    Sin' Habbie's dead.

And at horse races many a day,
Before the black, the brown, the grey,
He gart his pipe, when he did play,
    Baith skirl and skreed:
Now all such pastime's quite away
    Sin' Habbie's dead.

He counted was a waled wight-man,
And fiercely at football he ran;
At every game the gree he wan
    For pith and speed;
The like of Habbie was na than,
    But now he's dead.

And then, besides his valiant acts,
At bridals he wan many placks;
He bobbit ay behind folk's backs
    And shook his head:
Now we want many merry cracks,
    Sin' Habbie's dead.

He was a convoyer of the bride,
With Kittock hinging at his side;
About the kirk he thought a pride
    The ring to lead:
But now we may gae but a guide,
    For Habbie's dead.

So well's he keepit his decorum,
And all the stots of *Whip-meg-morum*;
He slew a man, and wae's me for him,
    And bore the feid;
But yet the man wan hame before him,
    And was not dead.

And when he play'd, the lasses leugh
To see him teethless, auld, and teugh:
He wan his pipes besides Barcleugh,
    Withouten dread;
Which after wan him gear eneugh;
    But now he's dead.

Ay when he play'd the gaislings gethered,
And when he spake the carl blethered;
On Sabbath days his cap was feathered,
    A seemly weid;
In the kirkyard his mare stood tethered,
    Where he lies dead.

Alas! for him my heart is sair,
For of his springs I gat a skair,
At every play, race, feast, or fair,
    But guile or greed;
We need not look for piping mair,
    Sin' Habbie's dead.

If the authorship of this poem is correctly attributed, then we must note that "game and grace" and the bells and hobby horse (*good play-meir*) as well as certain feast days, survived at Kilbarchan longer than they did in most other towns. The dance Trixie is doubtless a ring dance performed to the ballad chorus "Hey trix trim go trix," and The Maiden Trace is clearly a harvest processional dance.

The most important occasions for dancing and merrymaking which persisted throughout these times were weddings, harvest celebrations, and, of course, annual fairs. The penny weddings were very popular. Often these were attended by many people, as many as two hundred being not uncommon, who thought nothing of travelling great distances to attend. Each person was expected to contribute. Universal enjoyment on these occasions was a little conspicuous, too conspicuous to avoid the disapproving frowns of the Kirk. It is difficult to say when the custom began or, in fact, if weddings were ever otherwise, but the Kirk began to interfere with them soon after the Reformation.

In 1574 one Niel Laing was accused by the Kirk Session of Edinburgh of "making a pompous convoy and superfluous banqueting" at the marriage of Margaret Danielston "to the great slander of the Kirk."[6] The objection to "superfluous banqueting" at wedding feasts was founded on economic as well as moral grounds, and what was proscribed by the Kirk today was frequently proscribed by the civil authorities tomorrow. Parliament first passed an act limiting the expense of marriages and banquets in 1581 and similar enactments were made in the following century in 1621 and 1681.[7] Although many local Kirk sessions and regional presbyteries made independent efforts to control the more licentious habits of their parishioners, it was not until 1645 that the General Assembly of the Kirk saw fit to ordain the presbyteries to put the penny bridals under the severest restrictions.[8]

The general complaint was of "disorders that falls out at penny bridals." Andrew Edgar in *Old Church Life in Scotland* tells us that at Galston, Ayrshire, in 1635, there was disapproval of "the great multitudes of persons callit to brydells [which] *dearthis the contrie*, and taks men frae their labor." There is little said about excessive drinking, although occasionally, as at Rothesay, Bute, in 1658, there was to be no "sitting up to drink after ten o'clock at night."

The poor pipers, and to a less noticeable extent, other "minstrels," were an obvious target, and many Kirk sessions made efforts to prohibit them from bridals, thinking them the source of much "profanity and lasciviousness." Perhaps it was hoped by this measure to restrict the dancing, but what about the "loose speeches and singing of bawdy songs"? Faced with this problem, the next move was to limit the numbers attending. The most favoured limit appears to have been about forty, that is, not "above twenty persons on both sides"; but some presbyteries felt more comfortable with half that number. The presbyteries of Haddington and Dunbar declared, in 1647, that the paying of extravagant sums (one shilling Scots or eightpence sterling) caused "great immoralities — piping and dancing before and after dinner or supper," drinking after dinner and so forth. "Moreover, loose speeches, singing of licentious songs, and profane minstrelling in time of dinner or supper, tends to great deboshry . . . through all which causes, penny bridals in our judgment become seminaries of all profanation." They therefore ordained that not above twenty persons should ever gather on such occasions, and that all piping, dancing, singing, and loose speeches should cease.[9]

This was more or less the pattern of Kirk enactments at this time from Kilmarnock to Aberdeen, even in areas favourable to episcopacy.

In the case of musicians, the penalty for infringement was penance at Kirk, and in the case of the bridal party, forfeiture of the "consignation," (a deposit of a certain amount of money which varied according to the parish) in guarantee of serious intent and satisfactory conduct.

Baptisms, and lykewakes or burials, were also causes of "superfluous banqueting," and the various local restrictions found consummation in an act of Parliament in 1681 which endeavoured to limit attendance on these occasions.

[6] Quoted in Robert Chambers, *Domestic Annals of Scotland*, 2nd ed., vol. 1, p. 337.
[7] John Mackintosh, *History of Civilization in Scotland*, vol. 3, p. 280.
[8] Alexander Peterkin, *Records of the Kirk of Scotland*, p. 427.
[9] Chambers, *Domestic Annals*, 2nd ed., vol. 2, p. 162.

Marriages were restricted to the immediate family and no more than "four friends on either side, with their ordinary domestic servants."[10] The concern here, however, was economic rather than moral. Depending upon the region, the prohibitions had some effect, and it is sombre to read of a wedding with no musician, albeit with several lords and eight ministers, such as the wedding of James Somerville of Drum and Cambusnethan at Lesmahagow Kirk. That it was not to the bridegroom's liking we can gather from his own words: "At so solemn an occasion, which, if it be lawful at all to have them [musicians], certainly it ought and should be on a wedding day, for divertisement to the guests, that innocent recreation of music and dancing being more warrantable and far better exercise than drinking and smoking of tobacco, wherein these holy brethren of the presbyterian [persuasion] for the most part employed themselves, without any formal health or remembrance of their friends; a nod with their head, or a sigh, with the turning up of the white of the eye, served for that ceremony."[11]

Weddings, however, could not be stopped, and an observer remarked in 1665 that a good harvest was the cause "that a number of fee'd servants, both men and women, did marry at Martinimas by way of penny-bridals, both within the town of Edinburgh and other parts of the country." So was it to be on every good season, and many irregularities were thereby corrected. The penny wedding survived until economic conditions improved, but late in the next century, a stigma originating from snobbery fell upon them.

Where, it may be asked, were these bridal festivities held? Certainly not in the church, and there were no village halls. Many were held in alehouses or hostelries, and indeed, in some parts of the country, as in Inverurie and the Garioch, the lairds bound their tenants to hold all their marriages at an alehouse because this was the outlet for their bear (barley) crops in malt. The food was supplied free, but the consumption of ale probably more than compensated for this, especially when the festivities were prolonged. Otherwise, they were held in the green or the street if the weather permitted.[12] At Stirling in the sixteenth century, it appears to have been customary for the company at a wedding to resort to the market cross to dance and make merry.[13] The character of this merrymaking may be judged, perhaps, from an entry in the Kirk Session Records of Kilmarnock in the next century, on July 29, 1658, referring, however, to another class of public occasion: "There being a number of vaine wantoune lasses summondit for the lasciviouse and scandalous carriadge, in promiscuouse dancing with men, in mutual kissing and giveing ribbens as favours to the men, upon Whitsunday, in the town of Irvine, in the tyme of preaching . . . the forsaids women,

---

10 *Acts Parl. Scot.*, vol. 8, p. 350; Aberdeen Burgh Records, vols. 3 and 4. Also of Glasgow, cited in John Mackintosh, *History of Civilization in Scotland*, vol. 3, p. 281. This act applied also to baptisms and burials. The economic motives are revealed by the injunction "that neither bridegroom nor bride, nor their parents or relations, shall make above two changes of raiment at that time or upon that occasion."

11 *Memorie of the Somervilles*, quoted in Chambers, *Domestic Annals*, 2nd ed., vol. 2, p. 208. In September 1649, the Kirk session at Cambusnethan ordained that there should be no piping at bridals on penalty of forfeit of deposit and further punishment. [Chambers, *Domestic Annals*, 2nd ed., vol. 1, p. 338.]

12 The Glasgow Kirk Session enacted, on January 7, 1604, that "at Banquets, there should be no dancing openly on the street, playing on bagpipes, beating drums, or losing the Consignation Money."

13 At Stirling, October 30, 1600, the Kirk Session noted, "there has been great dancing and vanity publicly at the Cross usit by married persons and their company on their marriage-day." [Chambers, *Domestic Annals*, 2nd ed., vol. 1, p. 337.]

together with the piper, confessed, and were ordered to confess their sin from the public place before the congregation."[14]

Here we are faced with the celebration of a forbidden festival entrenched by long-established custom, but to celebrate "in the tyme of preaching" — this was too much! It is to another poem that we turn to illustrate the character of seventeenth-century bridal celebrations, a poem ascribed to Francis Sempill, son of the writer of "Habbie":

THE BLYTHESOME BRIDAL

Fy let us a' to the bridal,
  For there will be lilting there;
For Jockie 's to be married to Maggie,
  The lass wi' the gowden hair.
And there will be lang-kail and pottage,
  And bannocks of barley meal;
And there'll be good saut herring
  To relish a cog of good ale.

And there will be Sawney the souter,
  And Will wi' the meikle mou';
And there will be Tam the blutter,
  With Andrew the tinkler, I trow;
And there will be bow-leggèd Robbie,
  With thumbless Katie's goodman;
And there will be blue-cheekèd Dowbie,
  And Lawrie the laird of the land.

. . . .

And there will be Girn-again-Gibbie,
  With his glaikit wife Jenny Bell,
And misle-shinn'd Mungo Macapie,
  The lad that was skipper himsel.
There lads and lasses in pearlings
  Will feast in the heart of the ha',
On sybows, and rifarts, and carlings,
  That are baith sodden and raw.

And there will be fadges and brachan,
  With fowth of good gabbocks of skate,
Powsowdy, and drammock, and crowdy,
  And caller nowt-feet in a plate:
And there will be partans and buckies,
  And whitens and speldings enew,
With singèd sheep-heads and a haggis,
  And scadlips to sup till ye spew.

And there will be lapper'd-milk kebbucks,
  And sowens and farls and baps,
With swats and weel-scrapèd paunches,
  And brandy in stoups and in caps:
And there will be meal-kail and castocks,
  With skink to sup till ye rive,
And roasts to roast on a brander
  of flowks that were taken alive.

Scrapt haddocks, wilks, dulse and tangle,
  And a mill of good snishing to prie;
When weary with eating and drinking,
  We'll rise up and dance till we die.

[As published by Allan Ramsay, 1724]

The same poet has been credited with the vigorous song "Maggie Lauder" which interests us because it tells of a piper and his chance meeting with a merry dancer:

Then to his bags he flew wi'speed,
  About the drone he twisted;
Meg up and wallop'd o'er the green,
  For brawly could she frisk it.
Weel done, quoth he, play up, quoth she,
  Weel bob'd, quoth Rob the Ranter,
'Tis worth my while to play indeed,
  When I hae sic a dancer.

A number of anonymous lyrics from the seventeenth and eighteenth centuries add considerably to our knowledge of the habits and outlook of these times. Some of them

[14] Quoted in Andrew Edgar, *Old Church Life in Scotland*, p. 152.

are "The Wowing of Jok and Jynny," "Muirland Willie," "My Jo Janet," "Tak yer auld cloak about ye," and "The Barrin' o the Door." Most of these, and others, are included in Allan Ramsay's *Tea-Table Miscellany* (1724-32) or David Herd's *Scottish Songs* (1776). This form of literature, balladeering, versifying, and story-telling that belonged to the folk tradition, actually thrived during these troubled years; years which, as we can understand from the disturbed condition of society, were not conducive to the blossoming of formal imaginative literature, despite Drummond's admirable sonnets and Sir Thomas Urquhart's extravagant flights of prose. But among the hundreds of vagrants who trecked over moors and highways were many who carried the tales of their forebears and sang their songs. The travellers were by no means of genteel society, and their sentiments were hardly refined, but they were the unsuspecting transmitters of Scotland's treasures of rhyme, song, and music.

Most of the arresting events of the time, and there were many, found their way into ballad lore, and the classic verses of "Sir Patrick Spens" and "The Bonny Earl o' Moray" must then have been on innumerable lips.

Harvest customs are as varied as those of weddings, and fascinating as they are, we must restrict ourselves to those which involve dance. There is little direct evidence of harvest dancing in the seventeenth century. Too often, perhaps, there was nothing to dance about, but we can be sure that customs prevailing in the eighteenth century were certain to have been observed in the preceding one and even earlier. Many writers have been misled by a discussion of a harvest ring dance in Leyden's introduction to his edition of the *Complaynt* and thereby relate it to the shepherd's dance in that work. It is an unfortunate association of ideas. Leyden had seen a dance of reapers in which they danced in a ring after thrice shouting and thrice tossing their hooks into the air, a ceremony which survived over a century later to celebrate the binding of the last sheaf. Various customs are associated with it and it is steeped in the lore of antiquity. The sheaf, or last handful of corn reaped in the field, was often made up in the image of a human figure or doll, or under Christian influence, a cross. This image was commonly called the maiden, and was believed to be the habitation of the Corn Spirit. Plaited and adorned with ribbons, it was placed in the hands of one of the prettiest girls present. Then both were brought home in triumph to the music of fiddles or bagpipes, to inaugurate the harvest feast, often called kirn feast, maiden feast, or simply kirn. The "maiden" was prominently displayed and, after the feast and dancing which followed, it was hung up in some conspicuous place in the farmhouse.[15]

> The harvest treasures all
> Now gather'd in, beyond the rage of storms,
> Sure to the swain; the circling fence shut up;
> And instant Winter's utmost rage defied,
> While, loose to festive joy, the country round
> Laughs with the loud sincerity of mirth,
> Shook to the wind their cares. The toil-strung youth,
> By the quick sense of magic taught along,
> Leaps wildly graceful in the lively dance.
>
> [James Thomson, "The Seasons"][16]

[15] See F. Marian MacNeill, *The Silver Bough*, vol. 2.
[16] Thomson, born in 1725, was a native of Roxburghshire.

Just as I have found no evidence of church censure of dancing at kirn feasts, so have I found none of like merrymaking at annual fairs. Certainly the old celebrations of saints days were proscribed, but local fairs were of long standing as an economic necessity, even if they were normally associated with holy days, and have survived in many cases into modern times. Some evidence does show widespread concern, particularly in the Lowlands, with the licence associated with social occasions, but it by no means proves a widespread suppression of dancing. Various Kirk sessions developed their own attitudes to dancing and amusements generally, as we have seen in the case of penny weddings, but not until 1649 did the General Assembly act in the matter of dancing, and on this occasion it referred the censure of "promiscuous dancing" to the "care and diligence" of the individual presbyteries.[17] Here again, there is qualification: promiscuous dancing was the name given to mixed dancing, the implication being that dancing among men alone or women alone was acceptable. There are many instances of sets of men dancing, such as the country-dance hornpipe in England, and of course Scotch reels are often danced by men alone, even today.

Of course in the early years of the following century, there must have been many devout pillars of the Kirk who felt as Patrick Walker did when he earnestly wondered how anyone who had ever known what it was to bend a knee in prayer "durst crook a hough to fyke and fling at a piper's and fiddler's springs. I bless the Lord," he continues, "that so ordered my lot in my dancing days, that made the fear of the bloody rope and bullets to my neck and head, the pain of boots, thumbikens, and irons . . . to stop the lightness of my head and the wantonness of my feet."[18] Such men were tormented by feelings of guilt and a sense of perpetual sinfulness in everything human, even in walking in the fields before or after service on the Sunday.

This illustrates an extreme, if not uncommon, attitude and one that simply could not have been the dominant one. As regards promiscuous dancing, there was no more reason to doubt its sexual innocence than to doubt that of any concourse of young men and women. But, of course, there was a desire to avoid the incitement to license which the lusty-minded citizens of the period felt was implicit in the intermingling of the sexes in dancing schools. Promiscuous dancing was in disfavour even in England at this time. In judging of this, however, we must bear in mind that kissing found a conspicuous place in social dancing at this period. Partners customarily kissed before and after each dance, and there was also the kissing dance, Babbity Bowster, which was very popular in the countryside.

The magistrates of Lanark were apparently among those who took a stern view of promiscuous dancing — we cannot judge on what provocation — as the following pronouncement suggests: "The baillies and counsell takin into consideratioun the sin befoir God, and the abusis that has been formerlie and of lait comitit, within this burgh, by peoples intertaining of pyperis in promiscuis danceing, men and women together, not onlie the day tyme bot in the night; for remeid whairof; . . . ordeanes that no persone within this burgh suffer any pyper to play at thair houssis or yairds in tyme coming. . . ."[19]

17 Peterkin, *Records of the Kirk of Scotland.*
18 Quoted in Chambers, *Domestic Annals,* 2nd ed., vol. 3, p. 482.
19 R. Renwick, ed., *Extracts from the Records of the Royal Burgh of Lanark,* Scottish Burgh Records Society, Glasgow, 1893.

In view of this hardening of attitude, Satan's effrontery was all the greater when he met with John Douglas and eight women in 1659 on merry occasions when Douglas was piper to their dancing. His Satanic Majesty had two favourite airs which cannot now be identified: "Kilt thy coat, Maggie, / And come thy way with me" and "Hulie the bed will fa' " (*Spottiswoode Miscellany*, vol. 2, p. 68).

There can be no doubt that the populace as a whole did not miss an opportunity to drown their cares. One can well imagine how they seized upon the occasional days of national rejoicing. There was James VI's accession to the English throne and his subsequent solitary visit to his "ain countrie"; and the coronation of Charles I and later of Charles II at Scone. There was another visit by Charles I to Edinburgh, of three months' duration, and there was the restoration of Charles II. All these events, as well as royal birthdays, the naval victory over the Dutch, etcetera, gave occasion for official rejoicing during the dark years.

It is enlightening to read of the banquet given King Charles I and the English nobility on the occasion of his visit to Edinburgh in June, 1633. Spalding tells us that "after dinner, the provost, baillies, and councillors, ilk ane in others' hands, with bare heads, cam dancing down the High Street with all sorts of music, trumpeters, and drums."[20] It is easy to imagine what we would think of such a spectacle today.

Two weeks later, the king visited Perth, where he was received by a hundred armed men attired in white doublets and red breeches. Next day, "there was ane sword-dance dancit to his majesty the morn after his coming, upon an island made of timmer on the water of Tay, and certain verses spoken to his majesty by ane boy, representing the person of the river Tay. . . ."[21] This was the famous occasion of the performance of the Perth Glovers' dance described in chapter 2.

At the Restoration, the beautiful public fountain at Linlithgow was set flowing with "divers coloured wines of France and Spain." A symbolic representation of the Covenant as an old hag and "Rebellion" as a covenanting minister was set up in the market place. The charging of fountains with wine and the drinking of healths and breaking of glasses on such occasions were familiar practices in the Scots burghs. By 1661, some of the bizarre spirit of the Restoration in England seems to have found its way to the Scottish capital, for, in March, the *Caledonian Mercury* announced a variation on the horse racing which had recently become a weekly event on Leith sands, namely, a foot race to be run by twelve brewster wives in an advanced state of pregnancy, from Figgat Burn to the top of Arthur's Seat, for a "groaning cheese" and a "budgell" of Dunkeld whisky.[22]

The eye of authority does not seem to have rested too severely on these ploys, but what would it have done if a group of artisans had so diverted themselves? We would be wrong to conclude that these incidents were characteristic of the country as a whole, but they serve to correct an overly rigid impression of self-denial. None were more devout than the militant Covenanters, and even they were not above some innocent recreation.[23]

---

[20] John Spalding, *Memorials of the trubles in Scotland and England, A.D. 1624–1645*, quoted in Chambers, *Domestic Annals*, 2nd ed., vol. 2, p. 67.

[21] *Chronicles Perth*, quoted in Chambers, *Domestic Annals*, 2nd ed., vol. 2, p. 67.

[22] Chambers, *Domestic Annals*, 2nd ed., vol. 2, p. 273.

[23] James Barr, *The Scottish Covenanters* (Glasgow, 1947), p. 248.

Scotland, in the mid-seventeenth century, continued to be exposed to European influence. The gentry of the northeast, in Breadalbane and Strathspey, had enjoyed several generations of European-inspired civility. Their houses were finely furnished with tapestries and velvet cushions, and their cellars were stocked with French and Spanish wines.[24] Many of the gentry, notably the powerful Huntly-Gordons, had close family ties with France, and their sons were sent there to finish their education. The Erskines, Henry and Alexander, sons of the Earl of Mar, went to Paris to acquire a knowledge of polite usage — riding, sword play, and dancing — and from Saumur their tutor wrote: "Your lordships sonnis had spend ane yeir in dansing, eight munths in fensing, that Allexander dansis very properlie, he playis prettelie weil upon the lutt. . . . As for tennis, I did bargane with ane maister to lerne them so that they have also exercisit that pastym all this winter. . . ."[25] There was such a community of Scots in Bourges that Henry Erskine pointed out in 1617 that "if we had stayed still in Bruges we could not have learnit the Frence, in respek, of the great number of Scotsmen, that is there for the present, for we met every day together at our exercise, so that it was impossible for us not to speak Scotis."[26] There were not only Scottish students in France at that time, but also Scottish lecturers. Wodrow observed that, "most of the professors, in the academies at Samure, Montalban, Sedan and Lescar, were Scotsmen, and I recon it was so in several other Protestant academies . . . in France."[27] Scottish merchants, too, such as the noted Alexander Jaffray, burgess of Aberdeen, were encountered in Caen, Rouen, Paris, and Dieppe and, of course, in the Baltic ports.[28]

That many of the landed families and burgesses, most of whom were Episcopalian and some Catholic, of Perthshire, Aberdeenshire, the Mearns and Lothians, Moray, Sutherland, and Caithness had intimate contact with their class in France is highly significant from the point of view of the history of the dance. For, when Scottish dancing comes into clearer focus in the eighteenth century, its centre of influence is seen to lie in the very region we are discussing, and particularly in Breadalbane and Strathspey. This surely is no coincidence. Could it be, at a time when dancing was so much enjoyed in the social life of the English and French courts, and close commerce with these courts was enjoyed by the landed families of the north, that dancing was not freely practised in the recreational life of a region divorced from the more puritanical aspects of Protestantism? It would be very surprising if that were so, to say the least. Nor were even Glasgow's gentlefolks denied this recreation, as the minutes of November 21, 1662, of the Glasgow town council confirm. "In answer to a supplication given in by James Barnardon, Professor of the French tongue, dancing and fencing. After consideration had thereof, they grant to him license and libertis to hold and keep a schoole for that effect; and the lyk license is not to be grantit to any uthir persone for the space of fyve yeares. . . ."

Ten years later, in the most intense period of the covenanting troubles, two brothers

---

[24] See various inventories in Spalding Club proceedings.
[25] Collection of Mar and Kellie MSS, Supplementary Report (1930), letter dated April 21, 1618.
[26] Ibid., letter dater December 22, 1617.
[27] Robert Wodrow, *Collections upon the Lives of the Reformers and most eminent Ministers of the Church of Scotland*, vol. 2, Maitland Club, 1844, p. 27.
[28] John Barclay, ed., *Diary of Alexander Jaffray*, 2nd ed. (London, 1834), p. 44.

whom Chambers assumes to be English, Edward Fountain of Lochhill and Captain James Fountain, had their privileges, or patent, as Masters of the Revels proclaimed throughout Scotland, in virtue of which they were granted the right to license and authorize balls, masques, and plays.[29] Then in July, 1679, a month after the zealous army of persecuted Covenanters shed their blood against Monmouth and Claverhouse at Bothwell Brig, Privy Council Records reveal that the two Fountains petitioned the council against sundry dancing masters who made "public balls, dances, masks, and other entertainments in their schools, upon mercenary designs, without any licence or authority from the petitioners."[30] Thereupon the council ordered all dancing masters to desist from this practice and, in particular, prohibited "Andrew Devoe to keep any ball tomorrow, or any other time" without proper licence. Whether Devoe protested at this time is not known, but he did so two years later, saying that it was unheard of in Europe that a school ball should be regarded as an infringement of the patent of a master of revels. The council concurred and restricted the monopoly to *public* shows, balls, and lotteries. (Devoe's pupils were children of noblemen and gentlemen, and he seems to have emerged honourably from the amorous adventure revealed in 1677 by James Baynes, wright, who came before the Privy Council to petition the imprisonment of "one Monsieur Devoe, servant to the mountebank who was lately in this place" and who "hath, by sinistrous and indirect means, secured and enticed the petitioner's daughter and only child to desert her parents, and to live with him upon pretence of clandestine marriage.")[31] A few months afterwards, a bill was projected in Parliament against "oppressive monopolies" and "particularly of Mr. Fountain's gifts as Master of Revels by which he exacts so much off every bowling-green, kyle-alley, etc. through the kingdom, as falling under his gift of lotteries."[32] Apparently the Fountains stretched their powers to such an extent that Hugh Wallace, an agent for "the haill royal burghs of the kingdom," appeared before the council in the next year (1682), and accused these gentlemen of charging individuals daily "upon pretence of gaming at cards and dice and other games, or having such plays at their houses."[33] In reply to this the council requested specific evidence.

It appears that the Fountains had erected a playhouse in Edinburgh (the first of which there is notice), and were concerned with the loss of business caused by counter-attractions of any kind. No doubt it was their theatre in which the Irish theatrical company, recorded as visiting Edinburgh in 1681, performed.

In 1680, the Duke of York took up residence at Holyrood to escape the controversy concerning his right of succession to the crown which had arisen in London because of his professed Catholicism. It seems he was both popular and unpopular in Edinburgh. He and his daughter, the future Queen Anne, and their attendants held gay and brilliant court at the ancient palace which his brother, the king, had recently restored. The duke had many friends, including the Provost of Edinburgh, Sir James Dick, whose house was burned down by, it was suspected, students of the High School who had been dispersed from an antipapal demonstration on the High Street. At this

---

[29] Chambers, *Domestic Annals*, 2nd ed., vol. 2, p. 400.
[30] Ibid., p. 401.
[31] Ibid., p. 384
[32] Ibid., p. 401.
[33] Ibid.

very time, too, when tea was being introduced as a treat to Scottish ladies visiting the court, a good number of religious "phanatiques" as they were called, were hanged in the grassmarket. Three of these, of Cargill's Cameronian group, were offered reprieve, thanks to the Duke of York's intervention, if they would but utter the words "God save the King." This, unfortunately, they refused to do. Three months previously, in January, 1681, two women were hanged for the same offence along with four others who, to avoid the ignominy of the church pillory, had murdered their own children born out of wedlock. The duke, we are told, thought this punishment was entirely too severe.

His Royal Highness the duke and the princesses gave balls, plays, and masques, to the enjoyment of the nobility who attended them and to the horror of the more puritanical.[34] The duke played golf frequently on the Leith Links, an elephant was exhibited in Scotland for the first time, and an awesome comet appeared in the frosty night of the duke's first winter in Edinburgh and continued visible for a week. The devout Covenanter, Patrick Walker, wrote: "When Mr. McWard, who was then a-dying, heard of it, he desired Mr. Shields and other friends to carry him out, that he might see it. When he saw it, he blest the Lord that was now about to close his eyes, and was not to see the woeful days that were coming upon Britain and Ireland especially upon sinful Scotland."[35]

The royal party finally left Scotland by sea on May 15, 1682, and the celebrated Halley's comet appeared three months later. Lord Fountainhall reflecting on this, remarked: "I have seen a late French book, proving that comets prognosticate nothing that's fatal or dangerous, but rather prosperous things; yet, at the time it shone, the Duke of Lauderdale, that great minister of state, died." Then he expresses his own opinion that comets do not hold forth any prognostics of blood and desolation, "further than by their natural effects in infecting the air, so as to occasion sterility, pestilential diseases, and famine." There is a hint here of the growing interest in science which was to overtake the intelligentsia in Scotland within the next half century.

In the closing months of the century, the Glasgow Burgh Records of November 11, 1699, tell us that the magistrates and town council granted a licence to John Smith, dancing master, to teach dancing within the burgh subject to the following conditions: "That he shall behave himself soberly, teach at seasonable hours, keep no balls, and that he shall so order his teaching that there shall be no promiscuous dancing of young men and young women together, but that each sex shall be taught by themselves; and that one sex shall be dismissed, and be out of his house, before the other sex enter therein; and if the said John transgress in any of these, appoynts the magistrats to putt him out of this Burgh."

One encounters a similar entry in the Aberdeen Burgh Records for the very same year, which made a point of keeping the sexes separate. The directive to keep no balls seems to be at variance with the practice in Edinburgh, as evinced by the matter we have just considered. It was the practice for the burghs to employ or to license teachers of various kinds, as we have seen, and, later on, in 1728, a dancing master was contracted to teach dancing to the families of Glasgow artisans for a salary of twenty

---

[34] Ibid., p. 404.
[35] Ibid., p. 411.

pounds. Similar appointments continued to be made well into the eighteenth century.

As a bridge between this period and the next, one can do no better than mention Lady Grisel Baillie (1665–1746) who was eighteen years of age when the Duke of York returned to London from Holyrood, and who lived long into the next age, one of the most distinguished in a period of distinguished Scotswomen. Despite the deep religious convictions of her family which led to her helping her father, a Covenanter, to escape to Holland, she never at any time appears to have held any aversion to song or dance. On the contrary, her exiled father wrote to his wife to keep their many children "hearty and merry, laughing, dancing, and singing" and that if he were home he would aid them with the flute he was learning to play. Indeed, he wrote, "they ought not with right to pass a week-day without dancing; for lost estates can be recovered again...."[36]

As for Covenanters being antagonistic to secular song, Grisel wrote many lyrics in the Scots tongue including, of course, the well-known "Werena my hert licht I wad dee," so admired by Robert Burns. In easier days, Grisel Baillie's daughters became familiar figures at Edinburgh dance assemblies, and the singing of one (also Grisel, Lady Murray of Stanhope) was much admired at many a supper, not least by Allan Ramsay who inscribed to her Part Third of his *Music for the Scots Songs in the Tea-Table Miscellany* (1726).

These and like factors we must recall when we are tempted to adopt the oft-repeated view that the Kirk suppressed all dancing and song in the seventeenth century. The sedge may have withered from the lake, but the birds sang!

[36] Sarah Tytler and J. L. Watson, *The Songstresses of Scotland*, vol. 1, pp. 5–6.

6/The Century of Scotland's Most Various Life

Scotland's "most energetic, peculiar and most various life" – Edinburgh society – the public assembly – Horn Order – West Bow Assembly – Edinburgh Assembly – directresses – New Assembly – rival assemblies – Dunn's and Fortune's "Rooms" – oyster parties – Hunters' Ball – Capillaire Club – changes in dancing fashion – private parties – visitors' observations – customs – Miss Nicky Murray – George Square Assembly – spread of the public assembly – Aberdeen – Glasgow – Glasgow Gaelic Club – Northern Meeting – Duchess of Gordon – West Highlands – the dancing masters – Davie Strange – Edinburgh dancing masters – Francis Peacock – dancing school balls – Almack's – conduct of London assemblies – country dancing at London assemblies – Scotch Reel in the English assembly – birth-night balls – Caledonian balls

The eighteenth century was one of great vitality and originality everywhere, but nowhere more so than in Scotland. Now, at last, her travail done, Scotland moved into the period of her "most energetic, peculiar, and most various life."[1] It was to be Scotland's hour on the stage of mankind. Who could have guessed that this nation with a population of 1,500,000, with a revenue of about £160,000 when England's was £5,691,000, with a considerable section of the population living in the mountains and on islands remote from the arm of authority, with inferior methods of agriculture, and with few roads that could bear wheeled traffic, was soon to rank "in social, industrial and political virtues, at the very head of the British Empire"?[2]

It is no less remarkable that a nation which had so doggedly defended its independence and institutions against overwhelming forces for so long should now dissolve its own parliament and accept an incorporating union with its stronger neighbour. The long haul of cultural survival was now to begin, and doubtless it was some instinctive awareness of this that led the bellringer at St. Giles to awaken the people of Edinburgh on the fateful morning of 1707 with "Oh why should I be sad on my Wedding Day?" The impact of these events and the release of energy from preoccupation with the disputes of the previous century had a vitalizing effect on the social life of Scotland.

The personalities, philosophers, poets, scientists, engineers, preachers, and painters who rubbed shoulders in Edinburgh and Glasgow by the end of the century form a remarkable galaxy. And if there were eminent men, there were about as many women of like quality. As Henry Cockburn says, they sought no career, yet diffused an influence which may well have decided the fate of nations. The English Captain Topham wrote in 1775 that the "Scotch ladies speak French with great propriety, fluency

---

[1] This phrase was coined by Professor Masson, Edinburgh University, in the early years of this century.
[2] W. E. H. Lecky, *A History of England in the Eighteenth Century*, vol. 6, p. 44.

and with good accent, have an accurate and just knowledge of their own language, talk very grammatically and are great critics in the English tongue" (Letter xi). By the end of the century, these ladies of whom Topham wrote were of that "singular race of excellent Scotch old ladies" whom Henry Cockburn describes so eloquently in *Memorials of His Time*: "They were a delightful set, strong headed, warm hearted, and high spirited; the fire of their tempers not always latent; merry, even in solitude; very resolute; indifferent about the modes and habits of the modern world; and adhering to their own ways, so as to stand out, like primitive rocks, above ordinary society. Their prominent qualities of sense, humour, affection, and spirit, were embodied in curious exteriors; for they all dressed, and spoke, and did, exactly as they chose; their language, like their habits, entirely Scotch, but without any other vulgarity than what perfect naturalness is sometimes mistaken for" (pp. 61–62).

The spoken language of at least half the country was Gaelic. The Scots spoken in the Lowlands had lost the coordinating influence of a literature, but Henry Mackenzie tells us in *Anecdotes and Egotisms* that the upper classes, or what he called "genteel people," spoke a pure classical Scots which "had nothing of the coarseness of the vulgar patois of the lower orders." He mentions George Abercromby of Tullibody, an advocate and neighbour of his in George Square, who spoke the language "with a degree of eloquence and power of expression which I like extremely" (p. 15). Oliver Goldsmith writes in a letter of 1753: "Where will you find a language so prettily become a pretty mouth as the broad Scotch and the women here speak it in its highest purity."[3]

It was a hard-drinking age, and what would now be called stag parties were the fashion, at which the members would literally drink themselves under the table in gallant bumpers to the ladies they so coarsely neglected. Topham tells us that even the ladies at those popular suppers, which resembled the *petits soupers* of the French, would "drink more wine than an English woman could well bear," but, says he, "the climate requires it" (Letter ix, 1774). Port, sherry, and claret were the favourites at dinner and these had to be called for, "audibly naming the intended recipients who then acknowledged their fellowship by looking directly at each in turn and uttering the words 'Your good health,' accompanied by a respectful inclination of the head, a gentle attraction of the right hand towards the heart, and a gratified smile."[4]

In the country, and in the Highlands especially, whisky was by that time a staple drink. Elizabeth Grant tells us in *Memoirs of a Highland Lady* that even "decent gentlewomen" began the day with a dram. The bottle of whisky accompanied by a silver salver full of small glasses was placed on the side-table with cold meat every morning. There was a bottle in the pantry, with bread and cheese, for such callers as had business there, and even the poorest cottagers could offer it. Yet, she says, "except at a merry-making we never saw anyone tipsy" (p. 135).

The distinguished men of letters who comprised the Edinburgh literati were commended by Henry Mackenzie for "the free and cordial communication of sentiments, the natural play of fancy and good humour . . . very different from that display of learning — that prize-fighting of wit, which distinguished a literary circle of our sister country. The literary circle of London was a sort of sect, a caste separate from the

---

[3] Oliver Goldsmith, *Letters*.
[4] Henry Cockburn, *Memorials of His Time*, p. 42.

ordinary professions and habits of common life."[5] This opinion was well supported by Topham, whose letters provide many valuable observations on Edinburgh society:

A man who visits this country after having been in France will find in a thousand instances the resemblance which there is betwixt these two nations. That air of mirth and vivacity, that quick and penetrating look, that spirit of gaiety which distinguishes the French is equally visible in the Scotch. It is the character of the nation and it is a very happy one as it makes them disregard even their poverty. Where there is any material difference I believe it may be attributed to the difference of their religion. . . . Whenever the Scotch of both sexes meet, they do not appear as if they had never seen each other before or wished never to see each other again. They do not sit in solemn silence looking on the ground, biting their nails and at a loss what to do with themselves; and if someone should be hardy enough to break silence start as if they were shot through the ear with a pistol, but they address each other at first sight, an impressment that is highly pleasing. They appear to be satisfied with one another or at least if they really are not so, they have the prudence to conceal their dislike. To see them in perfection is to see them at their entertainments. . . . When the restraints of ceremony are vanished and you see people really as they are: And I must say in honour of the Scotch that I never met with a more agreeable people with more pleasing or more insinuating manners in my life. . . . Instead of that rudeness and uncouth mind that shyness and barbarism which is even cultivated by our peasants and which before I so much complained of, you find in the lowest kind in Scotland a compliant obsequiousness and softness of temper, an ambition to oblige and a sociability which charms you. . . . Even in Edinburgh the same spirit runs through the common people who are infinitely more civil, humanized and hospitable than any I ever met. Every one is ready to serve and assist a stranger. They show the greatest respect to a person superior to them and you never receive an impertinent answer, but after all this I wish I could say they were more happy. Not withstanding these many excellencies, I find lying, treachery, dissimulation, envy, detraction and vice have their respective significations. [Letter ix]

Topham remarks that the dress and taste of the upper classes in Edinburgh conformed more to those of Paris, a city with which these classes had as "constant a communication as with England." His esteem for the Scots ladies is a recurrent theme in his letters.

In many ways the late eighteenth century was a period of such contrasts that it is impossible to generalize with confidence. At the oyster parties which came into vogue, the conversation in mixed company could become very frank. How much the habit of swearing was given rein on these occasions is difficult to know, but in male society it was commonplace. Cockburn tells us that no admonition or indignation was considered seriously unless it was "clothed in execration," and the celebrated Lord Braxfield apologized to a lady whom he had damned at whist for bad play, explaining that he had mistaken her for his wife.

With so much variety, genius, and imagination abounding, it is easy to overlook the notorious and seamy side of Edinburgh life. Even the criminals, such as Burke, Hare, and Deacon Brody, cast up their quota of the bizarre. The poverty and insanitary state of the old town is easily overlooked in the face of such zest for life and knowledge.

---

[5] Henry Mackenzie, *An Account of the Life and Writings of John Home Esq.* (Edinburgh, 1822), pp. 22–23.

The people as a whole remained devoutly religious, albeit some of the conceptions of piety differed from those of former and later times. Sunday was now well established as the Sabbath, and a week of devotions always terminated the winter social season. The "Auld Lichts" and the "New Lichts," the Orthodox and the Moderates, engaged each other in interminable disputations, while the English Non-Conformists began to invade as the Industrial Revolution entered its most sordid phase, and the commercial pulse of the nation moved from Edinburgh to Glasgow.

No doubt English visitors to Scotland expected something very different from what they encountered, and nothing illustrates the prevailing contrast of pride and poverty more than Edward Burt's story in *Letters from a Gentleman* of visiting a laird and encountering a "parcel of dirty children, half-naked," whom he took to belong to some poor tenant and was surprised to find them part of the family. Yet the young laird, age fourteen, was attending university, and the eldest daughter of sixteen years "sat at table clean and genteely dressed" (Letter xxii). When Goldsmith moved to Holland in 1754, after studying medicine in Edinburgh, he remarked on one occasion that in Scotland "you might see a well dressed Duchess issuing from a dirty close and here a dirty Dutch man inhabiting a palace. The Scotch may be compared with a tulip planted in dung but I never see a Dutch man in his own house, but I think of a magnificent Egyptian temple dedicated to an ox."[6]

Although a good proportion of the transient population in the Lowland burghs was of Highland stock, more and more moved in permanently on account of overcrowding of the glens and the appalling and inhumanly disruptive policies of both government and land superior. Important movements of population now began which in time were to denude the Highlands and Islands of their ancient people to found communities and nations overseas and supply the labour demanded by the growing industrial complex. The displaced Gaels organized the first of their clubs or societies in the cities at the end of the eighteenth century. Those who were furthest away organized their clubs first, and London has this honour (1778), then Glasgow (1780) At these clubs the exiled Gaels could speak their native language and share with others the music and verse of their ancestors.

The Act of Union of the parliaments of England and Scotland in 1707 may have been a mixed blessing, and although it may not have been the best kind of union, nor well conceived, it did relieve Scotland of many burdens and free her from the possibility of physical strife with her ancient enemy. There were riots and one important constitutional rebellion; but the exigencies of growing commerce, industry, and education absorbed the national energy. Nevertheless, before the age of steam had truly dawned, there was time and need to garner the harvest of the song and story of Scotland and every opportunity and incentive for genteel society to flourish and emulate their counterparts in the other distinguished capitals of Europe.

THE PUBLIC ASSEMBLY

In the year 1703, Queen Anne went to Bath to take the waters and thereby attracted the attention of the beau monde to the possibilities of this pleasant old Roman town

---

[6] Goldsmith, *Letters*. Letter to Reverend Thomas Contarine, 1754.

as an agreeable resort for the idle rich. If this were not evident to all, it certainly was to one celebrated man of fashion, Beau Nash, who proceeded to establish a dance assembly there. From its opening in 1705, it was a very exclusive and formal assembly with strict regulations. The proceedings began in the evening at six o'clock with Nash himself leading the first Minuet, and continued to eleven o'clock, with an interval for tea and conversation at nine. The first two hours were devoted to Minuets, and the remainder of the evening was taken up by Country Dances. Then, precisely on the stroke of eleven, Nash would imperiously hold up his finger and the musicians would stop. This was not the first regular dance assembly in England, but it certainly became the most illustrious, with no serious competitor among the fashionable, not even Tunbridge Wells, until Almack's was founded some fifty years later. It was at Bath that many of the procedures adopted in the conduct of "polite" or select dance assemblies were initiated.

In England, the coffeehouse and the club were already established institutions some time before the Union. Coffeehouses were introduced to Edinburgh, but they did not thrive in the manner of their English counterparts. The first fashionable club to be constituted in Edinburgh seems to have been one founded in 1705 by a notable beau, John, the third Earl of Selkirk, known as the Horn Order. The name arose from the club's adopting a horn spoon as its insignia. The meetings were conducted very privately and, it is said, featured masquerades as well as formal dancing. "Promiscuous" dancing was sufficiently suspect by the puritan section of the population without promiscuous dancing in disguise which was associated with moral licence of a serious sort and which was actually prohibited in France — at least for a time — in the sixteenth century. The desire of the club's members to avoid publicity was understandable, but the secrecy probably increased the sinister apprehensions of the douce inhabitants of the burgh.

The first rays of the "enlightenment" were showing, however, and it was not long before Scotland's first public assembly was organized in Edinburgh, to be followed at intervals by others, as the century progressed. Public halls and house parties which included dancing in the jollifications became familiar events in the principal burghs until, by the 1770s, it was possible for Topham to say that, "I do not know any place in the world where dancing is made so necessary a part of polite education as in Edinburgh" (Letter xli).

Now the traditional dance forms of the central and northeast Highlands moved into the genteel Lowland assemblies and thence into the ballrooms of England and Europe. Marie Antoinette delighted in dancing *Écossaises* (that is, "Scottish fashion") with the young Lord Strathaven (later the ninth Marquis of Huntly), who visited France after 1783, and who by his agreeable personality and admirable skill in dancing became a favourite at the court of Louis XVI.[7]

Whether the club known as the Horn Order formed the foundation of the private assembly which John Maitland tells us in his *History of Edinburgh* was founded in

---

[7] Lord Strathaven was doubtless the original "Gay Gordon," although his famous ancestor, the second Marquis of Huntly, "Monsieur le Marquis de Gordon," cut a similar figure some one hundred and fifty years before. In the correspondence of Mirabeau with the Comte de La Marck we read: "On y parlait avec malignite de ce que la reine aimait a danser des ecossaises avec un jeune lord Strathavon aux petits bals chez Mme d'Ossum."

1710, or whether they were one and the same, is not clearly established. Contemporary newspapers did not remark on the beginning of any assembly in 1710, but since Maitland was then seventeen years of age, one must respect his statement. This assembly, called the West Bow Assembly, was conducted in an old mansion of the Somerville family "at the first angle of the Bow, on the west side of the street," later the site of St. John's Free Church. Chambers, quoting from Jackson's *History of the Stage*, tells us that on one occasion the company at the assembly rooms was assaulted by an infuriated rabble and that the door of their hall was perforated with red-hot spits.[8]

The steep curve of the West Bow with its castellated and garreted tenements precariously projecting over the roadway in picturesque piles is no longer with us; but several engravings of the old premises exist, and both Robert Chambers and Daniel Wilson, the celebrated antiquarians of the old town, drew sketches of the old assembly rooms before their demolition.

How long the West Bow Assembly survived is very uncertain; but it certainly came to an end before 1723, for in that year a dance assembly was projected, in circumstances which would indicate that it was an entirely new venture. The new assembly was to be held in premises at the rear of Patrick Steil's Close in the High Street and not in the picturesque location of its predecessor in the West Bow. The West Bow Assembly was a private affair, whereas the assembly projected in 1723 was more public and could be attended by people of acceptable social standing on the purchase of a ticket.

Allan Ramsay moved to support the proposal of having a public assembly by publishing his poem "The Fair Assembly" in June, 1723. Some passages from his prefixed address in his *Works* (vol. 1) are of interest here:

How much is our whole nation indebted to your Ladyships for your reasonable and laudable undertaking to introduce politeness among us, by a cheerful entertainment, which is highly for the advantage of both body and mind, in all that is becoming in the brave and beautiful. . . . It is amazing to imagine that any are so destitute of good sense and manners as to drop the least unfavourable sentiment against the Fair Assembly. . . . It is to be owned, with regret, that the best of things have been abused. The church has been, and in many countries is, the chief place for assignations that are not warrantable. Wine, one of Heaven's kindly blessings, may be used to one's hurt. The beauty of the fair, which is the great preserver of harmony and society, has been the ruin of many. Learning, which assists in raising the mind of man up to the class of spirits, has given many a one's brain a wrong cast. So places, designed for healthful and mannerly dancing, have, by people of an unhappy turn, been debauched by introducing gaming, drunkenness, and indecent familiarities. But will any argue from these, that we must have no churches, no wine, no beauties, no literature, no dancing? — Forbid it Heaven! Noble and worthy ladies, whatever is under your auspicious conduct must be improving and beneficial in every respect. May all the fair daughters copy after such virtuous and delightful patterns as you have been, and continue to be! That you may long be a blessing to the rising generation, is the sincere prayer of. . . Alan Ramsay. [P. 206]

The ladies to whom Ramsay refers were the Countess of Panmure and Ladies Orbiston, Drumelzier, Newhall, and North Berwick. The proceeds of the undertaking

---

[8] Robert Chambers, *Traditions of Edinburgh*, p. 44.

of a public dance assembly were to be directed toward the principal charities, for the poor and the sick; nevertheless, some ministers took the opportunity to publish admonitions and warnings against promiscuous dancing. Edward Burt also tells us "the ministers lost ground to their great mortification; for the most part of the ladies turned rebels to their remonstrances, notwithstanding the frightful danger" (Letter i).

The outcome of the preparations may be noted from an insert in the *Caledonian Mercury*, November 4, 1723: "The Edinburgh Assembly is to begin on Thursday next, the 7th inst., in the great hall in Patrick Steil's Close and tickets are given at Mr. Robertson's, Bookseller, opposite to the Cross."

Thus began an undertaking which was to continue with varying fortunes until the last quarter of the century, patronized by all the gentry, nobility, and people of consequence who visited the capital or who enjoyed city residence in the winter months.

No description of that first night has been left us. We must imagine the ceremony and greetings of arriving belles and beaux, the matronly chaperons converging on the narrow entrance to Steil's Close, and the dank, lamp-lit stairs which led up to the assembly room. Imagine the sedan chairs and horse-drawn carriages disgorging their sanguine occupants in buckles and taffetas, contrasting in all their elegance with the damp November shadows. The grey stone on stone. The courtesies and easy familiarity of Scottish manners ringing in rich Scottish accents, and the silent, curious bystanders, noting the laird of this and Miss Betty or Jane of that, with their genteel aunts or mothers, the ladies Eglintoun, Hamilton, Douglas, Cochrane, Dalrymple, Ramsay, Home and so on. Great names in Scotland's story contrast strangely with the unsavoury, if romantic and picturesque, Edinburgh closes, vennels, and frowning gables. Who among the plaid-shrouded women and tattered bairns watching this stately concourse would give a thought to the significance of the event, or that it would ever find a place in the annals of a town so charged with history?

There is no doubt, however, that this assembly was something of an innovation to the Spartan life of Edinburgh, and that it was a source of some anxiety to the devout of the Kirk. An anonymous pamphleteer attacked the enterprise with true Calvinistic horror of that which seemed to pander too much to worldly vanity:

Sir — I'm inform'd that there is lately a Society erected in your Town, which I think is call'd an Assembly. The speculations concerning this Meeting house of late exhausted the most Part of publick conversation in this Countryside. Some are pleased to say that 'tis only designed to cultivate polite conversation, and genteel Behaviour among the better sort of folks and to give young people an opportunity of accomplishing themselves in both; while others are of opinion, that it will have a quite different effect and tend only to vitiate and deprave the minds and inclinations of the younger sort. I happen'd the other day to meet with a Gentleman who had been lately in town, and, among other things, I presum'd to enquire his thoughts of this new Assembly; he was pleas'd to tell me that the people in town were as widely different in their opinions about it as we are in the country; some approving, others disapproving of it, but that for his part, he believed it would prove a Machine of Luxury to soften and effeminate the minds of our young nobility and gentry, and that in some measure it had already this effect that they, instead of employing themselves in the useful arts and sciences that might some time render them capable to serve themselves, their friends and their country, now made it their greatest care who should be the best equipped and dressed for an Assembly Night and to strain their fancies to invent some agreeable Love Tattle to tell the Belle Creatures whom they shall happen most to admire in the Meeting.[9]

But youth was not to be denied, and a young gentlewoman wrote to her friend:

They have got an assembly at Edinburgh where every Thursday they meet and dance from four o'clock to eleven at night; it is half-a-crown the ticket, and whatever tea, coffee, chocolate, buscuit, etc. they call for, they must pay as the managers direct; and they are the Countess of Panmure, Lady Newhall, the President's Lady [Lady North Berwick], and the Lady Drummelier. The ministers are preaching against it, and say it will be another horn order; it is an assembly for dancing only. Lord Crichton gave a ball lately, where there was a vast many ladys — Peggie Bell was queen.[10]

The English Captain Burt attended the assembly at this time and was impressed by the many beautiful ladies he saw there. Indeed, nowhere had he seen such an array! He tells us that the patrons were mainly people of distinction, and that "none are admitted but such as have at least a just title to gentility, except strangers of good appearance. And if by chance others intrude they are expelled upon the spot by order of the directrice or governess."[11]

The assembly season extended from mid–November to mid–April, averaging about twenty-six meetings annually, and of the five directresses, Lady Panmure ruled supreme until her death in 1731, then Lady Orbiston took over. The function of the directress was to ensure propriety and general good conduct, and that partners were placed with appropriate precedence in the Minuets which, as at Bath and elsewhere, opened the proceedings. The sets for the Country Dances which followed were as carefully arranged. Should a lady or gentleman be without a partner, the directress made the necessary introductions and so on, and of course, the strict protocol of genteel society prevailed. (For names of the directors and directresses of the Edinburgh Assembly, see Appendix C.)

There is an excitement and vitality surrounding the Edinburgh Assembly in its early years, and the effusions of Allan Ramsay and William Hamilton of Bangour go far to perpetuate this impression and to bear out Burt's comments on the beauty of the ladies which, it may be said, was still a matter of remark at the end of the century. In the early years, most of the assembly's illustrious patrons were Episcopalian, and consequently Jacobite in sympathy and Tory in politics. However, this pattern changed after the arrival of Prince Charlie, for at this time, Edinburgh society was spiritually ready for a Scottish court. Holyrood smiled again for a time with illusory joy, and even when the Highland army passed on its way north after the abortive sally into England, the leading Jacobite ladies gave a great ball which unfortunately coincided with the arrival of news of the battle of Culloden Moor. The first account of the battle was cheerful enough, but just when the ball had reached its sanguine height, the tragic tidings fell upon Edinburgh, and hearts and lights dimmed together as the gay assemblage dispersed in sorrow.

[9] *A letter from a Gentleman in the Country to his Friend in the City, with an Answer thereto, concerning the New Assembly*, quoted in James H. Jamieson, "Social Assemblies of the Eighteenth Century," *Book of the Old Edinburgh Club*, vol. 19, 1933, p. 40.

[10] Captain E. Dunbar, *Social Life in Former Days, chiefly in the Province of Moray*, 1865. Letter from Miss Anne Stuart, January 28, 1723. She was the niece of James, eighth Earl of Moray.

[11] Edward Burt, *Letters from a Gentleman in the North of Scotland*.

Hope still fired the breast of romantic Jacobites, however, when the assembly began its first season in 1732, and life was young for Willie Hamilton. He wrote a cheerful letter to his friend Henry Home, containing one of his satirical poems, in the vein of Pope, on the subject of the patch which Lady Jean Douglas wore on her brow, and told an amusing piece of gossip which sheds some light on the atmosphere of the assembly at that time:

Listen to the Relation of a Story which happened last Assembly but one. Mr. Cockburn the famous Countrydancer went to the Assemble obstinately resolved not to dance. What a Loss that was Every man that can dance is a sufficient judge. My Lady panmuir who prisided that Night observed him in a posture in which he was never befor at the Assemble viz Sitting. She asked him if he would dance and dance with Lady Jean Douglass. Who cou'd withstand so tempting an offer? His Resolution vanished and he Wou'd dance. Here Leave we him overjoy'd. I believe no body can guess his Transports but those who have had the same occasion. Were I accidentally on the Street when Mrs. Hume comes to Town I wou'd have much such the same Sensations too. . . . Lady panmuir cary'd him to Lady Jean. This putts me in mind of Venus taking Eneas by the Hand. . . . But how Surprised Was our heroe When instead of the Lady his ardent Expectations wished for the Reverse appear'd a daughter of the Earl of March. . . . What cou'd he do. He durst not fly and durst not Encounter the Serpent. Nothing remain'd but dancing with her which he did.[12]

Apparently Lady Panmuir (Panmure) had said simply "Lady Jean," in which case Mr. Cockburn[13] naturally thought of *the* Lady Jean, namely, Lady Jean (Jane) Douglas, the toast of his youthful contemporaries.[14]

William Hamilton was susceptible, as most poets are, to beauty in any form, but, in his case, especially in womankind. It is a pity that this, an admirable sensibility after all, receives so little respect.

Henry Home, the future Lord Kames of legal renown, was the recipient of Willie's "Interview of Miss Dalrymple and Miss Suttie between the Pillars at the Edinburgh Assembly," an amusing parody of the Glaucus–Diomed exchange of armour as translated by Pope. In this parody, Willie has Miss Suttie exchange her "bard of mean and poor device" for Miss Dalrymple's "Rothiemay, a gallant dear, who weigh'd full fifteen thousand merks a year." However, he continues:

> Like leaves on trees, frail beauty's race is found,
> Now green in youth, now with'ring on the ground,
> Extoll'd in song, or toasted deep in wine.
> Awhile, like lovely Jeanie Stewart shine;
> But swift decays the perishable grace,
> And Lady Orbieston scarce knows the face.
> Another year does other toasts restore.
> And Tibby charms, when Jeanie charms no more.

[12]Nelson S. Bushnell, *William Hamilton of Bangour*, pp. 14–15.

[13] Mr. Cockburn may well have been the advocate husband of Alison Rutherford, another of Edinburgh's famous women of the eighteenth century who loved the assembly.

[14] After an early disappointment, Jane Douglas married late in life, and it was only with considerable difficulty that the son she produced when she was fifty years of age was able to establish his right to the succession of the Douglas estates over the claims of his cousin, son of the Duke of Hamilton. This dispute, called the Douglas Cause, excited a great deal of heated partisanship among all ranks of people.

Jeanie was a famous beauty in the 1730s and joined the list of "toasts" which accumulated in the writings of Willie and others of the time. Thus she finds immortality along with her contemporaries, Ladies Mary and Eliza Montgomery, Jane Hume, Maria Dalrymple, Anne Cochrane, Charlotte Hamilton, and the "Katies four of beauteous name" — Stewart, Cochrane, Hamilton, and Hall — the principal belles whose presence or renown cast an aura over the early years of the assembly and drew the admiring comments of visitors.[15]

The first phase came to an end in the 1730s. The removal of the assembly to new premises on May 25, 1736, caused a change, or perhaps the change was too late to reverse a decline which had already started. Whatever the reason, there is little evidence of regular assembly meetings during the first ten years in the assembly's new home; we hear only of the occasional charity function.

This new home for the assembly was situated on the High Street, but a few closes along from the old one, between Bell's Wynd and Stevenlaw's Close "behind the City Guard." The access to the hall now came to be known as the New Assembly Close, to distinguish it from the Old Assembly Close. It is still there today, but the old close was destroyed in the fire of 1824.

The New (or "Bell's Wynd") Assembly's hour was yet to come. In the 1740s it showed only signs of decay and dissolution. This does not mean that all dancing had ceased; there were always the Hunters and Capillaire balls and the like, but the assembly apparently had lost its social place.

In 1745, when Prince Charlie came to "enjoy his own" again, the lease of the assembly premises was due to expire, a matter which was not unnoticed by Gavin Hamilton, bookseller, who was treasurer of the infirmary, and James Stirling, the merchant, who was treasurer of the workhouse. Possibly these gentlemen had been concerned at the loss of revenue which their charities may once have enjoyed from assembly donations, or perhaps they simply saw an opportunity to reorganize the assembly to the advantage of their charities. In any case, they looked into the matter and early in 1746 approached the owner of the property with an offer to lease the hall on condition that he would "whitewash the walls of the whole house . . . paint in size and colour the whole walls . . . mend all windows and make every other repair necessary to put the house in tenentable condition."[16] The entrepreneurs were not too certain of their expectations in the matter, however, for they asked the lease of the hall for only one season. This was agreed to by the proprietor, surprisingly enough; whereupon the sponsors called on another merchant, Hugh Clark, to join them. It was

[15] Jeannie Stewart, daughter of Archibald Stewart of Torrance, Lanark, married Thomas, eighth Earl of Dundonald; was at least proposed as assembly directress in 1753 and 1773. Mary Montgomery, daughter of the ninth Earl of Eglinton and his second wife, Anne, daughter of George, Earl of Aberdeen; married Sir David Cunninghame of Milnecraig. Bart. Eliza Montgomery, half-sister of Mary and daughter of Susanna Kennedy. Anne, Susan and Catherine Cochrane, the "graces three," daughters of the Earl of Dundonald. Anne married James, fifth Duke of Hamilton, February, 1723 and died in childbirth 1724; Susan married Charles, sixth Earl of Strathmore, 1725; Catherine married Lord Garlies, sixth Earl of Galloway (his second wife) 1729. She had numerous issue and died at Bath, 1786. Charlotte Hamilton, daughter of James, third Duke of Hamilton. Catherine Stewart, daughter of the fifth Earl of Galloway, and sister of Lord Garlies. Catherine Hall, daughter of Sir James Hall of Dunglass, married the poet, Hamilton of Bangour. Catherine Hamilton married Earl of Dundonald and thus became stepmother to the youngest of the Cochrane girls.

[16] First Assembly Minute Book, no. 1, February, 1746.

essential, however, to involve some distinguished people and to form a board of directors. They therefore approached Lords Minto and Drummore and the advocates John Hamilton and John Belsches of Invermay to this end and received their support.

Lord Minto (1693–1766), formerly Sir Gilbert Elliot (second Bart.), was then Lord of Justiciary, and Lord Drummore (1690–1755), formerly Sir Hew Dalrymple, was also a judge, although another of those rough-hewn personalities that chequer the Scottish scene. He was an enthusiastic piper, retained the famous Geordie Syme as his official minstrel, and was at his death governor of the Music Society. Alexander or "Jupiter" Carlyle, as he was often known, tells us that Drummore had two sons by Kate Vint, the "handsome" and "alluring" daughter of the landlady of Lucky Vint's, a popular tavern in the west end of the town of Prestonpans. Nevertheless, he raised a family of twelve legitimate children, was a pillar of the Kirk, and spoke often at the General Assembly.

The newly formed board of directors drew up a constitution on May 20, 1746, which included these regulations:

That all dancing in the Assembly Hall and everything relating thereto shall be under the inspection and management of Ladies Directresses not exceeding seven, who shall take their turn weekly, monthly, or according as they shall agree amongst themselves, the Lady Directress upon the night of their management to wear the badge to be made for that purpose.

That all the Ladies Directresses and Directors shall enter the Assembly at all times without tickets. The Lady Directress of the night to have four tickets sent to her for her disposal.

That the profits arising from the Assembly shall be divided into three equal shares, one whereof to be given to the Ladies Directresses to be by them placed in public or private charity as they shall think fit.

The hall might be let out at the rate of two guineas a night except that during the session time it shall not be let for charity balls.

The treasurer to contract with the musicians, and that if they appear there in drink or fail in giving punctual attendance, they shall be dismissed.

[First Assembly Minute Book,
May 20, 1746]

Nothing further occurred until August, when an orchestra was contracted. This orchestra comprised four fiddles, one bassoon, and two oboes. The fiddlers were John Reoch, James Cameron, John Wilson, and Robert Hutton; bassoon, John Thomson; oboes, Thomas Robertson and Charles Calder.[17]

The remuneration per musician was on a sliding scale: for an assembly not exceeding one hundred persons, each received six shillings; for an assembly of between one hundred and one hundred and fifty persons, each received seven shillings and sixpence; and for an assembly of over one hundred and fifty persons, ten shillings. It was the custom to supply the musicians with refreshments, but the directors were apparently at pains to ensure that this was carried out in moderation, having had some experience with inebriated musicians.

[17] John Thomson resided in Bailie Fyfe's Close in 1700, and in Old Assembly Close in 1796. Robert Hutton resided in the Old Assembly Close in 1768 and in Kennedy's Close in 1774.

There appears to have been no great hurry to start the venture, as the directors did not meet to appoint the directresses until November 29, when the following ladies were so honoured: the Countesses of Leven, Glencairn, and Hopetoun, and Ladies Minto and Milntoun. The ladies apparently convened and formally accepted the appointments, being, as the minutes put it, "convinced of the good effects of this undertaking upon the present intention both for polishing the youth and providing the poor." They submitted a set of rules for the conduct of the assembly, "which they desired to be wrote out fair and hung up in the Assembly Hall"; these were accepted and directed to be displayed.

No Lady to be admitted in a nightgown and no Gentleman in boots.

Dancing to begin precisely at 5 o'clock afternoon in the winter and 6 o'clock in summer.

Each set not to exceed ten couples to dance but one country dance at a time.

The couples to dance their minuets in the order they stand in their several sets.

No dancing out of the regular order but by leave from the Lady Directress for the night.

No dancing whatever to be allowed but in the ordinary dancing place.

No dance to begin after 11 at night.

No misses in skirts and jackets, robecoats nor stay-bodied gowns to be allowed to dance country dances but in a set by themselves.

No tea, coffee, negus nor other liquor to be carried into the dancing room.

It is expected no gentleman will step over the rail round the dancing place, but will enter or go out by the doors at the upper or lower end of the room, and that all ladys and gentlemen will order their servants not to enter the passage before the outer door with lighted flambeaux.

> [First Assembly Minute Book,
> December 16, 1746]

Someone had to be placed in charge of the kitchen and the cleaning of the premises, who, in turn, had the responsibility of employing and paying the necessary assistants — "not less than two." The directors thought, however, that the salary for this position had been too high in the past and that it should be reduced. The "Misses Robertson" who had formerly held the charge were given the opportunity of continuing on the new terms.[18] They were not very happy about the change, but they accepted nevertheless and went on to serve the assembly for a further eighteen years. Then one of the Misses Robertson died and the other, now very infirm, was retired, we are happy to say, with a pension. What a story they could have told us!

Special silver teaspoons were made for the New Assembly by James Ker, goldsmith, of which some are still in existence. They were attractively designed with a stem on which "Edr. Assembly" was inscribed, terminating in the shape of a fan.

The directresses' badge of office was changed from silver to gold, although the original oval shape was retained. The obverse of the new badge displayed a pelican on

---

[18] £ 15 sterling yearly, and the profits from the card tables and serving the refreshments. Not more than 2s. 6d. to be charged for each pack of cards.

a nest feeding her young and, on the reverse, a woman with a child leaning against her knee and the armorial bearings of the city.

Profits from the assembly, of course, were applied to the charities supported by its managers, and special balls were arranged to contribute toward such unexpected projects as the Peterhead and Kinghorn harbours, and in the early days especially, the subscribers were encouraged to wear linen and lace manufactured in Scotland as a means of promoting the home industries. The same mode of encouraging the home industries was attempted by the Marquis of Huntly at the Northern Meeting early in the following century.

The New Assembly rooms were, however, far from ideal, and the proprietor, or his agents, took little heed of requests for repairs. Around mid-century, serious attempts were made to obtain a site for a new hall, and in 1754 forces were joined with the Musical Society to petition the town council for an assembly and concert hall, but the proposed site was declared unsuitable by the celebrated architect Robert Adam himself. The old town, it should be remembered, was very congested, and the North Bridge had not yet been built to provide easy access to the new. An offer to purchase was made and rejected, but not until 1760 was hope of alternative accommodation abandoned and the requisite one thousand pounds given for the purchase of the hall. Redecorating and repairs were necessary, but an opportunity now arose to acquire accommodation on the opposite side of Bell's Wynd for a tea and card room. After some negotiations and difficulties, this tea room was built in 1766. Connected with the assembly room by an enclosed bridge across Bell's Wynd, its specifications are interesting. The inside dimensions were 32½ feet by 22½ feet, and sixteen feet high. The windows were to be of oak or fir, and glazed with crown glass. The floor joists were scantling 10½ feet by 3½ feet, and were supported by a beam with proper standards from the ground. The roof was blue slate.

The kitchens were situated in adjacent rooms converted to this purpose, and from these, tea, coffee, and "negus, fruit and cool tankard" were conveyed to the tea room by a waiter.

This improvement to the premises must have helped to offset some of the previous limitations, but still, as one critic observed, the dancing room was "neither elegant nor commodious." He remarked that "the door is so disposed, that a stream of air rushes through it into the room, and, as the footmen are allowed to stand with their flaxbeaux in the entry, before the entertainment is half over, the room is filled with smoke almost to suffocation. There are two tea or card rooms, but no supper room. When balls are given in the Assembly Room after the supper, nothing can be more awkward or incommodious to the company than the want of distinct apartments for supper and dancing. At present, upon these occasions, the table is covered in the dancing room before the company meets. Additional tables are set up, when room is made for them by the dancing being over. Chairs are to be brought in and waiters are pouring in with dishes, while the company are standing all the while on the floor."[19]

The contrast of highly bred ladies and gentlemen, in all their finery, against the crudity of their surroundings at the assembly is startling to modern eyes: the ladies in their hoops and lace negotiating the tortuous spiral up or down the stone stairs which

[19] Hugo Arnot, *History of Edinburgh*, new ed. (Edinburgh, 1816), p. 293.

reeked with the fumes from the twitching flambeaux of their servants; the dingy walls so often in need of redecoration, and the physical arrangements so inconvenient. But this contrast was characteristic of Scotland at that time. Nevertheless there is no question of the general quality of the people who brushed their way up the stairs and through the grey closes of Edinburgh's High Street. They were certainly not intellectually inferior to, or less handsome than, their counterparts in Paris or London; they were just born into a poorer environment with which a surfeit of comfort was at odds or not possible.

As the century progressed, there developed a movement of the more refined population out of the old medieval city into the new town, leaving the once aristocratic "lands" to the lower orders. This movement had repercussions on the Bell's Wynd Assembly, and because of this and its many competitors in the 1770s, it entered its final decline, and no one was surprised when it came to an end in 1784. In the following year the hall was sold to the town for the use of the Town Guard.

Meanwhile, in 1777, while the Bell's Wynd Assembly was still in existence, a rival assembly, finding its origins in the Royal Company of Archers, had built a hall in Buccleugh Street, near George Square. The dimensions of this hall, excluding the siderooms and offices, were forty feet by twenty-four feet. Assemblies consisting of one hundred subscribers, each of whom was entitled to bring a guest, were held every Tuesday.

From this assembly sprang that in Buccleugh Place, usually called the George Square Assembly, which opened on January 5, 1785, with a ball.[20] Subscriptions were invited, and it is interesting that balls were held, at least occasionally, for the children of these subscribers. Cockburn tells us in *Memorials of His Time* that "here were the last remains of the ballroom discipline of the preceding age" and that in his youth, "the whole fashionable dancing, as indeed the fashionable everything, clung to George Square" (p. 36).

This, however, was not the official successor to the Bell's Wynd Assembly. When the demise of the latter became inevitable, a committee was formed, under the presidency of the Earl of Moray, to found another assembly and to construct more commodious rooms in the new town on a site in George Street provided by the town council. This fine building was opened in 1787, and continues to be used at the present day as the George Street Assembly Rooms. The George Street Assembly regulations (January 12, 1789) were as follows:

That the ladies' subscription shall be one guinea.

That the subscriptions for gentlemen who are proprietors of the rooms shall be one guinea.

That the subscriptions for gentlemen who are *not* proprietors of the rooms shall be two guineas.

That each subscriber shall have twenty-four admission tickets.

Subscribers when absent to have the power of granting two of these tickets for each assembly, either to a lady or gentleman, and no more; when present, only one; and no ticket will pro-

---

[20] The George Square Assembly Hall was incorporated into a tenement in 1800.

cure admission unless dated and signed by the granter; and the tickets thus granted are not transferable.

Each non-subscriber to pay 3s. at the door on presenting his ticket.

Each director is allowed two additional tickets extraordinary for each assembly, which he may transfer, adding the word *Director* to his signature.

No admission without a ticket on any account whatever.

[James Grant, *Old and New Edinburgh*,
vol. 2, p. 149]

By the 1780s, however, some of the new hotels in the new town were providing accommodation for assemblies, particularly the "rooms" of John Dunn and Matthew Fortune. The latter was the son of the proprietor of Fortune's Tavern in the Stamp Office Close off the High Street. The tavern was a fashionable rendezvous in the period of 1760–70, and private balls were held there. Boswell records attending some of these, including, on February 18, 1768, "An Ayrshire ball."[21]

In 1786, Dunn ventured so far as to advertise a masquerade, as people called a masked ball, and one enterprising dressmaker publicized an appropriate stock of fancy dresses after the style of those in demand in London. But the ancient prejudice was still so strong and the opposition so vehement that Dunn felt it discreet to abandon the project and refund the ticket money.

A similar attempt by Digges, the manager of the Theatre Royal, some ten years previously, had met an equal fate; Digges, bowing to public opinion — to which he always paid "the utmost respect and attention" — rebounded with a ridotto which was so successful that he proposed to hold two each year thereafter. The ridotto was an entertainment of song followed by general dancing, introduced to England at the London Opera House in 1734,[22] and first attempted in Edinburgh at the Bell's Wynd Assembly Hall in 1760.

The masquerade suffered from associations which date back to the Roman mime, and Topham wrote in 1775 that it "was hitherto unknown in a public style" in Edinburgh and that in 1774 a gentleman had attempted a private performance at his own house, without success, owing to "want of proper variety of company" and also from "not understanding the nature and spirit of the diversion."[23]

About this time in Edinburgh, it was very fashionable to form parties to resort to a tavern for a repast of raw oysters and porter, usually followed by brandy or rum punch — as the ladies chose — with relaxed if not roisterous conversation and witty sallies appropriate to the scene. After the company tired of conversation, Topham observed, they began to dance reels, "their favourite dance, which they performed with great agility and perseverance" until, "on looking at their watches, the ladies now found it was time to retire. The coaches were therefore called and away they went" (Letter xvi). The men, of course, resumed drinking. Luckie Middlemass's tavern was the favourite howff and, according to Chambers, "the ladies would sometimes have the

---

21 James Boswell, *Boswell in Search of a Wife 1766–69*, ed. Frank Brady and Frederick A. Pottle (Yale, 1957), pp. 138–39.

22 Charles Burney, *A General History of Music.*

23 Edward Topham, *Letters from Edinburgh*, Letter xxx.

oyster-women to dance in the ball-room, though they were known to be of the worst character . . . under the convenient name of 'frolic.' "[24] These oyster-cellars as they are called, also became popular in Glasgow, but only Edinburgh could inspire the poem:

> When big as burnes the gutters rin,
> If ye hae catch'd a droukit skin,
> To Luckie Middlemist's Loup in,
> And sit fu' snug
> Owre oysters and a dram o' gin,
> Or haddock Lug.

In addition to the subscription assemblies and these diversions, there were the annual balls of the various societies. Topham observed (ca. 1775) that every week was "productive of something new." Perhaps the most distinguished ball was that of the Honourable Company of Hunters, usually held at Holyrood Palace. It was then customary to designate some beau as "king" and belle as "queen" of the ball, as was done in January 1730, when Lord Hope was chosen king and Lady Jean Leslie queen of the Hunters ball. Three hundred persons of distinction attended this ball, held at the Duke of Hamilton's Lodgings in the Abbey, and it did not finish until five o'clock in the morning. In 1736, the Honourable Charles Hope was designated king and Honourable Lady Helen Hope queen, and a table illuminated with 400 wax candles, at which 150 ladies sat at a time, was laid in the Gallery of the Kings.[25]

Another fashionable club, the Capillaire Club,[26] also held its annual ball at Holyrood; but after 1772, on account of the "dangerous state" of the palace, the Assembly Hall was used. Topham attended one of these and remarked on the supper at which were served "ices and everything that luxury can invent." He noted, too, the notorious practice of the gentlemen retiring after the withdrawal of the ladies to a private room where "each sacrifices his understanding and health to wishing in full bumpers the health of his fair partner." Some, indeed, changed into more suitable apparel for the affray.

There were also special occasions, such as the Bell's Wynd Assembly's Queen's birthday ball at which the lady directress represented the queen, and the public was allowed into the gallery, or the one given for the young unmarried ladies by the matrons and married ladies which is mentioned by Topham. For this ball, the ladies were given tickets for themselves and partner, and the gallant Topham writes: "You may be sure the old ones are not backward in their invitation, each of them is squired by some antiquated beau who, with his best clothes, brushes up his best minuet and revives in imagination the feats of ancient times" (Letter xlii).

Attempts made in the Edinburgh of the 1770s to establish imitations of the successful outdoor centres of entertainment at Vauxhall and Ranelagh Gardens in London seem characteristic of these times. In 1776 a Ranelagh Gardens was established in the

---

[24] Robert Chambers, *Traditions of Edinburgh*, p. 146, fn.

[25] Jamieson, "Social Assemblies of the Eighteenth Century," *Book of the Old Edinburgh Club*, vol. 19, 1933, p. 68.

[26] "Capillaire" is a syrup used to flavour drinks.

environs of Edinburgh. Signor Corri begged leave to inform the nobility and gentry that he had completed his ballroom and other parts of the plan of his garden at the Kirkbraehead, and that the opening would take place on Monday, May 9, at five o'clock. The annual subscription was to be one guinea, and the program was to include a musical entertainment lasting two hours and a ball which would commence at nine o'clock. The garden was to be illuminated "with transparent machinery and upwards of 400 lamps of various kinds." However, these ventures do not seem to have met with any lasting success; perhaps, as Hugo Arnot said of the Comely Gardens (a much less fashionable enterprise of the period 1750–80), because neither the climate nor the gardens were adapted to the purpose.

Then, as today, there was nothing so constant as change, and there were always those who recalled what was best in former days. Thus William Creech, douce bailie and publisher immortalized by Burns, contrasted the "public" assemblies of the 1780s with the assembly of former years. In 1763, he wrote, there was only one dancing assembly and there was "strict regularity with respect to dress and decorum, and great dignity of manners." The profits went to the support of the charity workhouse. Now, by 1787, there were at least three new elegant assembly rooms and one at Leith nearby, but the charity workhouse was neglected. In 1783, the public assemblies met at eight or nine o'clock, and the lady directress sometimes did not make her appearance until ten o'clock. "The young masters and misses," wrote Creech, "who would have been mortified not to have seen out the ball, thus returned home at 3 or 4 in the morning, and yawned and gaped, and complained of headaches all the next day." In a letter of about 1788 he commented on the rapid decline of dancing in this country, and particularly in the capital. "It is too well known that not above three or four assemblies have been attended this winter . . . and only two private balls. . . . The week of Preaching which generally terminates the amusements of this place, is past, and we must now look upon the season as irretrievably closed. . . . So negligent were the men, that one evening the ladies were driven to . . . footing it with one another."

By 1786 Minuets had disappeared with the old decorum, and "Country dances only used." "Dress," Creech continued, "particularly by the men, was much neglected; and many of them reeled from the tavern, flustered with wine, to an assembly of as elegant and beautiful women as any in Europe." He complained, "It is notorious that men have for several years been perversely obstinate in refusing to dance; even the limbs of the law decline the cause, and we no longer hear of an Advocate's Ball."[27] This, only fifteen years after Topham had written: "The gravest men here, with the exception of the ministers, think it is no disgrace to dance. I have seen a professor, who has argued most learnedly and most wisely in a morning, forgetting all his gravity in an evening, and dance away to the best of his abilities" (Letter xxxii). This combination of gravity and jollity has always been characteristic of Scotland. Who can say, too, that it was not characteristic of England prior to the eighteenth century?

In the last decade of the century, Creech could remark, "Although the Assembly Rooms are deserted (except on the Master of Ceremonies night), yet private balls, tavern dances, and oyster-cellar gambols have never been more frequent, or kept up

[27] William Creech, *Fugitive Pieces*, pp. 114–15.

to later hours." The private balls always closed with an elegant supper, and the clocks would strike four or five o'clock before the company parted. The ladies were usually accompanied by a man servant, and sedan chairs were used for transportation. A chaperon was required for the theatre, concerts, and balls in public assembly rooms, but at private balls, the lady of the house was thought sufficient.

Formal balls were not now so numerous, and it is this which Creech regretted:

This matter bears peculiarly hard upon my fair countrywomen, as they are thereby prevented from displaying attractions which nature has lavishly bestowed upon them. Perhaps in the fine texture of skins, and the brightness of bloom, the Englih ladies may equal ours; but I aver, that in the neatness of ankle, and prettiness of foot, the Scots women reign unrivalled. Sensible of these charms, whatever taste could invent, or art execute, has been employed in the decoration of the shoe. It has been stretched in the tambour, and has glittered with spangles and embroidery; every combination of colours has been used that could please or allure the eye, but all in vain, the men have continued motionless — long has it been the object of my thoughts to restore things to their ancient footing. . . .

I do not despair of seeing a couple of assemblies of 3 or 4 balls per week. During the season. These meetings have always been reckoned as the great mart for marriage.

It is fortunate that Topham, to whose observations we owe so much, visited Scotland when that ageless belle, Mrs. Rutherford, could write, "I have not seen Edinburgh so gay these 20 years."[28] Nevertheless, Mary Somerville remembered Edinburgh twenty years later (1798) as still "a gay, sociable place." Then, she tells us, girls walked together along the new Princess Street, the fashionable evening promenade of the last decades of the century, and often were joined by their "dancing partners." She describes an evening's entertainment: "We occasionally gave little supper parties, and presented the young men to our parents as they came in. At these meetings we played games, danced reels, or had a little music — never cards. After supper there were toasts, sentiments and songs. There was always one or two hot dishes, and a variety of sweet things and fruit."[29]

The better "confectioners" in Edinburgh, which were patronized by most of the aristocratic families, offered a complete catering service, including the decoration of the house, or rooms, the provision of food, dishes, and chairs, and even a band if necessary.

Dancing masters and teachers of music, especially of the German flute, violin, violincello, and guitar (for the ladies), had never been so numerous or enjoyed such prosperity. Publications of reels, strathspeys, jigs, hornpipes, and the "Auld Scots Sangs" appeared in quick succession in the shops of the various music-sellers. Here was a renaissance of the musical lore of Scotland.

The last part of the eighteenth century was a time of rapid change and restlessness: in 1763, the assembly and balls could be packed to the door; in 1783, a bad season, all seems in decline; then, in 1798, the spirit seems to have returned. Whatever Edinburgh may have been at this time, it was not indifferent, and never inactive.

[28] Alison Cockburn, *Letters and Memoirs of Mrs. Alison Rutherford or Cockburn* (Edinburgh, 1900). Letter to the Reverend Robert Douglas.

[29] Martha Somerville, *Personal Recollections of Mary Somerville*, p. 64.

CONDUCT OF THE ASSEMBLY

Before we review the rapid spread of the select public assembly for dancing in the late eighteenth century, it may be interesting to glean whatever information we can about the conduct of the assemblies. Some allusions have already been made concerning the deportment, particularly the rules for the New, or Bell's Wynd, Assembly set down by the directresses. How far these were modelled on the practice at Bath and how far on the exigencies of local circumstances it is not easy to say. The charitable purpose of the undertaking was perhaps as much, if not more, a matter of dignity — and sincere need — than any appeasement of the religious antipathy with which it was surrounded. This antipathy must substantially have abated with time, as will be remarked by those conversant with the liberality of outlook which was characteristic of Edinburgh of the latter half of that century.

The presence, as directress, of a matron of quality and rank was guarantee in itself of supreme respectability. Of course, many a distinguished mother, such as Grisel Baillie or Lady Eglintoun, escorted her charges to the assembly as did many a matronly aunt or guardian. The long procession of sedans containing Lady Eglintoun and her seven beautiful daughters halting to disgorge their lofty and graceful freight was one of the treasured spectacles of old Edinburgh. What a flurry of bongraces, lappets, hoops, petticoats, scarlet stockings, and clutched fans!

There was always the problem of returning home in the dark through somewhat unsavoury wynds, often with inadequate lighting. For although assembly dances originally began at four o'clock and lasted until about eleven, by the end of the century they could be as late as ten o'clock and continue until three in the morning.[30] Mary Somerville remarked that she often returned home from a ball in bright daylight, and although she was referring to balls held in the 1790s, it was not unknown for a private ball to go on until dawn before this time. So the ladies, sometimes escorted by their partners, were generally attended by manservants who carried the sedan chairs and who led the way with the jagged light of their flambeaux. The sedan chair took the place of the hackney carriage, or taxi in these days, and in the later years of the seventeenth century there were ranks of them in the principal streets. Their carriers were Highlanders to whom any young lady could be safely entrusted.

The accommodation of the assembly rooms did not permit all to dance at once. Thus it was that the directress issued tickets to each individual allocating not only a set which was composed of ten or twelve couples, but also a precise place in that set. In this way it fell to the directress to arrange the partners according to their rank or quality, and sometimes, within these, according to whether they were handsome or beautiful or unmarried, (the "beauty," "heartsome," or "maiden" sets).

The first set then took the floor, and each couple danced a Minuet in turn, after which they danced a Country Dance. This completed, the second set took the floor and repeated the procedure, and so on until all the sets had danced. Then the first set returned and resumed the sequence. This time, however, only Country Dances were performed. Topham tells us that the dancing set was surrounded by chairs to prevent interference from the rest of the company, although it may be noticed from the original regulations of the New Assembly that a rail surrounded the dancing space.

---

[30] Cf. Creech, *Fugitive Pieces*, pp. 114–15.

It is not surprising that a set rarely took the floor more than twice in an evening, and Topham observed that it was not unknown for there to be so many sets that some did not have any opportunity to dance at all! (Letter xlii). Mrs. Rutherford described taking a number of "misses" to the assembly in the 1770s. She remarked that she had never seen so "handsome" an assembly, and that there were seven sets, but she did not say whether they all danced more than once. She also told of holding a ball at her house: "On Wednesday last, I gave a ball. How do ye think I contrived to stretch out this house to hold twenty-two people, and had nine couple always dancing? Yet this is true, it is also true that we had a table covered with diverse eatables all the time, and that everybody eat when they were hungry, and drank when they were dry, but nobody ever sat down. . . . Our fiddler sat where the cupboard is, and they danced in both rooms; the table was stuffed into the window and we had plenty of room. It made the bairns all vastly happy."[31]

Topham reported that the mode of conducting the assembly was "much approved" of by the inhabitants of the city, and he agreed that it had "many conveniences"; but the young ladies, he added, complained that the lack of room deprived them of much dancing. Perhaps it was easier to find space for reels, as these were danced in separate parts of the room. One would expect the system of taking turns to offer the non-partici-pants a welcome opportunity for a chat, but this was not the case. Both Goldsmith and Topham, the one in 1753 and the other in 1774, remarked on this lack of social intercourse:

The men here have generally high cheek bones, and are lean, and swarthy, fond of action; danceing in particular: tho' now I have mention'd danceing, let me say something of their balls which are very frequent here; when a stranger enters the danceing hall he sees one end of the room taken up by the lady's, who sit dismally in a Groupe by themselves. On the other end stand their pensive partners, that are to be, but no more intercourse between the sexes than there is between two Countrys at war, the Ladies indeed may ogle, and the Gentlemen sigh, but an embargo is laid on any closer commerce; at length, to interrupt hostility's, the Lady directress or intendant, or what you will pitches on a Gentleman and Lady to walk a minuet, which they perform with a formality that approaches despondence, after five or six couple have thus walked the Gauntlett, all stand up to country dance's, each gentleman furnished with a partner from the afforesaid Lady directress, so they dance much, say nothing, and thus concludes our assembly; I told a Scotch Gentleman that such a profound silence resembled the ancient procession of the Roman Matrons in honour of Ceres and the scotch Gentleman told me, (and faith I believe he was right) that I was a very great pedant for my pains. [*Letters*, Letter to Robert Bryanton, 1753]

Topham's comments also reveal a lack of conviviality:

Were the Scotch gentleman disposed to gallantry, this manner [the company dancing one set at a time] of managing the dancing would afford them the finest opportunity they could wish as they are left the whole evening to furnish entertainment and conversation for their partners. But observations on the clothes and dancing of the party who are performing, too often fill up the vacant interval and instead of ogling eyes, protestations and endearments, the lady sits envying the more fortunate stars of her companion who is dancing whilst her partner yawns for the approaching period of his own exhibition. [Letter xlii]

31 Cockburn, *Letters and Memoirs of Mrs. Alison Rutherford*. Letter to Miss Cumming.

At the nobility's private balls in England, at this time, the ladies' fans were thrown upon a table; each man then drew a fan, and its owner became his partner for the evening. There is an allusion to this practice by Sir Alexander Boswell in his poem "Edinburgh or the Ancient Royalty." In this case, it appears, the partners for a particular assembly night — presumably among a particular group of acquaintances — were selected on some convenient occasion in anticipation of the event. Robert Chambers wrote that the ladies' fans were collected into a hat, but it is apparent that, whatever the method, all was not left to the hazards of chance, for, as Boswell remarked, the fan was selected "with care":

> The Assembly Closs received the Fair;
> Order and elegance presided there;
> Each gay Right Honourable had her place
> To walk a minuet with becoming grace;
> No racing to the dance with rival hurry —
> Such was thy sway, O fam'd Miss Nicky Murray!
> Each lady's fan a chosen Damon bore.
> With care selected many a day before;
> For, unprovided with a favourite beau,
> The nymph, chagrined, the ball must needs forego;
> But previous matters to her taste arranged,
> Certes, the constant couple never changed;
> Through a long night to watch fair Delia's will,
> The same dull swain was at her elbow still.
>
> [Alexander Boswell, "Edinburgh or the
> Ancient Royalty"]

As has been mentioned, it was always the prerogative of the directress to assign partners whenever necessary, and, of course, to determine the order of dancing. The personal qualities required to carry out these duties with the necessary authority and good sense were considerable, and consequently we have reason to stand in awe of the name of famed "Miss Nicky Murray" mentioned in Alexander Boswell's poem, for she alone, of all the many directresses who served the Edinburgh Assembly in its long history, has left her mark among the traditions of her city.

Miss Helen Nicholas Murray of Stormont was a sister of the Earl of Mansfield and lived with her sisters in one of the tenements at the head of Bailie Fyfe's Close where she received into her sagacious care numerous fair relatives and friends who sought a proper introduction to society. She was appointed directress in 1765, ten years before Topham visited Edinburgh. Topham admired the way in which she performed her duties; indeed, he asserted that the difficulties imposed by the limited space of the assembly room would have been insuperable without her. He described how, as she entered the room, a crowd surrounded her, clamouring for tickets for one of the first sets. Thus assailed by "the impetuous applications of chaperons, maiden aunts and the earnest entreaties of lovers," it was surprising how "with the utmost politeness, affability and good humour" she attended to everyone; "all petitions were heard and demands granted which appeared reasonable" (Letter xlii, May 19, 1775).

Nevertheless, Robert Chambers, who drew his information from the recollections of

Sir Walter Scott and the accretions of that avid social antiquarian, C. Kirkpatrick Sharpe, wrote that Miss Murray was "rather more marked by good manners than good nature."[32] Her good breeding, it appeared, did not extend to sparing the feelings of anyone if rank were not on their side. Introduced to a "Miss X," she is said to have asked imperiously, "Miss X of what?"[33] Yet even the gentry were not secure from the candour of her tongue, as one may judge from her comment to James Boswell after he had, as he put it, "harangued on Hibernia." "Ye're a great idiot," she said, much to his perplexity. It rankled sufficiently for him to refer to her (we take it to be her) as the "mistress of the Spuilhouse," *speelhuis* being Dutch for a low public dance hall.[34]

No wonder that other ladies feared to relieve Miss Murray or to succeed her. There were normally four directresses appointed to avoid difficulties which arose when, as so often happened, some of them lived out of town or fell ill. Those who were at least approached to serve during the period of Miss Murray's reign were the Countess of Dundonald, Lady Elphinstone, and Mrs. Campbell of Finab, and it is evident from the records that Mrs. Bruce of Kenet was appointed at the same time as Miss Murray, and Mrs. Johnston of Hilton appointed in 1776. Miss Murray died on November 7, 1777 (*Scots Magazine*, 1777, p. 627).

The last remains of the assembly system were preserved at the George Square Assembly attended by Cockburn. There, he tells us in *Memorials of His Time*:

No couple could dance unless each party was provided with a ticket prescribing the precise place in the precise dance. If there was no ticket, the gentleman, or the lady, was dealt with as an intruder, and turned out of the dance. If the ticket had marked upon it — say for a Country Dance, the figures 3.5, this meant that the holder was to place himself in the third dance, and fifth from the top; and if he was anywhere else, he was set right, or excluded. And the partner's ticket must correspond. Woe on the poor girl, who with ticket 2.7, was found opposite a youth marked 5.9! It was flirting without a licence, and looked very ill, and would probably be reported by the ticket director of that dance to the mother. Of course, parties, or parents, who wished to secure dancing for themselves or those they had charge of, provided themselves with correct and corresponding vouchers before the ball day arrived. This could only be accomplished through a director; and the election of a pope sometimes required less jobbing. When parties chose to take their chance, they might do so; but still, though only obtained in the room, the written permission was necessary; and such a thing as a compact to dance, by a couple, without official authority, would have been an outrage that could scarcely be contemplated. Tea was sipped in siderooms; and he was a careless beau who did not present his partner with an orange at the end of each dance; and the oranges and the tea, like everything else, were under exact and positive regulations. All this disappeared, and the very rooms were obliterated, as soon as the lately raised community secured its inevitable supremacy in the New Town. The aristocracy of a few predominating individuals and families came to an end; and the unreasonable old had nothing for it but to sigh over the recollection of the select and elegant parties of their youth, where indiscriminate public right was rejected, and its coarseness awed. [Pp. 36–37]

[32] Chambers, *Traditions of Edinburgh*.
[33] Ibid.
[34] Boswell, *Boswell in Search of a Wife* (1766–69), p. 199. Letter to Dempster, Edinburgh, February 2, 1769. Boswell was preparing to travel to Ireland on a matrimonial expedition.

SPREAD OF THE PUBLIC ASSEMBLY

By 1770, few towns of any consequence were without their formal subscription assembly. In Scotland, besides Edinburgh, there were the Aberdeen and Glasgow Assemblies, and only slightly less notable at this time, the assemblies of Leith (1777), Haddington (1788), and Dundee. In their conception they were exclusive institutions and showed in many ways the strong class dividing lines so much more strictly observed in English society.

Aberdeen

Alexander Jaffray has left us an interesting sketch of the assembly at Aberdeen in 1777 in *Recollection of Kingswells*:

When the weeks commenced, the Assemblies began as usual at that season, and continued at regular intervals for six months. Country dances were kept up with great spirit to the lively Scotch tunes, and formed a most agreeable amusement, free from ceremony, every one on terms of intimacy. The form was perfectly simple.

The gentleman sent a card to the lady he selected for the night, requesting the favour of her hand on the occasion, which was freely granted. The meeting of all parties took place at a certain hour in the evening at the assembly rooms, the ladies drew for places, and there was no change of partners for the night. After the dance, followed a supper, where cheerfulness and good humour prevailed. Those who could sing entertained the company, which remained to a late, or rather early hour. Each gentleman escorted his partner home, and several returned to drink the ladies health. The subscription was extremely reasonable, a guinea for the season each gentleman; non-residents in the town only half. I particularly noticed Mrs. Grant of Caron, a very pleasant sensible woman. Her two songs were "Yowie wi the crookit horn," and "Tibby Fowler in the Glen."

I had the pleasure of dancing at these assemblies with several of the fair damsels of Aberdeen, the former school acquaintances of our youthful days — Miss Besey Stevens of Broadlands, Miss Nelly Duncan, Miss Jenny Lagentwood of Tillery, Miss Meaves, the beautiful Miss Nancy Gordon, daughter of Sir Alex. Gordon, Miss Mary Anderson of Bountie. Next day the gentleman paid a visit at the house of his partner of the last night, and was always invited to tea in the evening. [P. 199]

As the new merchant class grew in numbers, they began to rival the landed gentry in importance and influence, particularly in Glasgow, so favourably placed for transatlantic trade, where the tobacco lords gradually gave way to the wealthy merchants or manufacturers who succeeded them.

Glasgow

Although Glasgow had none of the glamour of the capital, it was widely regarded as one of the most beautiful towns in Europe and, possibly for very practical reasons, it seemed cleaner and neater than Edinburgh. Travellers remarked on its appearance as early as 1650; Burt commented in 1725 that "Glasgow is to outward appearance, the prettiest and most uniform town that I ever saw; and I believe there is nothing like it in Britain."[35]

It is pleasant to re-create a picture of Glasgow at this time, with its wide streets, pastoral river, picturesque roofs and steeples, and to follow the burgh minstrels as they pipe the reveille from the Tron up the slowly curving echoes of the Heigh Gate, past the Drygate and Ratton Raw to the cathedral. The sun's hag fingers, scratching over the tiled roofs, castellated gables, and rich stone walls of history, warmed the medieval facade of Glasgow College. Perhaps there we would hear a cock crow from the hen-house in the Professors' Court, and the stir of weavers, millwrights, carpenters, coopers, blacksmiths, clerks, merchants, and stockbrokers setting about their business, in the rapidly growing town of twenty-four thousand people.

While grouse whirred across the fields of Cowcaddens and blackbirds sang in the orchards, shipowners would note intelligence of the arrival or departure of another cargo of tobacco, perhaps, or sugar or rum, from the Tail o' the Bank, and fishermen would haul their nets near the Kelvin. A packman setting off with his load across the narrow "auld brig" as others had done through four centuries before him would notice, perhaps, the vortice chains traced in the limpid waters of the river as they emerged from the shadows of the eight solid arches or from the shadows of the new bridge recently completed, and take for granted those which swirled gently from the wheels of the carts taking a quicker path through the stream at low tide.

The portentous cloud of smoke from the new iron works at Carron, near Falkirk, could not be seen, and the thunder, fire, and flash of hammers, furnaces, and welding rods, and the roar of automobiles and clang of tramcars that were to mark the Glasgow of the future would have seemed a vision of Hades. Yet, it was here at this time in the same pleasant town, in the university, commonly called Glasgow College, that James Watt and Professor Joseph Black were formulating the ideas and constructing the means which would lead to the transformation of the old town and the world.

Against such reflections, the graceful recreation and art of dancing seems unimportant, but many components, both spiritual and material, constitute life's fulfilment.

Glasgow's upper class, unlike Edinburgh's, was very limited in numbers in the early part of the century. At this period in Glasgow, the Duchess of Douglas was the most distinguished leader of fashion, and between 1728 and 1750, David Burrel was the sole teacher of dancing in the city, being subsidized and licensed by the town.[36]

Alexander Carlyle mentions attending "the dancing assembly" in Glasgow in 1743 and says it was held fortnightly during the winter, but he does not tell us where.[37] According to a manuscript subscription list which was originally in the possession of the Stirling library in Glasgow, the Glasgow Assembly Hall was not built until 1762. The first subscription on the list is dated 1757, and apart from Sir John Maxwell who heads it, there are no titled gentlemen among the 136 names. These are the names of distinguished or wealthy Glasgow citizens and neighbouring country gentry, some of which will strike a chord to those who know something of Glasgow: Dunlop, Glass-

---

35 Burt, *Letters from a Gentleman*, letter 2.

36 His terms were 25s. for seven months, 5s. for a ball, and 1s. for a "practising," when attended. [John Strang, *Glasgow and Its Clubs* (Glasgow, 1864), p. 12, fn.]

37 Alexander Carlyle, *Autobiography*, p. 84.

ford, Dreghorn, Buchanan, Dennistoun, Cochrane, Gordon, Ingram, Stirling, Speirs, Glen, and others better known to historians of the city.

The hall was situated near Glasgow Cross, and the usual hour for gathering was five o'clock later changed to six o'clock. By the late 1770s, a decline in support of the assembly was evident, and on reading the following advertisement in the *Glasgow Mercury*, March 25, 1779, one is reminded of the complaints expressed by Creech in Edinburgh some few years later:

The Assemblies of late have been so little frequented that it begins to be doubted whether that kind of diversion is agreeable to the Public, or whether the Gentlemen, by too intense an application to their *Glass*, may not have impaired their Locomotive Faculties. There is, however, to be a Dancing Assembly upon Thursday the first of April. If it will be well attended they will be continued as formerly.

Then, in the *Glasgow Mercury* on January 17, 1780, an announcement was made:

The Dancing Assemblies are to be carried on this year by a General Subscription, it being found of late that the money taken at the door will not answer the expense. They are to be held regularly at the Rooms on Tuesday evenings once a fortnight during the season.

A book is opened, where Gentlemen may subscribe at One Guinea each for the season, and lies for that purpose at Messrs. Campbell and Ingram's Insurance Office.

The ladies are to pay nothing. Stranger gentlemen will be admitted on paying 2s, 6d, at the door of the room. No town's Gentlemen will be admitted but subscribers. . . .

Senex tells us that rules were made for the purpose of excluding the "shopocracy" of the city from mixing in the Country Dances with the wives and daughters of the tobacco lords who were the directors of the assembly. He tells us that a Glasgow shopkeeper of wealth and respectability was refused tickets for his wife and daughters for the reason that "their rank did not entitle them to attend assemblies."[38]

Unfortunately for the "aristocratic" directors, they found that their assembly languished in financial embarrassment, while the balls held by various music teachers at the conclusion of their public concerts in the same hall, and at which no segregation of rank occurred, were extremely popular. To meet the challenge, they now inaugurated a series called "Rooms" instead of assemblies at which evening dress was optional and conduct nearly as free as at the music teachers' balls. The price of admission was reduced to two shillings, and tea was served.

Notwithstanding this relaxation, the Subscription Assemblies and the "Rooms" became increasingly neglected in favour of the balls. The fact was that the American War had begun to cripple too many of the great Virginian tobacco lords, and after this fateful event in the history of Britain and the world, the formerly ostracized merchants so increased in wealth and numbers on account of West Indian trade and manufacturing that the social barriers which had hitherto excluded them disappeared.

Meantime, however, the assembly directors took shares in the Tontine Society, formed in 1781, to build a coffeehouse and assembly room beside the existing assembly

[38] Senex, (pseud. Robert Reid), *Old Glasgow and Its Environs* (Glasgow, 1864), pp. 297–98.

hall at Glasgow Cross. An article in the *Glasgow Mercury*, November 21, 1782, stated that the Tontine buildings which resulted comprised "a large elegant room, to be occupied as a coffee room," and an assembly room, "with about twenty other apartments, to be occupied as a Tavern or Lodging Rooms."

A Mr. Smart acquired the lease and served dinner (called a Daily Ordinary) on the premises, at quarter-past three daily, before the coffee room was opened by the most splendid ball that had ever been seen in Glasgow, held on May 13, 1784. On this occasion "there was a complete mixture of the county nobility and gentry with the city aristocracy and shopocracy, graced by the presence of the Lords of Justiciary, Justice Clerk, and Hailes."[39] The brother of Senex attended this ball and described it as being so densely crowded that, although everything was orderly, there was scarcely room for dancing.

The New Assembly Hall now incorporated in the Tontine buildings was forty-seven by twenty-four feet, and twenty-four feet high, and until the assembly rooms in Ingram Street were built in 1796, it was the most fashionable hall in the city for general dancing assemblies and dancing school balls. The hall appears to have been used by dancing masters, for Senex added that soon after it was erected, he appeared on its boards at a dancing-school ball as a Jacky Tar Figurant. "I was dressed in the full costume of a sailor, with jacket and trousers, and a cudgel under my arm—all according to the dancing-school fashion of the time. Jacky Tar, with dress in character, was then a favourite dance for boys at the balls of Dick, Campbell, Fraser and Sellars."[40]

Of other halls in the city, Senex remarked that Frazer's Hall in King Street was not a fashionable place, but that the "price for a night's use of the room being small, secondary dances were frequently held there." He related that in his young days (1770s), the hall of the Merchants' House in the Bridgegate was beginning to become unfashionable and that the last dancing assembly held there was in October, 1780. This statement, however, is not correct, for the following notice appeared in 1783: "Mr. Smart presents his respects to the ladies and gentlemen who honour him with their company on Thursday evenings, and begs leave to inform them that . . . the rooms and assemblies are to be held at the Merchants' Hall, in Bridgegate . . . owing to the entry to the Tontine Assembly Rooms being under repair."[41]

By the 1790s, dancing was much in vogue among all classes, and the premier social event of the season was the Queen's Assembly in January at which the Lord Provost presided in full court dress and all the young belles of the city and neighbourhood

[39] Senex, *Old Glasgow and Its Environs*, p. 303.

[40] Senex, *Glasgow Past and Present*, vol. 1, p. 252.

[41] The Tontine Coffee House or Hotel was the centre of Glasgow legal and business life for several generations. One of its most interesting features was a reading room supplied with a large selection of newspapers (about sixty) which the waiter arranged in a heap and distributed by rushing into the middle of the room and throwing them to the ceiling. A general scramble of subscribers followed, particularly enjoyed by the underwriters, until all had secured a paper. This practice was changed after one of the gentlemen lost some teeth. Here it was that expectant crowds awaited the arrival of the London stage bearing dispatches of Trafalgar, Waterloo, and the passing of the First Reform Bill, and here all classes daily met in perfect equality. Nothing signifies the difference between life in Glasgow and Edinburgh better than the activities at the Tontine. It is a difference which remains to this day.

"came out." The Queen's Assembly of 1799, held in the Ingram Street Assembly Rooms, was attended by no less than four hundred and sixty people.[42]

The Glasgow Gaelic Club

About the time of the promotion of the Tontine Society, a group of Glasgow High-landers formed a club "to remind them of Ossian, the melodious and noble prince of poets, as well as to converse as friends in the bold and expressive language of heroes in ages past," as they phrased it in their first minute. This, the Glasgow Gaelic Club,[43] was formally established on March 7, 1780, the first president being George MacIntosh of Dunchattan and the first secretary, the Reverend Mr. MacDearmid. They procured a charter from the Highland Society of London, established 1778, which among other privileges delegated to them the power of awarding the annual prizes given by the London society at the Tryst of Falkirk for the encouragement of bagpipe music. Thus a committee of the Gaelic Club adjudicated a piping competition at that meeting for many years.

The meetings of the club, held in several taverns and hotels, were regular and numerous for the first ten years. At its first ball and supper, on March 7, 1792, there were twenty-nine members, ten stranger gentlemen, and forty-five ladies; however, after the club adopted a more exclusive membership policy, the numbers declined, until in 1805 there were only thirty. Members were at first obliged to appear at least in a tartan short-coat and preferably in as full Highland dress as possible, but later, a regulation male attire was adopted, possibly in emulation of the practice at the Nor-thern Meeting, comprising a coat of the Forty-Second Regiment tartan, with green velvet collar and gilt buttons, a waistcoat of plain white Marseilles quilting or kersey-mere, tartan trews or kilt, hose, and sporran.

At the first ball, the company met at seven o'clock to enjoy tea, coffee, and cards, and then danced to music provided by "McLachlan and his Bass." The evening closed with a hot supper at ten o'clock. This arrangement met with much criticism, and the club resolved that in future "a collation should be laid out in an adjoining room, whither the company might retire in sets, or small parties, in the course of the evening, leaving to all the liberty of quitting the ballroom and going decently home at any time one might think fit." The supper caused too long a delay and "exposed the company to cold while the table was covering."[44] It seems strange that the company did not anticipate the difficulty of finding sufficient sedan chairs when they rose together to go home.

As in Edinburgh, the sedan chair was the only practical "taxi" for ladies travelling from one part of town to another; the bearers were again usually Highlanders, wearing blue cloaks and carrying lanterns to help them pick their way through the mud-filled ruts of the unpaved streets.

---

[42] For more information on the Queen's Assembly, see John Strang, *Glasgow and Its Clubs*.

[43] Not to be confused with the Glasgow Highland Society, a benevolent society for Highland children, founded in 1729.

[44] John Strang, *Glasgow and Its Clubs*, p. 111.

The Glasgow Gaelic Club held a notable ball on March 7, 1806, at the Tontine Hotel, which contrasts dramatically with the one just described. It began at seven o'clock with the Reel of Tullochgorum, and from then until midnight chimed from the Tolbooth and the piper led the way to the refectory, country dance and reel alternated. The refection comprised the "delicacies of the season, and the choicest fruits and confectionery" then obtainable from "Baxter's Italian Warehouse." Then, after the usual Highland toasts, dancing continued until dawn.[45]

The balls were held at intervals of three years or so, and each surpassed its predecessor in numbers and brilliance. The last ball, held on January 24, 1841, was a fancy dress ball attended by three hundred guests displaying costumes of all nations. It was long remembered as the most splendid that ever took place in Glasgow.

The Northern Meeting

It seems an easy step from the nostalgic society of the sons of Ossian in Glasgow in the west to that of their aristocratic brethren converging on Inverness in the northeast. The Northern Meeting was established in 1788 as an annual week of social rendezvous for the notable families of the northern counties and was usually held on the last Monday of October.

Details of the original plan of the meeting can be gleaned from the prospectus, a reproduction of which is presented in Appendix D. About ninety members joined from the counties adjacent to Inverness. A unique feature was the imposition of a fine of two guineas upon absentees. It was soon found desirable to reduce the number of formal balls to two, however, and to intersperse them with undress dances and card parties. The gentlemen adopted a formal uniform consisting of "a grass green coat with buff edging, white metal buttons, black velvet cape with four silver embroidered or vellum buttonholes: buff or fancy waistcoat, buff or black silk breeches, the buttons having N.M. engraved thereon."[46] This gave way to Highland dress around mid-nineteenth century, and it was characteristic of the meeting to adapt itself to changing fashions and conditions. Horse races and concerts soon supplemented the balls, card parties, and dinners, and in 1841, piping and dancing competitions were instituted. These continue in some form to this day, although the round of balls and dinners has long since come to an end.

In its original form, the Northern Meeting had nothing to do with preserving the culture of the Gael. Indeed, many of its subscribers were actively clearing their glens of their population to make way for the "great sheep" and Lowland shepherds. Whatever the excuses and justifications for this, and there are many, it is the inhumanity that will live in history, and the shock of the betrayal of a people by those whom they honoured as their leaders and fathers. The warrior chief now was a landlord imbued with values learned at English colleges and only too conscious of the expensive posture expected of a man of fashion in southern society. The eccentric Macdonell of Glengarry, for all his ostentatious attachment to the trappings and ceremony of his forebears of old and his introduction of "games" at the conclusion of the Northern Meeting in 1822, presided over the evacuation of his people and, worst of all, to no

---

[45] Ibid., p. 118.
[46] Iain Colquhoun and Hugh Machell, *Highland Gatherings* (London, 1927), pp. 111–14.

purpose, for he squandered the fruit of his people's pain, so that his estates passed out of his family on his death in 1828.

At the end of the eighteenth century, the unquestioned leader of this northern élite was the celebrated Jane Maxwell, Duchess of Gordon, occupying in due season the retreat of the Huntly-Gordons in Strathspey, or entertaining the literati (Robert Burns among them in the winter of 1786–87) in her native city of Edinburgh, or residing in the aspiring burgh of Aberdeen. On occasion, she remained in the otherwise unglamourous train of her husband at the Hanoverian Court in London, where her portrait was painted by Sir Joshua Reynolds.[47] Although the duchess's influence on fashion and the fashionable was indisputable, Sir Walter Scott opined that her "sole claim to wit rested upon her brazen impudence and disregard to the feelings of all who were near her"; but Elizabeth Grant of Rothiemurchus held pleasant memories of her, calling her a beautiful and very cultivated woman.

It is a striking commentary on the easy manners of the Scottish gentry that she and her clever sister Eglintoun Maxwell were brought up by their mother in parsimonious circumstances in a house in Hyndford Close off the High Street of Edinburgh, and it was not uncommon to see Miss Eglintoun as a girl scurrying across the High Street to the Fountain Well to fill the kettle for tea. The story is told, too, of the high-spirited sisters riding on the backs of the swine which a nearby innkeeper allowed to forage in the street.[48]

This spirit never deserted them, and in time, when Jane Maxwell captivated the Duke of Gordon and became a celebrated duchess, she stimulated social activity wherever she halted. In her maturer years (ca. 1800), she spent each summer in Strathspey at what Elizabeth Grant described in her *Memoirs of a Highland Lady* as the "real old farmhouse of Kinrara." Then, Miss Grant goes on to tell us, "Half the London world of fashion, all the clever people that could be hunted out from all parts, all the north country, all the neighbourhood from far and near without regard to wealth or station, and all the kith and kin of both Gordons and Maxwells, flocked to this encampment in the wilderness during the fine autumns to enjoy the free life, the pure air, and the wit and fun the duchess brought with her to the mountains" (p. 32). Dance followed upon dance — they were "perpetual," remarks Miss Grant — in the drawing room or the servants' hall of an evening, with the footman, Long James, providing the music with his fiddle.

At an earlier stage of her life, we find her holding court at Aberdeen. One observer describes the scene:

We have had great doings here all this week. The town has been full of nobility and gentry. Monday, a great dinner at night; and so on alternately. There is sundry of the company

---

[47] Horace Walpole furnishes a diary of the duchess's movements during two days in 1791. "She first went to Handel's music in the Abbey; she then clambered over the benches, and went to Hasting's trial in the Hall; after dinner to the play; then to Lady Lucan's assembly; after that to Ranelagh, and returned to Mrs. Hobart's faro-table; gave a ball herself in the evening of that morning, into which she must have got a good way; and set out for Scotland next day." [Letter to Mary Berry, May 26, 1791. Horace Walpole's *Correspondence*, ed. W. S. Lewis (New Haven, Conn.: Yale University Press, 1944), vol. 2, pp. 272–73.]

[48] Chambers, *Traditions of Edinburgh*. Charles Kirkpatrick Sharpe's father told this anecdote. It was communicated to Chambers in a letter from Sharpe, June, 1824. See Alexander Allardyce, ed., *Letters from and to Charles Kirkpatrick Sharpe* (Edinburgh, 1888), vol. 2, p. 302.

gone. The Duchess of Gordon still remains, who is at the head of the whole company, who pay their devoirs to her. Colonel Lennox and Lady Charlotte are here; Lord Saltoun; the Earl of Peterborough; a Mr. Bissett, his brother-in-law; the Master of Forbes; Sir Wm. Forbes; the Countess of Kintore. They had all gone before now, but they waited for the motions of the duchess going away. Every day the company have been engaged in the Links at wicket. The Duchess of Gordon and Lady Charlotte Lennox all the time from twelve o'clock till five o'clock afternoon. Many ladies in their coaches, besides the gentlemen on horseback leaping over a five-barred gate. I suppose a great sum will be spent; and that at the public fare, and for private lodgings, I never remember such a full town before. Colonel Lennox looks very well. The Duchess has a cheerful countenance, and full of vivacity. No quarrels have happened amongst them, altho' they have been much intoxicated before the company broke up, at four, five, and six o'clock in the morning.[49]

These were the days when William Marshall, our great composer of Strathspeys, was butler at Gordon Castle, and the duke was no doubt regarding with satisfaction the first appearance in print of his verses to "Cauld Kail" (ca. 1780). The duchess's gaiety and spirit were inherited by her son who, as Lord Huntly, succeeded to her presiding charm at the Northern Meeting after her death in 1812. But Napoleon was now retreating from Moscow and times had changed.

The West Highlands

In some ways it is a relief to turn to the sea lochs and islands of the west. Obviously it was much more difficult to cultivate the elegancies of court and metropolitan society on the myriad islands of the Hebrides. Here there were fewer great houses than in the Central Highlands, and communication with the centres of fashion on the mainland was difficult. Yet the conduct of the laird's or chief's household was much the same as it was in Strathspey, as far as the environment would allow. The journals of Boswell and Johnson record many instances of this milieu from their tour to the Hebrides in 1773, just about the time of Topham's sojourn in Edinburgh.

It is pleasant to arrive with the intrepid travellers at Raasay, the pale sun shimmering from the ripples and eddies of their wake, and the creak and splash of the oars punctuating the chanting of their boatmen and of a group of reapers nearby, the only sounds disturbing the sharp calm of an October evening. All so deathly silent. The great literateur and Bozzy stepped ashore to be received by the illustrious MacLeod of Raasay and his family and escorted into their august mansion with due Highland ceremony.

"On a sideboard," Boswell wrote in his *Tour to the Hebrides*, "was placed for us, who had come off the sea, a substantial dinner, and a variety of wines. Then we had coffee and tea. I observed in the room several elegantly bound books and other marks of improved life. Soon afterwards a fidler appeared, and a little ball began. Raasay himself danced with as much spirit as any man and Malcolm bounded like a roe. Sandy Macleod, who has at times an excessive flow of spirits, and had it now . . . made much jovial noise. Dr. Johnson was so delighted with this scene, that he said, 'I know not how we shall get away' " (September, 1773).

[49] Private letter, October 9, 1789, quoted in Gavin Turreff, *Antiquarian Gleanings*, 2nd. ed., p. 198.

Here the residents danced every night of the year and did not allow the distinguished visitors to interrupt the custom. So happy were these occasions that Boswell "doubted whether unhappiness had any place in Raasay." The ball on the last evening of their stay befitted the occasion, with the eldest Miss MacLeod of Raasay, celebrated for her beauty, as queen of the ball. Two days before, Boswell and three other gentlemen had walked twenty-four miles over rugged ground to the top of the highest mountain on the island and there they "had a Highland dance," returning, he said, "not at all fatigued, and piqued ourselves at not being outdone at the nightly ball by our less active friends, who had remained at home."

A tantalizing glimpse, this, of Hebridean life at its most refined level, where the stresses which were producing emigration elsewhere were, as yet, scarcely felt. What a surprise for those who thought of all Hebrideans as savages and what a pity this existence had to pass away! Here, dancing was a domestic amusement, and the laird's tenants were considered merely an extension of his family, as had been the case from time immemorial in the clan system of the Highlands.

THE DANCING MASTERS

As far as dancing in Scotland is concerned, the difference between the seventeenth and eighteenth centuries lies not so much in the attitude of the Kirk as in the political and social environment. From the foregoing pages it appears that the nation suddenly began to dance in the eighteenth century, but this is a delusion. What, in fact, was different was not the enthusiasm for dancing, which the Scottish people had always shown, but the development of the art as "a necessary part of polite education" as Topham put it. At this stage, the dance streams of court and countryside had begun to merge in the genteel assemblies of the towns, and they coincided with an astonishing eruption of the nation's genius. The dancing master and the musician were now important craftsmen in moulding the nation's cultural fabric. Neither before nor since have they performed quite the same essential social role.

John Galt has his minister, through whom he wrote *Annals of the Parish*, attribute the appearance of a formal dancing school in an Ayrshire town to the demoralizing effects of "the smuggling"!

But a thing happened in this year (1761), which deserves to be recorded, as manifesting that effect the smuggling was beginning to take in the morals of the countryside. One Mr. Macskipnish, of Highland Parentage, who had been a valet-de-chambre with a Major in the campaigns, and taken a prisoner with him by the French, he having come home in a cartel, took up a dancing school at Irville, the which art he had learnt in the genteelest fashion, in the mode of Paris, at the French Court. Such a thing as a dancing school had never, in the memory of man, been known in our countryside; and there was such a sound about the steps and cottillions of Mr. Macskipnish, that every lad and lass, that could spare time and siller, went to him, to the great neglect of their work. The very bairns on the loan, instead of their wonted play, gaed linking and louping in the steps of Mr. Macskipnish, who was, to be sure, a great curiosity, with long spindle legs, his breast shot out like a duck's and his head powdered and frizzled up like a tappet-hen.

Macskipnish, with his French dance salon manner, would be a curiosity in the countryside, although itinerant dancing masters, that is, those who taught the native reels, could not have been unknown. Both Johnny McGill and James Gregg[50] were teaching in Ayrshire before 1761, and Galt is here referring to Ayrshire. I suggest Galt modelled Macskipnish on Davie Strange, an Ayrshire mason who, after studying under the famous Gallini in London and Maltere in Paris (teacher of the French royal family) and, under one of the notable Vestris dancing family, opened a dancing school in Ayrshire. He then opened another one in Edinburgh in Todrick's Wynd in the winter of 1764–65, and continued to practise there until possibly 1788.[51] Galt's description fits Strange in other ways too, and it is very possible that Strange's home town was Irvine, the Irville of Galt's novel. Henry Mackenzie has left an interesting memoir of the master and remarks that "his sister, as I was informed by a gentleman of Ayrshire who lived in the neighbourhood of their father, being so famous for her dancing that gentlemen used to go to penny weddings, on purpose to see her dance."

Mackenzie also tells us that Strange "used to employ high-sounding phrases for the illustration of his art, to the amusement of his scholars, but with a face of imperturbable gravity and importance himself"; and, above all, the author remarks, "he was an enthusiast and pedant in his profession, and thought dancing the paramount accomplishment in man or woman."[52] Another pupil, Mary Somerville, describes him as "exactly like a figure on the stage; tall and thin, he wore a powdered wig, with cannons at the ears, and a pigtail. Ruffles at the breast and wrists, white waistcoat, black silk or velvet shorts, white silk stockings, large silver buckles, and a pale blue coat. He had a little fiddle on which he played, called a kit. My first lesson was how to walk and make a curtsey. 'Young lady, if you visit the queen you must make three curtsies, lower and lower as you approach her. So ——— o ——— o,' leading me on making me curtsey. 'Now if the queen were to ask you to eat a bit of mutton with her, what would you say?' "[53]

Mary Somerville tells us also how Davie Strange supervised the practice of his pupils every Saturday afternoon in the George Street Assembly Rooms: "It was a handsome large hall with benches rising like an amphitheatre. Some of the elder girls were very pretty, and danced well, so these practisings became a lounge for officers from the Castle, and other young men. We used always to go in full evening dress. We learnt the minuet de la cour, reels and country dances. Our partners used to give us gingerbread and oranges. Dancing before so many people was quite an exhibition, and I was greatly mortified one day when ready to begin a minuet, by the dance master shaking me roughly and making me hold out my frock properly."[54]

Other Edinburgh dancing masters of note were MacQueen who taught in Skinner's Close in 1740; Lamotte, Le Picq, and Downie who practised in the mid-century; and Martin, Barnard, d'Egville, and Gallini who were established in the late 1700s. In 1775 Topham wrote: "For the number of inhabitants I suppose there are more dancing

[50] Gregg (Grig or Greig), the composer of "Gregg's Pipes" and other airs, taught dancing until he could scarcely see. He died at a very advanced age in 1817. See Stenhouse.

[51] Strange is listed in Edinburgh directories, 1733–88.

[52] Henry Mackenzie, *Anecdotes and Egotisms*, p. 75.

[53] Martha Somerville, *Recollections of Mary Somerville*, p. 41.

[54] Ibid., p. 42.

masters than in any other city; who gain large fortunes though they instruct on very moderate terms from the number of scholars who constantly attend. In general they may be said to be very good ones" (Letter xli).

Lamotte and Le Picq were French; the former, said Henry Mackenzie in *Anecdotes and Egotisms*, "had all the people of fashion for scholars but was thought not to make good *men* dancers . . . Le Picq was thought to teach males better . . . a grandfather or granduncle, of the celebrated dancer of that name who afterwards figured with so much éclat in London and was celebrated for his pirouettes." Le Picq's son lost his life in his calling: while dancing a "high dance" for the officers aboard a man o'war lying in Leith Roads, he made "what is called a 'cut' so high as to strike his head against a nail or staple in the ceiling of the cabin, which caused his death by a contusion of the brain" (p. 74).

Downie, the same writer reminisced, "was a muscular and powerful man who taught the strong active Highland Dances, but with little grace. When I was at Downie's, his school was in Niddry's Wynd underneath a room belonging to the Corporation of Mary's Chapel, in which was held a principal Mason lodge." There was an inner room "called the masking room, masks being at that time [ca. 1755] worn at the dancing school balls" (p. 74).

Martin's school was in Weir's Land, Todrick's Wynd, the same address, it will be noted, as that of Strange to whom Martin was assistant for twenty years. His first announcement occurred in 1783, and if the Edinburgh directory is correct, he must have begun to teach independently of Strange rather than in succession to him. This is not so important as the fact that he taught the "minuet and louvre, together with a variety of French, English and Scots high dances, also the different steps for country dances and cotillons."[55]

Barnard's rooms in Thistle Street were acquired by Laurie in 1794, and five years later a certain S. Wilson advertised his annual ball to take place in "Barnard's Rooms" under the patronage of the Duchess of Buccleugh and other ladies. He was not as important as d'Egville, late of the King's Theatre, London, who advertised a speciality of "Scotch Reels, Highland Flings and all Caledonian steps."[56] D'Egville also held classes in Glasgow.

Perhaps the most celebrated of the foreign dancing masters to practise in Edinburgh was Gallini who left a book on dance which dates from this period (ca. 1780). When the Bell's Wynd Assembly premises had finally exhausted the patience of its patrons, and thoughts were seriously turned to providing a more acceptable alternative, Gallini obtained the cooperation of the town council in purchasing a site in the new town for assembly rooms, but for some unknown reason nothing came of it. Gallini later established himself in London and, by what some called a combination of parsimony and assiduity, made a comfortable living.

We taste something of Georgian London with the announcement that Madame Bonnet (formerly Marcacci) would teach "fashionable and improved modes of dancing as taught by Gallini, Willis and others." Female dancing masters were uncommon

[55] Jamieson, "Social Assemblies of the Eighteenth Century," *Book of the Old Edinburgh Club*, vol. 19, 1933.
[56] Ibid.

as, in the words of one authority, they could not show the proper knee positions![57] Nevertheless there was a female dance teacher in Edinburgh early in the eighteenth century, Signora Violante,[58] but she taught ladies only. Her school was in Skinner's Close, a location obviously associated with dancing and near the assembly room. Alexander Carlyle, the civilized minister of Inveresk, referred to Signora Violante in his *Autobiography*:

I was very fond of dancing, in which I was a great proficient, having been taught at two different periods in the country, though the manners were so strict that I was not allowed to exercise my talent at penny-weddings, or any balls but those of the dancing school. Even this would have been denied me, as it was to Robertson and Witherspoon[59] and other clergymen's sons, at that time [1737], had it not been for the persuasion of those aunts of mine who had been bred in England, and for some papers in the Spectator which were pointed out to my father, which seemed to convince him that dancing would make me a more accomplished preacher, if ever I had the honour to mount the pulpit. My mother too, who generally was right, used her sway in this article of education. But I had not the means of using this talent, of which I was not a little vain, till luckily I was introduced to Madame Violante, an Italian stage dancer, who kept a much frequented school for young ladies, but admitted of no boys above 7 or 8 years, so that she wished very much for senior lads to dance with her grown up misses weekly at her practisings. I became a favourite of this dancing mistress, and attended her faithfully with two or three of my companions and had my choice of partners on all occasions, insomuch that I became a great proficient in this branch at little or no expense. It must be confessed, however, that, having nothing to do at Stewart's class, through the incapacity of the headmaster, and McLaurin's giving me no trouble, as I had a great promptitude in learning maths, I had a good deal of spare time this session which I spent, as well as all the money I got at a billiard table, which unluckily was within 50 yards of the college, I was so sensible of the folly of this, however, that next year I abandoned it altogether. [Pp. 53–54]

One of the endearing characteristics of "Jupiter" Carlyle is his droll manner of recalling anecdotes against himself. Whether he was sensible of this or not is difficult to say, but I cannot continue without sharing another with the reader:

My youth had been spent in a vain pursuit; for my first love, which I have mentioned as far back as 1735, had kept entire possession till 1753, by means of her coquetry and my irresolution. She was of superior understanding as well as beauty. In this last she would have excelled most women of her time, had she not been the worst dancer in the world, which she could not be prevailed on to leave off, though her envious rivals laughed and rejoiced at her persevering folly. Though she had a bad voice and bad ear, she was a great mistress

[57] G. Yates, *The Ball or a Glance at Almack's*, p. 36.

[58] Signora Violante and her husband gained fame as rope dancers, or performers on the high rope, travelling with their act to various British playhouses. In 1736, the Signora performed in the Old Assembly Hall. "It was announced that she danced a minuet on the rope, danced on a board placed loosely on the rope, danced on the rope with two boys fastened to her feet — danced with two swords at her feet — the rope being no thicker than a penny whipcord." [Chambers, *Domestic Annals*, 2nd. ed., vol. 3, p. 625.] She appears to have settled in Edinburgh, living at the foot of Carrubbers' Close, and taught gymnastics as well as dancing.

[59] The same Witherspoon who became president of Princeton University and one of the architects of the American constitution.

of conversation, having both wit and humour, and, with an air of haughty prudery, had enough of coquetry both to attract and retain her lovers, of whom she had many." [P. 421]

No town in Scotland could compare with Edinburgh in the distinction and numbers of dancing masters. Hence it is easy to overlook activities elsewhere. I do not suppose it really matters that Mr. Frazer advertised in October 13, 1783 that he would open his dancing school in MacNair's Land, King Street, Glasgow, or that a Mr. Sillars announced the opening of his school in Buchanan Close near the Exchange, also in Glasgow, on the same day; or that other two prominent Glasgow teachers were Messrs. Campbell and Dick; or that a Mr. Park announced the opening of his ballroom at the King's Arms, Trongate in 1799. The same listing could be done for every prominent town in Scotland, and it would not tell us very much except that dancing was popular and that there was a necessity to learn to dance correctly.

We cannot leave the subject of dancing masters, however, without saying something of Francis Peacock, the social and hospitable dancing master of Aberdeen. Peacock was a musician as well as a dancing master, and indeed the combination of the two roles was not unusual, as we have seen in France in the cases of Lully and Rameau. Peacock's claim to our attention arises from his book on dancing published in 1805. This was the first book on the subject written by a Scot and the first one to contain some kind of technical description of the setting and travelling steps of the reel as danced in the Highlands. At the time of the publication of this book, Peacock had been a teacher of dancing for sixty years, which means that he started his career in 1745, the year of the Jacobite rebellion. He held his classes in an old house called Pitfoddell's lodging, in the Castlegate, and if we can judge from the list of subscribers to his book, he counted among his pupils most of the gentry and nobility of the northeast, including the famous Duchess of Gordon to whom the book was dedicated.

Alexander Jaffray of Kingswells attended Peacock's dancing school, "the established dancing school of the city," in 1770, at the age of fifteen, and has left us one of the few accounts of Peacock's practice. "He was an excellent master, but stern and severe when a dull pupil came under his hands. . . . I went through the minuet but very indifferently, and declined exhibiting at the Ball, finding myself unequal to the task. The only part I took any pleasure in was the country dances, which were practised once every week. I declined attending the school after the first three months; tired of the practice of dancing, of which in after years I became very fond."

Peacock performed as a violinist and cellist at the concerts of the Aberdeen Musical Society; and for the occasion of the coronation of George III in 1761, composed an anthem which was sung by the gentlemen of that society in the Marischal College Hall before a distinguished gathering of five hundred people. "The audience was greatly delighted with the performance, being the best of the kind ever performed here."[60] He published also, in 1776, a collection of fifty Scottish airs,[61] and in the preface he says that he believed David Rizzio to be the composer of the best of them! He died in very comfortable circumstances, June 26, 1807, at the grand age of eighty-four, and left much of his estate to the charitable causes to which he had directed the proceeds of his

[60] Gavin Tureff, *Antiquarian Gleanings*, 2nd. ed., p. 264.

[61] *Fifty favourite Scotch Airs, for a Violin, German Flute, and Violoncello, with a thorough bass for the Harpsichord*. Dedicated to the Right Honourable Earl of Aberdeen.

book. He also left a memory of his continuing to organize his school balls until he was eighty years of age, balls which began at four o'clock and sometimes continued until four the next morning. Peacock's Close commemorates the name of this amazing gentleman.

Dancing school balls had long been customary, and were sometimes called the "finishing" balls because they came at the end of the instructional season. In the 1770s Topham mentions that these were very popular in Edinburgh and that the dancing masters who "swarm" in the town are "constantly exhibiting their scholars to the public." He points out that "it is a custom in London for some of the principal dancing masters to have balls for their benefit, but here it is a general thing from the one most in vogue to the humble teacher of a reel to the drone of the bag-pipe. Each has his ball and his public, or his two balls . . . and endeavours to show his own excellence and skill as a master by the execution and performance of his scholars" (Letter xli).

These were the days of disciplined and studied movement, in the finest traditions of the court dance. "*Dolcetti di movimente*" Dominico once intoned, and the Minuet was of this image, with Davie Strange and Francis Peacock its most devoted professors in Scotland.

LONDON DANCE ASSEMBLIES

In our preoccupation with Scotland, it is easy to overlook the example set by the great metropolis of London and perhaps also the close reciprocity of influence which it enjoyed in dancing, as well as in many other matters, with the "Athens of the North." It seems altogether appropriate that the most important assembly rooms in London should have been founded and owned by a Scotsman. His name was MacCall; the year, 1765. It was said that the enterprise was financed by the Duke of Hamilton, hereditary keeper of Holyrood Palace; this may be so, for MacCall had certainly previously married the duchess's maid. In view of the prevailing anti-Scottish sentiment of the city, MacCall found it expedient to transpose his name to Almack, and thus his premises, destined to become widely celebrated, were known to many generations as Almack's. The opening ceremony befitted this destiny, with many dignitaries in attendance, led by the Duke of Cumberland — the infamous "butcher" himself.

Many notable aristocrats paid the requisite subscription of ten guineas which entitled them to a ball and a supper once a week for twelve weeks. As one of the gentlemen explained to a friend, "The men's tickets are not transferable, so, if the ladies do not like us, they have no opportunity of changing us, but must see the same person for ever. . . . Almack's Scotch face, in a bay-wig, waiting at supper, would divert you, as would his lady, in a sack, making tea and curtseying to the duchesses."[62] For the period, the subscription was high, but this was not the only barrier; money alone could not ensure acceptance. It had to be supported by rank and aristocratic respectability.

As in Edinburgh, the assembly was directed by a committee of ladies who organized the balls. Soon the prestige of the establishment was such that it was far more of a social distinction to have entrée at Almack's than at court. In the Regency period, Almack's ballroom was described as measuring about one hundred feet by forty feet, "chastely

---

[62] Gilly Williams, in a letter to George Selwyn, quoted in John Timbs, *Club Life of London*, p. 74, and other sources.

decorated with gilt columns and pelastes, classic medallions, mirrors, etc., and [was] lit with gas, in cut-glass lustres. The largest number of persons ever present in this room at one ball was 1700."

Almack's Assembly Rooms, later called Willis's Rooms, after Almack's successor, are not to be confused with the club which he established in Pall Mall on the site of the British Institution in 1764, one of the several popular gambling clubs that thrived in eighteenth-century London.

The best account of Almack's in its heyday — the Regency period (ca. 1814) — comes from the eloquent pen of Captain Gronow. His description in *Recollections and Anecdotes* is too valuable and interesting to condense:

At the present time one can hardly conceive the importance which was attached to getting admission to Almack's the 7th heaven of the fashionable world. Of the 300 officers of the Foot Guards, not more than half a dozen were honoured with vouchers of admission to this exclusive temple of the beau monde; the gates of which were guarded by lady patronesses, whose smiles or frowns consigned men & women to happiness or despair. These lady patronesses were the Ladies Castlereagh, Jersey, Cowper & Sefton, Mrs. Drummond Burrell, now Lady Willoughby, and Princess Esterhazy, and the Countess Lieven.

The most popular amongst these grandes dames was unquestionably Lady Cowper, now Lady Palmerston. Lady Jersey's bearing, on the contrary, was that of a theatrical tragedy queen; and whilst attempting the sublime, she frequently made herself simply ridiculous, being inconceivably rude, and in her manner often ill-bred. Lady Sefton was kind & amiable, Madame de Lieven haughty & exclusive, Princess Esterhazy was a bon enfant, Lady Castlereagh and Mrs. Burrell de tres grandes dames.

Many diplomatic arts, much finesse, and a host of intrigues, were set in motion to get an invitation to Almack's. Very often persons whose rank and fortunes entitled them to entrée anywhere, were excluded by the cliqueism of the lady patronesses; for the female government of Almack's was a pure despotism, and subject to all the caprices of despotic rule; it is needless to add that, like every other despotism, it was not innocent of abuses. The fair ladies who ruled supreme over this little dancing and gossiping world, issued a solemn proclamation that no gentleman should appear at the assemblies without being dressed in knee-breeches, white cravat, and chapeau bras. On one occasion, the Duke of Wellington was about to ascend the staircase of the ballroom, dressed in black trousers, when the vigilant Mr. Willis, the guardian of the establishment, stepped forward and said, "Your grace cannot be admitted in trousers," whereupon the Duke, who had a great respect for orders and regulations, quietly walked away.

In 1814, the dances at Almack's were Scotch reels and the old English country dance; and the orchestra, being from Edinburgh, was conducted by the then celebrated Neil [*sic*] Gow. It was not until 1815 that Lady Jersey introduced from Paris the favourite quadrille, which had so long remained popular. I recollect the persons who formed the very first quadrille that was ever danced at Almack's. They were Lady Jersey, Lady Harriett Butler, Lady Susan Tyde, and Miss Montgomery; the men being the Count St. Aldegonde, Mr. Montgomery, Mr. Montague, and Charles Standish. The "mazy waltz" was also brought to us about this time; but there were comparatively few who at first ventured to whirl round the salons of Almack's; in course of time Lord Palmerston might, however, have been seen describing an infinite number of circles with Mme de Lieven. Baron de Neumann was frequently seen perpetually turning with Princess Esterhazy; and in course of time, the waltzing mania, having turned the heads of society generally, descended to their feet, and the waltz was practised in the morning in certain noble mansions in London with unparalleled assiduity.

The dandies of society were Beau Brummell, the Duke of Argyle, the Lords Worcester, Alvanley and Foley, Henry Pierrepant, John Mills, Bradshaw, Henry de Ros, Charles Standish, Edward Montagu, Hervery Aston, Dan Mackinnon, George Dawson Danier, "Rufus" Lloyd and others. They were great frequenters of White's Club in St. James's St., where, in the famous bay window, they mustered in force.

Drinking and play were more universally indulged in then than at the present time and many men still living must remember the couple of bottles of port at least which accompanied his dinner in those days. [Pp. 31–33]

If it is true that Niel Gow performed in 1814, then indeed it is a matter worthy of remark, for Niel had been dead seven years! However, Gronow undoubtedly alludes to Niel's son Nathaniel, who appears to have travelled to London on occasion with some of his associates to support his brother John (1764–1826), who had a music-selling business in London and performed at Caledonian balls in the city.

The method of conducting the dancing at these assemblies was very similar to that at Edinburgh. At court and very select assemblies, the company took their places in the dance according to social precedence; otherwise, each lady on entering the ballroom was presented by the Master of Ceremonies with a ticket which bore the number of her place in the dance, and which she was obliged to display conspicuously on her person. The balls usually opened with a promenade round the room followed by Minuets. When the Country Dances were to begin, the Master of Ceremonies called up the company and arranged them according to their numbers, the gentlemen taking the numbers of their partners. If the company was of sufficient size, it was divided into sets of up to eight or nine couples. Anyone requiring a partner could apply to the Master of Ceremonies to provide one, and two ladies or two gentlemen could dance together only if there were no alternative and if they received the permission of the Master of Ceremonies. The sets were about four and one-half feet wide with about two feet between the couples.

All assembled, couple number one had the privilege of "calling" the dance; that is, they declared the figures to be executed and the music to be played. If these gave reasonable grounds for complaint from the company, the Master of Ceremonies could object and ask the couple to call an acceptable substitute. Only the Master of Ceremonies was allowed to communicate with the musicians. If the musicians did not know the tune, they sometimes played something else, and often the caller did not know he or she had been duped. After the tune had been played once through, the dance was begun. When the dancing couple had progressed to third or fourth place, according to whether it was a two-couple or three-couple dance, the second couple started, and so on with all the couples in succession. There is no hint that the musicians varied the tune, a fact horrible to contemplate.

The next dance was called by lady or couple number two, couple number one now taking bottom place, and only after that dance was completed could the company normally expect a rest. If a couple did not know the figures specified, or disliked them, that couple could retire from the set.

About the time of Waterloo, and for a decade or so after, dancing was ardently indulged by all classes of the population. It takes us a little outside our period, but it may be appropriate to continue the discussion of dancing practices in the metropolis during the Regency. Teachers of dancing became very numerous in response to the demand, and soon the competition between them became very intense. The charlatans exploited their unsuspecting pupils, and even teachers of talent had to abandon their scruples and advertise to teach country dancing in six lessons, and submit to the caprices of influential pupils in perpetuating popular corruptions of the dance. Many became simply racketeers, holding balls for profit, and even charging no admission for these, but drawing their remuneration from the care of the hats. The majority of their pupils gained little more than a knowledge of a few trifling figures and practically no steps.

Thomas Wilson, from whose works I have drawn most of this information, tells us that "ten couples out of a hundred scarcely knew what they were about; being equally deficient in steps as in figures."[63] Frequent disputes arose in the ballroom among people performing a figure differently. Many danced so poorly, having little or no knowledge of steps, that they simply scurried to complete the figures of the dance as quickly as possible, without regard to the music. If the music tried to keep up with them, all the better, and then they would praise it as a merry tune. It was not uncommon, apparently, for the dancing couple to complete the figures ahead of the music and start again without giving it a chance to catch up. Nor was it uncommon for an unskilled person to call a dance with wrongly matched figures and music, say a four-bar figure to eight bars of music or vice versa, in which case the whole dance was soon out of phase. Indeed, Wilson also tells us that this could easily happen if the dance were taken from one of the many annual publications, as in these the figures were "very seldom found to be properly adapted to the music."[64]

"Calling-up" a dance could be a very exacting task, if taken seriously. Ideally, the caller should have been able to demonstrate the figures and the appropriate setting steps to the company, and so execute the dance that he could be referred to as a guide and example during its execution. Many, apparently, could not approach this ideal, yet they persisted in trying to carry it off. When, in these cases, the Master of Ceremonies was sufficiently competent to feel justified in complaining to the caller, he was sometimes given some such a retort as "I learnt dancing, Sir, when at school, and have lately danced at the assemblies at Bath and several others, equally, if not more fashionable, and have had the honour of having been selected to be partner and of dancing with my Lord or my Lady ———."

The notorious class consciousness of the English was never more acute than in the days of the Regency, and the lower orders drawn into the city by the pressures of the Industrial Revolution were sorely oppressed. The gulf between rich and poor was immense; labour and human life were cheap. Snobbery and affectation were by no means new to higher society, nor were the imposters and shams, but they were at no time more conspicuous. The sons of many a genial squire became infected by the dandyism of the metropolis — I almost said new dandyism, but it was not new, it was already there in the 1760s — and evident in what one writer called "contemptible groups of smirking quadrillers with unweaponed belts, stuffed breasts, and strangled loins! a set of squeaking dandies whose sex may be readily mistaken, or, I should

---

[63] Thomas Wilson, *A Companion to the Ballroom* (London, 1816); and *The Complete System of English Country Dances*.

[64] Wilson, *A Companion to the Ballroom*, pp. 203–29.

rather say, is of no consequence."[65] No doubt the Prince Regent and his companions, Beau Brummell and the like, gave the cult a glamorous impetus; but what was barely excusable in them was intolerable arrogance in their imitators. Perhaps it was just a peculiar adolescent effusion, for many of the dandies of the officer class in the Guards and in the cavalry distinguished themselves at Waterloo, but with the same sad, schoolboyish impetuosity for which they paid dearly.

It is not surprising, with such influences in the air, that the musicians at a ball were generally regarded contemptuously as mere fiddlers for hire, "frequently treated worse than their servants, and never, or seldom spoken to, but in an imperious haughty manner."[66] When indeed they were occasionally treated more familiarly and plied with liquor, it was too often for no other purpose than to make them drunk and appear ridiculous, a practice regarded as very amusing by some people. Then, in Wilson's words, "musicians are seldom paid for their labour, yet these employers never think that the musicians cannot find employment for more than five or six months in the year, and generally in the winter season, when the weather is bad. . . ." Now musicians' unions in some countries have reversed the situation to the other extreme. They extort the public to pay on occasion for musicians it neither wants nor requires, protect the most outrageous imposters, make life difficult for the true artist, and stand in the way of culture.

However, to return to our subject, the strictures levelled at the execution of Country Dances in Regency London were equally applied to the new Quadrille and Waltz and, from all accounts, the art of social dancing declined with the passing of the Minuet. Strangely enough the Scotch Reel became quite the rage and, as we have seen, was conspicuous on the program at Almack's in 1814.

The established dancing masters recalled with nostalgia the birth-night balls of George III's reign and the assiduous preparations for them. Counterparts of these balls were held at various assemblies throughout the kingdom, and the ceremonials of the occasion politely imitated.

At some suitable time previous to the birth-night ball, the Lord Chamberlain would invite applications from those who wished to attend, and no doubt the list of dancers which the Lord Chamberlain held in his hand on the evening of the ball was carefully compiled from these. When the ballroom was conveniently full, the doors were closed and, shortly thereafter, Their Majesties entered to the strains of the march from *Judas Maccabeus* played by the court band ensconced in the music gallery. They walked round a space in the centre of the room, passing a few words with the nobility near them, and retired to their chairs. Then, in the words of one observer:

The Lord Chamberlain advanced to the Prince of Wales and his royal sister, making his obeisance before them, on which they arose and performed the same ceremony before their Majesties, retiring backwards until they arrived at the opposite end of the open space, when the band immediately commenced playing a Minuet.

The court dancing-master (Mr. Desnoyer) spread the lady's train, which was exceedingly long and heavy with gold or silver, and which during the respectful preliminary, had been supported on a hoop. Having concluded a minuet the obeisance was repeated to their Majes-

---

[65] Jonah Barrington, *Sketches of his Own Times*, quoted in G. Yates, *The Ball*, p. 29.
[66] Wilson, *A Companion to the Ballroom*, p. 233

ties; and in the same manner proceeded the other members of the royal family and nobility according to precedence, going through the same ceremonies.

The gentleman did not go up a second time to make obeisance if he was required to dance another minuet (as was generally the case); but waited for another lady, who was under the necessity of going through the awful ceremony alone.

A country dance or two followed when the minuets were over; for cotillons or quadrilles were not then in fashion at court.

This observer goes on to say that the large court hoops were quite unsuited to the Country Dance, and that long custom could not divest the sight of its ludicrous aspects:

The jig measure, which corresponds to the canter in a horse's paces, produced a strong bounding up and down of the hoop — and the gavotte measure, which corresponds to the short trot, produced a tremulous and agitated motion. . . .

When the whole party was put in motion, but little trace of a regular dance remained; all was a perfect maze; and the cutting in and out of these cumbrous machines presented to the mind only the figure of a most formidable affray.

Then the numerous ornaments, tassels, embroidery, and so on which bespread the hoops were liable to become entangled with others of their kind, much to the embarrassment of the debutantes. However, as our observer so eloquently puts it:

This concatenation of petty distresses — the pretty suffusion of countenance incident to them — the attentive assiduity of the gentlemen to render assistance — the affable enjoyment of the whole scene by their Majesties, altogether disposed the company to an hilarity of tone, which was soon after enhanced by the opening of the buffets for refreshment, which took place on their Majesties retiring from the scene of action. The lips of the company were then unsealed, and the how d'yes, the friendly shakes and greetings of all sorts and kinds, flow about in unrestrained good humour, and in about an hour after, all had departed.[67]

There were Caledonian balls in London, even at that early date. The gentlemen wore tartan ribbon in their breast buttonhole, and the ladies wore white dresses with tartan sashes or scarfs. The scarf was not very wide and was tied with a loose knot under the left arm; it had fringed ends, one longer than the other. A sash, not long, was wound about the waist and tied behind.

Susan Sibbald records these facts in 1804 and remarks on the two giant thistles which reached from the floor to far above the orchestra which they flanked.[68] A supper interrupted the evening, and reels were danced almost exclusively.

[67] Yates, *The Ball*, p. 16–17.
[68] Susan Sibbald, *Memoirs of Susan Sibbald*.

7 / Scottish Dancing on the Eighteenth-Century Stage

Alexander Carlyle meets Violette on way to London – Scots in London – theatres – dance interludes – America – the denouement

Several English observers of dancing in the Scottish Highlands, such as Edward Topham, Thomas Garnett, and James Hall, compared it favourably with the stage dancing they knew. This would undoubtedly be the entr'acte dancing which was very popular in the theatrical entertainment of their time. It is of great interest that some of these stage dances were on a Scottish theme and presumably also in the Scottish traditional dance style, if not actually traditional dances. They were featured most frequently in the early decades of the sixteenth century and then, after a period of neglect between 1720 and 1750, they began to appear more regularly again despite the anti-Scottish feeling that then pervaded London. For one would not expect Londoners to have much attachment to things Scottish at that time, particularly after the Highland Jacobites had penetrated almost to the city itself. But Prince Charlie's forces retreated, and about the time they were harrying the government forces besieged in Athole and Fort William, that is, about the beginning of March, 1746, it is to our purpose to join our friend "Jupiter" Carlyle on his way to London aboard a packet from Holland.

He had a brisk crossing of about sixteen hours and, in common with the other passengers, was "heartily seasick." When the boat set out, Carlyle had noticed "three foreigners, of different ages, who had under their care a young person of about sixteen, very handsome indeed," whom he took for "a Hanoverian baron coming to Britain to pay his court at St. James's."[1] The young person was the only one of the strangers who had a berth in the cabin, which, as it happened, was directly opposite Carlyle's. At one anxious moment, the young person called out to him in French to ask if they were

[1] Alexander Carlyle, *Autobiography*, p. 192. This os the only evidence of Violette's mysterious early life that has come to us.

not in danger, but the voice was that of a woman! Carlyle reassured her, and not long after discovered that he was addressing "La Violette," who became celebrated for her dancing, and who was travelling to fulfil an engagement at the opera in the Haymarket. Carlyle befriended her party, saw them on their way to London, and received an invitation to attend her first performance at the opera, which he accepted with pleasure.

Carlyle makes no mention of it, but Lord Stafford remarks of that occasion, "She surprised her audience at her first appearance on the stage; for at her beginning to caper she showed a neat pair of black velvet breeches, with roll'd stockings; but finding they were unusual in England she changed them the next time for a pair of white drawers."

Eva Maria Veigel, "La Violette," became something of a celebrity of the London stage. She was the wife of the great actor-manager David Garrick to whom she remained devoted until, and indeed after, his death. As Mrs. Garrick she had occasion to entertain Carlyle in the company of John Home, the Scottish playwright, twelve years after their first meeting; but she did not recognize her early benefactor, and Carlyle, with his great-hearted tact, did not care to recall the occasion to her mind.

Garrick had brought Noverre, the great French choreographer, to London, for which bold enterprise the time was most propitious, for never had theatrical dancing enjoyed higher esteem in London nor been in greater demand everywhere. "Jupiter" Carlyle, himself a great enthusiast for the dance, was typical of the distinguished Scotsmen who visited London at this period, and who shared the general passion for the theatre. Surprisingly enough, the anti-Scottish feeling which pervaded the metropolis throughout the century did not stifle the growing popularity of Scottish songs and the occasional dance entr'acte on a Scottish theme, even if it made life a little uncomfortable for the Scots with whom Lord Bute seemed to fill his government and the Scots men of letters, physicians, and soldiers who rubbed shoulders at the Duke of Argyll's evening parties, or who discussed the topics of the day in the British Coffee House in Cockspur Street.

Dissatisfaction with the Hanoverian dynasty mitigated the anti-Scotch reactions to the Jacobite rebellion such that "the gay world at Bath and other parts of England" seemed "very fond of white rosed buttons, plaid or tartan," with which they decorated even the harness of their horses.[2]

The principal theatres were Drury Lane, Covent Garden, and the Royal Opera House in the Haymarket, all in energetic competition. The theatre-goers thronged to the doors at four o'clock in the afternoon for the curtain at six. They sat on backless benches and were by no means inhibited in showing displeasure or approval, sometimes, in extreme cases, tearing up benches and breaking chandeliers, to say nothing of attacking the players, who were protected from intrusions by a row of sharp iron spikes running along the front of the stage.

To calm this restive mass, it was necessary to fill the intervals with music and dance entertainment, and so it would happen that between acts of *Othello*, for instance, there might be billed "The Highland Reel: A New Comic Dance by Aldridge, Miss Valois, and Sga. Manesiere," a feature which entertained the patrons of Covent Garden on

---

[2] Carlyle, *Autobiography*, p. 199.

several occasions from March, 1768 to December, 1774; or perhaps "The Highland Laird and his Attendants," or "The Sailor's Song by Champnes and a Dance in character by the Sailor," features which appeared at Drury Lane in May, 1760. The nature of the play did not seem to matter, except, perhaps, in the case of *The Beggar's Opera*, where hornpipes, the New Country Dance, the Rustic Dance or the like were usual and appropriate. On October 23, 1760, Nancy Dawson made her first appearance on the stage of Drury Lane dancing a hornpipe at Act III in *The Beggar's Opera*, as she had formerly done at the rival Covent Garden, where, indeed, on the following evening the production of the same opera was adorned by a "New Hornpipe by Dr. Arne performed by Mrs. Vernon."

These dance interludes, reminiscent of the Elizabethan practice, were doubtless of considerable influence on the development of stage character dance in Great Britain, and it is of interest to us here to notice the dances on Scottish motifs which appear on London play announcements during the eighteenth century and earlier.

The earliest of these dances I have traced is called The Dance of the Bonny Highlander, performed at Drury Lane, July 6, 1700. The announcement tells us it had been performed "but once before on the English stage." One of the dancers in the company was Mr. Weaver, whom we encounter in his *Essay Towards an History of Dancing*, published in London in 1712. The next dance is simply entitled "Scotch Dance," performed by Mrs. Bignell or Bicknell (who also appears as an actress at Drury Lane, August 20, 1712) at Drury Lane on February 12, 1703, in January, 1706, and at other London theatres later. Whether this was the same dance as that entitled "Scotch Whim" and danced by Mrs. Bignell on July 19, 1703, we do not know, but it seems possible. A Mrs. Evans danced "Scotch Whim and Irish Trot" at Lincoln's Inn Fields on August 9, 1704.

At this same time, we find a dance called "Highland Lilt" among a number of dances, performed by a "Devonshire Girl never seen on the Stage before, with her Master." This item was first presented at Drury Lane, December 8, 1702. Other dances included in this recital were a "Genteel Round to the Harp alone, an Irish Humour," and "The Whip of Dunboyne." In June, 1703, at Drury Lane, one Claxton was billed to dance "The Highland" and "The Whip of Dunboyne," and a little over a year later, on October, 1704, we find, also at Drury Lane, "Country Farmer's Daughter" and "Highland Lilt" by Mrs. Mosee, and "The Whip of Dunboyne, an Irish Humour by Claxton, her master"!

All these items appeared during the years 1700 to 1704. The Scottish motif in the a "New Scotch Dance" of his own composition and performed it at Lincoln's Inn stage dance is not alluded to again until May, 1717, when a Mr. Newhouse introduced Fields with Miss Cross. It may only be coincidence that he reappears with a "Scotch Dance" exactly a year later, this time performing it with a Miss Smith. The principal dancers at Lincoln's Inn Fields at this time — the Salles, Mrs. Schoolding, de La Garde and sons, and later, Moreau — were brought over from the continent, but they shared the bills with such native talent as Mrs. Bullock, Miss Smith, and a few others, including, from time to time, Mr. Newhouse.

The de La Garde sons performed a new dance at Lincoln's Inn Fields called "Scotch Highlander," on April 7, 1719. A week later they introduced Mrs. Bullock into the act on the occasion of her benefit, April 25, this time calling their number simply

"Scots Dance." Perhaps it was a Threesome Reel. Doubtless it was this event which led Mrs. Bullock to prepare a "Scotch Dance" for herself, which she first performed on May 25, 1720 at the rival theatre, Drury Lane, in the next season, and repeated at regular intervals for some years at both Drury Lane and Lincoln's Inn. Her solitary performance of a "Highland Lilt" in November, 1723 was not repeated by her, unless this dance was the same as that billed "Scotch Lilt" in April of the following year. In May, 1722 she joined the dancers at Lincoln's Inn to perform a "Highland Dance," and indeed she appears to have played at two theatres for a time, unless we are dealing with two different ladies of the same name.

In the years 1750–57 there were occasional performances of "A New Scotch Dance in which will be introduced by Particular Desire the Scotch Measure and the Highland Reel by Froment and Mad. De La Cointrie." Here we have the first direct allusion to a dance called the Scotch Measure. The Scots Measure was performed by Fishar some twenty years later, on November, 1775, at the Haymarket, with no partner specified. The Highland Reel was a favourite number of Aldridge, Valois, and Manesière in the years 1768–74, about the time that this dance was moving into English ballrooms.

One looks in vain for a conspicuously Scottish name among the dancers of the London stage in the eighteenth century. The Irish are represented by Aldridge (whom we know was Irish) and doubtless also by that McNeil who made a specialty of a Fingalian Dance around mid-century. Nancy Dawson, who took up this dance in April, 1761, a few months, incidentally, before James Macpherson published his poems of Ossian, may have been of Scottish stock, but she did not perform Scottish dances.

One Middlemist, who performed dances in the presentations of Allan Ramsay's *Gentle Shepherd* at the Haymarket in the 1760s and 1770s was, in all likelihood, a Scot, as was James Lauder, whose singing was a special feature of these occasions.

One also looks in vain for many eye-witness accounts of the performance of dances with a Scottish motif on the London stage, and for reference to the music to which they were performed. However, a letter written by Ralph Bigland in 1749 gives one account of a song and dance interlude on the London stage, and mentions specifically the use of the bagpipe for musical accompaniment:

I have since I came here [London] been lately two or three times at the play and what invited me most was to see a new dance called the Scots Dance consisting of about 20 lads and lasses dress'd after the Highland fashion. The scene represents a very romantic, rocky, or mountainous country seemingly, at the most distant view you behold a glorious pair (which far surpass all the other actors) sitting among the rocks, while the rest are dancing below among groves of trees. Some also are representing with their wheels a spinning; all the while the music plays either Prince Charlie's minuet or the Auld Stewarts Back Again. At last descends from the mountains the glorious pair which to appearance is a prince and princess. Then all the actors retire on each side while the royal youth and his favourite dance so fine, in a word that the whole audience clap their hands for joy. Then in a moment the spinning wheels are thrown aside and every lad and lass join in the dance and jerk it away as quick as possible while the music briskly plays — Over the Water to Charlie, a bagpipe being in the band. In short it is so ravishing seemingly to the whole audience that the people to express their joy clap their hands in a most extraordinary manner indeed.[3]

[3] Bishop Forbes, *Lyon in Mourning*, vol. 2, p. 254. Letter from Ralph Bigland to Alexander Macmorland, Leith, March 3, 1749.

At the end of the century, Madame Frederick, a celebrated dancer, performed a pas seul to one of Marshall's Strathspeys. Indeed, in 1799, while she was performing at the Edinburgh Theatre Royal, she was prevailed upon to perform her dance during an interlude at the Edinburgh Piping Competition. And in the Watlen collection of circus tunes can be found the strathspey to which Mr. Lassells and Mrs. Parker danced the "celebration Strathspey Minuet" at the Royal Circus, Edinburgh and London, in 1793.

The terms "Strathspey" and "fling" began to appear on playbills only at the end of the eighteenth century, after which they appeared more frequently.

The interest in Scottish dance was now near its zenith, not only in the British Isles, but in the New World. It is of great interest to discover that the old American Company in Boston produced a "Scots Pastoral Dance — The Caledonian Frolic" in 1795, choreographed by William Francis who had recently arrived from England, and in which the celebrated American dancer, John Durang, performed. Durang himself presented a "Scotch ballet" entitled "Auld Robin Grey" about ten years later in which he danced "a Highland Fling" and in which he and his company danced "a strathspey, a *pas seul* and a garland dance." The self-portrait he left of himself dancing in this ballet is our earliest picture of a dancer performing a Scottish dance.

It would be interesting to discover if the companies performing in the Scottish towns earlier in the eighteenth century ever introduced some of the Scottish dance items which were so successful in London. However, one suspects that, had this occurred, it surely would have been remarked upon. Presumably the companies deemed it discreet to draw from their more general dance repertoire for Scottish audiences.

The song and dance interludes so essential to performances of plays in the eighteenth century gradually fell out of favour as the nineteenth century progressed.

8/ Dancing in the Countryside

*Penny wedding – wedding reels – Babbity
Bowster – The Bumpkin – The White
Cockade finishing dance of South Uist –
kissing in the dance – wedding parties –
fun at the fair – account from Ayrshire –
"penny reels" – harvest home – itinerant
dancing master – rockings – in the
Highlands – conditions of life – a ceilidh –
a dance in the farm-house kitchen – the
laird's ball – social dances*

        The subscription assemblies and private balls in the eighteenth century excluded the common people. There was, of course, in these times a much greater division between the classes, for the most part decided by birth or profession and, later, as we have seen in Glasgow, by wealth, until more recent times when the great middle class grew to bridge the gap. Then, too, in the nineteenth century, with the migration of the population to the towns — the centres of industry — the distinction between rural and urban society became more important. This distinction, however, was not so noticeable in the eighteenth century.

The wedding, fair, kirn, and even the funeral provided the most important occasions for dance among the common people. Despite the harshness of life in the countryside, young people found time to fall in love and marry, heedless of the consequences as in every age and every clime. A couple bespoke their wedding at a tavern, and then ranged the country to solicit guests who convened on the occasion to forget their cares for a day or two at their own expense.

This, the penny wedding described in chapter 5 as a notable institution in the seventeenth century, survived into the eighteenth and even the nineteenth century. The *First Statistical Account of Scotland* reveals the continued and widespread practice of this institution, despite the oft-quoted censure of the Kirk.

The wedding usually occurred on a Friday; in earlier times it was held on a Sunday. A barn was utilized for the dancing, and a house for the drinking. In other instances, the bride's house was the centre of celebrations. It was not always possible to find suitable indoor accommodation for dancing at weddings, especially in the Highlands, but everyone crowded into whatever shelter there was and took turns in the reels. If weather permitted, there was often some suitable location outdoors or else the company simply overflowed outside. W. Grant Stewart writes in his *Popular Superstitions of*

Scotland with respect to the Strathspey (ca. 1820): "The dinner being over, the 'shemit reel' is the next object of attention. All the company assemble on the lawn with flambeaux, and form a circle" (p. 274). Upon which:

The bridal pair and their retinue then dance a sixsome reel, each putting a piece of silver in the musician's hand. Those desirous may then succeed, and dance with the bride and the two maids of honour; and are gratified at the commencement and termination of each reel by the usual salutes.

On the floor, the dancers are beyond compare. Fired with emulation who shall "win the dance," every nerve and muscle is put into active service. [P. 277]

The Reverend James Hall has left an interesting description of a country wedding in *Travels in Scotland* (vol. 1) which he witnessed on a journey from Montrose to Aberdeen in 1805:

As I rode slowly along, I beheld, at a distance, on the banks of the Esk, a great number of people in their Sunday clothes dancing on a green, near a large tent covered with canvasses, blankets etc. It was a country wedding, where near four hundred people were assembled. There being a small inn in the neighbourhood, I put up my horse, and went to observe the rural scene. On a fine green or lawn the tent was stretched to the extent of forty or fifty feet; and a number of temporary tables of fir deal, with forms on each side. Two or three great cauldrons were boiling, filled with, I dare say, a hundred fowls, and a great number of mutton hams. There were pots also in which legs of mutton were stewed. The broth of the fowls and ham, boiled with onions, barley etc. was a dish fit for kings. At the cauldrons stood women with pitch-forks, stirring about the immense mass with both their hands, which seemed to require all their strength. A great number of gypsies, called in Scotland "Tinkers," and beggars, sat in groups at some distance, and sent deputations after dinner had begun for some time, to receive their portion in their own wooden dishes. This was sent without hesitation. It seemed to be considered as no more than their due on such a jovial occasion. The genteeler part of the guests were entertained in the tent, where there was wine. At the tables in the field, at one of which I seated myself, there was no wine, but great abundance of ale and whisky punch. This carousing at weddings is sometimes continued for three or four successive days, not by the company, but by new comers.

I find, that on such occasions, the new-married pair sometimes save fifty, sixty, or even an hundred pounds, each person paying five shillings at least, besides what drink they call for. I saw all kinds of rural mirth going on, some at reels, others at country dances, minuets, fandangos, highland capers, etc. [Pp. 299–301]

It is a pity we are not told the names of the bridal pair. The fact that there were some "gentles" in attendance marks the wedding as something special.

There is some confusion in the descriptions of the bridal ceremony that have come down to us, no doubt because there were local variations. The first reel, as Stewart tells us, was called the Shemit Reel, probably from the French *chez-mey*, best translated as "homecoming." This would be performed more appropriately at the bridal pair's home after they had been convoyed there by the guests in the ancient fashion, there being no "honeymoon." The term "shemit" is not known in the West Highlands, where the first dance of the bridal ball was, and is, a common Scotch Reel called the Wedding Reel (*Ruidhleadh na Banais*) which was danced by the bridal pair and the best man and bridesmaid.

Another custom which persisted long in the Catholic islands was the Stealing Reel

(*Ruidhleadh Ghoid*), in which first the bride then the bridegroom stole off to bed, their places in the reel being taken by others. This practice, it is said, was to cheat the fairies.

Lowland or Highland, the last dance of the bridal was Babbity Bowster or the Kissing Reel (*Ruidhleadh nam Pog*), known in England as the Cushion Dance or Joan Sanderson. This varied a little in form from region to region, especially in the West Highlands, but the basic idea was the same everywhere. The company was arranged in a circle, and one man whom we shall call the leader danced round within this circle carrying a handkerchief or, as it must have been originally, a cushion (bolster, or in Scots, bowster). This he placed on the floor opposite the lady of his choice and invited her to kneel with him upon it, but facing him so that they could kiss. This done, they rose and walked round in file or arm-in-arm, until the lady threw the handkerchief at some man of her choice. This man now lifted the handkerchief and ran after the lady, who gave some show of resistance, and casting the handkerchief round her neck, kissed her. In some regions he forfeited the kiss if the lady had already managed to link arms with the previous man. Then it was this second man's turn to continue the procedure and so on until all were on the floor or until there was room for no more. Finally, all joined in a ring with the last person "lifted" standing in the middle with the handkerchief. This person now selected and kissed someone of the opposite sex, kneeling as before, then left the ring. This procedure continued until only a few or no dancers were left. Then all took partners for a final reel.

The music to this dance in the West Highlands was "The White Cockade" for the processional part. In the Lowlands it was "Babbity Bowster." Many who have never danced Babbity Bowster know it as a party game in which the ring marches round singing "Bee Baw Babbity." In the instrumental version, a squeaky sound was made by bowing above the bridge of the fiddle to accompany the kissing. In the West Highlands, where the bagpipe was more common, the piper played a four-note phrase to accompany the words *pog an toiseach* (kiss first).[1] In most Lowland regions, the following duet accompanied the game:

Company:	Wha learnt you tae dance,
	Babbity Bowster, Babbity Bowster,
	Wha learnt you tae dance,
	Babbity Bowster brawly?
Reply:	My Minnie learnt me tae dance,
	etc.
Company:	Wha gi'ed you the keys tae keep,
	etc.
Reply:	My Minnie gi'ed me the keys tae keep,
	etc.
Company:	Kneel doun, kiss the grun'
	Kiss the grun', kiss the grun',
	Kneel doun, kiss the grun'
	Kiss the bonnie wee lassie (laddie), lassie, lassie. . .

[1] J. F. and T. M. Flett, "Some Hebridean Folk Dances," JEFDSS, vol. 7, no. 2 (1953).

The final "lassie" was chanted until the cushion had been placed on the floor before the selected lassie and the kiss transacted.

The tune, "Babbity Bowster," is one of the most common of Scottish tunes, and, like "Nancy Dawson" (Who'll come into ma wee ring), is yet on the lips of every Lowland child. It first appears on record in the Skene manuscript as "Who learned you to dance and a towdle," then as "Country Bumpkin" in Stewart's *Reels* (ca. 1768), and "Bab at the Bowster" in Aird's *Airs* (1782). The use of the term "Bumpkin" with respect to this tune arose in England from verses set to the air in an English ballad opera of the eighteenth century: "A country bumpkin who trees did grub, / A vicar who used the pulpit to drub."

Nor was this the only time the tune was used in this way; it appears in four other English operas of the period. Burns set "The Couper o'Cuddy" to it.

Perhaps the term "Bumpkin" became more acceptable among the genteel. William Creech refers to the "boisterous Bumpkin,"[2] and in a memoir of Norman Macleod, we are told of eighteenth-century dancing at New Year at Drumdrissaig, Knapdale, which always terminated in the Country Bumpkin.[3]

There is reason to believe that Creech and Macleod are not referring to the dance Babbity Bowster under another name, but that the Bumpkin was a different dance to the same tune. This dance is described first in Campbell's *Fourteenth Book of Strathspey Reels* (1799); in Gow's *Complete Repository*, part 4, page 38, although with a slightly different ending; and in *The Companion to the Reticule* (ca. 1820). It is included in the Blantyre manuscript (Sandeman Library, Perth, 1805) as The Bounky, and in several nineteenth-century ballroom handbooks, such as Anderson's *Ballroom Guide* (1886). In more recent times, the Bumpkin has been published by D. G. MacLennan in his *Traditional and Highland Scottish Dances* (1950) and by the Royal Scottish Country Dance Society (bk. 2).

The Bumpkin has also been called a Ninesome Reel, as indeed it qualifies to be, although the tune, of course, is a jig (Niel Gow uses "Elsie Marley"). To confuse matters a little further, J. Walsh used the tune "Bumpkin" for a Country Dance in his *Caledonian Country Dances* (1748–60) and, of course, calls his dance The Bumpkin, a dance of no importance.

We have been left a delightful vignette of The Country Bumpkin and dancing in the Borders at the dawn of the nineteenth century in the *Memoirs of Susan Sibbald*:

In those days, dancing was a favourite amusement, and regularly at Balls the last reel was a matter of contention, as to who should "keep the floor" longest. I was never beat although there were many girls who tried to conquer me. It was in the following manner. The last dance before breaking up was the "Country Bumpkin." Three gentlemen stood up with a lady in each hand, one trio before the other. Mr. John Riddell of Grahamslaw was generally my partner. I should have felt quite hurt if he should not have asked me to dance it with him. The gentleman in the middle set wore an Opera hat; there was a regular figure after the gentlemen had changed places and each worn the hat. The sets widened. Three other gentlemen sprang up to form three "foursome reels," taking plenty of room; then came the tug-of-war, and you would have been amused to see Niel Gow, the leader of the band, and

---

[2] William Creech, *Fugitive Pieces*, p. 338.
[3] Donald Macleod, *Memoir of Norman Macleod*, p. 22.

then so celebrated, come to the front of the orchestra, fiddle in hand, as if he would crush through it so excited he always was, and stamping with his feet and calling "high" as the music changed from strathspey to reel alternately.

You would see after a while ladies beckoning to young friends to take their places and gentlemen to do the same but I would never. Once at the Lamberton Races, perfectly without my knowledge until afterwards, a bet was made between a Mr. Scott and the Bishop of Durham's son (I forget his name), as to which should keep the floor longest, Miss Johnstone of Hutton Hall (to whom Mr. Scott was engaged) or myself. I was the last to sit down.

But the most trying time I ever had was at my last appearance at a public ball as a "dancing girl" . . . the last night of the Caledonian Races in the Autumn of 1807. The Honbl. Anna Maria Elliot, her sister Harriet, and many others continually changing with each other all trying to tire me out, fanning themselves and looking so warm while I never fanned myself at all, and thanks to my Bath dancing mistresses, Miss Fleming and Mam'selle Le Mercier, I had been taught such a variety of steps that dancing was not quite as fatiguing to me as to many.

At last the Earl of Dalkeith as my partner, when all had left the floor but ourselves, led me to a seat. . . ." [Pp. 246–47]

Here is Scottish love of movement at the ultimate, and at no rural harvest home, but at a Border ball of some distinction. The version of the Bumpkin described is clearly the same as that later published by Nathaniel Gow, ending in the three "foursome reels."

The sequel to Susan Sibbald's display of stamina was somewhat humiliating for her — she had actually worn a hole in the sole of each shoe, leaving her feet raw! To avoid her lameness being noticed, she persuaded her father to take her home in the morning before anyone had stirred.[4]

After this description, The White Cockade finishing dance enjoyed in the Hebrides seems almost delicate. A schoolmaster has left us a description of this version of the Cushion Dance from South Uist at the beginning of the present century:

The dance was held that night in the school despite the weather, and all seemed to enjoy it and to make little account of wind and rain. Immediately before the last dance the presentation to the retiring schoolmistress was made with many expressed good wishes and regrets at her departure. The last dance, called "The White Cockade" after Prince Charlie, was very much like our "Sir Roger de Coverley," yet was different. The girl dancers formed a rank with the same number of men forming another, both ranks facing each other. As far as I can remember the girl at the top of her rank, and the man at the bottom of his, advanced towards each other between the ranks and performed evolutions similar to those of the "Sir Roger." But at the end, when these two returned to their original places, the girl danced across and down the line behind the men. Without stopping on the way she placed a white handkerchief on the shoulder of the man of her choice as she passed. He then left the rank and followed, meeting her at the bottom where she waited for him; together they

---

[4] So much does dancing reveal the person that it comes as no surprise to learn that in 1853, when it certainly took a great deal of courage to cross the Atlantic, Susan Sibbald set forth to do so with her young son, to investigate the report that two of her emigrant sons were residing in a tavern! Arriving in Montreal, she proceeded on the long journey to the Toronto region, where she found that her fears had been unwarranted and that her sons were living decent, hardworking lives. She then hastened to her husband whom she had left in an ailing condition, but he died before she arrived. After settling her affairs, she returned to Canada and lived in comfortable distinction on Lake Simcoe.

danced out of the door. The dance now proceeded as before; and, as each girl departed from the dance with her chosen cavalier, the number of dancers became less and less till all had gone home and the dance was over.[5]

Other names for this dance in various regions were The Great Reel of the Bride,[6] The Bonny Lad, Pease Strae, The Bonnet Dance (possibly a bonnet used instead of a cushion), Country Bumpkin, Dannsa or Ruidhleadh nam Pog (Kissing Reel), and in Orkney, The Swine's Reel or the Lang Reel. Nor was the Cushion Dance or game reserved only for bridals. It terminated almost every convivial evening of dancing, whether at New Year, kirn, or casual evening party, such as that which Burns enjoyed on Loch Lomondside.

The custom of kissing one's partner before and after a dance was prevalent in eighteenth-century Scotland and perhaps has a much earlier origin, although there is no earlier mention of it except in England, where, as we have seen, the custom was well entrenched in Elizabethan times. Continental visitors to Scotland and England in the fifteenth and sixteenth centuries remarked on the freedom with which the ladies bestowed kisses as a salutation, even on a stranger, and this was still a matter of remark — this time by Englishmen — in eighteenth-century Edinburgh. It should not surprise us, therefore, that its practice in social dancing did not entirely die out in the countryside until the twentieth century.

Elizabeth Grant tells us that kissing was the practice at harvest home dances and like occasions in Strathspey in the late eighteenth century, and Alexander Carlyle in his *Autobiography*, refers to it in a story of a meeting with Lovat and Erskine of Grange in a tavern near Prestonpans, at which, he tells us, Lovat "grew frisky at last . . . and upon Kate Vint, the landlady's daughter coming into the room, he insisted on her staying to dance with him. . . . Lovat was at this time 75, and Grange not much younger; yet the wine and the young woman emboldened them to dance a reel, til Kate, observing Lovat's legs as thick as posts, fell a-laughing, and ran off. She missed her second course of kisses, as was then the fashion of the country, though she endured the first. This was a scene not easily forgotten" (pp. 66–67).

The "fashion of the *country*," remarks Carlyle — that is, of rural society — for kissing before or after the dance was no longer a custom associated with formal assemblies. The Duke of Gordon refers to the practice in an almost identical phrase in his verses to "Cauld Kail."

> "Now Piper lad, bang up the Spring;
> The Countra fashion is the thing,
> To prie their mou's e're we begin
> To dance the Reel of Bogie."

This, as other verses tell us, was a "fling" upon the grass "as they do in Stra'bogie" in Aberdeenshire around 1780.

The custom of kissing was still to be encountered in certain parts of the country within living memory, although perhaps the dancers kissed only at the beginning of a

---

[5] F. G. Rea, *A School in South Uist*, pp. 118–19.

[6] James MacKellar of Tayvallich, Argyll, a friend of the author, knew the dance by this name.

few reels during the evening when the fiddler would squeak out the necessary signal.

Markets, fairs, and in such towns as Mauchlin, Ayrshire, horse-racing meets, provided other important opportunities for indulging in the traditional dances. Some towns had an annual fair lasting a week or more, others had perhaps as many as three fairs and many markets. It was usual to have a fair on the farm term days to facilitate the hiring of labourers and servants. These in Scotland were Candlemas, Pentecost, Lammas, and Martinmas. Beltein was a term day in Ayrshire.

One fair was much the same as another in its games and practices, its vendors, players, and entertainers. William Aiton tells us of local fairs in Ayrshire, at which great numbers of lads and lassies foregathered in the afternoon and remained until midnight:

The country girls travel to the fair (unless in time of frost) without shoes or stockings, with their coats tucked up, and retire to the corner of the park, near the fair, where they put on their shoes and perform the labours of the toilette; after which, they stalk into the fair, make sham calls at shops, or saunter among the crowd, till their rustic admirers, who are also on the look-out, invite them to the change-house. This is done by tapping the fair one on the shoulder, treading on her foot, or by some pantomimic gesture which she understands, and readily obeys, unless a swain, more to her mind, shall then make similar signals. . . . A "sturdy fellow," having made his signals, struts off to the ale-house, his "clever hizzy," following at a short distance, proud of having gotten a "chance," and envied by such as have had none.

In the ale-house, the lad treats his lass with ale, whisky and sweet-meats, (called fairings), hugs her in his arms, tumbles her into a bed, if one can be found, though many persons be in the room, then, with one arm under her head, the other, and one of his legs over her, he enjoys a tête-a-tête conversation, longer or shorter, as the market happens to be brisk or slow. After a little time, they adjourn to some long-room, mason lodge, or barn, to dance reels. If the hall be much crowded at the time, they are obliged to maintain a struggle for the floor; which is done by the lad holding his partner by the sides, and pushing her forward to the front of the crowd.

Towards night, when John Barleycorn has obtained possession of the upper storey, these struggles for the floor often lead to blows. During the affray, the weak part of the company, with the fiddler, get upon the benches, or run into the corner, while the more heroic, or those who are most intoxicated, take the post of honour. Few blows are struck in these uproars; they only pull and haul, and make a hideous noise. A few minutes exhaust their rage; — new company arrives; — the fiddler becomes arbiter; — the tattered nymphs collect their shoes, and adjust their deranged dress; — the fiddler strikes up a reel; — the dance proceeds, and the affray ends as it began, no one can tell how.

If the lass has already been called for, the lad holds by her to the utmost; but if she has not been asked for, he soon becomes indifferent and ultimately leaves her. If she has many lovers, they press into the room, and even into the bed, where she is reclining; lay hold of her by the arm, leg, or any part of her dress which they can come at; and by dint of importunity, little short of compulsion, they obtain an audience. While one is pouring out his requests, in whispers into her ears, another fixes his talons on any part of her body, which he can reach; — she listens to him, till others arrive; — they jostle each other; and all of them roar out her name, like so many auctioneers calling a roup. She continues for a time, in a sort of passive uncertainty, yielding to the greatest force, sometimes getting upright, —at other times she is thrown upon the bed, till after enjoying several of these kind embraces, and hearing many supplications, one of the sturdiest of the chiels lays hold of her in his arms, whispers his prayer in her ear, and by main force, hurries her off holding her by the wrist, with one hand, and his other arm either round her neck or back, as a constable would keep hold of a thief, till he lodges her in a bed-side, in another ale-house; at all which "she is nothing loath." — The disappointed lovers follow and renew their applications; — a similar farce is gone through, till one of them hurries her to another ale-house, and to another bed, if one can be found.

This is what they call "holding the fair," and it is continued till about midnight, when the lads and lasses begin to pair off and return to the fair one's home, where they generally spend an hour or two by themselves, in the barn, byre, or cart shade, talking over the events of the day.[7]

There is no striking difference between the spirit portrayed in the description and that of fair activities some three centuries earlier. Certain it is, however, that the country fairs are very old and that dancing and music always formed a large part of their activities. One does not notice the Kirk particularly suppressing these occasions. It was probably recognized as impossible to do much about them. Even the so-called "holy fairs," which some presbyteries were wont to hold, at which preacher after preacher addressed the assembled country people from miles around, were not immune from the high spirits of youth liberated temporarily for the day. "Some were fu' o love divine and some were fu' o brandy," says Burns in "The Holy Fair," his satirical poem of such an occasion in Ayrshire.

The dancing at these events, to fiddle or bagpipe, in a barn or outdoors, was not of a refined sort. There were no Minuets, but there were the *licht* dances — possibly Loch Erichtside and the like which Burns danced, and especially the common reels, Babbity Bowster and Haymakers.

Sometimes some enterprising fiddler or local dancing master would rent a hall and conduct dancing there continuously during the fair, from some time in the afternoon until the small hours of the morning, a practice which became very common in the nineteenth century. The dancers were charged a penny for each dance ("penny reels") or, say, half-a-crown for the day, the ticket being a stamped imprint on the back of the hand so that the person was free to come and go. In some Border regions, the day was divided into three sessions, each of which required its own fee. We can see in this the beginning of the public dance halls of the twentieth century.

The kirn, often called harvest home or maiden feast, was held at the end of the harvest and was an affair for individual farms, although guests were often invited from neighbouring farms. Of course the granary was then conveniently empty and, after some cleaning up, it was decorated and prepared for the occasion (see also p. 75). And many mystic practices lost in antiquity were observed as befitted this most important occasion of the year, touching as it does the whole mystery of life and fertility. The last sheaf of the harvest, the "maiden," was decorated and given a place of honour in the farm house. The young girl who had cut the sheaf — preferably it was a young girl but sometimes a youth — reigned as a harvest queen or king. The feast was laid out, and always conspicuous on the groaning boards were ale crowdie, cream crowdie, and cheese. The late W. D. Cocker knew these occasions at first hand and has left us this vivid picture of them:

[7] William Aiton, *A General View of the Agriculture of the County of Ayr*, Board of Agriculture Report, 1811, pp. 572–74.

Hey! for the music o Bauldy Bain's fiddle!
   Redd up the barn, an' we'll gi'e ye a reel.
In till it noo, wi' a diddle-dum-diddle!
   Dod! that's the tune to pit springs in our heel.
Skirlin' o lassocks, an "hoochs" frae ilk fellow,
   Cheers when the gudeman himsel' taks the flair,
Leads Petronella wi' hellicate Bella,
   Brawest o dochters, though gey de'il-may-care.

Hey! for the music o Bauldy Bain's fiddle!
   Lads frae the bothies, an' herds frae the hill
Cleek wi' young lassies, sae jimp roun' the middle.
   Gosh! but some auld anes are soople anes still.
Lang Geordie Craddock, the grieve o Kilmadock,
   Widowed sae aft that he's fain to forget,
Wha would jalouse he could loup like a puddock?
   Faith! but there's spunk in the auld deevil yet!

Hey for the music o Bauldy Bain's fiddle!
   Syne we'll hae supper, for time's wearin' on;
Drinks for the droughty, an' scones frae the griddle —
   Bella's the lass that can bake a guid scone.
Bauldy's in fettle, an' sweirs he maun ettle
   Ae hinmaist hoolachan juist for the last.
Cast yer coats, callans, and joke tae't wi' mettle;
   Dancan an daffan days sune will be past.[8]

Sometimes party games were organized, and songs or solo dances learned from the itinerant dancing master or from a more accomplished friend were performed. Dr. Currie tells us that in Burns's time (and his too), ca. 1770, the Ayrshire peasantry were taught to dance "by persons generally of their own number, many of whom worked at daily labour during the summer months." Winter was the season for dancing instruction. Currie describes one dancing school: "The school is usually a barn, and the arena for the performers is generally a clay floor. The dome is lighted by candles stuck in one end of a cloven stick, the other end of which is thrust into the wall. Reels, strathspeys, country-dances, and hornpipes, are here practised. The jig so much in favour among the English peasantry, has no place among them. The attachment of the people of Scotland of every rank, and particularly of the peasantry, to this amusement, is very great. After the labours of the day are over, young men and women walk many miles, in the cold and dreary nights of winter, to these country dancing-schools; and the instant that the violin sounds a Scottish air, fatigue seems to vanish. . . ."[9]

Sometimes, too, there would be a dramatic interlude, a dramatic jig, appropriate to the occasion, and it was not uncommon for the company to break up just in time to set about the next day's chores. Rural social occasions altered little until World War I, after which traditional customs rapidly lost their ancient place.

8 W. D. Cocker, "The Barn Dance," reproduced by permission of Brown, Son and Ferguson Ltd., Glasgow.
9 James Currie, *The Life of Robert Burns* (Edinburgh, 1838), p. 8. Originally published *The Life of Robert Burns . . . with . . . Observations on the Scottish Peasantry* (Liverpool, 1800).

Since the kirns were domestic affairs involving the old as well as the young, the older dance forms persisted longer at these than at the public dances which were occasionally held in the villages and nearby towns in the later nineteenth century and into the twentieth century. The public dances in the Border valleys or Highland glens were usually arranged to coincide with the full moon, for often the young people who attended them had to walk many miles over hill track and rough road both there and back.

Although the ceilidh was an institution of Gaelic life, a similar custom still existed in Ayrshire in the seventeenth century called rocking (no doubt so named from the housewives meeting together with their spinning wheels called rocks). Later, in the eighteenth century, however, the rockings became entirely composed of young people who met and played games and danced in a neighbour's house.[10]

Turning again to the West Highlands, the English and Lowland travellers who ventured into the Highlands and islands of Scotland in the eighteenth and nineteenth centuries were appalled by the lethargy, dirt, and poverty of the inhabitants. In *Tour in Scotland* (vol. 1), Thomas Pennant described the inhabitants of Islay as "a set of people worn down with poverty; their habitations scenes of misery, made of loose stones, without chimnies, without doors . . . the inmates, as may be expected, lean, withered, dusky and smoke-dried. But my picture is not of this island only" (pp. 262–63).

"Savages" the southern travellers were wont to call the strange, lean, unkempt, begrimed people of the isles and glens. Yet, as Boswell and Johnson discovered, there was a warmth of hospitality and a generosity which were in striking contrast to the apparent poverty. The only sympathetic observers were those who were Highlanders themselves. They did not dwell on the superficial impressions of primitive life nor confuse it with destitution of mind as strangers were wont to do.

The unsympathetic observer remarked on the laziness of the Highlander; the observer who knew him remarked on the discouraging effect of the thin, stony soil, the hard weather, and the small returns for uncertain labour. The West Highlander, impulsive and fond of excitement, was a hunter and fisherman. When he could no longer maintain himself in this way, he degenerated. Certainly, the Hebrideans were worse off than their Grampian brethren in this respect. In Pennant's time, there were about forty-thousand cottagers in the Isles. The most common type of dwelling was the black-house, so called to distinguish it from the relatively rare white-house of stone and lime. It was a structure of some antiquity, comprising walls five or six feet thick and about the same in height, with an inner and outer facing of rough stones sandwiching a space filled with turf. The roof was formed by undressed branches of trees covered with straw thatch held down by heather ropes weighted with stones. There were no eaves, and the rain ran off into the turf-filled space, keeping the walls perpetually damp.

Wood was extremely scarce, and beds which were not recesses in the wall were formed of a framework of rough laths covered with straw and attached to four upright posts; sometimes a ceiling of divots protected them from leaks in the roof. The living

---

[10] John Mitchell, *Memories of Ayrshire about 1780*, Miscellany of the Scottish History Society, vol. 7, 1939, pp. 286–88.

room was separated from the byre by a wattle partition or a mere line of kerb-stones —
and in its centre smoked a peat fire. These black-houses did not have chimneys, and the
smoke from the fire oozed through the roof and impregnated the straw with soot,
giving the structure the appearance of a reeking dunghill from a distance. Sometimes a
hole in the roof above the fire served for a chimney.

Boswell and Johnson, it may be remembered, inspected such a house near Loch
Ness. The "old looking woman" of the house had raised five children there. Her husband, a man of eighty, was a goatherd, and the family subsisted on the proceeds of the
herd. She spoke little English and conversed through one of the guides who were
escorting the intrepid travellers. She offered them a dram and assured them that she
was as happy as any woman in Scotland.

The black-houses, springing out of the earth, rocks, and heather of the sea-girt isles
and ridges and loch-reflected hills, were hovels in the eyes of the southerner, but in the
eyes of such Highlanders as Norman Macleod who spent his youth among them, they
were bields and bowers of poetry:

The floor was clay; the peat-fire was built in the middle of the floor, and the smoke, when
amiable and not bullied by a sulky wind, escaped quietly and patiently through a hole in
the roof. The window was like a porthole, part of it generally filled with glass and part with
peat. One bed, or sometimes two, (with clean home-made sheets, blankets, and counter-
pane,) a "dresser" with bowls and plates, a large chest, and a corner full of peat, filled up the
space beyond the circle about the fire. Upon the rafters above, black as ebony from peat-reek,
a row of hens and chickens with a stately cock roosted in a paradise of heat.

Let me describe one of these evenings [a *ceilidh*]. Round the fire are seated, some on
stools, some on stones, some on the floor, a happy group. Two or three girls, fine, healthy,
blue-eyed lassies, with their hair tied up with ribbon snood, are knitting stockings. Hugh,
the son of Sandy, is busking hooks; big Archy is peeling willow-wands and fashioning them
into baskets; the shepherd Donald, the son of Black John, is playing on the Jews' harp;
while beyond the circle are one or two herd boys in kilts reclining on the floor, all eyes and
ears for the stories. The performances of Donald begin the evening and form interludes to
its songs, tales and recitations. He has two large "Lochaber trumps," for Lochaber trumps
were to the Highlands what Cremona violins have been to musical Europe. He secures the
end of each with his teeth, and, grasping them with his hands so that the tiny instruments
are invisible, he applies the little finger of each hand to their vibrating steel tongues. He
modulates their tones with his breath, and brings out of them Highland reels, strathspeys, and
jigs, — such wonderfully beautiful, silvery, distinct, and harmonious sounds as would draw
forth cheers and an encore even in St. James's Hall. But Donald, the son of Black John, is
done, and he looks to bonny Mary Cameron for a blink of her hazel eye to reward him,
while in virtue of his performance he demands a song from her. Now Mary has dozens of
songs, so has Kirsty, so has Flory, — love songs, shearing songs, Prince Charlie songs, songs
composed by this or that poet in the parish; and therefore Mary asks, What song?. So until
she can make up her mind, and have a little playful flirtation with Donald, the son of Black
John, she requests Hugh, the son of Sandy, to tell a story. Although Hugh has abundance
of this material, he too protests that he has none. But having betrayed his modesty, he starts
off with one of those which are given by Mr. Campbell. . . . When the story is done, improvisation is often tried, and amidst roars of laughter the aptest verses, the truest and most
authentic specimens of tales, are made, sometimes with knowing allusions to the weaknesses
or predilections of those round the fire. Then follow riddles and puzzles; then the trumps
resume their tunes, and Mary sings her song, and Kirsty and Flory theirs, and all join in

chorus, and who cares for the wind outside or the peat-reek inside! Never was a more innocent or happy group.

This fondness for music from trump, fiddle, or bagpipe, and for singing, story-telling, and improvisation, was universal, and imparted a marvellous buoyancy and intelligence to the people.[11]

No occasion was more joyfully observed than Hogmanay, and the father of the writer of the foregoing passage has left us a revealing description of it as it was known to him in the West Highlands in the late eighteenth century. He alludes to dancing in this description:

After the songs the dancing began, very different from the slow, soft, silken steps of the present day. First came in a smart dame, dressed like a housekeeper, with a bunch of keys jingling by her side; strong, sturdy, and active she looked. The woman sang *Port a Beul*, [*sic*] (i.e. a tune from the mouth) selecting Cailleach an Dudain, (the old wife of the mill-dust), and it was she who capered and turned, and sprang nimbly. After this they danced the *Dubh-Luidneach* (Black Sluggard). But the best fun was when the Goat Dance, "Weave the Gown," (*Fidh an Gunn*), and the "Thorny Croft" (*Croit am Droighin*) were danced.[12]

These are ancient dramatic dances which had almost entirely disappeared by the end of the nineteenth century. No doubt they are remnants of a tradition of dramatic jigs, traces of which had been left even in the Lowlands in the eighteenth century, as, for instance Auld Glenae, the one which Burns describes as having been performed at weddings. Cailleach an Dudain, indeed, is the most frequently mentioned of these old jigs.

In the days before easy communications, cinema, radio, and television, the ceilidh was the public forum for the discussion of news and for the transmission of culture from one generation to another. There was always time for dancing, and when the moon and weather were fair, the company, particularly the younger members, eagerly resorted to some favourite spot on the green or on the road for this purpose, a practice which is still to be encountered in the Hebrides. All the better if there were a piper or fiddler, otherwise there was puirt-a-beul (the Gaelic "mouth music"), or deedling, or an enthusiastic exponent of the Jews' harp, or more recently, the melodeon.

It is quite evident that there was little room even for dancing a Threesome Reel in the typical Highland house of the eighteenth and nineteenth centuries. Some of the large farmhouses occasionally had a suitable kitchen with flagged floor and a huge fireplace, such as that in which Alexander Smith witnessed an evening of dancing during his celebrated visit to Skye in the summer of 1860:

There was a huge dresser near the small dusty window; in a dark corner stood a great cupboard in which crockery was stowed away. The walls and rafters were black with peat smoke. Dogs were continually sleeping on the floor with their heads resting on their outstretched paws. . . . The fleeces of sheep which had been found dead on the mountain were

---

[11] Dr. Macleod, under the pseudonym "Finlay the Piper" in the first Gaelic magazine, ca. 1830. Translated and reproduced by his son Norman Macleod in *Reminiscences of a Highland Parish* (London, 1867), pp. 144–48.

[12] Ibid., pp. 348–49.

nailed on the walls to dry. Braxy hams were suspended from the roof; strings of fish were hanging above the fireplace. The door was almost continually open, for by the door light mainly entered. . . .

When Peter came with his violin the kitchen was cleared after nightfall; the forms were taken away, candles stuck into the battered tin sconces, the dogs unceremoniously kicked out, and a somewhat ample ballroom was the result. Then in came the girls, with black shoes and white stockings, newly-washed faces and nicely smoothed hair; and with them came the shepherds and men-servants, more carefully attired than usual. Peter took his seat near the fire; McIan gave the signal by clapping his hands; up went the inspiring notes of the fiddle and away went the dancers, man and maid facing each other, the girl's feet twinkling beneath her petticoat, not like two mice, but rather like a dozen; her kilted partner pounding the flag floor unmercifully; then man and maid changed step, and followed each other through loops and chains; then they faced each other again, the man whooping, the girl's hair coming down with her exertions, and with a cry the dancers rushed at each other, each pair getting linked arm in arm, and away the whole floor dashed into the whirlwind of the reel of Hoolichan. It was dancing with a will, — lyrical, impassioned; the strength of a dozen fiddlers dwelt in Peter's elbow; McIan clapped his hands and shouted, and the stranger was forced to mount the dresser to get out of the way of whirling kilt and tempestuous petticoat. . . .

Chief among the dancers on these occasions were John Kelly, Lachlan Roy and Angus-with-the-dogs. . . .[13]

The dance combination here was apparently Strathspey and Reel o' Tulloch (that is, Hoolichan), since there was a change of tempo as the dancers swept into the Hoolichan (see chap. 11). The Country Dance was not known in the Hebrides until the late nineteenth century. There were many reels enjoyed in the Hebrides apart from the so-called Highland Reel or the Reel o' Tulloch, some of them simple folk dances almost as easily called games, and these are described in chapter 15. We cannot assume that the few Hebridean reels that have survived into our own times are all ancient, for many reels were composed and passed out of fashion over the years just as dances do today; but others, for some reason, remained local favourites through many generations.

Certainly, by the late eighteenth century, it became customary for the laird to hold a ball for his tenants and neighbours, a practice continued today by the queen at Braemar. By the late nineteenth century, these balls were somewhat formal occasions, requiring all to wear their "Sunday clothes." The dances were then mainly reel, Strathspey, and Reel of Tulloch, singly or in combination, and Country Dances, such as Flowers of Edinburgh, Triumph, Petronella, Rory O'More, Haymakers, Speed the Plough, the popular Strip the Willow, Polka, and Highland Schottische.[14] Quadrilles and Waltzes made little progress in the Highlands, and the Eightsome Reel did not make its appearance there until very late in the nineteenth century.

The stream of traditional dances and the introduction of the new ones were perpetuated in the countryside by the itinerant dancing masters. They usually followed a recognized circuit, and remained in each place for a number of weeks to hold classes

---

[13] Alexander Smith, *A Summer in Skye*, introd. by W. Forbes Gray (London: Sampson Low, Marston and Co., n.d.), pp. 107–9.

[14] J. F. and T. M. Flett, *Traditional Dancing in Scotland*, appendix by F. Rhodes.

for social and solo dancing. They gave their public classes in a barn or village hall which served as a studio, and, in addition, they held private classes in the houses of those who requested them.

The title "Professor" or "Dancie" was given to the dancing master, and occasionally he was a person of the quality of J. Scott Skinner of Elgin or David Anderson, the celebrated dancing master of Dundee, who had a headquarters in his home town and who published a ballroom handbook to aid his pupils. He taught a Highland Fling, Gille Callum, "Jacky Tar" or similar hornpipe, and sometimes Seann Triubhas and other solo dances in the Scottish tradition. He also, of course, taught the social dances, the common reels and Country Dances, and as the nineteenth century closed, he taught the Highland Schottische and a variety of dances not in the Scottish tradition, such as the Quadrille, Pas de Quatre, Varsovienne (La Va), and the Polka.

There were dance teachers on the islands, of course, including the occasional Lowland teacher who had migrated there. One noted Hebridean master and choreographer of the nineteenth century, McLachlan, had spent some years in France. Generations of dancing masters have come and gone shrouded in anonymity — including those who were responsible for the superlative dancing of Strathspey — although recently an attempt to acknowledge many of those who are recalled within living memory has been made by J. F. and T. M. Flett.[15] Almost every participant at the growing number of Highland Dance competitions became a teacher in due course.

---

[15] Ibid., see List of Informants.

9 / Dawn of a New Age

*Passing of the Minuet – introduction of
the Quadrille – triumph of the Quadrille,
Polka, and Waltz – the Schottische –
popularity of the Foursome Reel and Reel
of Tulloch – decline of reels and country
dancing*

As the nineteenth century dawned, the world had entered a new age and the poised life of the leisured classes was threatened by the fires of great forges, by the clamour of a million hammers, and by the ideas which accompanied them, thrown up, as it were, with the fossil remains of the primeval forests of Britain.

In both England and Scotland, the Minuet passed away with the life from which it drew its being. All the dancing masters who put pen to paper at this time attest to its elegance and grace. Elizabeth Grant joined them in lamenting the passing of "the good old minuet style of moving" which, in 1860, she wished from her heart were the fashion again for, she thought, the manner of the time was not so graceful, "nor the carriage by any means so good, nor the gestures so easy as in the days of stately sinkings and risings and balancings of the body required in the Minuet."[1] G. Yates, a noted London dancing master, praises the Minuet in *The Ball*: "It helps wear off anything of clown-ishness in the carriage of the person, and breathes itself even into the most indifferent actions, by promoting a gentle and agreeable manner of performing them. In short, all the graces that characterize a good execution of a minuet will insensibly influence every part of the person, and communicate a certain freedom and agreeableness of motion easier to be conceived than defined" (p. 79).

In the 1780s, William Creech described in *Fugitive Pieces* the dances enjoyed at the various Edinburgh balls: "The minuet with its beautiful movement, the cheerful country dance, the joyous jigg, the riotous reel, the boisterous bumpkin, the sprightly strathspey, and the courtly cotillion" (p. 338). Fifty years later, he would have had to delete the Minuet, the "jigg," and the Cotillion and add the courtly Quadrille, the

---

1 Elizabeth Grant, *Memoirs of a Highland Lady*, p. 87.

dizzy Waltz and the bubbling Polka! Was Creech's "joyous jigg" the twosome jig alluded to by Scott in his novel *Redgauntlet?*

The Cotillion was brought to England from France in 1780. Originally a French folk dance, it was performed in a square set. New Cotillions appeared from about 1780 in the Country Dance collections in England, but the dance was never more than a novelty in Scotland. Its relative, the Quadrille, met with like resistance, but was more successful. The Quadrille was first danced publicly in Edinburgh in the winter of 1816, a year after its introduction to Almack's.[2] Elizabeth Grant described in her *Memoirs of a Highland Lady* the impact of the Quadrille:

A much more pleasant style of smaller parties had come into fashion with the new style of dancing. It was the first season of quadrilles, against the introduction of which there had been a great stand made by the old-fashioned respectables. Many resisted the new French figures altogether, and it was a pity to give up the merry country dance, in which the warfare between the two opinions resulted; but we young people were all bit by the quadrille mania, and I was one of the set that brought them first into notice. We practised privately. . . . Finlay Dunn[3] had been abroad, and imported all the most graceful steps from Paris; and having kept our secret well, we burst upon the world at a select reunion at the White Melvilles: the spectators standing on the chairs and sofas to admire us. People danced in those days . . . we did not merely stand and talk, look about bewildered for our vis-a-vis, return to our partners either too soon or too late, without any regard to the completion of the figure, the conclusion of the measure, or the step belonging to it; we attended to our business, we moved in cadence, easily and quietly, embarrassing no one and appearing to advantage ourselves. We were only eight; Mr. White Melville and Nancy Macleod opposite to Charles Cochrane and me, Honnie Melville and Charles Macleod with Fanny Helland and Miss Melville. So well did we all perform that our exhibition was called for and repeated several times in the course of the evening. We had no trouble in enlisting co-operators, the rage for quadrilles spread, the dancing master was in every house, [that is, every house of the gentry] and every other style discarded. Room being required for the display, much smaller parties were invited. Two, or at most, three instruments sufficed for band, refreshments suited better than suppers, an economy that enabled the inviters to give three or four of these sociable little dances at less cost than one ball; it was every way an improvement. [Pp. 236–37]

These were private parties, however, and not to be confused with the more public dancing assemblies. The advance of the Quadrille was gradual. John Lockhart writes in a strangely similar passage in *Peter's Letters* (vol. 3, 3rd ed.) of its being hailed "as a kind of wonder" in Glasgow, where, he says, it "seems to have made still less progress . . . than in Edinburgh." He goes on to say of a private ball in the Buck's Head Inn, "The moment the set was formed in a smaller apartment, communicating with the great dancing-room, the whole of the company crowded in to see it, and soon formed a complete serried phalanx of gazers all about the performers. Nay, such was the

---

[2] Cf. *Memoirs of a Highland Lady*, p. 212. Although the introduction of the Quadrille to Almack's was the signal of its entrance into the repertoire of the public assembly, it had been danced privately in London over thirty years before. Horace Walpole writes in a letter to Lady Ossory, March 27, 1773, of several balls held at the residence of the French Ambassador in London at which Quadrilles were danced. One of the dancers was Lady Sefton whom Gronow mentions as an important directress of Almack's in his time.

[3] Could it be that this should be Barclay Dun who published a book of Quadrilles entitled *Translation of Nine Quadrilles* (London, 1818)? Finlay Dun, born in Aberdeen, taught music in Edinburgh.

enthusiastic curiosity of some of the ladies in particular, that they did not scruple to get upon their feet on the benches and sofas all around the wall. . . . At some of the pauses in the dance, the agility of the figurantes was rewarded, not with silent breathings of admiration . . . but with loud roars of hoarse delight, and furious clapping and drumming of heels all about" (pp. 235-36).

Originally, the Quadrille required the command of a wide range of steps and movements: jette, assemble, balotte, pas de Zephyr, pirouette, glissade, pas de basque, emboîte, entrechat, pas brize, fleuret, pas bourre, chasse, and coupe. Some of these movements were beyond the capabilities of the majority of dancers, and in time it became possible to execute the Quadrille with no knowledge of dancing, its execution being simply a matter of walking or sliding through the figures. The North American Square Dance is a rustic version of this.

A study of Quadrilles is not our concern here. Suffice it to explain that the original Quadrille was a square dance in five distinct sections for four couples. These were Le Pantalon (2 × 32 bars); L'Ete (4 × 24 bars); La Poule (4 × 32 bars); La Pastourelle (4 × 32 bars); and La Finale (4 × 32 bars). Many other combinations of figures were developed, of which The Lancers became a firm favourite, but not in Scotland until near the close of the nineteenth century. Another popular Quadrille, The Caledonian, sounds as though it could exhibit Scottish influence, but does not particularly do so, while the "Scotch Reel Quadrille" does.

During the nineteenth century, variants of the Country Dance, such as the Écossaises and the "Spanish" Country Dances, joined forces with the Quadrille in the city assemblies, but all fell in time to The Lancers and the energetic Polkas, Waltzes, Mazurkas, and their many derivatives. The execution of the Quadrille, which originally made considerable technical demands on its dancers, began, like that of the Scotch Reel, to deteriorate as less exacting dancing skills were cultivated. In 1847, Henri Cellarius, a French dancing master, wrote in the *Drawing Room Dances*, "As to the French quadrille, as it is now generally executed, one can not dissemble that its reign, as a dance, seems well nigh at an end, and that it will be a long time before it becomes other than what it is at present — an opportunity, that is, for gossip rather than for dancing, a sort of necessary halting-place amidst the waltzes and polkas" (p. 20).

This, of course, could be regarded as one of its advantages, as Edward Ferrero, an American dancing master of the same period, pointed out in *The Art of Dancing*: "The quadrille commends itself to the lovers of dancing, for various reasons. It admits of the display of great taste in the presentation of the hands, and gracefulness in the walk; it is a happy relief from the more fatiguing polka, redowda and similar dances; and it allows those who are not familiar with them, to share in the pleasure of the dance, from which they might otherwise be debarred. It affords, too, an opportunity for pleasant conversation and interchange of civilities, which could not perhaps be otherwise detained" (p. 121).

A New England gentleman visiting London in 1845 has left a description of a society ball held at Almack's for the benefit of Polish exiles which was, in effect, a repeat of a fancy dress ball held previously under the patronage of Queen Victoria and intended to counterfeit the dress and manners of the court of George II. The Duchess of Bedford presided and two Scottish duchesses, Roxburgh and Sutherland, were conspicuously in attendance. He found "the old figure dances very pleasing" and, of course, there were not only Minuets but also Highland Reels and the more recent Quadrilles and Waltzes. "Two very large rooms for dancing were opened, besides the side rooms," he tells us, "and yet they were greatly crowded." Many expensive costumes were worn, and the writer remarks on their "becoming modesty," but, oh, "the Highland gentlemen in their country costume, with their legs bare above the gaiters and extending some ways above the knees, especially when they sat down, were perfectly disgusting." He hoped the Minuet would come into fashion again, but could not be reconciled to the Waltz, which seemed to him to "border upon indelicacy — except among brothers and sisters or members of the same family."[4]

By this time, the palmy days of exclusiveness at Almack's, now called Willis's Rooms, had passed, and the institution had reached the end of its glittering career. The English Country Dance was no more after a reign of over two hundred years, and the world of Smollett and Jane Austen, although fondly remembered by many of the older generation, had disappeared forever.

The new couples' dances, such as the Waltz, overcame the prejudice against their more intimate character, but they were slower in finding acceptance in Scotland. But a Scottish version of the Schottische, a Nordic Polka performed to an imitation of the Strathspey, became very popular and was called the Highland Schottische. Queen Victoria remarked that this was "much liked" at the ball held in her honour at Inverary in 1875. The other dances at that ball, incidentally, were mostly reels and Country Dances, and it ended with La Tempête.[5]

Love of movement continued to be a characteristic of Scottish dancers. The Foursome Reel and Reel of Tulloch, separately or together, were still their classic favourites, along with the Eightsome Reel, as the twentieth century dawned, and this was true not only of the countryside but of the rapidly growing industrial or urban areas. The Country Dances survived more prominently in the Lowland countryside and along the Highland Line. David Anderson's *Ballroom Guide*, published in the 1890s, gives some indication of prevailing fashion; it contained about eight Country Dances and only a few Quadrilles, Pas de Quatre, "party" dances including the new style of Cotillion with its various antics and the like which made no inroads in Scotland, and a selection of "circle" (or couples') dances and "miscellaneous."

Of these, the reels and Country Dances were recognized as indigenous forms: their music and their heritage belonged to Scotland in a way that could not be claimed for the Caledonian Quadrille. Improved communications, twentieth-century city dwelling, and change of manners and values, along with a catastrophic, if victorious, war, destroyed the environment from which the native dance forms and their music drew their sustenance. They sickened and nearly died. Social dancing became cosmopolitan, and sports and athletics became healthier outlets for physical exercise and recreation, for women as well as men. Scottish traditional dancing, like forms of life facing extinction, had to find a new way of survival.

[4] Henry Colman, *European Life and Manners*, vol. 1, pp. 352–54.
[5] Queen Victoria, *More Leaves from the Journal . . . 1862–1882*.

10 / Scottish Dance Tradition

*French contacts – reeling – earliest record
of use of word "reel" – Country Dance –
Highland Reel – female dancing – male
dancing – high dances – hornpipe stepping
among Scots countryfolk – tradition in
Cape Breton – stage dance – Hill MS –
Ewen MacLachlan's dances – balletic
influence*

We have already noted considerable evidence of the rich inheritance of dance surviving everywhere in Scotland in the eighteenth century. Dramatic folk dances belonging to a culture that reached far back into the mists of antiquity still found a place in the social life of the West Highlands, the islands, and the southwest Lowlands. The social reels abounded everywhere in their various local forms and in their most sophisticated flowering in the Central Highlands from whence that particular and celebrated reel, variously called the Scotch Reel or the Highland Reel, burst upon the ballrooms of the world. Mrs. Grant of Laggan indicates in her *Poems* the geographical concentration of the latter's two rhythmical forms as "the source of Tay" and "by rapid Spey" respectively. No evidence refutes this. The *licht* dances of the Lowlands, those of the Border valleys and by the shores of the North Sea, were blood relatives of the rural dances of northern England — "the good old Country Dances of England" — the survivors of the *licht* dances which largely comprise the catalogues in the *Complaynt of Scotland* and *Colkelbie's Sow* (cf. chap. 2). Add to these the high dances which remain the distinctive glory of the culture of the Gael, and we span a considerable range of artistic resource. It will be the purpose of most of the succeeding chapters to consider this resource in greater detail.

As we have seen, there was a vexatious dearth of careful description of Scottish dance until recent centuries. The Frenchman, de Lauze, is really not helpful when he writes in 1623 in his *Apologie de la Danse*, "Every nation and province has its favourite dance; thus the English have Measures and Contre-dances, the Scots have the Scots Brawls." Scots Brawls, indeed — this comes as a surprise. But was the Brawl or Branle so popular in Scotland at this time? There is no other hint of it unless some of the popular ring dances, to which there are many allusions in the seventeenth century, were Branles. We have seen, certainly, that Branles were probably the most familiar of the French dance forms in fifteenth- and sixteenth-century Scotland, but there is no reference to them in subsequent periods, with the possible exception of a Branle in Sutherland in the late nineteenth century, apparently known there as the "Brail."[1] One suspects, however, that de Lauze was generalizing on the strength of the Branle d'Écosse, which may not have been a native Scottish Branle at all.

We have seen how the dance forms and fashions of the fifteenth-century French court spread into all the courts of Europe, including that of Scotland, years before Mary Queen of Scots was born. The French court itself was indebted to the Italian and the Spanish, and all three were indebted to the dances of their folk. There is evidence of some passing of dances from the Scottish court downwards in the allusions we have drawn from Scottish literature of the time, but I think we can safely limit this to the environs of the court — the Lothians and Fife — and the regions of Norman infiltration. Some of the latter, however, take us into the Central Highlands and as far north as Sutherland and Caithness, the Gordons and the St. Clairs (Sinclairs) particularly coming to mind. We have seen, however, that by the late sixteenth century and even through the turbulent years of the seventeenth century, the Scottish nobility — and landed families and even scholars — shared the general attitude to dance as an essential part of polite education and sought to finish their education in France. These families were largely concentrated in the northeast, but also in the Central Highlands. Manuscript lute books compiled by some of them have survived,[2] containing references to Galzearts, Volts, Sarabands, Currants, Almons, Brails, Canaries, Pavens, Basse Dances, Bourrées, Passamezes, Balletes, and Robinettes. Many are original compositions, such as Aberdein's Currant and My Lord of Marche Paven, both composed by James Lauder in 1584, and which appear in several manuscript collections.

These dances as well as their music surely graced the ballroom of many a Scottish noble house or merchant's country seat. Yet the only direct mention of the performance of a dance in such circumstances from the seventeenth century occurs in a report of the trial of Lady Rothiemay in the celebrated Frendraught case, 1634, in which the ubiquitous Babbity Bowster or Cushion Dance is referred to: "She dancit with the licht horsemen in the place of Rothiemay, the cushion dance, (bearing the cushion upon her shoulders)."[3]

There is no doubt, however, about the place of the Minuet. It was the most important dance in polite assemblies in Scotland, as it was elsewhere during the eighteenth century. Its distinguished contemporaries, the "Sprightly Rigadoon and Louvre slow . . . and smooth Bretagne," do not seem to have had much of a run there, although some Edinburgh dancing masters of the period included these in their advertisements. Judging from the fact that both John Riddell and Robert Mackintosh composed and published Gavottes along with their Reels and Strathspeys (in 1782 and 1783 respectively), the Gavotte may have enjoyed some favour as a dance in Scotland at that time, but there is no evidence to support it.

It is easy, then, to see from these facts how French influence on dancing could infil-

---

[1] Mabel Dolmetsch, *Dances of England and France.*

[2] Skene MS (1615–20), National Library, Edinburgh. *Ancient Scottish Melodies*, transcribed by William Dauney, 1838. Rowallan MS (1612–28), University of Edinburgh Library. Gordon of Stralloch MS (1627–29), National Library, Edinburgh. Panmure MSS, 1622 et seq., Brechin Castle, Angus.

[3] Robert Chambers, *Domestic Annals of Scotland*, 2nd ed., vol. 2, p. 78.

trate Scotland. This infiltration perhaps explains the cultured foot and leg movements which characterize what is called Highland dancing, distinguishing it in refinement and elaboration from other dances of the British jig or hornpipe tradition to which it belongs. As we have noted in chapter 2, there is a strong resemblance between the Galliard, with its variety of capers alternating with travel, and the Scotch Reel. There are also great differences between them, however. The music is vastly different, and only one or two steps are alike in kind; it is in spirit and culture that they are blood brothers.

The use of the word "Reel" as the name of a specific dance creates some confusion, for, in Scotland, "reel" was originally a generic term for the social dances of the countryside, such as the Reel of the Black Cocks, Reel of Tulloch, Whalsay Reel, and Reel o'Bogie. It has also the meaning of tracing a zig-zag path: "Athir throu other reland [reeling]," as we read in the following passage from Gavin Douglas's translation of the *Aeneid* (ca. 1520), in which the related word "revellyng" is also used.

> And gan do dowbill brangillys and gambatis,
> Dansys and roundis traysing mony gatis
> Athir throu other reland, on thar gys:
> Thai fut it so that lang war to devys
> Thar hasty fair, thar revellyng and deray,
> Thar morysis and syk ryot, quhil neir day.[4]

In England the French word *hey* was used for the reel figure, a *haye* being a woven fence. Thus to dance "hey-de-guize" or "go the haye" was compressed to "hydegy," and testifying to the fundamental character of the figure in English folk dancing, "hydegy" became synonymous with any rustic or country dance. This, of course, is exactly the function of the word "reel" in the Scottish languages, it being both a generic term for social folk dance and the name of a serpentine figure. In Scotland, and Ireland too, the word "reel" is used also of the characteristic common-time dance music of the countryside.

The affinity of the reel, as a figure, to Celtic scroll designs has suggested an obvious relationship. The word, however, appears to be Gothic and is even used by the Danes of their own native dances.

A favourite early example of the use of reel in connection with dance occurs in the report of a trial of four women and a man accused of witchcraft in 1590. We have already referred to this event. One of the "confessions" recorded at the trial avers that the witches took hands and "daunced this reill or short dance, singing all with one voice 'Cummer go ye before.'" A report published in London tells us "she confessed that this Geilles Duncan did go before them playing this reill or daunce upon a small trump, called a Jewes Trump, until they entered into the Kirk of North Barrick. These confessions made the King in wonderful admiration, and sent for the said Geillis Duncan, who upon the like trump did play the said dance before the Kings Majesty."[5] In the Constable manuscript cantus of the seventeenth century there are the

---

[4] Gavin Douglas, Virgil's *Aeneid* 13, in *The Poetical Works of Gavin Douglas*.

[5] Trial of Johnny Mowbray, June 7, 1591. Records of the Court of Justiciary, in manuscript. (See Dalyell, *Musical Memoirs of Scotland*, p. 182). The English report was published in a broadsheet entitled *Newes from Scotland*, 1591. See also the trial of Agnes Sampson, January 27, 1591, in Chambers, *Domestic Annals*, 2nd ed., vol. 1, p. 214.

first lines of a song containing the word used in this sense: "The Reill, the reill of
Aves / The joliest reill that ever was." These are the only examples from that period.

It is curious that in the glossary included in the edition of Gavin Douglas's *Aeneid*,
published in Edinburgh in 1710,[6] the word "reel" is discussed with reference to the
passage from that work which we have quoted above. Here we find the reel described
as a dance "where three dance together." There is indeed every indication that this
was an early popular form of the reel, and we shall discuss this in chapter 11.

The specific dance called the Scotch Reel or Highland Reel in the eighteenth and
nineteenth centuries and later was of a linear form involving only the interlacing reel
figure, alternating with setting, and performed by four dancers. This was the supreme
social dance of Scotland. Its widespread popularity in the eighteenth and nineteenth
centuries led to its appropriating the word "reel" to itself. It is performed to the traditional common-time dance music of the country, which is given the general name
"reel" also. The rhythms of this music vary somewhat, the most distinctive being that
which reached fruition in Strathspey and is so named. We will return to these matters
when we consider the dances in a little more detail.

The use of the word "reel" in Scotland as a generic term for group social dance
leads to some anomalies, as when dances to jig or hornpipe music are called reels.
Country Dances performed to reel music are referred to as reels, while those to strathspey rhythms are called Strathspeys, and those to jigs are called jigs! So is the confusion of the terminology compounded.

As we shall see in more detail in later chapters, the term "country dance" was
originally English and became identified in Scotland, during the eighteenth century,
with the longwise "progressive" form of the dance for any number of couples which
prevailed in seventeenth-century England. The most characteristic of these were then
danced to 3/2 hornpipe, 9/8 and 6/8 jig rhythms, and were, to an increasing extent,
devised by dancing masters.

It is a striking fact that the same Scots who, Topham says, held their dances sacred
and would "bear no innovation on that point," and who were sufficiently conservative
to evince no interest in the Allemandes, Cotillions, and other French dances which
were so fashionable in eighteenth-century England, took to the longwise Country
Dance remarkably easily. Would they have done so if there had not been something
about the dance which belonged in some measure to their own tradition? Despite the
undeniable and overwhelming popularity of the native Reels, Country Dances are
most prominently featured from the very first public dance assembly in Scotland,
which, as we have seen, was about the year 1710.

The longwise formation of the prevailing English Country Dances of the time was
not in itself an innovation to Scotland; the evidence indicates that many Scottish reels
were of this formation, but the device or principle of progression, and the system of
figures associated with it were now highly developed in the English dance assemblies.
Thus it came to pass that the longwise, indefinitely progressive dance to the traditional
dance music exclusively assumed the classification of Country Dance and became
widely regarded as England's most characteristic dance form. The Country Dance
will be discussed in greater depth in chapters 19 and 20; suffice it here to say that it

[6] *Virgil's Aeneid, translated into Scottish verse by G. Douglas,* glossary by T. Ruddiman (Edinburgh,
1710).

found ready acceptance at all levels of Scottish social life in the growing towns and their precincts in the Lowlands, and there merged with the native strain of *lycht* dances. Alexander Ross, in his poem "Helenore" (1768), mentions the Country Dance in the Aberdeenshire countryside: "An' throw an' throw, they lap they flang they ran: / The cuintray dances, an' the cuintray reels."

Only a few references to the names of Scottish dances come to us from the seventeenth century. A dance called Gillatrypes is mentioned in a witch trial early in that century: "The Divil alwayis takis the Maiden in his hand nix him, quhan we daunce Gillatrypes. . . ."[7] It is also mentioned a few years earlier in the Elgin Kirk Session Records, June 2, 1596, in a note stating that three servant lasses confessed to having been "in ane dance callit gillatrype singing a foull hieland sang." There is a suggestion of something sinister about this dance; was it a recognized witches' dance? Its name establishes it as a dance from the Gaelic-speaking community.

Then, in his poem "The Highland Host" (ca. 1680), Robert Cleland alludes to Highland warriors dancing Donald Couper. "Trumpets sounded, skenes were glancing / Some were Donald Couper dancing." This could mean simply some kind of reel danced to the tune "Donald Couper" — a *lycht* dance. The tune appears to have been well known in seventeenth-century England, and is to be found, with dance figures, in John Playford's *The Dancing Master* (1657).

As the eighteenth century dawned, Country Dances of the English pattern were being set to Scottish Reels or Rants in addition to the 3/2 hornpipes of the Borders and 6/8 and 9/8 jigs from England and Ireland. By the end of the eighteenth century, 3/2 hornpipes and 9/8 jigs no longer found a place in Scottish country dancing. There were still, of course, *lycht* dances of the Scottish countryfolk performed to 9/8 jigs — although they were called reels — and some, as we have remarked, survived into recent times. But the 3/2 hornpipe measure seems to have had no hold on Scottish sentiment in general.

The great Scottish dance of the eighteenth century, however, was the Highland Reel, belonging to that tradition of highly cultivated virtuosity of footwork which places it on a technical plane far above normal folk dance and even above the "cultivated" Country Dance.

Francis Peacock, the celebrated eighteenth-century Aberdeen dancing master, in his *Sketches relative to Dancing*, had this to say of the skill bestowed on this dance in the Highlands: "Our colleges draw hither, every year, a number of students from the Western Isles, as well as from the Highlands, and the greater part of them excel in this dance; some of them, indeed, in so superior a degree, that I, myself, have thought them worthy of imitation" (p. 86). And again, "The fondness of the highlanders for this quartet or trio (for it is either the one or the other) is unbounded, and so is their ambition to excel in it. . . . I once had the pleasure of seeing, in a remote part of the country, a reel danced by a herd boy and two young girls, who surprised me very much, especially the boy, who appeared to be about twelve years of age. He had a variety of well-chosen steps, and executed them with so much justness and ease, as if to set criticism at defiance" (p. 85).

---

[7] Robert Pitcairn, *Criminal Trials in Scotland*, vol. 3, pt. 3, appendix, p. 606.

Nor did this enthusiasm remain isolated to the Highlands or to Scotland. The passion for dancing which developed in the Scottish capital during the eighteenth century brought the Highland Reel (or Scotch Reel) very dramatically to the attention of the ever-increasing flow of foreign visitors who came to savour the heady vigour of the northern intellect. We have seen the reactions of Topham; but while he was letter-writing, other Englishmen were introducing the Highland Reel to the assemblies of London itself, to Almack's and to Bath, so that by the turn of the century many dancing masters in the English capital were advertising their qualifications for coping with the vogue. Peacock tells of two London dancing masters travelling to Edinburgh by coach to take lessons in the Highland Reel from the most "fashionable" master in the city (probably Strange) who was so busy with the preparations for a ball that he was obliged to refer them to Peacock's assistant who happened to be in town, and with whom they pursued a course of instruction of three lessons a day during their sojourn. Peacock assumed from the fact that these gentlemen possessed their own coach that they were teachers of means and consequence.

Some few years later, Thomas Wilson, whose works on English country dancing are a mine of information, wrote in the *Complete System of English Country Dancing*: "No species of Dancing has ever been so universally danced, nor has ever become so great a favourite, either in this Country or any other, as Reels; not even Country Dancing, most persons, whether in possession of knowledge of Country Dancing, or not, are able to dance Reels, and particularly the Scotch" (p. 139). In another place in the same work, he mentions that the Scotch Reels "have been introduced into most of the foreign Courts of Europe, and are universally practised, in all our extensive colonies . . ." and that "assemblies are very frequently held for the purpose of dancing them only" (p. 135).

The aristocratic Captain Gronow tells us that in 1814 the dances of Almack's were Scotch Reels and the "old English country dance," and that the orchestra was from Edinburgh. This, of course, was the year preceding that which saw the public introduction of the Quadrille; but despite the great vogue of the latter, the Reel and Strathspey Reel were very popular "all over Great Britain" as late as 1852.[8]

Perhaps Queen Victoria's unbounded love of the Highlands had some influence on this affection for the Highland Reel; her diaries bear testimony to her enjoyment of Highland dancing, and although she did not dance — not even a Country Dance by the time she sojourned regularly in the Highlands — many of the royal family participated in Reels. Indeed, no other dances, she tells us, were performed amidst the Braes of Mar. This we gather from her remarks on her memorable visit to Inverary in September, 1875, during which she attended a ball held for the tenants and townspeople by the duke: "It was not like the Highland balls I have been accustomed to," she wrote in *More Leaves from the Journal*, "as there were many other dances besides reels" (p. 303).

It may not be out of place to recall the lavish displays with which Victoria was welcomed on her visits to Perthshire, the bonfires, fireworks, and Highlanders dancing reels by torchlight. Hers was the Scotland of Landseer, of shaggy Highland

---

[8] John T. Surenne, *The Dance Music of Scotland*.

cattle in peat-stained reflections of misty, frowning mountains in heavy gilt picture frames; of bellowing stags and the salute of pipers in far-flung outposts of empire. The favourite dance of the Highlanders for the entertainment of Queen Victoria, other than reels, was Gille Callum (commonly called the Sword Dance), the "double" Sword Dance, and what was probably the Argyll Broadswords.

In 1890, David Anderson wrote in *Ballroom Guide*: "Now-a-days most dancing masters devote much of their attention to teaching the walking and glisade steps, which are invaluable as imparting graceful carriage, but which are not to be compared in the least to our Scotch steps, which combine gracefulness and muscular culture. The latter only went out of fashion on account of the difficulty of mastering them; but it is satisfactory to see them once more coming to the front and sought after by the highest of our land, as was evinced by the enthusiasm with which they were received at the Paris Exhibition Highland Gathering" (p. 13).

The Reel could be danced by couples or by men or women only, and both sexes employed the virtuoso steps involved. In the ballroom, custom and practical exigencies dictated a more decorous style for the ladies, but lads and lassies barefoot on the green knew no such restraints. If the "virtuoso" steps are strung together, we have a kind of hornpipe to which males and females can give their own unique character. In Strathspey style these become what we know as a Highland Fling.

Step dances of the fling variety and the Gille Callum and other Pyrrhic dances so dear to the heart of a society of mountaineers and warriors certainly strengthen the legs, and this was no bad thing for those to whom fleetness of foot and hardiness of limb were beyond price. For this reason, perhaps, the male has put his own particular character on these dances, but "Highland capers" were by no means eschewed by the female. It will be recalled that our earliest notices of solo dancing in Scotland refer to girls — the lasses who danced before James IV at Forres and Dingwall — and a century later to Maggie Lauder who danced in Fife and who was immortalized in song. Alexander Jaffray, born near Aberdeen in 1755, recalled a "female servant in the family, a Highland girl named Lizzie Althash who was an excellent dancer; and was often called to exhibit a *pas seul* before the company when they happened to visit."[9] Thus we have examples of the female propensity for dancing from both Lowland and Highland society, and we have not exhausted all the evidence.

Nevertheless, in Scottish Highland society, male dancing proficiency was every bit as much esteemed as male athletic prowess. We read of Lord Lovat in the late sixteenth century organizing such recreational exercises as swimming, archery, football, putting the stone, throwing the bar, fencing, wrestling, and dancing among the young members of his clan and being joined in them by other nobles and gentry and members of adjacent clans on certain days in the chapelyard at Inverness.[10] Such exercises, of course, were not exceptional in the accomplishments of a typical gallant of the period. We noted this with reference to the "Admirable" Creighton (see p. 57). The tradition persisted long in the Highlands, and Donald Sage's description in *Memerobalia Domestica* of Donald Gunn in Sutherland in the eighteenth century exemplifies the

---

9 Alexander Jaffray, *Recollections of Kingswells.*
10 Wardlaw MS, Fraser Chronicles, p. 171, Scottish History Society (Edinburgh, 1905).

epitome of the Highland peasant: "He had a face full of expression which conveyed most unequivocally the shrewdness, cunning, acuteness, and caustic humour so strongly characteristic of his race. Donald Gunn surpassed his whole neighbourhood and, perhaps, the whole parish, in all rustic and athletic exercises. At a brawl, in which, however, he but seldom engaged, none could exceed him in the dexterity and rapidity with which he brandished his cudgel; and though many might exceed him in physical strength, his address and alert activity often proved him more than a match for an assailant of much greater weight and size. Then in dancing he was without a rival. With inimitable ease and natural grace he kept time, with eye and foot and fingers, to all the minute modulations of a Highland reel or Strathspey. He was also a good shot, a successful deer stalker, angler, smuggler, and a poacher" (p. 178). A catalogue worthy of the "Admirable" Creighton himself! Alas, however, Sage continues, "despite these peculiarly Highland recommendations, Donald was a notorious thief and made some hair-breadth escapes from the gallows!"

There are some allusions to Scotsmen dancing in Elizabethan and early Jacobean times — "a Scotch-man's dance" or "a Scottish jig," but never a "Highland Fling" — and in a letter from John Chamberlain to Alice Carleton quoted by John Nichols (*The Progresses of King James I*, vol. 2, London, 1828), we read, "yesterday there was a medley Masque of five English and five Scots, which are called the high Dancers, among whom Serjeant Boyd, one Abercrombie, and Auchmouty [one of the Grooms of the King's Bedchamber] that was at Padua and Venice, are esteemed the most principal and lofty. . . ." (p. 725).

The passion of the Highland warrior for dancing to his native music is certainly of long standing, and Mr. Gib, Master of the Household to Prince Charlie during the '45 Rebellion, an Edinburgh man, thought it a matter of remark how the Highlanders with the prince would, at the end of the day, forget the fatigues of their long marches as soon as they heard the pipes play a dance tune. Up they got, to dance "as nimbly as if they had not been marching at all. . . . I believe the devil is in their legs."[11]

From their natural habitat, the high dances of the Highlands found their way into the studios of the city dancing masters. Topham often alludes to this in his letters from eighteenth-century Edinburgh, and has some particularly interesting remarks to make on one of the numerous dancing masters' finishing balls:

At these balls the children dance minuets; which would be very tiresome and disagreeable, as well from the badness of the performance, as from the length of time they would take up were they regularly continued, but the dancing masters enliven the entertainment by introducing between the minuets their high dances (which is a kind of double hornpipe) in the execution of which they excel perhaps the rest of the world. I wish I had it in my power to describe to you the variety of figures and steps they put into it. Besides all those common to the hornpipe, they have a number of their own which I never before saw or heard of; and their neatness and quickness in the performance of them is incredible; so amazing is their agility that an Irishman, who was standing by me the other night, could not help exclaiming in his surprise "that by Jesus he never saw children so handy with their feet in all his life."

The motion of the feet is indeed the only thing that is considered in these dances as they rather neglect than pay any attention to the other parts of the body; which is a great pity,

---

[11] Bishop Forbes, *Lyon in Mourning*, vol. 2, p. 171.

since it would render the dance much more complete and agreeable, were the attitudes of the hands and positions of the body more studied and understood by them. From the practise of these high dances, one great advantage is derived to the young men, in giving prodigious powers to their ankles and legs; but I cannot say it is an ornamental advantage either to them or to the ladies; as it makes them too large in those parts for the proportion of the rest of the body. [Letter xli]

We would like to know if the dances Topham saw had names. It is odd to think that an English army officer interested in dance had never seen the Scottish high dances before his visit to Edinburgh in 1775. What a change there has been since his time! Only the motion of the feet seemed to matter, arms and body were neglected, neatness and agility were required in abundance, and the best way he could describe the dances was to call them "a kind of double hornpipe" which included all the figures and steps of the hornpipe (as known to him) and a number of others he had never seen before.

The traditional hornpipe was obviously an elementary step dance, that is, a dance in which rhythms are beaten out by the feet as in tap dancing; but the extension of shuffles and beats into kicks, rockings, sheddings, shakes, balances, bourrées, etcetera, is easy to comprehend, and thus Highland dancing joins with pure hornpipe dancing in natural alliance. All Scottish high dances are of the nature of step dances. Attitudes and bodily deportment are restricted; emphasis lies in the feet and legs. Nevertheless the kinship of this dance form with the stage hornpipe of the eighteenth century is very evident.

The word "hornpipe" has a very limited meaning today, but in the eighteenth century, its connotation was much wider (see chap. 16). Thus Topham, we can accept, was certainly talking of what we would call Highland dancing. To a person accustomed to the hornpipes (or jigs) of the theatre, as Topham undoubtedly would be, the simple arm positions of Highland dancing, possibly not very well delineated at that, would appear too inert and rudimentary. Hence Topham's comment implying that arm movements were employed more artistically in the hornpipe dancing with which he was familiar.

The dance Seann Triubhas and enchainments of reel steps would comply with Topham's remarks, and perhaps if we had accompanied Topham, we would have recognized some of the reel steps in Strathspey rhythm as Highland Fling steps. Seann Triubhas was referred to as a well-known "double" hornpipe at the end of the eighteenth century, but the evidence is that it was more of a high dance than a pure step dance.

Nevertheless, hornpipe stepping was basic to the country dancing master's curriculum. This is well exemplified by John MacTaggart's account in *The Scottish Gallovidian Encyclopedia* of a country dancing master's syllabus from the southwest Lowland corner of Scotland — Kirkcudbright and Galloway — early in the nineteenth century.

The first step taught was "Peter a Dick's Peatstack." This was the beating out of the rhythm "peter dum dick," well known by all my own contemporaries who practiced on the "clappers" in the 1930s in Dunbartonshire. The complete phrase "uttered" by the feet was "Peter a Dick, Peter a Dick, Peter a Dick's Peatstack." Our informant explains that the taps were executed by giving three "flegs" (flutterings with a swing-ing step) and two stamps with the heel alternately. When this was reasonably mas-tered, the pupils were taught to "fleup through the sidestep." To "fleup" means to dance without lifting the feet, probably shuffling, or trebling (or tripling).

Then, in MacTaggart's words:

Jack on the Green,[12] *Shawintrews,* and other *hornpipes,* with the *Highland Fling,* mayhap; these dances were all got pretty well by the feet in the *first month,* with sketches of *four-some,* eightsome reels and some country dances; but if the scholars attend the *fortnight* again of another *month,* they proceed at great length into the labyrinths of the art.

A light heel'd souter is generally the dancing dominie; he fixes on a barn in some *clauchan* to show forth in; he can both fiddle and dance, at the same time; he can cut double quick time, and *trible Bob Major;* he fixes on and publishes abroad when his *trial night* is to come on, so the young folk in the neighbourhood doff their clogs, and put on their *kirk-shoon,* these being their *dancing-pumps;* off they go to the trial, which, if it be a good turn-out, he tries no more, but begins teaching directly; if not, he has a second and even a *third* trial; . . .

They learn the "Flowers of Edinburgh" mayhap; *Sweden* and *Belile's Marches,* with other hornpipes, and country dances many; such as *Yillwife and her Barrles — Mary Grey — The Wun that shook the barley,* &c. with the famous *Bumpkin Brawley;* yes, and they will even dare, some times to imitate our Continental neighbours over the water, in their *waltzing, alimanging,* and *Cotillion* trade; ay, and be up with the Spaniards too, in their *quadrilles, borellos,* and *falderalloes* of nonsense; so out-taught, they become fit to attend *house-heatings, volunteer and masonic-balls,* and what not. [P. 263]

There is evidence that step dancing in the Irish manner was by no means confined to Galloway, but was well rooted in the West Highlands and the Hebrides at that time. An English traveller, Colonel Thornton, alludes to this in his description in *A Sport-ing Tour through the Highlands of Scotland* of a dancing master's ball held at the Dalmally Inn during his stay there in 1804:

They were dancing a country-dance when we entered. The company consisted of about fourteen couple, who all danced the true *Glen Orgue Kick.* I have observed that every district of the Highlands has some peculiar cut; and they all shuffle in such a manner as to make the noise of their feet keep exact time. Though this is not the fashionable style of dancing, yet, in such dancers, it had not a bad effect.

But I shall never forget the arrogance of the master; his mode of marshaling his troops, his directions, and other manoeuvres were truly ridiculous; he felt himself greater than any adjutant disciplining his men, and managed them much in the same manner. [Pp. 265–66]

The Glen Orchy Kick (Glen Orgue is another spelling) is no longer identifiable and may have passed away with its exponents. The step-dance manner of setting and travelling in social dances was apparently carried to Canada, where, in the Scottish settlements on the eastern seaboard, it conspicuously survived into modern times. Of course, this manner of dancing is peculiarly associated with Ireland and not with Scotland; hence the obvious suspicion that the step dancing four- and eight-hand reels

---

[12] Jack on the Green is a 9/8 jig Country Dance in the Bodleian MS and also in Walsh's *Caledonian Country Dances* (London, 1745). The "Jack in the Green" is the young man adorned in leaves and foliage in the May revels, simulating the fertilizing spirit of spring.

of Cape Breton are somehow of Irish derivation, and, if not, a legacy of the original French settlers of these parts. There certainly was a substantial influx of Ulster-Scots in the late eighteenth century, and the Acadian French had clog dances of their own; but how can we explain the apparently entire loss of the native dancing of the Gael in Cape Breton where he has preserved his language, music, poetry, and customs so tenaciously? No, we must strongly suspect that he has preserved his dancing, too, at least the dances or the dance style favoured by his forefathers, who left their native land in the early nineteenth century. The implication is that in the regions of Scotland from whence these early emigrants were drawn, the technique of "Highland Dance" was not indigenous. These regions would embrace mainly the West Highlands and the Hebrides, but also Sutherland. Yet we know from contemporary sources that what we call Highland dancing was known in the Western Isles (as we are told by Peacock in the passage quoted earlier in this chapter) and certainly in Sutherland, in the eighteenth century. It is nevertheless evident that only the slightest trace of this is detectable in all that is known of Cape Breton dancing in the past century. However, we shall return to this topic in chapter 15, as it properly belongs to the discussion of West Highland reels.

One can see some analogy in the dance music of Cape Breton with that of Scotland; it is mainly a mixture of Scottish, Irish, and French music, and is predominantly of common-time hornpipe character which, of course, embraces the various classes of the Scottish Reel. The strathspey is comparatively ignored by most performers, although it is certainly far from being unpopular with Cape Breton fiddlers today. But their mode of playing is identifiably different from the native Scottish style and exhibits characteristics which are more common among Irish fiddlers. Other Scottish settlements in Canada, notably in the Ottawa Valley, the Glengarry settlement in Ontario, and the Red River settlement in Manitoba, have retained a tradition of fiddling Scottish (and Irish) dance music, exhibiting characteristics peculiar to each region. These characteristics range from a recognizable affinity with the native Scottish style, as in Cape Breton and Glengarry, for instance, to what is commonly called Western music, a style of playing wedded to the square dancing of pioneer frontier life. The style of playing is an indicator to the style of dancing with which it is associated; bearing this in mind, it is clear that hornpipe stepping has been the characteristic dance technique of most, if not all, Scottish settlements in Canada. I was interested, however, to discover that stepping is today regarded as an alien intrusion in the Glengarry settlement. As we have seen, too, it was not unfamiliar in Scotland. It was performed in North Argyll, as suggested by Thornton's remarks on the dancing class ball at Dalmally Inn in 1800, and it was certainly familiarly encountered in reel and Country Dance at many a Lowland hop in barn or village hall in the nineteenth century. Hornpipe stepping was also encountered in country dancing in England and certainly in New England at this time; but it was a style of dancing associated with the vulgar, and strictly taboo among the cultivated, as far as more formal social dance was concerned. It was probably a product of overcrowded dance floors.

The solo hornpipe or stage dance was another matter and, of course, stepping in all its complexity is the substance of Irish dancing. Yet one suspects that the employment of beating techniques in social dance must derive from dancing in hard shoes on a resounding surface, and hence can hardly predate the use of wooden flooring in dancing places (to say nothing of the hard shoes). Not many barns or inns in Scotland — or Ireland — had suitable wooden floors prior to the eighteenth century. For the solo performer, of course, a tabletop or a board sufficed.

We have seen something of the influences at work on the eighteenth-century dancing master in the principal Scottish towns. The accomplished and even sophisticated native dance technique of the Central Highlands was often joined in the same person with a classical dance training — at least of sorts. These dancing masters may often have devised dances which were products of such a union for their pupils. Archibald Duff, who seems to have succeeded Peacock in Aberdeen, was one of these, judging from the contents of his *Choice Selection of Minuets; favourite airs, hornpipes and waltzes etc.* (Edinburgh, 1812). In this collection there are a number of arrangements of tunes obviously devised to accompany dances composed by Duff for his pupils, such as:

Pas Seul danced by Miss Margaret Burnett of Leys
Pas Seul danced by Miss Allardyce of Dunnotter
Pas Seul danced by Miss Francis Urquhart

Then there are some titles with the term "danced by" omitted:

Pas Seul Miss Jane Forbes
Pas Seul Miss Anne Mitchell
Miss Eliza Low's High Dance
Carleton House High Dance

and many more.

Most of these dances are in three parts. For instance, Miss Jane Forbes' Pas Seul comprised "Pomposo" 4/4, "Slow — Bonny Jean of Aberdeen," "Presto — Speed the Plough." They usually comprised a selection of reels, strathspeys, jigs, and airs in 9/8 and 2/4, with the occasional allemande or tune by Ignaz Pleyel. Obviously these were not necessarily dances of a peculiarly Scottish cast. However, two are mentioned that are of interest because they are known to us: The Graces — à Pas Trois (the music allegretto 6/8) and the Marquis of Huntly's Highland Fling.

Duff's dances devised for his pupils were, for the most part, obviously of the character of the stage dances which were in popular demand at the theatre of the day. It is easy to understand how these should influence the repertoires of fashionable dancing masters in the principal towns and perhaps even those of the itinerant dancing masters.

The Scotch Whim (1703), Highland Lilt (1702), various Scots Dances (1719 et seq.), and Highland Dances (1722 et seq.) which were introduced occasionally to London theatre audiences from the beginning of the eighteenth century were, presumably, the creations of professional dancers drawing on the Scottish dance idiom. Perhaps some, at least, of the dances were what could be called traditional, but if not, one would expect them to be derived from the traditional. One suspects the presence of a cultivating influence on Scottish Highland Dance, of course, even earlier than this. A few observers, as we have seen, compared the native high dancing of the Scots, at both dancing school and social Highland assembly in the late eighteenth century, very favourably with stage dancing; so the native strain at its most sophisticated was relatively highly evolved.

Sir John Sinclair refers to certain "slow Highland dances" in a letter to the Duke of Atholl's factor in 1806: "There are one or two persons at Dunkeld who dance slow Highland dances, emblematical of war or courtship — Neil [*sic*] Gow knows who they are and the tunes."[13] The letter is endorsed with "The Battle, Mc An Fhorsair played by Donald Dewar." These latter dances were obviously of the Pyrrhic variety and, apart from a few recorded allusions to Mc An Fhorsair and its tune, are unknown today. There is a total absence of written record of traditional Scottish dances, or of dances in the traditional Scottish style, up to this period. Dances were handed down from one dancer or teacher to another by demonstration. It was difficult to describe them in writing, although some dancers undoubtedly took notes to serve as a kind of aide-mémoire, just as they do today. A few such notebooks survive, but only Frederick Hill's contains descriptions of the steps of solo dances as distinct from social dances.

The discovery of the Hill manuscript is an intriguing story, and I pass it on just as Isobel Cramb told it to me.

A few years ago, an Aberdeen doctor attending an elderly patient noticed by his patient's bedside a notebook which, because of its apparent age and his patient's evident interest in it, excited his curiosity. On inquiring what it was, the doctor was told that it was a collection of dances made by the patient's father, Frederick Hill, and was called *Frederick Hill's Book of Quadrilles and Country Dances, 22nd March, 1841*. The doctor recalled this when, some time after the patient's death, he was speaking to Isobel Cramb, whom he knew to be an ardent student of Scottish dance. Mrs. Cramb contacted the family concerned, only to find that the book had probably been destroyed. She was disappointed, but Mrs. Lorimer, the great-granddaughter of Frederick Hill, continued the search, and eventually found the book. What a treasure-trove it proved to be! It included three Highland Flings and several other dances. Of these, The Earl of Erroll, The King of Sweden, and Scotch Measure have been published, and it is to be hoped that the remainder will follow before too long.

Mr. Hill had evidently noted these dances as he learned them; the problem remained to interpret their manner of performance and, crucial to this, to find their music. Fate, however, had not finished with the matter and again took a hand when Mrs. Cramb decided to have the Earl of Erroll performed at a concert in honour of the Princess Margaret. In the audience at this concert was a Miss Flora Cruickshank, of Peterhead, last of a long family line of dancing teachers in Aberdeenshire. At the close of the evening, Miss Cruickshank sought out Mrs. Cramb to tell her how much she had enjoyed the performance of the Earl of Erroll, and how much its execution differed from that which she had known. Thus it came about that Isobel Cramb had many sessions with Miss Cruickshank in the latter's home, going over the steps of the dance. Miss Cruickshank, supporting herself between two chairs, demonstrated the technique, and this enabled Mrs. Cramb to interpret the terms used by Mr. Hill in his notes and thus the execution of the other dances in his collection.

When this was accomplished, Miss Cruickshank revealed that she "had mair," and so we come to have Flora Macdonald's Fancy as taught to Miss Cruickshank by her

---

[13] John Murray, *Chronicles of the Athol and Tullibardine Families.*

grandfather, a beautiful dance for ladies which has found its way to the Highland Games platform.[14] The tune for this dance was "I Ha'e Laid a Herrin' in Salt," but Mrs. Cramb substituted the appropriate airs, "The Last Measure Prince Charles danced with Flora Macdonald" and "Wha'll be King but Charlie."

Miss Cruickshank had her grandfather's copy of the tune for the Earl of Erroll, a "double" hornpipe, but the King of Sweden was still without music. Then Mrs. Cramb found "Charles the Twelfth King of Sweden's March" in the Gillespie manuscript (1768); it was a "double" hornpipe, which had the same number of parts as the dance. This seemed too much of a coincidence to ignore. We know, of course, that the King of Sweden's March was a familiar hornpipe in the late eighteenth-century country dancing schools in the southwest of Scotland. The association of Charles XII of Sweden with Scotland can arise only through the many Scottish officers who served with him, as they did with his more famous ancestor, Gustavus Adolphus. Both of the dances have steps and a structure resembling the Irish hornpipe and a refrain of single and double trebles. Each step, of course, is performed beginning right, then repeated, beginning left, in the manner of Scots and Irish step dances.

One of the most important earls of Erroll was the fifteenth Earl, who, as Hereditary High Constable of Scotland, attended the coronation of George III — the handsomest man present on that occasion, or so Horace Walpole tells us. He was a great patron of the arts, and it was to him that Francis Peacock dedicated his "Fifty Favourite Scotch Airs, for violin, German Flute, and Violoncello, with a thorough bass for the harpsichord" in 1762. This dedication suggests that Peacock composed the dance, The Earl of Erroll.

It is very possible that the Earl of Erroll and the King of Sweden figured in the dancing-school concerts attended by Topham, but whereas they demand facile and neat footwork, their range is too limited to fit all aspects of his remarks. Arm movements are not specified for either dance; ladies would hold their skirts, and Mrs. Cramb regards the King of Sweden as undoubtedly a woman's dance and treats it as such. It could as easily be treated in a more masculine way.

Other solo dances which have come down to us in one way or another are The Scottish Lilt and Miss Forbes, recorded and published in D. G. MacLennan's *Traditional and Highland Scottish Dances*. He tells us that the Lilt originated in Perthshire. Both are regarded as ladies' dances. Then there are the dances of Ewen MacLachlan, who studied dancing while attending the Scots College at Douai, France. The best known of these are Tullochgorm, Highland Laddie, O'er the Water to Charlie, and Blue Bonnets. They were composed after their creator returned to South Uist, where he spent the last thirty years of his life, (from 1855 to 1885). They have been recorded by Jack MacConachie, who took them down in 1949 from the dancing of John Mac-Leod of Eochar. MacLeod had learned them from Archie MacPherson, one of MacLachlan's pupils whom MacLennan had seen performing these dances in 1925. Different versions of the dances have since come to light: a Hielan' Laddie was published by David Anderson in his *Ballroom Guide* where he calls it a "Woman's Solo"! A dance called Hielan' Laddie existed prior to MacLachlan's time, however, as is

---

14 This dance was more widely remembered than Mrs. Cramb realized. Janet T. MacLachlan, a noted Scottish dance teacher in Ontario, tells me that she recalls an itinerant dancing master in Lanarkshire teaching a set of this dance in the early 1930s.

revealed by a letter sent to the Edinburgh Gaelic Society in the early 1830s (cf. p. 246), as well as one named Over the Hills and Far Away, a very un-Scottish title but another name for "The win' has blawn my kilt awa'," an old Scottish song.

One dance about which there is some mystery is the Scotch (or Scottish) Measure. MacLennan tells us in *Traditional Scottish Dances* that it was a twosome in the eighteenth century, and Isobel Cramb followed MacLennan's statement in arranging the Hill manuscript version as a twosome. One wishes that MacLennan had told us how he came by this information. Since the Scottish Measure, as music, is a class of hornpipe, we shall return to it when we discuss the hornpipe in chapter 14.

It is interesting to notice the solo dances performed by Mr. and Mrs. J. Scott Skinner's dancing classes in the late nineteenth century: "Highland Fling, Ghillie Callum, Cane Hornpipe, Three Graces [apparently a solo], Jack O'Tar, Sailor's Hornpipe, Scotch Jig, Scotch Medley," some of which are unknown to us. The classes were held in numerous towns in the northeast and notably in Elgin, Forres, and Nairn. Today, there are still new step dances in the Scottish tradition being composed, some of which, in time, may become favourites; but these do not belong to our present study.

This discussion leads us to the Scottish high dances now so familiar on the Highland Games platform — the Highland Fling, the Seann Triubhas, and the Gille Callum — which, together with the Reel, form the basic corpus of Scottish Highland Dance. The ballet technique so evident in these dances and in the Reel in its allegro and Strathspey forms has apparently come from European sources. The obvious connection is with France, although the spirit is more Italian. It is likely that the balletic influence has become even more marked as the eighteenth-century, and later dancing masters, trained in the principles of the French Academy, have exerted their influence. But the germ of that style must have been present long before that time.

It has been suggested that the Highlanders had formerly developed their most characteristic dances for the purpose of strengthening the legs of the young warriors. I would suggest something of the reverse: that in a society of strong-legged mountaineers, the active use of the legs in dancing would be most natural and inevitable. Perhaps, however, these two ideas are complementary.

11 / The Scotch Reel

*Reel of four – threesome – medley –
technique and execution – printed sources
– Peacock – travelling steps – footwear –
setting steps – arm and finger positions –
"hooch" – the Strathspey – first record
of word in allusion to dance – alternative
to reel – Strathspey Minuet – Cummings
of Strathspey – native land of Highland
dancing – other reels in the tradition –
"four-handed" and "eight-handed" reels –
Cape Breton style – Reel of Tulloch –*

*Hullachan – Ninesome, Sixsome, and
Eightsome Reels – Shetland and Orkney
reels*

Of the Scottish dances, or dances based on a Scottish motif which appeared on the eighteenth-century stage (see chap. 7), only the Highland Reel can be related with assurance to a dance we know today. It is, nevertheless, very possible that some of the Scotch dances, so called, were none other than Seann Triubhas Willichan, for instance, mentioned in Scottish sources of the time, or what would now be identified as a Highland Fling.

The Highland Reel, or Scotch Reel, as the same dance was variously called, is the kernel of the classical art of Highland dancing. We have already noted that there are many reels among the native social dances of Scotland, but *the* Reel is that particular dance for four, or three, in which the performers cut the figure of the reel with each other and alternate this with a variety of setting steps.

When performed by four dancers, the formation is as indicated below, with two inner dancers back to back and the outer dancers looking inward.

If the dance is performed by two couples, the men usually take the inner positions.

The dance begins with all dancers executing the figure, using the appropriate travelling step, for eight bars, the two dancers in the centre exchanging positions on the last step. Now all set for eight bars, then execute the figure again for eight bars, set for eight bars, and so on. The two central dancers exchange positions at the end of each travelling section. There need be no limit, other than physical endurance, to the number of times this sequence is repeated, but in practice it is usually restricted to thirty-two, forty-eight, or sixty-four bars. Sixty-four bars was thought "quite sufficient" by David Anderson.

When performed by three dancers, the figure can be executed such that a new dancer takes the central position for the eight bars of setting, or the same dancer can return to the central position each time.

One very old and widely encountered form of the Threesome Reel is that in which the dancers are linked to each other by cloths held in the hands, a device which is of ancient origin, and was a common feature of ritualistic and mumming dances in medieval times. A version of this reel, collected in Perth and Angus, is described in the Royal Scottish Country Dance Society (RSCDS) collection (bk. 1), and the Fletts also have collected a version of it in the field.[1] Mary Isdale MacNab published another version which she entitled The Shepherd's Crook.[2] This is a very pretty dance in Strathspey style, but since no source is declared, our suspicions are confirmed that, whatever the original, the published dance is largely of Mrs. MacNab's own devising.

The earliest surviving reference to the Reel as a specific dance alludes to it as a dance for three. This information is in the glossary to an edition of Douglas's translation of the *Aeneid*, printed in 1710.[3] Some sixty years later, Sir John Gallini likewise describes the Scotch Reel as a dance for three.[4]

Three, however, is a "crowd," while multiples of couples form a company. Thus it befell that in the eighteenth- and nineteenth-century dance assemblies, the Foursome Reel was favoured to the exclusion of the threesome versions. The objection to the Threesome Reel was overcome by developing it as a round-the-room dance, the result being a simplified variant ambiguously called the Highland Reel in the RSCDS collection. Another of the same kind is the well-known Dashing White Sergeant which appeared in English ballrooms around the middle of the nineteenth century.

In the case of the Foursome Reel, the conventions of social dancing made it preferable to start with the couples vis-à-vis, the ladies moving in to begin the reel, and the men following after a two bars' pause. In D. G. MacLennan's version outlined in *Traditional and Highland Scottish Dances* the men step into the middle after a preparatory chord and proceed.

The celebrated Aberdeen dancing master, Peacock, tells us in *Sketches relative to dancing*, published in 1805, that in many parts of the Highlands the strathspey style of music was preferred to the common reel, but that the latter was generally chosen for the dance on account of its greater liveliness. And Barclay Dun, who taught dancing in Edinburgh (ca. 1798–1838), wrote in 1818 in his preface to *Translation of Nine Quadrilles*, "There are two kinds of music to which the Scotch Reel is danced, viz. the reel properly so called, and the Strathspey." The style of dance and music associated with Strathspey, however, gained favour in the eighteenth-century dance assemblies. It accorded well with the sophisticated dancing tastes of the time, and soon there grew a tendency to combine the two styles by performing the dance first in Strathspey, then in common reel style. This combination, in fact, became what was

---

[1] J. F. and T. M. Flett, *Traditional Dancing in Scotland*, p. 173.

[2] *Scottish Country Dance Book of Four Set Dances*, collected by Mary Isdale MacNab (London, 1948).

[3] *Virgil's Aeneid, translated into Scottish verse* by G. Douglas, glossary by T. Ruddiman (Edinburgh, 1710), p. 246.

[4] John Gallini, *A Treatise on the Art of Dancing* (London, 1772).

generally understood by the term Foursome Reel in the nineteenth century, but it was also widely known as the Strathspey and Reel, Scotch Reel, and Highland Reel.

The pairing of Strathspey and Reel and Jig and Reel occurs in some late eighteenth-century publications of Scottish dance music,[5] and is given the name "medley." The medley found some use in country dancing, in which connection the term is mentioned in Susan Sibbald's *Memoirs*, page 249.

There is difficulty in executing the reel of four to common reel music, and it has been known for musicians to play an extra two bars to allow the dancers to get back to place without an ungainly scramble.[6] It has also been known, in some localities, for the reel figure to be reduced to an oval for the same reason. This, however, approximates the form of the dance known in the Hebrides to which we shall turn presently. The only way to complete the reel of four elegantly in eight bars of common reel music is to keep the figure very slender, with the dancers rotating their shoulders to pass almost back-to-back. Much skill is required to make this look tidy and easy, surely a practical indication that the threesome is the natural combination for the Scotch Reel in allegro form.

The earliest written descriptions of the Scotch Reel appear in the period 1811–21.[7] The earliest use of the term "foursome reel" is probably that in the Duke of Gordon's version of "Cauld Kail," "In foursome reels the Scots delight." Burns, too, uses the term in his poem "The de'il cam fiddlin thro' the town": "There's threesome reels, there's foursome reels, / There's hornpipes and strathspeys man." It was not until the following century that the term "foursome reel" was used in a publication of dances or music and decidedly associated with a combination of Strathspey *and* Reel.

Technique and Execution of the Scotch Reel

It has been easier to describe the Scotch Reel as being performed by two couples, but the sex of the dancers is really immaterial. Dancing, in this reel, is for the sake of dancing, the dancers performing to and for each other, inspiring each other, as Topham noticed so long ago. When all the dancers were male, the reel was sometimes referred to as a Ram Reel.[8]

The first published description of the technique of the Scotch Reel was that of the Aberdeen dancing master already introduced, Francis Peacock. His book, *Sketches relative to dancing*, was published in 1805, but he was, in fact, drawing upon a long career as a dancing master extending over sixty years. He describes two travelling steps and seven setting steps, and these are given verbatim in appendix B. These could be combined or modified in any way the dancer pleased. "You have it in your power," Peacock says, "to change, divide, add to, or invert, the different steps described, in whatever way you think best adapted to the tune, or most pleasing to yourself."

---

[5] For instance, *Part First of the Complete Repository of Original Scots Slow Strathspeys and Dances by Niel Gow and Sons* (Edinburgh, 1799), pp. 8–38.

[6] Flett, *Traditional Dancing in Scotland*, p. 148.

[7] These are: Thomas Wilson, *An Analysis of Country Dancing*, 2nd ed. (London, 1811), p. 257; *Contre-Dances a Paris 1818*, MS 3860, National Library, Edinburgh; Barclay Dun, *Translation of Nine Quadrilles*, p. 205; and Thomas Wilson, *The Complete System of English Country Dancing*, p. 137.

[8] John Jamieson, *Etymological Dictionary*.

A proliferation of variations on these basic themes must have existed even in Peacock's time. Every dancer and dancing master contributed his quota, large or small, over the years, while the sifting of natural selection proceeded correspondingly, stimulated especially by the growth of competition dancing. The best of these steps are to be found in the dancing manuals of the late nineteenth century, particularly in David Anderson's *Ballroom Guide* and *Universal Ballroom Guide*, in J. G. Atkinson's *Scottish National Dances*, and in D. R. Mackenzie's *The National Dances of Scotland*. Then, in an attempt to free the art from its more alien or degenerative accretions and to offer a standard for competition dancing, the Scottish Official Board of Highland Dancing was formed in 1954 under the guiding hand of Mr. Jack Muir, third in a line of a family of dancing masters in Motherwell. The board directed its attention to the steps of those dancers who were distinguished students of former great dancers or teachers (particularly J. L. Mackenzie and Bobby Watson) and published a textbook which is now the manual of every competition Highland dancer. A most valuable contribution has been made by J. F. and T. M. Flett in *Traditional Dancing in Scotland*. The Fletts recorded all they could discover of the technique and style of the Scottish traditional social dances as these survived in living memory, roughly in the decade 1950–60.

The Scotch Reel is rarely performed with any excellence today except in Highland Dance schools and at the occasional Highland Dance competition, and possibly its sophisticated technique will continue to militate against it as a social dance. Its manner of performance in the eighteenth century, when every Scot worthy of the name could perform at least a few steps, is difficult to imagine relative to modern standards as exhibited at Highland Games. Eighteenth-century observers leave us glowing accounts of the high level of skill of the average Scottish dancer in his native reel, but it is certain that just as Highland Dance standards have improved within living memory, so also has the technical execution of the reel. For one thing, the complexity of the steps has increased, if Peacock's descriptions of them in 1805 are any guide, although it may be wrong to take these as a standard. Nevertheless, the standard of reel dancing at balls today can hardly be discussed for there is scarcely such a thing, except occasionally at functions associated with Highland societies or Scottish Country Dance balls, in which case I have no doubt that, with few exceptions, the eighteenth century takes the plum.

The reel steps described by Peacock (see Appendix B) are mere rudiments of the steps which have come down to us. Certainly, the first of the two progressive travelling steps is clearly the so-called skip-change-of-step: advance R., close L., advance R., and hop, advance L., etc. The second travelling step, however, is not so familiar: spring gently forward on R. and close L., (repeat three times), spring R., and bring L. through on hop. Repeat beginning spring L., etc. The body is turned to left with the right foot advancing and to the right with the left advancing. Peacock does not call this springy step an alternative; he says that it may be used instead of the first step in the repeat of the first measure. That is, the first step for four bars, the alternative for the next four bars. These steps bore the Gaelic name *Ceumsuibhail* (Kemshoo'hl) which Peacock translates as "step to glide with rapidity," but which is probably only "step to proceed." Otherwise it may be *Ceumsuibhloch*, (nimble step, or to traverse nimbly).

Peacock makes no suggestion that different steps were used for strathspey rhythm, but he leaves us with the decided impression that the travelling and setting steps he describes could be performed to reel *or* strathspey music, and that although the strathspey style of music was preferred in "many parts of the highlands," the reel, being the more lively, was "more generally made choice of in the dance."

These remarks were published in 1805, and in 1818, Dun, in his preface to *Translation of Nine Quadrilles*, remarks that in strathspey rhythm the steps are danced with "alacrity and promptitude on the points of the toes," while the reel is danced in more of a "running and flowing style." Here then is confirmation, not of the use of different steps, but of a difference in style in the performance of possibly the same steps. As early as 1780, Creech's description in *Fugitive Pieces* of the reel as "riotous" and the Strathspey as "sprightly," is consistent with the Dun's remarks — and with the music — but there is still no suggestion of any more than a difference in style rather than of substance.

Two comments from the same period attract our attention, one by the English dancing master, Thomas Wilson, and the other by that superb dancing gentlewoman, Elizabeth Grant. Wilson writes in 1821 in *The Complete System*, only fifteen years after Peacock, that "strathspeys, from the nature of their *steps* will be uniformly Andante; Reels will be quicker, and consequently Allegro" (p. 302). Miss Grant tells us in *Memoirs of a Highland Lady* that in 1810, on one of her family's visits to London, she attended the dancing classes of a Mr. Blake and that on one occasion, she and her sister "so far forgot the English regular four-in-a-bar style of evenly goose-stepping the Scotch reel, as in our happy excitement, to revert to good Mr. Grant's Strathspey fashion of springing through in time to the music, at which, as both Jane and myself were exceedingly admired by the elders of the company, no remark was made by Mr. Blake or his assistant, but we received a sufficient lecture during our next lesson for so disgracing his teaching" (p. 89). Miss Grant does not say whether the music was strathspey or not; all she says is that she danced "Strathspey fashion" to a reel.

Wilson seems to say there were steps peculiar to the strathspey rhythm, and Miss Grant to say that there was a "Strathspey fashion" of travelling in the Reel which involved springing through "in time to the music," whereas the fashion in London was an even "four-in-a-bar" goose-stepping. This may well have been the step which was commonly used in country dancing within living memory, that of the step-close-step-through. There is a hop as the foot is passed "through" to fourth position, and this is essentially the RSCDS step of today.

Anderson's description of the *Kemshoo'hl* in *Ballroom Guide* some eighty years later is the same as Peacock's first travelling step, except that the foot on coming through is brought up in front of the supporting leg on the hop. This is essentially the approved reel travelling step today. He used the same step for Strathspey. He says that "in the Scotch Reel (Strathspey time only), the common Polka steps may be used, but bring the foot up in front instead of behind, with the hop each time." It was easier for Anderson to illustrate his meaning through a well-known step, but it does not follow that the step was derived from the Polka! By 1910, this step, which Mackenzie says resembled the "polka spring," was used mainly at Highland Games. The influence of the contemporary dancing is revealed in the travelling step proposed for the ballroom in Mackenzie's *National Dances of Scotland*: "(1) Slide R. F. toe out to 4th pos.; (2) Slide L. F. toe out to 4th pos.; (3) Slide R. F. toe out to 4th pos.; (4) Raising L. F. toe in 4th inter. pos. before hop on R. F. toe. (1 bar). Do this alternately for the 8 bars." This is a sad degeneration of an elegant step. Atkinson describes the step in *Scottish National Dances* thus: "(1) R. to 4th pos.; (2) L. to 5 rear; (3) R. to 4th pos.; (4) hop R. and pass L. over instep of R.; Repeat L."

Mackenzie describes the travelling step for the ballroom reel as chasse: "(1) Slide R. F. toe out to 4th pos.; (2) Slide L. F. toe up to back, 5th pos.; (3) Slide R. F. toe out to 4th pos. (1 bar). Do this alternately for the 8 bars." Here there is no hop and the feet "skliff" over the floor. He adds, however, that some substitute "light springs from foot to foot (jettes) — two to each bar" for chasse, but that neither was effective if badly performed.

In these examples there is a decided modification to suit prevailing conditions. Heeled shoes were standard in the ballroom, and the reel had now taken on the aspect of a domesticated plant or animal, its wild beauty and native vigour softened. If the only alternative were crudity and incompetence, then the change was to be preferred; but one recalls with some nostalgia the sight of the dancers at a market-day ball in Strathspey which Dr. Hall described so glowingly a century before (cf. chap. 18).

In the natural original state, the reel was a dance of the open air, the dancers unfettered by encumbering stiff-soled shoes. Their feet were bare and if they wore shoes, they were flexible "brogs" of hide. Footwear in the ballroom, the hay loft, or the barn was a matter of economics and fashion rather than suitability for dancing, and no one thought the subject of sufficient importance to mention it. But undoubtedly such factors as well as contemporary dancing fashions had an influence on the reel in the ballroom.

It is interesting to turn to the reel travelling steps approved today. The Anderson Strathspey step, as we may call it here, may still be seen, but it is not included in the steps approved by the SOBHD. These are:

1) Progressive Strathspey Movement: Beginning with the right foot in 3rd Aerial, step with that foot along the line of travel to 4th (inter); close ball of L to 3 or 5 (rear) extending R to 4 (inter-aerial); spring on R on line of travel bringing L to 3 (rear aerial); hop on R with slight forward travel, passing the L as in shedding (i.e. from rear to front) to 3 (aerial). On the first two counts the body is at 45° to the line of travel with the left shoulder leading. The head is always directed along the line of travel.

2) Progressive Reel Movement: Hop on L taking R to 3 (aerial low), step R along line of travel to 4 (inter) (count "& 1"); close the ball of L to 3 or 5 rear, then, with slight elevation, spring R along line of travel (count "& 2"). The body is turned as for Strathspey.[9]

Flett tells us that the above Strathspey travelling step, a very spirited one, is said by D. G. MacLennan to have been introduced about the year 1900 by James A. Gordon, a well-known Highland dancer.[10]

The setting steps, the glory of the Scotch Reels, are wonderful in their variety. Some are performed on the spot, while others involve some lateral travel. Those steps used in strathspey rhythm, involving no travel, are associated also with the solo Highland Fling and are called fling steps accordingly. Anderson suggests that "Fling"

---

[9] *Textbook of the SOBHD*, 1st ed., 1955, p. 32.
[10] Flett, *Traditional Dancing in Scotland*, p. 97.

steps be used by "Gentlemen Beginners" in the common reel, in which case they would be performed at half speed.

Other Strathspey setting steps involve lateral travel, such as that now commonly associated with The Glasgow Highlanders by the RSCDS, or with those called Common Schottische or Highland Schottische.[11]

Although it is not possible here to present details of the many reel setting steps, it is worth noting that in the Borders, at the end of the eighteenth century, the three favourite reel setting steps were what were called the double shuffle, cut-the-buckle, and pigeon's wing.[12] The double shuffle is probably the shuffle "in-out," twice with each foot alternately; it is a familiar step within living memory. The cut-the-buckle is surely the same as cover-the-buckle, familiar in Irish dancing in the early nineteenth century, apparently used of double or triple shuffles.[13] Pigeon's Wing or *Ailes de Pigeons* has been used of high cuts by some Scottish dance teachers, although it is used of very different movements by others.

In the matter of deportment, Peacock does mention that, in travelling, the body is turned to the left when the right foot leads and to the right when the left foot leads. This is still the practice today. In fact, the figure cannot otherwise properly be executed, being of necessity very close to a straight line and not a figure of eight. Present practice is for the arms to be held up in third position during the figure, while in the ballroom the ladies hold their skirts, and, judging from several old prints, this is close to eighteenth-century practice.

Mackenzie illustrates his book with an engraving of two couples travelling in a reel of four. The men are holding their arms in third position, and the ladies have each

5 The Highland Reel. Reproduced from Mackenzie, *The National Dances of Scotland*.

[11] For more details on the reel setting steps, see ibid. and *Textbook of the SOBHD*.
[12] Susan Sibbald, *Memoirs of Susan Sibbald*, p. 153.
[13] Patrick Kennedy, *On the Banks of the Boro*; and F. O'Neill, *Irish Minstrels and Musicians* (Chicago, 1913).

raised their right hand from their skirt to clasp gently the near hand of the gentleman in passing. The author refers to this as the good old way of touching hands for luck, although its obvious practical purpose is to ensure that all cut the reel in the same way, that is, passing their partners giving right shoulders. A painting dated 1832 shows two couples touching hands in this way in what may be a reel, performed in the grounds of Crathes Castle. This touching of hands is practical only when the reel is performed in the Strathspey style.

The arm positions of the dancers in the Scotch Reel and in Highland Dance generally were probably more carefully formulated in the nineteenth century than in previous times. Ladies were permitted to raise their arms as did the men, to place them akimbo or, as Atkinson expresses it in 1900, to have "one hand to dress the other akimbo, or both to dress."[14] David Anderson states in *Ballroom Guide* that the arms, when held up, should be bent at the elbow such that the hands project only about four inches "above the head." This is consistent with Sir Iain Colquhoun's statement in *Highland Gatherings* that "for the best form" in the dancing of reels in the ballroom, the hands should not extend above the level of the head! (p. 74) . The practical limitation, here, is that the cut of the evening jacket does not permit the hands to be raised very high without an unseemly disarray. The SOBHD now accepts that the arms should form a graceful curve from the shoulder to finger tips, the fingers being grouped in a relaxed way with the thumb on the extreme joint of the middle finger. The fingers, in this position, are said to represent the antlers of a deer, and indeed, with the fingers stiffly extended (as some dancers favour), the position is a Hindu miming symbol for a deer. The right arm is up when the left leg is "flinging" and vice versa, the other arm is akimbo.

Eighteenth-century prints, such as David Allan's *Penny Wedding*, do not show arm positions with clarity in the reel, but some of the nineteenth century do. The grouping of the fingers arises from the practice of snapping them, at least in reels. This same grouping with the thumb on the middle finger is seen very clearly in at least one ninth-century Anglo-Saxon drawing of a dancer performing to the music of timbrel and wind instruments. Indeed, snapping of the fingers in Scottish dancing is referred to as early as the seventeenth century, as in the poem "Patie's Wedding."[15] The custom survived into the present century, although it is no longer encountered.

That a lady's dress, unlike the kilt, can be used as an adjunct to artistic movement is well illustrated in old engravings of Scottish dancing. Such use of the dress, or apron, has little to do with utility. Arms akimbo may suit some steps; eloquent use of the skirt, whether the skirt is ankle-length or not, may suit other steps. Some steps are more suitable for ladies, and others are also suitable if executed with decorum. The lasses that danced "barefoot on the green" may not have observed such restraint, but in the ballroom, some modification would seem appropriate.

The occasional shout of "hooch," particularly on the change from one tempo or tune to another, was accepted by most Scottish dancing masters, although it was re-

---

14 J. G. Atkinson, *Scottish National Dances*. See also Flett, *Traditional Dancing in Scotland*, p. 148.

15 "They danced as weel as they dow'd wi a crack o' their thooms and a happie." [David Herd, "Patie's Wedding" in *Ancient and Modern Scottish Song* (Glasgow, 1777).] Elizabeth Grant writes of her brother and the fiddler's son "dancing the fling with all their hearts and cracking their small fingers." [*Memoirs of a Highland Lady*, p. 200.]

garded with increasing disfavour by some as the twentieth century dawned. In *Companion to the Ballroom*, Thomas Wilson, the erudite London dancing master of the Regency period, ruled out entirely both snapping of fingers and shouting, at least for the English. "Snapping of fingers, in Country Dancing and Reels and the sudden howl or yell too frequently practiced, ought particularly to be avoided, as partaking too much of the customs of barbarous nations; the character and effect by such means given to the Dance, being adapted only to the stage, and by no means suited to the Ball Room" (p. 244). He acknowledged in a footnote, however, that the "howl or yell" was "introduced in some Scotch parties as partly national with them." It is interesting to note that the word "hooch" occurs in the sense of executing a hey in the description of a wedding dance in a sixteenth-century English ballad, "Abowghte with howghe let us wynde."

THE STRATHSPEY

The strathspey, musically, is a way of playing common-time reels with a peculiar snap or jerk in the rhythm and at a slower tempo. The rhythm of the strathspey is peculiar to Scotland although, strangely enough, it is not possible to claim that the rhythm is peculiar to the district of Strathspey, for it has an obviously ancient hold on the vocal dance music of the Gael. However, it is indisputable that during the eighteenth century and later, the overwhelming majority of composers in the idiom were domiciled in the northeast or Strathspey region of the country.

Whatever the origin of the musical style, the dance style was certainly a product of those regions in the broad "strath" of the River Spey. When this dance or dance style was widely introduced to Lowland society in the eighteenth century, it was naturally named after its place of origin, Strathspey. The first appearance of the word in written record with reference to dance is comparatively recent. The earliest reference has been erroneously quoted by the *Oxford Dictionary* as occurring in a passage in Zachary Boyd's "John Baptist," written about 1653, and included in his unpublished work, "Flowers of Zion." The vital passage was contrived to read:

> To please the King, the Morrice dance I will;
> Stravetspy, and after, last of all,
> the Drunken Dance I'le dance within that hall . . .

This read so unsatisfactorily that I took an opportunity to consult the manuscript itself in Glasgow University Library. The orthography presents some difficulties, but it is clear that the punctuation in the above passage is almost entirely spurious. What has been interpreted as "Stravetspy" is almost certainly the phrase "strive to essay" with the "i" undotted.[16] This conclusion is supported by the punctuation and the sense:

> And after that with measure and with skill
> To please the King the Morrice dance I will
> Strive to essay, and after last of all
> The drunken dance I'le dance within that Hall . . .

[16] This conclusion was reached independently of Flett who also pursued this matter with the same result.

This is an instance in which the dotting of an "i" would have avoided a serious error, but it is difficult to explain the insertion of the punctuation. Indeed, it is not until the eighteenth century that the word "strathspey" first appears with reference to music or dance; it occurs in the Menzies manuscript (1749) in which The Montgomerie's Rant is described as "a strathspey reele." The first appearance *in print* that I have been able to find is "A New Strathspey Reel" in James Oswald's *Caledonian Pocket Companion,* volume 3 (Edinburgh, 1751).

The first title page to include the term "Strathspey" would appear to be that of Daniel Dow's collection, *Thirty-Seven New Reels and Strathspeys* [1776]. Then in the 1780s several important collections appeared with the term "Strathspey Reels" on the title pages. Some of these are: Alexander McGlashan, *A Collection of Strathspey Reels* [1780]; Angus Cumming, *A Collection of Strathspey or Old Highland Reels* (1780); Robert Ross, *A Choice Collection of Scots Reels or Country Dances and Strathspeys* [1780]; William Marshall, *A Collection of Strathspey Reels* (1781); McGlashan, *A Collection of Reels, consisting chiefly of Strathspeys, Athole Reels. . .* [1786]; Joshua Campbell, *A Collection of New Reels and Highland Strathspeys* (1788); and publications of Malcolm McDonald, Niel Gow, and John Bowie of approximately the same date. Other later publications use "Strathspey Reels" in their titles. In fact, henceforth the word "Strathspey" is seldom absent from a collection of Scottish dance music.

We have seen how the Scotch Reel was and is performed to strathspey rhythm as well as to the other common-time rhythms loosely designated as reel. We have seen, too, how Francis Peacock, the Aberdeen dancing master whose career began in the middle of the eighteenth century, clearly states in his *Sketches relative to dancing* that, in the dance, the strathspey rhythm was an alternative to that called reel. It is evident from the context of his remarks that the dance he refers to is the Scotch Reel for four dancers. This is consistent with the term "Strathspey" as it was generally used of dance from the nineteenth century to the present day. There is a lack of evidence to enable us to extend our remarks with certainty into the eighteenth century, but Peacock does not lead us to believe that the usage then was different.

In the notes to his poem *The Grampians Desolate,* published in 1804, Alexander Campbell wrote, "Highlanders excel in those steps and figures called Reels and Strathspeys which they still exhibit with that vivacity, firmness, grace, and agility, for which they are noted." Then, in his *Albyn's Anthology,* (vol. 2, 1818), in a footnote to the tune "Donald Caird's come again," he stated, "This air is a dancing measure, or slow strathspey, danced by two highlandmen with appropriate gesture, but without the fling or gambol peculiar to the quicker strathspey or reel."

There is some ambiguity in this remark; but it is consistent with what we know to interpret it as referring to a twosome performed to a slow strathspey air — in this case to the tune "Donald Caird" — and to the Strathspey Reel for four, or three, dancers. Alexander Campbell tells us also, in another note to *The Grampians Desolate,* that the term "two-some" was a Lowland term for "dances of two," that they were performed generally by a male and female, and that the tunes played during the dance were various and changed at pleasure (p. 263). This does not tell us whether the various tunes were always strathspeys, or reels, or jigs, or an alternation from one to the other. The term "twasome" is mentioned by the Duke of Gordon (husband of the

1 Illustration of dancing figures from an early Anglo-Saxon manuscript. Reproduced from Strutt, *Sports and Pastimes*.

2 Morris dancers from an ornament engraved by Israhel Van Meckenem in the fifteenth century. [British Museum]

3 Festival costume of the Perth Glovers, Photograph by Star Photos, Perth. [Courtesy of City of Perth: Art Gallery and Museum]

4 Characters of the May Games, about 1470, taken from an ancient window in a house at Betley, Staffordshire. Reproduced from Alford, *English Folk Dances*.

18 *Grown Gentlemen Taught to Dance* by John Collet, engraved and printed for Robert Sayer, September, 1768. The notice on the wall reads, "Grown gentlemen taught to dance and qualify to appear in the most brilliant assemblies at the easy expence [*sic*] of 1 11s.6d."

17 Engraving of a theatrical Highland dancer, ca. 1846. [Courtesy of the Harry T. Peters Collection, Museum of the City of New York]

15 Susanna, Countess of Eglintoun (1689-1780). Susanna Kennedy of Culzean was a celebrated beauty of eighteenth-century Edinburgh who carried her stately form – she was all of six feet tall – with an elegance and poise long remembered as the "Eglintoun Air." She was the third wife of the ninth Earl of Eglintoun. Reproduced from Grant, *Old and New Edinburgh* (London, 1882).

16 A Country Dance in an English Assembly Room, 1790, by Thomas Rowlandson

14 Badge of office worn by the lady directresses of the Edinburgh Assembly in the old Bell's Wynd off High Street. Reproduced from Jamieson, *Book of the Old Edinburgh Club*. [Courtesy of the Museum of Antiquities]

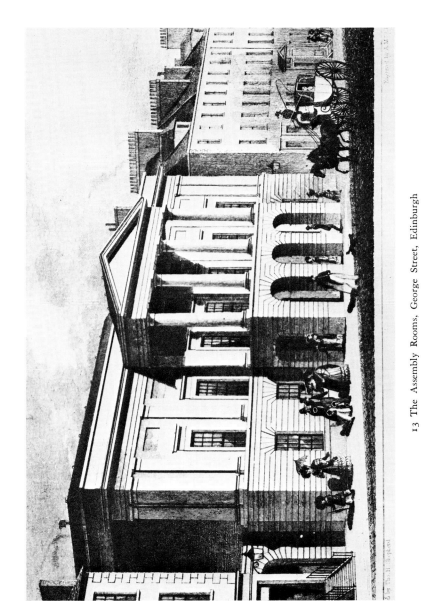

13 The Assembly Rooms, George Street, Edinburgh

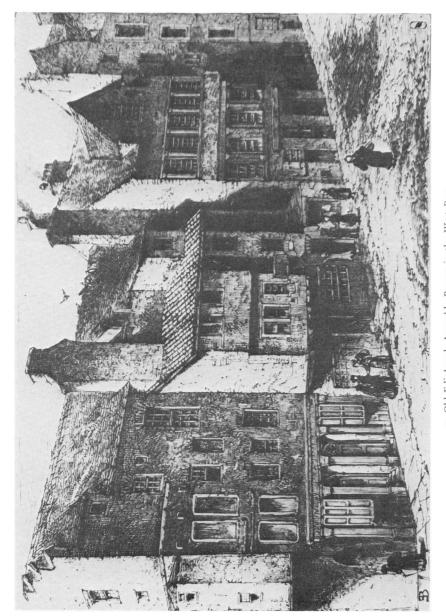

12 Old Edinburgh Assembly Rooms in the West Bow

11 *A Highland Wedding* by De Witt, in the Clerk of Penicuik Collection. The artist resided in Scotland from 1673 to 1687, but actual year of painting is not known. Photograph by Tom Scott, Edinburgh. [Courtesy of the Scottish National Portrait Gallery]

10 Engraving of painting *Village Festival* by F. Goodall. Note dancers doing "four hands across." Reproduced from J. S. Virtue, *The British Schools of Art.*

9 *The Kermess of St. George*, painting attributed to Peter Breughel ca. 1560. Note dancers in the lower right and the sword dancers in the middle of picture. Activities depicted here are not dissimilar from those typical of any festival day in the burghs of England and Scotland at this period. Reproduced from Sharp and Oppe, *The Dance*.

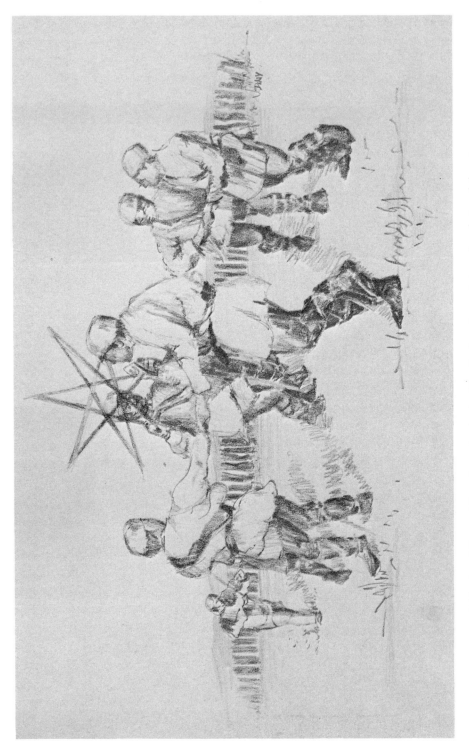

8 The Sword Dance of Papa Stour, drawing by Diny Bentley, after a photograph early twentieth century.

6 Illustration of fifteenth-century French peasants dancing a *carole* taken from a prayer-book in the Bibliothèque Nationale, Paris. Reproduced from Alford, *English Folk Dances.*

7 Engravings of dancing and tumbling. The dance minstrel, gleeman, or entertainer of Saxon England was an acrobat; hence, in Saxon manuscripts dealing with the dance of Herod's daughter, she is represented as tumbling.

5 Engraving by J. Brooks, ca. 1834, showing May Day celebrations at Arthur's Seat, Edinburgh. There appear to be four classes of dance. *Top right*, a twasome, and beneath that, the **Cutty-Hunker** (?); to the left of the top-hatted figures, a Foursome Reel, with the fiddler on a bank beside this. *Centre*, a ring or processional dance. An ornamented tree in the background seems to be what the artist refers to as a maypole. The Highland soldier beside it is merely a spectator. [Courtesy of Edinburgh Public Libraries]

19 *A Dancing Lesson at Hopetoun House*, a painting showing the Macdonald sisters, daughters of the third Lord March. [Courtesy of the Scottish National Portrait Gallery]

20 *The Penny Wedding* by David Allan. [Courtesy of the National Galleries of Scotland.]

21 Highland dancing at Crathes Castle, Deeside, 1834. [Reproduced from *Clans, Septs, and Regiments of the Scottish Highlands*, courtesy of Johnston and Bacon, publishers]

22 A sketch showing a Highland family returning from a fair after a dance, 1829. Reproduced from Campbell, *Popular Tales of the West Highlands*.

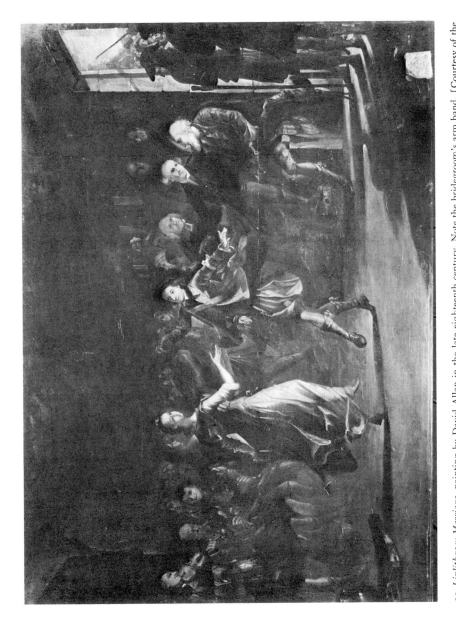

23 *Linlithgow Marriage*, painting by David Allan in the late eighteenth century. Note the bridegroom's arm band. [Courtesy of the Countess of Erroll and the National Galleries of Scotland]

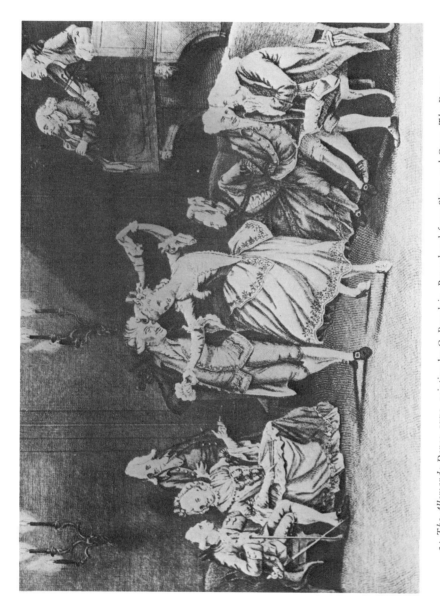

24 *The Allemande Dance*, 1772, painting by C. Brandoin. Reproduced from Sharp and Oppe, *The Dance*.

25 Frontispiece from Wilson's *Ballroom Guide* showing the Scotch Reel, Country Dance, and Waltz

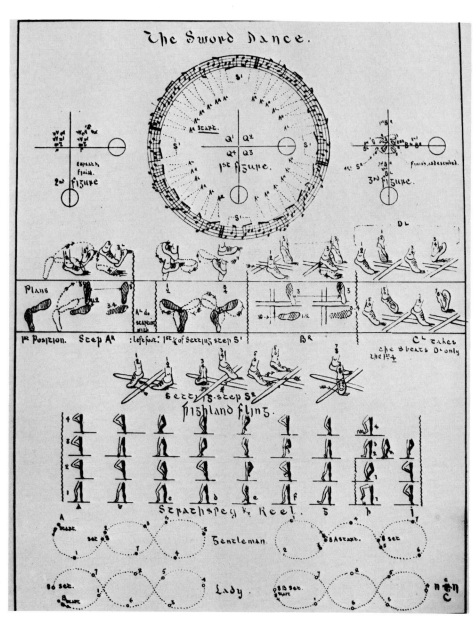

26 Description of the Gille Callum, Fling, and Reels. Reproduced from North, *The Book of the Club of True Highlanders*.

27 *Gille Callum*, painting by R. R. McIan. Reproduced from R. R. McIan, *Gaelic Gatherings* (London, 1848).

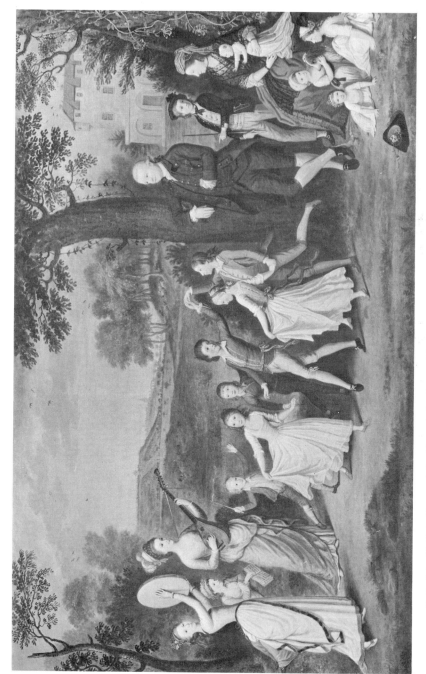

28 *Sir John Halkett, Bart. and Family,* painting by David Allan, 1784. [Courtesy of the National Galleries of Scotland]

29 A sailor and a wench jigging in a tavern. Reproduced from Sharp and Oppe, *The Dance*.

30 A jig at an Irish wedding, an engraving after Wrightson. Reproduced from Lily Grove et al., *Dancing* (London, 1895).

31 John Durang, in character of a hornpipe. A drawing by Diny Bentley after Durang's self-portrait.

32 Nancy Dawson. [Courtesy of the Dance Collection, New York Public Library]

33 Bobby Watson performing the Sailors' Hornpipe, 1958. Photograph by Scarborough and District Newspapers Limited, Scarborough.

34 Sketch showing Highland sports at Burnbank, September 13, 1884. Reproduced from A. S. Boyd, *Glasgow Men and Women* (London, 1905).

35 The end of the Reel o' Tulloch danced at Braemar, 1966. *Right*, dancer is Billy Forsyth, former Cowal "world champion." [Courtesy of the *People's Journal*, Dundee, and D. C. Thomson and Company]

36 Young dancers performing the Gille Callum at games in Ontario in 1962. The girls are dressed in the mock Highland dress so popular with them, while the boy eschews this for more appropriate dress.

37 Flora Macdonald's Fancy being beautifully performed in the Aboyne costume at St. Ann's, Nova Scotia, in 1963

38 Bobby Watson dancing at the Sorbonne, Paris, May, 1954. [Courtesy of
Les Reportages Photographiques de France, Paris]

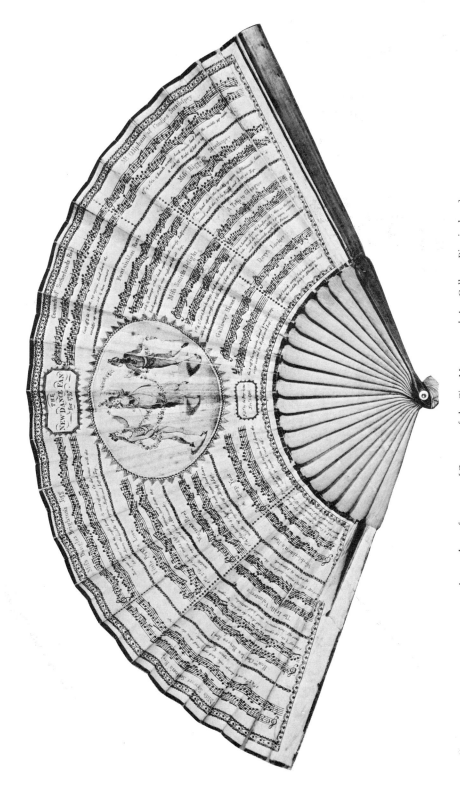

39 A new dance fan, 1797. [Courtesy of the City Museum and Art Gallery, Birmingham]

celebrated Duchess, Jane Maxwell, and employer of the illustrious composer of Strathspeys, William Marshall) in his verses to "Cauld Kail":

> In cotillons the French excel;
> John Bull, in contra dances,
> The Spaniards dance fandangoes well
> Mynheer in Allmande prances;
> In foursome reels the Scots delight,
> The threesome maist dance wondrous light;
> But twasome ding a' out o' sight
> Danc'd to the reel of Bogie.

There are references to the Scotch Jig as a dance for two, and some hint (though little more) of the Scottish Measure as a dance for two,[17] and there are also references, such as that above, to the Strathspey as a dance for two.

Indeed, John Jamieson in his *Etymological Dictionary of the Scottish Language* describes a Strathspey as "a dance in which two persons are engaged, otherwise called a *twasum dance*. Denominated from the country of Strathspey as having been first used there." This supports Topham's reference, in 1775, to the "Straspae" as "a kind of quick minuet" (Letter xxxiii). "We in England," he adds, "are said to walk a minuet; this is galloping a minuet. The French one is esteemed by all people at the Opera, as peculiarly elegant, and affording the greatest opportunity possible for a fine woman to display her figure to advantage. In this of the Scotch, however, every idea of grace seems inverted, and the whole is a burlesque; nothing of the minuet is preserved, except the figure; the step and the time most resemble a hornpipe — and I leave you to dwell upon the picture of a gentleman full-dressed, and a lady in a hoop, lappets, and every other incumberance of ornament, dancing a hornpipe before a large assembly."

Undoubtedly this, the Strathspey "twasum" was the same as the Strathspey Minuet which is said to have been danced by Prince Charlie at Holyrood in 1745,[18] and which is mentioned by Mrs. Calderwood in 1756.[19] It is referred to also in Watlen's *Celebrated Circus Tunes performed at Edinburgh this season* (1798), in which a Strathspey entitled "Miss Bigg's (of Newcastle) Delight" is described as "the celebrated Strathspey Minuet as danced by Mr. Lassells and Mrs. Parker at the Royal Circus, London and Edinburgh." But nowhere else in the numerous publications of Scottish dance music from that period is there any allusion to the Strathspey Minuet or twasum. This should not surprise us, for the music for the Strathspey twasum was of course what the publications termed the Strathspey Reel.

The Strathspey twasum, called simply Strathspey in the Highlands, was featured at the Edinburgh competition of piping and dancing during the early nineteenth century. There, however, since women did not then participate in competitions of any kind, the dance was performed by two men. This fact was deplored by Dalyell in

---

[17] D. G. MacLennan, *Traditional and Highland Scottish Dances*.

[18] "Prince Charlie at Lude House took share in minuets, High Reels and Strathspey minuet." [Bishop Forbes, *Lyon in Mourning*.]

[19] Coltness Collections (Maitland Club, Edinburgh, 1842), pp. 195–96. Two Scots at Spa in Belgium danced a Strathspey Minuet at a ballroom owned by a Scot.

his *Musical Memoirs of Scotland*. "Can anything blunt our sympathies more," he asks, "than beholding two brawny sons of Terpsichore leading up each other in measured time and space . . . where the genuine partnership should be shared as nature directs?" (p. 103). Perhaps this was the reason that in the successive competitions, 1838, 1841, and 1844 (they were held triennially at this period), no "two could be found . . . to execute the Highland Strathspey, a dance for two."

In the latter half of the nineteenth century, another Strathspey twasum, this time a Strathspey Polka rather than a Minuet, the Highland Schottische, became very popular in the ballrooms of the British Isles.[20] Could it be that this couples' dance of alternating and travelling to sprightly strathspey tunes was of the character of its predecessor? It is very probable that it was.

To add a further complication, it is now the habit to refer to Country Dances to strathspey tunes as simply "Strathspeys," but it should be remembered that this usage dates only from the 1920s.

Let us leave the last ambiguous word to the genial Henry Mackenzie, that great literary figure of eighteenth-century Edinburgh, who wrote at the end of a long life in 1825 in *Anecdotes and Egotisms*: "Strathspey is the native land of Highland Dancing, as the name of the dance most admired in the Highlands denotes. Tho' as danced there it seems a violent exercise, yet it appears rather to recruit the wearied limbs than to add to their fatigue."

OTHER REELS IN THE SCOTCH REEL TRADITION

In the Hebrides and on the adjacent mainland, certainly in the districts of Moidart and Knoydart, the reel figure in the Foursome Reel was unknown until the late years of the nineteenth century. The Fletts tell us in *Traditional Dancing in Scotland* that there the travelling figure was a circle. The two couples started from the vis-à-vis position, the ladies crossing in front of their partners on the first two bars, then all travelling in a circle, right shoulders to the centre, but *not* forming "hands across." On bars seven and eight, the men moved into the centre where, back to back, they faced the ladies, as in the usual Scotch Reel, and set for eight bars before proceeding in a circle again and repeating the sequence. As recollected, strathpsey music alternated with reel at the discretion of the musician, and doubtless local variations were to be encountered in the past (pp. 156-59).

It is satisfying to note that this is the form of the Cape Breton "four-handed" reel named Ruidhleadh Cheathrar (Foursome Reel) or Ruidhleadh Beag (Small Reel), the term "small reel" presumably distinguishing it from the "eight-handed" or Ruidhleadh Mor (Big Reel). These two forms of circular reel have variations occurring in the "travel" section. For instance, instead of the opening circle figure, the ladies (starting from the vis-à-vis or "square" position, with the ladies on their partners' right) may change places, passing right shoulders, followed by the men doing the same; the ladies likewise return to place, followed by the men. All then set to opposites for eight bars, then repeat the "crossing" figure and set to partners, and so on.

[20] For a description of the Highland Schottische in its original form, see Edward Scott, *Dancing* (London, 1894), pp. 137–42. Scott tells us that this dance was originally known as the Balmoral Schottische.

Sometimes, instead of setting, the partners, or opposites, swing each other at will. This figure bears a strong similarity to a dance called Ruidhleadh nam Coileach Dubha (Reel of the Black Cocks), collected in South Uist in 1956 by Frank Rhodes, to whom we are much indebted for the results of his field research in Cape Breton.[21] In Cape Breton, hornpipe stepping was used for setting; this comprised simple shuffling and beating; but in the Hebrides, reel steps were used within living memory. As the Cape Breton dances were recollected, the "swinging" was performed with a Waltz or Polka hold (it is likely that this was a nineteenth-century development), with a walking or a pivot turn. A favourite style of pivot turn is well known to us through the Reel of Tulloch, which is a like variant of the Scotch Reel.

The Reel of Tulloch (*Ruidhleadh Thulachain*) is a very thrilling dance, even more thrilling, and certainly more judiciously designed, than the common Scotch Reel. It is unique in having its own tune, known throughout the Highlands in the eighteenth century as Righ nam Port (King of Airs). There are a few stories purporting to tell how the dance originated, all probably spurious, the most plausible being that it was devised as an impromptu dance among a number of the congregation of the church in Tulloch, near Ballater in Aberdeenshire, when they found themselves marooned there without their minister during a period of heavy snowfall. Certainly it would serve the purpose of keeping warm very well, especially when danced in its round-the-room form.

The first known mention of the Reel of Tulloch as a dance is in a notice in the *Caledonian Mercury*, March 27, 1819, recording that four of the office bearers of the Edinburgh Society of Highlanders opened the society's ball with it. But nothing like the Reel of Tulloch appears in any dance manual until 1844, when, under the name of the Duchess of Sutherland's New Highland Reel, its round-the-room form is described in *The Ballroom Annual*, published in London in 1844. Its next appearance seems to be as Hullachan — an Anglification of the Gaelic pronunciation — in H. D. Willock's *Manual of Dancing* (1865). This differs in some respects from the Reel of Tulloch in Anderson's *Ballroom Guide*. Anderson tells us that when this reel was first introduced, the figure was described as for the standard reel of four, the tune being performed slowly and with steps to suit. These remarks correspond with the Hullachan as described by Willocks and by J. F. Wallace in *Excelsior Manual of Dancing* (1872). Anderson adds that at his time of writing (ca. 1890), it was danced to "reel time" throughout and that this tempo was considered much better.

The Reel of Tulloch is recorded by the Fletts in *Traditional Dancing in Scotland* as having been performed at the Edinburgh piping and dancing competitions in 1829, 1832, 1838, and 1844. A letter written to the Edinburgh Gaelic Society in 1835 contains the reference, "The Breadalbane Ball reel mostly termed the reel of Tulloch," which, as the Fletts point out, suggests that the Reel of Tulloch was developed at the Breadalbane balls, just as a little later the Eightsome Reel was developed at the Atholl Meeting and Skye balls (p. 134).

A number of versions of the Reel of Tulloch gained currency, and, of course, there was a natural tendency to combine the different foursome reels in a sequence dictated by the Master of Ceremonies or by the musician.

---

21 See Flett, *Traditional Dancing in Scotland*, appendix by F. Rhodes, pp. 267–85.

If the tune "Reel of Tulloch" is "King of Airs," then there should be no hesitation in claiming the combination of Strathspey and Reel of Tulloch as the "King of Reels," for this combination is surely supreme in the sheer art of Scottish Highland reeling. More elaborate combinations have been attempted, particularly in the late nineteenth-century ballroom, such as the Eightsome Reel continuing into a Strathspey Reel (three times), then Reel (once), concluded by Reel of Tulloch — an incredible test of stamina and fitness which makes one suspect the quality of the execution. Like combinations were still a feature of such balls as the Perth Hunt right into the present century.

The Reel of Tulloch was subjected to local variations in form as well as habit, and the details of some of these are found in the Flett work so often cited in this chapter. Its basic form, however, is executed in this manner. The two couples face each other some eight or nine feet apart. The dance begins with the ladies dancing towards each other and setting to each other (pas de basque step) (eight bars). They then swing each other, taking right arms in a hold commonly called the Tulloch hold (four bars) and then with left arms (four bars). The men and ladies, now facing each other in line as for foursome Scotch Reel, set for eight bars, then they execute the swing or turn (as above) for eight bars, ending with the men now in the centre, the ladies standing at the extremities. The men now set to each other, while the ladies stand still (eight bars), execute the Tulloch turn (eight bars), and end facing their original partners with whom they perform the same set-and-turn sequence, leaving the ladies in the centre. The ladies now set and turn as before and so on until all reach their original positions.

The "Tulloch" turn is executed with each grasping the other's elbow, the foot belonging to the held arm being used as a pivot, the other foot, in second position, moving round as the pivot foot is moved. The dancers almost face each other and hold the free arm in second position. Six beats are used for the turn, each way. Beats seven and eight are used to change arms, the men high-cutting, the ladies using spring points, and on beats fifteen and sixteen they break to face new vis-à-vis.[22]

A ballroom alternative is that the dancing couple stand with like shoulders together, their hands clasped behind their backs. Each dancer places left arm across small of back (palm out), extending right arm sideward (palm in) under extended right of other, and grasping left of other with right.

The term "Roon aboot Hullachan" used in connection with this dance comes from a version in which the dancers are arranged in a circular file round the room facing each other — the ladies all facing to move the same way, and the men likewise in the opposite direction. Then alternately setting and turning with their consecutive opposite numbers, the dancers progress round the circle. The Fletts remark in *Traditional Dancing in Scotland* that in the Borders the tune was usually "The Irish Washerwoman" or similar double jig, and the dance was called the Hullachan Jig. A "double" Reel of Tulloch was also popular in the early years of this century (pp. 153–54).

It seems inevitable that variations on the classical "linear" reels, such as the Ninesome, Sixsome, and Eightsome Reels, would suggest themselves. Thomas Wilson knew of no other reels than the basic two, and consequently devised several for five

---

[22] See ibid. and *Textbook of the SOBHD*.

or six dancers to be performed to common-time hornpipe tunes. These are explained in his *Complete System of English Country Dancing*. He apparently did not know of the Ninesome Reel or Country Bumpkin as a much superior reel to those he devised himself, involving the set-turn-reel sequence of the Scottish Country Dance.

Another variation of the linear reel is the Sixsome Reel. In this, as it is described in 1830,[23] four women stand at the corners of a square and two men, back to back, in the middle describe a reel with two corners along one diagonal, while the other two corners exchange places across the reel and back to place. This is repeated along the other diagonal. The men then set for four bars to the corner they are facing then repeat to the corner on their right.

Another Sixsome Reel was popular in Shetland and was danced by three of each sex, a man between two ladies facing a lady between two men. No hands are given, and there is the characteristic setting and reeling, the setting occurring first. This reel is danced to jig or reel tunes and is very similar to one popular in Orkney, although the latter is also danced to strathspey tunes. The Shemit Reel danced at weddings was of this form.

Probably the most popular Scottish dance during the early twentieth century was the Eightsome Reel; no Scottish party was complete without it and, indeed, it is the only reel known to many Scots now living.[24] Had it not been for the revival of the Scottish social dance in the 1920s by the Royal Scottish Country Dance Society, the Eightsome might well have had the whole field to itself, and been very corruptly executed at that.

As recorded by the RSCDS, the dancers take up a square formation. There is an introduction or chorus of forty bars with which the dance begins and ends, comprising eight hands round and back (slip step for eight bars); ladies with right hands in wheel with men on outside holding their left hand (four bars); then men still holding their partners by the right hand wheel back again with left hands across (four bars); all set to, and turn partners (eight bars); these manoeuvres are followed by Grand Chain (sixteen bars), the partners giving right hands to begin and the women advancing clockwise. All finish in original places. The middle section of the dance now begins with the first lady setting in the centre, while the remaining seven slip round and back (eight bars). This could be called the chorus. Then the figure: first lady sets to and turns partner, the same to opposite man, then performs a reel of three with the two men (sixteen bars). The chorus and figure are repeated, this time beginning the figure with the man who was originally on the lady's right. The chorus and figure sequence is now repeated with each of the ladies and men in turn, and the dance concludes with the chorus and introduction repeated.

A note to this dance in RSCDS (bk. 2) reads: "It is said that this dance was worked up by the late Earl of Dunmore and several friends from their recollections of Round Reels. They spent a week in the early 1870's evolving this dance at the time of the

---

[23] W. Smyth, *A Pocket Companion*, 1830. See also Elizabeth MacLachlan, ed., *The Border Dance Book*; and Hugh A. Thurston, *Scotland's Dances*, p. 38.

[24] A good friend of the author, the late Jamie MacKellar of Tayvallich, Knapdale, used to tell how he introduced the Eightsome Reel to that district in the later years of the nineteenth century. He learned it at a dance in Lochgilphead, a larger town nearby. Another dance he recalled obtaining in this way was the Country Dance, The Queen's Welcome.

Atholl Gathering Ball. Later that season, or possibly the following year, it was introduced at the Portree Ball, and at Perth. It caught on throughout the country and is
now danced in all parts of Scotland. There are examples of round Country Dances to
be found in old books, but none with quite the same figure."

The writers of this note obviously looked for the origin of the old "round reels" in
the long extinct round Country Dances in Playford, and were struck by the lack of
similarity. Hugh Thurston, however, rightly draws attention to the Irish round jigs
and reels which have a similar form: introduction, chorus, figure, and finale. Doubtless these belong to the family of round reels, but more probably the old round reels
were kin to the West Highland reels.

There are three reels for eight dancers in the Blantyre manuscript (1805) and two
in the National Library manuscript 3860 (1818); one of the latter being the same as
the introduction to the modern Eightsome Reel; and the first published version in
W. Smyth's *A Pocket Companion for Young Ladies and Gentlemen* (1830) has the
square formation, the eight hands round, and the double hands wheel of the one
we know. Its first published description (with minor differences) is found in David
Anderson's *Ballroom Guide*; the next published reference is in J. G. Atkinson's
Scottish National Dances, and the third is in Donald Mackenzie's *National Dances of
Scotland*. A more detailed comparison of some of these and several others is contained
in Thurston's *Scotland's Dances*, but since the publication of this book in 1954, an
attractive variant in the northeast of Scotland has been published by the RSCDS (bk.
21) under the title of Buchan Eightsome. This, in most respects, is a more satisfactory
Eightsome than any of the other versions.

Whatever the weaknesses in the original version of the Eightsome Reel which led
to the several variations, the dance is a masterpiece of its kind and will long remain
with us. It represents, as Thurston has pointed out, the merging of at least three traditions: the Reel, the Round Reel, and the Country Dance. Above all, its spirit and
technique is that of the Reel.

According to Thurston's *Scotland's Dances*, from the Eightsome has evolved the
"double" Eightsome, described in the RSCDS book 6, and a further development,
originally for display purposes, the "Quadruple" Eightsome or "Thirty-two-some."[25]

Another strain of social or group dances or reels survived until recent times in the
West Highlands, and these are discussed in chapter 15.

---

[52] For descriptions of less well-known reels from various parts of Scotland, see Flett, *Traditional Dancing
in Scotland*, pp. 156–86.

12/The Familiar High Dances

Highland Fling – Seann Triubhas – Gille Callum – broadsword exercise – Dirk Dance – Gille Callum finishing dance – mention of Scottish "Sword Dance" at Drury Lane – broadsword dances

THE HIGHLAND FLING

The word "fling" is often applied to dance in the Scottish Lowland tongue. The connotation is one of high and violent movement in the same sense as to fling up one's heels or to fling out one's arms. An appropriate example of this usage occurs in John Knox's account of one of his famous interviews with Queen Mary: "for in fiddling and flinging they are more exercised than in reading or hearing of God's most blessed word. . . ."

There are many other examples to be found in Scottish literature, of which the following must serve as typical: "Now ilka lad has got a lass / And ta'en a fling upon the grass"[1] and "He took a spring and danced a fling."[2]

Today, we are familiar with the Highland Fling as the name of a specific solo dance performed to strathspey rhythm, but we look in vain for a reference to a dance of this name prior to the early 1800s. The earliest usages of the term "Highland Fling" have more the appearance of referring to a specific step or class of step. For instance, toward the end of the eighteenth century, d'Egville advertised in an Edinburgh newspaper that he makes a specialty of "Scotch Reels, Highland Flings and all Caledonian steps." Here, perhaps, there is some ambiguity, but around 1805 the Reverend James Hall writes in *Travels of Scotland* (vol. 2) of his attempting to join a dance on Speyside: "For my part, I tried what I could do, and called up some steps I had learned in the south, and what is called the polished parts of Scotland: but finding the highland fling, as it is termed, more natural than my stiff see-saw method of dancing, I adopted it as

[1] James Johnson, ed., *The Scots Musical Museum*, Song no. 162.
[2] James Hogg, *Jacobite Relics*, vol. 1, p. 81.

well as I could . . ." (p. 388). Here, "Highland Fling" is decidedly used as a step, as it is when Susan Sibbald refers in her *Memoirs* to an elderly friend at the same period dancing a reel, "cracking his fingers; 'Highland Fling,' 'Pigeon's Wing,' and 'Cut the Buckle,' all performed most wonderfully for so stout a person" (p. 188).

Yet there are other allusions which suggest that there were a *number* of steps which came into the category of "flings." Elizabeth Grant remarks in *Memoirs of a Highland Lady* (1804) how Highlanders never lost an opportunity of acquiring a few more flings and shuffles, and in another place in the same work, she talks of a "single" and "double" fling step: "We children sometimes displayed our accomplishment on these occasions in a prominent manner to the delight at any rate of our dancing master. Lady Jane was very clever in the Gillie Callum and the Shean Trews, I a little behind her in the single and double fling, the shuffle and heel-and-toe steps" (p. 34).

In John Jamieson's *Etymological Dictionary of the Scottish Language*, Highland Fling is defined as "one species of movement" in dancing, "species" or class of movement, not just one particular movement.

What, then, were the steps called flings? Certainly the image conjured by the word is one of vigorous kicking: "Loupan and flingan on a crummock," wrote Burns — of the very stuff of the setting steps in the Reel. Chambers helps us a little when he remarks in 1842 that "Highlanders dance reels with great agility and are fond of introducing the steps ordinarily called the Highland Fling, which is of the character of dancing on each foot alternately, and flinging the other in front and behind the leg which is dancing."[3] Elizabeth Grant tells us that her father, in dancing a reel, does a "turn-about" which "he imagined was the fling."[4] Then, too, Lady Binks in Scott's *St. Ronan's Well* (1823) makes the company "alternately admire, smile, and stare, by dancing the highest Highland Fling."

Whatever the precise details, we are clearly dealing with a class of reel setting step associated with the Highlands; in all probability the reel in Strathspey style. In any case, we may reasonably conclude that the use of the term "Highland Fling" often meant what we have called Highland "capers" or what Mrs. Grant in her poem "Roy's Wife of Aldivalloch" (ca. 1770) refers to as the "Highland walloch": "I wat she was a cantie quean / And weel could dance the Highland walloch." This interpretation is reinforced by Lord James Murray in a letter to his mother in 1814: "He a guest from Russia was very anxious to see the Highland Fling and accordingly I got Moon who dances very well, and some others to figure in a Reel."[5]

There is ample testimony of the excellence of dancing in the Highlands in the eighteenth and nineteenth centuries, and particularly of the singularly cultured style of dancing prevailing in Strathspey which naturally came to be identified with that region and named after it. Perhaps it is not going too far to suggest that to Lowlanders the terms "Strathspey" and "Highland," as they applied to dance, were synonymous. There is every suggestion that this was so.

It seems inevitable that dancers would develop enchainments of reel steps as solo dances — "Highland wallochs" indeed — with arbitrary arrangements without names, and that some specific arrangements, such as The Marquis of Huntly's Highland

---

[3] Robert Chambers, *Chambers Information* (Edinburgh, 1842), p. 560.

[4] Elizabeth Grant, *Memoirs of a Highland Lady*, p. 147, referring to the year 1813.

[5] John Murray, *Chronicles of the Athol and Tullibardine Families*.

Fling, would emerge in the course of time. The tune of this title was composed by Jenkins, some time before 1806. Perhaps, indeed, this tune was devised for, or inspired by, the specific arrangement of steps which bore the same name — a Highland Fling, as James Logan expresses it in *The Scottish Gael* (1831) "in that style called the Marquis of Huntly's" (p. 440). The steps of The Marquis of Huntly's Highland Fling are included with other two arrangements or "Flings" in the Hill manuscript (Aberdeen, 1841). The steps involve much more pointing and turning than the Highland Fling approved by the Scottish Official Board of Highland Dancing today.

It is certainly noteworthy that, unlike Gille Callum and Seann Triubhas, Highland Fling has no Gaelic name. An arbitrary arrangement of reel steps would warrant no distinguishing title among the Gaels themselves, but would acquire some distinguishing appellation when introduced to Lowland society. This seems to be what gave rise to the name.

In *Glasgow and Its Clubs*, John Strang tells us that on January 20, 1804, when the Gaelic Club of Glasgow entertained the Stirling Militia then training in the city, several of the club members danced the "Highland Fling" to the music of the pipes, and showed "a dexterity and grace that even astonished" the commanding officer, the Duke of Montrose (p. 115). One is left uncertain, however, as to whether Strang would have used the term "Highland Fling" in that way in 1804, since he wrote his passage much later.

When one considers the central position accorded the Highland Fling among Highland Dances today, it is remarkable that it was not introduced to dance competitions until around 1840!

It is, of course, frustrating that written record of the steps employed in Scottish dancing is so scarce. The Hill manuscript provides us with much useful material, but what distinguished the Lonach Highland Fling taught by J. Scott Skinner?

The earliest published description of a specific Highland Fling is that in Mozart Allan's *Guide to the Ballroom*, which slightly antedates the fuller, but similar, description in David Anderson's *Ballroom Companion* (1894). The latter is recognizably the same as the Highland Fling defined by the SOBHD in 1955. The shedding or round-the-leg movements of the working foot in certain steps is called swinging, and the preceding spring onto both feet is called the spread, the feet six inches apart and sharing the weight equally. The spread is no longer approved, having been replaced by "second position" — the weight on the supporting foot and the working foot on the point, extended to the side. This was introduced in the late nineteenth century[6] and was quickly adopted by other dancers. Anderson's arm positions are as for the reel.

It is customary to seek romantic reasons for the characteristics of Highland Dance, such as the Fling's being a warrior's dance of victory performed upon his targe. This reasoning may well be nonsense, like most of these tales, but it serves to highlight a characteristic of the dance, namely, that it is performed on the spot, with no travel. Anderson confirms this supposition, as does the SOBHD. Nevertheless, certain army versions of the Highland Fling involve some steps with lateral travel; doubtless, this practice harks back to the conception of a Highland Fling as any arbitrary collection of reel steps.

[6] D. G. MacLennan, *Traditional and Highland Scottish Dances*, p. 20.

Elizabeth Grant's remark about the "turn-about" or whirling, in the Fling is, perhaps, coincidental to the fact that this whirling was a distinguishing feature of the jig as it is characterized in Elizabethan times.

It will be recalled, too, that the movement of the working foot from second to third aerial (pied croise), so characteristic of the Fling, is conspicuous in the Branle d' Écosse, and hence must have been associated with Scotland even in medieval times — associated indeed with Highland "capers," "walloch," "spring," and "fling" or — dare we say — "Scottish Jygge," as the same exercise is variously described.

The Highland Fling familiar to us on the Highland Games platform of today is generally regarded as a dance for men. It certainly puts a premium on the strength of the legs, and the continued hopping on the ball of the foot, with no relaxation onto the heels, tends in time to thicken the calves of the legs. As we shall see in chapter 17, Highland Dance competitions, and indeed all physical competitions, were for males only until the early years of the present century. The male tradition in Highland Dance thereby enjoyed prominence, and the masculine elements of the dances were thus emphasized. There is nothing more certain, however, than that the women of Scotland enjoyed dancing every bit as much as did their sisters in Ireland, for instance, where a similar tradition of "flinging" prevailed. Manners and customs, of course, are not static, and the norms of one period may not be those of another; but certainly eighteenth- and nineteenth-century conceptions of decorum, even in the rustic communities of Scotland and Ireland, emphasized grace and restraint in the dancing of girls, particularly with regard to social dancing.

Doubtless it was for this reason that David Anderson included in his *Ballroom Companion* of the 1890s a ladies' Highland Fling, a "fling" of low elevation comprising the steps a lady could use with propriety in the Strathspey Reel. There is no reason to suppose that there was a traditional Highland Fling for ladies, nor that there was ever a taboo against their performing those dances we consider male today. Thus P. R. Drummond, in his recollections of Perthshire, could write in the 1870s in *Perthshire in Bygone Days* that "no gypsy of old Spain, was ever more attached to her grotesque 'Fandango' than these two maidens were to their 'Shantruse' their 'Hulochan' and 'Highland Fling'" (p. 312).

The execution of the Highland Fling is all very much a matter of style based not only upon attitudes to male and female but also upon the decidedly differing physiques and sexual roles.

SEANN TRIUBHAS

The Seann Triubhas, pronounced "Shan Trews" and literally meaning "old trousers," is a close relative of the Fling but, unlike the latter which is danced on the spot, this dance involves many travelling steps. In its present form, it has many graceful movements and, as usually performed, it displays an overall spirit of elegance. There has been a widely accepted story that the kicking or sweeping movements of the legs in the first step represented the attempt of the dancer to shake off the despicable trews, but D. G. MacLennan writes in *Traditional and Highland Scottish Dances* that "this first step has nothing to do with the idea of kicking off the trews, but . . . is new to the dance and was composed by myself" (p. 27). Of course there are, and were, many other kicking movements in the dance, and since the subject is old trousers, this should not surprise us. It is habitual to embroider simple facts of this kind with romantic fiction, and it is a great temptation to explain the dance as a demonstration of resentment on having to eschew the kilt after the '45 Rebellion. But trews are a very ancient Celtic garment.

The Seann Triubhas, then, is simply associated with a pair of old trews which may or may not be a subject of distaste or fun to the wearer, and may or may not have something to do with the '45 Rebellion. This suggestion of comic undertones in the dance is supported by Alexander Carmichael, who wrote in 1900 in *Carmina Gadelica* that Seann Triubhas was formerly danced with much more acting than now. Robert Tannahill, too, at least a century before, describes it as "merry" in his poem, "The Kebbuckston Wedding": "And gie us three wallops o' merry shantrews / With the true Highland Fling of Macrimmon the piper." The element of humour has practically disappeared from the dance as it is now performed.

One is inclined to regard the present elegant character of Seann Triubhas enhanced by the balletic arm movements as a recent acquisition, but Logan, in 1831, writes that it "is danced with much grace," and the circling arm movements were a characteristic of the Seann Triubhas as described by Anderson in 1890. Anderson's version is very different in detail from that described by the SOBHD textbook (1955), but it is recognizably the same dance with the initial movement of the working foot from third aerial, through fifth to fourth aerial (called chasse by Anderson), with rotating arm movements, and with the pirouette and balance movements. Also both versions conclude with two quick steps which can be Highland Fling steps. The high cutting, side cutting, double beats back and front, and entrechat in the version approved by the SOBHD were innovations accountable to the celebrated William MacLennan prior to 1890;[7] the spread-eagle leap, now one of the optional closing steps of the dance, is also of recent addition, but was disapproved of by William MacLennan's brother "D.G."

One of the reel setting steps described by Mackenzie in *National Dances of Scotland* is called the Seann Truis step, which is a spring to fifth on point right; slip right on point to second; slip left point to fifth rear; and repeat. The sequence is repeated, beginning with a spring to fifth on point left. Close with springs to fifth, right and left (rocking). Neither Anderson nor the SOBHD describes such a step. In the quotation from Elizabeth Grant given on p. 182, "Gillie Callum" and "Shean Trews" are mentioned in a way that could be taken to refer to them as steps, but I think it is evident that they are dances, and that the "single and double fling, the shuffle and heel-and-toe step" are steps in these. In another place Miss Grant refers to Lady Jane as she "who danced the Shean Trews."

The Seann Triubhas is today invariably danced to the tune "Whistle o'er the lave o't," which suits it admirably; the tune is so intimately associated with the dance that it is now commonly known as "Seann Triubhas." Anderson gives the tunes of his version as "Whistle o'er the lave o't / Wha widna fecht for Charlie. . . ." Why these tunes should have displaced "Shaun Truish Willichan," which appears certainly to have been the original tune of the dance, is open to conjecture. Stenhouse wrote (ca.

[7] Ibid., p. 27.

1820) that this tune had been known "at all our dancing schools for many generations," and Cunningham wrote about the same time in *Scottish Songs* that "Shaun Truish Willighan" was "a popular hornpipe air, to which all the youth of Nithsdale have danced."[8] "Seann Triubhas Willighan" (or Willie's auld Trews) first appeared under that name in print in Bremner's *Second Collection of Scots Reels or Country Dances* (1768) and is a set of "Deil stick the minister."[9]

"Whistle o'er the lave o't" was also the title of a song in the seventeenth century, the ribald words of which can be found in David Herd's *Ancient and Modern Scottish Songs*. Robert Bremner published the tune in his 1756 edition, and James Dick remarks that the tune is said to be in the Blaikie manuscript (1692), although Burns attributes it to John Bruce, a Highland fiddler who lived in Dumfries around 1720.

It is evident that the two principal tunes associated with Seann Triubhas have a long history and no doubt the dance has also.

GILLE CALLUM AND PYRRHIC DANCES

"The ancient Caledonians," wrote James Logan in *The Scottish Gael*, "had a sort of Pyrrhic dance over swords, which is not yet entirely unknown but the Gilli-Callum, which generally terminates a ball, is supposed to have but a faint resemblance to the ancient sword dance" (p. 438). This is an arresting statement in many ways, raising at least the following four important points: the Caledonians had a military dance over swords; this dance was not "entirely unknown" when Logan wrote in 1830; the dance called Gilli-Callum only faintly resembled it; and the Gilli-Callum generally terminated a ball.

Logan does not give his authority for his statement that there was an ancient Caledonian sword dance, and many writers since have attributed the authority to Tacitus and even Julius Caesar. All are wrong, for the only reference to such a dance in the writings of the Roman historians is that already quoted in chapter 1, in which Tacitus describes European tribesmen dancing amidst swords and spears that are levelled at them. These tribesmen were not Celts, they were Germans. The Caledonians may well have had such a dance, but no one ever reported seeing it. Traces of such a Pyrrhic dance were yet in existence, says Logan, but he could quite easily be referring to the ritualistic sword dances we have discussed earlier. However, as we have seen, these are not Pyrrhic dances, although they may be easily mistaken for them, and indeed have commonly been so mistaken.

The ritual hilt-and-point sword dance was perhaps not so widespread in Scotland as it was in England, but we have noted the examples recorded in Shetland and Perth and references to it elsewhere. That other examples survived to the early nineteenth century is implied by Logan's remark.

General Stewart of Garth quotes the following passage showing that the Earl of

---

[8] Thomas Wilson writes in his *Companion to the Ballroom*, 1816, p. 59, that Shon Truish Willichan consisted of "a number of steps necessary to be taught by a master."

[9] At the circuit court at Stirling, June 5, 1683, a man was tried for reviling a parson by causing the piper to play "The Deil stick the minister." Sundry pipers were present as witnesses and declared it was the name "of ane spring." [Robert Chambers, *Domestic Annals of Scotland*, 2nd ed., vol. 2, p. 453.]

Crawford danced a variant of a Pyrrhic dance ca. 1753: "He was not more remarkable for his elegance in dancing than in his noble way of performing the Highland Dance, habited in that dress and flourishing a naked broadsword to the evolutions of the body."[10] This indeed was a kind of Pyrrhic dance. "Its name," says Stewart, "was Mackinorsair," (that is, Mc an Fhorsair). He writes that he had seen it performed by old men, but that it had by then (ca. 1825) disappeared, and that in later times a staff replaced the sword.[11]

Mc an Fhorsair, we may surmise, is what was referred to as the "Broad Sword Exercise." Stewart also relates how two privates of a Highland regiment, on being presented to King George II (who had never seen such a regiment before) "performed the broadsword exercise and that of the Lochaber Axe or Lance."[12] The Inverness Press remarked in 1816 that at a meeting of the Society of True Highlanders at Inverlochy, "cudgelling, the Broadsword exercise, and the Dirk Dance, especially the last two in great style by McDonald, Ross and Gunn, gave much satisfaction." And in 1817 there is the allusion "broadsword played. . . ."

The Dirk Dance involved two dancers, each armed with dirk and targe, who went through the motions of combat with step dancing interspersed. Its Gaelic name was Bruicheoth or Battle Dance. Logan wrote in 1831 in *The Scottish Gael* that this dance was still executed by a few and that it and the Gilli-Callum were exhibited in London some years previously by one Mac Glassan. He also said that he knew a person who, at the age of 106 saw the Dirk Dance performed and declared it was not at all like the one he had formerly known (p. 439). The Dirk Dance was performed at the Edinburgh competition in 1841, and in *Musical Memoirs of Scotland* Dalyell describes it as it appeared then:

A dancer appears brandishing a dirk or poniard, lays it on the stage and dances around it. While he is describing a wide circuit, another coming forth snatches up the weapon. The owner having a second in reserve they fight: one is stabbed, and falls; the victor, dragging him to a suitable place, dances around his body in a very savage style, then slaps one foot, which begins to quiver, next a hand, which quivers also, after this the other hand, which quivers — and as all three members quiver a farther slap on the other foot produces symptoms of animation. Whisky is now offered to the resuscitent, who proving incapable of the draught, most of it is swallowed by the victor himself. He raises the wounded man, then able to share the proffered beverage, restoration follows, and both dance together. [P. 106]

The familiar resurrection theme is encountered in such dramatic dances as Carlin of the Mill Dust (cf. chaps. 16 and 19).

A Dirk Dance involving a single dancer is known in the Isle of Man, where some other dances related to the Hebridean and Irish dramatic or mimic dances can still be found. In this version the dancer carries the dirk round in a circle at arm's length, forward, point upward, then lays it down, salutes it, and dances round it. Then he picks it up and does side steps and leaps, kicking the dirk at head level, lays it down again, dances round it, and salutes four times. After this, he lifts it and makes slashes over his

[10] David Stewart, *Sketches of the Highlanders*, appendix, 2nd ed., vol. 1.
[11] Ibid., 2nd ed., vol. 1, p. 258.
[12] Ibid.

head and about his body, passing the dirk between his legs. Finally, he carries the dirk round again, and finishes kneeling to it.[13]

The tune of this dance was apparently noted as a lullaby in Skye, although it was a virile air as it was played in Man.[14] According to Logan, the tune for the combative Dirk Dance was "Phadric MacCombish," [15] which is probably none other than the well-known pipe tune *Biodag air MacCombaish* (MacCombish's Dirk).

D. G. MacLennan knew one version of the dance as it was handed down to him from his grand-uncles who, he tells us, were, in 1850, about the only people acquainted with it,[16] and Thurston mentions a Dirk Dance found in Canada, similar to the Manx version, except that the dirk is always flourished in the hand and never placed on the ground.[17]

There are ritualistic undertones to the Dirk Dance which dilute its Pyrrhic aspects, and it may be that a similar process has once been associated with the dance over crossed swords we know so well today, and also know by the name of its tune, "Gille Callum." In the passage quoted earlier from her memoirs, Elizabeth Grant there described how she and "Lady Jane" danced "Gillie Callum" and "Shean Trews," and how she was a "little behind" Jane in certain steps. The passage is ambiguous and can be interpreted as referring to Gille Callum and Shean Trews as the names of the steps; but Miss Grant refers later to Lady Jane as "she who danced the Shean Trews" (p. 37) and to herself actually performing the dance, wearing yellow shoes (p. 34). Thurston finds it difficult to imagine two small girls dancing the Gille Callum sword dance in a nineteenth-century drawing room, and consequently believes it to have been a different dance; but it was a Highland drawing room, and when, for that matter, did girls wear trews? No, I do not think it would be unseemly for young girls to dance the Gille Callum sword dance we know over sticks in a Highland drawing room. As we shall see, however, there was in fact another usage of this dance as a preliminary to the Kissing Reel, which certainly was appropriate to the drawing room.

Alexander Campbell, in his notes to *The Grampians Desolate*, states that "Gillie Callum da' pheigin is generally danced by one man who performs it with great address over a naked broadsword laid on the floor," and that it "is sometimes danced by two, three, or four men, but when so done they do not reel, but only change places." It is also styled by the writer as one of the "national dances which are daily becoming more obsolete." Dalyell tells us in *Musical Memoirs of Scotland* that the Gille Callum "had no place among the more modern entertainments of the Lowlands" (although it was "said to be common in the Highlands") until it was exhibited by John MacKay at two successive Highland Society piping and dancing competitions at Edinburgh in 1832 and 1835. By 1841, it was a regular feature of these meetings. In this case the dance was performed over "two naked swords laid across" (p. 105).

In 1844, the King of Saxony toured Scotland and was entertained by the Marquis of Breadalbane at Taymouth Castle in a manner by no means so lavish as, but reminiscent of, the reception given Queen Victoria on her famous visit of two years

---

[13] Mona Douglas, "Manx Folk Dances," *JEFDSS*, vol. 3, no. 2 (1937), p. 114.

[14] Ibid.

[15] James Logan, *The Scottish Gael*, p. 439.

[16] D. G. MacLennan, *Traditional and Highland Scottish Dances*.

[17] Hugh Thurston, *Scotland's Dances*, p. 45.

before. The queen never forgot the display on that occasion, associating it with memories of her happiest days — bonfires, fireworks, and "highlanders dancing reels by torchlight" — and was sufficiently struck by the novelty to record in *Leaves from the Journal* that at Dunkeld, Charlie Christie, steward to the Duchess of Atholl, "danced the 'sword dance' (Two swords crossed are laid upon the ground, and the dancer has to dance across them without touching them)" (p. 21). The King of Saxony must have been equally impressed by the performance of the sword dance, for he also gives a description of it:

The Company moved into another room, and several men immediately entered, dressed in full Highland costume. The piper commenced his enlivening strains, and a young man in Scottish garb first appeared with two naked swords. He laid them crosswise on the floor, and with a peculiar jerking motion of his legs and arms, began to dance to the music of the bagpipes. With a certain rhythm, he stamped with both feet on the ground, quicker and quicker, tred now on this side and now on that, of the naked sword blades, without ever touching them – threw up his arms in the air, and one while assumed the attitude of an attacking and at another of a defending warrior. At length he seized the swords again — swung them over his head, and disappeared. The whole exhibition had something savage, but, at the same time, natural and primitive, in its character, which made a lively impression on my mind; and the movements of the youth were so bold and vigorous, that it was impossible to avoid participating in the spirit which he displayed."[18]

Here, and in Queen Victoria's comment, there is reference to the crossed swords step dance we know today which, apart from the final flourish of the swords (no longer practised), involves no wielding of the weapons. It is not unlikely that the alternating of the arms from first to second or third positions would appear to represent fighting and defending attitudes to an untutored onlooker. There is no mistaking the style of the performance — "savage," "natural and primitive," "bold," "vigorous," "stamped with both feet on the ground" — a much severer style than that approved today, although the best performance is still bold and vigorous. We have no way of evaluating Breadalbane's performer, however, and I am reminded of a similar display presented by a muscular young man performing this dance in a small chalet in Ontario to the evident distress of its structure and supports, and to which the epithet "savage" could well have applied; yet it was regarded by the authorities present as a manifestation of the inferiority of the dancer!

This was the dance, no doubt, to which Norman Macleod referred in *Reminiscences of a Highland Parish*, when he wrote in 1867: "A poor remnant of the 'Sword Dance' is still preserved among us, and may be often witnessed on the stage; sometimes on the decks of steamers, and even on the streets of our large towns, burlesqued by idle vagabonds who assuredly disgrace 'the garb of old Gaul' by exhibiting it in such contemptible performances" (p. 349, fn.). Dr. Macleod apparently also confused this dance with the ritual hilt-and-point sword dance about which he had read in Brand's *Antiquities*.

In view of what we know and have observed of the Gille Callum, surely Logan must be mistaken when he says it usually terminated a ball. Here, however, we meet

18 C. G. Carus, *The King of Saxony's Journey through England in 1844* (London, 1846).

with an unexpected and curious link with the Cushion Dance or Babbity Bowster. In a version of Babbity Bowster, current at least as late as 1890, the dance was preceded by the first man taking the handkerchief which he was to use instead of a cushion and, twisting it into a rope, he laid it on the floor and danced round it a few steps, in the manner of the Gille Callum, before proceeding round the room. A bonnet was often used instead of a handkerchief, and MacLagan describes a dance, Am Bonaid Ghorm (The Blue Bonnet), as given him by a native of Sutherland, in which two sticks were laid crosswise with a bonnet at their intersection, the dancer dancing over them, lifting, and replacing the bonnet several times. The bonnet would then be used in place of a handkerchief. The dance was "slow in some movements and rapid in others."[19]

The Fletts carried out much valuable research on this topic in the Highlands and Borders, and found that the practice of opening the Kissing Reel with a sword dance over a twisted handkerchief had apparently persisted longer in the West Highlands than in the Islands, while the piper's playing of *pog an toiseach* when the couples kissed was peculiar to the Isles.[20]

Perhaps "Gille Callum" was the original tune of the Kissing Reel, and certainly the words are appropriate: "Gillie Callum, two pennies, two pennies, two pennies, Gillie Callum one bodle. I shall get a wife for twopence, twopence, twopence, a useless one for one bodle. I shall get a sweetheart for nothing, for nothing, for nothing, my pick and choice for one bodle."

On the other hand, there is a story that the song was composed on the occasion of Malcolm (Callum) Canmore's introduction of the "bodle," or in derision of his tax gatherer, and again that the dance was inspired by one of his victories. But we have seen how much nonsense can sometimes be embroidered into tradition. Nevertheless the tune "Gille Callum" has a primitive ring about it, especially when chanted to the dance with hand clapping; and if the sense of its words, the typical nonsense words of puirt-a-beul, fits the spirit of the Kissing Reel, its rhythm fits the vigour of a dance over swords. Nonetheless, one need only compare it with the tune of "Bab at the Bowster" to be struck by a family resemblance. It is very easy to run from one tune into the other. There is a very similar rhythm and repetition of phrase in the two tunes, but one could say the same of the Northumbrian tune "Keel Row." The earliest written record of the tune "Gille Callum" is to be found in the Drummond Castle manuscript of Highland Dance music (1734). The earliest published version is that in Bremner's *Second Collection of Scots Reels* (1768), where it is attached to a Country Dance under the phonetic title "Keelum Kallum toa fein."

The earliest reference to a solo Scottish "Sword Dance" that I have yet encountered appears on a playbill for Drury Lane Theatre, December 31, 1733: "A New Scotch Sword Dance by Baker in a Highland Character." This is a curious item, for there was no dancer named Baker then employed at Drury Lane, nor is a "Scotch Sword Dance" ever again featured, at least under that name. The performance, too, was a "benefit" for "Baker." One can only surmise that the beneficiary was Job Baker, the popular kettledrummer, a conjecture that is supported by the Vivaldi concerto and harp solo on the program. Did Job Baker perform this "Sword Dance" as a novelty?

[19] R. C. MacLagan, *The Games and Diversions of Argyleshire*, p. 103.
[20] J. F. and T. M. Flett, "Some Hebridean Folk Dances," *JEFDSS*, vol. 7, no. 2 (1953).

To such straits are we driven, however, by the lack of written record, that we must pounce on this comparatively recent evidence of a known association of Highlanders with a solo sword dance. We shall never know what caused Job Baker the kettledrummer to dance this particular dance at his benefit.

Another allusion to a solo sword dance from the same period occurs in an anti-Jacobite song composed between 1745 and 1760:

> When you came over first frae France,
> You swore to lead our King a dance,
> And promis'd on your royal word,
> To mak the Duke *dance o'er the sword*.[21] [Italics mine.]

Here, as in Campbell's reference in notes to *The Grampians Desolate* quoted earlier, a single sword only is mentioned. But, as we have seen, two swords were certainly involved in the Gille Callum in the nineteenth century. We must allow for a confusion of two different dances however.

We have to wait until 1881 for a technical description of the Gille Callum over crossed swords, and this is given in Charles North's *Book of the Club of True Highlanders*. In this account, contrary to present practice and to the description published by Anderson in 1894, the dancer moves clockwise round the swords. Otherwise, the dance has varied very little over the years.

The Gille Callum performed by two dancers over one pair of swords is now called the "double" Sword Dance, but this is simply an extension of the solo dance.

Another version of the "double" Sword Dance is known today as the Argyll Broadswords. It is distinctly different from the Gille Callum, although as one would expect, similarities in step-work inevitably arise. The Argyll Broadswords dance is performed by four dancers over a cross formed by four broadswords. The dance begins with the dancers placed at the sword hilts and comprises arrangements of travelling steps round the swords and spring-points, heel-and-toe steps, and springs over them, all done in concert to strathspey rhythm. It concludes with two steps in common reel tempo. One can encounter several versions of this dance that differ in the arrangement or order of the steps or in the nature of certain steps, depending on the taste of the dancing master who has taught it. According to D. G. MacLennan, the dance was resuscitated in 1888 by his brother William, an outstanding dancer and piper in his day, and from this source it passed into the repertoire of various Scottish regiments.[22]

The Argyll Broadswords as we know it is a Pyrrhic dance, whatever its progenitors may have been. Likewise the Gille Callum within recent memory. If the Gille Callum were a ritualistic dance of antiquity, we would expect it to have been part of some kind of communal dancing experience, for it has no dramatic connotations which could establish it as a dramatic jig. The ritualistic sword dances involve a circle of dancers and terminate in a symbolic sacrifice. Could it be that the Gille Callum was originally a central episode in a unique version of the ritualistic sword dance with,

---

[21] Printed by Donaldson and Reid in 1761, under the title "Highland Laddie." See Stenhouse, *Illustrations of the Lyric Poetry*, vol. 2, p. 11.

[22] Letter from D. G. MacLennan to Hugh Thurston, *Scotland's Dances*, p. 89. See MacLennan, *Traditional and Highland Scottish Dances*, for a description of William MacLennan's dance.

perhaps, each of the performers taking turns in the dance over the swords? There is the suggestion of such a link in what is known of a dance called the Lochaber Broadswords, reputedly a kind of Gille Callum for two dancers, in which the tiring dancers were replaced by a fresh pair four times in succession. Perhaps, indeed, this was the identical dance seen in the Highlands in 1879 by an English correspondent of Douglas Kennedy: "Two swords were placed on the ground. At the points two dancers took their places. Six others formed a circle with their swords pointed toward the dancers, whom they ringed in. The dance began slowly to pipe music, and grew faster and faster, the dancers avoiding the ring of swords and never touching the swords on the ground. When one grew exhausted, he danced to the place of one of the six swordsmen, who took his place, and so the dance continued until all eight had taken part, when the two swords were taken up swiftly, and seven formed a ring round the eighth man with their swords pointing at his throat."[23]

The sacrificial character of the final formation confirms the ritualistic derivation of the dance. It is easy to accept that the Gille Callum has been drawn from this source, and this accepted, one wonders if the crossed swords has any Christian significance, or if indeed it is simply a natural symmetrical figure into which two swords would inevitably be arranged. No other sword dance of this kind has survived to be recorded, although there are some instances in which the final lock of swords characteristic of these dances is laid upon the ground. The Sword Dance of Papa Stour is one of these, but in this the dancers do not dance to the shield of locked swords; instead, they simply extricate their swords "by a figure directly opposite to that by which it had been formed."[24]

In the Bacchu-Ber Sword Dance performed at Cervières in the Hautes-Alpes, the dancers in one figure lay down their swords radiating outwards from the centre and salute them in turn,[25] but they do not dance over them. Otherwise, the Gille Callum survives with no apparent antecedents or close relatives.

[23] Douglas Kennedy, "Observations on the Sword Dance and Mummers' Play," *JEFDSS*, 2nd ser., no. 3 (1930), p. 22.
[24] Samuel Hibbert, *A Description of the Shetland Islands*. See also appendix A.
[25] *Folklore Journal*, vol. 5 (1887).

13/The Jig

Derivation of jig – Scottish Jig – Scottish Measure – Old Scots Jig – Auld Glenae – Wooing of the Maiden – Rinnce Fada – Irish Jig – rhythms – jig and Galliard – Pepys and jig

It has often been suggested that the word "jig" is derived from the old French name *gigue* meaning a small fiddle, and certainly the first recorded use of the word in English in John de Garlandia's *Vocabulary* (ca. 1225) seems to confirm this supposition. On the other hand, its most characteristic meaning is that of lively movement, in which case the root would seem to be the Norse *geiga* meaning anything round or revolving as in "whirligig," with the verb *giguer* meaning "to caper." Pulver has pointed out that dialects of the Romance languages have the noun *gigue*, meaning the small fiddle, and those of Norse origin use the verb *giguer*.[1] The Norman dialect, for instance, has the latter but not the former. There is a strong argument, therefore, that the English word "jig" — variously spelled in early writing as jigge, gigge, gig, and jeg — is from the Norse and refers to sprightly movement, especially to whirling.

Thus we find "jig" used to pertain to ditties or verses with a lively rhythm and recurring refrain, and to dances in similar vein with much turning or spinning:

> He daunces very finely, very comely,
> And for a Jig, come cut and long tail to him,
> He turns ye like a Top.
>> [Beaumont and Fletcher, *The Two Noble*
>> [*Kinsmen*, act 5, scene 2]

or

> Our Enemies to Starling-bridge
> (Like a whirlegig, did dance a jig).
>> [*Bagford Ballads*, 1, 333]

[1] Jeffrey Pulver, "The Ancient Dance Forms," *Proceedings of the Musical Association*, vol. 40, no. 80, February 17, 1914.

The latter is from a ballad concerning Charles II's campaign against Cromwell in 1641 and is apparently composed by a Scot.

Fabyan, in his celebrated *Chronicles* (1516), refers to a "jig" which was sung "in daunces, in caroles of ye maydens and mynstrellys of Scotlande."[2]

Such jigs were indeed early associated with Scotland. John Foxe, in the second edition of his *Actes and Monuments* (1570) presents certain lyrics under the head of "Scottische Gigges and rymes," and the terms "Scotch jig" and "Northern jig" are frequently encountered in Elizabethan literature with reference to verses, and particularly to combined song and dance acts or dialogues.

In *The Elizabethan Jig*, Baskervill quotes a satirical pamphlet of 1641 in which the Governor of Edinburgh Castle is represented as keeping a fool and a fiddler to entertain his household when they were drinking:

Then they goe to singing of Scots jigges, in a jearing manner, at the Covenanters, for surrendering up their castles. The fiddler he flings out his heels and dances and sings:

> Put up thy Dagger Jamie,
> and all things shall be mended,
> Bishops shall fall, no not at all
> When the Parliament is ended,

Then the Foole he flirts out his folly and whilst the Fidler playes he sings:

> Which never was intended,
> but only for to flam thee;
> We have gotten the game,
> wee'll keep the same,
> Put up thy Dagger Jamie.   [P. 56]

The fiddler dancing while playing is a very common phenomenon, and I am told that fiddlers in Ireland within living memory rarely stood while playing, which brings to mind the Scottish outlaw MacPherson who lived in the late seventeenth century:

> Sae rantinly, sae wantonly,
> Sae dauntinly gaed he,
> He play'd a spring, and danc'd it round
> Below the gallows tree.

Entertainment of this kind was customarily presented at the close of a play in Elizabethan times. Thus we come by what scholars refer to as the Elizabethan Jig, a light dramatic interlude or finale involving song and dance.

The noted Elizabethan musician, Thomas Morley, in his *Plaine and Easie Introduction to Practicall Musicke* (1597), alludes to the "Scottish Jig" as a class of tune which had a very simple musical form but a unique flavour or "qualitie" which made it difficult to imitate. "And I dare boldly affirme," he writes, "that looke which is hee who thinketh himselfe the best descanter of all his neighbors, enjoin him to make but a

---

[2] Robert Fabyan, *Chronicle* (1516). *The New Chronicles of England and France*, ed. H. Ellis (London, 1811), p. 398.

Scottish Jygge, he will grossly err in the true nature and qualitie of it." It is tantalizing to be left in the dark as to the identity of Morley's "Scottish Jygge." Florio, about
twenty years earlier, described the Italian *chiarantana* as a "kinde of Caroll or song
full of leapings like a Scotish gigge," in *The World of Words*, and Shakespeare, in
Much Ado about Nothing, describes a kind of wooing as "hot and hasty, like a Scotch
jig and full as fantastical" (act 2, scene 1). Again we are left in doubt. At least it is
clear that Morley was referring to a class of tune. Florio and Shakespeare may or may
not be referring to the same class of tune, but it is more likely that they are referring
to a dance.

That the term "Scottish Jig" was used of a dance or of a class of dance, performed
by Scots at this period seems clearly to be confirmed in a passage in Robert Greene's
play, *James the Fourth* (1598). In this, Oberon explains to Bohan, a Scot, that the antic
dancers, among whom he has been conjured to appear, were intended to show him
"some sport in dancing." To which Bohan replies:

Ha, ha, ha, thinkest thou those puppets can please me? Whay I have two sons, that with one
Scottish jig shall break the neck of thy antics.
Oberon: That would I fain see.
Bohan: Why thou shalt, ho boys.
Enter Slipper and Nand
Haud your clacks lads, trattle not for thy life, but gather up your legs and dance me forth-
with a jig worth the sight. [Induction, ll. 75–85]

A century later, a French writer, Menage, remarked that in Scotland the word "jig"
was used to signify a very merry dance air, and of course, we have written evidence of
what was called a jig in Scotland at that time — the same indeed as is called jig today.
One style of this, of which the well-known "The Campbells are Coming" is a familiar
example, was in fact often described as "Scottish Jig" in the eighteenth-century music
collections, but the character of this air scarcely tallies with Florio's or Shakespeare's
remarks. There are, however, many examples of the class of ditty which was referred
to as "Scottish Jig" in the sixteenth and seventeenth centuries, such as a "New Scotch
Jig" which appeared in England in mid-seventeenth century and "The Bonny Cravat"
which was sung to the tune of "Jenny come tye my Cravat":

> As Johnny met Jenny a going to play,
> Quoth Johnny to Jenny, I prithee love stay:
> Since thou art my honey, my joy, and delight,
> I'le love thee all day, and I'll please thee at night.
>   Jenny come tye my Jenny come tye my,
>   Jenny come tye my bonny Cravat.
>   I have tyed it behind, and I've tyed it before,
>   I've ty'd it so often, I'le tye it no more.

There is nothing in the language here which betrays a Scottish origin for the lines,
except the use of Johnny and Jenny, the perennial wooers of Scottish balladry. A song,
"Jamie come try me,"[3] was written, we are told, by Burns from a single line or title of

3 James Johnson, ed., *The Scots Musical Museum*, item no. 229.

an old song and set to a tune of Oswald's printed in his *Curious Scots Tunes* (1742). That this tune, like so many of Oswald's, is of too wide a compass for ordinary voices, leaves us in no doubt that it was not the original.

The metre of this "New Scotch Jig" certainly corresponds to 6/8 jig and fits, "like a glove," the "Scottish Jig" as it is known in the eighteenth century. So evident is this from the words that it comes as a surprise that the tune "Jenny come tye my Cravat" in Playford's *Apollo's Banquet* (fifth ed.) should turn out to be not quite a jig but a corranto, originally named "The Scotch Currant."

This warns us to be careful about classifying a tune with no more guide than the words set to it.

We cannot easily judge whether this tune complies with Morley's remarks, for it is difficult for us to hear it through the cultured English ear of his time. On the other hand, if the tune had been a strathspey, we could see his point quite clearly, but no tunes of the nature of strathspeys appear in the seventeenth-century music publications. The characteristically Scottish tune at this time, as far as English publications indicate, was what later was called the Scottish Measure, a class of slow common-time hornpipe. Nevertheless, the character of some of the reel and "fling" steps, and particularly the whirling in some of the latter, is decidedly jig-like.

The music for a "Scotch Man's Dance" from a comedy entitled *The Northern Lass* by Richard Brome, first performed at the Globe Theatre in London in 1632 and revived in 1684, was published by Playford in *Apollo's Banquet*. This is a Scottish Measure, not unlike the tune we know as "Dumbarton's Drums," and by no means a strathspey.

A dance called the Scots Jig, however, was taught in eighteenth-century Edinburgh dance schools, according to Darsie Latimer's remarks in Sir Walter Scott's *Redgauntlet*:

The dance to be performed was the old Scots Jigg, in which you are aware I used to play no sorry figure at La Pique's, when thy clumsy movements used to be rebuked by raps over the knuckles with that great professor's fiddlestick. The choice of the tune was left to my comrade Willie, who having finished his drink feloniously struck up the well-known and popular measure,

> "Merrily danced the Quaker's wife,
> And merrily danced the Quaker."

. . . .

My partner danced admirably, and I like one who was determined, if outshone, which I could not help, not to be altogether thrown into the shade.[4]

[4] Sir Walter Scott, *Redgauntlet* (Edinburgh, 1867), pp. 226–27.

From this extract, it seems that the "old Scots Jigg" was a couple's dance. One is tempted to call it a "twasum" but, later in the same passage, Latimer describes the dances performed as "Scottish jigs, and reels, and 'twosome dances,' with a strathspey or hornpipe for interlude." He thus distinguishes jigs from "twosome dances," and, incidentally, omits the Country Dance, although Darsie Latimer's partner preferred it to the Minuet.

The choice of the tune "The Quaker's Wife," which is of the category of tune known as "Scots Jig" in the eighteenth century, had dramatic significance in Scott's novel, and brings to mind Elizabeth Grant's description in *Memoirs of a Highland Lady* of how, at Doune in 1804, she and her brother "did merrily dance the quaker's wife together quite to the satisfaction of the servants . . ." (p. 31). One suspects that this dance was the same as that danced to the tune of "The Quaker's Wife."

The question remains, of course, as to whether Sir Walter Scott was knowledgeable in dancing matters, for one recalls his lameness and his poor ear for music. However, since Lockhart relates in his *Life of Sir Walter Scott* that Scott attended the Assembly Rooms as a young man in the 1790s (p. 48), I think it can be assumed that Scott was talking from experience.

As mentioned before, the jig was used as a dramatic interlude. There is a tune in William Ballet's manuscript "Lessons for the Lute" (Trinity College, Dublin) dated in the reign of James VI and entitled "A Scotis gig, Ye owld Man." This title suggests the dramatic jig best known in the southwest of Scotland by the name of Auld Glenae. Robert Burns was familiar with this jig, which he says was performed at country weddings. He describes it as follows:

A young fellow is dressed up like an old beggar; a peruke, commonly made of carded tow, represents hoary locks; an old bonnet; a ragged plaid, or surtout, bound with a straw rope for a girdle; a pair of old shoes, with straw-ropes twisted round his ankles, as is done by shepherds in snowy weather; his face they disguise as like wretched old age as they can; in this plight he is brought into the wedding house, frequently to the astonishment of strangers who are not in the secret, and begins to sing:

> O, I am a silly auld man,
> My name it is auld Glenae, & c.

He is asked to drink, and by and by to dance, which, after some uncouth excuses he is prevailed on to do, the fiddler playing the tune, which here is commonly called Auld Glenae; in short, he is all the time so plied with liquor that he is understood to get intoxicated, and with all the gesticulations of an old drunken beggar, he dances and staggers until he falls on the floor; yet still in all his riot, nay in his rolling and tumbling on the floor, with some or other drunken motion of his body, he beats time to the music, till at last he is supposed to be carried out dead drunk.[5]

"Auld Glenae" is apparently a version of the song best known as "An the Kirk wad let me be," set to a 9/8 jig, which has been used for a number of songs including "The Blythesome Bridal." It is also used for a Country Dance in Walsh's *Caledonian Country Dances* (ca. 1750) under the title "Silly old man." I have been unable to find

---

[5] Davidson Cook, "Annotation of Scottish Songs by Burns," *Burns Chronicle*, no. 31, January, 1922. Rpt. in James C. Dick, *The Songs of Robert Burns* (Hatboro, Penn.: Folklore Associates, 1962).

the continuation of the lines quoted by Burns, but those collected by Herd in *Ancient and Modern Scottish Songs* run as follows:

> I am a puir silly auld man,
>   And hirplin' ower a tree;
> Yet fain, fain kiss wad I,
>   Gin the kirk wad let me be.
>
> Gin a' my duds were aff,
>   And guid haill claes put on,
> O, I could kiss a young lass
>   As weel as ony man.

Alan Cunningham (1784–1842) also was familiar with the dance Auld Glenae, referring to it in *Scottish Songs* as "a Nithsdale interlude" (p. 152). He believed that it was originally performed by two persons, one the "sinner" and the other a minister of the Kirk, the humour being sustained by the contrast of arch simplicity and grave admonition; but he had never seen it so performed. At the time of his writing this in 1825, Auld Glenae and other similar dramatic jigs which had been familiar in the southwest corner of Scotland had "fallen into disuse or discredit." Of these, Cunningham was familiar with two: The Wooing of the Maiden, which "seemed designed as a humorous portraiture of the vicissitudes of courtship," and The Roke and the wee pickle tow, which was a kind of morality on the theme of idleness and waste against industry and thrift.

The Wooing of the Maiden was performed at weddings:

Just before the time of stocking-throwing, the door of the barn was opened, and a youth and maiden entered, keeping time to the sound of the fiddle which commenced the air that gave a name to the entertainment. The youth was a lively peasant with no small share of inventive humour, and dressed in the extremity of the fashion; while the damsel personated with very good grace a fantastic old maid, flourishing in ancient finery, with a sharp shrill voice and a look of great importance. They advanced to the middle of the floor beating time to the tune, and smiling upon each other, and mimicking the appearance of delight and joy. This pantomime having lasted some five minutes, the maiden sang part of a song adapted to the music, which praised the charms of opulence, and laid the scene of domestic love and endearment among bags of gold, in the middle of many acres, and concluded with extolling the wisdom and discretion of age. This was answered by a song from her lover, which, with the usual enthusiasm of youth, spoke with great contempt of charms which were rated by the acre — of attractions which were weighted by gold; and laid the scene of true love endearment at the time when maidens step out of their teens. As the charms of the rustic actress happened to be far from considerable, and as she had in all appearance overstepped her teens a good score of years, she considered this lyric declaration of her lover as somewhat personal, and proceeded to resent it in very passable pantomime. — She strode round the floor with the stride of an ogress, and shivered all her finery with anger and pride as a fowl ruffles its feathers. Her lover seemed by no means desirous of soothing her; he mimicked her lordliness of step, and the waving of her mantle, and stepped step by step with her and the music round the floor. He then took an empty purse out of his pocket, shook it before her face, threw it into the air and caught it as it fell, and burst out into another verse of song in contempt of riches and all who possessed them. This was answered by a corresponding verse from the maiden, in which she laughed at empty pockets, and scorned poverty, in the way the world has ever done. He then turned from her in great anger. And now began the more dramatic part of the entertainment: he danced round the company, and having singled out a young woman, the most beautiful he could find, he saluted her, took her hand, danced with her into the middle of the floor, and made earnest love as far as the silence of pantomime would allow. This excited the anger and jealousy of the other; and as the nature of the dance required the music still to be obeyed by the feet, we had a very good dance; a very good song from the slighted lady, in scorn of her landless rival; a song in reply from the other, vindicating the supremacy of youth and beauty against the influence of moorlands and meadows; and, finally, a verse from the hero of the entertainment, rejoicing in the choice of his heart in opposition to that of avarice. This kind of contest continued some time — one moment limited to pantomime, and the next breaking out into satiric verse: it ended, however, as all contests of that kind generally do, in the triumph of her of the houses and land, and with her success the representation terminated. I may add, that I have seen it acted without the assistance of song, and that the addition of the verse, though a great improvement by lending the voice to action, impeded the operations of the dance and rendered it subordinate. [Pp. 149–51]

The Roke and the wee pickle tow begins with the musician playing the tune, upon which a "staid and thrifty-looking dame" appears

with a roke or distaff in her bosom replenished with flax, from which she twines or seems to twine thread. She is joined in the dance, but not in the industry, by a joyous, middle-aged man, somewhat touched, it may be, with liquor: he holds a candle in his hand, and dances with her round the floor, beating accurate time all the while to the music. He of the candle sings a verse to the air of the music, in which he laughs at thrift, and counts industry a colder companion than pleasure. She of the roke replies to this, and tells him in song that idle pleasure ends in sorrow and repentance, while homely industry brings peace and happiness, and shuts the door on pain and on poverty. The music, played purposely slow for the sake of the song, bursts out more boldly, and the dance, like that of the witches in Tam O'Shanter, grows fast and furious; for the man endeavours to set the roke on fire with his candle, while the woman eludes him with great activity, and all the while the music and the feet echo to each other. This contest continues for the space of five minutes or more, and then they renew the bickerings between idleness and thrift in satiric song. On the side of Industry, many proverbs pressing the necessity of thrift are woven into verse, while all the curious sayings which ridicule labour, and paint pleasure lying idle among beds of lilies, are at the command of him who would have been the "Unthrift" in one of the old moralities. Fire prevails however at last against its combustible opponent, and the pleasure of the audience is measured by the duration of the strife; for it requires no small management and agility to preserve the "Roke and the wee pickle tow" amid the evolutions of the dance. This dramatic entertainment . . . is sometimes represented without song, and it is not at all improbable that it forms only a portion of some more important performance. [Pp. 151–52]

The similarity of these song and dance dramas to those of the West Highlands discussed in chapter 16 is obvious. They are all of the same genre of dramatic jigs. In a very similar vein is the Irish Washerwoman, familiarly known as the Irish Jig by Scottish dancers and practised today in their dancing schools. Here the tantrums of an irate washerwoman are vehemently displayed, or, if it is a man, an irate Paddy complete with shillelagh. The tune is a superb set of variations, usually published under the title of "Paddy's Leather Breeches," which, in the hands of a good piper, can sound absolutely fascinating.

The Irish Jig, properly so called, is a very different style of step dance with no dramatic overtones, nor any whirling or leaping so characteristic of the Irish Washerwoman and the Elizabethan Jig.

"Fading" was a term used of jig dancing in Elizabethan times, and associated with Ireland.[6] In Ben Jonson's "Irish Masque," twelve Irishmen danced fading. Probably this was the celebrated Irish folk dance Rinnce Fada (Long Ring) with its intermittent refrain of steps or capers. Indeed the word "fa-ding" was used as a refrain in English song. In one well-known Elizabethan play, *The Knight of the Burning Pestle* by Beaumont and Fletcher, one of the characters orders a boy to dance fa-ding: "Fa-ding is a fine jig, I assure you," he says, and goes on to urge the boy thus: "Now a'capers, sweetheart! cannot you tumble youth?" (act 3). To dance fading, then, was to caper in a particular manner.

The Faddy or Furry Dance preserved in Cornwall was a processional dance similar to the Rinnce Fada, in which the participants proceeded hand in hand, in and out various streets and houses of the village.

The Rinnce Fada in its original processional form has all the characteristics of antiquity. It was a ceremonial dance associated with the Beltane festival and was performed widely throughout the southern counties of Ireland. A ballroom form of the dance, in longwise country dance formation, evolved during the eighteenth century. In this version, the stepping began at one end and gradually worked through the rows until all participants were stepping. It was used as a finishing dance at both private and public balls in southern Ireland.

The stepping tradition of the Irish Jig may well have evolved from the capers of the Rinnce Fada. Jig stepping should not be confused with that of reel or hornpipe, but it is in the same vein, and the variety of steps employed is now very great. Our principal interest is in Scottish dance, but where the jig is mentioned, we may pay particular attention to the Irish forms.

William Chappell and Jeffrey Pulver both regarded the jig as a newcomer to Ireland in the seventeenth century. Chappell says that he found no Irish Jig bearing that name before the latter part of the seventeenth century. But Grattan-Flood calls attention to a letter from Sir Henry Sidney to Queen Elizabeth in 1569 containing a reference to the dancing of jigs by the Anglo-Irish ladies of Galway.[7] The same author claims an antiquity for the Irish Jig of more than a thousand years, although his earliest authorities do not use the name jig but port, which in Gaelic signifies an air, either vocal or instrumental. Whether or not these early ports were played with the rhythm of the Irish Jig is not clear. There are two rhythms, single and double, respectively thus:

and

[6] Charles R. Baskervill, *The Elizabethan Jig*, p. 358; and W. H. Grattan-Flood, "Notes on the Irish Jig," *Musical Opinion*, 1914.

[7] Grattan-Flood, *A History of Irish Music*, 4th ed. (London, 1927), p. 160.

None of the ports I have examined meet with these requirements. Rather, they are slow airs, adagios for the harp in common time. Burns set "Ae Fond Kiss" to Rory Dall's Port as it appeared in James Oswald's collection, and here it is in 6/8 in the rhythm:

However Burns directed it to be played "slow and tender." The reader may notice how this rhythm coincides with that of "Pibroch of Donuil Dubh," another very old air which has the pronounced rhythm of the Single Jig. When such close affinities exist, it is difficult to be dogmatic about differences. Variations on any port may well have fallen into jig rhythm.

The Italian Giga is in the rhythm of running triplets of the style of the Irish Double Jig. It is presented here in 12/8:

When we recall that Irish harpers were known in Italy[8] and indeed in other parts of Europe in the thirteenth century, there is some plausibility to Flood's suggestion that the Giga thereby comes from the Irish prototype. The same authority informed Pulver that the earliest *printed* Irish tune, taken from *Parthenia Inviolata* (ca. 1613), is an Irish Jig, but gives no further details.

The characteristic English jig has the rhythm:

Its spirit is light and tripping. Many composers gave it the time signature 2 because of its beating two to the bar, or 3 in 1. Its form was the common one of two measures each of four or eight bars, repeated, and was written in 3/8, 6/8, 3/4, 6/4, 12/8, etcetera. Sometimes, it seems, it was the spirit of the music which justified the title "jig," as there are, in the *Fitzwilliam Virginal Book*, two jigs in common time, "Nobodyes Gigge" and "Giles Farnaby's Gigge," a not unusual occurrence in Elizabethan times. This recalls, as Pulver points out, those sixteenth- and seventeenth-century "marches" in 3/4 which are marches only in spirit.

The jigs appearing in Playford's *Dancing Master* — "Kemp's Jegg," "Millison's Jegg," "Lord of Carnarvan's Jegg" and many more — conform to the rhythm:

The rhythm of the jig must have been known in the British Isles long before it was named. Pulver believes that the jig reached Ireland from England by way of the

---

[8] Vincenzo Galileo (Dialogo di Vincenzo) gives Dante as his authority: "This most ancient instrument was brought to us from Ireland (as Dante says) where they are excellently made in great numbers, the inhabitants of that island having practised on it for many and many a century." [Quoted in Sir John Hawkins, *A General History of the Science and Practice of Music*, vol. 3. Also quoted in Grattan-Flood, *The Story of the Harp* (London, 1905), pp. 55–56.]

Anglo-Irish community. He based his thesis mainly on the probable Norse origin of the word "jig," but overlooked the fact that the Anglo-Saxons were not the only bearers of Norse influence to the British Isles. Certainly, as far as written music goes, many jigs appear in English publications of the sixteenth and seventeenth centuries, whereas there were no printed collections of music from Scotland or Ireland until much later. In the light of what we know of the spirit of Irish music, even as early as Giraldus's reference in the twelfth century, I can see no reason to entertain the idea that the jig came to Ireland from England.

In the normal Irish Jig the measures are of eight bars and each measure is repeated once. A number of Irish tunes in jig rhythm are peculiar in that they have a first measure of eight bars and a second of six, but these are not suitable for the ordinary dance. The Irish Jig may be danced as a solo or by one or more couples. A series of steps are first executed, beginning with the right foot, for the first measure; then repeated, beginning with the left foot, for the second measure. In a solo, the dancer now travels in a circle for the next sixteen bars. With a couple, or two couples, the partners give right hands across, or "wheel" to the right (six bars), fall back to place and shuffle (two bars), then repeat giving left hands across.

The Hop-Jig is in 9/8 with the musical measures in eight bars and repeated as in the normal jig; but the dance does not follow the usual pattern of repeats and comprises a measure of stepping alternating with a measure of travelling. It is usually danced by one or more couples, each couple dancing independently. The travel is in a semicircle, and the step is a peculiar glide which is very pleasing: the toe of the right foot is moved about two feet to the right; the toe of left is brought up behind right heel; and the same is repeated with four-inch travel (one bar). This action is repeated for two bars, then the dancers turn on the fourth bar, beating time, one long, four short, and return by same semicircle to place during the next four bars. The dancers pass back-to-back, exchange places, and return.

In all the Irish step dances, the dancers hold their arms inertly by their sides and thus enforce attention on the feet and the movement.

In England there were jigs in the antic dances of the grotesqueries of the May Games. The characters of the Morris danced solos and trios and so on. The Morris Jig, known in recent times as a solo step dance, was often performed by one or more dancers in turn, with music, steps, and hand movements typical of the Morris.[9] The dividing line between this jig and the hornpipe is obscure, as far as step technique is concerned, but, of course, the music is distinctive, though the triple-time hornpipe (3/2) is obviously related to both 6/8 and 9/8 jigs.

In Elizabethan London, the jig and hornpipe (3/2) were included among the dances in vogue. According to Barnaby Riche, who wrote in 1581, these were "measures, galliards, jigs, brauls, rounds, and hornpipes."[10] One suspects that, at a later date, the jigs, rounds, and hornpipes would have been lumped together under the term "Country Dance," but there were also jigs and hornpipes.

Pepys made some entertaining remarks on the subject of the solo jig in his diary. Of a party at Woolwich, for instance, on October 11, 1665, he wrote: "My wife and

[9] Cecil J. Sharp, *The Morris Book* (London: Novello, 1912).
[10] Barnaby Riche, first preface to *His Farewell to Militairie Profession*.

Mercer and Mrs. Barbara danced, and mighty merry we were, but especially at Mercer's dancing a jigg, which she does the best I ever did see, having the most natural way of it and keeps time the most perfectly I ever did see." Then again, on August 14, 1666, he related that Mercer donned "a suit of Tom's, like a boy ... and danced a Jigg." On another occasion he mentioned that King Charles II had been entertained by Moll Davis dancing a jig. A solo jig was also taught by Johnny McGill, the Ayrshire fiddler and dancing master in the eighteenth century.

An affinity between jig and Galliard is to be inferred from numerous allusions in English literature from the period of Elizabeth. One writer refers to the "artificial curious Galliards, Jigs or Corantoes, learned with much pains and practise at a Dancing-Schoole, as ours are."[11] Jig and Galliard shared a certain virtuoso quality, and in John Cleiveland's *Mixed Assembly* [1648] a jig is described in which a couple are said to tread "cinquepace," the five basic Galliard steps. There is also an association between the Galliard and the Irish Country Dance Trenchmore. "Among a number of these Country daunces," wrote Nicholas Breton in *Wits Trenchmour*, "I did light on such a Galliard, as had a trick above Trenchmour."[12] A broadsheet balled entitled "The West Country Jigg: Or a Trenchmour Galliard" has come down to us. It is interesting to see what was involved in this:

> The Piper he struck up
>   and Merrily he did play,
> The shakeing of the sheets,
>   and eke the Irish hay
> Then up with Aley, Aley,
>   Up with Priss and Prue:
> In came wanton Willy,
>   amongst the jovial crew.

> To a Merry Scotch Tune, or Up with Aley, Aley, & c.
>   [*Roxburghe Ballads*, 7, pp. 342–44]

A song, "Up wi't, Aily, Aily," is referred to by Burns in a letter to Ainslie, July 29, 1787. The rhythm suggests a 9/8 jig and "The Shakeing of the Sheets" and the "Irish Hey" are celebrated Irish tunes.

The "country measures rounds and jigs" danced by the "mad lads" and "country lasses" of England found their way into Playford's hands and appeared in *The Dancing Master* as "Country Dances." In *Fugitive Pieces*, Baillie (William) Creech of Edinburgh, Burns's publisher, with reference to eighteenth-century Edinburgh assemblies and balls distinguishes between the "merry country dance" and the "joyous jig" (p. 338). This agrees with Scott's same distinction in *Redgauntlet*, and supports Scott's description of the "joyous jig" as a couple's dance called the Scots Jig. Perhaps the Scots Jig is the same as the "north countrey Jigg" which, it is suggested in a book of conduct, *Mysteries of Love and Eloquence* (1658), "will please the ladies better than all your French whisks and frisks. . . ."

---

[11] William Prynne, *Histriomastix*, p. 252, quoted in Baskervill, *The Elizabethan Jig*, p. 356.
[12] A. B. Grosart, ed., *Work of Nicholas Breton*, vol. 2 (London, 1879), p. 20.

14/The Hornpipe

Characteristics of "Jacky Tar" hornpipe –
triple-time original – "double" and "single"
hornpipes – Scottish Measure – Nancy
Dawson – enthusiasm for entr'acte dances
in the eighteenth century – jig and
hornpipe as taught by Johnny McGill in
1750 – step dancing in the English and
and Irish alehouses – stepping in Nova
Scotia and New England – John Durang
hornpipe "in the character of a sailor" –
Fishar and Aldridge – The Wapping

Landlady – Durang and Francis in Phila-
delphia – Sailors' Hornpipe – hornpipes
aboard ship – earliest notices of hornpipe –
English hornpipes – origin of term
hornpipe

The word "hornpipe" is, today, popularly associated with a dance for sailors. Popularly, that is, outside Ireland, for the Irish have a native hornpipe of their own which, for all its similarities, is very different in character, musically and choreographically. The Sailors' Hornpipe is performed to common-time tunes of a particular cast, most bearing the word "hornpipe" in their title, such as "College Horn-pipe," "Fishar's Hornpipe," "West's Hornpipe," and "Aldridge's Hornpipe." This is the class of tune familiarly recognized as hornpipe today, which, for convenience here, we shall call the "Jacky Tar" class of hornpipe.

The "Jacky Tar" class of hornpipe tune is characterized by staccato quaver runs punctuated by the stressing of the second and third beats within the bar at regular intervals. These intervals are not the same in every tune, but the phrases always end with this double stressing: pom! pom! Since the first beat of the bar is stressed anyway, the tune's phrases seem to end pom! pom! pom!, often on the same note. The effect is brilliant and exciting. The reader is doubtless very familiar with examples of this class of tune. The three strong beats at the end of the phrases are claimed to be an Irish characteristic, and certainly they are present in the so-called Irish hornpipe; but the Irish hornpipe tune is slower and very jaunty, with a rhythmic characteristic comparable to that of the strathspey. As a dance it is a pure step dance, that is, the technique of the dance lies in the beating of rhythms by the feet, with those steps we know as trebles, brushes, shuffles, etcetera.

While the Sailors' Hornpipe we know employs like steps, it is much more of a character dance, a high dance performed in soft shoes and bearing a strong relationship to the Scottish high dances. The Irish are not at all interested in this dance, and, in any case, despite Nelson's Irish ancestry, the British Jack Tar exerts no claim on republican Irish sentiment.

Nowhere is the Sailors' Hornpipe more assiduously studied today than in the Scottish Highland Dance schools. Dance teachers regard it as an excellent means of cultivating nimble foot movements and rapid changes of balance. But what were called jigs and hornpipes were certainly basic fare in Scottish dance schools in the eighteenth century, alongside the Highland Reel and, in the centres of fashion, the Minuet!

At this point, however, we must note that prior to the middle of the eighteenth century, if we judge from the music collections in print and in manuscript, the tunes called "hornpipes" in Scotland and England were not of the same category as the "Jacky Tar" variety which usurps the name today. Indeed the "Jacky Tar" class of hornpipe tune comes into prominence only toward the end of the eighteenth century. The earlier "hornpipe" was a peculiar syncopated limping-gait of a tune in triple-time — 3/2 or 6/4 or 12/8 — a rhythm which Purcell and Handel regarded as peculiarly English. In *Illustrations of the Lyric Poetry*, William Stenhouse has written, ca. 1824, that tunes of the category of 3/2 hornpipes had been played in Scotland "time out of mind, as a particular species of the double hornpipe," and that James Allan, onetime piper to the Duke of Northumberland, had assured him that this "particular measure originated in the borders of England and Scotland." This suggestion is supported by the large number of triple-time hornpipes embraced in the standard repertoire of the Northumbrian small-pipes and among Border songs. Some examples are: "Go to Berwick Johnnie," "The Dusty Miller," "Jockey said to Jenny," and "Robin Shure in Hairst."

The rhythm peculiarly lends itself to comic or jaunty verses, and many a nurse has dandled the baby on her knee to "Dance to y'r Daddie" or "Wee Totum Fogg." The words give out the characteristic rhythm of the triple-time hornpipe:

> Dance to your daddie,
> My Bonnie laddie,
> Dance to your daddie, my bonnie lamb;
> And ye'll get a fishie,
> In a wee wee dishie,
> An' ye'll get a fishie when the boat comes hame!

and:

> Wee Totum Fogg
> Sits upon a creepie:
> Half an ell o' gray
> Wad be his coat and breekie.

No other class of tune is designated "hornpipe" in music collections in England or Scotland until the advent of the "Jacky Tar" class of tune at the end of the eighteenth century. Step dances to common-time dance tunes, such as Seann Triubhas, were sometimes referred to as "double" hornpipes in eighteenth-century Scotland, and although the tunes associated with these dances were sometimes called "double hornpipe airs," they were never designated as such in the music collections.

The Irish use the terms "single" and "double" of their hornpipes, reels, and jigs. In the case of the Irish hornpipe and reel, the single is in 2/4 and employs simpler steps than the double which is performed in 4/4. The single Irish hornpipe was a ladies' dance employing light shuffles and batters performed in an easy and graceful style; the double was a male dance exploiting the more difficult trebling steps with much "drumming" and "grinding."

The distinction indicated by the use of "single" and "double" with reference to step dancing in Scotland was thus very different; the one was the hornpipe so-called in dance and music, a triple-time measure, and the other a step dance to Rants.

A slightly different style of Scottish double hornpipe air — though the difference is not dramatic — was called the "Scottish Measure," a term which first appears in print in Playford's collection of Scots tunes (1700) — "Full of the Highland Humours" as he put it. Prior to this, tunes of the character of the Scottish Measure appeared in English publications (there were no like Scottish publications in the seventeenth century) simply as "Scots tunes," particularly in Playford's *Apollo's Banquet* and its editions. Two examples are "Dumbarton's Drums" and what is known since Burns's day as "Corn Rigs."

D. G. MacLennan, who came of a dancing family, describes the dance Scottish Measure in *Traditional and Highland Scottish Dances* (1950), as a twasome dance of the Lowlands, but does not declare his authority. The earliest of the very few recorded allusions to the Scottish Measure as a dance that I have discovered occurs in a Covent Garden playbill dated April 24, 1749, advertising a performance of *The Beggar's Opera* —"*A New Scotch Dance* in which will be introduced by Particular Desire the *Scotch Measure* and the *Highland Reel* by Froment and Mad De La Cointrie."

A year later, "The Scotch Measure and Highland Reel by Froment" were advertised, with no partner mentioned; these items continued to be repeated at intervals between 1750 and 1757. Then at the Haymarket Theatre, November, 1775, Arnold Fishar performed a dance called The Scots Measure in a presentation of *The Gentle Shepherd*, but no partner was advertised. These items do not clarify the matter, although the use of the word *the* in *the* Scots Measure suggests that the dance was an established character of Scottish dance, as *the* Highland Reel, for instance. Nevertheless, these playbill references are the only allusions to the Scottish Measure as a dance that have come to my attention prior to the description of a dance of the name in the Hill manuscript (ca. 1840). The Hill manuscript does not note that the dance is a dance for two, although Tibbie Cramb re-created it as such.

Couples' dances in the traditional idiom were certainly known in the Scottish countryside in the eighteenth century. We have noted elsewhere allusions from that period to what was called a twasome and the Strathspey Minuet. It is surely a dance of this kind we see being executed in the painting catalogued in the Penicuik House collection in 1724, as *A Highland Wedding* by De Wit. De Witt is known to have spent some time in Scotland between the years 1673 and 1687, and his painting must therefore be expected to belong to this period. It is a strangely austere picture, reflecting something of the crudity and simplicity of Scottish life along the Highland line. There is a mixture of Lowland and Highland dress styles among the bystanders, who are watching a man and woman dance vis-à-vis to the music of the bagpipe. The dancing man carries a sword, which surely distinguishes him as one of the upper class, and the woman wears rude shoes tied with ribbons. (Women of the lower orders rarely wore shoes in those days.) The attitude of the dancers suggests that they are stepping to each other. The piper is dressed in tartan and wears trews, another gentlemanly distinction at that period.

Here, certainly, we have a twosome dance, and a hornpipe style of dance at that, from all appearances. It is conceivable that this was performed to the category of Scottish hornpipe tune which became identified as Scottish Measure (or was it a Scotch Jig?). Since a bagpiper provides the music, we can discount the possibility that a court dance is being performed.

We are left to ponder whether the word "Measure" in the term "Scottish Measure" refers to the rhythm of the class of tune of that name or to the dance, as in "treading a Measure." As we have seen, Pavanes and Basse Dances were referred to as "the Measures" in Elizabethan England and were couples' dances. Could it be that the characteristic Scottish twosome received the name "Scottish Measure" by analogy with the courtly "measures"? Certainly, the Scottish Measure, *as music*, suggests nothing so sedate. "The White Cockade," "Whaur Gadie Rins," and "Flooers o' Edinburgh" are Scottish Measure tunes which may be familiar to the reader.

The "double" hornpipe tunes of Scotland are to all appearances, the ancestors of those tunes we call hornpipes today, tunes of the class of "College Hornpipe" and "Jacky Tar," to which, as mentioned earlier, the Sailors' Hornpipe is danced. This was the new style of hornpipe tune which first became noticeable toward the end of the eighteenth century, which, it has been suggested, was created by Thomas Arne with the two instrumental dances of this kind he composed for his version of Purcell's "King Arthur" in 1767.[1]

The Irish hornpipe, of course, belongs to the same family, and, indeed, this class of dance music in the British Isles reminds one of the selective processes of the evolution of species in nature. Darwin's finches in music! In time, with migration, a certain mixing of the breeds of British hornpipe tunes has become noticeable, particularly between the Irish and Scots, but the original rhythmical distinctions persist.

When Nancy Dawson, at the height of her celebrity as an entr'act dancer, went over to David Garrick at Drury Lane to dance in his production of *The Beggar's Opera*, she was replaced at Covent Garden by Mrs. Vernon who, on the evening of October 24, 1760, danced to a "New Hornpipe" composed by Thomas Arne. The occasion demanded something special as a counterattraction to the popular Nancy, and one wonders if this "New Hornpipe" of Arne's was the first of the new genre of common-time hornpipe.

The tune to which Nancy Dawson danced to fame in *The Beggar's Opera* was, it seems, that which bears her name in many publications; a tune which will be known to most readers of these pages. It is, or was, familiar in Scotland as the tune of "Who'll come intae ma wee ring?," and among other English-speaking peoples as "Here we go round the Mulberry Bush." It enjoyed an immense popularity in its day, was introduced to other plays and set to variations for harpsichord as "Miss Dawson's Hornpipe." But, musically, it is not a hornpipe, it is a jig!

This brings us to the fact that in earlier times any step dance fell under the definition of hornpipe, whatever the music. The hornpipe clearly was the ancestor of the modern tap dance, and it was very popular on the eighteenth-century stage. The

[1] Sir George Grove, *Dictionary of Music and Musicians*, ed. H. C. Colles, 4th ed. (London, 1940).

eighteenth century was the great age of Harlequin and Columbine and of dances in that vein. These dances were performed as entr'act entertainment during the performance of plays and at the close.

Sometimes the dances were in character with the play: in *The Beggar's Opera*, there would be a hornpipe and a country dance; in *Love in a Village*, a country dance or peasant dance; and in the few London performances of *The Gentle Shepherd*, something in a rural and Scottish vein. But perversely enough, one could find the French Minuet or Louvre danced after a patriotic play entitled *Brittania*! Of course many of the dancers were French.

John Weaver classified the theatrical dances as "Serious, Grotesque and Scenical."[2] Carlo Blasis terms them "Serious, demi-Caractere and Comic."[3] There could be a Minuet or The Dutch Skipper, Irish Lilt, Scotch Dance, French Sailor's Dance, Sailor and His Lass, Mad Man's Dance, Grand Wedding Dance and so on. The Sailor and His Lass with some modification could be the French Sailor and His Wife or the Fisherman and His Wife, and so also could other themes lend themselves to variations. From time to time there would be the simple notice: "Hornpipe by Mathews," or "by Aldridge," "by Miss Pitt," or "by Fishar," and so on.

The first mention of a hornpipe in the playbills of the eighteen century that I have discovered is that from Drury Lane, June 10, 1713 — "Hornpipe by a Gentleman for his Diversion" — a single performance which was not repeated. At Southwark Fair held in September, 1717, the rural connotation of the hornpipe was emphasized when "Esq. Timothy's Countryman" performed "The Lancashire Hornpipe with much applause." Then in the 1720s, one Tom Jones made a specialty of a "Hornpipe" and performed it at several theatres. After this, the word "hornpipe" appears regularly on London playbills, and it is not until after 1740 that one finds it at all associated with a nautical theme. Certainly, Nancy (or Miss) Dawson's Hornpipe in the 1760s was in no way related to sailors.

Nancy Dawson is of interest to us on other grounds, however. In his *Illustrations of the Lyric Poetry*, William Stenhouse publishes a note from C. Sharpe that Sharpe had it from a lady connected with Dr. Smollet, the novelist, that Nancy Dawson "cut her first capers near Kelso, where she was born, the daughter of a humble cottager," and that "Miss Nancy's relatives continued farmers in the same vicinity" forty years prior to this (p. 306).

Although a memoir published in Nancy's lifetime describes her as having been born in poor circumstances in London, the daughter of Emmanuel Dawson, a porter, she names her father in her will as William Newton, a staymaker at Martlet Court. Her mother, described in the memoir as having died, is named in her will along with a brother, William.[4] The memoir is obviously suspect, and it is very likely that William Newton was of a Scottish Border family. It is understandable that Nancy should not reveal her Scottish origin in the anti-Scottish London of her day.

Her celebrity is remarkable. She was a relatively unknown dancer for some years, and it was not until she was twenty-nine and dancing with Rich's company at Covent Garden that she was called upon to substitute for the regular dancer in a revival of

[2] John Weaver, *An Essay Towards an History of Dancing* (London, 1712).
[3] Carlo Blasis, *The Art of Dancing*, p. 88.
[4] Cf. "Nancy Dawson," *Dance Perspectives*, no. 25 (September 1966).

The Beggar's Opera (1759). In this she was an immediate sensation. She drew the theatre-lovers from Garrick's serious drama at Drury Lane and the following squib on Garrick's discomfiture was written to the tune of her dance:

> Her easy mien, her steps so neat,
> She foots, she trips, she looks so sweet,
> Her every motion is complete,
> I die for Nancy Dawson.
>
> See how the op'ra takes a run,
> Exceeding *Hamlet, Lear* or Lun,
> Tho' in it there would be no fun,
> Was't not for Nancy Dawson.
>
> Tho' Beard and Brent charm every night,
> And female Peachum's justly right,
> And Filch and Lockit please the sight,
> 'Tis crowned by Nancy Dawson.
>
> See little Davy strut and Puff,
> P... on the op'ra and such stuff,
> My house is never full enough,
> A curse on Nancy Dawson!
>
> Tho' Garrick he has had his day
> And forc'd the town his laws t'obey,
> Now Johnny Rich is come in play,
> With help of Nancy Dawson.

Garrick, however, exploited Miss Dawson's notorious respect for the highest bidder and managed to engage her for Drury Lane in the following year. There she made her first appearance in her usual hornpipe in the third act of *The Beggar's Opera* on October 13, 1760, and continued in Columbine roles. She retired in 1763, the devoted inamorata of Ned Shuter, a Falstaffian figure, whom Garrick described as "the greatest comic genius ever seen." Nancy died but four years after her retirement.

Who, may we ask, remembers the Granier family of dancers, the Shawfords, or even Aldridge or the popular Miss Baker who succeeded to Nancy's celebrity? Here is a caprice of immortality!

The enthusiasm and zeal of the theatregoers of the eighteenth century and their partisanship for favourite actors, actresses, and dancers has never been exceeded. The theatre doors were opened at four for curtain at six. The patrons sat on backless benches and the more fashionable in the pit and lower gallery and even in boxes encroaching on the stage itself. They were vociferous and responsive in the extreme and restive to a degree that made any intermission hazardous. Hence the dances between the acts of *Richard III* or *King Lear,* serving a similar purpose on occasion to that served by the fringe of sharp spikes along the front of the stage. The principal competing theatres were Covent Garden and Drury Lane, Lincoln's Inn Fields, and later the Haymarket Theatre, the Pantheon, and King's Theatre.

Entr'acte dancing was for the most part greatly relished, and Edinburgh audiences do not appear to have differed from this characteristic of other theatregoers, for James Dibdin tells us in *The Annals of the Edinburgh Stage* that on one occasion, after putting up with several discreditable performances, they took violent exception to the omission of the advertised hornpipe in *The Beggar's Opera* (p. 136).

The distinction between the jig and the hornpipe as dances is a fine one, and the slightest evidence of what may have been taught in this vein in the dancing schools is of considerable interest. Not much of this evidence survives, but we have a tantalizing glimpse of a jig and hornpipe as taught by a dancing master, the celebrated Girvan fiddler, Johnnie McGill, in a southwest Scottish town around the year 1750. This information is given by a contributor to *Notes and Queries*[5] who communicated some of the contents of manuscript instructions written by his father's dancing master. The instructions were entitled "The Dancing Steps of a Hornpipe and Gigg. As Also, Twelve of the Newest Country Dances, as they are performed at the Assemblys and Balls. All Set by Mr. John McGill for the use of his School, 1752."

There were sixteen steps in the hornpipe and fourteen in the jig, but the contributor did not think the instructions would be intelligible, so he made a selection to illustrate his point. It is clear that the second, third, and fourth steps of the hornpipe are "slips and shuffle forward," "spleet and floorish backwards," and "Hyland step forwards." Elsewhere, he says, there are directions to "heel and toe forwards," "single and double round step," "slaps across forward," "twist round backward," "cross strocks aside and sink forward," "short shifts," and "back hops," — steps we can recognize as of the character of the modern Sailors' Hornpipe. He appears to give us only the last step of the jig, "happ forward and backward."

One discerning correspondent advised that a transcript of this manuscript be placed in the Advocates' Library, Edinburgh, but to our great loss, this was not done. The dancing master concerned was undoubtedly Johnnie McGill.

The hornpipe described here is what might be called a high dance as distinct from the pure step dance. Doubtless the "stage" hornpipe was of this character. The step dances, or hornpipes, which were a living part of the English heritage as recently as the nineteenth century, had more in common with the Irish strain in being purely step dances. The Lancashire clog dance must surely have been what was otherwise known as the Lancashire Hornpipe.

In many parts of England, it was a common feature at feasts and wakes and on Saturday nights for men, and women too, to take turns at "stepping" to the music of the country fiddler in the village alehouse. Many of the dancers used stepping shoes or light clogs, and a favourite surface was, as in Ireland, the top of a large table. In Ireland, the table was often soaped. Nimbleness and clatter, we are told, were essential, and often, when there was no music, the tunes could be identified from the audible pattern of the dancer's stepping. Our informant describes the village step dancing in *Notes and Queries*:

What were the village step dances of the earlier half of the nineteenth century like? A Nottinghamshire woman of fifty, when lamenting to me the disappearance of various forms of village merry-making described to her by her elders, said she had known a few people who

---

[5] *Notes and Queries* (September 1, 1855), p. 159.

were excellent step dancers and could make the time of the dance "come out of the floor like with the beating of their feet." The women "would draw up their skirts short, and pull the back of the skirt forward between their legs, to show their feet and ankles. Then you could see the steps well."

It is assumed by those who disapprove of John Wesley that early Wesleyanism killed the hereditary amusements of English village life; but is not this rather unjust? There were still excellent fiddlers and their cronies were acquainted with old songs, dance tunes, and games, which the younger people might have picked up too, had not changed social conditions given them tastes and ideals foreign to the traditional sports of country life.[6]

To which another correspondent from Worksop replies:

There were many men step dancers, and a few women ones, well into the later half of the nineteenth century in most villages, and step dancing displays were usual incidents at feasts and wakes. On Saturday nights also "stepping" would suddenly break out at village ale houses, when two or three men would pit themselves against each other in short spells, hardly of the nature of contests. When a lad I saw many such steppings, and step dancers are by no means dead, though gone out of village life, maybe. A good dancer was one capable of taking any step music, or without any music whatever. Many of the dancers used stepping shoes or light clogs — the latter preferred in the clog-wearing localities. Nimbleness and clatter were essentials, with a good "crowdy" to give the music. There were a number of men who were good "crowdies" — fiddlers, playing from ear the tunes to which the dancers stepped. The dancing was always on wood — a floor or large table: the latter preferred as the steppings and beats could be seen to the better advantage. Some danced without the crowdy, but it was to music which they knew by heart and carried in their feet.

When the dancing was done without a crowdy, the listeners could tell the tunes by the steps and beats on the boards. Sometimes there would be a couple of dancers on the table. When one had gone through an arranged number of steps, he stopped, the other taking his place; and this was done so deftly that there was no break in the music whilst the change was made. The old fiddlers were hard to tire, and one crowdy with intervals "to wet his whistle," could keep it up for hours.[7]

This, then, was the native English hornpipe of the countryside, and doubtless it was carried to New England. We must remember this when we consider the step-dancing tradition of the eastern provinces of North America.

Chapter 12 discussed the peculiarity of what appears as an Irish tradition of stepping, firmly established in Cape Breton, and how stepping in social dancing was obviously familiar in the west of Scotland and Lowlands at one time. Indeed. we shall have occasion to notice that hornpipe stepping was familiarly employed in Country Dances wherever these were enjoyed in the British Isles,[8] although it was regarded as vulgar in the more select assemblies.[9]

In every community in which stepping was enjoyed, there were occasions for the solo dancer to exhibit his prowess, as in the instances described above. Improvisation was a feature of every good exponent's performance, but most of the steps were pre-

---

[6] Ibid. (April 6, 1907), p. 269.
[7] Ibid. (May 11, 1907), pp. 378–79.
[8] John Gallini, *Treatise on the Art of Dancing.*
[9] See Thomas Wilson, *A Companion to the Ballroom*, p. 223.

conceived and were identified by names. A folklore collector in Lunenburg County, Nova Scotia, recorded, as recently as 1950, the following interesting conversation with a subject:

One time I was at my uncle's and there was a violin player there. He asked if anybody could dance. They pointed to me and said, "There's Reuben."
So he said, "How many steps can you dance?"
I said, "About fourteen or fifteen."
He said I couldn't, so I said, "I'll give you a different step every time and at the end of each a double back step."
I danced fifteen different steps and he laid a $5 gold piece down. I'd learned to dance when I was in America. If I saw a dancer I caught on. These are some of the steps: Double back shuffle, cross steps, shingle, strip the willow, dodging six, hunt the squirrel, American eight, sliding step, lift your leg, rustic dance and triple shuffle.[10]

Dodging Six and Hunt the Squirrel are the names of English Country Dances known in the seventeenth century and no doubt also in colonial America. Strip the Williow is a Scottish 9/8 reel.

Two of the set dances — or bouts as the Irish call them — of which the same collector heard at Mahone Bay, Nova Scotia, bore the names of well-known tunes, the Scottish "De'il Among the Tailors," and the eighteenth-century English "Fishermans [Fishar's?] Hornpipe."

The theatrical dancer was not likely to be content to limit himself to the close stepping of the traditional hornpipe dancer, and we must not be surprised, therefore, if the theatrical hornpipe grew to embrace the embellishing contributions of trained dancers. Sir John Gallini writes in 1772 in *Treatise on the Art of Dancing* that dancers from France and Italy studied hornpipe dancing in England and introduced it to continental audiences with great success. The American dancer, John Durang, tells us how he contrived to learn what he called "the correct stile of dancing a hornpipe in the French stile," from a French dancer Foussel who visited Durang's hometown, Philadelphia, with a touring company around 1780. The French, Durang remarks, seldom did "many real ground steps." In other words, the French dancers entertained a more balletic conception of the hornpipe, and doubtless so also did the ballet-trained native dancers of the British theatre.

Foussel introduced Durang to the curious step called "The Pigeon's Wing," but could not show him "the principle and the anatomy of the figure of the step." Nor, adds Durang, could any other dancer he ever met. He took great pride in the fact that he succeeded where others apparently failed, for he broke down the step and communicated it to his pupils.

The Sailors' Hornpipe of Scottish dancing schools today is clearly of the eighteenth-century theatrical character dance tradition and retains many of its features, as a comparison with the steps of the Sailors' Hornpipe performed by Durang can testify. It would be interesting to discover what the eighteenth-century London playbills have to tell us about this dance.

[10] Helen Creighton, *Folklore in Lunenburg County, Nova Scotia*, National Museum of Canada, bulletin 117, 1950, p. 73. (Lunenburg County is of Yankee-German foundation.)

These playbills testify to the popularity of hornpipe dancing. As many female dancers as male performed hornpipe dances, and it is evident that these dances were not always on a nautical theme, for the fact is mentioned when they are. The first of these occurs at Drury Lane, May, 1740, when Yates, who was frequently billed to perform hornpipes prior to this date, is suddenly billed to perform a "Hornpipe in the Character of a Jacky Tar." There is no mention then or later of anyone performing *the* or *a* Sailors' Hornpipe. It is always a hornpipe "in the character of a sailor" — or of a Jacky Tar.

6 A dancer in the character of Jack Tar, ca. 1817. Reproduced from Wilson, *Ballroom Guide.*

In the August following Yates's nautical hornpipe, at the rival Covent Garden there was billed "a Hornpipe by a Gentleman in the Character of a Sailor"! These instances occur about twenty years before the period which has been regarded as seeing the introduction of the class of tune now associated with the Sailors' Hornpipe.

The reason for the sudden interest in the naval theme is not difficult to find, particularly when we notice that the song "Rule Britannia" was given its first performance at this time (August, 1740) in a masque at the close of an entertainment given before Frederick, Prince of Wales, at Clivedon House. The words were by the Scottish poet James Thomson and the music by Thomas Arne. The occasion of this outburst of patriotic sentiment sprang from the imperialistic fervour of the British people on the occasion of the war with Spain in dispute of access to the South Americas — the so-called War of Jenkins' Ear.

Sailors' dances were familiar among numerous other character or comic dances on the eighteenth-century stage, but the practice of distinguishing hornpipes seems to suggest that these "Sailors' Dances" were not necessarily hornpipes.

At Covent Garden, April, 1755, there was a notice, "In the Sailor's Dance by desire will be introduced a Hornpipe by Poitier." Poitier, whose son and daughter also danced, was French. A very similar notice occurs eight years later at the same theatre: "A Sailors' Dance in which will be introduced a Hornpipe by Miss Twist, Miss Pitt and Miss Daw." These notices surely establish that a Sailors' Dance was not necessarily a hornpipe.

There is, however, one notice from Drury Lane, May 9 and 19, 1760, which is curious: "Hornpipe by a sailor from The Royal Sovereign." This was the year following the Year of Victories, the "glorious year" of Garrick's *Hearts of Oak*: "Hearts of Oak are our ships," he says, "Jolly tars are our men." The Royal Navy had restored its glory at Lagos, Quiberon Bay and Quebec, and doubtless the *Royal Sovereign* had returned to port for refitting. Britain's security and her growing empire were now seen to rest upon the "hearts of oak" and their "jolly tars." Here was a theme that was a growing part of British life, and one, as we know, which was to reverberate with trumpet sounds with Nelson and echo on to the mid-twentieth century.

Again, at Covent Garden, May, 1765, a notice reads, "A New Hornpipe by Miss Snow (in character of a sailor)," which was repeated once or twice, and then disappears from the bills. Meantime hornpipes — with no allusion to sailors — are billed with somewhat increasing regularity.

Miss Poitier's Hornpipe at this period certainly could not have been in the character of a sailor, as we may judge from the following intriguing comments published in the *Theatrical Review* of January 1, 1763, concerning a performance at Covent Garden in the presence of Their Majesties two nights before:

Would any person suppose she could have the confidence to appear with her bosom so scandalously bare, that to use the expression of a public writer, who took some moderate notice of the circumstance, the breasts hung flabbing over a pair of stays cut remarkably low, like a couple of empty bladders in an oil-shop. One thing the author of that letter has omitted, which, if possible, is still more gross; and that is, in the course of Miss Poitier's hornpipe one of her shoes happened to slip down at the heel, she lifted up her leg, and danced upon the other until she had drawn it up. This had she worn drawers, would have been more excusable; but unhappily, there was little occasion for standing in the pit to see that she was not provided with as much as a fig leaf. The Court turned instantly from the stage — the pit was astonished! and scarcely anything, but a disapproving murmur, was heard, from the most unthinking spectator in the twelvepenny gallery.

In all justice to Miss Poitier's name, it must be noted that she denied the impropriety. The press had exceptional freedom in those days.

It is surely significant that most of the new hornpipe tunes are named after dancers who figured on the late eighteenth-century and early nineteenth-century London stage, tunes such as "Fishar's Hornpipe," "Aldridge's Hornpipe," "Richar's Hornpipe," "Miss Baker's Hornpipe," "West's Hornpipe," and "Durang's Hornpipe." The inference is plain; these are not traditional hornpipe tunes in the pure sense, but a theatrical development of the traditional stream, likewise the dances performed to them.

Arnold Fishar and Robert Aldridge were particularly active in London in the period 1762–1775. Fishar was a ballet master at Covent Garden. Aldridge "a dancer of ease," as he was described in a doggerel poem in *Gentleman's Magazine*, January, 1772, appeared at both Covent Garden and Drury Lane, but was as much esteemed in his native Dublin as in London. Some idea of the tunes to which Aldridge danced can be found in Alexander McGlashan's *Collection of Scots Measures, Hornpipes, Jigs, Allemands etc.* (Edinburgh, 1781) where a number of items are marked "as danced by Aldridge." Aldridge would appear to have resided in Edinburgh at this date, and is noticed as founding the Boar Club with Schetky senior.[11]

John Durang, to whom we have already referred, has been styled the "first American dancer."[12] He was born in Lancaster, Pennsylvania, of German parents in 1768 and made his debut with Lewis Hallam's company in 1784. Hallam had just returned from England after an absence from the colonies encompassing the revolutionary years. Durang's first dance with Hallam was a Peasant's Dance and later, in another show, he danced a comedy number La Fricasse and a hornpipe.

Durang was of a theatrical family and perhaps this is how he came by his first dancing knowledge. It is apparent from his memoirs that he was substantially self-taught and picked up a great deal from observation of other dancers. Of interest to us here is his dancing on November 7, 1790, of "a Hornpipe on thirteen eggs Blindfolded, without breaking one,"[13] which recalls the fact that the tune "Fishar's Hornpipe" was also known as the "Egg Hornpipe." Another connection with Fishar occurred a few days later when Durang made his first appearance in The Wapping Landlady. Now, this ballet, or "Pantomimic Dance" as it was styled on Durang's playbills, was first choreographed by Arnold Fishar and was first performed at Covent Garden, April 27, 1767, at a benefit night for Fishar and the principal danseuse, Sga Manesiere. Two of Fishar's young pupils performed prior to the main ballet, and the program was billed to conclude with Fishar and Manesiere dancing a "Double Hornpipe." It is evident from these advertisements that the term "double" means in this case a hornpipe for two dancers.

The Wapping Landlady was a very popular comic ballet on the London stage, being presented at frequent intervals over a period of years. Occasionally something novel was introduced to it, depending, one supposes, on the dancing skills available. In the 1770s for instance, "a New Hornpipe by Six Principal Dancers" was introduced, and a competitive ballet called The Sailors Revels on a similar theme was staged at Drury Lane at the same time. The Wapping Landlady, it should be explained, was on the theme of Jack Tar ashore — "Come ashore Jolly Tar" indeed! The characters were described as Jack (in distress), the Landlady, A Milk Woman, (or Orange Woman or Nosegay Woman), supported by sailors and sundry women. The theme is Jack in trouble ashore, particularly with his landlady. It was doubtless a topical situation with the conclusion of the Seven Years War.

Again, we do not know how Durang came by this ballet, for he was never in England. Perhaps William Francis, a Dutchman who settled in Philadelphia in 1772 and who was noted for specializing in rustic and comic ballets after his return from a visit to England (1787–93), is the source. Certainly, Durang danced in Francis's ballets,

[11] Robert Chambers, *Traditions of Edinburgh*.

[12] Lillian Moore, *John Durang, The First American Dancer*, Chronicles of the American Dance, ed. Paul Magriel (New York, 1948).

[13] This was known as the Egg Dance. The dancer stepped in and about the eggs.

which included such items as "Scots Pastoral Dance — The Caledonian Frolic" (ca. 1795), and went into a teaching partnership with him (ca. 1794–1806).

In 1796, Durang was engaged by John B. Ricketts, a Scots immigrant, to direct the pantomimes at the circus Ricketts had established in Philadelphia some six years before. Durang remained in this capacity until the enterprise was destroyed by fire on December 17, 1799.

Another theatre proprietor in Philadelphia at that time who interests us was Alexander Reinagle whose father and family established themselves as professional musicians in Edinburgh in the 1770s. Reinagle was born in England, raised in Edinburgh, and moved to America in 1786. He is remembered as the founder and conductor of the Philadelphia City concerts.

Durang has a special claim on our attention through his identification with the Sailors' Hornpipe. This became his recognized forte, even when the zenith of his dancing days was behind him. Can we doubt that this dance was prominent in The Wapping Landlady? It is clear from Durang's memoirs that some city dancing masters (he specifically mentions one in Boston) were making a specialty of a hornpipe in the character of a young sailor not yet out of his teens. Certain it is, however, that the Sailors' Hornpipe became synonymous with the term "hornpipe" in the nineteenth century, and the "College Hornpipe," to which it was predominantly performed, the musical motif associated with sailors in the popular mind. Only Durang, however, of the early performers of this dance, has left any identifiable record of his steps. This was published by his son Charles who followed his father as dancer and actor:

PAS DE MATELOT

A Sailor Hornpipe Old Style

1. Glissade round (first part of tune)
2. Double shuffle down, do
3. Heel and toe back, finish with back shuffle
4. Cut & buckle down, finish the shuffle
5. Side shuffle right and left, finishing with beats
6. Pigeon wing going round
7. Heel and toe haul in back
8. Steady toes down
9. Changes back, finish with back shuffle and beats
10. Wave step down
11. Heel and toe shuffle obliquely back
12. Whirligig, with beats down
13. Sissone and entrechats back
14. Running forward on the heels
15. Double Scotch step, with a heel Brand in Plase (*sic*)
16. Single Scotch step back
17. Parried toes round, or feet *in* and *out*
18. The Cooper shuffle right and left back
19. Grasshopper step down
20. *Terre-a-terre* (*sic*) or beating on toes back
21. Jockey crotch down

22. Traverse round, with hornpipe glissade
    Bow and Finish[14]

Each step takes up one strain of the tune. There are a variety of other shuffles, but the ones quoted in Durang's hornpipe are the principal steps with their original names.

The following extract was published by Elias Howe, a Boston dancing master, in 1858 in his *Complete Ball-Room Handbook* as the steps of Sailors' Hornpipe and "music — Durang's Hornpipe." It expands upon Durang's hornpipe, from which it is obviously derived:

Double shuffle and gliding step round — heel and toe back, finish with back shuffle — double shuffle and gliding step round – slide shuffle right and left, finishing with beats — repeat first change — pigeon wing going round — repeat first change — rocking step forward on the toes — repeat first change — wave step down — repeat first change — changes back, finish with back shuffle and beats — repeat first change — wave step down — repeat — heel and toe shuffle obliquely back — repeat &c — whirligig, with beats down – repeat &c — sissone and entrechats back — repeat &c — double scotch step, with a heel brand in place — repeat &c — single scotch step, back — repeat &c — parried toes round, on toes in and out — repeat &c — cooper shuffle right and left back — repeat &c — grasshopper step down — repeat &c — beat on the toes back — repeat &c — Jockey crotch step down — repeat &c — traverse step round, with hornpipe gliding step, bow and finish.

The tune "Durang's Hornpipe," still in the repertoire of exponents of this class of music, was composed in 1785 by Hoffmaster, a talented German musician and prominent member of New York's artistic circles, who had the striking peculiarity of being but three feet tall.

A study of the steps of Durang's Sailors' Hornpipe reveals it to be the dance we would recognize today, but the absence of nautical motifs is puzzling. Apart from the instructions "Heel and toe haul in back" and possibly "Wave step down," there are no allusions to the characteristic actions of the sailors' occupation. Where are "climbing the rigging," "rowing ashore," "land ahoy!," "pay day," "hauling in the line"? They may be there, but if they are, it is not easy to identify them.

I think we can take it that the nautical motifs were introduced in varying degree by various dancers. One would distinguish his specific hornpipe as The Binnacle Hornpipe, another as Jacky Tar, and give his own slant to the basic hornpipe technique. What we see today is the natural selection of this wide range of steps, not a traditional dance of sailors.

The affinity with the Scottish high dances is plain and the relationship of both the Binnacle Hornpipe and Jacky Tar to the hornpipe taught by Johnny McGill in 1755 is also plain. Senex, the notable Glasgow reminiscer, recalls dancing "Jacky Tar" in Campbell's dance classes (ca. 1790) and, in his *Old Glasgow and its Environs* (Glasgow, 1864), he describes his appearing at a dancing school ball in the Tontine Assembly Hall "as 'a Jacky Tar Figurant,' dressed in the full costume of a sailor, with jacket and trousers, and a cudgel under my arm — all according to the dancing-school fashion of the time. Jacky Tar, with dress in character, was then a favourite dance for boys at

---

14 Charles Durang, *The Ballroom bijou and art of Dancing* (Philadelphia, 1855).

the balls of Dick, Campbell, Fraser, and Sellars" (p. 302). The "Jacky Tar" hornpipe has been in the repertoire of Highland dancers ever since.

There remains, however, the suspicion that there may have been some kind of nautical step dance or jig which emanated from the seafaring community and became familiar among sailors. But it is altogether more likely that sailors simply resorted to the performance of the landlubbers' step dances for exercise and recreation on a ship becalmed or in a long spell of fine weather. What more natural than the familiar jig or hornpipe to fiddle or pipe in the confines of the main deck? Captain Cook is said to have encouraged this recreation on his long voyages in the 1770s.[15] It is perplexing that there is practically no reference to the practice in the naval or seafaring journals and memoirs of the period. The only reference I have so far encountered is in the diary of a young Scottish lady, Janet Schaw, who describes the activities of her ship during a spell of fine weather near the Azores on a voyage to the West Indies in 1774: "The effect of this fine weather appears in every creature . . . even our Emigrants seem in a great measure to have forgot their sufferings . . . and if we had anything to eat, I really think our present situation is most delightful. We play at cards and backgammon on deck; the sailors dance hornpipes and jigs from morning to night. . . ."[16]

There is no reason to believe that the sailors danced hornpipes or jigs that were any different from those they knew ashore or that the fiddler who accompanied them did not play the music of the country fiddler. Undoubtedly, many sailors became well practised in the hornpipe step dance, and G. Yates, a noted London dancing master, goes so far as to write in *The Ball* in 1829 that few English seamen were to be found who were not acquainted with the hornpipe, some indeed, "dancing it in perfection" (p. 175). Schoolboys then destined for a naval career, he tells us, generally made a point of learning the hornpipe, and it appears to have been included in the training of naval cadets in the nineteenth century. The tradition grew in the Royal Navy rather than in the merchant marine. One merchant seaman, whose sailing ship career embraced the last years of sail, writes that he never saw a hornpipe performed under the Red Ensign.[17]

There is an alleged reference[18] by Pepys to learning the tune of the "Seaman's Dance" which I have so far failed to locate. A tune of this name, however, is in the Blaikie manuscript, 1692. There is some suggestion of a sailors' jig or "Jig of the Ship" said to be a tune of the seventeenth century, which, one is ready to accept, may have been the tune of the sailors' jig performed at Drury Lane on June 30, 1712, "by a gentleman for his diversion" — possibly the same gentleman who performed a hornpipe at the same theatre a year later, and to whom we have already alluded.

Purcell, however, introduces a "Sailors' Dance" to his *Dido and Aeneas* (1688) which is a jaunty tune in common time to a rhythm which does bear a resemblance to the "Jacky Tar" style of hornpipe. But Purcell does not call it a hornpipe nor a jig. Certainly, Purcell had written "Scotch Tunes" which were in imitation of the Scottish Measure, and it is probable that Arne was led to compose his new hornpipes under

---

[15] Blasis, *The Art of Dancing*, p. 26.

[16] Andrews, ed., *The Journal of a Lady of Quality, in 1774–1776* (New Haven, Conn.: Yale University Press, 1923), p. 68.

[17] Frank Hubert Shaw, *White Sails and Spindrift* (New York, 1947), p. 34.

[18] Correspondent to the *Mariner's Mirror*, vol. 7 (1921), p. 352.

the inspiration of some of these tunes by Purcell, for Arne was very familiar with Purcell's music. However, this remains conjecture.

If one goes back to Shakespeare, one may or may not wish to attach significance to the skipper in *The Tempest* making a "caper" at one point in the play; or to the appearance of "twelve skippers in red cappes, with short cassocks and long sloppes, wide at the knees of white canvas striped with crimson, white gloves and pomps and red stockings to dance a brave and lively dance, shouting and triumphing after the manner of the sea," a scene introduced by Campion into one of his masques around this same period.[19] I am inclined to accept the latter as no more than a ballet of roistering skippers.

The word "hornpipe" is English, and as well as being the name of a species of dance, it is the name of a particular style of rural shepherd's reed pipe which in the Celtic tongue is called the *piobcorn*. In the Scottish Lowland tongue it was called the *stoc'n horn*. There must be some significance to the fact that the Celtic-speaking peoples do not use their word piobcorn for the dance or its music. The Irish use the English word "hornpipe" for this purpose. The obvious conclusion is that the English were the first to use hornpipe of dance and music, and the word has been adopted by the Gaelic-speaking people to describe their own dances of the same style.

The earliest notices of the hornpipe in English literature allude to it as a round.[20] An English traveller in 1609 likens the dancing of American Indians to "our Darbyshire Hornpipe, as man first and then a woman, and so through them all, hanging all in a round."[21] And Richard Barnfield's *Shepherds Content* (1594) shows how a shepherd

> Leads his Wench a Country Horn-pipe Round
> About a May-pole on a Holy-day.

Spenser paints a delightful picture in his *Shepherd's Calendar* (May):

> Before them yode a lustie tabrere,
> That to the many a horn-pype playd,
> Whereto they dancen eche one with his mayd.
> To see those folks make such jovysaunce,
> Made my heart after the pype to daunce.

The English counties conspicuously associated with the word "hornpipe" in the sixteenth and seventeenth centuries were Derbyshire, Nottinghamshire, and Lancashire.

An English ballad, probably of the late sixteenth century, describes a hornpipe at a wedding, the like of which was never seen "in all the northe lande." All are urged to dance for company, and the first to "break the stroke" must pay the piper a penny:

> Halfe torne, Jone, haffe now Jocke
> Well dansyd, be sent Denny.

[19] C. I. Elton, *William Shakespeare, His Family and Friends*, ed. A. Hamilton Thompson (New York, 1904), p. 402.
[20] See William Chappell, *Popular Music of the Olden Time*, vol. 2, p. 545.
[21] See *Antiquary*, vol. 12, p. 252.

In with fut, Robsone, owt with foot, Byllinge.
Torne rownde Robyne, keep trace Wylkyne,
Make churchye pege behynde.   [peek]
Set fut to fut a pas quod Pylkyne   [pace]
Abowghte with howghe let us wynde.   [hey]
Kepe in Sandar, holde owt Syme,
Nowe Gaff hear gome abowt me mat   [Matt]
Niccoll well dansyde and tryme.
A gambold, quod Jocky, stand asyde,
Let ilk man play his parte,
Mak rom my mastars, stand mor wyde,
I pray youe with all my harte.[22]

A dance of men indeed; continuous, winding, sustained, hearty. In the sixteenth-century play *James IV*, by Robert Greene, Slipper, after dancing with some others says: "Nay, but my friends, one hornpipe further! a refluence backe, and two doubles forward! What! not one crossepoint against Sundayes?" (act iv, scene iv). This is one of the only allusions to the technique of the dance that we have from this early period. Remember, of course, if Playford is any guide, these English hornpipes were of the triple-time variety.

A quotation from a passage published in 1609 is referred to by William Chappell in his *Popular Music of the Olden Times* in which the peculiar dancing or musical attributes of the various English counties are set forth: "The courts of Kings for stately Measures; the city for light heels and nimble footing; the country for shuffling dances, Western men for gambols; Middlesex men for tricks above ground, Essex men for the Hay, Lancashire for Hornpipes, Worcestershire for bagpipes, but Herefordshire for a Morris dance, puts down not only all Kent, but very near (if one had line enough to measure it) three-quarters of Christendom."

In Westmorland, Anne Gilchrist tells us, hornpipes were danced both solo and in rows in the nineteenth century and had many special steps known by curious names. The itinerant dancing master would teach each pupil a special step which remained the exclusive property of that pupil and was exhibited during the dance at the country assembly when all the dancers advanced down the room side by side in a row.[23]

By the 1680s, Isaacs and Beveridge, the court dancing masters, started to devise long-wise country dances of a distinctive kind to triple-time hornpipe tunes. These were called maggots, from the Italian *maggioletta*, meaning a plaything, and were often named in honour of someone. They became quite a vogue, even passing to France, and if Rameau is any guide, exhibited more boisterousness and crudity than dancing finesse. We will have occasion to comment on this when we come to discuss the Country Dance (see chaps. 19 and 20). The triple-time hornpipe Country Dance did not survive long into the eighteenth century.

The Irish hop-jig rhythm (in 9/8) which came to our attention in our discussion of the jig seems to fall between the triple-time hornpipe and the jig. It has a similar bob-wheel rhythm, and it is satisfying to notice that a tune of this kind (although

---

[22] "Our Jockye sale have our Jenny," *Songs and Ballads*, ed. Wright, Roxburgh Club, pp. 123–24.
[23] Anne G. Gilchrist, "Old Fiddlers' Tune Books of the Georgian Period," *JEFDSS*, vol. 4 (1940), p. 19.

marked 9/4) is to be found in Playford's *Apollo's Banquet* described as a "hornpipe-jig." A very appropriate classification, one thinks. The syncopation of the hornpipe is missing from the 9/8 jig; only the bob-wheel rhythm is shared.

The hornpipe, then, appears as a "country round" and a solo step dance. The question arises: Do both uses of the word come from the musical instrument? The herd-boys and shepherds of the British Isles in the Middle Ages used the hornpipe, but it must find its origins in a greater antiquity. It is essentially the keyboard, or chanter, of the bagpipe. If the horn-piper danced, he would be constrained to beatings of the feet, and there would be some air or airs more suitable for this than others. A characteristic dance tune could well have emerged in a pastoral region of the country. This would exclude most of Scotland, and the facts do not refute this if it is the triple-time air we are referring to.

However, another origin of the use of the word "hornpipe" in dance has been propounded. It is suggested that the word comes from a ritual harvest dance called Herne Pipe, herne being the god of harvest, "gerne" or "grain" being other forms of the word. W. G. Raffé in his *Dictionary of the Dance* styles this dance as a pre-Saxon ritual performed to pipe and tabor and employing "the long-remembered tummy-patting motions signifying delight after a good meal."[24] His authority for this is not quoted, nor have I discovered it. He states, however, that some of the Cotton manuscripts carry pen-pictures of dancers performing the "Herne-Piping."

Now, anything pre-Saxon in the British Isles is most likely to be Celtic, particularly in England. "Herne" is a Germanic word. Certainly the Celtic root for corn is *gran*, Latin, *granum*, while that for horn is *corn*, Latin, *cornu*. The etymology of the Gaelic word *piobcorn* is clearly to be sought in horn and not in grain. Whether horn should be tied to the horn of plenty, the cornucopia, frequently attributed to local deities of abundance, is anybody's guess. The fact is that it is used of bony projections from the head of goats, cows, sheep, and other animals, and that these have been used as musical instruments called horns or, with a reed, what is called in the *Complaynt* "ane gait horn and ane reed." Cow-horns are certainly referred to by several Scots writers in the Middle Ages.

How the dancers in the Cotton manuscripts can be said to be performing the "Herne-Piping" is not evident. In any case the manuscripts are Saxon and do not predate the eighth century.

The evidence does not support the "Herne-Piping" theory, much as I would like to accept it.

It is perhaps significant that we can quote evidence, as above, that the Derbyshire Hornpipe was a social round and that Steele in *The Tatler* (no. 106, 1709) can have Florinda dancing "the Derbyshire Hornpipe in the presence of several friends." The suggestion here is that the two forms, communal and solo, coexisted.

We have much the same today. Scottish Country Dances are performed to music in the traditional idioms which is otherwise related to solo dances, of which a few are hornpipes, although among solo dances, only that "in the character of a sailor" carries the word "hornpipe" into its name.

---

[24] W. G. Raffé, *Dictionary of the Dance* (New York [1965]).

15 / Folk Dances and Reels of the Highlands and Isles

Boswell in Skye – nineteenth-century puritanism – recording of surviving memory of folk dances of the Isles and Highland emigrants – weaving and pantomimic dances – West Highland social reels – Shetland and Orkney Reels – cudgel dance – ritualistic remnants and affinities with Ireland, Isle of Man – Norse influence

In October, 1773, Boswell and Johnson were entertained at Armadale in Skye and on a Saturday evening, Boswell tells us, "the company danced as usual. We performed with much activity, a dance which I suppose the emigration from Skye has occasioned. They call it 'America.' Each of the couples after the common involutions and evolutions, successively whirls round in a circle, till all are in motion; and the dance seems intended to show how emigration catches, till a whole neighbourhood is set afloat. . . . We danced to-night to the musick of the bagpipe, which made us beat the ground with prodigious force."[1]

Here is a recorded instance of the invention of a social dance in the Western Isles inspired by a topical event. We can hardly accept that this was a unique occurrence. One wonders what Boswell meant by the "common involutions and evolutions"; doubtless these terms included reeling. One imagines that in the "whirling" of which he speaks, the couples would hold hands, facing each other, and employ a pivot step. The Waltz or Polka or Schottische were yet a long way off, and any closer proximity of the couples would surely have been a matter of remark to Boswell.

Between these days and the twentieth century, the old way of life and economy of the Highlands collapsed. The suffering and hardship were often aggravated by a deliberate policy of disruption and the inhumanity of callous land superiors and agents. The oppressive poverty and insecurity fostered a morbid religious fervour and an intense, if ambiguous, puritanism which swept through the affected regions of the West Highlands and Western Islands, just as the nonconformist religious revival took root about the same period in the black miseries of the industrial towns.

[1] James Boswell, *Journal of a Tour to the Hebrides*, Saturday, October 2. Ed. F. A. Pottle and Charles H. Bennett, Toronto, 1936.

The severity of the puritanism which swept through the West Highlands was un-
believable in a society so devoted to music and poetry, and took its direction from the
most uncompromising branch or splinter of the Church of Scotland in the nineteenth
century. Alexander Carmichael in *Carmina Gadelica* (vol. 1) describes the reaction of
one old woman in the "Lews":

The good men and the good ministers who arose did away with the songs and the stories, the
music and the dancing, the sports and the games that were perverting the minds and ruin-
ing the souls of the people. . . . If there was a foolish man here and there who demurred, the
good ministers and the good elders themselves broke and burnt their instruments, saying:
"Better is the small fire that warms on the little day of peace than the big fire that burns on
the great day of wrath."

These were the days of foolish doings and of foolish people. . . . In my young days there
was hardly a house in Ness in which there was not one or two or three who could play the
pipe or the fiddle or the trump. And I have heard it said that there were men, and women
too, who could play things they called harps, and lyres, and bellow-pipes, but I do not know
what these things were. [P. 26]

Many emigrants took this puritan zeal with them to Canada — to Nova Scotia, Upper
Canada, and Manitoba, where the privations of pioneer life put a premium on the
philosophy of unremitting "useful" work and the introspection encouraged by Calvinistic precepts. It is easy to exaggerate this attitude and its regressive influence on the
folk music, dancing, and lore of the Gaels at home and abroad — whatever it did for
science and philosophy — for the most outrageous examples of suppression are the
most widely publicized; but there is no doubt that it has left some legacy of loss in the
Protestant communities.

The nineteenth-century Catholic communities danced and sang with less feelings of
guilt on the whole, although in Cape Breton at least one instance is reported of the
eight-handed reel's being proscribed by priests and fiddles being destroyed.[2] Nevertheless, it is evident that in the Hebrides the Catholic islands have been the most fruitful
sources for collectors of the folk arts of the Gael.

The collecting and recording of the traditional dances from the past still remembered by an ever-decreasing number of elderly Gaels in the Scottish western seaboard
have been pursued by but a handful of enthusiasts only very recently. The Fletts and
Frank Rhodes have published their discoveries, an immensely valuable contribution;
otherwise, we must lean on sundry and desultory descriptions — most often merely
titles — or reconstructions of dances which have passed out of ken.

Many of these dances belong to particular localities, such as The Eight Men of
Moidart from Moidart, An Dannsa Mor from Eigg, and Long Bharrach from Barra.
Other dances have had a wider currency, such as the circular reel and, of course, as we
have seen, the Cushion Dance, which varies only slightly in form and name from
place to place. Still other dances have moved from the Hebridean or Shetland fringe
into the mainland, such as the Foula Reel and Strip the Willow.

The Foula Reel, a version of the Norwegian or Scandinavian Country Dance known
in the late nineteenth-century ballrooms, was a substantial modification of the old

---

[2] F. Rhodes. See J. F. and T. M. Flett, *Traditional Dancing in Scotland*, p. 271.

Swedish weaving dance called Vava Vadmal.[3] This genre of Norse weaving dance has probably been known wherever the Vikings settled and was certainly familiar in the Hebrides, Shetland, and Orkney. Through the Royal Scottish Country Dance Society, Mary Isdale MacNab published a version of the Vava Vadmal called Hebridean Weaving Lilt which, she tells us, was collected from a Canadian whose Norwegian ancestors had settled in Iona. Unfortunately, Mrs. MacNab did not publish the raw material from which she fashioned her many attractive re-creations; it is to be hoped that this will be made available some day.

The Hebridean Weaving Lilt is much closer to the Vava Vadmal than is the Foula Reel, with accented running steps pounding the rhythm, and alternating under and over movements through arched arms simulating the action of the loom. As published, it is set to a schottische-type strathspey tune, although this was not the tune, according to Thurston, to which it was danced in Canada, nor would we expect it to be the original rhythm of the dance. In David Anderson's *Universal Ballroom Guide*, the Foula Reel is in 6/8 and the Scandinavian ballroom version to "any mazurka 3/8 tune."

A similar corruption has occurred with Strip the Willow, a dance of the weaving genre, with accented running steps to 9/8 rhythm. The delightful tune "Drops of Brandy" is often associated with it, and it is under that name that the dance is known in England, although it is performed there to "schottische" tunes.[4] Today, Strip the Willow can be encountered danced to marches or to reels with Country Dance steps, or more often with unbridled abandon.

The weaving dance brings us to other group folk dances of a pantomimic or dramatic variety which, at one time, were a concomitant of social gatherings or balls in the Hebrides and West Highlands. Dances of this kind were known also in Ireland and in the Isle of Man within the past century, and undoubtedly they are a remnant of the primitive ages of mankind. They are the earliest of the social dance forms known to man. Alongside the pantomimic group dances, there were the solo dances of a dramatic kind which we shall discuss presently. Suffice it to say here that references to both are encountered occasionally in nineteenth-century descriptions of social life in the Highlands and that the most comprehensive list of these to date is that compiled by D. G. MacLennan in *Traditional and Highland Scottish Dances*. He refers to them as "now forgotten" and is able to describe only a few. He actually saw some performed, however, but made no effort to record them.

Carmichael refers to five of these pantomimic dances in his *Carmina Gadelica*: Cath nan Coileach (The Combat of the Cocks); Turraban nan Tunnag (Waddling of the Ducks); Ruidhleadh nan Coileach Dubha (Reeling of the Black Cocks); Cath nan Curaidh (Contest of the Warriors); and Cailleach an Dudain (Carlin of the Mill Dust). The last named is the most frequently mentioned in other works, but it is not a social dance. The first three or four are group dances, and the Fletts were fortunate enough to find, around 1951, old people who recalled some of them from their youth. According to an old piper, Neil MacNeil of Barra who was taught The Combat of the Cocks and The Reeling of the Black Cocks by one "Ronald-the dancing-master," these

---

[3] Patrick Shuldham-Shaw, "Folk Music and Dance in Shetland," *JEFDSS*, vol. 5, (1946–48).

[4] Hugh A. Thurston, *Scotland's Dances*, p. 14.

dances at that time had not been danced for sixty years on the island, although prior to this they had been very popular.

The Combat of the Cocks is a jig for two couples, performed in the formation of a wheel. First, all four set on the spot, forming four hands across for sixteen bars, then travel for sixteen bars in a clockwise direction with a kind of hop-step-step. The tempo quickens, and all set with a backstep for sixteen bars. Then, using a pivot step, they spin in a clockwise direction. This sequence is repeated as often as desired.

The Reel of the Black Cocks as collected by the Fletts was also for two couples who begin by facing each other, the men on their partners' left. One couple goes down on one knee, while the other couple sets to them with "any Reel steps" for eight bars, and so on as often as desired. The words of the song are roughly: "Reeled the black cocks, and danced the ducks / Reeled the black cocks, on the bank up there." The kneeling couple apparently represents the ducks, and in one version danced by children two girls "cooried" or crouched on their hunkers, with their hands held to represent beaks, and imitated ducks, while two boys reeled with them continuously with no setting.

Another dance of the same name was collected by Rhodes in South Uist. This was very similar to that version of the Cape Breton four-handed reel in which the partners and "opposites" swung with a Waltz hold.[5]

Turraban nam Tunnag (Waddling of the Ducks) was a dance or game in which the dancers assumed a hunkered posture and proceeded in file or in a circle, or even cut a reel figure, in imitation of the manner of ducks. Young and old both at one time joined in this dance. It testifies to the agility of the islanders, for the posture is a tiring one. The hands were placed under the thighs, and the waddling would continue sometimes for as long as half an hour. One is reminded of Cuttymun and Treeladle, familiar in the Lowlands at one time.

We owe the precision of some of these details to the Fletts, who obtained descriptions in Benbecula and Eigg, but were unable to ascertain the tune.[6] R. C. MacLagan also refers to this dance as known in Argyll.[7]

A dance, Dannsadh nan boc or Dance of the Bucks (he-goats) was of a similar kind and performed by three men "who reel fantastically, leap, bound, and bleat as he-goats do; and stopping on all fours, they jump alternately over each other, causing by this means much merriment."[8] Another description of this dance tells us that "at Harvest home in some parts of Skye, the crofter, instead of sending a sheaf from his own field, went into his neighbour's field, where there was still standing corn, and made up a fanciful stook, which was called *Gobhar-bacach*, 'the lame goat'; and this was repeated by each crofter in succession until all had finished cutting. Among the ceremonies associated with the sheaf was the *Dannhsadh-nam-boc*, dance of the goats...."[9]

By no means all Hebridean social dances are of this ancient variety; some indeed have no pantomimic or dramatic overtones and are more in the nature of singing games. Examples of dances of this kind are Coille Bharrach (The Barra Wood) and The Pin Reel described by the Fletts.[10]

---

[5] Rhodes. See Flett, *Traditional Dancing in Scotland*, p. 271.
[6] J. F. and T. M. Flett, "Some Hebridean Folk Dances," *JEFDSS*, vol. 7, no. 2 (1953).
[7] R. C. MacLagan, *The Games and Diversions of Argyleshire*, p. 103.
[8] Alexander Campbell, notes to *The Grampians Desolate*, p. 264.
[9] A. R. Forbes, *Gaelic Names of beasts (Mammalia), birds, fishes etc.* (Edinburgh, 1905).
[10] Flett, "Some Hebridean Folk Dances."

Coille Bharrach begins with any number of people holding hands and dancing round in a ring, leaving one man in the centre who selects first one lady then another to link arms with him; then another man links up with these to complete a ring of four. The four then release arms and dance a reel of four while the encircling ring dances round them, after which they rejoin the outer circle, while another man jumps in to repeat the dance.

The Pin Reel is similar. In this, any number of couples form the ring, dancing round with a skip step, while one odd lady, the "pin," occupies the centre. When the music stops, the ladies step into the circle and form an inner ring; then, when the music stops again, all rush for partners and a new "odd" lady is left as the pin. After the ladies endure a run of this, the dance is repeated with the men in the inner ring and a man as pin. The Pin Reel seems to have been one of those dances which were more widely diffused,[11] and is possibly one of the variety of round reels which are said to be among the progenitors of the Eightsome Reel. In fact, both Coille Bharrach and the Pin Reel bear similarity to parts of the modern Eightsome Reel.

Another dance, An Dannsa Mor, is described by MacLennan, who saw it twice in 1911 on the Island of Eigg, as a kind of representation of the trial of a girl accused of fraternizing with one of Cumberland's soldiers. A ring of eight men dance round a solitary girl with a simple step-hop movement, stopping periodically to fire questions at her. This, however, is an abbreviated version of the dance of that name which Flett tells us is still performed on Eigg and which is reputed to have originated in Skye.[12]

In this case, any number of men participate (some say twelve) and form a ring with arms extended at shoulder level. Two of the men diametrically opposite each other move into the ring where, with elbows bent, they jauntily walk backwards and forwards on the balls of the feet in time to the music, eyeing each other the while, and, as they do so, they sing a verse each in succession. Meanwhile, the ring remains still with spaces reserved to receive the singers when they return to the circle for the chorus. During the chorus, the dancers hop round on the left foot with their right legs extended toward the centre of the circle, their feet held about eighteen inches from the ground. There are eight lines to the chorus and four hops to each line, and the second half of the chorus is sung at a faster tempo than the first. The singers then repeat the performance with the next two verses and so on. In what may be called the second part of the dance, the song concerns "the miller's daughter," and in this, the first singer acts the part, covering his eyes and shaking from side to side while the other walks about quietly, repeating the refrain "said the daughter of the miller" after each line. The sense of the lines is: "Alas, alas, alas, / Alas, alas, alas, / What harm have I done? / I lay with a soldier, / Has not many a girl done it?" This obviously is the part of the dance noted by MacLennan. Its persistent rhythm is suggestive of a mill wheel.

There is evidence that the An Dannsa Mor has been subject to variations in performance over the years and possibly also to the usual additions and deletions to which all folk dances are subject in course of time.

A dance for three, Fidhan Gunn (Weave the Gown) of which no trace has been

---

[11] Traced in Eigg, Uist, Barra, Shetland. Cf. Shuldham-Shaw, "Folk Music and Dance in Shetland," p. 76; and Flett, "Some Hebridean Folk Dances," p. 126. A version of The Nine Pins is given in David Anderson, *Ballroom Guide*.

[12] For full details of this interesting dance and its music, see Flett, "Some Hebridean Folk Dances."

found, was mentioned by Alexander Campbell in the notes to *The Grampians Desolate*. He tells us that this was a common Threesome Reel, but with this difference: the dancers all faced in the same direction throughout the dance!

In Shetland and Orkney, where Norse influence is indisputably paramount, one is struck by the similarity of some of the older dances, as these are described for us by repute, to those we have just discussed. Marian MacNeill in *The Silver Bough* (vol. 3) depicts the "Trow Dance" as "very ungainly and laughter-provoking," the "Selkie's (Seal's) Dance" as "more of a game than a dance," and the "Merry Man's Reel" as "quite a pretty one — evidently inspired by a poet's vision of the Aurora Borealis" (p. 134). The trows, incidentally, are the Norse trolls who were believed to enjoy dancing. These dances have not been collected.

What are called the Shetland Reels employ the same system of alternating setting and travelling as those of the mainland. The best known forms were those for three couples, still to be encountered at weddings and the like. They are essentially adaptations of the Threesome Reel in which couples act as units and begin from a set as for a longwise Country Dance. In one version, the middle couple is "improper." Each lady is followed by her partner, and the reel begins with the first lady casting down and the second dancing up and the third joining in to cut a reel of three. All finish in their original places and set to partners, usually with the back step ending with three quick stamps.

Other reels were for two and for four couples, but are not now so well known. The setting steps were a form of back step, pas de basque, side steps, shuffles, stamps and the like.[13] Patrick Shuldham-Shaw opined that the dance tunes of Shetland are largely from the mainland and Ireland, but were played in a peculiar Shetland style.[14] There is, however, a considerable corpus of native Shetland Reel tunes.

Another class of Shetland Reel, the Auld Reel, recollected in such names as the Auld Reel from Whalsay and the Auld (or Muckle) Reel o' Finnigarth have been familiar for some time only as the names of tunes. They were last danced around the first decade of the present century. Their common characteristic was the absence of setting, and, as in the three-couple reel, the couples danced as units. Combinations of the Auld Reel and the Shetland Reel of Three are remembered, a union reminiscent of the Eightsome and Foursome Reels for instance.[15]

Surprisingly enough, the dances of Orkney, as they have been collected, show more affinity with the mainland dances than with those of Shetland. A Sixsome Reel was very popular, and the Axum Reel is known to country dancers through the version published by the RSCDS (bk. 18). Flett has published what he claims to be the correct version.[16]

Whether we look to the Hebrides, Shetland, Orkney, Ireland, or the Isle of Man, we detect traces of a strain of group dances with pantomimic and ritualistic overtones and another strain of social dances with no such overtones, but with special steps and figures and called reels or jigs.

There is some record of stick and cudgel dances which are of the Pyrrhic rather than

---

[13] Flett, *Traditional Dancing in Scotland*, pp. 199–229.
[14] Shuldham-Shaw, "Folk Music and Dance in Shetland."
[15] Flett, *Traditional Dancing in Scotland*, p. 222.
[16] Ibid., pp. 187–98.

the ritualistic order. The English Cotswold Morris is of this kind; there is no hilt-and-point formation, but there is a striking of sticks which marks it as a Pyrrhic dance. A Manx dance, Mylecharane's March, however, involves six dancers, each carrying two thick sticks, who execute quick, intricate figures with difficult steps, with two additional characters in attendance — a "fiddler" and a white "mare." The fiddler is "killed" and "resurrected" in the manner of the "sacrifice" in sword dances. This is very different from the Irish Droghedy's March from county Wexford described in 1812 by Patrick Kennedy in *On the Banks of the Boro*:

The tune called Droghedy's March was occasionally danced to among the hornpipes, by a performer furnished with a short cudgel in each hand, which he brandished and clashed in harmony with the tune. But we had the good fortune to see it performed in a complete fashion on the borders of the barony of Bargy, in the old manor-house of Coolcul, whose young men, joined by the stout servants and labourers on the farms, were well able, in country parlance, to clear a fair. Among these the present chronicler was initiated into the mysteries of mumming, and was taught to bear his part in that relic of the Pyrrhic or Druidic dance, "Droghedy's March." We practised it in one of the large parlours, and this was the style of its execution: Six men or boys stood in line, at reasonable distances apart, and six others stood opposite them, all armed as described. When the music began, feet, and arms, and sticks commenced to keep time. Each dancer, swaying his body to the right and left, described an upright figure of 8 with his fists, both of them following the same direction, the ends of the sticks forming the same figure, of course. In these movements no noise was made, but at certain bars the arms moved rapidly up and down, the upper and lower halves of the right-hand stick striking the lower half of the left-hand stick in the descent of the right arm, and the upper half of it in the ascent, and *vice versa*. At the proper point of the march each man commenced a kind of fencing with his *vis-a-vis*, and the clangs of the cudgels coincided with the beats of the music and the movements of the feet. Then commenced the involutions, evolutions, interlacings and unwindings, every one striking at the person with whom the movement brought him face to face, and the sounds of the sticks supplying the hoochings in the reels. . . . The steps, which we have forgotten, could not have been difficult, for *we* mastered them. . . . This war dance is (or was) performed to a martial tune resembling Brian Boru's march. . . . [Pp. 231–32]

This is surely something of the same kind as the cudgel play in which, Logan relates in *The Scottish Gael*, the Scottish Highlanders indulged "as a necessary preparation for the management of the broad-sword . . . used in certain dances to exhibit their dexterity" (p. 440). Another writer tells us that in the early nineteenth century, in the higher parts of Aberdeenshire, "the young farmers, like their fathers, are very expert in dancing and managing a cudgel without a master."[17]

It is striking that although the ritual sword dance was evidently brought to Britain by the Scandinavians (although its wide distribution throughout Europe, Spain, Portugal, Italy, the Balkans, etcetera, argues against a Germanic, still less a Norse, origin for the sword dance), the Scandinavians have left little trace of it outside Shetland, the Isle of Man, and the Danish parts of England. Whatever Hebridean dance elements we may be disposed to attribute to the Vikings, it is arresting to notice that the Vikings did not establish in the Hebrides the most notable dance ascribed to them elsewhere, namely, the hilt-and-point sword dance.

[17] Reverend Skene Keith, quoted in James Logan, *The Scottish Gael*, p. 440.

The Hebrides, it must be repeated, have always been markedly resistant to innovation; this characteristic is assisted by their remoteness and the peculiar magic of the Hebridean life. It is a great pity that no dance scholars paralleled the work of the song and music collectors of the nineteenth century in recording the lore of the past, but we must be thankful that so much has been collected, even if only in the nick of time.

16 / Dramatic Folk Jigs of the Highlands and Isles

*Cailleach an Dudain and other folk jigs –
death and resurrection theme – dance
of death – dramatic play as an intrinsic
part of Hebridean social life*

In the dramatic folk dances known, in some cases within living memory, in the Hebrides, and which, we can be sure, once enjoyed widespread popularity dating back into the mists of time, the primitive union of dance and drama attracted the prejudiced censure of the early Christian Church of Rome. Mention has been made of the puritanical forces which eroded many of the simple joys of the past in the Highlands during the early nineteenth century and of the equally important changes in ways of life which contributed a destructive force hardly less great. Nevertheless, dramatic jigs were still performed on several islands, such as Eigg, Uist, Skye, and Eriskay in the early years of the present century. Some people who saw them and whom one would have been expected to be equipped to record and describe them with technical insight, such as D. G. MacLennan, unfortunately failed to do so. Thus, we have to turn to the superficial descriptions occasionally included in published recollections and to the valuable investigations carried out more recently in the field by J. F. and T. M. Flett, and Frank Rhodes.

The most frequently mentioned of these old dances is Cailleach an Dudain[1] (Carlin of the Mill Dust), but it is apparent that it is often confused with a different dance, a'Cailleach (Old Wife). In the former, a man and woman take part; in the latter, only a woman. It is easy to see how confusion could arise, for a'Cailleach seems, from Alexander Campbell's description subscribed, to have had a variable character, depending on the performer. Two of the tunes which Campbell heard played and sung to it are sometimes given as the names of other dances: Cailleach an Dudain mentioned above, and Cailleach a' Stopan-falaimh (Old Woman of the Empty Choppan). It

---

[1] The earliest mention of Cailleach an Dudain is in the preface to Campbell's *The Grampians Desolate*. The tune "Cailleach an Dordon" is in the Mac Farlane MSS (ca. 1740) in the National Library of Scotland.

seems possible that these were variants of the "Old Woman" dance, depending upon the role assumed by the dancer.

Norman Macleod's description of Cailleach an Dudain is almost identical to Campbell's description of a'Cailleach in the preface to *The Grampians Desolate*:

The person who dances is dressed in a very grotesque style, having a huge bunch of keys hanging by her apron-string, and a staff to support her, for she affects to be very stiff, and lame of one leg. When the tune strikes up, she appears hardly able to hobble on the floor; by degrees, however, she gets on a bit, and as she begins to warm, she feels new animation, and capers away at a great rate, striking her pockets, and making her keys rattle; then affecting great importance as keeper of the good things of the storeroom, ambry, and dairy. Meanwhile some of the company present join the person who plays the tune, and sing words suitable to the character the dancer assumes — generally some nonsense of a comic cast with which the matron, or Cailleach seems wonderfully delighted. The names of the tunes and words that I have heard played and sung to this dance, are, "A 'Sean Rong mhor," "Cailleach an Durdan," "Cailleach a' Stopan-falaimh," and several others that I do not at present recollect.

One suspects that the puirt-a-beul example, "Ruileadh cailleach sheatadh cailleach" (old woman would reel, an old woman would set), which Francis Collinson collected in Barra and which he reproduced in his *Traditional Music of Scotland* (p. 100) was one of the tunes Campbell could not recollect.

Several good descriptions of Cailleach an Dudain are extant, and one by Father MacDonald from nineteenth-century Eriskay is especially complete. He describes it as a "Punch and Judy" dance:

Two take part in the dance — an old man and an old trembling shivering hag (a man dressed in punch attire does her part). The old hag comes in trembling and quivering with a stick in her hand and her husband similarly armed. They fight with the sticks — dancing all the time. Finally the old man thrusts his stick into her body and she falls down dead. The old man beats his hands and howls most atrociously as it occurs to him that he has murdered the old woman. The sudden change from anger and animosity to broken-heartedness for the loss of his partner in life is ridiculous. He bends down over her only to find out more surely that she is dead. The lamentation is heart-rending. Again and again he bends over her and again his sorrow is only intensified. He bends down and touches her boot and the foot rises a little and quivers away most singularly. The old man regains a little confidence. He bends down again and touches the other foot, and it too begins to shake incessantly. At these signs of returning life he bursts out into hysterical laughter. He touches the hands one by one. They too begin to quiver. The old carlin stretched out on the floor with her two feet and two hands quivering looks ridiculous to a degree and the spectators nearly drown the piper with their uproar. The old man then bends down and touches her hair and up she springs with renewed life and they both rush into each other's arms most gleefully.[2]

Alexander Carmichael's version from Uist, described in his *Carmina Gadelica* (vol. 1), differs from this only in being less violent and more mystical. I cannot agree with Flett in concluding that it is therefore less pure — possibly it is more pure! In *Traditional and Highland Scottish Dances* (2nd ed.), the dance D. G. MacLennan describes

---

[2] Quoted in J. F. and T. M. Flett, "Some Hebridean Folk Dances," *JEFDSS*, vol. 7, no. 2 (1953), p. 115.

under the same name, also from Uist, is just as mystical, but differs in several respects from the others: A man is found dead after a quarrel during general dancing. He is covered by a white cloth. "Laments arose, the local wise woman suddenly appeared, to walk round and round the body muttering an incantation; she then began a dignified dance, withdrawing the cloth and always gazing on the 'dead' face. She touched his hand, his foot, his arm, his leg, and all in turn began to shake. She bent to touch his forehead and up jumped the dead man to dance again while — so great had been the tension — the wise woman was frequently carried out in a faint" (p. 33).

The Fletts, however, have recorded some details of the step used in a degenerate version of Cailleach an Dudain in Benbecula. Their informant knew the dance well, although it had scarcely been performed since the early 1900s, and declared that it was not a step dance. The step used by the husband in dancing round the "dead" Cailleach is described in "Some Hebridean Folk Dances":

Bar 1   Count "and ONE"   Full step forward on right foot
         "and"   Small step of about three inches forward on left foot
         "TWO"   A similar step forward on right foot
Bar 2   Repeat the "and TWO" of bar 1 twice
Bars 3 and 4   Repeat bars 1 and 2 with opposite feet

Several versions of the tune have been published,[3] one of which is the following:

The words for Cailleach an Dudain from the Carmichael manuscripts, Edinburgh University, are:

Chailleach an dudain (repeated three times)	Carlin of the mill dust
Cum do dheireadh rium!	Keep thy rear to me!
Chailleach an dudain (repeated twice)	Carlin of the mill dust
Cum do chul rium,	Keep thy back to me,
Cum do cheathramh rium!	Keep thy quarter to me!
Chailleach an dudain (twice)	Carlin of the mill dust
Null e! Nall e!	Over with it! Back with it!
Cum do cheathramh rium!	Keep thy quarter to me
Chailleach an dudain (twice)	Carlin of the mill dust
Sios e! suas e!	Down with it! Up with it!

[3] Norman MacDonald, *Gesto Collection of Highland Music*; William Ross (Pipe Major), *Third Collection of Pipe Music*, Edinburgh, 1940; and Francis Collinson, *The Traditional and National Music of Scotland*.

Nuas na beirearan!	Let it not be brought down!
Cum do chul rium!	Keep thy back to me!
Cum do cheatheamh rium!	Keep thy quarter to me!

In a popular corruption of Cailleach an Dudain a youth would lie as dead on the floor while the company danced round him, chanting a verse urging him to rise and choose a partner. It is told, more than once, how the youth, to the horror of the merrymakers, has been found to be actually dead.[4]

We have noted in chapter 12 the "resurrection" of a victim in the Dirk Dance and we can see that it is a common theme arising from some ancient origin. The Cailleach an Dudain as a woman's solo seems logical, but it was certainly widely known as a "Punch and Judy" dance in the nineteenth century. The Punch and Judy pantomime itself was a novelty in Scotland in the late eighteenth century.

The "resurrection" of a youth pretending to be dead is probably a different dance drama, and indeed it is identical in theme to a game which was formerly played at wakes in many parts of Europe. Lincoln Kirstein described this game in his *Book of the Dance*: One of the young men sank to the ground, pretending to be dead. "The girls and women danced round him, in graceful parody of mourning gestures. At the same time they sang a hilarious dirge, then one after the other, bent over the dead man and kissed him back to life" (p. 86). Then all danced a round dance and the procedure was repeated with a girl as the dead person. Kirstein also remarked that in medieval Hungary, for example, at wakes "one of the mourners lay down with a handkerchief over his face. Bagpipes struck up a dance of death. Then men and women, half singing, half wailing, crossed his hands on his chest, trussed him up, turned him over, played tricks with him. . . . Once indeed, God punished such foolery and when they went to rouse the player, he was dead indeed" (p. 86).

This is similar to an eighteenth-century — not a medieval — incident described by Charles Rogers in *Scotland Social and Domestic*. The incident took place at Monifieth, Forfarshire, where at a lykewake one of the elders thought to chasten the hilarity by replacing the corpse with one of his confederates and have him rise to startle the company. He managed to remove the "mourners" and carry out his plan, but when the hilarity resumed the substitute "corpse" did not rise and was in fact found to have died (p. 22).

The theme of resurrection is widespread, but its purpose — the laying of the ghost of the deceased, the expulsion of demons, the release of the spirit or whatever — is forgotten. The "Old Woman of the Mill Dust" danced her way from primitive antiquity and lingered in the Hebrides with her companions until our own times.

There was dancing at these wakes, which lasted sometimes for many days, depending on the opulence of the deceased. The dances began on the night after the death, and in the words of Dr. Thomas Garnett in *Tour through the Highlands*: "All the neighbours attend the summons; and the dance, accompanied by a solemn melancholy strain called a lament, is begun by the nearest relatives, who are joined by most of those present; this is repeated every evening till interment" (p. 119).

Elizabeth Grant tells us of an instance in which the corpse fell out of the bed,[5]

---

[4] T. Sinton, *Places, People and Poetry of Dorres in Other Days*, trans. Gaelic Society of Inverness, vol. 26, 1910.

[5] Elizabeth Grant, *Memoires of a Highland Lady*, p. 143.

and J. G. Frazer relates another strange occurrence: "About 100 years ago [ca. 1783,] a young man attending a funeral was told that after the funeral there was a dance, and that he was to dance with the widow. He was to ask her to name the tune. Her answer was 'It would need to be a merry one for my heart is very sair.' She appeared in full weeds and the guests were arranged for a country dance. She and her partner stood at the top of the dance, went down the middle hand-in-hand and out at the door of the room. The dancing was continued by the other guests. This was thought to show honour to the deceased."[6]

Of the other dances mentioned by Dr. Macleod in *Reminiscences of a Highland Parish*, the Goat Dance and Weave the Gown are described with the group dances. The Thorny Croft (*Croit am Droighan*) remains, and this concerns the lamentations of a farmer whose ground was covered with thorns and briars. It contained much dolorous recitative and was devised to excite the compassion of "some fair spectator."

Both Carmichael and MacLennan refer to Marabh na beiste dubh, the death or killing of the black beast (otter), but neither describes the dance, although Mac-Lennan mentions seeing it. As it is remembered now on Eigg, it is not a dance at all but a short one-man drama enacting the capture and killing of an otter. The otter is represented by a cushion or a sack of straw which someone manipulates such that the otter appears to be hiding behind various obstructions, such as a table leg, poking its head out, cannily looking about and sharply withdrawing as the hunter's cudgel falls. The hunter continues to stalk his prey until he "stuns" it, then he throws it over his shoulder in triumph, holding it by the "tail." The animal "revives" and "bites" the hunter on the buttock at which the hunter howls, drops his captive, but falls back onto it. A few more blows with the cudgel finish the poor animal, and the performance is completed, having lasted about half an hour.[7]

One can imagine children enjoying such an interlude in an evening's entertainment, but we must remember that in such play, people who live close to nature are close to children, their imagination is alive and unspoiled. This is well illustrated by a story told by an artist who happened to be visiting in Barra at Halloween some years ago. He was asked by some boys to make false faces for them. This he did out of a roll of cotton, painting in the features as necessary. The boys insisted on his joining them, and in his own words: "The first black-house we went into was crowded, but on our appearance the crowd backed before us, the women screaming and throwing themselves on the ground in an ecstacy of fear. I threw back my mask, and the effect was electric. They all yelled with laughter. I pulled my mask down again, and they were convulsed with terror."[8]

Another dramatic solo dance, Dannsadh na Goraig (Crazy Woman's Dance) was seen by Keith MacDonald at the end of the nineteenth century. He describes the dance in *Puirt-a-Beul* as a "sort of circular jig round the room, which might or might not be accompanied by the 'port-a-beul,' ending with a sudden rush out of the room." It was danced by a woman who held the skirt of her gown with both hands, the arms being stretched above her head, so as to hide head and face.

The Dannsadh a' Chroig Leith was danced by one man assuming the character of

[6] J. G. Frazer, *Folklore Journal*, Folklore Society, London, 1883.

[7] Flett, "Some Hebridean Folk Dances."

[8] From an account written by Mr. John Duncan for F. Marian MacNeill, *The Silver Bough*, vol. 1, notes to chapter 1.

a rustic or day labourer with a flaughter spade and doubtless this was the dance known as the Flaughter Spade Dance which was performed to the tune of "Sior bhuain culaig"[9] and the dance named the Speyde in the *Complaynt of Scotland*. The man sings of his hard day's work.

Very little is known, except the names, of many of the others. Dannsadh an Dubh Luidnaich (dirty, drenched) is described as a comic or grotesque dance for one person.[10] A Chuthaich Chaol Dubh (the thin, black, little woman) is described as a kind of wild fantastic dance that required great strength and agility for its various steps and movements, and was danced by a man.[11] Dannsadh an Chleoca (The Cloak Dance) was about a young laird just returned from abroad with his servant:

The young laird comes in, as if newly arrived, looks round the company with seeming wonder, and after rambling through the appartment while the tune is playing, he all at once stops, throws off his mantle, plaid, or cloak, and away his staff, affecting at the same time considerable emotion; his servant, who is by, picks up the cloak and staff, and puts on the one, and places the other in his hand, endeavouring at the same time to quiet his master, who seems to be pacified, and foots it away again to the same tune, till he tires, and throws away his mantle and staff again; which his man takes up, and presents them as before, repeating the same several times, till at last the servant recollecting that he has a letter, pulls it out of his pocket, and offers it to his young master, who says he is unable to read, owing to a phlegmon on his posteriors, which marvelously affects his eye-sight![12]

Dannsadh Fear Druim o Chairidh was for a male dancer, but we do not even know as much as that about Dannsadh Chrioskaidh, Flail Dance (Tiree), Fisherwive's Creel Dance, and Shane Dance, all listed by D. G. MacLennan; or Tri-Croidhan Caorach (Three Sheep's Trotters).

The most complete descriptions we have of one of these dances is of Crait an Dreathan (The Wren's Croft). The mention of the Battle of Bothwell Brig dates this drama from the comparatively recent period of the late seventeenth century. It was performed by one man, dressed as a crofter in a tartan plaid, who relates an episode from his life in a series of verses interspersed by dances. He stops short after each verse and calls on the piper or fiddler to play up the tune for his dance.[13] The recital proceeds as follows:

CRAIT AN DREATHAN	THE WREN'S CROFT
Bha mise roimh so mo thuanach,	I was formerly the farmer of
an Craig an Dreathan: agus ma bha,	the Wren's croft; and if I was,
ma' ta bha i duileach treabha'	indeed it was very difficult to
Bhai i go fiadhaich balcach, clochach,	labour; it was wild, balky, stony,
carnach, claen-foidach, ack duleach	cairney, and the furrow ill to clear;
treabha mar bha i, threabh misi i.	yet difficult as it was, I laboured it.
Seid suas!	Blow up!

---

[9] Trans. Gaelic Society of Inverness.

[10] Alexander Campbell, preface to *The Grampians Desolate*; and D. G. MacLennan, *Traditional and Highland Scottish Dances*, 2nd ed.

[11] Ibid.

[12] Campbell, *The Grampians Desolate*, pp. 264–65.

[13] Ibid. Campbell writes that it was more often a fiddler, especially in the Braes of Athole.

*An deigh sin thainig buidh-
eann mhor, mhor saigheadoirin
feabh na duicha, agus thug iad
leabha mi, agus cha do stad iad
leam riabh, gus an d' thainig
iad cean Bhotel-brig.*
                    Seid suas!

After that there came a
great company of soldiers to
the country, and they forced
me to join them; and they never
halted till they brought me to
Bothwell-brig.
                    Blow up!

*Ach an uair a biodh cach ri
saighdearach, bhidhinsa anns na
peasarehan.*
                    Seid suas!

But when the rest would
be soldiering, I would be
always found among the pease.
                    Blow up!

*Bha mi laeth' mach spaisdeir-
each, agus thachair truir bhain-
tighearnan orm, and thug mi treis
do dhithis dibh, agus suadha an
treas te a ton re cnoc.*
                    Seid suas!

I was one day out strolling;
and I met three ladies; I
pleased two of them, and I
let the third ********
                    Blow up!

*Nuair cha cach thun a bhlair,
theasamh mi fhein ann a' croabh
mhor sgithich a chunnaig mi
thall, agus tharuing mi mho
chlaidhiomh, agus rinn mi mar
sud, agus mar sud.*
[draws sword or stick and strikes
at legs and shoulders of the company]
                    Seid suas!

When the rest went to the
battle, I myself stood in a
large thorn tree I saw over the
way; and I drew my broad-sword,
and I laid about me thus, thus,
and so, so.
                    Blow up!

*Nuar thainig me do-thigh,
rinn Fionghol Donn agam fhein
an Cath-ta so damh,* [displays plaid]
*agus chuiri andeargan' cridhghuirm,
agus an gorm an' crithe'n uaine,
agus cearsle dhubh na cheann
deire, agus chaithe mi mar sud
fhein e.*
                    Seid suas!

When I came home, my own
brunette Flora made this tartan here;
and she put the red into the heart
of the blue, and the blue into the
heart of the green, and a clue
of black at the end, and I wear it
as you now see.
                    Blow up!

*An deigh sin, bha Crait an
Dreathan abaigh; agus bhuain
mi i; agus bha cearamh corna
inn te, agus rinn mi cearamh
brudhaist dheth, agus ma bha
mi buidheach, bha; 's mar robh,
leig dha; — cha robh tulle ggam
re faighinn.*
                    Seid suas!

After that the *Wren's Croft*
was ripe; and I cut down the crop;
and I had a quarter of barley on
it; of which I made a quarter of
brose; and if I was satisfied —
well — if I were not – I had no more
to get.
                    Blow up!]

[Alexander Campbell, *The Grampians
Desolate*, pp. 226–68]

In the Germanic languages, the same word frequently signifies both dance and play, and in some it also embraces the ideas of sacrifice or festival. We can see here that the Germanic word "dance" is used by the Gaels in this sense. The social dances are called "Reels" (also a Germanic word), but those that imitate animals or fowls, as in the dances of the goats or ducks, are called "dances"; and, of course, these kinds of dances are very primitive and are found all over the world. The impersonation of characters or human situations is comparatively recent. The prowess of the hunter is an appropriate subject in a predatory society as are the actions of weaving or spinning in a herdsman's society, and the sowing, delving, and planting in an agricultural society. Elements of all these motifs appear in the West Highland dances.[14]

This chapter would not be complete without some mention of the well-known Seann Triubhas. We have already discussed this old "hornpipe" in chapter 12, where it was remarked that there was some reason to classify this dance as a dramatic jig. Carmichael tells us in his *Carmina Gadelica* ca. 1860 (vol. 1) that Seann Triubhas was danced at the St. Michael's Day balls in South Uist along with some of the many dramatic dances now lost, and he remarks that it once "contained much more acting" than it did in his time (pp. 208-9). The sophistication of the technique of Seann Triubhas sets it apart from the general run of Scottish dramatic jigs known to us. Of course, we know little of the technique of most of these, but there is no indication that it involved anything but the most rudimentary movements.

It is significant that Seann Triubhas is known only by its Gaelic name. This would seem to establish the dance as belonging to the Gaelic-speaking region. Its full title was no doubt originally the same as that of the old Rant to which it was performed — "Seann Triubhas Willichan" (Willie's Auld Trousers) — a title which can be traced back at least to about 1745, although the germ of the air can be traced from an even earlier time. Printed or manuscript records of Highland Dance airs do not carry us much further into the past.

The style of the dance asserts that it is a product of Perthshire and Strathspey, the home of Highland art dance. Its appearance in the Hebrides must be suspected to arise from its migration there, as also must the Hebridean appearance of the Reel of Tulloch which Carmichael mentions among the dances at the St. Michael's Day balls in the nineteenth century.

We must remember, however, that Francis Peacock in the eighteenth century included dancers from the Isles in his praise of Highland dancing prowess. Whether the possession of this more sophisticated technique influenced the execution of at least some of the old dramatic jigs and produced a remnant in the cultivated shape of Seann Triubhas is an intriguing question. But no scholar could doubt that the simple steps of such survivals as Cailleach an Dudain are close to the primitive style, placing much more emphasis on the drama than on the form.

The St. Michael's Day balls which Carmichael describes in so much detail were very similar to the West Highland ceilidhs we have discussed in chapter 8. Song, dance, and merriment were continued all night with "many curious scenes being acted, and many curious dances performed" (207-9). The largest house with the

---

[14] Some pantomimic dances of this kind, such as The Planting Stick and The Butchers' March from Limerick and Coolagurra from Cork, survived also in Ireland into recent times.

evenest floor was generally selected for the dancing. The music was provided by a series of pipers, fiddlers, and "players of other instruments" until the dawn. If the musician was a married man, a collection of money or grain was taken up for him.

This great occasion in honour of the patron saint of boats and boatmen, and of horses and horsemen, Carmichael tells us, fell into a decline from the sudden termination of the athletic contests and horse races associated with it in 1866.

17/ From Highlands to Lowlands- The Highland Games

Falkirk Tryst – first bagpipe competition – Edinburgh "exhibition of martial music"– dancing introduced – Strathspey twosome – Reel of Tulloch – Gille Callum – Highland Fling – Dirk Dance – other dances suggested – Strathfillan Games – Braemar – Northern Meeting – Brig o' Tilt – other old gatherings – Luss – Cowal – distinguished dancers – competitive female dancing – competitive dancing dress – the Highland vogue

By the beginning of the eighteenth century, the cattle fair at Crieff was the great annual rendezvous of Highlander and Southerner, the former to sell his cattle, the latter to purchase it. In 1723, at least thirty thousand head of cattle changed hands, mostly to English drovers. But in the latter half of that century, for reasons which do not concern us, the Crieff Fair declined in favour of the Falkirk Tryst, which, together with the Dumbarton Tryst, became the most important annual event in the West Highland calendar.

Norman Macleod tells us that every glen was moved by these trysts. "What a collection of cattle, of drovers, and of dogs," he writes in *Memories of a Highland Parish*. "What speculations as to how the market would turn out. What a shaking of hands in boats, wayside inns, and on decks of steamers by the men in homespun cloth, gay tartans, or in the more correct new garbs of Glasgow or Edinburgh tailors! What a pouring in from all the glens, increasing at every ferry and village, and flowing on, a river of tenants and proprietors, small and great, to the market!" We can imagine how many youths, impatient for the day, would come each year, wide-eyed to the scene of the fabulous adventures which had formed much of the substance of the conversation of their elders. There they would meet, perhaps, those of their relatives who had already migrated to the growing towns of the Lowlands, the first of that immense body of Highland exiles who turned their backs on their native glens for a better living in the towns and farms of the south, and filled the ranks of the new Highland regiments in the British army.

The émigré Gaels now looked with concern upon the impending loss of their culture along with their way of life. Even the Great Pipe was in apparent danger of extinction, and hence the Gaelic Society of London (founded 1778) turned its attention to encouraging the preservation of the Great Music. It seemed obvious that one of the great cattle fairs would offer the most convenient opportunity for arranging an assemblage of pipers from various parts of the Highlands to participate in a competition devoted to the performance of pibroch. Thus it came to pass that the Falkirk Tryst became the scene, in 1781, of the first of the modern bagpipe competitions so familiar at Highland Games. According to J. Graham Dalyell, who is the principal source of this early information,[1] there were thirteen competitors on this first occasion who each played four pieces. The competition took three days and met with considerable approval. The venture was repeated in the following year, but at the third competition, the superintendence of which had been delegated by the Highland Society of London to its Glasgow branch, the adjudicators selected thirteen of the seventeen entrants as being almost equally worthy and were unable to arrive at an acceptable decision. Many of the competitors found this most unsatisfactory, and doubtless there were other causes of dissatisfaction that were not recorded. The upshot was that the disaffected pipers immediately arranged a repeat of the competition in Edinburgh, under the patronage of Macdonald of Clanranold, and this was held on the three days beginning Wednesday, October 22, 1783.

The "elegant and numerous company" who attended the Edinburgh competition expressed an earnest desire that a committee be formed immediately to establish a "Highland Society" at Edinburgh who, "in imitation of that at London, might have it in their power to give the necessary assistance and encouragement to the numerous body of people from the Highlands residing in the city and neighbourhood, to whose labours we are so much indebted in every branch of manufacture and agriculture." This society was instituted in 1784.

Possible conflict was avoided when the Falkirk Tryst was that year unexpectedly postponed, and the "gentlemen of the Highlands, the proper judges on this occasion, could not be had without waiting a longer time than was convenient," whereupon the competition was permanently transferred to Edinburgh. It was held here annually until 1826, then continued triennially until 1844.

On the first occasion in Edinburgh, 1783, "by desire of the company, several of the pipers afforded no small entertainment by giving a specimen of their agility or spirit in Highland dancing." The managers apologized to the public for the deficiency of dress of the participants, excusing it on the grounds that having set out to perform at Falkirk, where dress was of no moment, none had expected to appear "before so magnificent and great a company." The giving of two awards of "an elegant Highland dress with silver epaulettes, double silver loops, buttons, and feathers in new bonnets" was a forerunner of things to come, for after 1785 candidates were warned to appear in "the Highland habit."

Three prizes were awarded on this first occasion: a bagpipe, forty merks, and thirty merks.[2] In 1809 these were augmented to five prizes. Three extra prizes, Dalyell tells us, were awarded in 1835: a gold medal to the highest qualified of any who had previously won the competition was awarded to John Mackenzie, piper to the Marquis of Breadalbane; a silver medal to Donald Macra, an eighty-year-old piper who had come first in 1791; and a silver medal to a promising youth of fourteen, John Macdonald. This is possibly the first occasion on which medal awards were presented; but

---

[1] Graham Dalyell, *Musical Memoirs of Scotland*, pp. 93–107.
[2] 1000 marks is equivalent to £55 6s. 8d. sterling.

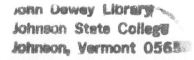

the first prize was always a bagpipe "with a suitable decoration, such as a flag, formerly bearing the Scottish thistle, as a very appropriate emblem," and later "the coat armorial of the Highland Society of London." A silver plate, suitably inscribed, was attached to the pipe, and the winner was expected to lead a victory march through the streets at the close of the Edinburgh exhibition.[3]

In 1785, the Exhibition of Martial Music as it was now called, was held on August 30, in Dunn's Assembly Rooms. There were twenty-five competitors, and these performed between them forty-eight different salutes, marches, gatherings, laments, etcetera, "the wildness and martial style of which had a very pleasing effect."[4] The finalists competed publicly on the last day, and dancing was introduced as a divertissement at suitable intervals during the long succession of pibrochs and marches. Thus the Edinburgh exhibition of piping became a fascinating attraction for visitors to the capital, particularly to the growing body of European travellers, one of the most celebrated being Felix Mendelssohn, who was escorted to the performance by Finlay Dun, a prominent Edinburgh musician of the time.

After 1826, the Edinburgh piping competition was held every three years rather than annually and this, noted Dalyell, induced a decline in the quality of the pipers who competed, although there was no decline in their numbers — usually about twenty-five. The decline presumably led to the discontinuance of the competition in 1844, by which time, of course, the growth of Highland gatherings may have been attracting the interest of the best pipers.

The dancing at the Edinburgh piping competition was always subordinated to the piping; nevertheless the idea of extending the competition to embrace dancing was soon suggested,[5] but was not carried into effect until about 1795,[6] by which time there were dancers performing who were not also competing pipers. All the participants were reimbursed from the proceeds of the public part of the competition, and it is evident that the public was especially interested in the dance exhibitions, no doubt to the chagrin of the promoters who wryly conceded in 1817, that two-thirds of the audience came "merely to see the dances."[7] As with the pipers, the eliminating rounds of the dance competition were disposed of in the first two days. Indeed it seems that the dancing at the public part of the competition was primarily for entertainment, all but the very poorest dancers performing once, and the winners and runners-up several times. The dancers were all males, and between 1816 and 1846 over one hundred and seventy names are recorded, of which only a few repeatedly appear over long periods. The number of dance competitors varied from eighteen in 1819 to forty-four in 1844, the last year of the competition.

There were two or three adjudicators, and they restricted their comments to "very good" and "indifferent." Only occasionally did they extend their comments to more critical remarks, such as "takes too big a reel," made in 1829, or "dances too high," a remark made in 1832.[8]

---

[3] Dalyell, *Musical Memoirs of Scotland*, pp. 93–107.

[4] Twenty-four pipers offered "Failte a' Phrionsai" ("The Prince's Welcome"), and, along with "Glass Mheur" and "Grim Donald's Sweetheart," it was a long-standing favourite.

[5] Cf. *Scots Magazine*, vol. 49 (1787), p. 360.

[6] Cf. *Scots Magazine*, vol. 57 (1795), p. 476.

[7] MS of the Highland Society, letter to the secretary, 1817.

[8] See J. F. and T. M. Flett, "Some Early Highland Dancing Competitions," *Aberdeen University Review*, vol. 36, no. 115 (1956), pp. 345–58 for adjudication of the competitions.

A criticism of the lighting and visual effects is contained in a letter dated July 14, 1817, preserved among the manuscripts of the Highland Society, addressed to Henry Mackenzie, the eminent "man of Feeling" himself, who was secretary for a time:

Having been informed that you are a member of the Highland Society under whose patronage the Competitors in Highland Music hold their annual exhibition — I beg leave to suggest to you (as a man of taste), that the dances which accompany the music are susceptible of a very simple and obvious improvement — viz. *by lighting the lamps in front of the Stage*, in place of introducing light from the window on the side of the Stage opposite to the audience, as at present. At present only the dark side of the dancers is visible, without the smallest variety of shade. In consequence the limbs of the dancers resemble, to my fancy, those of the black-legged highland sheep when collected together . . . and their monotonous appearance together with the clattering noise produced, do . . . detract . . . from the true effect of that highly energetic dance. . . .

There is just one other point . . . that on account of the manner in which the light is introduced, the exposed limbs of the dancers are sometimes exhibited to view in a manner altogether superfluous, and highly offensive to every *lady* of correct taste and feeling — and not a little so, to some of the other sex, who may not perhaps be entitled to express themselves according to their true sensations on the subject. Were this matter, Sir, properly regulated, I am satisfied that many of the fair would think it no offence to attend the exhibition, *which is not the case at present*. And the increased attendance would far more than repay the additional charges of wax candles and lamps.[9]

As Flett suggests, "the clattering noise" produced by the dancers probably indicates that they wore hard shoes; one can scarcely claim, however, that this practice was traditional.

In the dances performed at the Edinburgh competition, reports of the early years refer only to Highland Reels[10] and in certain instances, at least, it is clear that no other dances were involved. In 1797, Madame Frederick, a celebrated danseuse of the time, was appearing at the Edinburgh Theatre Royal, featuring in her repertoire a dance performed to one of Marshall's strathspeys — probably that later named after her.[11] The promoters of the competition had the happy inspiration of asking her to perform during one of the interludes. This she did, "dressed in an appropriate garb." Her program, we are told, comprised "Strathspeys, Jigs, and other dances."[12] Highland Reels and Strathspeys are reported as being danced in 1802. "Strathspey" could refer to the foursome Strathspey or to the twosome; the latter certainly was performed in the competition at a later stage.

The idea of introducing variety to the dances at the competition was followed up in 1806, as is suggested by a letter from Sir John Sinclair to the Duke of Atholl's factor:

Sir John Sinclair's compts. to Mr. Palliser. There are one or two persons at Dunkeld who dance slow Highland dances, emblematical of war or courtship. The Committee of the

---

9 Quoted in ibid., p. 350.

10 *Scots Magazine*, vol. 50 (1788), p. 359; vol. 51 (1789), p. 410; vol. 53 (1791), p. 360; vol. 57 (1795), p. 476; and vol. 60 (1798), p. 574.

11 MacKay, *A Collection of Ancient Piobairreachd* (Aberdeen, 1838), p. 17.

12 David Stewart, *Sketches of the Highlanders*, appendix, p. 53.

Highland Society wish much to have these dances exhibited at the Edinburgh Theatre on Tuesday next, and wishes that the men should be sent so as to be in Edinburgh on Monday night, or early on Tuesday morning.

Neil [sic] Gow knows who they are and the tunes that ought to be played, the names of which they should bring with them. Let them call for Lord James Murray at Dumbrech's Hotel, or Sir John Sinclair, Charlotte Square.

An endorsement in pencil on the letter reading "Alexr. Gow — Peter Robertson, The Battle, Mc an Fhorsair — played by Donald Dewar," suggests the reply.

There is no evidence that these dances were ever performed at Edinburgh. "The Battle" does not suggest a dance "emblematical of courtship," and we know the dance Mc an Fhorsair (The Forester's Son) from two or three references to it which identify it as a "war dance" in which a naked broad sword was flourished to the evolutions of the body.[13]

By 1813, however, another dance had appeared on the program, not the Gille Callum, not a Highland Fling, but the mysterious Strathspey Twosome. It had a tenuous existence, and no wonder, for it was essentially a couple's dance and no doubt accounts for Dalyell's remark, "Can anything blunt our sympathies more than beholding two brawny sons of Terpsichore leading up each other in measured time and pace."[14] Only seventeen names are associated with it in the records between 1816 and 1844.[15] It appears to have been danced by two couples at a time. A Robert Gunn and a James MacGregor are prominently linked with it, but Gunn retired in 1832 and MacGregor could not find a partner in 1835. In 1838 the committee lamented that "the Highland Strathspey seems to have disappeared," and it is vexatious that the Highland Society of Edinburgh should have allowed it, and no doubt other dances, to disappear without some detailed record of them.

The Reel of Tulloch was introduced in 1829 by two sets of four men. It is strange to say that, although at the next competition all the competitors danced it, no one danced it at all on the following one. However, it reappeared in 1838 and in 1844.[16]

The Gille Callum was not introduced to the Edinburgh competition until 1832, when five men competed: James MacGregor from Tomintoul; John MacKay, piper to Lady Gwydyr at Drummond Castle; Roderick Mackay, piper to Abercairney; William MacLeod from Lochbroom, and William Stewart from Athole. The winner was John MacKay as the minutes record: "The ancient Ghille Challaim or sword dance over two naked swords was peculiarly gratifying, and was performed by John MacKay with a degree of precision and ease altogether extraordinary, considering the intricacy of the figure and the rapidity of the motions." The Gille Callum was repeated with ever-increasing popularity at each competition thereafter and is firmly established today.

Of the five finalists in 1844, Dalyell tells us, some avoided quick steps very cautiously from "apprehension of touching the swords, which impaired the effect of the performance." There was obviously no standard "three or four slow — two quick" in those days! Originally, too, the orchestra employed for the dancing played also for

[13] Dalyell, *Musical Memoirs of Scotland*, pp. 93–107.
[14] Ibid.
[15] Ibid.
[16] Ibid.

the Gille Callum, but this was mercifully changed to the bagpipe in 1838, the champion of the pipers being granted the privilege.

In 1834, one dancer, Allan Cameron Mackay of Strontian, wrote a letter to the organizers: "A. C. Mackay took the liberty — to suggest . . . to have some old highland hornpipes . . . danced on Wednesday — he had also the pleasure ———— have liberty from some of your ———— able members to have the Breadalbane ball reel ———— mostly termed, the reel of Tulloch danced — he moreover begs liberty to have the sword dance hornpipe played to by his native music — Edinburgh musicians may play well enough for Quadrilles and Micolanzes. But they are certainly insufficient to play Gillie Callum. Highland Laddie and highland fling — with — over the Hills and far away — are in his humble opinion worth the viewing."[17] Mr. Mackay was obviously a Gaelic speaker. His use of "hornpipe" as a generic term for step dance is interesting, as are his references to Highland Fling, Highland Laddie, and Over the Hills and Far Away. The existence of a Highland Laddie at this date establishes that Ewen MacLachlan's version of some twenty or thirty years later was not the first. This is a most valuable letter.

Mackay's remark in 1834, however, seems to preclude the likelihood that the "Strathspey Dance" performed by John Grant in 1832 was identical to the Highland Fling; obviously a dance known as Highland Fling existed. A solo "Strathspey Dance" figured in the competitions of 1841 and 1844, however, and it is significant that in the manuscript of the printed list of winners in 1844, there is a note against the name Peter Comrie who "gained first prize for Highland Fling." Now, Comrie had won first prize for the "Strathspey Dance" at the previous competition, which lends support to the idea that the "Strathspey Dance" of the competition records was what we might call a Highland Fling. Curiously enough, the printed list of competition winners usually contained no reference to the dances performed, and indeed the reference to Highland Fling in the reporting of Peter Comrie's prize is crossed out in the manuscript draft.

It is strange, however, that Dalyell, writing his account about that time, makes no reference to a Strathspey solo dance or Highland Fling. He does make reference, however, to a Dirk Dance performed in 1841 by John MacBeth, piper to the Highland Society of London, and John Thomson, piper to Alexander MacAlister of Torrisdale.

The Edinburgh exhibitions cannot be referred to as Highland Games, for the latter embrace not only piping and dancing, but at least some of the ancient athletic contests so dear to the Gael. The first of what we may call our modern Highland Games were those of the Strathfillan Society, established by Lord Gwydir in 1819 on his Drummond estate in Perthshire. James Logan describes these events in *The Scottish Gael*: "The annual meetings are held in a romantic spot, and are attended by numerous noblemen, gentlemen, and ladies, with a large assemblage of Highlanders. The effect of their gaudy costume, the bagpipes, and the various sports exhibited amid highly picturesque scenery, is extremely fine. A beautiful lake affords the pleasure of a boat race, and a recital of Gaelic compositions relieves the fatigue of the athletic exercises, while prizes of bagpipes, dirks, suits of tartans, snuff mulls, etc., send the competitors

[17] Ibid.

home in high delight" (p. 445). Although Logan has omitted dancing from his list, Highland Reels were featured at the Strathfillan Games, as well as adult and juvenile competitors in the "Ancient Scotch Sword Dance."[18] Prizes were offered by the society and by private members.

The early Strathfillan Society Games came to an end around the 1840s; meanwhile the most celebrated of our Highland Games today, Braemar, came into being. The first Braemar Games were held in 1832 under the auspices of the Braemar Highland Society founded in the summer of 1826. The first patrons were the Earl of Fife and James Farquharson of Invercauld. The Marquis of Carmarthen (later Duke of Leeds) became an honorary member and took a nineteen year lease of Mar forest. He dressed all his retainers in full Breadalbane tartan and thus established a fashion that was soon copied by other lairds.

Braemar, of course, is especially famous for its association with Queen Victoria. When she first came to that magnificent country in September, 1848, the games were held at Invercauld, and she was graciously pleased to attend. Next year they were held at Braemar Castle, and in 1859 a special private gathering was held for the queen who was then entertaining members of the British Association. She remarked that "we gave prizes to the three best in each of the games. . . . Last of all came the dancing — reels and Gillie Callum. The latter the judges could not make up their minds about, it was danced over and over again; and at last they left out the best dancer of all! They said he danced 'Too well!' "[19]

In 1853, the dancing at Braemar included the Highland Fling, Reel of Tulloch, and Seann Triubhas. These dances, along with the Gille Callum and Highland Reel, have been the staple competition dances ever since, although in recent times the Sailors' Hornpipe has been added and, even more recently, the ladies' dance, Flora Macdonald's Fancy.

Another of the great Highland gatherings was the Northern Meeting, as it was called, held in Inverness. This was instituted in 1798 to enable the gentry and nobility of the northeast to enjoy an annual week of social intercourse. Balls, dinners, and card parties were held in glorious succession. Races and concerts were added to the social round, but it was not until 1841 that piping and dancing were introduced. To encourage competitors from afar, travelling expenses for one day's journey were granted. The dances at the first competition were the Highland Fling, Reels, and Gille Callum. It is notable that the prize for the Fling was three guineas, whereas that for the others was two guineas. In 1841, James Grant from Strathspey won the Fling and John Macallister from Tulloch won the Reels — making a piquant play with names.

By 1848, the fame of the Northern Meeting was attracting many observers from the principal cities. Steamers ran special services from Glasgow, Leith, and London, and coaches ran from Dingwall, Perth, Aberdeen, and other towns in the vicinity. In 1865 the balls were attended by about six hundred people. The balls were held on the two nights following the games, the Thursday and Friday, and the champion piper was expected to play for the Highland Reels. At the beginning of the present century,

[18] From a handbill preserved among the manuscripts relating to the Edinburgh competitions, quoted by Flett, "Some Early Highland Dancing Competitions."

[19] Queen Victoria, *Leaves from the Journal.*

the Northern Meeting was still one of the great events in the life of Inverness. Large crowds of people congregated on Church Street to watch the horse-drawn buses arrive at the Rooms with their festive freights of dancers. One can imagine what a week of piping and singing and dancing this great parade concluded. The tradition still lives, although the piping and dancing competitions are held in the comfort of the Rooms, and no longer in the Northern Meeting park, at the mercy of the elements.

An interesting description made by Catherine Sinclair of dancing at the Brig o' Tilt Meeting in Blair-Atholl in 1840 alludes to the Gille Callum, performed over sticks, and to the Reel of Tulloch: "All that feet can do, these Highlanders did, and more than I ever saw any feet attempt before, but we all looked on in solemn silence, as if watching an execution. . . . Nothing ever looked more like insanity than the reels at last. Four stout Highlanders, in full dress, raised on a wet slippery wooden platform, dancing in the open air, under a torrent of rain, cracking their fingers to imitate castanets, shuffling, capering, cutting, whirling round, and uttering the sudden yell, customary here, during a very animated dance, to encourage the piper."[20] Miss Sinclair obviously found this performance something of a novelty, although she was a descendant of the famous Sir John Sinclair of Statistical Account fame, who, as we have seen, was active on the Committee of the Highland Society in the early years of the century.

7 Program of the Luss Highland Games, 1893

[20] Catherine Sinclair, *Shetland and the Shetlanders* (London, 1840), pp. 416–17.

Some of the old gatherings, even in the heart of Strathspey, such as the Badenoch and Rothiemurchus Highland Games at Kingussie, have been discontinued, but the Braemar, Oban, and Glenfinnan gatherings are happily still with us and loyal to their old traditions. That at Glenfinnan is opened by a Gaelic song and an address by the Chief which, if it is in English, is followed by another in Gaelic as seems appropriate in that historic and beautiful mountain-mirrored spot where Prince Charlie's standard was exultantly raised so many sad years ago.

In the Lowland fringe in Dumbartonshire and Argyll, the Luss Highland gathering is held in the land of the Colquhouns. Even in these days of proximity to the industrial belt of the Clyde, it retains a great deal of character which sets it apart from other Highland Games. The Luss gathering was established by the enthusiasm of local farmers and sportsmen in 1875, and this cosy intimate local atmosphere pervades it still. The Luss Games are, unfortunately, not important from a dancing point of view. As in so many other gatherings of the kind, dancing is there regarded more as colourful window-dressing, but the athletic contests are diversified and characteristic. Not so very long ago, the Loch Lomond steamers provided the principal means of transportation; now even clumsy double-decked buses from Balloch can charge their way along the twisting road. But the bonnie banks of Loch Lomond are still worthy of their name, and the peace and the green, the rocks, the burns, and the clouded hills round the broad islanded water diffuse a spirit that endures.

➤ PROGRAMME. ➤

LOCAL.	PRIZES—1st	2nd	3rd
1. High Leap (running),	15/	7/6	5/
2. Long Leap (running),	15/	7/6	5/
3. Hop, Step, and Leap (or Two Hops),	15/	7/6	5/
4. Light Ball,	15/	7/6	5/
5. Hammer,	15/	7/6	5/
6. 100 Yards Race,	15/	7/6	5/
7. Hurdle Race (Twice Round),	15/	7/6	5/
8. Boys' Race (under 12, entry free),	4/	3/	2/
9. Half-mile Handicap Race,	15/	10/	5/
10. Boys' Race (under 14, entry free),	5/	3/	2/
11. Hurdle Sack Race (Committee provide Sacks),	15/	10/	5/
12. Bolster Bar (for Boys under 16),	6/	4/	2/

OPEN.	PRIZES—1st	2nd	3rd
13. Heavy Ball,	30/	20/	10/
14. Hammer,	30/	20/	10/
15. Caber,	30/	20/	10/
16. Scotch Wrestling (all Weights),	50/	30/	20/
17. Do. (14 Stones and under),	30/	20/	10/
18. Pole Vaulting,	30/	20/	10/
19. High Leap (running)	30/	20/	10/
20. One Mile Handicap Race,	40/	20/	10/
21. 440 Yards Handicap Race,	30/	20/	10/
22. 220 Yards Handicap Race,	30/	20/	10/
23. Hop, Step, and Leap (or Two Hops),	25/	15/	10/
24. Pibroch Playing (to commence at 10 a.m. prompt),	50/	30/	20/
25. Highland Fling Dancing,	30/	15/	5/
26. Do. for Boys under 16,	20/	10/	2/6
27. Do. for Girls under 16,	20/	10/	2/6
28. Ghillie Callum,	30/	15/	5/
29. Reel Dancing,	30/	15/	5/
30. Do. for Boys,	15/	10/	2/6
31. Sailors' Hornpipe,	20/	10/	5/
32. March Playing,	30/	15/	10/
33. Reel Playing,	30/	15/	10/

A Handsome Prize will be given for

A HILL RACE FOR SHEPHERDS.

Local Competition only.

The Winners will be indicated by Flags—1st, Red; 2nd, White; 3rd, Blue.

KNITTING.

LOCAL.	PRIZES—1st	2nd	3rd	4th
Best Pair Hose, Hand Knitted (Alloa Yarn),	15/6	10/6	7/6	5/6
Best Pair Sox, Hand Knitted (Fingering 4-Ply),	12/6	7/6	5/	3/

OPEN.	PRIZES—1st	2nd	3rd	4th
Best Pair Hose, Hand Knitted,	20/	15/	10/	7/6
Best Pair Sox, Hand Knitted,	20/	15/	10/	7/6

Two Special Prizes will be given by Mr Lumsden of Arden (Open to Dumbartonshire) for Gentlemen's Knitted Neckties.

CROOKS AND WALKING STICKS.

LOCAL.	PRIZES—1st	2nd
Shepherds' Crooks,	10/	7/6
Fancy Crooks,	10/	7/6

LOCAL.	PRIZES—1st	2nd
Plain Walking Sticks,	10/	7/6
Fancy Walking Sticks,	10/	7/6

Special Prize will be given by Mr Lumsden of Arden for the Best Shepherd's Crook ; also for Best Plain Walking Stick shown.
The Exhibitor must be resident in the Parishes of Luss or Arrochar, or Landward part of Row Parish.

Rossdhu, Luss, July, 1908.   ARCHIBALD WILSON, Hon. Secy. and Treas.

8 Program of the Luss Highland Games, 1908

In the early days, dancing bulked larger on the program at Luss, or, rather, it had greater variety, no doubt because there were fewer competitors. In 1893 the dances featured were Highland Fling, Gille Callum, Reel, Sailors' Hornpipe, Irish Jig, and Seann Triubhas. There was a Highland Fling contest for boys under fourteen, and in 1908, separate contests in this dance were held for boys and girls under sixteen years of age.

We have now come into the times of the Cowal gathering which began in 1894. To those acquainted with this event in recent years, it will come as no surprise that the first gathering was blighted by rain. The attendance was so poor that the Dunoon burgh crier was asked to go through the town proclaiming a reduced price of admittance (1s. 6d.). Cowal was mainly an athletic meeting, and not until about 1910 did dancing begin to receive much attention. In that year the first challenge cup for juvenile dancing was awarded. The early regulations, strange to relate, permitted girls to enter certain solo piping events, but excluded them from open dancing competition.

Girls have come into competitive Highland dancing only since the early years of the century. No doubt it was the juvenile events which first introduced them, as certainly it was the two major wars which depleted the ranks of the male dancer. All through the nineteenth century most of the competitive pipers were also dancers. Of course, there were not then the scores of dancers competing that we see today, but there were never less than a dozen stalwart male dancers, and even just prior to the Second World War, although the young ladies already dominated in numbers, the great event for all the young aspiring dancers was the appearance of the "big yins" — graceful A. D. Cameron, elegant Sydney Black, immaculate J. L. Mackenzie and the incomparable Bobby Cuthbertson.

The competitive Highland Dance platform has thrown up its quota of celebrities, but these do not really start to make some claim to fame until about the middle of the nineteenth century. One name which comes down to us from that early period is John MacNeill of Edinburgh, who died in 1890. Of lesser fame were David Anderson, the notable Dundee dancing master, and J. M. MacLeod of Kirkaldy. Other dancers made at least a local impression which in some cases has been recorded by writers of local history. One such writer, Henry Dryerre, in his *Blairgowrie and Strathmore Worthies*,[21] mentions Nottman as the best step dancer of the day (ca. 1853), and writes affectionately of Tam Cramb of Wolfhill, Perthshire, whose fifty years of service as a fiddler and dancing master embraced this period. Cramb, who cultivated a long well-groomed beard, was a true Highlander in that he competed not only in dancing, but in throwing the hammer and putting the stone, a not uncommon versatility among early competitors in the Highland Games. Likewise James Paton of Murthly was not only one of the best all-round athletes of his time, but, according to Dryerre, "one of the finest, most graceful dancers ever seen."

One cannot but be impressed by the appreciative way these early commentators write of dancing prowess. Athletic achievements had their honour and thus names like Donald Dinnie survive from the early period, but athletics did not transcend dancing in importance as they unfortunately do today. In the nineteenth century there was, of

21 Henry Dryerre, *Blairgowrie and Strathmore Worthies* (Edinburgh, 1903), pp. 422–23.

course, a considerable public reasonably skilled in dance. The reel in its several forms was still the supreme social dance of hall and hay loft, and command of a battery of reel steps was an important social accomplishment among all classes. The gifted dancer, then, enjoyed a fairly knowledgeable and certainly appreciative gallery.

D. R. Mackenzie, a notable judge and teacher of Highland dancing around the beginning of this century, tells us that the best dancers he had seen were John MacNeill and William MacLennan of Edinburgh,[22] both pupils of John MacNeill of Edinburgh, mentioned above. "The characteristic dancing syles of these two gentle-men," Mackenzie tells us, "were truly Highland, artistic, and without any affectation." This is echoed by Angus MacPherson, a celebrated piper, who remarks of William MacLennan (ca. 1960): "It can be truthfully said his deportment, hand and foot work were a picture of artistic splendour so different from the modern acrobatic stunts introduced by some dancers of to-day."[23]

William MacLennan, in the nineteen-century tradition of versatility, distinguished himself as a piper as well as a dancer, and his memory is reinforced by his tragic early death from meningitis while on tour of North America with Scott-Skinner and company in 1890. He studied ballet with Cecchetti and Barratti and certainly was responsible for the introduction of certain balletic embellishments to the competition Highland dances, particularly the Seann Triubhas. His brother "D.G." has identified most of these, and tells us also that William was the only Highland dancer of his time to employ the entrechat. Both his brothers, "D.H." and "D.G.," carried on the tradition and were among the best dancers of the early decades of the present century. In *National Dances of Scotland*, D. R. Mackenzie names the best contemporary High-land dancers (ca. 1910) as D. H. MacLennan, Edinburgh; John Mackenzie, Glasgow; Graham McNeilage, Alloa; and Charles McEwan, Langcroft. D. G. MacLennan adds George Melvin, J. A. Gordon, Neil and Malcolm Cameron, A. D. Cameron, J. Mc-Lean, R. Massie, Don Gordon from Finab, and Mearns and Cardownie from Dundee.

Great competition dancers of the northeast at that time were Johnnie Pirie of Aberdeen and Willie Sutherland of Thurso, while Angus MacPherson recalls with pleasure from his native Strathspey "the humorous Peter Stewart; Peter Mackay of Kingussie and Lawson and Murray from Granton-on-Spey."

J. L. Mackenzie, a former pupil of Pirie's, is well known to all interested in Highland Dance today, although in the twilight of a long and illustrious dancing career. His elegant dancing is familiar to many at home and abroad through personal appearances and to some extent caught for posterity through the illustrations of the SOBHD textbook.

When we turn at length to Bobby Watson, we see him as the last of that line of great male Highland dancers who made Highland dancing their business and kept actively competing through the years. Watson is very well known indeed through his frequent performances on stage and television. None of his famous predecessors or competitors have come to the attention of as wide a public. He is of a short, strong, stocky build, and has the advantage of astonishingly small feet. His cuts and round-the-leg work can be remarkably neat and rapid. His Sailors' Hornpipe, performed in

---

[22] Donald R. Mackenzie, *The National Dances of Scotland*.
[23] Angus MacPherson, *A Highlander Looks Back*, 3rd ed. (Oban, 1966).

striped naval shirt, bell-bottomed trousers, and bare feet on a spacious stage, is a tour de force in the best traditions of the entr'acte hornpipe dancer of the late eighteenth century. Likewise his performances of such character dances as Highland Laddie or Wiltu Gang tae the Barracks Johnnie? have the stamp of dramatic authenticity, a rare quality among competitive Highland dancers. Yet, on the competition boards, he can shed this bent, as is appropriate, stabbing his feet in nimble thrusts round the swords, and reeling in vigorous restraint with the rest. Other young male dancers have danced their hour on the stage, then retired from it, and many excellent dancers have not felt the compulsion to compete at Highland Games.

The tradition of male dancing in Scotland is as unmistakable as that among the Cossacks or Spaniards or Greeks. This soon showed itself in the activities of the Highland regiments in the British army. The Pyrrhic dances, of course, were most favoured in the army, apart from the reel, and were used in exhibitions of dancing soldiers.

There have been many distinguished female Highland dancers in recent times, but few continue competitive dancing into womanhood, and, of course, like female athletic competition, female competitive dancing is a comparatively recent phenomenon. We have noticed that at Luss in 1908, girls and boys competed in separate sections, which is right and proper, for the dancing of boys and girls is not precisely comparable, the disparity increasing as they grow older. If the numbers of interested boys had been able to support this competitive dancing, and the games organizers had had wit and concern to prevent a decline, the contemporary dearth of young male Highland dancers might have been avoided. Unfortunately also, the admirable combination of piping and dancing is no longer encouraged; a Willie MacLennan is hardly possible today.

As we have remarked elsewhere, it must not be assumed that Scottish girls have not traditional claim on Scottish dance. Obviously the Pyrrhic dances — Gille Callum, Mc an Fhorsair, Argyll Broadswords and the like — were decidedly male dances. Seann Triubhas also, from its title alone, predicates the male. The Highland Fling as a pas seul is a male dance, but in the respect that it is an enchainment of reel steps, it has no particular gender, as would be the case with any enchainment of reel steps, for women dance reels as well as men. This does not mean that men would dance reels like women or vice versa; the styles would be different, and should be different!

The best-known female dancer of recent times is Miss Jessiman of Huntly. She is a particular and precise dancer and continues to give pleasure to many at the Games. Other brilliant female Highland dancers have reached the top, then retired to family life and teaching; their names are, unfortunately, too readily forgotten. Angus MacPherson, who has been familiar with Highland Games before and since ladies danced in them, tells us that the best lady dancer he has known was Miss Mary Aitken of Aberdeen.

Braemar, Oban, and a few other annual Highland Games do not permit ladies to compete in their dancing competition, and this has done much for the encouragement of male dancers. The introduction of female dances, such as Flora Macdonald's Fancy, however, offers the girls an opportunity to participate in the future. If it is true that the art of Highland Dance would have died out without female support, then indeed, to that extent, we must be grateful to the hundreds of girls who have pursued it.

Dress regulations first grew out of the desire of the Edinburgh exhibition authorities to encourage the preservation of Highland dress, and they offered prizes at an early stage for the best dressed competitor, although as Dalyell remarks, it was difficult to define a criterion of dress supported by history. Since all the competitors were then male, it was therefore the male dress which was specified. Military dress was the only obvious ceremonial standard, based upon what antiquaries had gleaned of the well-dressed chiefs of the late medieval and seventeenth-century clans, and it was this which was adopted or emulated as a standard. Naturally, the child competitors imitated the dress of their adult counterparts and adorned themselves as miniature replicas of the warriors of old — a new and artificial cult. Then when the girls grew into young ladies, they continued to counterfeit the warrior's dress, complete with feathered bonnet, plaid, sporran, and kilt. In due course, as more and more girls entered the competitions, the incongruity of the military dress became more obvious and, in 1952, the committee of the Aboyne Games therefore sponsored a special costume for girls.

This costume was based upon the seventeenth- and eighteenth-century dress of Highland women, versions of which are to be seen in portraits of Flora Macdonald, sometimes retaining the plaid called the arisaid which reached from the neck to the heels, tied before on the breast, with a broad buckle adorned with engravings of animals and a crystal or cairngorm. Below the breast it was held by a pleated leather belt, laced with pieces of silver. The tartan of the arisaid was almost always white — hence the dress Stewart tartan which was an arisaid sett of the Royal tartan.[24]

The Aboyne dress had a loose tartan skirt gathered at the waist, a close-fitting bodice and loose-sleeved blouse, and an arisaid. A very becoming dress indeed, but one which reveals only too starkly the impropriety of girls dancing the Sword Dance and an elevated Highland Fling. For this reason, probably, the SOBHD dress has gained greater favour. This comprises a white blouse with lace-ornamented front, and a tartan skirt reaching to the centre of the knee. A shaped velvet jacket or waistcoat with ornamental buttons may be worn, and hose is optional. This, too, is a big improvement, but some girls feel that it still gives them a masculine look and prefer the Aboyne dress which, of course, is immeasurably superior as attire for the dance Flora Macdonald's Fancy. Other girls tenaciously cling to all the overadornment of their sham warrior's regalia. I suspect that it is as an excuse to dress up that many girls trek round the various games, for there can be little pleasure in dancing with all these encumberances flapping about them.

Male dancers are increasingly favouring the Montrose doublet as competition dress, although it is really formal evening wear; but it is good to note that the SOBHD has ruled that a plain shirt and tie be accepted as suitable for male dancers. This, with belted kilt, tartan or plain hose, and with or without bonnet, is eminently suitable attire for a dancer, particularly in hot climates.

Returning to the competitions themselves, it is sufficient for our purpose to note the trends represented by the select group of Highland gatherings that have attracted our attention. There are innumerable gatherings or games held annually in many parts of the world. There is not a Saturday throughout the summer in Scotland that

---

[24] Frank Adam and Innes of Learney, *The Clans, Septs and Regiments of the Scottish Highlands.*

does not see several take place in sundry towns. Most of these events are of no great age, and range in character from what we may call the authentic, as at Braemar or Glenfinnan or, in athletic aspects, at Luss, to the purely athletic track meet with some far-off dancers and pipers to add but a taste of tartan, as at Edinburgh (Murrayfield).

Much the same can be said of Highland gatherings in Australia, New Zealand, South Africa, Canada, and elsewhere. What it all means in terms of the art of dancing is a vexing question that after a time must confront everyone interested in Scottish dancing as an art. Is Highland dancing today an art, a sport, or a business?

Highland dancing began simply enough, as we have seen. There was a natural desire of the Highlander to perpetuate his traditions of athletic, musical, and dancing prowess. In addition to this came the discovery of the romance and richness of Gaeldom by the Lowland Scot, Englishman, and European alike, stirred first by James Macpherson's poems of Ossian and expressing itself in the historical novels of Sir Walter Scott. Then George IV visited Edinburgh in the autumn of 1822, wrapped a kilt and plaid round his ample form, held a levee and enjoyed himself immensely. Sir Walter Scott was master of ceremonies, with the town council panting in his train. It is strange that at this period, the kilt had acquired a stigma in the eyes of many Lowlanders, particularly, one suspects, of the upper classes in Edinburgh. To someone objecting to this dress, particularly on so large a man as George IV, Lady Saltoun is reported to have said: "Nay, we should take it very kind of him; since his stay will be so short, the more we see of him the better."[25] It was a gay ten days, and everyone who was anyone strained to be presented. Not everyone would have recognized the king had they seen him, and one stout gentleman, Sir William Curtis, standing near His Majesty, was repeatedly mistaken for him. Among those who so erred was John Hamilton Dundas, who kneeled to kiss Sir William's hand and "finding out his mistake, he called 'Wrong, by Jove!' and rising, moved on undaunted to the larger presence."[26]

Some twenty years later Queen Victoria discovered the Highlands for herself. How she loved them, and their gracious, intelligent, culturally rich, if primitive people! Successive generations of her descendants have continued to find solace each autumn in the Highland retreat she established for them, and the spirit of Victoria and Albert pervades the deer-abounding Braes of Mar to this day. This glamour cast its rays over the land of tartan and pibroch, and a new dimension entered the attitude toward everything Highland. Perhaps even yet, in these days of bus tours and realism, some may, on viewing the Trossachs, thrill to the recollection of Scott's outdated but unaccountably lingering lines:

> The stag at eve had drunk his fill
> Where danced the moon on Monan's rill,
> And deep his midnight lair had made
> In lone Glenartney's hazel shade.

Alas, there is but little poetry in the lives of most of the organizers of the Highland gatherings of today.

---

[25] Elizabeth Grant, *Memoirs of a Highland Lady*, p. 261.
[26] Ibid.

18/Taste and Style in Scottish Social Dancing

Topham's observations – Scots' love of movement – Lockhart in Glasgow – Hall in Strathspey – Elizabeth Grant in Strathspey – Jaffray in Aberdeenshire – the poet's view – footwear – the itinerant dancing master's program – enjoyment of technique

Despite the "swarm" of dancing masters in the town and the assiduous study of the art of dance, the Scots in the eighteenth century did not impress English visitors with their grace in the ballroom. The most severe criticism, since it comes from one who was not ill-disposed to the Scots, is that made by Edward Topham:

But I cannot say they are any great proficients in any style of dancing that requires grace. The Scotch are perfect strangers to it in any part of their life. Agility and strength are most natural to them, and their darling delight, which they endeavour to improve from their earliest infancy and in which they arrive at much perfection. But as many people take the greatest pains to accomplish what they will never obtain; so the inhabitants of this country exhaust much time in learning a minuet, the most requisite part of which they never arrive at, namely, that elegant and graceful air which is the very essence of it, and of which the Italians and French are the only complete masters.

At least he does not say the English had mastered the Minuet. However, by way of compensation he goes on to say:

If the Scotch are deprived of this advantage to their persons, all provident nature has bestowed in them others, which are of much greater use to themselves and society. The want of grace is abundantly recompensed by a superiority of strength and manliness and that sinewy arm the very sight of which is sufficient to make a pampered offspring of the south stand amazed and tremble. [Letter xli]

In another letter, he says much the same thing in another way:

But without partiality to our own, or any other country, I shall not hesitate to say, the Scotch dance more ungracefully than any other people I have yet seen. The Swiss, who are far from being a refined or polished nation, dance naturally, in the most graceful style imaginable to young peasants, with no other ornaments but cheerful, healthy looks and sprightly countenances. . . . The Scotch, however, have nothing but their enthusiasm and activity to recommend them. It is no civility to attempt to show them anything new; they hold their dances sacred, and will bear no innovation on that point. Cotillons, and other French dances, have not travelled so far north — and you may tell them . . . that they might as well stay where they are.

The ladies, however, to do them justice, dance much better than the men. But I once had the honour of being a witness to a reel in the Highlands, where the party consisted of three maiden ladies, the youngest of whom was above fifty, which was conducted with gestures so uncouth, and a vivacity so hideous, that you would have thought they were acting some midnight ceremonies, or enchanting the moon. [Letter xxxii]

Topham returns to this theme whenever the subject of dancing arises. The taste of the Scots for dancing *per se* as distinct from a means to promote social intercourse intrigued him. "A Scotchman," he says, "comes into an assembly room as he would into a field of exercise, dances till he is literally tired, possibly without ever looking at his partner, or almost knowing who he dances with."

No student of Scottish dancing can avoid leaning on Topham; he is not only the most voluble observer of social dancing in Edinburgh during its golden age, but almost the only one of any kind. For this reason, too, we must be careful. Here is what he says in the earlier part of Letter xxxii:

The dances of this country are entirely void of grace, which appears to me to be the first principle, unless we consider it, as the savages do, merely as an exercise.

The general dance is a Reel, which requires that particular sort of step to dance properly, of which none but people of the country can have any idea. All the English whom I have seen attempt it, were very deficient in their imitations, although the Scots were too polite openly to ridicule of grown gentlemen learning to dance.

The perseverance which the Scotch ladies discover in these Reels, is not less surprising, than their attachment to them in preference to all others. They will sit totally unmoved at the most sprightly airs of an English Country Dance, but the moment one of their tunes is played, which is liquid laudanum to my spirits, up they start, animated with new life, and you would imagine they had received an electric shock, or been bit by a tarantula. A lady, who, for half an hour before, has sat groaning under the weight of a large bahoop and a corpulent habit of body, the instant one of these tunes is applied to her ear, shall bounce off her feet, and frisk and fly about the room to the great satisfaction of all the spectators.

By the "sprightly airs of an English Country Dance," Topham was doubtless referring to jigs.

A Scot could be equally puzzled with Topham's being able to "sit totally unmoved" at the most riotous airs of a Scottish reel, or at the most sprightly airs of a strathspey. Topham had neither a dancing nor a musical appreciation of reels, nor did he share the Scot's ability to shed his inhibitions. There is no doubt about how the Scot felt about dancing — he liked to move — and the native dances suited this taste.

Obviously, Smollett (a Scot) took the Scottish view when he made Humphrey Clinker write from Edinburgh, "The lady directress of the ball, thinking she (Liddy) was overcome by the heat of the place, had her conveyed to another room, where she soon recovered so well as to return and join in the country dances, in which the Scotch lasses acquit themselves with such spirit and agility, as put their partners to the height of their mettle."

Topham certainly conceded that the Reel was a dance which "none but a native of Scotland can execute in perfection. Their great agility, vivacity and variety of horn-pipe steps," he says, "render it to them a most entertaining dance, but to a stranger, the sameness of the figure makes it trifling and insipid though you are employed during the whole time of its operation which indeed is the reason why it is so peculiarly adapted to the Scotch who are little acquainted with the attitude of standing still" (Letter xlii).

Lockhart, Sir Walter Scott's son-in-law, says much the same thing in his *Peter's Letters to His Kinsfolk*, and one suspects that he has been influenced by Topham:

It is a great mistake under which the Scotch people lie, in supposing themselves to be excellent dancers; and yet one hears the mistake re-echoed by the most sensible, sedate, and dance-abhorring Presbyterians one meets with. If the test of good dancing were activity, there is indeed no question, the northern beaux and belles might justly claim the pre-eminence over their brethren and sisters of the south. In an Edinburgh ballroom, there appears to be the same pride of bustle, the same glorying in muscular agitation and alertness ... but this is all; — the want of grace is as conspicuous in their performances, as the abundance of vigour. We desiderate the conscious towerlike poise — the easy, slow, unfatiguing glide of the fair pupils of D'Estainville. To say the truth, the ladies in Scotland dance in common pretty much like our country lasses at a harvest home. They kick and pant as if the devil were in them; and when they are young and pretty, it is undoubtedly no disagreeable thing to be a spectator of their athletic display; but I think they are very ignorant of dancing as a science. Comparatively few of them manage their feet well, and of these few what a very insignificant portion know anything about that equally important part of the art — the management of the arms. And then how absurdly they thrust out their shoulder blades! How they neglect the undulation of the back! ... As for the gentlemen, they seldom display even vigour and animation, unless they be half-cut — and they never display anything else.

It is fair, however, to mention, that in the true indigenous dances of the country, above all in the reel (the few times I have seen it), these defects seem in a great measure to vanish, so that ambition and affectation are after all at the bottom of their bad dancing in the present day, as well as of their bad writing. [Letter xix]

This final paragraph touches on the truth of the matter. Essentially, the native tradition was at odds with the terre à terre grace of the Minuet. The grace of the Highland Strathspey or of the Allegro Reel is of a different kind, a kind which looks back to the Galliard and the Coranto for its close relations.[1]

It is a pity that Lockhart did not tell us what he meant by "the true indigenous dances of the country" of which he obviously regarded the Reel as only one. Could it be that he included Country Dances in that category? What were the dances for which the "towerlike poise" or "unfatiguing glide" were "desiderate"? The Minuet we know

---

[1] The following comment from a French source illuminates this point: "La dance Ecossaise, ou Reel, est extrêmement difficile à suivre pour étranger: la mesure en est si précipitée et si différente des contredanses Françaises, qu'on voit fort peu qui révississent, mais les habitants les dansent avec beaucoup de grace et de légèreté." [*Promenade autour de la Grande Bretagne par un officier francais émigré*, Edinburgh, 1795.]

about, but we would be surprised to find it still in vogue around 1818 (the year in which Lockhart began *Peter's Letters*). Perhaps he was thinking of the Quadrille which was now coming into favour in the cities. He does comment, in the same passage, on the heavy-footed "big, lazy, clumsy fellows one sees lumbering cautiously" in the evolutions of that dance and on the comparative aptitude of the girls. The "lugubrious gravity" of their performance, however, reminded him of a "prayer meeting," and one is again reminded of Topham when he adds, "and yet these good people, put them fairly into a reel, can frisk it about with all possible demonstrations of hilarity."

It is really not surprising that people raised on a thriving dance tradition of vigorous complexity and ornament of steps should encounter difficulty in capturing the precise poise and constraint of the Minuet. But numerous critical comments warn us to avoid the implied conclusion that dancing in the English assembly was more accomplished. It was not. This varied, certainly, according to circumstances, but Thomas Wilson and others leave us some hair-raising pictures of formal dancing in England in the Napoleonic period.[2] The experts, both amateur and professional, were difficult to please, of course, for good dancers are always even more scarce than good musicians in any age.

The celebrated Mrs. Grant of Laggan, who lived in Strathspey most of her life, turns the tables on Topham and others when she refers to the fashionable, aping "with air constrained, the rural balls!"

> The nymph that wont to trace the source of Tay,
> Or lead the sprightly dance by rapid Spey,
> With conscious triumph smiles aside to see,
> This 'faint reflection of the rural glee.'
> Short pleasure languid imitation feels,
> While polish'd courtiers pant in active reels.
> [Ann Grant, *Poems*, pt. 3]

That a Scotsman could have some idea of grace is implied by Creech's comment in *Fugitive Pieces* that by 1786, "Minuets were given up and country dances only used, which had often a nearer resemblance to a game of romps, than to elegant and graceful dancing" (p. 114).

Whatever the accomplishments of dancers in Edinburgh, there is no question in the Reverend James Hall's mind, twenty-five years later, of the high quality of dancing in Strathspey. Hall was every bit as English as Topham. While visiting Castle Grant, he accompanied Sir James Grant into Grantown to attend the livestock auction sale. Dinner was provided and about twenty gentlemen sat down to it, when it was announced that there was to be a "ball and dance" in the town hall, if any chose to attend." I found," writes Hall in *Travels in Scotland* (vol. 2), "some of the gentlemen, instead of rising to go to the dance, draw nearer the table, and fill their glasses . . . I set out to see the ladies."

When I arrived at the ballroom large, nearly filled with dancers of all ages, from gentlemen and ladies of 80 to 8, all dancing: Hons. and Rt. Hons., and people from 1000's a year to

---

2 Thomas Wilson, *Companion to the Ballroom*.

those not worth sixpence, all dancing and happy. I have heard some of the finest music in London, Edinburgh, York and Bath and seen the dancers at the Opera House, the Royal circus, Saddlers Wells etc. I have seen Italian, French, German, Dutch, Fandango dancers etc., but never any to exceed, I had almost said equal the musical grace, and airy lightness of the dancers here. All seemed life, innocence, and happiness; every one seemed familiar and easy, yet propriety of conduct was uniformly and strictly preserved. [P. 324]

This of course brings us right into the world of Elizabeth Grant who has left us so many valuable sketches of social life in Strathspey at this time. Some of her remarks are, I think, relevant at this point. For instance, in her *Memoirs of a Highland Lady*, she describes a harvest home at Rothiemurchus in 1813 and a Christmas ball:

When the gentlemen joined us the parlour was prepared for dancing. With what extasies we heard the sweep of that masterly bow across the strings of my father's Cremona! The first strathespey was danced by my father and Mrs. Macintosh [a twosome?]; if my mother danced at all, it was later in the evening. My father's dancing was peculiar — a very quiet body, and very busy feet, they shuffled away in double quick time steps of his own composition, boasting of little variety, sometimes ending in a turn-about which he imagined was the fling; as English it was altogether as if he had never left Hertfordshire. My mother did better, she moved quietly in Highland matron fashion . . . like . . . Mrs. Macintosh, for however lightly the lasses footed it, etiquette forbade the wives to do more than "tread the measure." William and Mary moved in the grave style of my mother: Johnnie without instruction danced beautifully; Jane was perfection, so light, so active, and so graceful; but of all the dancers there, none was equal to little Sandy . . . the son of Duncan Macintosh. . . . After the more stately reels of the opening of the dance were over . . . the servants and labourers and neighbours of that class came by turns into the parlour. . . . We were accustomed to dance with all the company, as if they had been our equals; it was always done. There was no fear of undue assumption on the one side, or low familiarity on the other; a vein of good-breeding ran through all ranks influencing the manners and rendering the intercourse of all most particularly agreeable. [Pp. 147–48]

At this time, the forest of Rothiemurchus was falling to the woodsman's axe, and the Christmas ball of the foresters was a great event:

So large a party, so many strangers, some splendid dancers from Strathspey, the hay loft, the straw loft, the upper floor of the threshing-mill all thrown open en suite; two sets of fiddles playing, punch made in the washing tubs, an illumination of tallow dips! It is surprising that the floors stood the pounding they got; the thumping noise of the many energetic feet could have been heard half a mile off. . . . When a lad took a lass out to dance, he led her to her place in the reel and pree'd her mou' — kissed her — before beginning, she holding salute, and he giving a good sounding smack when the lass was bonnie. [P. 151]

Elizabeth Grant's accounts of the busy dancing activity of her region of the Highlands and Strathspey give us no reason to believe that Country Dances were danced there in her time, although Haymakers was a favourite. The Northern Meeting was a different matter. There, fashions of the metropolitan assemblies found a place, and Miss Grant wrote of joining "the long country dance" forming in the assembly room.

Through his mother, Henry Mackenzie was connected with most of the chief familes of Speyside and he married a daughter of the House of Grant. In his *Anecdotes and Egotisms*, he comments on the enthusiasm of the dancing in Strathspey:

Strathspey is the native land of Highland dancing, as the name of the dance most admired in the Highlands denotes. Tho' as danced there, it seems a violent exercise, yet it appears rather to recruit the wearied limbs than to add to their fatigue. The post at Castle Grant who travelled three days in the week to Forres, a distance of 22 miles, for the letters and returned in the evening, besides many extra errands in that town and neighbourhood, I have seen in the hall, after his return, dancing for several hours with admirable agility, and, as Goldsmith says, "dancing down" some of the stoutest of his partners. [P. 75]

It is fortunate for us that Elizabeth Grant was so much a product of this vigorous dancing environment, and one wonders what Topham would have said if she had told him how "old Neil Gow" was sent for when her family stopped over at Inver on their journey north in 1804, and how her father had to take her for a walk by the riverside in the moonlight to calm her excitement after hearing the great fiddler. In her *Memoirs*, she related that a dancing master (she does not tell us who) "taught us every variety of wonderful Highland step" and that she and her brother William did "merrily dance the quaker's Wife together quite to the satisfaction of the servants, who all took lessons too, in common with the rest of the population, the Highlanders considering this art an essential in the education of all classes, and never losing an opportunity of acquiring a few more flings and shuffles" (p. 31).

Perhaps a great deal of this skill was absent from the Lowland assemblies. Alexander Jaffray writes from Aberdeenshire in *Recollections of Kingswells*: "Even among the peasants there are many good, though untaught dancers. The Scottish Highlanders are particularly remarkable for good taste in dancing both as to time and measure, whether in slow or quick movements; and many show a variety and neatness of natural steps which would not disgrace some of the best stage dancers" (pp. 146-47). This echoes Francis Peacock's comment in *Sketches relative to dancing*: "This pleasing propensity, one would think, was born with them, from the early indications we sometimes see their children show for this exercise. I have seen children of theirs, at five or six years of age, attempt, nay even execute, some of their steps so well as almost to surpass belief" (p. 85).

Dr. Garnett, the English scholar, conceded the superiority of the Highlanders in the art of dance in commenting on a ball he attended at Dunkeld, 1798, at a dancing school: "In the evening there was a dancing school ball at the inn, to which we were politely invited, and where we had again an opportunity of hearing Neil [*sic*] Gow, and observing the superiority of the highlanders to our countrymen in dancing; some of the children we saw dance this evening, would have cut no disgraceful figure on the stage."[3]

His words almost reiterate those of Dr. Hall, Elizabeth Grant, Peacock, and Jaffray which we have quoted earlier. Of course, the English Captain Topham and the literary Lockhart were restricted to comments on the Lowland assemblies and were comparatively circumscribed in the matter of musicality. Certainly, Topham had some disparaging remarks to make about the boisterous execution of a Reel by three middle-aged Highland women on the green, but the reader can be left to evaluate the importance of these as a reflection on dancing standards in the Highlands.

[3] Thomas Garnett, *Observations on a Tour through the Highlands of Scotland*, vol. 2 (London, 1800), p. 74.

One would be surprised, however, if there were not some dramatic differences in style between the formal dance assembly and the informal kirn.

The spirit and style associated with the kirn may be deduced from these extracts from some lively poems:

> He dances best that dances fast,
> And loups at ilka reesing o't,
> And claps his hands frae hough to hough,
> And furls about the feezings o't!
>
> [Alexander Ross, "The Bridal o't,"
> ca. 1770]

> The lasses bab'd about the reel,
> Gart a' their hurdies wallop,
> And swat like ponies when they speel
> Up braes, or when they gallop.
>
> [Quoted in David Stewart,
> *Sketches of the Highlanders*]

But there is something more elegant about this:

> The bonniest sight I ever saw
>   Was by the brig of Johnstone,
> For 'midst a rank of rosie queans
>   I saw my dearie dancin':
> Snow white stockings on his legs,
>   And siller buckles glancin',
> A gude blue bonnet on his head,
>   And O, but he was handsome.
>
> [Alan Cunningham, "The Ploughman"]

The *Banffshire Journal*, published in the late nineteenth century, describes the spirit of the kirn among the fisher-folk at Collieston on the Aberdeen coast: "On the green-sward under the blue canopy of heaven on a sweet afternoon in summer — the music of the violin, the song of the lark ... right overhead, the ringing guffaws of the juvenile spectators, the clapping of hands, the loud 'hoochs' and 'whoops' of the dancing fisher-men, all commingling and commingled with the murmur of the billows breaking among the rocks."

We can judge for ourselves, however, from the few engravings and painting avail-able to us, that the poet was inclined to heighten the feeling of gaiety at the expense of the good dancers. He has no space for the stylish deportment of the lady making grace-ful use of skirt or apron or the cat-like spring and easy cutting of the youth with the spirit of the music in his bones. The artist had an eye for this, as a glance at David Allan's several dance scenes and David Wilkie's *Penny Wedding* will show.

In "The Ploughman" the dancing youth is wearing buckled shoes and white stockings; but almost immediately we recall Ramsay's lines: "Down to ilk bonny singing Bess/Wha dances *barefoot* on the green."[4] [Italics mine.]

---

[4] Allan Ramsay, *The Tea-Table Miscellany*, vol. 2 (Edinburgh, 1823), p. 202.

This brings us to the influence of footwear upon dance style. There is no doubt that for a large part of their lives, the generality of youths and children in Scotland did not wear shoes of any kind until comparatively recent times, whether they lived in the Highlands or the Lowlands. In the Highlands, when some covering of the feet was required, it was an old practice to wrap an oval piece of raw hide neatly round the foot by means of thongs passed through holes in the material. Martin, Burt, and other travellers describe footwear of this kind in the eighteenth century. The hairy side was usually outwards, and the skin was pierced with small holes to allow drainage of the water taken up in the crossing of rivers and wet ground. They were called brogs, the prototype of the brogues and gillies of today.

Heeled and stiff-soled shoes were an alien style to Highlanders in general throughout the eighteenth century. From this fact, we may confidently surmise that, as far as Highland dancing was concerned, such shoes were an encumbering innovation.

Thomas Morer remarked in his *Short Account of Scotland* that the tradition was staunchly held that "it was founded upon ancient law, that no males should wear shoes till they were 14 years of age, that they might be hardened for the wars" (p. 14). He also observed in the Lowlands that though the menfolk were shod, the ordinary women and children even of the better class went barefoot, especially in summer.

In Ayrshire, around 1742, we are told that "young women wore woolen cloaks; with hoods of the same kind of cloth. . . . They had no buckles on their shoes; these were tied with a piece of red or blue tape. The women in general, and particularly the younger part of them seldom put on shoes and stockings excepting to go to the church, or to a fair or market."[5] We may add to this Sunday and holidays, or during frost and snow, as occasions for wearing shoes by both men and women in the eighteenth century. Even at that, the women particularly seemed so unaccustomed to their shoes that they hobbled as they walked, and usually, in going to kirk on Sunday, carried their shoes until they came within sight of the church. Likewise house wives travelling to town would walk barefoot to the environs, and then would wash their feet and don their shoes and stockings.

By mid-eighteenth century, ladies' shoes were leather soled, with uppers of floral silk brocade to match the dress. Men's shoes were of morocco or leather, with heels of medium height and metal buckles. As the eighteenth century drew to a close, shoes became more and more a status symbol with the common people, particularly in the towns. In formal dancing assemblies, ladies' dancing slippers of a heelless variety or with a very slight heel and of pastel-shaded uppers were fashionable in Scotland, as in England and France. Creech relates in *Fugitive Pieces* that, sensible of their superior neatness of ankle and prettiness of foot, the Scottish ladies employed "whatever taste could invent, or art execute" in the decoration of their dancing shoes. They were stretched in the tambour, they glittered with spangles and embroidery, and every combination of colours "that could please or allure the eye" was used (p. 339).

In the nineteenth century, low-heeled shoes were customary in European and American ballroom dancing for both male and female; consequently the tendency was to walk or slide through the dance steps. Which was the cause and which the effect is perhaps a little vague, but doubtless the change in dress fashion contributed its

[5] Thomas Pollock in Kilwinning Statistical Account, xi, 156–57.

influence on social dance style, as indeed it has always done. It was customary, however, to change into these dance shoes or slippers for formal dancing, while in the countryside many could not afford special dance shoes and wore instead their best outdoor shoes. In due course, one can see it was considered a mark of refinement for males to wear dancing slippers and hence in the usual confused way, this fashion came to be regarded by the common people as an affectation. Thus, even today, it has been reported from parts of Scotland and Nova Scotia that males have shown a marked disinclination to wear gillies when they are introduced to Scottish country dancing!

J. F. Flett consulted a number of people who took lessons from itinerant dancing masters in Lowland Scotland during the late nineteenth century and in *Social Dancing in Scotland*, she remarked: "These old dancing masters do not seem to have put great emphasis on technique. It was much more important to learn the figures of the dances, and, while they taught steps, they were not greatly worried if their pupils did not attain great precision or polish. Indeed great precision was impossible since many of their pupils wore ordinary outdoor shoes. The emphasis throughout traditional dancing in Scotland, was, as one would expect, much more on enjoyment than technique" (pp. 153-63).

Now, we cannot let this last remark pass without comment. It was *enjoyment of technique* that inspired people to go to watch Davie Strange's sister dance at penny weddings in eighteenth-century Ayrshire; it was enjoyment of technique which caused Elizabeth Grant to remark so often on beautiful dancing, none being equal, it may be remembered, to "little Sandy" the grieve's son; and it was the "exquisite" dancing of "Jupiter" Carlyle's "fair Caledonian" friend which "carried off all hearts," and not the superior beauty and intellectual qualities of her competitor in the company.[6] In the dances of that period, and the Scotch Reel was then a great favourite, a precise technique and its associated deportment were fundamental. Indeed, without technique the Scotch Reel is nothing, for there is no interest in the figure, as Topham accurately remarked. Thus it was in every way consistent with the tradition and the dance style of the period that in praising Maria's dancing, Robert Burns should have had a special word for her stepwork:

> How gracefully Maria leads the dance!
> She's life itself. I never saw a foot
> So nimble and so elegant; it speaks,
> And the sweet whispering poetry it makes
> Shames the musician.[7]

The itinerant dancing master had much to teach in a limited time, his approach was utilitarian — so many different dances to cover, and more figures than ever before. Nor could he make silk purses out of sows' ears, if that should have been his material. Furthermore, we must recognize the change of emphasis in the performance and style of the contemporary dances. And that the tradition of accomplished dancing was stronger in some parts of the country, particularly in the northeast and Central Highlands, than in others. One may question the validity of the style of execution asserted

---

[6] Alexander Carlyle, *Autobiography*, p. 461.
[7] J. Logie Robertson, ed., *The Poetical Works of Robert Burns* (London, 1904), p. 304.

for the Scottish Country Dance by the Royal Scottish Country Dance Society as to whether one regards it as a dance of the Lowland barn or assembly hall. But there is more than one dance tradition in Scotland and, without question, that tradition which is most individualistic, most vital, and most peculiar to Scotland, places a marked emphasis on the technique of the dance. It is Highland Dance *tradition* that is the fertilizing force in Scottish dancing; and the Scottish Country Dance is all the richer because of it, and indeed may have little peculiar identity without it.

19/The Country Dance

Country Dance in Elizabethan times –
contrapassi – Chiarenzana – "Court"
Country Dances – longwise formation and
progression – Playford and The Dancing
Master *– vogue in Europe – contredanse –*
Rameau – antics – time of Charles I –
kissing in the dance – Walsh and other
publishers – increasing use of Scottish
tunes – Thomas Wilson and the English
Country Dance

In that interesting sixteenth-century work, *The Complaynt of Scotland*, the dances of the countryfolk were called *licht* dances to distinguish them from the serious or grave dances of high society. Among these were rounds or carols, processionals, and winding heys. Dance activity of this kind was called reeland (reeling) in Scotland, and if the hey was the dominating figure in reeling, one can see how the figure itself would come to be called a reel. Thus, as we have also seen, the word "hey" was used in England in exactly the same sense as the word "reel" in Scotland. Both referred to the same interweaving figure and both referred to a social folk dance.

By the end of the sixteenth century, these dances in England were often referred to as Country Dances. One suspects that this term must have developed from an increasing distinction between the dances of the town and the dances of the country, perhaps arising from the growth of London as a great metropolitan community in which court dancing was *de rigueur*.

Country Dances became a favourite diversion at the court of Queen Elizabeth. There are frequent references to them in Elizabethan plays and poems, and there was a corresponding interest in their music on the part of serious musicians. The temper of the times, it seems, called for some counterpoise to the more disciplined forms in music and dance and especially one which appealed to the growing national spirit of the English Elizabethans.

It was characteristic of many a Tudor squire to share some of these jovial dances with his servants and retainers, and this is exactly what happened at Elizabeth's court where, as John Selden tells us in *Table Talk*, after the court dances were kept up "with Ceremony," Trenchmore and the Cushion Dance were performed. He points out that "all the Company Dance, Lord and Groom, Lady and Kitchen-Maid, no distinction."

The dances seen at a typical village celebration in England were named by Nashe in 1596 as Rogero, Basilena, Turkeyloney, All Flowers of the Broom, Pepper is Black, Greensleeves, and Peggy Ramsay. Basilena and Turkeyloney were Estampies.[1] (The Estampie was one of the earliest of the court dances for couples and threes.) The jigs, Greensleeves and Peggy Ramsay, were favourite "Northern" tunes, and certainly, at a later date, they were regarded as Scottish tunes. Whether the dances, that is, their peculiar combinations of figures, were of "Northern" origin we have no way of determining. Nor, of course, do we have any record of figures to Country Dances prior to the publication of John Playford's *Dancing Master* in 1651. One of the most frequently mentioned dances in the second half of the sixteenth century is Trenchmore.[2] This name is probably a corruption of the Irish Rinnce Mor (Great Ring), and there is every indication that it was, like the Cushion Dance, clearly distinguishable from the general run of Country Dances. It was apparently characterized by capers and stamping (with hands on hips) akin to the Galliard.[3] Playford published Trenchmore in his second edition of *The Dancing Master* as a longwise dance for any number, reminiscent of Strip the Willow in its figuration, but this version could not have been its original form.

In 1602, Irish tunes were very much in favour at court, along with "Mutche dauncing in the privi chamber of contrey dawnces before the Q.M."[4] By this time there were what were referred to as "new" Country Dances, as we gather from a remark in the Sidney papers: "Her Majestie is in very good health, and comes much abroad these holidays: for almost every night she is in the presence, to see the ladies daunce the old and new Country dances, with the taber and pipe."[5]

It has been conjectured that the "new" Country Dances were the products of a combination of the traditional English (and Scottish and Irish) country dance form and the Italian figured court dances of the similar form called *contrapassi*, of which Fabritio Caroso presented a few in his *Il Ballarino* (1581), a widely used dance manual of the time. One of the contrapassi described by Caroso is the Chiarenzana, a favourite wedding dance of the early Renaissance.[6] In the Academia di Belle Arti, Florence, there is a painting on a cassone of this dance being performed at the wedding of a daughter of the Adimari family (ca. 1450), showing it to be a longwise dance for several couples. This corresponds with Caroso's description which, according to Melusine Wood,[7] runs as follows:

All facing up, honour the Presence,
All up and back twice
Top couple faces down and the rest repeat the previous figure to them
Second couple face down and repeat,

[1] Melusine Wood, *Historical Dances*.

[2] See J. P. Cunningham, "The Country Dance: Early References," *JEFDSS*, vol. 9, no. 3 (1962).

[3] See Margaret Dean-Smith and E. J. Nicol, "The Dancing Master," *JEFDSS*, vol. 4, no. 5 (1944), p. 226.

[4] Letter from the Earl of Worcester to the Earl of Shrewsbury, quoted in John Nichols, *The Progresses and Public Processions of Queen Elizabeth*, vol. 3, p. 40.

[5] Quoted in E. K. Chambers, *The Elizabethan Stage*, vol. 4, 1923, p. 115.

[6] Otto Gombosi, "About Dance and Music in the Late Middle Ages," *Musical Quarterly*, vol. 27, no. 23 (1941), p. 291. See also Florio, *The World of Words*, 1598.

[7] Melusine Wood, "Some Notes on the English Country Dance before Playford," *JEFDSS*, vol. 3, no. 2 (1937), p. 97.

Third couple etc.
First man leads his partner through the second couple and in such a way that he faces the
second woman and his partner faces the second man. Hey three changes and pass on to the
next. [This could mean a figure of eight round the second couple.]
When the first couple comes to the top again all dance forward [up?] and back twice as at
the beginning. First and second couple four hands half round to left and back. Honour.
First couple raise their arms, second couple pass under and up to first place while first couple
continue to progress.

We are told, says Miss Wood, that many more figures can be done. The following coda
finished the dance:

All face up and honour.
Top couple faces down, take hands and, raising arms, move down outside the lines so that
all the other pass under. Each couple does likewise as it comes to the top. Arriving at the
bottom, release hands, cast, and lead up to original places.
First couple turn, both hands, half round and back, and honour.
First man repeats with second woman while first woman repeats with second man, and so
on with third etc. to bottom of set, where first couple take hands and dance back to lady's
seat.

The steps were comparatively simple, and the progression was once through the dance,
after considerable elaborations, to the bottom of the set.

   Some other contrapassi for a fixed number of couples are described by Caroso —
Pizochara, for instance, for four couples, and Anello, for two couples. The progression
in Pizochara is contrived by the last couple dancing up the middle to top place. There
is no progression in Anello.

   We can see from this evidence, then, that it is quite conceivable that the Italian
figured dances suggested a line of development of the native Country Dance, in
longwise formation particularly, so producing a new genre of "Court" Country
Dance to the native dance tunes. The longwise formation, however, did not predom-
inate among the Country Dances in the first edition of *The Dancing Master*. The
majority of the 105 dances in that collection were rounds for three and four couples and
any number, and squares for two and four couples. The longwise sets were for three
and four couples and "for as many as will." These were a mixture of progressive and
non-progressive. Progression, when it occurred, was accomplished in three ways. One
was that the top couple, after proceeding once through the dance, finished at the
bottom of the set, a method which was more favoured for the fixed three or four
couple sets and was not so suitable for the indefinitely long sets. Another was progression by one place at a time in two-couple and three-couple dances (or "duple
minor" and "triple minor" sets, as Cecil Sharp called them) involving "as many as
will." The third method did not conduce to a very active dance; in this, the top woman
ended at the bottom of the ladies' side, the other ladies moving up one place, while the
men retained their original places throughout the dance.

   The square dances for four couples exhibited the most elaborate figures, and one of
the best of these in the first edition of *The Dancing Master*, Fain I Would, is marked
"as in Oxford," which seems to identify it with the court of Charles I, Oxford being

the seat of the Royalist government during part of the Civil War. Some of these dances, indeed, as has been suggested, may be modified masque dances.[8]

Playford does not describe the technique of execution of these dances. What were their steps? How did partners turn? How were hands held? These questions are not to be found answered in Playford's publications. Cecil Sharp made an admirable attempt to find the answers and to transcribe Playford's dance descriptions into a more intelligible form in his *Country Dance Book*. His task was prodigious, but he was worthy of it and achieved great success. His objective was to restore the original "country" style of the dances, knowing well that their manner of execution did not remain constant throughout the seventeenth and eighteenth centuries, the degree of formal movement varying according to fashion.

The majority of the tunes in *The Dancing Master* were of 6/8 jig and common-time varieties; but in the eighth, ninth, and tenth editions (1690–98), a number of dances called maggots, whims, delights, and fancies, to triple-time hornpipe (3/3), appeared in some profusion. These, the inventions of the royal dancing masters, Messrs. Isaacs and Beveridge, were of the form of an introduction followed by one or more figures, harking back to the Italian Chiarenzana.[9] Mme la Dauphine introduced them to French society, and we can judge their popularity from the fact that Raoul Feuillet, the author of a famous treatise on choreography, compiled a collection in *Recueil de Contredanses* of thirty-two of these longwise Country Dances, sixteen of which are traceable to Playford's tenth edition and the remainder composed "after the English model." He defined their handing, deportment, and steps after the French style, and this in turn was taken up in England as a new fashion.

The English Country Dance now enjoyed a considerable vogue in the European centres of fashion. Lady Mary Montagu wrote from Vienna in 1717: "The ball always concludes with English Country Dances to the number of thirty or forty couples, and [they are] so ill danced that there is very little pleasure in them."[10] In 1749 Walpole wrote from Italy that the Italians were "fond to a degree of our Country Dances,"[11] — a comment which reveals a happy repayment of a debt from the past.

Thus the Country Dance developed as a dance of the assembly room and the grand ball. It was called *contredanse* in France and *contretanz* in Germany. The longwise form of Country Dances exclusively prevailed in the eighteenth century and this, combined with the fact that ballroom dances in general came to Britain from France, and that the Country Dance had then no apparent identity with rusticity, led to the widely held presumption that the term "country dance" was a manifest corruption of the French *contredanse*. This reasoning led some to seek without success the origin of the Country Dance in a possible *contredanse* imported by the Normans. The longwise Country Dance "for as many as will" with progression by one place at a time and engaging minor sets of two or three couples progressively down the long, opposing lines of gentlemen and ladies was now everywhere identified with England and was

8 Dean-Smith and Nicol, "The Dancing Master."

9 Ibid.

10 Quoted in Cecil J. Sharp and A. P. Oppe, *The Dance*.

11 Ibid. The Italians called the longwise dances "indeterminata," that is, an indeterminate number of people took part; for square dances, the term "determinata" was used.

Newcastle   *Round for eight*

Meet all, back againe, fet to your owne, and to the next ⌣ That againe ∴

Armes all with your owne by the right, men all fall with your left hands into the middle, We. go round them to your places ⌣ Armes againe with your owne, and We. left hands in, men goe about them towards the left to your places ∴

Sides all with your owne, and change places ⌣ Sides with them ⌣ Sides with the next, and change places with them —

The firft man and 3. Wo. take hands and meet, the firft Wo. and 3. man, lead out againe then holding up your hands, the other foure caft off and come under your armes to their places ⌣ The other foure the like ∴

Armes all with your We. and change places ⌣ Armes with the next and change places ∴ Now every man is with his owne Wo. in the Co. place.

Fall back from each other, foure and foure a breſt to each wall. turn and change places with your oppofites ⌣ Fall back from each other foure and foure along the roome, turne S. change places with your oppofite ∴ So each falls into his place as at firſt.

9 Facsimile of a page from Playford's *The Dancing Master* (3rd ed.), describing the dance, Newcastle

universally understood to be the specific dance form referred to when the term "Country Dance" was used.

Thus, in Scotland, such dances as Haymakers or Sir Roger de Coverley which were for a fixed number of couples, were distinguished from Country Dances, and were called simply Haymakers, or Bumpkin (Ninesome Reel), or reels.

The practice of using the French term *contredanse* for country dance became fairly widespread in the English-speaking world in the nineteenth century, particularly in North America. The French, however, used the term to describe their Quadrille, which displaced the Country Dance in English and European assemblies in the nineteenth century. Rameau is credited with devising the first Quadrille for one of his ballets in the early eighteenth century.

It was also Rameau who complained in 1725 in *Le Maître à Danser*: "All the perfection of these Country Dances is by a distorting of the body in turning about, and stamping with their feet as if they had wooden shoes on, and putting themselves in several ridiculous postures. . . ." This description represents some deterioration from Feuillet's ideal, and reminds us of the tendency to introduce antics and pantomime into many English Country Dances in the eighteenth century. The following injunctions are given in G. Waylett's *Country Dance Collection* (1749 and 1751): "Clap hands — strike hands across — snap fingers — beckon your partner — stamp four times — give three jumps — give a little jump — hold up finger — pull your partner — peep three times — peep down and up — hit your right elbows together and then your left — act the cobler. . . ."

These antics, however, were not really new. Among the dances in the first three editions of Playford, of about a century before, there are a few injunctions for peeping, shaking, winding, clapping hands, snapping fingers, etcetera. Then, of course, there were dances involving kissing (these may be called "game" dances), such as Kemp's Jig, Bobbing Joe, Trenchmore and some others, to say nothing of the widespread Cushion Dance or Babbity Bowster that never grew old. From all acounts, the height of this frivolity was reached, not as one would suspect in the time of the Merry Monarch, but in the time of his father, King Charles I. This was the period which Selden described as turning away from the things "pretty well" of James's reign to "Trenchmore and the Cushion Dance, hoity-cum-toity omnium gatherum." No doubt Charles II was too much of a dancer to mix his kissing games with the art he loved.

Certainly by the end of the sixteenth century, and probably long before, it was customary in England for the gentleman leading a lady into a dance to salute her with a kiss. Shakespeare alludes to this practice in *Henry VIII* when he has that monarch say to Anne Boleyn as he leads her into a dance, "Sweetheart, I were unmannerly to take you out, and not to kiss you." Kissing between partners as a salutation prior to, and often after, a dance survived into the eighteenth century in many parts of the British Isles.

The various editions of *The Dancing Master* suffered no rivals in the publication of Country Dances until around 1686 when the first tentative competitors ventured into the field. John Walsh, in particular, published annual collections of twenty-four dances for many years after 1705. These have the appearance of being original figures set to favourite tunes of the time. Sometimes, the composers are identified, as, for instance, one Nathaniel Kynaston in the years 1710–18, and, for the year 1721, Mr. Birkhead of the Theatre Royal in London. Walsh occasionally published groups of the annual collections in single volumes, and has been taken to task for his plagiarism of the Playford productions in the early editions of his best-known compendium, *The Compleat Country Dancing-Master* (first series 1719, second series 1731). Of special interest to us, however, is his collection of nearly seventy dances entitled *Caledonian Country Dances*, published in 1733, and the eight subsequent volumes of this series published by his son from 1737 to about 1760.[12]

The variety of published collections now markedly increased; they were all from London houses and most ran to several editions often supplemented by annual collections. Notable among these were: Waylett (1749); Thompson (1751); Dukes (1752); Rutherford (1756); Bremner (1756); Welch (1767); Werner (1785); Campbell (ca. 1785); Preston (1786); and many others, ending with Burton and Whitaker and, greatest of all, Thomas Wilson in the early nineteenth century. Most dances were styled as being performed "at Court, at Bath, Tonbridge, Carlton House, Prince of Wales, . . . and all public assemblies."

There was a marked increase in the number of Scottish tunes employed, and of course, in this period, the dances were named after the tunes. It is likely that a number of the dances emanated from Scotland, but it is not possible to distinguish these from the English dances except, perhaps, where they contain the figures reel of three at the sides and set to and turn corners, figures which became popular in Scotland.

Unfortunately, apart from the works of Nicholas Dukes and Welch, none of the numerous books of Country Dances contained specific directions on the subject of execution until Thomas Wilson wrote his important books (ca. 1820), just at the peak of the Country Dance's popularity and complexity in England after the Napoleonic Wars. Wilson now referred to "The English Country Dance," although he did not explain why he inserted the word "English." The inference is that he felt a need to distinguish the English from the Scottish and Irish Country Dances.

But, alas, the Country Dance was on the eve of its long eclipse; the Minuet had fallen deep in the shadow, and the sun rose on a new day of the Cotillion, Quadrille, Waltz, Polka, Varsovianna, Lancers, and their relatives.

---

[12] The dates of these have now been established by William C. Smith (see Flett, *The Scottish Country Dance*, Scottish Studies, vol. 11, 1967, p. 10): bk. 1, 1733, 1735, 1736; bk. 2, 1737; bk. 3, ca. 1740; bk. 4, 1744; bk. 5, 1748; bk. 6, 1751; bk. 8, 1757; and bk. 9, ca. 1760.

20 / The Scottish Country Dance

English Country Dance fashion – English longwise dance – Scottish MS collections of Country Dances – restorations by RSCDS – identification of Country Dances – contents of Drummond Castle MS, Holmain MS, Menzies MS, Bodleian MS – Walsh's Caledonian Country Dances – other sources of Scottish Country Dances – Robert Bremner – John Bowie – Bremner's Reels or Country Dances – Scottish figures – Scottish contribution to the Country Dance – teaching of itinerant dancing masters – Robert Burns and Loch Erichtside – centres in the nineteenth century – field researches of J. F. and T. M. Flett – strains of dances in the Country Dance style – Country Dance in nineteenth-century Scotland – David Anderson – principal printed sources – practice of dancing masters

There are several plausible ways in which the fashion of Country Dances at court could have been passed to polite society in Scotland in the later seventeenth century. There were numerous Scottish noblemen acquainted with court life, and it seems certain that the sojourn of the Duke of York at Holyrood for nearly two years, 1688–90, would provide occasion for country dancing after the current English manner and introduce the latest favourites to many of the Scottish gentry invited to private palace occasions. The goings-on in the palace were very discreet and little is recorded of them.

There is no hint of Country Dances being taught in the Glasgow and Edinburgh dancing schools of the time, and not until 1710 is there any suggestion of a regular dance assembly in any town in Scotland. A number of Scottish noblemen compiled their own collections of Country Dances to Scottish tunes and a few of these have survived, the earliest being that compiled for the Jacobite Duke of Perth, dated 1734 and called the Drummond Castle manuscript.[1]

Such dances as the weaving dances, of which Strip the Willow is a familiar example, comprising a fixed longwise set of four couples, and various reels of the same structure have obviously long been known in Scotland. Where there is progression in these, it is of that class whereby the top couple finishes at the bottom of the set after one execution of the dance. The round and the reel figure are also prominent in Scottish dance.

It is very possible that some of the dances published by Playford to Scottish tunes in the seventeenth century were of Scottish origin, or, more plausibly, based on a Scottish original; but this cannot be proved one way or the other.

It is also possible that some examples of Italian *contrapassi* were introduced to the

---

1 A copy is held in Glasgow University library.

fifteenth- and sixteenth-century Scottish court; one at least is mentioned in *Colkelbie's Sow*, as we have noted. But the Scottish dance fashion leaned more heavily on the French than did the English, and the French evinced no interest in contrapassi. Nevertheless, it is conceivable that this class of figured social dance was not unknown in Scotland in the early or the late sixteenth century, at least in court circles. James VI, after all, possessed Caroso's book in which contrapassi were described.

There is, however, no suggestion, prior to the eighteenth century, of a development of the social folk dance in Scotland of the kind which produced the ballroom Country Dance in England; nor of any propietory claim on that form of Country Dance which appropriated the name exclusively to itself, namely, the longwise dance "for as many as will" with duple and triple minor sets. Nevertheless, dances of this structure were taught by itinerant dancing masters in the Scottish Lowlands by mid-eighteenth century, and were found at all levels of Lowland society, at least later in that century. The earliest identifiable association of one of these dances with Scotland is the manuscript description of one called John Anderson, dated 1704, and first commented upon by William Dauney in *Ancient Scottish Melodies*. To this description is appended the curious remark, "The tune is to be played even through once over every time so the first couple has time to take their drinks to be danced with as many pairs you please."

Of the manuscript collections of Country Dances surviving from this period in Scotland, the Drummond Castle manuscript is probably the earliest. Other important manuscripts are the Holmain (ca. 1730–50), the Menzies (1749), and the Bowman (ca. 1760). The Drummond manuscript was written for the Duke of Perth by David Young, undoubtedly the same D. A. Young who compiled the manuscript, "A Collection of the Newest Country Dances Performed in Scotland," 1740, in the Bodleian Library, Oxford.

None of the titles included in the Drummond manuscript appears also in the Bodleian manuscript, and comparing titles with the Holmain and Menzies manuscripts, the same absence of duplication is striking. Three, This is not my own House, Argyle's Bowling Green, and Lennox Love appear in both the Drummond and Holmain, and one, The Menzies Reel (*Ruidhle daoine na Marachan*) appears in both the Holmain and Menzies. In most of the descriptions, the word "reel" is used, where "hey" would be used in the English versions. The Royal Scottish Country Dance Society has reconstructed the three named from the Holmain manuscript, and the versions in the Drummond correspond very closely to these.

The Menzies manuscript contains two dances called Strathspey reele, one of the earliest uses of the term "Strathspey" with respect to dance. One of these, The Montgomeries' Rant, is set to a tune of another name by the RSCDS, a reel, "Lady Eglintoun" (the Eglintouns, of course, are Montgomeries).

With some exceptions in the early Playford collections, Country Dances were named after their tunes until recent times, when the RSCDS and others found it more desirable to associate the name of the dance with its figures and select a suitable tune for it regardless of name. Most of the old dances restored by the RSCDS are still associated with their original tunes and bear the names of these tunes. It does seem questionable, however, to retain the original title of a Country Dance when the tune giving its name to the dance is a well-established one and is no longer used in association with it. For instance, "This is no my ain hoose" is a celebrated old song to a set of an old tune. The Country Dance of that name taken from the Holmain manuscript was set by the RSCDS to another tune entirely which presumably was thought more suitable for the dance. It can be argued that at least this keeps the old names and their associations alive. Nevertheless, it prevents our using the old tune for another set of figures more appropriate to it and naming the dance after it.

Such considerations did not trouble the eighteenth-century collectors and publishers. It is not unusual to find in their works more than one set of figures associated with the same tune and bearing the same name, or indeed the same sequence of figures set to different tunes and accordingly bearing different names. The titles of the dances included in the manuscript collections mentioned are nevertheless of interest.

DRUMMOND CASTLE MANUSCRIPT

Whip Her and Gird Her 6/8
Jack Leighton 4/4
Drummond's Rant 4/4
Athol Braes 4/4
Argyle's Bowling Green 4/4
Fairly Shot of Her 12/8
Allastor 4/4
New Bigging 6/8
Drops of Brandy 9/8
Hey to Cowpar 6/8
The Maltman 9/8
Wee're all forsaken for want of silver 9/8
A Wife of my Own 9/8
Euphie McNab 6/8
My own Kind Dearie 4/4
Lady Jean Hum's Reel 12/8
Lady Susan Montgomery's Hornpipe 3/2
Rams Horns 4/4
Camstronnan's Rant 9/8
Lady Christian Montgomery's
    Hornpipe 3/2
Drouth 6/8
Hey my Nanny 9/8
Kirkcudbright 4/4
Kiss'd Yestreven 6/8

Lucky Black's Daughter 4/4
Highland Laddie 4/4
Lennox Love 4/4
Wattie Laing 4/4
You'll ay be welcome back again 4/4
Up and Worst them all Willy 4/4
Because I was a bonny lad 4/4
A ranting Highland Man 4/4
Countrey Kate 9/8
Laddie with the Yellow Coatie 4/4
Tibbie Fowler in the Glen 4/4
Rob Shore in Harvest 3/2
Old Age and Young 3/2
Braes of Mar 4/4
This is not my own House 4/4
King of Damascus 4/4
The Old Wife Beyond the Fire 4/4
O'er Bogie 4/4
Kick the World Before You 9/8
Unfortunate Jock 6/8
Drunken Wives of Fochabers 4/4
Border Reel 12/8
Confederacy 4/4
Drummond Castle 6/8

HOLMAIN MANUSCRIPT

Green Sleeves
Cald Kale
Hunt the Squiril
The Dusty Millar
This is not my own House
Argile's Bouling Green

The Birks of Abergeldie
Lennox's Love to Blanter
The Old Way of Killiecrankie
Bathget Bogs or Pease Straw
Miss Hyden
Reel a Down a Mereken

MENZIES MANUSCRIPT

The Menzies' rant or Reel don ne
   Marachan
O'er the watter to Charly
General Stuart's reel or The new Way
   of Gil Don
The Montgomeries' rant — a strathspey
   reele
Conteraller's rant — a strathspey reele
You'r welcome, Charly Stuart
Saw you Charly coming or Fye father
   see him, etc.
He'll aye be welcome back again

Open the door to three
Cope's march
The infare or Will ye marry Kitty
The mighty pretty valley or Reel of
   Tulloch
The Priest and his books
Lady Mary Menzies's Reel
Thirtieth of Aprile
Miss Clemy Stuart's reel
Mr. Jack Stewart's reel
The blew ribon

BODLEIAN MANUSCRIPT

"A Collection of the Newest Country Dances Performed in Scotland written at Edinburgh by D. A. Young, W.M. 1740."

Bung your Eye   6/8
Caberfei   4/4
The Collonel   9/8
The Braes of Balquhidder   4/4
The Drummer   4/4
A' Body Loo's Me   4/4
The Drunken Wives in Pearson's
   Closs   4/4
The Ragged Sailor   6/8
The Cadger o' Crieff   4/4
Down on Yon Bank   4/4
The Holly Bush   6/8
Stick the Minister   4/4
The Lads of Leith   6/8
Welsh Fusileers   6/8
Mairi Allan   4/4
Arthur's Seat   4/4
Mumping Nelly   4/4
A Kiss for a Half Pennie   4/4
The Gimlet   9/8
Drunken Meg Young   6/8
The Miller of Drone   6/8
The Kingdom of Fife   9/8
I'll Ne'er Leave Thee   4/4
The Coronet   4/4

The Lads of Air   4/4
The Key of the Cellar   3/2
Hakie   4/4
Cock a Bendie   4/4
Simon Brodie   4/4
McPhersons Rant   4/4
Stuarts Rant   4/4
Castle Stuart   4/4
Duncan Mackay   4/4
Castle Grant   4/4
The Shire of Air   9/8
Jack on the Green   9/8
Cromdel Hill   4/4
Up in the Morning Early   6/8
O'er the Muir Among the Heather   4/4
The Wood of Fyvie   4/4
What Meikle Sorrow Ails You   4/4
The Fire Side Reel   4/4
Macdonald's Rant   4/4
Lancaster Hornpipe   3/2
The Piper   9/8
Eccles's Rant   4/4
Captain Ross   4/4
Kate McFarlan   4/4

Not all the tunes are Scottish, and some of the titles are decidedly English, such as "Hunt the Squirrel," "Jack Leighton" (a popular Northumbrian air), and "Welsh Fusileers" (a tune familiar to Scottish country dancers today as "Maid of the Mill"). The manuscripts embrace the period 1730–50, and the Menzies manuscript helps to date itself by the inclusion of so many titles alluding to the '45.

Since the Drummond Castle and the Bodleian manuscripts were drawn up by the same hand, it is worthwhile to compare them. The Drummond contains forty-eight and the Bodleian forty-eight dances and no titles are duplicated. The dances are, for the most part, somewhat rudimentary, and many of the tunes are 3/2 hornpipes or 9/8 jigs. The Drummond has seven of the former and eight of the latter. The Bodleian, only two and six. Of 6/8 jigs, the Drummond has eight, the Bodleian eight. The latter has one tune of the nature of a strathspey, with the snap conspicuous and with the unlikely name of "The Coronet." "Down on yon Bank" is the tune which later was called "Roy's Wife of Aldivalloch," a very popular air, earlier known as "The Ruffian's Rant."

Jack McConachie, in publishing the contents of the Bodleian manuscript,[2] has taken a great deal of licence, most of it necessary to make the dances interesting today and, of course, has had to replace the 9/8 and 3/2 tunes. He has retained the original titles and has omitted a few dances altogether.

These manuscript collections of Country Dances set to Scottish tunes indicate a need which was not being satisfied by the published collections. They also represented a fruitful source of new dances for the English publishers. John Walsh apparently just perceived this fact earlier than most and brought out his first book of *Caledonian Country Dances* in London in 1733.

The Walshes brought out nine books altogether in the series. In some, the title page describes the collection as, "of all the celebrated Scotch country dances now in vogue," and in others, "of all the celebrated Scotch and *English* country dances now in vogue" [italics mine].

There is an effort made in book 3, third edition (ca. 1750) to distinguish the Scottish dances both by presenting their titles in a table and by designating them in the text as "Scotch" or "A Scotch Country Dance." As Thurston remarks, it is difficult to detect anything Scottish about such titles as Boscomb Bucks, Meillionen, Huzza, and Ragg, or about their tunes. On the other hand, some others with obviously Scottish tunes are not specifically marked "Scotch." One suspects much carelessness on the part of the compiler, perhaps even indifference. Meillionen (pronounced Methlionen) is the Welsh name for clover, and is the title of a Welsh tune. The Country Dance set to it by Walsh had a clapping routine between partners — "both hands, each others, right hands against one another, both hands, left hands, both hands, breasts," etcetera.

Blouzabella (a jig), which is also designated "Scotch" by Walsh, seems also a curious Scottish title, but as Blousy Bella, as it appears in a British Museum manuscript (Add 34204, ca. 1708 by G. B. Buononcini for unacc. Flute), its pedigree, as a title, seems legitimate.

Lovers of Scottish country dancing today are familiar with The Border Reel, The Reel of Glamis, John Black's Daughter, and The Yellow-Haired Laddie, drawn by the RSCDS from Walsh's *Caledonian Country Dances*.

Many dances to Scottish tunes — bearing the titles of these tunes — were included in other London publications, a good number of which have been restored by the RSCDS for inclusion in its collections, along with some which are not danced to

[2] Jack McConachie, *Scottish Country Dances of the Eighteenth Century*, Imperial Society of Teachers of Dancing, London, 1960.

Scottish tunes. Of special interest to Scottish dancers are the publications of Thompson, Rutherford, and Bremner (ca. 1760 and later), Preston, Campbell, and Wilson (ca. 1786–1816) who supplied such favourites as Miss Nancy Frowns and She's ower Young tae Marry Yet (Thompson); Gates of Edinburgh, Grants Reel, Machine Without Horses (Rutherford); Hamilton House (Campbell); Monimusk (Preston); and many others. John Johnson's *Caledonian Country Dances* (1744 and 1748) is a plagiarism of Walsh's.

The printing and publishing of music of all kinds was now a thriving business, and Robert Bremner, who had developed a successful music-selling business in Edinburgh in the 1750s, was impelled by his business instincts to move his centre of operations to the very heart of this amazing outpouring, London. There he established his shop in 1762 under the sign of the "Harp and Hoboy" opposite Somerset House in the Strand, and speedily became the most important music-seller and publisher in the country.

One of his first enterprises had been the publication of a collection of Scottish Reel tunes in several numbers. Now, on his arrival in London, he published another volume, this time including figures for twenty-eight Country Dances set to well-known Highland Reels. It is noteworthy that there were no collections of Country Dance figures published in Scotland prior to 1774, in which year there is a tantalizing record of a lost work entitled: *The Dancer's Pocket Companion, being a Collection of Forty Scots and English figures of Country Dances, with two elegant copperplates showing all the different figures made use of in Scots or English Country Dancing. Properly explained by William Frazer, Dancing Master, Edinburgh.* (See Stenhouse, *Illustrations of the Lyric Poetry.*) The earliest surviving Scottish publication of the kind is John Bowie's *Collection of Strathspey Reels and Country Dances*, Perth, 1789. Of the six dances in this, only Miss Murray of Ochtertyre has so far found acceptance by the RSCDS. The William Frazer referred to above is doubtless the same as he who taught dancing in McNair's Hall, King Street, Glasgow, in the 1780s.

The contents of Bremner's second collection of *Reels or Country Dances* are of great interest as they are all Scottish:

The New Town of Edinburgh	Mount your Baggage
Miss Betty MacDonald's Reel	Col. MacKay's Reel
Col. McBain's Reel	Miss Cahoon's Reel
Ross House	The Nether Bow has Vanished
Glenlyon's Rant	Drumsheugh
The House of Gray	The Bridge of Nairn
The Deacon of the Weavers	The Wives of Kilwinnon
Lady Betty Hay's Reel	Open the Door to Three
Kheelum Khallum tao Fein	Straglass House
(Gille Callum)	Robin Shore in Herst
Ephie McNab	We'll all to Kelso go
The Whigs of Fife	Invercauld's Reel
Caper Fey (Caber Feidh)	The Cross Well of Edinburgh
The Waterman's Rant	Croagh Patrick
The Sailor Lassie	

Three of these dances, Miss Cahoon's Reel, The Bridge of Nairn, and Straglass House have been restored by the RSCDS (bk. 13).

It is striking, and probably indicative of the public for whom the collection was intended, that Bremner uses such English terms as "hey," whereas the Scottish word is reel, and "foot" instead of set.

The question that now arises is whether or not these Country Dances set to Scottish tunes and preserved in Scottish manuscripts or in publications of the period exhibited characteristics which would distinguish them as Scottish dances. As far as figures or formations are concerned, there was only one for which a Scottish origin can be claimed: set-to-and-turn-corners-and-reel-of-three on the sides, a figure which is obviously derived from the Scotch Reel. It makes its appearance in no uncertain fashion in the Bowman manuscript (ca. 1760, Laing Collection, Edinburgh University), in which 78 dances out of a total of 122 end in this figure. It also appears among the Bremner dances mentioned above. Otherwise, the figures in these dances were little different from those in the Drummond manuscript. In the latter there is setting to partner, casting off, four hands round with third or second couple, setting in line across or up-and-down the dance, and a figure called right and left. A common opening figure in the Bowman collection is "First man set to and turn second lady, first lady likewise with second man." Such figures as allemande, promenade, and poussette had not yet been introduced.

Another feature of the Country Dance in Scotland is the absence of game dances or dances introducing the frivolous nonsense familiar to English dancers of the period. The Scots had evidently a greater respect for dancing.

Nevertheless Hugh Thurston writes in *Scotland's Dances* that "there is no hint of any Scottish influence on the figures, steps, style or technique [of the Country Dance] until well after 1800, when Wilson mentions a Scottish step. . . ." By this comment he presumably means Scottish influence on the Country Dance in England, which is not to say that the Scots had no Country Dances of their own or that they did not perform them in their own way before this time. The fact that a Scottish setting step is mentioned by Thomas Wilson, around 1816, as being used in country dancing in England only confirms the obvious suspicion that such steps were used in country dancing in Scotland.

As we shall see, the technique of the Country Dance was very arbitrary, fashion alone prescribing the steps. If the Scottish contribution to the figures of the Country Dance could be considered slight in the eighteenth century, there can be little doubt that the difference between the Scottish and English manner of executing the Country Dance was at least as great as the difference between the dancing characteristics of the two peoples. The evidence of several observers, some of which has been quoted in chapter 18, confirms this.

We have been told of the electric effect of the music of the reel on the Scots. Who can believe, then, that in a dance performed to this music and involving the sequence set-to-and-turn-corners-and-reel, for instance, a sequence so similar to that of their favourite dance, the Scots would not naturally set and travel as they would do in a reel to the same music? What have we to say, too, about the probable steps employed in strathspey rhythm for Country Dances? As we have noted, the word itself appears in connection with a Country Dance for the first time in the Menzies manuscript, and its first similar appearance in a published collection occurs in Bremner where the dance Straglass House is labelled Strathspey.

Here, then, we have the true nature of the Scottish contribution to the longwise progressive Country Dance; it is to be found in the music and the steps. The Scots developed the form after their own fashion, just as the English had done with the Italian contrapassi a little over a century before, drawing upon their native traditions of dance and music to make something of their own. In a similar fashion, the Irish gave the Country Dance many jig tunes and, above all, those elegant tunes in 9/8 with which, as Wilson directs, Irish steps were requisite. A British tradition emerged with fertile combinations of local colours superimposed on a common background of *licht* dances: the English Country Dance in England; the Scottish Country Dance in Scotland; and the Irish Country Dance in Ireland.

The evidence does indicate that, in the eighteenth century, the innovations to the Country Dance form were emanating from the formal dance assemblies, of which every town of any consequence could boast at least one by the 1770s — Edinburgh, Aberdeen, Glasgow, Dundee, Leith, and Haddington being the most prominent in Scotland. The published collections, too, must have enjoyed considerable patronage. As we have seen, however, the Scot preferred his native Threesome and Foursome Reels, although other dances of the ring and longwise forms were known in many parts of the country, dating from the distant past and danced in the open air in bare feet at kirn feasts, penny weddings, Beltane, Yule, fairs, trystes, rockings, ceilidhs, and the like, as of old.

The particular longwise "for as many as will" *progressive* dance form, known as the Country Dance, was restricted to the Lowland areas until comparatively recent times; but it did there find its way out of the assembly room and private ballroom into the barn. The itinerant dancing masters, professionals such as Johnny McGill, fiddler and dancing master of Girvan and Dumfries, were important in increasing the popularity of the Country Dance. It is altogether revealing that McGill taught Country Dances in the 1750s in his largely rural circuit.

A set of manuscript instructions written by McGill for his pupils in 1752 included "Twelve of the newest Country Dances." These were set to the following tunes: "Up and war them a' Willy," "Because he was a bonny lad," "Old age and Young," "My wife's a wanton wee thing," "Rattling roaring Willy," "Cadgers of the Cannongate," "Ephey McNab," "The Corral or Backel," "The Lads of Dunse," and "Jock of the Green." The correspondent who revealed this information to *Notes and Queries* in September 1, 1855, did not complete the list and he did not preserve the manuscript, as far as I can discover.

It is easy to see how a rural strain of Country Dances not derived from printed sources could emerge from this activity. Certain dances became favourites in particular regions, such as those in sprightly strathspey rhythm which survived into the present century in the Borders. Notable in these is the employment of what we call the High-land Schottische setting step in such dances as Haughs of Cromdale, Braes of Busby (RSCDS, bks. 4 and 9), and Loch Erichtside (MacLachlan, *Border Dance Book*). We have to thank Ian C. B. Jamieson for collecting these dances, although not all of them are well conceived.

Loch Erichtside of the *Border Book* recalls to mind that Robert Burns mentions a dance of this name in a letter written on his way down Loch Lomondside at the end of his Highland tour: "On our return, at a Highland gentleman's hospitable mansion, we fell in with a merry party, and danced till the ladies left us, at three in the morning. Our dancing was none of the French or English insipid formal movements; the ladies sung Scotch songs like angels, at intervals; then we flew at Bab at the Bowster, Tullochgorum, Loch Erroch Side, etc. like midges sporting in the mottie sun, or craws prognosticating a storm in a hairst day. When the dear lasses left us, we ranged round the bowl till the good-fellow hour of six; except a few minutes that we went out to pay our devotions to the glorious lamp of day peering over the towering top of Ben Lomond."[3]

In the 1780s, it will be recalled, William Creech deplored the decline of the Country Dances to a "game of romps." He undoubtedly was alluding to conditions prevailing in the Edinburgh assemblies, and perhaps it is this degenerative trend which is reflected in the motley group of alien titles published by Niel Gow as "a few of the most fashionable dances danced in Edinburgh" in the season 1787–88:

Greenwich Hill 2/4	Madam Cassey 6/8
The Harriot 2/4	Good Morrow to your Night Cap
Royal Circus 6/8	(very old) 2/4
Les Piedmontese 6/8	The Nymph 2/4
Captain Macintosh 2/4	La Belle Catherine 2/4

A similar selection published by Nathaniel Gow as the "favourite dances performed at the annual ball of the George St. Assembly Rooms, Edinburgh," in 1813, is just as curious:

Cawdor Fair	The Legacy ("Waltz time") Irish
Caledonian Hunt's March	La Fantasia (6/8)
Paddy's Frolic ("Waltz time")	Carfrae Frolic (6/8)
Manont's Retreat (6/8)	

There is some reassurance, however, in that the same author quotes Fight about the fireside and Kenmure's on and away among the five favourite dances of 1822. The former, especially, is an excellent dance and an excellent tune, and both have found a place in the RSCDS collection.

When we recall how the repertoire of reels and strathspeys of the band used for the Edinburgh Highland Dance competition in the 1830s had declined to an appalling state, we must conclude that the really active centres of country dancing were then in those regions of Perth, Kincardine, and Aberdeen, particularly, in the north, and Ayr and the Border counties in the south, where the fiddler still reigned supreme.

There is fortunately a great deal of data available to us on the subject of rural dance activity in the nineteenth century, thanks to the field researches of J. F. and T. M. Flett, recorded in *Traditional Dancing in Scotland,* to which the reader is referred for a wealth of valuable information. Suffice it for us to observe that while the English Country Dance fell before the glamorous Quadrille and the heady sophistication of the Waltz, the Scottish Country Dance continued to hold a substantial place in its own countryside, alongside the new dances, and in company with the Reel, until the dawn of the twentieth century.

[3] Letter to Mr. James Smith, Linlithgow, June 30, 1787.

It is not unexpected that the Quadrille should exert some influence on the native dance strain. Indeed, there was a great deal of mutual borrowing of characteristics between the Country Dance, Reel, and Quadrille to produce new dances, of which the outstanding examples are the Eightsome Reel and Glasgow Highlanders. The Quadrille figure, ladies' chain, also found its way into the Country Dance.

There were other influences at work, however, during the nineteenth century, and these were the new strains of dance in the Country Dance style which first appeared in the London social centres in the early 1820s: the "Écossoises," "Spanish Dances," "Circassian Circles," and "Swedish Dances." The Écossoises were progressive longwise dances. The Spanish Dances were also longwise dances, but were danced to Waltz music, and apart from the first couple being reversed ("improper") and certain special allemande figures, they were no different from Country Dances. In fact they were also called "Waltz" Country Dances and were often danced in Circassian Circle formation, that is, in opposing couples round the room. Examples of both are included in the RSCDS books.[4] In the so-called Swedish Dances, invented by G. M. S. Chivers,[5] each man has two partners, one on either side, and the company is arranged with opposing trios facing each other. Two well-known examples of these in Scotland are The Dashing White Sergeant (RSCDS, bk. 3) and a similar dance ambiguously called The Highland Reel (RSCDS, bk. 13) which was collected in Angus.

Some Scottish Country Dances show evidence of having started life as one or other of these special types of progressive dance. The task of detecting and cataloguing these is a fascinating one, and one which Hugh Thurston has gone far to accomplishing in his *Scotland's Dances*.

By the 1870s the Country Dance was clearly losing ground in fashionable Scottish society in the principal cities; but it survived more securely in the rural areas in many parts of the country, nourished by the periodical visitations of itinerant dancing masters. It only began to reach the West Highlands and Hebrides in the 1850s[6] and even more recently, the Orkneys.[7] Many people still alive in these areas can remember the introduction of Quadrilles.

David Anderson, whose dance books have been of such value to students of Scottish dancing, conducted a dancing school in Dundee from about 1870 to 1905. He also visited other towns as a "professor" of dancing at various times of the year, travelling as far north as Dingwall and Inverness. The extent of his travels is reflected in the titles of the Country Dances he composed for the communities he served: Abernethy Lasses, Badenoch Fancy, Brechin Fancy, Broughty Ferry Castle, Grantown Favourite, Inverness, Kingussie Flower, Monifieth Star, Perth Inch, and Tayport Beauty. These, of course, were in addition to many other dances he taught which were not of his own composition. They are also found in books other than his own.

In the past few decades, many of these dances have been collected from the countryside, along with a good number which are not to be found in any printed sources. The so-called Border dances are in this latter category, along with such examples as Peggy's Love from the county of Moray.

[4] Waltz Country Dance (or La Guaracha), RSCDS, bk. 4. Circassian Circle, RSCDS, bk. 1.
[5] G. M. S. Chivers, *The Modern Dancing Master*.
[6] J. F. and T. M. Flett, *Traditional Dancing in Scotland*.
[7] Ibid., p. 159. Country Dances were first performed in Flotta as late as 1891.

The principal printed sources of Scottish Country Dances of the nineteenth century are: J. P. Boulogne, *The Ballroom* (1827); W. Smythe, *A Pocket Companion for Young Ladies and Gentlemen* (1830); Joseph Lowe, *A Selection of Popular Country Dances* (ca. 1840); W. E. Allan, *New Reference Guide to the Ball Room* (ca. 1870); and David Anderson, *Ballroom Guide* (1886). A remarkably high proportion of these dances are thirty-two bar, two couple dances to reel music, and end with the sequence "down the middle and up and poussette."[8] The allemande had disappeared and strathspey tunes were not used, except in the Border counties.

No doubt the people of the rural areas learned more from one another and from the itinerant dancing masters than they did from any ballroom guide. It is, therefore, of great interest to learn what the dancing masters taught and their manner of teaching. Much emphasis, it appears, was placed on deportment and ballroom etiquette. In Kincardineshire, around 1886, a Mr. Lilly held classes for children of ten to fourteen years one afternoon a week for three months. The boys, we are told by the Fletts, were taught how to make a bow and how to ask the girls to partner them. When the end-of-season ball was imminent, each boy had to find his own partner and seek the permission of her mother to escort her daughter to the ball.[9]

We are indebted to the same authority for a reconstruction of the procedure of R. F. Buck, the best known itinerant dancing master of the Borders in the late nineteenth century:

To begin his first lesson he selected either a simple Country Dance such as The Nut, or a "couple" dance such as the Common Schottische or the Polka. The Country Dances he taught included Blue Bonnets, Bonny Breastknots, Bottom of the Punchbowl, Corn Rigs, Cumberland Reel, Drops of Brandy, Duke of Perth, Flowers of Edinburgh, Haymakers, Highland Laddie, Jessie's Hornpipe, Meg Merrilees, Petronella, Rifleman, Rory O'More (also known as the American Dwarf), Roxburgh Castle, Speed the Plough, and the Duchess of Gordon's Fancy. . . .[10] Mr. Buck also taught the Foursome Reel and the Reel of Tulloch (the latter either in sets of two couples or in one large circle round the room), the Highland Fling, the Sword Dance and the Sailor's Hornpipe. He taught also Quadrilles and Lancers (giving his pupils one figure of these each evening until they knew the entire dances), Circassian Circle and a number of "couple" dances.

Mr. Buck also held classes in towns like Selkirk, but there he restricted himself to the standard half dozen Country Dances. His complete repertory was given only to the country folk who would appreciate it.[11]

Thus it arose that in the towns, where fashion exerted a greater influence and the way of life was more exclusive, the Country Dances included on ball programs diminished to a mere half dozen or so favourites. If D. R. Mackenzie's *National Dances of Scotland* is any guide, these were, in 1910: Rory O'More, Petronella, Triumph, Flowers of Edinburgh, The Duke of Perth, and a trivial thing called Mary Queen of Scots. The performance of these was clumsy in extreme in comparison to the standards set by the

---

[8]Hugh A. Thurston, "The Development of the Country Dance as Revealed in Printed Sources," *JEFDSS*, vol. 7, no. 1 (1952).

[9] J. F. and T. M. Flett, *Social Dancing in Scotland, 1700–1914*, p. 162.

[10] See Elizabeth MacLachlan, ed., *The Border Dance Book*, and the RSCDS books for details of favourite versions of most of these dances.

[11] Flett, *Social Dancing in Scotland, 1700–1914*, p. 160.

RSCDS or even by the past. "Down the middle and up" had become a walk, and instead of a poussette, the couples did a "two-step waltz" round each other. In Rory O'More the first couple "Irish trot down centre, and up backwards."

A few other Country Dances held their place in fashionable circles — Petronella and The Duke of Perth, for instance — alongside the Foursome Reel, Reel of Tulloch, Eightsome Reel, Haymakers, and Strip the Willow; but with the exception of these it seems that the Circassian Circle, Quadrille, Lancers, Schottische, Polka, and Waltz were preferred to Country Dances and the native reels.

The Foursome Reel, Reel of Tulloch, Glasgow Highlanders, and the indestructible Eightsome Reel also held their own in fashionable circles in to the early 1920s. Strip the Willow, performed to a reel rather than its original 9/8 jig, remained a favourite party dance and, with the Eightsome Reel, is one of the two enduring remnants of Scottish traditional social dance surviving today among the untutored population in general. A modified Highland Schottische is still performed at rural hops, but the Circassian Circle, Quadrille, and Lancers, so conspicuous in the ballrooms of the early part of the century, scarcely survived the First World War. The Scottish Country Dance and the Scotch Reel in its several mutations seemed destined to go the way of all the national antiquities and, worse still, to take their heritage of music along with them.

21/Technique of the Country Dance

English comments in the seventeenth century – Cecil Sharp's interpretation of Playford – Minuet and Rigadon interpolations – Feuillet's contributions – Rameau's criticism – Dukes on English dancing – Wilson on technique – pas de basque – Scottish Reel tastes – English corruptions in the Regency period – Wilson on Strathspey steps – Border step – influence of Waltz – task of RSCDS – dance of assembly room versus dance of countryside – technique adopted by RSCDS – "treepling" – evolution of figures

Despite the great popularity of the Country Dance in English and Scottish dance assemblies over so many years, it is remarkable that so little has been written about its execution, whether of figures or steps. It must be acknowledged, however, that the Country Dance is not unique in this particular among British traditional dance forms. We have seen how the earliest written technical description of the Highland or Scotch Reel dates from as recently as 1805, and even this account is not particularly detailed. There are, however, some superficial observations that shed some light on the matter, although mainly with reference to country dancing in England. These, nevertheless, are of interest to Scottish dancers and are worth some attention here.

On thing is clear. The Country Dance of the seventeenth-century English ballroom retained its country spirit. One writer in 1602 alludes to it thus:

> . . . the youth must needs go dance,
> First, galliards; then larousse; and heidegy;
> "Old lusty gallant"; "all flow'rs of the bloom" [broom?]
> And then a hall: For dancers must have room.
>
> And to it then, with set, and turn about,
> Change sides, and cross, and mince it like a hawk,
> Backwards and forwards, take hands then, in and out,
> And, now and then, a little wholesome talk,
> That none could hear, close rowned in the ear.

Then he gives us a view of the manner of dancing, revealing that dancers may claim a kiss before and after the dance, although it "goes sore" when kiss upon kiss is taken! He continues:

> But to behold the graces of each dame!
> How some would dance as though they did but walk;
> And some would trip, as though one leg were lame,
> And some would mince it like a sparrow hawk;
> And some would dance upright as any bolt;
> And some would leap and skip like a young colt!
>
> And some would fidge, as though she had the itch;
> And some would bow half crooked in the joints;
> And some would have a trick; and some a twitch;
> Some shook their arms, as they had hung up points,
> With thousands more that were too long to tell,
> But made me laugh my heart sore, I wot well.[1]

This description presents a not unfamiliar picture.

Playford did not describe steps nor comment on the manner of execution of the dances he published, and this lack of description and comment is also characteristic of the many Country Dance books published in England in the succeeding century. The omission means, presumably, that the steps were well known, or that they were left to be described by dancing masters. It could also mean that the steps were copied by one generation of dancers from another. Cecil Sharp made a study of Playford's dance steps and concluded that they were walking, running and skipping, the double hop and the "slip." Playford does refer to a slip step, but he rarely goes any further than to describe, for example, "forward a double and back, set and turn single"; but what was involved in "set"? (The other word used for "set" was "foot.") It would be no surprise if, in a court which enjoyed the Galliard and Coranto, setting steps from these dances were employed; the Country Dance must at many times in its history have reflected the dancing tastes of its environment.

The triple-time hornpipe tunes which enjoyed an upsurge of favour in the 1680s lent themselves to the use of the step of the Minuet, now entering its period of ascendancy. Indeed, the seventh edition of Playford's *Dancing Master* (1686) included Country Dances to Minuet and Rigadon music, and in later editions Minuet and Rigadon steps are occasionally specified (cf. *The Dancing Master*, compiled by John Young, vol. 2, 4th ed., 1728: in a reference to Kelways Maggot, "the first Man and 2d. Wo. make the first New Rigadon Steps," and in a reference to Mademoiselle Dupingle, "the first Cu. Hands all four round the Minuet Step.") Raoul Feuillet had then published his attempt to polish the technique of the Country Dance in *Recueil de Contredances*, and Essex and Weaver had translated this book into English, Essex in 1710 and Weaver in 1712. The Essex translation commented on the Country Dance: "Of ye feet, steps, Hands and Armes. Tho' my designe is not to mark any steps in Country Dances, being willing to leave the Dancers ye liberty of composing the same as they please, there are notwithstanding some motions of ye Feet, Hands and Armes which

---

[1] Nicholas Breton, "A Mother's Blessing," (1602) from *Works of Breton*, ed. A. B. Groshart, vol. 1 (New York: AMS Press, 1966).

I can't omit inserting here" (p. 7). It continues with a discussion of a variety of Country Dance steps:

Advice concerning ye steps that best suite with Country Dances. The most ordinary steps in Country Dances (those excepted that are upon Minuet Airs) are steps of Gavot, drive sideways Bouree step and some small Jumps forward on either Foot in a hopping manner, or little hopps. In all round Figures as the preceeding and following are, one may make little hopps or Bouree steps but little hopps are more in fashion. . . . As it is ordinary that every figure of a Dance ends at every cadence or end of the Aire, it will be proper to make a small Jump upon both Feet.

In all figures that goe forwards and backward, or backwards and forwards, you must always make gavotte steps. . . . In all figures that goe sideways you must always drive sideways. . . .

When it will be requisite to make other steps than them wee have mentioned, as Rigadoon steps, balances &c, they shall be mark'd upon ye figures. [Pp. 15–16]

Nevertheless, some fifteen years later, in 1725, Rameau declared in *Le Maître à Danser*:

All the perfection of these Country Dances, is by a distorting of the body in turning about, and stamping with their feet as if they had wooden shoes on, and putting themselves in several ridiculous postures. . . . Is it not possible to make dances for several persons to dance together in regulated steps after the manner of the German dances?

That the degree of refinement depended upon the rank of society is voiced by Kellom Tomlinson who remarked in *Art of Dancing* (1735) that country dancing had "become as it were the Darling or favourite diversion of all Ranks of People from the Court to the Cottage in their different manners of Dancing." Nicholas Dukes, in 1752, opined that "every Gentleman or Lady who is desirous of performing Country Dances in a Genteel, free and easy manner [is under] the necessity of being first duly Qualified in a Minuet, that beautiful dance being so well calculated and adapted as to give room for every person to display all the Beauties and Graces of the body which becomes a genteel Carriage."[2]

As the Minuet declined in favour, so did the deportment associated with it. Despite the fact that a "lady of distinction" could write by the end of that century that "the characteristic of our English country dance is that of gay simplicity" and that "the steps should be few and easy, and the corresponding motion of the arms and body unaffected, modest and graceful,"[3] chaos seems to have been then no uncommon concomitant of country dancing in English centres of fashion.

Dukes make a further brief allusion to Country Dance steps in England around 1750, stating that the dancers kept "continually footing as in casting off, crossing over, or any other part of figuring." He continues with the advice, "You may foot it forwards or backwards or sideways as the case requires." But again, we may ask, how did one "foot it"?

Then Wilson's *The Complete System of English Country Dancing* was published in 1821, the most thorough exposition of the Country Dance in England. Even here,

---

[2] Nicholas Dukes, *A Concise and Easy Method of Learning the Figuring Part of Country Dances.*
[3] Quoted in Barclay Dun, *Translation of Nine Quadrilles.*

however, no precise definitions of steps are given, only names. Wilson refers to a chasse and a side step for travelling. A typical instruction would be: "Top couple join hands with second lady and turn completely round to places; which requires four bars, and *three chasses one Jetté and Assemblé.*" "Down the middle and up" in Wilson's treatise is always down for two, back for two (with "slip step") with or without a cast off to second place for four ("three chasses Jetté and Assemblé"). The instruction "down for four and back for four," common in Scottish country dancing, was objectionable to Wilson because it carries the dancing couple out of the set; but he acknowledged a marked tendency for people to favour this. On the subject of setting, the following direction by Wilson for "set to corners" is informative: "Gentleman at C sets to Lady at A, with back, or Scotch setting step — four bars." From another instruction it is evident that one "Scotch step" took two bars and one "back step" took one bar. It would be satisfying if the Scotch step were the pas de basque, the principal setting step in Scottish dancing today; it certainly takes the same number of bars. There is not much doubt about the back step; this must be the reel setting step described by Peacock in 1805 as "an easy familiar step much used by the English in their Country Dances." This was a simple back step which occupied one bar and was called the Minor Kemkossy.

Wilson also makes the interesting remark that the cast off step is "one of the greatest ornaments that can be exhibited in a Country Dance," but leaves us guessing as to its precise nature. This is a pity because some such step would be an asset in Scottish country dancing today.

It is surprising that the term "pas de basque" does not appear in descriptions of Scottish dancing until Atkinson's *Scottish National Dances* (1900) in which he describes a pas de basque derrière. D. R. Mackenzie, in his *National Dances of Scotland* (1910), applies the term to the step used in Petronella, and indeed, David Anderson, in his *Ballroom Guide* of some twenty years before, refers to it as the Petronella Step. He described it as "stand in first position, hop out on right foot in 2nd, bring left in front 5th, beat behind with right. Repeat to left." Nevertheless, he depicts a pas de basque among the reel steps in his book, but does not use this name. Of the Petronella Step Anderson adds, "This step may also be used for Contra Dances, Circassian Circle etc. in setting to partners, but must *never* be used for Quadrilles." Nevertheless, the pas de basque was certainly used in Quadrilles in Scotland within living memory. It is, of course, a step which is widely used in different forms in the folk dances of many countries. Even in Scottish dancing today it is used in at least three or four forms and doubtless has long been known, though perhaps by another name. Certainly, Susan Sibbald, a most enthusiastic dancer in the period around 1800, includes the pas de basque among a number of steps used in Cotillions, although she tells us that she could make out only that it was "pas de something" — what she had heard an Irish girl call "paddy busk."

There is no reason to believe that the Scots employed the same steps as the English in the ballroom Country Dance in the eighteenth and nineteenth centuries, and much reason to believe, as was expounded at some length in the previous chapter, that they would favour the same steps — both travelling and setting — as they employed in the reel. However, toward the end of the eighteenth century, Alexander Gibb, "dancing master of Edinburgh and Haddington," informed his "friends and public that he had not been to Paris this year, but that he had as many modern dances, and fashionable reel and country dance steps, as any of his line in town."[4] This remark seems to indicate some adoption of steps by Edinburgh dancers from fashionable society elsewhere.

It is evident from various comments that the Country Dance was subjected to some corruptions in England during the Regency period. Just what "steps" meant to dancers in London at this time is rather scathingly described by Thomas Wilson, who writes in *A Companion to the Ballroom* that dancers in general either did not know "proper steps" or thought them unnecessary. He adds that few dancers had "ever been taught any *sort* of steps," and of these, few had been taught well enough to apply them properly. The result he describes is one of complete disregard of steps and of phrasing, and as an example, he tells us that in "set and change sides — set and back again" the dancers "generally *run* across as fast as they can, without stopping to 'set' out the time; and with the exception of sometimes making a sort of turn or ridiculous antic, run back directly, intirely [*sic*] leaving out the *setting*." Consequently, the dancers completed the figure prematurely. The dancers, he relates, "not knowing what to do with their feet or themselves to fill up the time (as they cannot perform any proper steps for that purpose) in the hope of avoiding detection, enter into some other figure, without waiting to finish the strain, and by this means continue out of time the whole dance." To cope with this, the musicians were instructed to play "as quickly as possible," regardless of the character of the tune. Those who could perform the dance properly were at the mercy of the ignorant and were unceremoniously dragged into the figures (pp. 217-18).

Then there were others who had acquired "a few Hornpipe steps" and would introduce them at every opportunity without discrimination. Wilson stated that these steps were "very improper for a Country Dance; and persons so using them must be ever considered, as being unaccustomed to good company and of very vulgar habits" (p. 223). At this time, the Country Dance was equally popular in America. Howe, in his *Complete Ball-Room Handbook*, remarked that Quadrille steps were used and that the "Pigeon's Wing or some other flourish" was introduced as often as possible (p. 23). Wilson's "Hornpipe steps" were doubtless what was called treepling in Scotland.

Tunes in 9/8 were another matter. Here "Irish steps" were recommended, 9/8 being a favourite Irish metre. Wilson complained, however, that these steps were almost unknown to English dancers in 1816, and "shuffling and grotesque movements" were substituted "to fill up the time" (pp. 220-21).

STRATHSPEY STEPS

In discussing the tempi of the dances presented in his *Companion to the Ballroom*, Wilson remarks on Strathspey steps: "Since Dancing has become a Science, various Steps have been introduced, with a view to display the skill of the dancers and as these require more time to perform them with elegance, it follows of course, that the

---

[4] Quoted in John Glen, *Glen Collection of Scottish Dance Music*, Biographical Sketches, Edinburgh, 1891 and 1895.

time in which they ought to be played will be considerably slower than before their invention. Strathspeys from the nature of their steps, will be uniformly *Andante*: Reels will be quicker; and consequently *Allegro*: and Airs in 6/8, having similar steps to those in common time, will naturally be slower, or *Moderato*" (pp. 220–21). None of the airs included in the *Companion*, however, is marked andante and, although a number of the "Scotch" tunes are really strathspeys, they are marked allegro; in other words, they were apparently to be played as reels. One of these, for example, is the tune known as "Auld Lang Syne," from Burns's setting of it. This air is one of a number of variants of a strathspey "The Miller's Wedding" which first appeared in print in Bremner's *Reels* in 1759, a tune which Burns referred to as "a common Scots country dance."

This is confirmation of what one would suspect, that Country Dances to strathspey airs really found no place in English country dancing unless they were disguised as reels. Wilson, in alluding to the Strathspey, must be referring to the Foursome Reel, or Scotch Reel as he calls it, which was enjoying some vogue in the London of his day.

There can surely be no doubt that the Scots would use the appropriate "Strathspey" reel steps to their Country Dances set to strathspey airs. This is confirmed by the known mode of performance of the "Strathspey" Country Dances which survived in southern Scotland within living memory.[5] "Professor" R. F. Buck, a noted itinerant dancing master in the Border counties, taught the normal Strathspey reel travelling step, of that version in which the dancing foot is brought through and up to the front of the leg instead of round the leg. The sequence is: Step R, close L, step R and bring left foot through and up in front of R leg (third aerial) with a hop R, then repeat with L leading. Most of the Border people apparently omitted the third aerial position and simply swung the travelling foot through on the hop ready to step forward on it. This is the basic reel travelling step described by Peacock, which becomes the "skip-change-of-step" in reel or jig rhythm.

The setting step in the Border Strathspeys was that used by the Royal Scottish Country Dance Society today. This is often referred to as the Common Schottische setting step, but this name is unfortunate, for the step is at least as old as the Branle d'Écosse. It is certainly not the form of the step which is recent, but the name "Schottische."

In some other dances, the Highland Schottische setting is used, the Highland Schottische being a Scottish twosome employing a Highland Fling motif.

Before discussing these steps as they are treated today by the RSCDS, we must note the influence of the Waltz. Just as there were Country Dances to Minuet tunes at one time, so also were there "Waltz" Country Dances.[6] By the early twentieth century, the poussette was executed in Scotland by the couples waltzing round each other, once or twice or one-and-a-half times, according to whether or not progression was required.[7] The Waltz hold was used, although in the countryside the older form, with the man's hands on his partner's waist and her's on his shoulders, was preferred.

---

[5] J. F. and T. M. Flett, *Traditional Dancing in Scotland*.

[6] An example of a "Minuet" Country Dance is the Yellow-Hair'd Laddie, RSCDS, bk. 12; and an example of the "Waltz" Country Dance is a dance of the same title, RSCDS, bk. 4.

[7] Donald R. Mackenzie, *The National Dances of Scotland*. The earliest description of the waltz-poussette is in MS 3860 (1818) National Library, Scotland.

This hold was used also in turning corners. It is well established, however, that the original method was for the partners to hold hands — the figure, in fact, was called the draw, that is, drawing one's partner out of and into line.

TASK OF THE RSCDS

The love of movement which, as we have seen, was ever a characteristic of Scottish dancing, combined with a loss of technical skill, of knowledge, and of favourable environment, had reduced such dances as the Eightsome Reel, or any other reel, to rowdy romps. Such Country Dances as were still countenanced were danced only in certain regions and corruptly at that. Thus it seemed that certain standards of performance had to be established by the Scottish Country Dance Society and most vigilantly preserved from any encroachment of rowdyism, or contempt for the art of the dance.

As can well be imagined, the task facing the creators of the society in 1923 was greater than anticipated. The laudable desire was to restore the "authentic" Scottish Country Dance, in form and execution, to its former place of honour in the social dancing of Scotland. What, indeed, were the "authentic" form and execution of the Scottish Country Dance? The student of this subject, familiar with the contents of these pages, will appreciate the difficulty — or impossibility — of this task. The form of the dance as expressed in its figures and system was relatively easier to establish than its style and mode of execution, in that these have varied so much throughout the years, and possibly also throughout the country.

Very wisely, the creators of the society turned to the recollections of old people and to those dances which yet survived, not all of which were Country Dances in the strict sense. The hope was that some tradition had been established and still lived in the memory of the countryfolk. The alternative was to take as models the major part of the population, who had danced on the green, in the barn, on the threshing floor, barefooted or in outdoor shoes, and accept the folk spirit of Lowland Scotland which they diffused, a spirit as riotous as their favourite reel could be. Yet, on the other hand, Elizabeth Grant and her associates and servants in Rothiemurchus expressed something more than this in their dancing, which was as authentically Scottish, although they did not then dance Country Dances in their part of the Highlands, unless Haymakers is included.

The following poem which I came across sheds an interesting light on the subject of dance styles in the Highlands. It was sung by Lachlan Gorach of Mull, a "half-witted natural" as he was described by Alexander Stewart writing in *Nether Lochaber* in 1883.

> First the heel and then the toe,
> That's the way the polkas go;
> First the toe and then the heel,
> That's the way to dance a reel,
> Quick about and then away,
> Lightly dance the glad Strathspey
> Jump a jump and jump it big,
> That's the way to dance a jig;

Slowly, smiling as in France,
Follow through the country dance,
And we'll meet Johnny Cope in the morning.

The element of graciousness, conspicuous in the dance assemblies of the eighteenth century, fostered by the Minuet, and retained in more recent times in Quadrille dancing, was now deliberately fostered in the Country Dance. Elegance and grace were conceived as its very essence, and if we are tempted to recall the comments of those who deplored the absence of this in the dancing of the Scots, we must also recall Dr. Hall's eulogy of these characteristics in the vigorous dancing in Strathspey and the observations expressed on this subject already in these pages.

Much misunderstanding has arisen from the confusion of the Country Dance with the Reel and its relatives of the countryside — and indeed from a recollection of how Country Dances were treated or ill-treated within living memory. Certainly, the Scottish Country Dance, along with the Reels, was danced in many a barn and hayloft, and here its terre à terre character, so assiduously cultivated in the ballroom, was manifestly impractical, although high elevation is by no means incompatible with grace and elegance, as visitors to Strathspey so often testified over a hundred years ago.

Whether those responsible for the restoration of the Scottish Country Dance were aware of all these considerations, in the early years especially, is doubtful. But somehow, a synthesis of the various elements has been achieved. The Scottish Country Dance Society did not attempt to revive the *licht* dances, or reels, of the Scottish countryfolk, nor the rural adaptations of the Country Dance form prevailing in the nineteenth century; its primary aim was to restore the Country Dance as a dance of the eighteenth-century Scottish assembly room. There is every justification for this as these pages must show, and the style of the restored Scottish Country Dance is very much in character with the eighteenth-century attitudes that saw the finest flowering of traditional Scottish dance and music and that pervaded the Scottish dancing schools of the nineteenth century. Nor was the Scottish Country Dance restored to some particular state in its past, for this really could not be done; it was, instead, re-created.

RSCDS TECHNIQUE

Scottish Country Dances are set to four basic classifications of traditional dance rhythm: reel (4/4) (including Rant and Scottish Measure); Strathspey (4/4 and 2/4); jig (6/8); and common-time hornpipe. Those jig and hornpipe rhythms, in 3/2 and 9/8 and multiples thereof, not so intimately associated with Scottish dance, are omitted by the RSCDS. The step technique essentially comprises a travelling and a setting step common to reel, jig, and hornpipe, and another for Strathspey.

Taking the reel group first, the travelling step is called the skip-change-of-step (hop–step R — close — step R — hop — step L) and the setting step is a pas de basque. The skip-change-of-step is the first of the two kemshoo'le reel steps described by Peacock. It is of the form of step commonly called chasse, but chasse is still associated in the minds of many with step-close-step without the hop, as used in the Quadrille. Why not give the skip step its Gaelic name *kemshoo'le*? There are other kemshoo'les, but so also are there several pas de basques. The skip step as taught today by the RSCDS is a forward gliding movement with a skip and a sense of flight, a character entirely consistent with the meaning of kemshoo'le, "to glide with rapidity."

The pas de basque is done on the spot except when travel is specified, as in poussette or set-to-and-turn-corners. It comprises a spring onto the right foot in first (count 1); place left in third with heel just touching the edge of the instep (count 2); beat right and jette left between second and fourth inter (count 3 and); spring on left bringing it into third (count 1) as the right is brought low over the ankle into third as in the previous count 2 (count 2), beat left and jette right (count 3 and). The step is executed on the balls of the feet, and the toe is pointed and low to the floor. The rhythm is exactly that of the Scottish Measure.

Employing this step in jig rhythm, the count must be modified from the three equally spaced "1-2-3-and" to "1-and-2-3 and-a" or "1-2 and 3 and-a." The first rhythm is favoured by the RSCDS, and the latter is rejected as approximating too closely to the "two-beat" pas de basque. In the two-beat corruption, both feet land together on count one and separate with a jette on count three. This step is clumsy and is not used in Scottish dance.

A pas de basque in the rhythm "12-3" is used in the Highland dance Gille Callum, both "closed" and "open" (fourth opposite fifth); otherwise it is mostly an equally spaced three-beat pas de basque which is used, although often with lateral travel.

Some observations have been made on Strathspey steps. The RSCDS adopted the travelling step long remembered and danced especially in the Border country. Thurston associates it with the Schottische, and Flett has sought the origin in a Quadrille step described in books as early as 1822. Surely, as Suphy Johnston would have expressed it, "This is great nonsense sir!" Three variants are commonly known; and in addition to the simple step-through which has now become the standard in the Country Dance, there is the step in which the foot is brought up behind, then round, the leg. The latter is now adopted by the Scottish Official Board of Highland Dancing as their standard. All are very beautiful steps when performed well.

The key to the form of the Strathspey travelling step used in the Country Dance by the RSCDS lies to a great extent in Jean Milligan's lyrical tastes and passion for Scottish song. Her feeling for the Strathspey was expressed long ago by Robert Burns: "The kindlan bauld Strathspey," he rhapsodied, "lento largo in the play." (The word "kindlan'" is derived from the verb "to kindle," meaning to set alight; the word "bauld" means bold.) Burns's comment expresses the tempo exactly. There is no point in digging up evidence of a faster tempo from the past and protesting that Miss Milligan's tempo is slower than tradition supports. A trend toward a slower tempo has kept pace with improvement in dancing standards in Highland dancing as well as in the Country Dance.

From this inspiration has grown the beautiful, lento largo "kindlan bauld" step Miss Milligan has now taught several generations of dancers. It has evolved with these dancers, and it takes a well controlled, poised, and musical dancer to execute it to perfection. Dance style, however, is extremely dependent on the music, and if there is no "lento largo in the play," there is no "lento largo" in the dance. The subtle legato beauty of this step, so dependent upon the placing of the body, is a disadvantage for the majority of dancers, who consequently resort to a jumpy step and find themselves, unless the music is equally erratic, with too much time on their hands (or their feet?), reminiscent of the dancers in Thomas Wilson's London so many years ago.

The slow Strathspey setting step, the Common Schottische, as taught by the RSCDS corresponds to the smooth undulation of the travelling step.

The "legato" Country Dance Strathspey steps, travelling and setting, are of great beauty, and fill a gap in the range of expression of the native social dancing of Scotland. Perhaps the step used for the Strathspey Minuet, which was performed to the "slow" Strathspey, was not unlike the legato steps, but, in any case, it was undoubtedly subjected to some artistic refinement, though perhaps not more than that to which all Scottish reel steps have been subjected. One perplexing problem is raised by the legato step, however, and that is that not all strathspey airs are of the "kindlan bauld" variety. To smooth out many of the sprightly strathspey tunes is to destroy their character, and the slow Strathspey step is not compatible with them. It is in these cases that the Highland Strathspey step in the form in which the travelling foot is raised in front of the supporting leg, with a hop, would be more appropriate, as would some such step as that used for "addressing the swords," in the Argyll Broadswords, for setting. In fact as it is in many cases, the Highland Schottische setting is used.

The principal objection to the employment of the appropriate range of technique in Strathspey Country Dances would be its increase in the demands on the skill of the dancer. If this could be overcome, surely it would constitute an enrichment of the art.

No other steps, apart from the slip step in reels and jigs etcetera, are used by the RSCDS in the Scottish Country Dance. Highland Reel setting steps are used in the Eightsome and its relatives and also in Glasgow Highlanders, a delightful dance of the late nineteenth century. These dances contain elements of Reel and Country Dance. A running step is used in Strip the Willow, a Minuet step in The Yellow-Hair'd Laddie; and a Waltz step in Waltz Country Dance.

The hornpipe stepping (treepling as it was called in Scotland), much used by the commonality in the nineteenth century in country dancing and even in reel dancing in many parts of the countryside, English as well as Scottish, has no place in the Scottish Country Dance as a dance of the ballroom, nor in the classical art of Scottish Reel dancing.

EVOLUTION OF FIGURES

The figures of the Scottish Country Dance as restored by the RSCDS differ in many respects from those described by Wilson in his treatise on the English Country Dance, and it is interesting to compare them. This task has been excellently accomplished by Hugh Thurston in his pioneering book *Scotland's Dances*.

One of the hazards in transcribing a Country Dance from an old collection is that certain figures have changed, and the same name has often been used for different figures. One of these, for instance, is the allemande. In Scottish country dancing today, the allemande is a progressive promenade figure for two couples, executed with a particular hand hold — the gentleman's arm reaching over the lady's shoulder to her right hand, her left hand in his — and terminating in the lady's turning under the gentleman's arm, a characteristic of the dance called the Allemande. To Thomas Wilson, allemande meant dos-à-dos, but its usual meaning was an under-arm turn, both taking four bars. Thurston points out the significant fact that in the dances published by the RSCDS which were collected in the field as distinct from being transcribed from printed sources, the allemande appears only in Strathspeys, and he very justly questions whether this graceful figure should ever be used in a dance to reel tempo, suggesting that in these cases an erroneous interpretation has occurred.

A figure which appears often in the Drummond Castle manuscript is called right and left. Today, this is a chain figure for two couples just as it was in Playford's time, but sometime in the eighteenth century a diagonal figure appeared with the same name, and the two figures existed side by side thereafter. In the diagonal figure, the ladies and men exchange places with their diagonal partners and return. This figure is encountered in some dances performed today, but it no longer has any particular name.

Perhaps no figure has been subjected to so many variations as the poussette. As already explained, it was at one time called the draw, but then the term "poussette" was introduced and this name has persisted in Scotland. Today, the couples follow a square path round each other with pas de basque or, in Strathspeys, a diamond path with the slow setting step. The figure may be progressive or nonprogressive, and partners face each other and hold hands in the original manner of the movement.

It is not our concern here to examine the figures of the Scottish Country Dance in greater detail, although it can become a strangely absorbing study for an enthusiast.[8] What now amounts to a considerable number of new dances have been composed, which introduce some ingenious variations on the basic system of figures.[9] The Royal Scottish Country Dance Society has accomplished wonders, on the whole, in formulating and disseminating knowledge of the system. Imperfections exist, but it is satisfying that so much has been achieved that is worthwhile.[10]

[8] In addition to Thurston's *Scotland's Dances*, there is a useful analysis of the dances in the early Scottish manuscript collections in Flett, *The Scottish Country Dance*, Scottish Studies, vol. 11, 1967, pp. 1–11 and 125–47.

[9] Cf. Hugh Foss, *Roll up the Carpet*, published in serial form in *The Reel*, newsletter of the Scottish Country Dance Society of London, 1965.

[10] For more details of the Scottish Country Dance today, see Jean C. Milligan, *Won't You Join the Dance?* and *Introducing Scottish Country Dancing* (Glasgow, 1968); and Allie Anderson and John M. Duthie, *Complete Guide to Scottish Country Dancing*.

22 / Apotheosis of the Scottish Country Dance

Decline of the Scottish Country Dance – founding of the Scottish Country Dance Society – plan of restoration – advantage for Scottish children – work of the RSCDS – favourite dances of the sixties – modern trends – contemporary practice at Scottish Country Dance balls

In the years following World War I, what survived of the Scottish social reel and Country Dance tradition could be seen at the Perth Hunt and the Glasgow Police balls and like occasions — exotic survivals in an era of jazz and its derivatives. Even at the celebrated Northern Meeting in Inverness, with its incomparable pedigree, the music for the ball was provided, in 1923, by an ensemble known as the Yahoo Jazz Sextet. Nothing can mark more dramatically the decline of the place of the traditional dances and their music in the social life of Scotland. The Eightsome Reel, Strathspey, and Reel of Tulloch were interspersed with the waltzes and fox trots in deference to the illustrious history of the occasion, and perhaps a piper played for the reels as had been the practice for a few decades before the war, but it seems altogether appropriate that when the ball ended at five o'clock in the morning, it was with the "Stirring galop, John Peel."

But "the darkness is deepest before the dawn," and it seems peculiarly propitious that in this very winter, a public meeting was called in Glasgow by Mrs. Stewart of Fasnacloich and Jean C. Milligan, then a lecturer in physical education at Jordanhill Teacher Training College, to found the society which was destined to make Scotland dance again to her own music, the Scottish Country Dance Society. The Country Dance was now to find that new way of survival to which we alluded, but in the 1920s, that wished-for outcome did not appear at all certain for the restoration of the Scottish Country Dance was in itself a sufficiently daunting task, let alone the grandiose idea of reintroducing it to the social life of Scotland!

How well these aims have been accomplished is there for everyone to see today. Perhaps the grand objective of *total* acceptance of the Country Dance in modern Scottish social life has not been achieved, but that seems altogether too much to expect in these times. As it is, the achievement has been considerable, certainly in excess of the most sanguine expectations of the founders of the society on that murky winter's night not so very long ago.

When we take the Country Dance Society to task for various things, we must remember that it began its work with very little to guide it and had to begin collecting dances and investigating the technique of their execution with a great deal more urgency than was conducive to the avoidance of error and misconception. The wonder is that so much solid worth was accomplished in these circumstances.

Very wisely, a start was made with those dances best recollected in living memory. These were published, and a system of teacher-training was established. This alone, however, would not have achieved so much had it not been for the exceptional endowment of Jean Milligan as a leader and as a teacher. Uncompromising fidelity to the style, to the tradition — as she conceived it — to the honour of Scotland, and to the precepts evolved by the society have been the themes of her forceful utterances. She has carried these also furth of Scotland to Canada and to the United States where centres of considerable enthusiasm are to be found, and via her disciples or emissaries, to Australia and New Zealand and other outposts of Scotland's "empire."

Of particular significance has been Miss Milligan's influence, through her field of physical education, on the young of Scotland. This is not only of the most vital importance to the preservation of the cultural identity of Scotland but is also of the greatest benefit to the children. As the philosopher Locke says in his *Essay on Education*: "Nothing appears to me to give children so much confidence, and so to raise them to the conversation of those above their age, as dancing. I think they should be taught to dance as soon as they are capable of learning it; for though this consists only in outward gracefulness of motion, yet I know not how, it gives children manly thoughts and carriage more than anything." The Country Dance is ideally suited to these ends and by its means an easy and courteous relationship between boys and girls can early be insinuated. All who have enjoyed the experience of teaching children and young people Scottish country dancing can testify to the truth of this and to Locke's insight in the matter.

Happy is the nation indeed which has such a superb social dance form at the service of its young. Scottish educators must not ignore this or fail to develop it.

The Scottish Country Dance Society has regularly published collections of dances since its foundation. Each book has been received with enthusiasm, its peculiar problems of phrasing and execution vigorously discussed and earnestly studied. A most successful summer school for the society's teachers and candidate teachers was organized and has been conducted annually at the University of St. Andrews with most beneficial results under Miss Milligan's direction. There the work has embraced the broader spectrum of Scottish dance through the teaching of Highland Dance to interested adult males, for many years under the direction of Bobby Watson, as excellent a teacher as he is a dancer. These procedures are all very commendable and must all be placed on the considerable asset side of the society.

Classes and clubs devoted to the performance of Scottish Country Dances according to the precepts of the Royal Scottish Country Dance Society (it now has the royal prefix) have proliferated in some profusion throughout the British Isles and Commonwealth, and bands of musicians who enjoy playing the traditional music have found new purpose and an increasingly appreciative public.

What of the dances? The reader may be interested in a list of what we may consider the favourite Country Dances of the nineteen sixties, and this I subscribe:

Cadgers in the Canongate	The Dashing White Sergeant
Montgomerie's Rant	The Linton Ploughman
General Stuart's Reel	Duchess of Atholl's Slipper (S)
The Glasgow Highlanders	Cameronian Rant (S)
The Eightsome Reel	Red House Reel
Miss Nancy Frowns (Jig)	Miss Mary Douglas
The Birks of Invermay (Strathspey)	Madge Wildfire (S)
She's Ower Young to Marry Yet (S)	None So Pretty
Lochiel's Rant (S)	Corn Rigs
Braes of Tulliemet (S)	Fergus MacIvor (J)
The Deuks dang ower my Daddy (J)	The White Cockade

In recent years, a number of dances composed in this period have enjoyed much favour. These include: Mairi's Wedding, Reel of Mey, and White Heather Jig which, set to attractive music, and employing only the travelling step and interesting figures, have much to commend them to less able dancers. Those interested in preserving the Scottish characteristics of the dances, however, may look on this trend with disquiet.

Kingussie Flower by Anderson (1890) has been revived with success, although demanding a higher order of dancing skill, as has the new Hamilton Rant, a dance emanating from Canada. Among Strathspeys, my own favourites are an obscure, earlier one, The Widows, and a more recent one, The Stoorie Miller, which give much scope for good "Strathspey" dancing in the Country Dance lyrical style.

Scores of Country Dances have been devised, and many of these have been published in recent years. Originality is difficult to achieve, and none of the new dances can really claim superiority over the best of the old, although there is every indication that the thought going into the dances is becoming increasingly more tutored. Hugh Foss, in particular, has exercised his mathematical bent, for instance, in constructing a series of dances on the idea of a counterpoint of movement — fugues, he calls them. He has also given much thought to the matching of music and movement in his Country Dances. Nan Hill, a gifted teacher of movement, has begun teaching the application of the theories of Labban to the structure of Country Dances, thus educating teachers of Scottish country dancing to see patterns of time, space, and mood with new insight. The consequences of this development could be considerable.

The most notable innovations to the vocabulary of figures are the new figures of progression: Robert Campbell's Tournet and particularly John Drurie's Rondel, and the so-called double figure of eight which seems to have been introduced (or reintroduced) by Hugh Foss. Of course, on the face of it, there are countless possible configurations, but complexity must be avoided in the interests of the utility of the Country Dance in its social role. A standard way of executing the principal figures seems essential. There are certainly examples in the RSCDS collection of dances which run contrary to the standard form in some respect, such as setting first to second corner, but, for instance, one never gives left hand to a first corner. The same cannot be said of all new dances, for the quest for originality leads to departures from the norm, a norm, admittedly, which has sometimes been established by the RSCDS and not altogether by tradition, but which has nevertheless been of immense value in the promotion and social use of the dances.

The fact that a large proportion of the new dances involves all four couples simultaneously presents practical difficulties in the dance assembly and dispenses with the very useful advantages of the three-couple dance, one of which is the opportunity of a rest afforded each couple in turn. Certainly, as proficiency and experience have increased, taste has turned to the more complicated dances. The key to the successful Country Dance, nevertheless, remains the same; it is embodied in the word "flow" or "phrasing," and this in turn is related to the music.

Let us turn now to the etiquette and conduct of contemporary Scottish Country Dance balls or "dances." Ladies can always dance together. Sets are limited to four couples, or five if there is an extra couple, and are arranged in long lines down the hall, each couple joining the end of the line as it is formed. The men's and ladies' sides of the dance are usually about seven feet apart, about two to three feet separating the couples longitudinally. Stewards, or some helpful persons, "count" out the sets, so that before the dance begins, every dancer knows his or her place, that is, first or second couple or whatever. The dance is performed twice through by each couple. Gone are the days — fortunately — referred to nostalgically in a letter to the editor of the *Aberdeen Evening Express*, January 18, 1886, when one could "go o'er twenty couples in the Merry Lads o' Ayr without stop." "It made one feel very comfortable," the writer declares.

There are indications of a decline of the original enthusiasm for the Country Dance in Scotland itself, although something of the reverse is manifest in the Commonwealth countries at the time of writing. The most threatening trend is the noticeable dearth of male dancers, but this is no new phenomenon in our sophisticated society. It occurred at the end of the eighteenth century, and arose then, as now, from the manners and values of the times. Good male teachers are also in short supply in both Highland and country dancing and, while this is a result of the general shortage, it also contributes to it. Perhaps the lack of male dancers is now the natural order of things, but it should not apply to the Scots. Like the Cossacks, the Tartars, the Sikhs, the Spanish gypsies, and many others, the Scottish male is heir to a grand tradition of dance. If he ignores this inheritance, it is largely because he has been caught up in that same force of Western conformity which makes the new office buildings and flats of Glasgow so little different from those of Manchester, Montreal, or San Francisco.

Scottish Country Dance balls or "dances" may be formal or informal. Formal attire for the men is Highland dress; informal attire calls for a white shirt, plain tie and hose, and kilt. The kilt, although not traditional in the Country Dance, gives necessary freedom to the limbs and shape to the technique, which is the glory of the form. After all, normal male apparel in earlier centuries was based on stockings and breeches which gave like freedom. Modern trousers are uncomfortable for the energetic style of the dance and are lacking in character in any case.

The subject of footwear has already been discussed. In practice, today, men wear gillies, and women, gillies or ballet slippers. In certain instances where the ball program is sprinkled with other kinds of dance, the ladies may prefer to retain their heeled, dress shoes. This, of course, limits their movement, but older women in particular seldom consider this a hardship.

When all this colourful, well-trained, well-ordered, accomplished array — where these are appropriate terms — begins to move to a superb band such as Stan Hamilton's which exhibits all the intuitive zest and skilled musicianship this unique combination can bring to it, the performance is a joyful sight, a thrilling aural and visual experience. Brooches thrusting rapier shafts of red, blue, and green through waves of tartan sashes and kilts, coming and going through the music.

Thomas De Quincey regarded this spectacle of "free, fluent and continuous motion above all the scenes of this World"; a spectacle which presented for him "a sort of masque of human life, with its whole equipage of pomps and glories, its luxury of sight and sound, its hours of golden youth, and the interminable revolution of ages hurrying after ages, and one generation treading on the flying footsteps of another; whilst all the while the over-ruling music attempers the mind to the spectacle, the subject to the object, the beholder to the vision."

The Scottish Country Dance ball is all of this and more. Long may it remain a crowning glory to the social life of Scotland and the Scots.

Appendix A

THE SWORD DANCE OF PAPA STOUR

The earliest detailed account of the sword dance preserved on the Island of Papa Stour, Shetland, dates from the nineteenth century, and is found in Samuel Hibbert's *A Description of the Shetland Isles* (Edinburgh, 1822). Sir Walter Scott acquired a description of the dance when he visited Scalloway during his voyage round the northern coasts and islands in August, 1814* and published what he collected of the dialogue of the play in the notes to his novel, *The Pirate* (Edinburgh, 1822), by which time he had read Hibbert's account. Then, about twenty years later, James Wilson published an account and text in his *A Voyage Round the Coasts of Scotland and the Isles* (Edinburgh, 1842, pp. 356–66). Wilson's dialogue is very close to Hibbert's, but he gives a more picturesque description of the action based upon his own eye witness.

Hibbert introduces his account thus:

Papa Stour is the only island in the country where the ancient Norwegian amusement of the sword dance has been preserved, and where it still continues in Thule, to beguile the tediousness of a long winter's evening. . . . We shall suppose Yule to be arrived, which is always announced at break of day by the fiddles striking up the Day-dawn, an ancient Norwegian tune, that, being associated with gaiety and festivity, is never heard without emotions of delight. As the evening approaches, piles of turf are lighted up in the apartment where wassail is to be kept; young and old of each sex make their appearance, and, after the whisky has gone liberally round, it is announced that the sword-dancers are making their appearance. . . . The company then seat themselves on the forms, tubs, beds, and benches, that serve the place of chairs, leaving a large space in the middle of the room for the exhibition. The fiddle strikes up a Norn melody, and at the sound of it a warrior enters in the character of St. George, or the master of the Seven Champions of Christendom, a white hempen shirt being thrown over his clothes, intended to represent the ancient shirt of mail that the Northmen wore, and a formidable looking sword being girt to his side, constructed from the iron hoop of a barrel. St. George then stalks forward and makes his bow, the music ceasing while he delivers his epilogue.

Sir Walter Scott adds some details to this account in the diary of his tour:

At Scalloway my curiosity was gratified by an account of the sword-dance, now almost lost, but still practised in the island of Papa, belonging to Mr. Scott. There are eight performers, seven of whom represent the Seven Champions of Christendom, who enter one by one with their swords drawn, and are presented to the eighth personage, who is not named. Some rude couplets are spoken (in English, not Norse), containing a sort of panegyric upon each champion as he is presented. They then dance a sort of cotillion, as the

* W. G. Lockhart, *Memoirs of the Life of Sir Walter Scott*, 2nd ed. (Edinburgh, 1839), pp. 217–18.

ladies described it, going through a number of evolutions with their swords. One of my three Mrs. Scotts' readily promised to procure me the lines, the rhymes, and the form of the dance. I regret much that young Mr. Scott was absent during this visit; he is described as a reader and an enthusiast in poetry. Probably I might have interested him in preserving the dance, by causing young persons to learn it. A few years since a party of Papa-men came to dance the sword-dance at Lerwick as a public exhibition, with great applause.

Wilson remarks on the jovial and hearty manner of performance:

During the dance they "give utterance to wild unearthly cries, or sudden shouts and screams, and such a turmoil takes place that we at one time deemed ourselves rather in bedlam than Papa Stour.... The exhibition was ... not deficient in a certain wild gracefulness, in spite of the occasional prevalence of exuberant and uncouth glee.

The differences between the texts of the dialogue collected by the three authorities whose works are drawn upon here are not serious. But in the interests of compiling as complete a text as possible, it seems advantageous to lean heavily on Hibbert and supplement his version from the other two sources. The lines that occur in Scott's version but not in Hibbert's are enclosed in brackets [ ]. Those lines that occur in Hibbert's version but not in Scott's are in parentheses ( ). Quotations from Wilson are marked (W). This is the system followed by Alfred W. Johnston in his article "The Sword Dance of Papa Stour," in the *Old Lore Miscellany of Orkney, Shetland, Caithness and Sutherland*, vol. 5, (London, 1912), in which he attempts a like synthesis of the same three versions.

Text

Enter the master, St. George, "with a straightened portion of herring hoop in his hand to represent a sword. Bowing his head and body and scraping the ground with one of his hind legs." (W)

> Brave gentles all, within this boor,
>   If ye delight in any sport,
> Come see me dance upon this floor,
>   (Which to you all shall yield comfort.
> Then shall I dance in such a sort,
>   As possible I may or can;)
> You, minstrel man, play me a porte,
>   (That I on this floor may prove a man.)

He then toddles about the floor for a few seconds, with a shifting motion of the feet, the toes turned well inwards, and making a low sweeping reverential bow . . . the music ceases. (W)

[He bows and dances in a line]

(The minstrel strikes up; the master bows and dances)

Now have I danc(e)d with heart and hand,
　　Brave gentles all, as you may see,
For I have been tried in many a land,
　　(As yet the truth can testify:)
In England, Scotland, Ireland, France, Italy and Spain,
　　Have I been tried with that good sword of steel.

[*Draws and flourishes*]

Yet I deny that ever a man did make me yield;

(*Draws his sword, flourishes it, and returns it to his side*)

For in my body there is strength,
　　As by my manhood may be seen;
And with that good sword of length,
　　Have oftentimes in perils been,
And over champions I was king
　　And by the strength of this right hand,
Once in a day I killed fifteen,
　　And left them dead upon the land.
Therefore brave minstrel do not care,
　　But play to me a porte most light,
That I no longer do forbear,
　　But dance in all these gentles' sight:

(*The master then bows, and while the music plays, again dances and thus, after having "Rid his prologue like a rough colt, knowing not the stop," he gives notice of the further entertainment that is intended*)

Although my strength makes you abased,
　　Brave gentles all be not afraid,
For here are six champions, with me, staid,
　　All by my manhood I have raised.

(*He dances*)

Since I have danced I think it best
　　To call my brethren in your sight,
That I may have a little rest,
　　And they may dance with all their might:
(With heart and hand as they are knights.)
　　And shake their sword of steel so bright,
And show their main strength on this floor,
For we shall have another bout
Before we pass out of this boor,
Therefore, brave minstrel do not care
　　To play to me a porte most light.
That I no longer do forbear,
　　But dance in all these gentles' sight.

[*He dances, and then introduces his knights as under*]

(The minstrel obeys: the master again dances, and then, with much polite discretion, introduces into the room six formidable looking knights, each with a white shirt over his clothes in the place of a shirt of mail, and a good sword girt to his side, their respective names and deeds being announced in well set verse)

> And champion Dennis, a French knight,
>   Who stout and bold is to be seen;
> And David a (brave) Welshman born,
>   Who is come of noble blood:
> And Patrick, also, who blew the horn,
>   An Irish knight amongst the wood.
> Of Italy, brave Anthony the good,
>   And Andrew of (fair) Scotland King.
> St. George of England brave indeed,
>   Who to the Jews wrought muckle tinte.
> Away with this! — Let us come to sport,
>   Since that ye have a mind to war,
> Since that ye have this bargain sought.
>   Come let us fight and do not fear
> Therefore, brave minstrel, do not care
>   To play to me a porte most light,
> That I no longer do forbear,
>   But dance in all these gentles' sight.

[*He dances, and advances to James of Spain*]

(The master, after shewing his brethren a specimen of the sort of pas seul that they will be required to exhibit before the company, draws his sword, and addresses all the knights in succession)

> Stout James of Spain, both tried and stour,
>   Thine acts are known full well indeed,
> Present thyself within our sight,
>   Without either fear or dread.
> Count not for favour or for feid.
>   Since of thy acts thou hast been sure;
> Brave James of Spain, I will thee lead,
>   To prove thy manhood on this floor.

[*James dances*]

(James of Spain draws his sword, and on the fiddle being heard, he proves his manhood on the floor by a pas seul)

> Brave champion Dennis, a French knight,
>   Who stout and bold is to be seen,
> Present thyself here in our sight,
>   Thou brave French knight, who bold hast been,
> Since thou such valiant acts hast done,
>   Come let us see some of them now;

With courtesy thou brave French knight,
Draw out thy sword of noble hue.

[Dennis dances, while the others retire to a side]

(The minstrel strikes up; Dennis draws his sword and dances)

Brave David a bow must string, and (big), with awe,
Set up a wand upon a stand,
And that brave David will cleave in twa.

[David dances]

(David draws and dances)

Here is, I think, an Irish knight,
Who does not fear, or does not fright.
To prove thyself a valiant man,
(As thou has done full often bright:)
Brave Patrick, dance, if that thou can.

[He dances]

(Patrick draws and dances)

Thou stout Italian, come thou there;
Thy name is Anthony, most stout;
Draw out they sword that is most clear,
And do thou fight without any doubt;
Thy leg (thou) shake (bow), thy neck thou lout
And shew some courtesy on this floor,
For we shall have another bout,
Before we pass out of this boor.

(Anthony draws and danes)

Thou kindly Scotsman, come thou here;
Thy name is Andrew of Fair Scotland;
Draw out thy sword that is most clear.
Fight for thy King with thy right hand;
(And aye as long as thou can stand.)
Fight for thy king with all thy heart;
And then, for to confirm his band,
Make all his enemies (for) to smart,
(And leave them dead upon the land.)

[He dances, Music begins]

(Andrew draws and dances)

Formations

"Figure. The six stand in rank with their swords reclining on their shoulders. The master (St. George) dances, and then strikes the sword of James of Spain, who follows George, then dances, strikes the sword of Dennis, who follows behind James. In like manner the rest — the music playing — swords as before.

"After the six are brought out of rank, they and the master form a circle, and hold their swords point and hilt. This circle is danced round twice.

"The master runs under the sword opposite, which he jumps over backwards. The others do the same. He then passes under the right-hand sword, which the others follow, in which position they dance, until commanded by the master, when they form into a circle, and dance round as before. They then jump over the right-hand sword, by which means their backs are to the circle, and their hands across their backs. They dance round in that form until the master calls 'Loose,' when they pass under the right sword, and are in a perfect circle.

"The master lays down his sword, and lays hold of the point of James' sword. He then turns himself, James, and the others, into a clew. When so formed, he passes under the midst of the circle; the others follow; they vault as before. After several other

"The minstrel now flourishes his bow with spirit, and the sword-dance commences. The master gives a signal to his brethren, who stand in rank with their swords reclined on their right shoulders, while he dances a pas seul. He then strikes the sword of James of Spain, who moves out of line, dances and strikes the sword of Dennis; then Dennis sports a toe on the floor, and in the same manner brings David out of line, and thus each champion is successively made to caper about the room.

"The Champions hold their swords in a vaulted direction, and, headed by the master, successively pass under them: they then jump over their swords, — this movement bringing the weapons into a cross position, from which they are released by each dancer passing under his right hand sword. A single roundel, hilt and point, is then performed as before.

"The roundel is interrupted by the master, who runs under the sword of his right hand, and then jumps over it backward; his brethren successively do the same. The master then passes under his right hand sword, and is followed in this movement by the rest. Thus they continue to dance, until a signal is given by their director, when they form into a circle, swords tended, and grasping hilts and points as before. After a roundel has been danced, the champions jump over their right hand sword, by which means their back is to the circle, and their hands across their backs, and in this form they dance round until the master calls 'loose!' They then respectively pass under their right hand swords, and are in a circle as before.

"The master now lays down his own sword, and seizing hold of the point of James sword, turns himself, James, and the rest of the champions into a clue, and their swords being held in a vaulted position, he passes under them and thus comes out of evolutions, they throw themselves into a circle, with their arms across the breast. They afterward form such figures as to form a shield of their swords, and the shield is so compact that the master and his knights dance alternately with this shield upon their heads. It is then laid down upon the floor. Each knight lays hold of their former points and hilts with their hands across, which disentangle by figure directly contrary to those that formed the shield. This finishes the Ballet."

the circle being followed in the same manner by the other knights. A repetition of all or part of the movements already described, then ensues. The master and his brethren, in the next place throw themselves into a circle, each holding his arms across his breast, and with their swords, form a figure intended to represent a shield; this being so compact that each champion alternately dances with it upon his head. The shield is then laid down upon the floor, when each knight laying hold of the hilt and point which he before held, and placing his arms across his breast, extricates his sword from the shield by a figure directly opposite to that by which it had been formed. The movement finishes the sword dance. The master then gravely steps forward and delivers the following."

Epilogue

Mars does rule he bends his brows,
  He makes us all aghast
After the few hours that we stay here,
  Venus will rule at last.
Farewell, farewell, brave gentles all.
  That herein do remain,
We wish you health and happiness
  Till we return again.

Appendix B

HIGHLAND REEL STEPS BY FRANCIS PEACOCK

This account of reel steps is taken from Francis Peacock's *Sketches Relative to the history and theory but more especially to the practice and art of dancing* (Aberdeen, 1805), pp. 85-98.

1) Kemshóole,* or Forward Step. [*Ceumsuibhail*, step to glide with rapidity.] This is the common step for the *promenade* or figure of the reel. It is done by advancing the right foot forward, the left following it behind: in advancing the same foot a second time, you hop upon it, and one step is finished. You do the same motions after advancing the left foot, and so on alternately with each foot, during the first measure of the tune played twice over; but if you wish to vary the step, in repeating the measure, you may introduce a very lively one, by making a smart rise, or gentle spring, forward, upon the right foot, placing the left foot behind it: this you do four times, with this difference, that instead of going a fourth time behind with the left foot, you disengage it from the ground, adding a hop to the last spring. You finish the *promenade*, by doing the same step, beginning it with the left foot. To give the step its full effect, you should turn the body a little to the left, when you go forward with the right foot, and the contrary way when you advance the left.

2) Minor Kemkóssy — Setting or Footing step. [*Cèum-coisiche*, from *Cèum*, a step, and *Coiseachadh*, to foot it, or ply the feet.] This is an easy familiar step, much used by the English in their Country Dances. You have only to place the right foot behind the left, sink and hop upon it, then do the same with the left foot behind the right.

3) Single Kemkóssy — Setting or Footing step. You pass the right foot behind the left to the fifth position, making a gentle bound, or spring, with the left foot, to the second position; after passing the right foot again behind the left, you make a hop upon it, extending the left toe. You do the same step, by passing the left foot twice behind the right, concluding, as before, with a hop. This step is generally done with each foot alternately, during the whole of the second measure of the tune.

4) Double Kemkóssy — Setting or Footing step. This step differs from the Single Kemkossy only in its additional number of motions. You pass the foot four times behind the other, before you hop, which must always be upon the hindmost foot.

5) *Lemastrást* [*Lèum*, a leap, a spring]. Cross Springs — These are a series of *Sissonnes*. You spring forward with the right foot to the third or fifth position, making a hop upon the left foot; then spring backward with the right, and hop upon it. You do the same with the left foot, and so on, for two, four, or as many bars as the second part of the tune contains. This is a single step; to double it, you do the Springs, forward and backward, four times, before you change the foot.

---

* The spelling is Peacock's.

6) *Seby-trast* [*Siabadh*, to slip; *Trasd*, across]. Chasing Steps, or Cross Slips — This step is like the *Balotte*. You slip the right foot before the left; the left foot behind the right; the right again before the left, and hop upon it. You do the same, beginning with the left foot. This is a single step.

7) *Aisig-thrasd*. Cross-Passes — This is a favourite step in many parts of the Highlands. You spring a little to one side with the right foot, immediately passing the left across it; hop and cross it again, and one step is finished; you then spring a little to one side with the left foot, making the like passes with the right. This is a minor step; but it is often varied by passing the foot four times alternately behind and before, observing to make a hop previous to each pass, the first excepted, which must always be a spring, or bound, by these additional motions, it becomes a single step.

8) *Kem Badenoch*, a Minor Step — You make a gentle spring to one side with the right foot, immediately placing the left behind it; then do a single *Entrechat*, that is, a cross *caper*, or leap, changing the situation of the feet, by which the right foot will be behind the left. You do the same beginning with the left foot. By adding two cross leaps to three of these steps, it becomes a double step.

9) *Fosgladh*, [An opening]. Open Step — Slip the feet to the second position, then, with straight knees, make a smart spring upon the toes to the fifth position; slip the feet again to the second position, and do a like spring, observing to let the foot which was before in the first spring, be behind in the second. This is a minor step, and is generally repeated during the half, or the whole, measure of the tune.

10) *Cuartag* [from Cuairt, a round]. Turning Step — You go to the second position with the right foot; hop upon it, and pass the left behind it; then hop, and pass the same foot before. — You repeat these alternate passes after each hop you make in going about to the right. Some go twice round, concluding the last circumvolution with two single cross capers. These circumvolutions are equal to four bars, or one measure of the tune. Others go round to the right, and then to the left. These, also, occupy the same number of bars.

Combined or Mixed Steps

These are an association of different steps, and which are necessary to add variety to the dance. For example: You may add two of the sixth step (Seby-Trasd) to two of the third (Single Kemkóssy). This you may vary, by doing the first of these steps before, instead of behind; or you may add two of the second step (Minor Kemkóssy) to one single Kemkóssy. These steps may be transposed, so that the last shall take the place of the first. Again: — Two of the sixth step (Seby-Trasd) may be added to the fourth step, (Double Kemkóssy) in going to either side.

Another variety, much practised, is to spring backward with the right foot instead of of forward, as in the fifth step, and hop upon the left; then spring forward, and again hop upon the same foot, and add to these two springs, one single Kemkóssy, passing the right foot behind the left. You do the same step, beginning it with the left foot. In short, without particularising any other combinations, I shall only add, that you have it in your power to change, divide, add to, or invert, the different steps described, in whatever way you think best adapted to the tune, or most pleasing to yourself.

Appendix C

DIRECTORS AND DIRECTRESSES
OF THE EDINBURGH ASSEMBLY

Abstracted from James H. Jamieson, *Social Assemblies of the Eighteenth Century*, Book of the Old Edinburgh Club. The figures after each name indicate the date of appointment. Previous to 1746 the assembly was directed solely by ladies.

Directors

JOHN BELSCHES (1746). Advocate, son of Alexander Belsches of Invermay, Sheriff-Clerk, Edinburgh. Died December 29, 1777.

HUGH CLARK (1746). Merchant, Edinburgh. Died November, 1750.

HEW DALRYMPLE of Drummore (1746). Son of Sir Hew Dalrymple or North Berwick, Bart., who was president of the Court of Session. Admitted an advocate, 1710, and appointed a Lord of Session with the title of Lord Drummore, 1726. Died June 18, 1755.

WILLIAM DOUGLAS (1746). Merchant, Edinburgh. Treasurer of both the Assembly and the Musical Society.

SIR GILBERT ELLIOT (1746). Second baronet of Minto; appointed a Lord of Session with the title of Lord Minto, 1726; Lord Justice-Clerk, 1763. Died April 16, 1766. His father, who bore the same name, also sat on the Bench as Lord Minto.

GAVIN HAMILTON (1746). Bookseller, Edinburgh.

JOHN HAMILTON (1746). Advocate, the second son of Thomas Hamilton, sixth Earl of Haddington. Died February 11, 1772.

JAMES STIRLING (1746). Merchant, Edinburgh; carried on a grocery business at the Black Bull, below the Tron Church. According to the *Edinburgh Evening Courant*, 1758, he sold tickets for the Assembly at his shop. Treasurer of the Charity Workhouse. Died February 17, 1764.

GILBERT LAURIE (1755). Son of Gilbert Laurie of Crossrig, an Edinburgh surgeon. An apothecary and Commissioner of Excise; Lord Provost of Edinburgh, 1766–68 and 1772–74.

ROBERT PRINGLE of Edgehill (1755). Son of Thomas Pringle, W.S.; admitted advocate 1724; appointed a Lord of Session with the title of Lord Edgehill, 1754. Died April 8, 1764.

ROBERT BRUCE (1766). Son of Alexander Bruce of Kennet; appointed a Lord of Session with the title of Lord Kennet, 1764. Died April 8, 1785.

JOHN DALRYMPLE (1772). A younger brother of Lord Hailes. Lord Provost of Edinburgh, 1770–72 and 1777–78. Born 1734, died 1779.

HONOURABLE JAMES ERSKINE of Alva (1772). Son of Charles Erskine of Tinwald, Lord

Justice-Clerk; appointed a Lord of Session with the title of Lord Barjarg, 1761. A brother of Mrs. Campbell of Finab. Born 1722, died May 13, 1796.

JAMES EDGAR (1774). Collector of Customs at Leith. Died February 6, 1799. (Interesting particulars about him are found in Kay, *A Series of Original Portraits* [Edinburgh, 1838], vol. I., p. 385.)

SIR WILLIAM FORBES of Pitsligo, Bart. (1774). Well-known banker. Born April 5, 1739, died November 12, 1806.

Directresses

This list includes lady directresses from 1723 to 1746; also those who held office along with the directors from 1746 onwards. Those marked with an asterisk were invited to serve, but whether they did so is not apparent from the Minutes.

COUNTESS OF PANMURE (1723). Margaret, youngest daughter of William, Duke of Hamilton, and wife of James Maule, fourth Earl of Panmure, one of the Privy Councillors of James VII. The countess, who was a directress till at least 1728, was a prominent leader in Edinburgh society. Died December 6, 1731.

LADY DRUMELZIER (1723). Elizabeth, daughter of Alexander Seton, first Viscount Kingston, and wife of the Honourable William Hay of Drumelzier.

LADY ORBISTON (1723). Probably Margaret, daughter of Sir Archibald Hamilton of Rosehall, Bart. and wife of James Hamilton of Dalziel and Orbiston.

LADY NEWHALL (1723). Katherine, daughter of Johnston of Hilton and wife of Sir Walter Pringle, Lord Newhall, one of the Lords of Session.

LADY DALRYMPLE of North Berwick (1723). Marion, daughter of Sir Robert Hamilton of Pressmennan, a Lord of Session, and wife of Sir Hew Dalrymple of North Berwick, Lord President of the Court of Session (1698–1737).

COUNTESS OF GLENCAIRN (1746). Elizabeth, daughter of Hugh Macguire of Drumdow, Ayrshire, and wife of William, twelfth Earl of Glencairn. Died June 24, 1801.

COUNTESS OF HOPETOUN (1746). Lady Anne Ogilvy, second daughter of James, fifth Earl of Findlater and Seafield, and first wife of John, second Earl of Hopetoun. Died February 8, 1759.

COUNTESS OF LEVEN (1746). Elizabeth, daughter of Alexander Monypenny of Pitmilly and second wife of Alexander, fifth Earl of Leven. Died May 15, 1783.

LADY MILNTOUN (MILTON) (1746). Probably Elizabeth, daughter of Sir Francis Kinloch of Gilmerton and wife of Andrew Fletcher of Milton, Lord Justice-Clerk (1735–48). Died November, 1782.

LADY MINTO (1746). Helen, daughter of Sir Robert Stewart of Allanbank, Bart. and wife of Sir Gilbert Elliot of Minto, second baronet. [See SIR GILBERT ELLIOT.] Miss Jean Elliot, authoress of one of the versions of "The Flowers of the Forest," was her daughter. Died June 22, 1774.

HONOURABLE LADY JEAN FERGUSSON (1747). Only child of James, Lord Maitland (eldest son of James, Earl of Lauderdale), and wife of Sir James Fergusson, Bart., a Lord of Session with the title of Lord Kilkerran. Born December 7, 1703, died March 29, 1766.

LADY HENRIETTA CAMPBELL* (1750). Daughter of John, second Earl of Breadalbane. She was one of the ladies of the Bedchamber to the Princesses Amelia and Caroline, daughters of George II. Died unmarried, January 27, 1766.

MRS. GRANT of Prestongrange (1750). Grizel, only child of Reverend John Millar, minister of Neilston, and wife of William Grant, a Lord of Session with the title of Lord Prestongrange. Born 1708, died September 30, 1792.

MRS. FERGUSON of Pitfour (1753). The Honourable Anne Murray, daughter of Alexander, fourth Lord Elibank, and wife of James Ferguson of Pitfour, who sat on the Bench as Lord Pitfour. Died January 2, 1793.

LADY KELLO* (1753). Christian, daughter of Sir Francis Grant of Cullen and wife of George Buchan of Kello. Died August 4, 1784.

MRS. SCOTT of Gala* (1753). Elizabeth, daughter of Colonel John Stewart of Stewartfield and wife of Hugh Scott of Gala. Died 1784(?).

LADY SINCLAIR of Longformacus (1753). Sydney, daughter of Robert Johnston of Hilton and wife of Sir John Sinclair of Longformacus, fourth baronet. Died May 25, 1777.

MRS. BRUCE of Kennet (1765). Helen, eldest daughter of George Abercromby of Tullibody and wife of Robert Bruce, Lord Kennet. [See ROBERT BRUCE.]

HONOURABLE MISS NICOLAS HELEN MURRAY of Stormont, better known as Nicky Murray (1765). Died November 7, 1777.

LADY NAPIER (1768). Henrietta-Maria, daughter of Major George Johnston, cadet of the Hilton family, and second wife of Francis, fifth Lord Napier. Died September 20, 1795.

MRS. CAMPBELL of Finab (1773). Susan, daughter of Charles Erskine of Tinwald, Lord Justice-Clerk, and wife of Robert Campbell of Finab and Monzie. She was sister of the Lord of Session who went by the title of Lord Barjarg. [See JAMES ERSKINE.]

COUNTESS OF DUNDONALD* (1773). She was also proposed in 1753. Jean, daughter of Archibald Stuart of Torrance, Lanarkshire, and wife of Thomas, eighth Earl of Dundonald. Died March 21, 1808.

LADY ELPHINSTONE (1773). Lady Clementina Fleming, daughter of John, sixth Earl of Wigton, and wife of Charles, tenth Lord Elphinstone. Died January 1, 1799.

COUNTESS DOWAGER of Moray (1773). Margaret, second daughter of David, third Earl of Wemyss, and wife of James, eighth Earl of Moray. Died August 31, 1779.

MRS. JOHNSON of Hilton (1776). Probably daughter of Major George Johnston and sister of Lady Napier.

Appendix D

CHARTER OF THE NORTHERN MEETING

At Inverness, the 11th June 1788 —— In a Meeting where the under mentioned Gentlemen were present,

Colonel *Hugh Grant* of Moy,
Mr *Cumming of Altyre*,
Mr *MacLeod of Geanies*,
Mr *Munro of Culcairn*,
Mr *Fraser of Relick*,
Mr *Fraser of Culduthel*,
Captain *Alexander Mackenzie*, 71st.

Captain *William Wilson*, 39th.
Mr *Baillie of Dochfour*,
Captain *Gregor Grant*,
Baillie *Alexander Shaw*,
Lieutenant *John Ross*,
And,
Doctor *John Alves*,

They, after a Conversation at length on the Subject, came to the following Resolutions, viz.

1. That an ANNUAL MEETING of Gentlemen, Ladies, and their Families, shall hold in this Place for the Space of One Week, to commence on the last Monday of October first, and thereafter on the last Monday of October Yearly, and that for Purpose of promoting a Social Intercourse.

2. That the Meeting shall be named the NORTHERN MEETING.

3. That a List be made out of those Gentlemen who it is thought would chuse to be Original Constituent Members of this Meeting, and that a Copy thereof and of the proposed Plan as hereafter expressed, shall be transmitted to each of the Gentlemen and Ladies therein named, with a Request, that they will, with their earliest Convenience, specify to the Secretary of the Meeting, whether they chuse to remain nominated Original Constituent Members, or decline the Offer.

4. That every Gentleman or Lady, being the Head of a Family, who is or shall become a Constituent Member of this Meeting, shall pay in to the Secretary, the Sum of ONE GUINEA Yearly, for the public Purposes of the Meeting; and that all such Members as shall absent themselves shall pay double that Sum, (excepting Officers below the Rank of Field Officers, who may be necessarily absent on Duty.)

5. That out of this Fund, the Notices to the Members, the Printed Tickets of Admission to the Ball Room, the Music, Lights, Door Keepers, Tea and Negus at the Ball shall be paid; and that the Debursement thereof, shall be committed to the sole Charge of the Secretary and Stewards to be now named.

6. That this meeting do name the Stewards and Secretary for the Year, and do accordingly nominate and appoint *A. Penrose Cumming* of *Altyre*; *James Fraser* of *Culduthel*; *Edward Fraser* of *Relick*, and *Donald MacLeod* of *Geanies*, Esqs; to be Stewards for the first Meeting; and Doctor *John Alves* Physician here to be Secretary – Which Offices the Gentlemen being present did agree to accept.

7. That the whole Business of the Meeting, shall be conducted by the Stewards and

Secretary, conformable to the General Regulations now laid down, or that may here-after be resolved on. That they shall alternately act as Toast-master and Croupier at the Entertainments, and as Masters of the Ceremonies at the Ball Room; and that the whole Gentlemen and Ladies of the Meeting, shall support the Authority of the Stewards.

8. That a Book shall be immediately purchased and kept by the Secretary, in which these Resolutions shall be entered, and all the future proceedings of the Meeting; and that the Gentlemen now present, do pay to the Secretary, their Subscription of a Guinea each, to enable him to get these Resolutions, and the List of proposed Members Printed and distributed, which the Gentlemen present agreed to and paid accordingly.

9. That the whole Company, Ladies and Gentlemen, do Dine together, and that it is to be understood as a Regulation, that they do all come to Table dressed for the Ball in the Evening.

10. That the Company do meet and Dine the first Day at Mr *Beverly's Inn*; the fol-lowing Day at Mr *Ettles's Hotel*, and thereafter at the Inns alternately.

11. That Dinner be on the Table each Day precisely by Four o'Clock. That ladies having retired, the Bill shall be called for by the Two Stewards, who do not act as Toast master and Croupier for the Day, at Half past Six o'Clock, and he proportioned by them, and collected by the Secretary, as soon as it can be proportioned.

12. That in proportioning the Bill, all the Members present, shall, individually pay for their own Ordinary, and for that of every Lady they introduce; and that the Gentle-men shall pay equally, for the whole Liquors consumed.

13. That it shall be in the Power of the Stewards to introduce Strangers, both to the Entertainment and Ball; but not in the Power of any private Individual of the Meeting.

14. That the Ordinary, etc. of all Strangers introduced, shall be proportioned on the Members who are present at large, at the time of collecting the Bill.

15. That there shall be no Allowance for Servants of the Company, it being under-stood, that every Gentleman puts his Servants on Board Wages.

16. That immediately after the Bill is settled and paid, the Gentlemen do adjourn to the Ball Room.

17. That the Dancing do commence each Night precisely by Eight o'Clock, and stop precisely by Twelve.

18. That Mr *Cumming* of *Altyre*, be directed to write to Captain *Graham*, Master of the Ceremonies at *Edinburgh*, for a Copy of the Regulations adopted there, as to the order of Dancing and conduct of the Balls, and that they shall be adopted by this Meeting: a Copy of them to be Printed and hung up in the Public Rooms of each Inn, and in the Dancing Room.

19. That the Provost of *Inverness* be applied to, for the Use of the Town Hall for the Balls, and the Room above for a Tea Room, by the Secretary in the Name of the Meeting.

20. That there shall be a Public Breakfast prepared next Morning, at the Inn where the Company dined the Day before, for as many Ladies and Gentlemen as chuse to resort there, at the Hour which will appear most agreeable to the Company.

21. That the Meeting shall commence on Monday the Twenty-Seventh of *October*, and continue to have an Entertainment and a Ball on that Day, the *Tuesday, Wednes-day, Thursday*, and *Friday* following; and that on the Forenoon of *Saturday*, the

Gentlemen of the Meeting, shall assemble at *Beverly's*, receive the Secretaries Accounts, chuse new Stewarts and Secretary, appoint the following Years Meeting, determine any Petitions for Admission of New Members, and do any other Business that may respect the Meeting.

22. That those who wish to become Members after the Meeting is fully constituted, must apply by Petition, to be lodged with the Secretary, at least One Week before the first Day of Meeting annually; and the Question shall be determined by Ballot, of those Members who are in Town, the first Day immediately after the Ladies retire from Dinner; and that Five Black Balls shall exclude any Person so Petitioning. That the Secretary do provide a Ballot Box and Balls, before the first Day of Meeting.

23. That no Subscription Paper for any public or private Work or Undertaking, shall, under any pretext whatever, be obtruded on the Company when met collectively; and that whoever presumes to infringe on this Regulation, shall be subject to a Fine of *One Guinea*.

24. That as the Object of the Meeting is Pleasure and Innocent Amusement, and that it is thought the having One or more Packs of Hounds here, with which such Gentlemen as are so inclined, might hunt every Morning of the Meeting; Mr *Brodie of Brodie*, and Mr *MacLeod of Geanies*, Members, be requested, the first to apply to His Grace the Duke of *Gordon*, and the latter to Sir *Hector Munro*, for the favour of permitting their Huntsmen and Packs to attend here during the Week of the Meeting, (provided they do accede to the Plan of the Meeting), that Gentlemen may hunt with them alternately.

Thereafter, the Gentlemen present, made up a List of such Gentlemen belonging to the Three Counties, as they thought might chuse to accede to the Plan of Meeting, which was delivered to the Secretary to be classed by him and Printed.

Bibliography

GENERAL

ABERDEEN RECORDS. *Extracts from the Records of the Burgh of Aberdeen, 1643–1747.* Edinburgh: Burgh Records Society, 1872.

Accounts of the Lord High Treasurer of Scotland, vols. 1–4. Ed. T. Dickson and Sir J. Balfour Paul. Edinburgh, 1877–1902.

Acts of the Parliament of Scotland. Edinburgh, 1844.

ADAM, FRANK, and INNES [of Learney]. *The Clans, Septs and Regiments of the Scottish Highlands.* 4th ed. Edinburghs W. and A. K. Johnston, 1952.

ALEXANDER, WILLIAM. *Notes and Sketches of Northern Rural Life in the Eighteenth Century.* Edinburgh, 1877.

ALFORD, VIOLET. *English Folk Dances.* London: A & C Black, 1923.

———. "What Folk Song Says of Folk Dance." *JEFDSS,* vol 2, 1935

———. "Morris and Morisca." *JEFDSS,* vol. 2, 1935, pp. 41–48.

ALLAN, W. E. *New Reference Guide to the Ball Room.* Glasgow [1870, 1880, and 1890].

ANDERSON, ALLIE and DUTHIE, JOHN M. *Complete Guide to Scottish Country Dancing.* Edinburgh: MacDougall, ca. 1930.

ANDERSON, DAVID. *Ballroom Guide.* Dundee, 1886, 1891, and 1894.

———. *Universal Ballroom Guide and Solo Dance Guide.* Dundee, 1900, 1902.

ANDERSON, MATTHEW SMITH. *Europe in the Eighteenth Century.* New York: Holt, Rinehart & Winston, 1961.

ARBEAU, THOINOT [pseud. Tabourot]. *Orchesographie.* [Paris], 1588. Trans. C. W. Beaumont and preface by Peter Warlock. London: Beaumont, 1925.

ARNOT, HUGO. *History of Edinburgh.* Edinburgh, 1779.

ASHTON, JOHN. *Modern Street Ballads.* London, 1888.

———. *A History of the Chap-Books of the 18th Century.* London [1880].

———. *Social England under the Regency.* London, 1899.

ATHOLE COLLECTION. Ed. James Stewart-Robinson. Edinburgh, 1884. Rpt. Edinburgh: Oliver and Boyd, 1960.

ATKINSON, J. G. *Scottish National Dances.* Edinburgh, 1900.

Ayrshire at the Time of Burns. Ayrshire Archeological and Natural History Society, 1959.

BACKMAN, E. LOUIS. *Religious Dances in the Christian Church and in Popular Medicine.* Trans. E. Classen. London, 1952.

The Bagford Ballads. Ballad Society. 1878.

BAILDON, H. B. *Poems of William Dunbar.* Cambridge, 1907.

BALDERSTON, KATHARINE C., ed. *Collected Letters of Oliver Goldsmith.* Cambridge: The University Press, 1928.

BANNATYNE MANUSCRIPT. Ed. George Bannatyne. 4 vols. Vol. 1, ed. W. Tod Ritchie. Edinburgh: Scottish Text Society, 1928–34.

BAPTIE, DAVID. *Musical Scotland Past and Present.* Paisley, 1894.

BARING-GOULD, S. *Old Country Life.* London, 1889.

BASKERVILL, CHARLES R. *The Elizabethan Jig.* Chicago: University of Chicago Press, 1929.

BEAUMONT, CYRIL W. *Bibliography of Dancing.* London: Dancing Times, 1929.

BEDE, THE VENERABLE. *Ecclesiastical History of the English Nation.*

BEUEVAL. *Les Fils de Henry II.* Paris, 1898. (Pp. 316–24 contain information on dances in vogue at the French court.)

BLASIS, CARLO. *The Art of Dancing.* London, 1831.

———. *Notes upon Dancing.* London, 1847.

BOECE, HECTOR. *The Chronicles of Scotland.* Trans. into Scots by John Bellenden, 1531. Ed. R. W. Chambers and Edith C. Batho. Edinburgh: Scottish Text Society, 1936.

BONWICK, JAMES. *Who are the Irish?* London, 1880.

BOOK OF THE OLD EDINBURGH CLUB. Edinburgh Club, Edinburgh.

BOSWELL, JAMES. *The Journal of a Tour to the Hebrides* (London, 1785). Ed. Frederick A. Pottle and Charles H. Bennett. Toronto: University of Toronto Press, 1936.

BOULOGNE, J. P. *The Ballroom, or the juvenile pupil's assistant.* Glasgow, 1827.

BRAEMAR BOOK. *The Scottish Annual and The Braemar Gathering Book.* Issued annually by the Braemar Highland Games Society, Arbroath.

BRAND, JOHN. *Observations on the Popular Antiquities of Great Britain.* London, 1849.

BRANTOME, PIERRE DE BOURDEILLES. *Oeuvres Completes.* Paris, 1876.

BREMNER, ROBERT. See Bibliography of Dance Music Collections.

BROWN. See Salusbury, Sir John.

BROWN, PETER HUME. *Survey of Scottish History.* Glasgow: James Mac-Lehose & Sons, 1919.

———. *Scotland in Time of Queen Mary.* London: Methuen, 1904.

———. *Scotland Before 1700* (from contemporary documents). Edinburgh: David Douglas, 1893.

BUCHANAN, GEORGE. *History of Scotland* (1582). Trans. Aikman. Edinburgh, 1821.

BUKOFZER, MANFRED F. *Studies in Medieval & Renaissance Music.* London: Norton, 1951.

BURGH RECORDS SOCIETY. *Extracts from the Records of the Burghs of Aberdeen, Edinburgh, and Glasgow.* See Aberdeen Records, Edinburgh Records, and Glasgow Records.

BURNET, GILBERT. *History of His Own Time.* London, 1838.

BURNEY, CHARLES. *A General History of Music.* London, 1789.

BURNS, ROBERT. *Letters.* Ed. J. Delancey Fergusson. Oxford, 1931.

BURT, EDWARD. *Letters from a Gentleman in the North of Scotland.* 1754.

BURTON, A. *Rushbearing.* London, 1891.

BURTON, ELIZABETH. *The Elizabethans at Home*. London: Secker & Warburg, 1958.

BUSHNELL, NELSON S. *William Hamilton of Bangour*. Aberdeen: Aberdeen University Press, 1957.

BYRNE, M. ST. CLARE. *Elizabethan Life in Town and Country*. London: Methuen, 1925.

CAHUSAC, LOUIS DE. *La Danse ancienne et moderne, ou Traité historique de la danse*. 1754.

CAMPBELL, ALEXANDER. *The Grampians Desolate*. Edinburgh, 1804.

CAMPBELL, JOHN. *A full and particular description of the Highlands of Scotland, Manners and Customs, etc.* London, 1752.

CAMPBELL, JOHN F. *Popular Tales of the West Highlands*. New ed., Paisley, 1893.

Wm. Campbell's —th Collection of Country Dances and Strathspey Reels . . . . London, 1786– ca. 1805.

CARLYLE, ALEXANDER [1722–1805]. *Autobiography*. Ed. J. Hill Burton. London: T. M. Foulis, 1910.

CARMICHAEL, ALEXANDER. *Carmina Gadelica*. Edinburgh: Constable, 1900.

CARNS, C. G. *The King of Saxony's Journey through England in 1844*. London, 1846.

CAROSO, FABRITIO. *Il Ballarino*. Venice, 1581.

———. *Della Nobilita di dame*. Venice, 1602.

CARRUTHERS, ROBERT. *The Highland Notebook*. Edinburgh, 1843.

CELLARIUS, HENRI. *The Drawing Room Dances*. London, 1847.

Celt & Saxon Studies in the Early British Borders. Cambridge: Cambridge University Press, 1963.

CHALMERS, GEORGE. *Poetic Remains of Some of the Scottish Kings*. London, 1824.

CHAMBERLAIN, JOHN. *Correspondence with Sir Dudley Carleton and others (1573–1632)*. Select items published by the Camden Society, 1861.

CHAMBERS, E. K. *The Medieval Stage*. 2 vols. London, 1903.

CHAMBERS, ROBERT. *Domestic Annals of Scotland*. 2nd ed., Edinburgh, 1859.

———. *Popular Rhymes of Scotland*. Edinburgh, 1826, 1841.

———. *Traditions of Edinburgh*. Edinburgh, 1868.

———, ed. *Life and Works of Robert Burns*. Rev. William Wallace. Edinburgh, 1896.

CHANCELLOR, E. B. *Life in Regency and Early Victorian Times*. London: B. T. Batsford, 1926.

CHAPPELL, WILLIAM. *Popular Music of the Olden Time*. London, 1859.

———. *Old English Popular Music*. Ed. H. Ellis Woolridge. London, 1893.

CHEAP, JOHN. *The Chapman's Library*. Glasgow, 1877.

CHESTER, ROBERT. See Salusbury, Sir John.

CHILD, FRANCIS J. *The English and Scottish Popular Ballads*. Harvard, 1882–98.

CHIVERS, G. M. S. *The Modern Dancing Master*. London, 1822.

CLELAND, JAMES. *Annals of Glasgow.* Glasgow, 1816.

CLEUGH, JAMES. *Love Locked Out.* London: Tandem Books, 1963.

COCKBURN, HENRY [Lord]. *Memorials of His Time.* New York, 1856.

————. *Circuit Journeys.* Edinburgh, 1889.

COLLINSON, FRANCIS. *The Traditional and National Music of Scotland.* London: Routledge and Kegan Paul, 1966.

COLMAN, HENRY. *European Life and Manners.* Boston, 1850.

COLQUHOUN, Sir IAIN, and MACHELL, HUGH. *Highland Gatherings.* London: Heath Cranton, 1927.

[*The*] *Complaynt of Scotland* (1548). Ed. J. Leyden. Edinburgh, 1801.

COPLAND, ROBERT. *The Maner of dauncynge of bace daunces.* London, 1521. (Bodleian Library.)

COULTON, GEORGE GORDON. *Medieval Panorama.* Cambridge: Cambridge University Press, 1938.

COWIE, R. *Shetland.* Edinburgh, ca. 1879.

CREECH, WILLIAM. *Fugitive Pieces.* Edinburgh, 1815.

CROMEK, ROBERT HARTLEY. *Remains of Nithsdale and Galloway Song.* London, 1810.

CUMMING, C. F. GORDON. *In The Hebrides.* London, 1886.

CUNNINGHAM, ALAN. *Scottish Songs.* London, 1825.

DALYELL, Sir J. GRAHAM. *Musical Memoirs of Scotland.* Edinburgh, 1849.

DANIEL, GEORGE. *Merrie England in the Olden Time.* London, 1841.

DARLING, FRANK FRAZER, ed. *West Highland Survey* (1955). Development Commission, West Highland Survey.

DAUNEY, WILLIAM. *Ancient Scottish Melodies from a Manuscript of the Reign of King James VI.* Edinburgh, 1838.

DAVIES, Sir JOHN. *Orchestra, a poem of dancing, (1596).* Ed. Tillyard. London: Chatto & Windus, 1945.

DEAN-SMITH, MARGARET. "A Fifteenth Century Dancing Book." *JEFDSS,* vol. 3, no. 2, 1938, p. 106 et seq. (Article on *Sur l'art et instruction de bien dancer* by Michiel Toulouse. Printed before December 30, 1496.)

————, and NICOLE, E. J. "The Dancing Master." *JEFDSS,* vol. 4, nos. 4, 5, and 6, 1943, 1944, and 1945.

DE GRAMMONT [Count]. *Memoirs.* Trans. Horace Walpole. London, n.d.

DE LAUZE, F. *Apologie de la Danse.* 1623.

De Maisse's Journal. Ed. G. B. Harrison. London: Nonesuch, 1931.

DEWAR, JOHN. *Manuscripts of West Highland Tales.* Ed. John MacKechnie. Glasgow: MacLellan, 1964.

DIBDIN, JAMES C. *The Annals of the Edinburgh Stage.* Edinburgh, 1888.

DICK, JAMES C. *The Songs of Robert Burns.* Hatboro, Penn.: Folklore Associates, 1962.

DICKINSON, W. C. *A New History of Scotland.* vol. 1. London: Nelson, 1961.

DILLON, MYLES, and CHADWICK, NORA K. *The Celtic Realms.* London: Weidenfeld and Nicolson, 1967.

Discours du Grande et Magnifique Triomphe & c. Rouen,, 1558. Rpt. Roxburgh Club, 1818.

DOLMETSCH, MABEL. *Dances of England and France* [1450–1600]. London: Routledge and Kegan Paul, 1949.

———. "Sixteenth Century Dances," *Musical Times,* vol. 57, 1916, pp. 142–45.

———. "Dances in Shakespeare's England," *Musical Times,* vol. 57, 1916, pp. 489–92.

DOUGLAS, GAVIN. Virgil's *Aeneid* (1553), in *The Poetical Works of Gavin Douglas.* Ed. John Small. 4 vols. Edinburgh, 1874.

DOUGLAS, Sir G. *Scottish Poetry — Drummond to Fergusson.* Glasgow: Maclehose, 1911.

DOUGLAS, MONA. "Manx Folk Dances: Their Notation and Revival." *JEFDSS,* vol. 3, no. 2, 1937, pp. 110–16.

DRAKE, NATHAN [1766–1836]. *Shakespeare & His Times.* London, 1817.

DRUMMOND, P. R. *Perthshire in Bygone Days.* Edinburgh, 1879.

DUKES, NICHOLAS. *A Concise and Easy Method of Learning the Figuring Part of Country Dances.* London, 1752.

DUN, BARCLAY. *Translation of nine of the most fashionable Quadrilles, consisting of fifty French country dances as performed in England and Scotland.* Edinburgh, 1818.

DUNBAR, WILLIAM. *The Poems of William Dunbar.* Ed. H. Bellyse Baildon. Cambridge: The University Press, 1907.

DUNN, CHARLES W. *Highland Settler.* Toronto: University of Toronto Press, 1953.

DURANG, JOHN. *The Memoirs of John Durang* (1785–1816). Ed. A. S. Downer. Pittsburgh: University of Pittsburgh Press, 1966.

EDGAR, ANDREW. *Old Church Life in Scotland.* Paisley, 1886.

EDINBURGH RECORDS. *Extracts from the Records of the Burgh of Edinburgh.* Ed. J. D. Marwick. Edinburgh: Scottish Burgh Records Society, 1869 et seq.

EGAN, PIERCE. *Life in London.* London, 1821.

EINSTEIN, DAVID LEWIS. *The Italian Renaissance in England.* New York: Columbia University Press, 1902.

ELYOT, SIR THOMAS. *Boke named the Governour.* London, 1531.

———. *The Castel of Helth.* London, 1537.

EMMERSON, GEORGE S. *Rantin' Pipe and Tremblin' String.* London: J. M. Dent & Sons, 1971.

ERSKINE, HENRY. *His Kinsfolk & Times.* Edinburgh, 1882.

ESPRIELLA, MANUEL ALVAREZ. *Letters from England.* London, 1814.

EVELYN, JOHN. *Diary.* Ed. William Bray. London: J. M. Dent & Sons, 1907.

FARMER, HENRY G. "Music in 18th Century Scotland." *Scottish Art & Letters,* no. 2, Glasgow, ca. 1950.

———. *A History of Music in Scotland.* London: Hutchinson, 1947.

FERGUSSON, ROBERT. *Poetical Works.* Ed. Robert Ford. Paisley: Gardner, 1905.

FERRERO, EDWARD. *The Art of Dancing.* New York, 1859.

FEUILLET, RAOUL AUGER. *Recuil de Contredances.* Paris, 1706. Trans. John Weaver, 1712; John Essex, London, 1710.

——. *Choreographie.* Paris, 1701. Trans. J. Weaver, London, 1706.

FLETT, J. F. and FLETT, T. M. *Traditional Dancing in Scotland.* Appendix by F. Rhodes. London: Routledge, 1964.

——. "Some Hebridean Folk Dances." *JEFDSS*, vol. 7, no. 2, 1953.

——. "Some Early Highland Dancing Competitions." *Aberdeen University Review,* vol. 36, no. 115, pp. 345–58.

——. *Social Dancing in Scotland, 1700–1914.* School of Scottish Studies, Edinburgh University, 1956, pp. 153–63.

FLORIO. *The World of Words.* London, 1598.

FORBES, BISHOP. *Lyon In Mourning.* Scots Historical Society, Edinburgh, 1895.

FRASER, GORDON. *Sketches and Anecdotes of the Royal Burgh of Wigtoun.* Wigtoun, 1877.

FRASER, Captain SIMON [of Knockie]. *The Airs & Melodies Peculiar to the Highlands of Scotland and the Isles.* Edinburgh, 1816.

GAELIC SOCIETY OF INVERNESS. Transactions, from 1871 et seq.

GALLINI, JOHN [Giovanni-Andrea]. *Treatise on the Art of Dancing.* London, 1772.

GALT, JOHN. *Annals of the Parish.* Edinburgh, 1821.

GARNETT, THOMAS. *Tour through the Highlands.* London, 1811.

GEORGE, DOROTHY M. *England in Johnson's Day.* New York, 1928.

GLASGOW RECORDS. *Extracts from the Records of the Burgh of Glasgow.* Vols. 1–3, ed. J. D. Marwick; vols. 4–6, ed. Robert Renwick. Glasgow: Scottish Burgh Records Society, 1876–1911.

GOLDSMITH, OLIVER. *Collected Letters of Oliver Goldsmith.* Ed. Katharine C. Balderstone. Cambridge: The University Press, 1928.

GOMBOSI, OTTO. "About Dance and Dance Music in the Late Middle Ages." *Musical Quarterly,* vol. 27, no. 3, 1941.

GOODMAN, WILLIAM. *The Social History of Great Britain during the Reigns of the Stuarts.* 2nd ed., New York, 1845.

GORDON, JAMES F. S., ed. *Glasgow Ancient and Modern.* Glasgow, 1874.

GOW, NIEL, and SONS. *Collections (Six Books) and Repositories (Four Parts).* Edinburgh, 1784–1817.

GRAHAM, HENRY G. *Scottish Men of Letters in the Eighteenth Century.* London, 1901.

——. *Social Life of Scotland in the Eighteenth Century.* 2nd ed., Edinburgh: A. & C. Black, 1900.

GRAMONT, Comte de. *Memoirs.* Trans. Horace Walpole. London, n.d.

GRANT, ANN [of Laggan]. *Poems.* Edinburgh, 1803.

GRANT, ELIZABETH. *Memoirs of a Highland Lady 1797–1827.* Ed. Lady Strachey. London, 1898.

GRANT, JAMES. *Old and New Edinburgh.* London, 1882.

GRAY, ALEXANDER. *Historical Ballads of Denmark.* Edinburgh: University of Edinburgh Press, 1958.

GRAY, M. M. *Scottish Poetry from Barbour to James VI.* London: J. M. Dent, 1935.

GRAY, W. F., and JAMIESON, J. H. *A Short History of Haddington.* Edinburgh: East Lothian Antiquarian and Field Naturalists' Society, 1944.

GRONOW, [Captain]. *Recollections and Anecdotes.* London, 1864.

HALL, JAMES. *Travels in Scotland.* London, 1807.

HAMBLY, W. D. *Tribal Dancing and Social Development.* London: H. F. & G. Witherby, 1926.

HAMILTON, WILLIAM [of Bangour]. See Bushnell.

HANDLEY, JAMES E. *Scottish Farming in the Eighteenth Century.* London: Faber & Faber, 1953.

HARTMANN, CYRIL HUGHES. *La Belle Stuart.* London: Routledge, 1924.

HARVEY, WILLIAM. *Scottish Chapbook Literature.* Paisley: Gardner, 1903.

HAWKINS, Sir JOHN. *A General History of the Science and Practice of Music.* 5 vols. London, 1776.

HENDERSON, T. F. *Mary Queen of Scots.* London: Hutchinson, 1905.

——. *Scottish Vernacular Literature.* 3rd ed. Edinburgh: John Grant, 1910.

HERD, DAVID. *Ancient & Modern Scottish Songs, Heroic Ballads, etc.* Edinburgh, 1776.

HERON, ROBERT [1764–1807]. *Observations made in a Journey through the Western Counties of Scotland in Autumn, 1792.* Edinburgh, 1793.

HETT, FRANCIS PAGET, ed. *Memoirs of Susan Sibbald.* London: Bodley Head, 1926.

HIBBERT, SAMUEL. *A Description of the Shetland Isles.* Edinburgh, 1822.

HILLGROVE, THOMAS. *A Complete Practical Guide to the Art of Dancing.* New York, 1864.

HOGG, JAMES. *Jacobite Relics.* Edinburgh, 1819.

HOWE, ELIAS. *Complete Ball-Room Handbook.* Boston, 1858.

HUBERT, HENRI. *The Rise of the Celts.* New York: Alfred A. Knopf, 1934.

HUGON, CECILE. *Social France in the XVII Century.* London: Methuen, 1911.

JACKSON, HOLBROOK. *The Eighteen Nineties.* London: Grant Richards, 1913.

JAFFRAY, ALEXANDER. *Recollections of Kingswells* [from 1755–1800]. The Miscellany of the Third Spalding Club, vol. 1, 1835.

JAMES VI. *Papers Relative to the Marriage of James VI* for Bannatyne Club, Edinburgh, 1828.

JAMIESON, JAMES H. "Social Assemblies of the Eighteenth Century." *Book of the Old Edinburgh Club,* vol. 19, 1933.

JAMIESON, JOHN. *An Etymological Dictionary of the Scottish Language.* Edinburgh, 1808.

JENNINGS, SOAME [pseud. Soame Jenyns]. *The Art of Dancing,* a poem, 1729.

JOHNSON, JAMES, ed. *The Scots Musical Museum,* (issued in six parts from 1787–1803). With *Illustrations of the Lyric Poetry and Music of Scotland* written for *The Scots Musical Museum* by William Stenhouse, ed. David Laing. Edinburgh, 1853. (See Stenhouse, William.)

JOHNSON, SAMUEL. *Journey to the Western Islands of Scotland*. Ed. R. W. Chapman. London: Oxford University Press, 1924.

JOHNSTON, ALFRED W., and AMY JOHNSTON, eds. "The Sword Dance of Papa Stour," in *Old Lore Miscellany of Orkney, Shetland, Caithness and Sutherland*, vol. 5. London: The Viking Club, 1912.

JOHNSTON, THOMAS. *A History of the Working Classes in Scotland*. 4th ed. Glasgow: Unity Publishing Company, 1946.

JONES, EDWARD. *Musical and Poetical Relics of the Welsh Bards*. London, 1794.

KENNEDY, DOUGLAS. *England's Dances: Folk Dancing Today and Yesterday*. London: G. Bell & Sons, 1949.

KENNEDY, PATRICK. *On the Banks of the Boro*. Dublin, 1867.

KINNEY, TROY, and KINNEY, MARGARET. *The Dance*. New York: Tudor, 1914.

KIRSTEIN, LINCOLN. *The Book of the Dance*. New York: Garden City, 1942.

KNOX, JOHN. *History of the Reformation in Scotland* (5 vols., 1584). Ed. W. C. Dickinson, 2 vols. Edinburgh: Nelson, 1949.

KOHL, J. G. *Travels in Scotland* (1842). London, 1844.

LAING, DAVID. *Early Scottish Metrical Tales*. London, 1889.

LANARK RECORDS. *Extracts from the Records of the Royal Burgh of Lanark*. Ed. R. Renwick. Glasgow: Scottish Burgh Records Society, 1893.

LANE, JANE. *The Reign of King Covenant*. London: Robert Hale, 1956.

LANG, ANDREW. *History of Scotland*. London, 1892.

LECKY, W. E. H. *A History of England in the 18th Century*. New York, 1891.

LELAND, JOHN. *Collectanea*. London, 1774.

LENNARD, REGINALD V., ed. *Englishmen at Rest and Play, 1558–1714*. Oxford, 1931.

LEYDEN, J. ed. *The Complaynt of Scotland*. Edinburgh, 1801.

LINDSAY, Sir DAVID. *The Works of Sir David Lyndsay of the Mount (1409–1555)*. Ed. Douglas Hamer. Scottish Text Society, 3rd ser. Edinburgh, 1931–33.

LITTLE, BRYAN. *The Building of Bath*. London: Collins, 1947.

LOCKE, JOHN. *Locke's Travels in France 1675–79*. Ed. John Lough. Cambridge, 1953.

LOCKHART, JOHN GIBSON. *Life of Sir Walter Scott*. London, 1848.

———. *Peter's Letters to His Kinsfolk*. 3rd ed. Edinburgh, 1819.

LOCKHEAD, MARION. *The Scots Household in the Eighteenth Century*. Edinburgh: Moray Press, 1948.

LOGAN, JAMES. *The Scottish Gael*. 1st ed., Edinburgh, 1831; 5th American ed., Hartford, 1847.

LOWE, JOSEPH. *A Selection of Popular Country Dances*. Edinburgh, ca. 1840.

LYTHE, S. G. E. *The Economy of Scotland in its European Setting 1550–1625.* Edinburgh: Oliver & Boyd, 1960.

MACDONALD, KEITH NORMAN. *Gesto Collection of Highland Music.* Ed. Keith Norman MacDonald. Edinburgh, 1895.
————. *Puirt-a-Beul.* Glasgow, 1901.
MACKENZIE, AGNES MURE. *The Foundations of Scotland.* Edinburgh: W. & R. Chambers, 1938.
————. *The Rise of the Stewarts.* London: Alexander Maclehose, 1935.
————. *The Scotland of Queen Mary.* London: Alexander Maclehose, 1936.
MACKENZIE, DONALD R. *The National Dances of Scotland.* Glasgow: MacLaren, 1910.
MACKENZIE, HENRY. *Anecdotes and Egotisms.* Ed. Harold William Thompson. London: Humphrey Milford, 1927.
MACKENZIE, JOHN. *Sar-Obar Nam Bard Gaelach.* Introd. by J. Logan. Glasgow, 1841.
MACKENZIE, PETER. *Reminiscences of Glasgow.* Glasgow, 1865.
MACKENZIE, W. C. *The Races of Ireland and Scotland.* Paisley, n.d.
MACKIE, R. L. *King James IV of Scotland.* Edinburgh: Oliver & Boyd, 1958.
MACKINNON, JAMES. *Culture in Early Scotland.* London, 1892.
MACKINTOSH, JOHN. *The History of Civilization in Scotland.* Paisley, 1895.
MACLACHLAN, ELIZABETH, ed. *The Border Dance Book.* Edinburgh: McDougall's Education Company, 1932.
MACLAGAN, R. C. *The Games and Diversions of Argyleshire.* London: Folklore Society, 1901.
MACLENNAN, D. G. *Traditional and Highland Scottish Dances.* 1st ed., 1950; 2nd ed., 1953. Edinburgh: Oliver & Boyd.
MACLEOD, DONALD. *Memoir of Norman Macleod.* Toronto, 1876.
MACLEOD, NORMAN. *Reminiscences of a Highland Parish.* London, 1867.
MACNEILL, F. MARIAN. *The Silver Bough.* 4 vols. Glasgow: MacLellan, 1959–70.
MACQUEEN, MALCOLM A. *Skye Pioneers.* Winnipeg: Stovel, 1929.
MACTAGGART, JOHN. *The Scottish Galovidian Encyclopedia.* 1824.
MAITLAND FOLIO MANUSCRIPT. [Sir John Maitland.] Ed. W. A. Craigie. Edinburgh: Scottish Text Society, 1913, 1927.
MANCHESTER, Duke of. *Court and Society from Elizabeth to Anne.* London, 1864.
MATHEW, DAVID. *Scotland Under Charles I.* London: Eyre & Spottiswoode, 1955.
MCELWEE, WILLIAM. *The Wisest Fool in Christendom.* New York: Harcourt Brace, 1958.
MCURE, JOHN. *Glasgow Ancient and Modern.* Glasgow, ca. 1867.
MELLOR, HUGH. *Welsh Folk Dances.* London: Novello, 1935.
MELVILLE, Sir JAMES of Halhill [1535–1617]. *Memoirs of his own Life.* (1st pub. London, 1683.) Edinburgh: Bannatyne Club, 1827.

MILL, ANNA JEAN. *Medieval Plays in Scotland*. St. Andrews: St. Andrews University Press and Blackwood, 1924.

MILLIGAN, JEAN C. *Won't You Join The Dance?* Glasgow: Paterson, 1951.

MORER, THOMAS. *A Short Account of Scotland*. London, 1702.

MORLEY, THOMAS A. *Plaine and Easie Introduction to Practicall Musicke*. London, 1597. Shakespeare Association Facsimiles, no. 14, London, 1937.

MURRAY, JOHN [Seventh Duke of Atholl]. *Chronicles of the Athol and Tullibardine Families*. Edinburgh, 1908. (Privately printed.)

MURRAY, AMY. *Father Allan's Island*. Edinburgh: Chambers, 1936.

NEGRI, CARLO. *Nuove invenzione di balli*. Milan, 1604.

NICHOLS, JOHN. *The Progresses and Public Processions of Queen Elizabeth*. London, 1823.

NORTH, CHARLES NIVEN MCINTYRE. *Leabhar Comunn nam Fior Ghael* (The Book of the Club of True Highlanders). London, 1881–82.

O'DELL, A. C. and WALTON, K. *The Highlands and Islands of Scotland*. Edinburgh: Nelson, 1962.

O'KEEFE, J. G., and O'BRIEN, ART. *The Handbook of Irish Dances*. Dublin: M. H. Gill & Sons, 1944.

OLRIK, AXEL. *A Book of Danish Ballads*. Trans. by E. M. Smith-Dampier. New York: American-Scandinavian Foundation, 1939.

PATERSON, JAMES [1825–76]. *Origin of the Scots and the Scottish Language*. N.d.

PATTISON, BRUCE. *Music and Poetry of the English Renaissance*. London: Methuen, 1948.

PEACOCK, FRANCIS. *Sketches relative to the history and theory but more especially to the practice and art of dancing*. Aberdeen, 1805.

PEARSON, LU EMILY. *Elizabethans at Home*. Stanford: Stanford University Press, 1957.

PENNANT, THOMAS. *Tour in Scotland and Voyage to the Hebrides*. London, 1774–76.

PENNECUIK, ALEXANDER [of New Hall]. *Works*. Leith, 1815.

PEPYS, SAMUEL. *Diary*. 1st pub., London, 1893–99.

PETERKIN, ALEXANDER. *Records of the Kirk of Scotland*. Edinburgh, 1843.

PIGGOTT, STUART, ed. *The Prehistoric Peoples of Scotland*. London: Routledge, 1962.

PINKERTON, JOHN. *History of Scotland*. London, 1797.

PITCAIRN, ROBERT. *Criminal Trials in Scotland*. Bannatyne Club, Edinburgh, 1833.

PLANT, MARJORIE. *The Domestic Life of Scotland in the Eighteenth Century*. Edinburgh: Edinburgh University Press, 1952.

PLAYFORD, JOHN. *Apollo's Banquet*. London: 1st ed., 1663; 5th ed., 1687; and 6th ed., 1691.

———. *The Dancing Master*. London: 1st ed., 1651; 2nd ed., 1665; 3rd ed., 1670; and 4th ed., 1686.

PREBBLE, JOHN. *The Highland Clearances*. London: Secker and Warburg, 1963.

PRESTON. *24 Country Dances for the Year*. . . . London, 1786–1800.

PRIDDIN, DEIRDRE. *The Art of the Dance in French Literature*. London: A. & C. Black, 1952.

PRYDE, GEORGE S. *Scotland from 1603 to the Present Day*. Edinburgh: Nelson, 1962.

———. *Social Life in Scotland since 1707*. Historical Association, Pamphlet no. 98.

PRYNNE, WILLIAM. *Histriomastix*. 1629.

PULVER, JEFFREY. "The Ancient Dance Forms." *Proceedings of the Musical Association*, vol. 40, no. 80, February 17, 1914.

———. "The Gigue." *Proceedings of the Musical Association,* vol. 40, no. 80, February 17, 1914.

RAMEAU, PIERRE. *Le Maître à Danser*. [Paris?], 1725. Trans. by Essex, 1728.

RAMSAY, ALLAN. *Works*. Edinburgh, 1848.

RAMSAY, EDWARD B. [Dean of Edinburgh]. *Reminiscences of Scottish Life and Character*. 6th ed. Edinburgh, 1860.

RAY, JOHN. *Itinerary*. 1661.

REA, F. G. *A School in South Uist* (from 1890–1913). Ed. John Lorne Campbell. London: Routledge and Kegan Paul, 1964.

REESE, GUSTAV. *Music of the Middle Ages*. London: J. M. Dent & Sons, 1940.

REID, ROBERT. [Senex]. *Glasgow Past and Present*. Glasgow, 1851.

———. *Old Glasgow and its Environs*. Glasgow, 1864.

REYHER, PAUL. *Les Masques Anglais* (from 1512–1640). Paris: Hachette et Cie, 1909.

RHYS, Sir JOHN, and JONES, DAVID BRYNMOR. *The Welsh People*. 4th ed., London: T. F. Unwin, 1906.

RICHE, BARNABY. *His Farewell to Militairie Profession*. Shakespeare Society, London, 1846.

RITCHIE, R. L. GRAEME. *The Normans in Scotland*. Edinburgh: Edinburgh University Press: 1954.

ROGERS, CHARLES. *Scotland Social and Domestic*. London, 1869.

RUTHERFORD. *Compleat Collection of 200 . . . Country Dances*. . . . 3 vols. London, 1749, 1756, and 1760.

RYE, WILLIAM B. *England as Seen by Foreigners in the Days of Elizabeth and James I*. London, 1865.

SACHS, KURT. *World History of the Dance*. New York: Norton, 1937.

———. *The Commonwealth of Art*. London: Dobson, 1955.

SAGE, DONALD. *Memerobalia Domestica* or Parish Life in the North of Scotland. Edinburgh, 1889.

SALUSBURY, Sir JOHN, and CHESTER, ROBERT. *Poems*. Ed. Brown. Published for the Early English Text Society by K. Paul, Trench, Trübner and Co. 1914. (Extra series no. cxiii.)

SCHOLES, PERCY A. *The Oxford Companion to Music*. London: Oxford University Press, 1939.

SCOTT, EDWARD. *The ABC of Dancing*. London, n.d.

Scottish Art and Letters. 6 numbers. Glasgow: Maclellan, 1945–51.

SCOTTISH COUNTRY DANCE BOOKS. Edinburgh: Royal Scottish Country Dance Society, 1923 et seq.

SELDEN, JOHN. *Table Talk*. Ed. Edward Arber. London, 1868.

SENEX [pseud.] See Robert Reid.

SHARP, CECIL J. *The Morris Book* (in five parts). London: Novello, 1907–1913.

——. *The Country Dance Book*, parts 1 to 6. London: Novello, 1909–22.

——. *The Sword Dances of Northern England* (in three parts). London: Novello, 1911–13.

——, and OPPE, A. P. *The Dance*. London: Halton & Truscott Smith, 1924.

SHARPE, CHARLES KIRKPATRICK. *Letters from and to Charles Kirkpatrick Sharpe*. Ed. Alexander Allardyce. Edinburgh, 1888.

SHULDHAM-SHAW, PATRICK. "Folk Music and Dance in Shetland." *JEFDSS*, vol. 5, 1946–48, pp. 74–80.

SIBBALD, SUSAN. *Memoirs of Susan Sibbald*. Ed. Francis Paget Hett. London: Bodley Head, 1926.

SINCLAIR, Sir JOHN, ed. *The Statistical Account of Scotland*. Edinburgh, 1791–99.

SKELTON, JOHN. *Maitland of Lethington*. Edinburgh, 1888.

SKENE, W. F. *Celtic Scotland*. Edinburgh, 1880.

SMITH, ALEXANDER. *A Summer in Skye*. London, 1865.

SMITH, GEORGE GREGORY, ed. *Elizabethan Critical Essays*. Oxford: Clarendon Press, 1904.

SMYTHE, W. *A Pocket Companion for Young Ladies and Gentlemen*. Edinburgh, 1830.

SOBHD. *Textbook of Highland Dancing*. Edinburgh: Thomas Nelson & Sons, 1955.

SOMERVILLE, MARTHA. *Personal Recollections of Mary Somerville*. Boston, 1874.

SOUTHEY, ROBERT. *Journal of a Tour in Scotland in 1819*. London: John Murray, 1929.

Spottiswoode Miscellany. Ed. James Maidment. The Spottiswoode Society, Edinburgh, 1844.

STENHOUSE, WILLIAM. *Illustrations of the Lyric Poetry and Music of Scotland*. Ed. David Laing. 2 vols. Edinburgh, 1853. (See Johnson, James.)

STEPHENSON, CARL. *Medieval History*. 3rd ed., New York Harper, 1951.

STEWART, ALEXANDER. *Nether Lochaber*. Edinburgh, 1883.

STEWART, General DAVID [of Garth]. *Sketches of the Character, Manners and Present State of the Highlanders of Scotland*. 2 vols. Edinburgh, 1822.

STEWART, WILLIAM GRANT. *The Popular Superstitions and Festive Amusements of the Highlanders of Scotland*. Edinburgh, 1823.

STODDART, JOHN. *Remarks on the local scenery and manners in Scotland during the years 1799 and 1800*. London, 1801.

STRANG, JOHN. *Glasgow and Its Clubs*. Glasgow, 1856. 2nd ed. rev. and enl., London and Glasgow: R. Griffin, 1857. 3rd. ed. enl., Glasgow: John Tweed, 1864.

Strathbogie Presbytery Book (1631–54). Extracts from Spalding Club, Aberdeen.

STRICKLAND, AGNES, and STRICKLAND, ELIZABETH. *Lives of the Queens of Scotland and English Princesses*. New York, 1852.

STRUTT, JOSEPH. *Sports and Pastimes of the English People*. London, 1801.

STUBBES, PHILIP. *The Anatomie of Abuses,* London, 1583. Ed. F. J. Furnivall, 8771–82 (New Shakespeare Society Series VI, nos. 4, 6, 12).

STEENSTRUP, J. C. *The Medieval Popular Ballad*. Copenhagen, 1891. Trans. E. G. Cox, Boston: Ginn, 1914.

SURENNE, JOHN T. *The Dance Music of Scotland*. Edinburgh, 1852.

SYDNEY, WILLIAM CONNOR. *Social Life in England 1660–1690*. London, 1892.

TACITUS. *Agricola Germania*. Trans. H. Mattingly. London: Penguin, 1948.

TANNAHILL, ROBERT. *Poetical Works*. Ed. David Semple. Paisley, 1874.

TAYLOR, JOSEPH. *A Journey to Edinburgh in Scotland (1705)*. First printing Edinburgh: Brown, 1903.

TEIGHMOUTH. *Sketches of Scotland*. London, 1836.

TERRY, WALTER. *The Dance in America*. New York: Harper, 1956.

Thompson's Compleat Collection of 200 Country Dances. . . . London, 1751.

Thompson's 24 Dances for the Year. . . . London, 1762–1817.

THORNTON, THOMAS. *A Sporting Tour through the Highlands of Scotland*. London, 1804.

THURSTON, HUGH A. *Scotland's Dances*. London: Bell, 1954.

———. "Country Dances of the Recent Past." *JEFDSS*, vol. 7, no. 3, 1954.

———. "The Development of the Country Dance as revealed in Printed Sources." *JEFDSS*, vol. 7, no. 1, 1952.

TIMBS, JOHN. *Club Life of London*. London, 1866.

TOMLINSON, KELLOM. *Art of Dancing*. London, 1735.

TOPHAM, EDWARD. *Letters from Edinburgh*. London, 1776.

TOULOUSE, MICHIEL. *Sur l'art et instruction de bien dancer*. Paris, 1482–96. Facsim. rpt., Royal College of Physicians, London, 1937.

TREVELYAN, G. M. *The History of England*. London: Longmans, 1926.

TURREFF, GAVIN. *Antiquarian Gleanings from Aberdeenshire Records*. 2nd ed., Aberdeen, 1871.

TYTLER, P. F. *History of Scotland*. Edinburgh, 1841.

TYTLER, SARAH and WATSON, J. L. *The Songstresses of Scotland*. 2 vols. London, 1871.

URLIN, ETHEL L. *Dancing Ancient & Modern*. London, n.d.

VICTORIA, QUEEN. *Leaves from the Journal of Our Life in the Highlands from 1848–1861*. Ed. A. Helps. London, 1868.

————. *More Leaves from the Journal of Our Life in the Highlands from 1862–1882.* Ed. A. Helps. London, 1883.

VUILLIER, GASTON. *A History of Dancing from the Earliest Ages to Our Own Times.* Trans. into English, New York, 1898.

WAINWRIGHT, F. T., ed. *The Problem of the Picts.* Edinburgh: Thomas Nelson & Sons, 1955.

WALLACE, J. F. *Excelsior Manual of Dancing.* 1872, 1881.

WALSH, JOHN. *Caledonian Country Dances.* London, ca. 1744.

WARRACK, JOHN. *Domestic Life in Scotland (1488–1688).* London: Methuen, 1920.

WATT, LAUCHLAN MACLEAN. *Scottish Life and Poetry.* London: James Nisbet, 1912.

WEAVER, JOHN. *Orchesography* (translation of Feuillet's *Choregraphie*). London, 1706.

WHITELAW, ALEXANDER. *The Book of Scottish Song.* London, 1844.

WILLCOCKS, H. D. *Manual of Dancing.* Glasgow, 1865.

WILSON, JAMES. *A Voyage Round the Coasts of Scotland and the Isles.* Edinburgh, 1842.

WILSON, ROBERT. *An Historical Account and Delineation of Aberdeen.* Aberdeen, 1822.

WILSON, THOMAS. *A Companion to the Ballroom.* London, 1817.

————. *The Complete System of English Country Dancing.* London, 1821.

WOLFRAM, RICHARD. *Deutsche Volkstänze.* Leipzig: Leipzig Bibliographisches Institut, 1937.

WOOD, MELUSINE. *Some Historical Dances.* London: Imperial Society of Teachers of Dancing, 1952.

————. *More Historical Dances.* London: Imperial Society of Teachers of Dancing, 1956.

————. "Some Notes on the Country Dance before Playford." *JEFDSS*, vol. 3, no. 2, 1937, pp. 93–99.

WYCHERLEY, WILLIAM. *The Complete Works.* Ed. Montague Summers. London: Nonesuch, 1924.

WYLIE, J. A. *Early History of the Scottish Nation.* London, 1886.

YATES, G. *The Ball or A Glance at Almack's in 1829.* London, 1829.

DANCE MUSIC COLLECTIONS IN TEXT

BOWIE, JOHN.   *A Collection of Strathspey Reels and Country Dances.* Edinburgh [1789].

BREMNER, ROBERT.   *A Collection of Scots Reels or Country Dances.* Edinburgh, 1751–61.

————.   *A Second Collection of Scots Reels or Country Dances.* London, 1768.

CAMPBELL, JOSHUA.   *A Collection of New Reels and Highland Strathspeys.* Glasgow, 1788.

CUMMING, ANGUS.   *A Collection of Strathspeys or Old Highland Reels.* Edinburgh, 1780.

DOW, DANIEL. *Thirty-Seven New Reels and Strathspeys*. Edinburgh [1776].

Fitzwilliam Virginal Book (ca. 1650). Ed. J. A. Fuller Maitland and W. Barclay Squire. London, 1894.

GOW, NIEL. *A First Collection of Strathspey Reels*. Edinburgh [1784].

MARSHALL, WILLIAM. *A Collection of Strathspey Reels*. Edinburgh, 1781.

MCDONALD, MALCOLM. *A Collection of Strathspey Reels*. Edinburgh [1788].

MCGLASHAN, ALEXANDER. *A Collection of Strathspey Reels*. Edinburgh [1780].

————. *A Collection of Reels, consisting chiefly of Strathspeys, Athole Reels.*...Edinburgh [1786].

OSWALD, JAMES. *A Collection of Curious Scots Tunes*. London [1742].

ROSS, ROBERT. *A Choice Collection of Scots Reels or Country Dances and Strathspeys*. Edinburgh [1780].

SOCIETY PUBLICATIONS CONSULTED

Burns Chronicle (annual publication). The Burns Federation, Kilmarnock

Dance Perspectives (periodical). New York

English Folk Dance and Song Society. London

Gaelic Society of Inverness (proceedings). Inverness

Mariner's Mirror (Journal of Society for Nautical Research). Cambridge

The Book of the Old Edinburgh Club. Edinburgh Club, Edinburgh

Saltire Review (periodical). Edinburgh

Scottish Historical Review (bi-annual publication). Edinburgh

Scottish Studies, University of Edinburgh, publication of the School of Scottish Studies

General Index

Aberdeen, 68, 72, 78, 111n.3, 146, 155, 160, 166, 174, 229, 247, 281; Midsummer fire, 13; Lords of Bonaccord, 19n.25; Bringing in the May, 19, 20; prohibition of "choree" in church and churchyard, 19, of May festival, 24; Aberdeenshire, 78; dancing master's license *1699*, 80

Almack's, 87, 118, 119, 146, 147, 154

Angles, 4; Anglo-Saxons, 3; Anglo-Normans, 4

Angus, 166

Argyll, 3, 226, 249

Arisaid, 253

Assembly: Aberdeen, 105, 280; Bath, 86, 271; Carlton House, 271; Dundee, 105, 280; Edinburgh, 88–91, 93–97, 101, 115, 243, 280; Glasgow, 105, 107, 108, 117; Haddington, 105, 280; Leith, 105, 280; London, 120, 271; Tonbridge, 87, 271. *See also* Almack's, Balls, Northern Meeting

Atholl (Blair Athol), 248

Australia, 298

Ayr, 281

Ballads, 33

Balls. *See also* Assembly: Duchess of Portsmouth's Supper, 64; An Ayrshire Ball, 97; Hunters' Ball, 98; Capillaire Club, 98; Topham attends, 98; Queen's Birthday, 98; private and public, 99; Advocates, 99; Glasgow Tontine, 108; Glasgow Gaelic Club, 109, 110; Dancing masters' "finishing", 118; Inveraray, 148; Edinburgh, 156; Dalmally Inn, 158; Dunkeld, 260; King's Birth Night, 122; Caledonian (London), 120, 123, (Borders) 135; Lamberton Races, 135; Lairds', 143; Balmoral, 143; Perth, 180, 297; Atholl, 180; Portree, 180; St. Michael's Day (S. Uist.), 238; Grantown, 258; Rothiemurchus, 259; George St. Assembly (Edinb.) 281; Glasgow Police, 297.

Baltic, 78

Baptisms, 72

Barra, 224, 227n.11, 232

Bath, 86

Beltane. *See* Festivals

Benbecula, 226, 233

Blairgowrie, 250

Book of Sports, 25

Borders, 281

Boston, 129, 217

Breadalbane, 78

British Isles, cultural affinities, 4–5

Britons, 3

Burials. *See* Wakes

Caen, 78

Caithness, 78, 150

Caledonia, 3

Caledonians, 1, 7, 28, 186

Canada, Scots stepping in, 158–59, 176, 224, 225, 263, 298, 299

Cartuaitheail, 12

Ceilidh, 140, 142, 238

Celtic (Celts), 3, 11, 186

Christ's Kirk, 23, 37, 51

Church (Roman), 70

Clog Dance, 209, 211

Cornwall, 200

Covenanters, 77, 79, 81. *See also* Kirk

Dalserf, 25

Dancers (Highland): Mary Aitken, 252; Lizzie Althash, 155; David Anderson, 134, 144, 155, 162, 166, 168, 169, 172, 225, 250, 282, 288, (book) 177, 180, 183, 185, 283; Sydney Black, 250; A. D. Cameron, 250, 251; Allan Cameron, 246; M. Cameron, 251; N. Cameron, 251; Cardownie, 251; C. Christie, 189; P. Comrie, 246; Tom Cramb, 250; Bobby Cuthbertson, 250; Don Gordon, 251; J. A. Gordon, 170, 251; James Grant, 247; John Grant, 246; Gunn, 187; B. Jessiman, 252; Maggie Lauder, 155;

Lawson (Granton), 251; John Macallister (Tulloch), 247; John MacBeth, 246; McDonald, 187; C. McEwan, 251; MacGlassan, 187; J. MacGregor (Tomintoul), 245; P. Mackay (Kingussie), 251; J. MacKay (piper), 245; R. Mackay (piper), 245; Ewen MacLachlan, 162; J. L. Mackenzie, 168, 250, 251; John Mackenzie, 251; J. McLean, 251; D. G. MacLennan, 134, 162, 163, 166, 170, 184, 185, 188, 207, 225, 227, 231, 232, 235, 236; D. H. MacLennan, 251; William MacLennan, 185, 251, 252; John MacLeod (Eochar), 162; J. M. MacLeod (Kirkaldy), 250; W. MacLeod (Lochbroom), 245; Graham McNeilage, 251; John MacNeill, 250, 251; Neil MacNeil (Barra), 225; Archie MacPherson, 162; George Melvin, 251; Murray (Granton), 251; Nottman, 250; J. Paton (Murthly), 250; J. Pirie (Aberdeen) 251; Ross, 187; J. Scott Skinner, 144, 163, 183, 251; Peter Stewart, 251; William Stewart (Athole) 245; Willie Sutherland, 251; John Thomson (Torrisdale), 246; Bobby Watson, 168, 251, 298

Dancers (Stage):
Robert Aldridge, 126, 128, 205, 209, 210, 215; Miss Baker, 210; Baker, 190; Bignell or Bicknell, 127; Mrs. Bullock, 127; Claxton, 127; Miss Cross, 127; Miss Daw, 214; Nancy Dawson, 127, 128, 134, 208–10; Mad. De La Cointrie, 128, 207; de La Garde, 127; John Durang, 129, 213, 216, 217; Mrs. Evans, 127; Arnold Fishar, 207, 209, 215; Foussel, 213; William Francis, 216, 219; Madame Frederick, 129, Froment, 128, 207; Granier, 210; Tom Jones, 209; Mr. Lassells, 129, 175; McNeil, 128; Sga. Manesiere, 126, 128, 216; Mathews, 209; Middlemist, 128; Moreau, 127; Mrs. Mosee, 127; Mr. Newhouse, 127; Mrs. Parker, 129, 175; Miss Pitt, 209, 214; Poitier, 214; Salles, 127; Mrs. Schoolding, 127; Shawfords, 210; Miss Smith, 127; Miss Twist, 214; Miss Valois, 126, 128

Dancing Masters (Scottish), 113; itinerant, 139, 143, 144, 263; syllabus of, in Galloway, 157; at Dalmally, 158; recollections of in Ayr, 139, W. E. Allan (book); D. Anderson, see Dancers (Highland); J. G. Atkinson (book), 168, 172, 180, 288; Barnard (Edinb.), 114; James Barnardon (Glasgow), 78; Madame Bonnet (formerly Marcacci), 115; R. F. Buck, 283, 290; Colin Campbell, 47; Joshua Campbell (Glasgow), 117, 174, 218; Miss Flora Cruickshank, 161; D. Egville, 114, 181; Andrew Devoe, 79; Messrs. Dick (Glasgow), 117, 219; Downie (Edinb.), 114, 115; Archibald Duff (Aberdeen), 160; Barclay Dun (Edinb.), 166; William Fraser (Edinb. & Glas.), 117, 219, 278; Sir John (Giovanni) Gallini, 114, 115, 166, 213; Alexander Gibb (Edinb.), 288; Guillian, 47; James Gregg (Grig), 114; Lamotte (Edinb.), 114, 115; Laurie, 115; Le (La) Picq (Edinb.), 114, 115, 196; Mr. Lilly, 283; Joseph Lowe (book), 283; Jack MacConachie, 162, 277; D. R. Mackenzie (book), 168, 180, 251, 283, 288; Ewen MacLachlan, 162, 246; D. G. MacLennan, see Dancers (Highland); Mary Isdale MacNab, 166, 225; MacQueen (Edinb.), 114; Macskipnish (Galt's character), 113–14; Johnny McGill, 114, 211, 218, 280; Martin (Edinb.), 114, 115; Jack Muir (Motherwell), 168; Mr. Park (Glasgow), 117; Francis Peacock (Aberdeen), 117, 118, 153–54, 160, 162, 166–67, 174, 238, 260, 288, (book), 310; Ronald (Barra), 225; Mr. Sellars (Glasgow), 117, 219; John Smith (Glasgow), 80; W. Smythe (book), 283; David Strange (Edinb.), 114, 118, 154, 263; Signora Violante, 116, J. F. Wallace, 177

Dancing masters (Non-Scottish): Thinot Arbeau, 34, 41, 44; Arena, 45; Beauchamps, 65; Beveridge, 221; Mr. Birkhead, 270; Mr. Blake, 169; Carlo Blasis, 209; Fabritio Caroso, 35, 266, 274; Henri Cellarius, 147; C. M. C. Chivers, 282; Robert Copland, 58; Desnoyer, 122; Domenico di Piacenza, 34, 44, 118; Nicholas Dukes, 287; Gugliemo Ebreo, 34; Essex, 286; Edward Ferrero, 147; Raoul Feuillet, 268, 270, 286; Miss Fleming, 135; William Hudson, 58; Thomas Hutsoun, 58; Isaacs, 221, 268; Nathaniel Kynaston, 270; Lully, 65; Negri, 35; Noverre, 126; Pecour, 65; Rameau, 221, 270; Kellan Tomlinson, 287; Michiel Toulouse, 34; Weaver, 127, 209, 286; Willis, 115; H. D. Willock, 177; Thomas Wilson, 121, 154, 169, 173, 258, 271, 278, 287, 289; G. Yates, 145, 214, 219

Danes, 3, 33
Deasil, 12
Dieppe, 78
Dingwall, 247, 282
Dublin, 216
Dumbartonshire, 249
Dunbar, 72
Dundee, 68, 144, 282

Edinburgh: bringing in May, 19; festival dance, 20; Kirk session, 68, 72; visit of Charles I, 77; dancing masters, 79; first playhouse, 79; Duke of York at Holyrood, 79; oyster parties, 85, 97; seamy side, 85; coffee houses, horn order, dancing in, 87; West Bow Assembly, New Assembly (Bell's Wynd), 88; ready for Scottish Court, 92; tavern parties, 97; Ranelagh and Comely Gardens, 98-9; Creech and the Assembly, 99-101; Mary Somerville, 101; dancing masters, 114-116; dancing school balls, 118
Edinburgh Exhibition of Piping: 129, 175; established, 242; dancing at, 242-3; dress at, 242; awards at, 242-3; attraction of, 243; Mendelssohn at, 243; decline of, 243; criticism of, 244; Madame Frederick at, 244; Strathspey Twosome, 245; decline of Strathspey, 245; Reel of Tulloch, 245-6; Gille Callum, 245; orchestra at, 246
Edinburgh, Highland Society of, 23, 86, 109, 146n.3, 245; visit of George IV, 254. See also Assembly, Balls, Dancing masters
Edinburgh Musical Society, 95
Eigg, 224, 226, 227, 231
Elgin sword dance, 19; 23; Kirk, 153; 163
Eriskay, 232
Essex, 221

Fair (Tryst), 76, 137, 138, 241
Falkirk, 241, 242
Festivals: Pre-Christian and medieval occasions, 11, 23; Beltane (Beltein), 11-13, 21, 23, 26, 70; Church, 11, 14; Corpus Christi, 26; Hallowe'en, fire at Buchan, 13, 17; Hogmanay, 17; Kirn (Harvest Home), 70, 75, 138, 139, 259, 261; Lammastide (*Lugnasad*), 11; May Day, 11-14, 17-19, 21, 23-25, 69; Michaelmas, 11; Midsummer, 11, 13; Samhain, 11; St. Barchan Feast, 70; St. Obert (Perth bakers' saint), 26; Whitsun, 25; Yule, 11, 12, 14, 17, 18, 24, 48, 69
Flemings, 4
Forfar, 234
Forres, 163
France, 4, 41, 70; influence on Scots, 51, 52, 150; Scottish students and merchants in 17th c., 78

Gaelic Club (Glasgow), 109-10
Galston, 72
Galway, 200
Games: "te-he", 22; Barley Break, 25
Garioch, 73
Germans, 3, 11, 186
Gillatrypes, 153
Glasgow, 68, 105, 247; no dancing in streets, 73n.12; terms of dancing master's license, 80; dancing master for artisans, 80; Gaelic Society (or Gaelic Club), 86, 109, 110, 242; oyster-cellars, 98; Assembly, 107; Tontine Society, 107; Tontine Hotel, 110; Tontine Coffee House, 108n.41, 124; Frazer's Hall, Merchant's House Hall, Queens Assembly, 108; Ingram St. Assembly, 109; Park's Ballroom, 117; 18th c. dancing masters, 117; Quadrille at Buck's Head Inn, 146
Goidels (Gaels), 3
Guizers (grotesques or mummers), 14, 15, 17, 23, 48

Haddington, 72, 105, 280
Harvest Home. See Festivals: Kirn
Hebrides, 3, 112, 140, 142, 167, 224-30; dramatic jigs, 231-39; finishing dance, 135; and Cape Breton, 159

Hertfordshire, 221
Highland (s), 84, 140, 184, 223–24, 263
Highland Dress, 253–54
Highland Games (Gatherings), 180, 242, 246–54
Highland Society (London and Edinburgh), 241–44, 248
Highlanders: 28, 155–56
Holy Days, 10, 19. See also Festivals
Holyrood, 48, 49, 53
Hungary: Dance of Death, 234

Inns of Court: Masque for Princess Elizabeth, 61; revels, 62
Inverness, 282
Inverurie, 73
Ioculatores, 9
Ireland, 11, 158, 200, 201, 220, 225, 228
Irvine, 73
Islay, 140
Isle of Man, 225, 228, 229
Italy, 201

Janglers (Jongleurs), 9
Jew's harp: dancing to, 38, 39, 142; Lochaber Trump, 141; witches dance to, 151

Kent, 221
Kilbarchan, 70
Kilmarnock, 72, 73
Kincardine, 281, 284
Kingussie, 249
Kirk, the, 68–73, 76
Kirkcaldy, 70
Kissing, 76, 136, 285
Knapdale, 134
Knoydart, 176

Lanark, 76
Lancashire, 221
Leith, 247
Linlithgow, 77
London, 216, 247; dancing school 16th–17th, c., 61; dancing school in 1669, 63; Highland Society (Gaelic Society), 86; dance teachers, 120, 121; King's Birth Night Ball, 122; anti-Scottish feeling, 126; 18th c. theatres, 126; entr'acte dancing, 126. See also Assembly, Almack's

Lothians, 78
Lowlander, 28
Lusitani, dance of, 7

Manuscript collections of dances: Blantyre MS, Nat. Lib. 3860 (1818), 180; Bodleian MS, 274, 276; Bowman MS, 274, 279; Drummond Castle MS, 190, 273–5, 277, 295; Hill MS, 161; 183, 207; Holmain MS, 274; 275; John McGill MS, 280; Menzies MS, 274, 276, 279
Masque, 49, 50, 61–63
Masquerade, 87, 97
Master of the Revels, 18, 19, 24, 48, 79
Mauchlin, 137
Mearns, 78
Middlesex, 221
Minstrels, 9
Moidart (Moydart), 176, 224
Moray, 78
Motherwell, 168
Mummers. See Guizers

Nairn, 163
New England, 212
New Zealand, 298
Normans, 4, 150
Norse, 3, 4
North Berwick, 40, 58
Northern Meeting: 95, 110–12, 247, 259, 297, 315–17, Appendix C
Northumbria, 3

Orkney, 179, 225, 228

Pageant for Queen Anne (James VI), 24
Paris, 78
Penny Wedding (or Bridal), 71, 73–74, 131
Perth, 23, 26, 30, 68, 77, 78, 166, 238, 246, 247, 281
Philadelphia, 213, 216, 217
Picts, 3
Piobcorn (stoc'n horn or hornpipe), 220
Port a Beaul, 142
Promiscuous dancing, 76, 87
Punch and Judy, 232, 234
Puritans, 59, 60, 62

Rants, 207
Reformers (Protestant), 24–25

Resurrection theme, 187, 234
Ridotto, 97
Robin Hood: 14, 19, 20, 24
Rocking, 140
Romans, 3, 11
Rothesay, 72
Rothiemurchus, 291
Rouen, 78
R.S.C.D.S. (Royal Scottish Country Dance Society), 171, 179, 225, 228, 264, 274, 275, 277, 278, 280, 281, 284, 290, 291–95

St. Andrews, Magistrae and scholars in May at, 19; 23
St. Kilda, 39
Schottische: 148, 223, 284; Common Schottische, 283; Highland Schottische, 143, 144, 148, 171, 176, 280, 290
Scotland: Scots, 3; language of, 4, 84; medieval population, 27; in 17th c., 68–69; in 18th c., 83–86
Scotsmen dancing at English Court, 156
S.O.B.H.D. (Scottish Official Board of Highland Dancing), 168, 170, 172, 183, 185, 251, 253, 293
Selkirk, 283
Shetland: 179, 225, 227n.11, 228, 229
Skye: dance in kitchen, 142; 231
Stirling, 68, 73, 107
Stoc'n horn, 220
Strathclyde, 3

Strathmore, 250
Strathspey (place), 78, 132, 238, 258, 259, 260, 292
Sunday observance, 70
Sutherland: 78, 150, 159, 190

Taverns: Fortune's, 97; Lucky Middlemist's, 98; Tontine Hotel, 110; Buck's Head Inn, 146
Theatres: Covent Garden, 126, 127, 209, 210, 214, 215, 216; Drury Lane, 126–28, 190, 208, 210, 214–16; Globe Theatre, 196; Haymarket Theatre, 126, 207, 210, 218; King's Theatre, 210; Lincoln's Inn Fields, 127, 128, 210; Pantheon, 210; Royal Circus, 129; Theatre Royal, Edinburgh, 129, 244
Tryst (see also Fair): Dumbarton, 241; Falkirk, 241, 242

Uist, 231, 232, 238
United States, 298

Wake, 72, 234, 235
Westmorland, 221
Witches, 40; dance at North Berwick, 58, 151; John Douglas and eight women, 77; dance Gillatrypes, 153
White's Club, 120
Withershins, 12
Worcestershire, 221

Index of Names

(*See also* General Index: Dancers and
Dancing Masters)

Adam, Robert, 95
Aiton, William, 137
Allan, David (artist), 172, 261
Allan, James (Border piper), 206
Alvanley, 120
Anderson, Miss Mary, of Bountie, 105
Anne d'Este, Duchess of Guise, 55
Anne of Denmark, nuptial welcome to
    Edinburgh, 58
Anne, Queen of Britain, 79, 86
Antoinette, Marie, 87
Aquinas, Thomas, 10
Argyll (Argyle), Duke of, 120; evening
    parties, 126
Aristotle, 9
Arne, Thomas (musician), 127, 208, 214,
    220
Aston, Hervery, 120
Atholl, Duchess of, 189
Augustine, 9

Baillie, Lady Grisel, 81, 101
Baker, Job, (musician), 190
Ballet, William, 197
Bedford, Duchess of, 147
Belsches, John, of Invermay, 93
Black, Joseph, 106
Boswell, Sir Alexander, 103
Boswell, James, 97, 103, 104, 140, 141, 223;
    and Johnson, at Raasay, 112, views of
    Highlanders, 140, at Loch Ness, 141, at
    Armadale, 223
Bowie, John (publisher), 174, 278
Bradshaw, 120
Brantôme, 42, 54
Braxfield, Lord, 85
Breadalbane, Marquis of, 188
Bremner, Robert (publisher), 186, 190, 271,
    278, 279, 290; Collection, 278

Bruce, Mrs., of Kenet, 104
Bruce, John (fiddler), 186
Brummell, Beau, 120, 122
Buccleugh, Duchess of, 115
Burns, Robert (poet), 70, 81, 111, 136, 138,
    139, 167, 182, 186, 197, 201, 203, 207,
    263, 280, 290, 293; description of Auld
    Glenae, 142
Burt, Edward (Capt.), 89, 90, 262
Burton and Whitaker (publishers), 271
Bute, Earl of, 126
Byrd, William, 59

Caesar, Julius, 186
Campbell, Mrs., of Finab, 104
Campbell, Alexander (poet), 174, 228, 231,
    232, 237
Campbell (publisher), 271, 278
Campion, 220
Carlyle, Alexander ("Jupiter"); love of
    dancing, 116; meets Violette, 125; at
    Garrick's, 126; dance with Lovat, Ers-
    kine and Kate Vint, 136; 263
Carmarthen, Marquis of (later Duke of
    Leeds), 247
Carmichael, Alexander: 185, 224, 225, 232,
    235, 238
Castlemaine, Lady, 63
Castlereagh, Lady, 119
Cecile, Lady, 50
Chamberlain, John, 156
Chambers, Robert, 103, 182
Chappell, William, 200, 221
Charles I, King of Britain, 25, 26, 62, 67,
    77, 270
Charles II, King of Britain, 63–65, 77, 203,
    270
Charles XII of Sweden, 162
Charles Edward Stewart (Prince Charlie),
    135, 156, 175, 249
Cicero and dancing, 9
Claverhouse, 79
Cleland, Robert (poet), 153

Cochrane, Anne and Katie (Assembly belles), 92
Cockburn, Mr. (country dancer), 85, 91, 96
Cockburn, Sir Henry, 104
Cocker, W. D. (poet), 138
Collinson, Francis, 232
Colquhoun, Sir Ian, 172
Cook, Captain, 219
Corri, Signor, 99
Cosmo, Grand Duke, 64
Courtin (French Ambassador), 64
Cowper, Lady, 119
Cromwell, Oliver, 25, 63, 67
Crighton (or Creighton), "The Admirable", 57, 92, 155, 156
Creech, William, 99, 145, 203, 258, 281
Crawford, Earl of, 186, 187
Cramb, Isobel, 161–63, 207
Cumming, Angus (fiddler), 174
Cunningham, Alan (poet), 198, 261
Currie, Dr., 139

Dalkeith, Earl of, 135
Dalrymple, Maria, 92
Dalyell, J. Graham, 175, 188, 242, 243, 245, 246, 253
D'Angoulême, Henri, 42–44
Danier, George Dawson, 120
Dauney, William, 37
De Flamarens, Marquis de, 65
De Lauze, 149
De Lieven, Mme, 119
De Maisse, 59
De Medici, Catherine, 44, 52
De Neumann, Baron, 119
De Quincey, Thomas, 301
Derby, Countess of, 64
De Ros, Henry, 120
De Vitry, Cardinal Jacques, 10
Dewar, Donald (piper), 245
De Witt, 207
Dibdin, James, 211
Dick, James, 186
Dinnie, Donald, 250
Diodorus, 7
Douglas, Duchess of, 106
Douglas, Lady Jean, 91
Dow, Daniel (fiddler), 174
Dowland, John, 59

Drumelzier, Lady, 88, 90
Drummond, 75
Drummond, P. R., 184
Drummore, Lord (Sir Hew Dalrymple), 93
Dryerre, Henry, 250
Dukes, Nicholas (publisher), 271
Dun, Finlay, 146, 169, 243
Dunbar, William (poet), 50
Duncan, Geilie (danced a reill), 58, 151
Duncan, Miss Nelly, 105
Dundonald, Countess of, 104
Dunmore, Earl of, 179
Dunn, John, 97

Eglinton, Lady, 101, 274
Eleanor of Aquitaine, 29
Elizabeth, Queen of England, 55, 58, 59, 61, 200, 265
Elphinstone, Lady, 104
Elyot, Thomas (poet), 59
Erroll, 15th Earl of, 162
Erskine of Grange, 136
Esterhazy, Princess, 119

Farquharson, James, of Invercauld, 247
Fergusson, Robert (poet), 13, 70
Fife, Earl of, 247
Fleming, Lady (mother of Henri d'Angoulême), 42
Flett, J. F. and T. M., 144, 168, 170, 177, 190, 224, 225, 226, 231, 232, 244, 263, 283
Flood, W. Grattan–, 200, 201
Foley, 120
Forbes, Sir Wm., 112
Fortune, Matthew, 97
Foss, Hugh, 299
Fountain, Edward and James, Masters of Revels, 79
Fountainhall, Lord, 80
Frazer, J. G., 235
Frederick, Madame, 244

Galileo, Vincenzo, 201
Galt, John, 113
Garden, Beatrix, 54
Garnett, Thomas, 125, 234, 260
Garrick, David, 126, 208, 210, 215
Gay Gordon (Lord Strathaven), 87, 124
Geddes, Jenny, 67

George III, 122
George IV, visit to Edinburgh of, 254
Gilchrist, Anne Geddes, 221
Giraldus Cambrensis, 202
Glen, 107
Glencairn, Countess of, 94
Goldsmith, Oliver, 84, 102
Gordon(s), 107, 150
Gordon, Duchess of (Jane Maxwell), 111, 112, 175
Gordon, Duke of, 136, 167, 174
Gordon, Miss Nancy, 105
Gosson, 62
Gow, Alexander, 245
Gow, John, 120
Gow, Nathaniel, 120, 135, 281
Gow, Niel, 119, 120, 134, 161, 174, 245, 260, 281; at Border Ball, 134
Grant, Elizabeth, 84, 111, 136, 145, 146, 169, 182, 184, 185, 197, 234, 259, 260, 263, 291
Grant, Sir James, 258
Grant, Mrs., of Caron, 105
Grant, Mrs. of Laggan, 149, 258
Gregg (of Gregg's Pipes), 104n.50
Gregory (Pope), 9
Gronow, 120, 154
Gwydir, Lora, 246
Gustavus Adolphus, 162

Hall, Rev. James, 125, 170, 181, 258, 260, 292; at a country wedding, 132; comment on dancing in Strathspey, 258; at a ball in Grantoun, 259
Hall, Katie (Belle of Assembly), 92
Hallam, Lewis, 216
Hamilton, Gavin, 92
Hamilton, John, 93
Hamilton, Katie (Belle of Assembly), 92
Hamilton, Stan, 301
Hamilton, William, of Bangour, 90, 91
Handel, 206
Henry II, King of England, 41
Henry VIII, King of England, 50, 52, 58
Herd (ballad collector), 198
Hetzner, 59
Hibbert, Samuel, in Shetland, 303
Hill, Nan, 299
Hoffmaster (musician), 218
Home, Henry, 91

Home, John, 126
Hopetoun, Countess of, 94
Huntly, Lord, 112
Huntly, Marquis of, 95, 124

Jaffray, Alex., of Kingswells, 105, 117, 155, 260
James I, King of Scots, 21
James IV, King of Scots, 20, 47, 48, 50, 155
James V, King of Scots, 21, 52
James VI of Scotland and I of Britain, 25, 26, 57, 58, 61, 77, 197, 274
Jamieson, Ian C. B., 280
Jenkins, George (musician), 183
Jersey, Lady, 119
Johnson, Samuel, 112, 140, 141, 223
Jonson, Ben, 62
Johnston of Hilton, Mrs., 104

Kelo, John (bellman, Aberdeen), 24
Kennedy, Douglas (folkorist), 192
Kennedy, Patrick, 229
Kintore, Countess of, 112
Kirstein, Lincoln, 234
Knox, John, 9, 41, 53, 54, 181

Labban, 299
Lagentwood, Miss Jenny, of Tillery, 105
Landseer, 154
Lauder, James (Scots singer), 128
Lauder, James (Composer, 16th c.), 150
Lauderdale, Duke of, 80
Lennox, Lady Charlotte, 112
Lennox, Colonel, 112
Lieven, Countess of, 94, 119
Lloyd, "Rufus", 120
Locke, John (philosopher), 298
Lockhart, John G., 146, 197, 257-58
Logan, James, 183, 185, 186, 187, 189, 229, 246
Louis XIV, King of France, 65, 87
Long James (footman fiddler), 111
Lovat, Lord, 136, 155
Lucian, on dance, 9

MacBeth, John (piper to High. Soc. London), 246
MacDearmid (Minister to the Glasgow Gaelic Club), 109
Macdonald of Clanranold, 242

MacDonald (Father), 232
Macdonald, John, 242
MacDonald, Keith, 235
McDonald, Malcolm (fiddler), 174
Macdonnell of Glengarry, 110
McGlashan, Alexander (fiddler), 174, 216
Mackenzie, Henry, 84, 114, 115, 176, 244, 259
Mackenzie, John (piper to the Marquis of Breadalbane), 242
Mackinnon, Dan, 120
Mackintosh, Robert (fiddler), 150
McLachlan (fiddler), 109, 144
MacLeod of Raasay, 112, 113
Macleod, Rev. Norman, 134, 141, 189, 232, 235, 241
MacNeill, Marian, 228
MacPherson, Angus (piper), 251, 252
Macpherson, James (poet), 128, 194
Macra, Donald, 242
Macskipnish (fictitious dancing master), 113-14
Malcolm III (Canmore), King of Scots, 4, 190
Margaret, Queen (spouse of James IV), 48
Marlowe, Christopher, 59
Marston, 60
Martin, 262
Martin, Martin, 39
Mary of Guise, 52
Mary, Princess, 64
Mary, Queen of Scots, 20, 35, 41, 50, 52-55, 150, 181
Mary, Virgin, Festival of, 26
Maxwell, Miss Eglintoun, 111
Maxwell, Jane. See Gordon
Maxwell, Sir John, 106
Marshall, William (fiddler), 112, 129, 174, 175, 244
Megallotti, Count, 64
Melville, Sir James, 55
Mendelssohn, Felix, 243
Milligan, Jean C., 293, 297-98
Milntoun, Lady, 94
Mills, John, 120
Minto, Lady, 94
Minto, Lord, 93
Monmouth, Duke of, 63, 64, 79
Montagu, Edward, 120
Montagu, Lady Mary, 268

Montague, Mr., 119
Montgomery, Eliza, 92
Montgomery, Mary, 92
Montgomery, Miss, 119
Morer, Thomas, 262
Morley, Thomas (composer), 59, 194, 196
Meaves, Miss, 105
Murray, Lord James, 182, 245
Murray, Miss Helen Nicholas, of Stormont, "Nicky," 103-4

Nash, Beau, 87
Newhall, Lady, 88, 90
North Berwick, Lady, 88, 90
Northbrooke, John, 59

Orbiston, Lady, 88, 90, 91
Oswald, James (musician), 201

Palmerston, Lord, 119
Panmure, Countess of, 88, 90, 91
Parr, Catherine, dancing in her chamber, 60
Pennant, Thomas, in Islay, 140
Pepys, Samuel, 63, 203, 219
Perth, Duke of, 273
Pierrepont, Henry, 120
Plato, 9
Playford, Henry (publisher), 62
Playford, John (publisher), 62, 64, 153, 180, 196, 201, 203, 221, 222, 266-68, 286, 295
Plutarch, 9
Preston (publisher), 271, 278
Pulver, Jeffrey, 200, 201
Purcell, Henry (composer), 206, 219
Pytheas, 3

Ramsay, Allan, 81, 88, 90, 128, 261
Ramsay, Schir Johne, 49
Reinagle, Alexander, 217
Reynolds, Sir Joshua, 111
Rhodes, Frank, 177, 224, 226, 231
Riche, Barnaby, 202
Richmond, Duchess of (La Belle Stuart), 64
Ricketts, John B., 217
Riddell, John (fiddler), 150
Riddell, Maria, 263
Rizzio, David, 52, 117

Rob the Ranter, 74
Robertson of Lude, 54
Robertson, Peter, 245
Rogers, Charles, 234
Ross, Robert (fiddler), 174
Rothiemay, Lady, dances Cushion Dance, 150
Roxburgh, Duchess of, 147
Rutherford, Alison, 91n.13, 100, 102, 271
Rutherford (publisher), 278

Sage, Donald, 155
St. Aldegonde, Count, 119
St. Augustine, 10
St. Clairs (Sinclairs), 150
Saltoun, Lady, 254
Saltoun, Lord, 112
Saxony, King of, 188
Schaw, Janet, 219
Schetky, 216
Scott, Sir Walter, 17, 104, 111, 135, 303; attended Assembly, 197; and Scots Jig, 203; and visit of George IV to Edinburgh, 254
Sefton, Lady, 119
Selkirk, Earl of, 87
Sempill, Robert, of Beltrees, 70
Sempill, Francis, 74
Senex (pseud. Robert Reid), 107, 218
Shakespeare, William, 59, 220, 270
Sharp, Cecil, 267, 268, 286
Sharpe, Charles Kirkpatrick, 104, 209
Shuldham-Shaw, Patrick, 208
Shuter, Ned, 210
Sibbald, Susan, 123, 134, 135, 167, 288
Sidney, Sir Henry, 200
Simpson, Habbie, 70
Sinclair, Catherine, 248
Sinclair, Sir John, 161, 244, 248
Smith, Alexander, 142
Smollet, Tobias, 209, 256
Somerville, James, of Drum, 25, 73
Somerville, Mary (physicist), 100, 101, 114, 115
Spenser, Edmund, 59, 220
Spiers, 107
Standish, Charles, 119, 120
Steel, Richard, 222
Stenhouse, William, 185, 206, 209
Stevens, Miss Besey, of Broadlands, 105

Stewart, Jeanie (Assembly Belle), 91
Stewart, Katie, 92
Stewart of Fasnacloich, 297
Stewart of Garth, 186
Stirling, 92
Strang, John, 183
Strathaven, Lord (the "Gay Gordon"), 87, 124
Sutherland, Duchess of, 147
Suttie, Miss, 91
Syme, Geordie (piper), 93

Tacitus, 7, 11, 186
Tallis, Thomas (composer), 59
Tannahill, Robert (poet), "The Kebbuckston Wedding", 185
Thompson (publisher), 271, 278
Thomson, James, 214
Thomson, John (piper to Alexander MacAlister of Torrisdale), 246
Thornton, Colonel, 158
Thurston, Hugh, 180, 188, 225, 277, 279, 293
Topham, Captain, 83, 87, 101, 102, 103, 112, 113, 114, 118, 125, 152, 162, 258, 263; at Capillaire Club Ball, 98; at Assembly ball, 98; at dancing master's ball, 156; describes high dances, 156–57; describes "straspae", 175; on Scottish dance style, 255–56, 260; on Scottish dances, 256; on the Reel, 257, 263; sees three Highland women dance, 260
Tyde, Lady Susan, 119

Urquhart, Sir Thomas, of Cromarty, 57, 74

Victoria, Queen, 147–48, 154, 188, 247, 254
Vint, Kate, 136
Violette (Eva Maria Veigel, Mrs. Garrick), 125–26

York, Duke of, 63, 79, 273
Young, David (publisher), 274
Young, John, 62

Walker, Patrick, 76, 80
Walpole, Hugh, 268
Walsh, John (publisher), 134, 270, 271, 277

Watlen (publisher), 129
Watt, James, 106
Waylett, G. (publisher), 270, 271
Welch (publisher), 271
Wellington, Duke of, 119
Werner (publisher), 271

Wesley, John, 212
Wilkie, David (artist), 261
William and Mary, 68
Wilson, James, 303
Wood, Melusine, 266
Worcester, Lord, 120

Index of Dances

Allemande (Almain, Almon), 50, 58; Haye, 59, 150, 152, 175, 283
Argyll Broadswords. *See* Broadsword

Babbity Bowster, 76, 133, 134, 138, 150, 190, 270
Ballad, 33. *See also* Festival Dance
Ballete, 150
Balleti (Balli), 34
Basse Dance, 34, 35, 38, 39, 49, 50, 58, 150, 208
Battle Dance. *See* Pyrrhic
Bee Baw Babbity, 133
Blue Bonnet, The (Am Bonaid Ghorm), 190
Bounky, The (*See* Bumpkin), 283
Bourée, 46, 65, 150
Brail (Branle), 150
Branle (Braul, Bransle, Brail, 33, 38, 53; Bransle, 63; Braul, 45, 59, 202; Branles d'Avignon, 41; Branle de Bourgogne, 34; Branle de Champagne, 41; Branle Double, 34, 151; Branles d'Ecosse, 41, 42, 44, 150, 184, 290; Branle Gai, 34; Branle du Haut Barrois, 34; Branle de Poitou, 41, 42, 65; Branle Simple, 34; Miming Branles, 41, 55; Scots Brawls, 149
Bretagne (Brittagne), 65, 150
Broadsword: Argyll Broadswords, 155, 191, 252, 294; Broadsword Exercise (Mc an Fhorsair), 161, 187, 229, 245, 252; Lochaber Broadswords, 192
Bruicheoth. *See* Pyrrhic
Buffons, 23, 31, 38
Bumpkin, The Country ("Bounky"), 134, 136, 158, 179, 270, 283

Canary, 44, 45, 59, 150
Carol. *See* Ring Dance
Cascarde, 44
Chacoune, 46
Chiarenzana. *See* Contrapassi

Cinquepace. *See* Galliard
Contrapassi, 35, 266, 273; Chiarenzana, 266–68; Anello, 267; Pizochara, 267
Contredanse, 149, 175, 268, 270
Coranto (Courante, Currant), 44, 45, 59; refined in 17th c., 63, 150, 203, 257
Cotillion, 41, 55, 115, 145, 146; new style of, 148, 152, 175, 271, 288
Country Dance, 61–63, 120–23, 143, 152, 264–74, 278–87, 290–92, 294, 297–300. *See also* Contredanse.
Cushion Dance, 133, 135, 136, 150, 190, 224, 265, 266, 270
Cuttymun and Treeladle, 38, 226

Dannsa nam Pog. *See* Ruidhleadh Nam Pog
Dance of Death (Deid Dance), 39, 234
Dirk Dance (Phadric MacCombish), 234; in Highlands, 8; at Edinburgh and London, 246; Isle of Man, 187; tune, 188; Canada, 188
Dirrye Dantoun (Dirrydan), 50
Duck Dance, 38

Écossaises, 147, 282
Egiptiane Dance (Gypsy Dance), 26
Estampie, 266

Faddy (Furry) Dance, 200. *See also* Festival Dance, Rinnce Fada
Fading. *See* Festival Dance, Rinnce Fada
Fandango, 175, 184
Farandole, 32, 34
Festival Dance (Ring, Round, Carol), 10, 19, 31–33, 35, 40, 58, 202–3, 265
  Farandole, 32, 34
  Harvest (Kirn), 75
  Maiden Trade, 70
  Mylecharane's March (Manx), 229
  Processionals, 265
  Rinnce Fada ("Long Ring"), 32, 62, 200
  Rinnce Mor (Great Ring), 266

Rinnce Teampuill (Temple Round), 32
Trixie, 70
Figures (Country Dance), Allemande, 35; Ladies' Chain, 282; Poussette, 283; 290; Rondel, 299; Tournet, 299
Fling. *See* Highland Fling
Florilia (dance of spring), 10
Furry Dance. *See* Faddy

Galliard, 34, 38, 53, 55, 58, 59, 150, 151, 202, 203, 257, 266, 285; cinquepace, 44, 203; Arbeau's description of, 44; comes into its own, 44, 45; Barnaby Riche's complaint, 60; "Curio," 60; subdued in 17th c., 63
Gavotte, derivation of, 46, 150
Gay Gordons, 35
Giga, 201
Gillatrypes, 153
Gille Callum, 2, 8, 38, 144, 155, 163, 182, 183, 185, 188–92, 245–48, 250, 252, 293
Grand Wedding Dance, 209
Gypsy Dance (Egiptiane Dance), 26

Haymakers, 259
Hey (haye), 35, 40
Highland Fling, 2, 129, 144, 157, 158, 163, 170, 245, 246, 250, 252, 283; and Reel, 155; introduction to competitions, 183; Ladies', 184; Lonach, 183; Marquis of Huntly's, 160, 182
Highland (Hielan') Laddie, 162, 246, 283
Highland Schottische, 284
Highland Walloch, 182
Hornpipe (*see also* Steps, Stage Dance, Scottish Measure), 40, 127, 151, 157, 159, 197, 202, 214, 216
  Aldridge's, 205, 215
  Baker's, 215
  Binnacle, 218
  Cane, 163
  College, 205, 208, 217
  Derbyshire, 220, 222
  Double, 216
  Durang's, 156, 157, 215, 217, 218
  Egg, 216
  Fishar's, 205, 213, 215, 216
  Irish, 205

Jacky Tar, 144, 163, 217, 218, 247, 250, 251, 283
  Lancashire, 209, 211, 220
  Nottinghamshire, 220
  Richar's, 215
  Sailors', 205, 214, 215, 217, 219
  Single (triple-time), 205, 206, 221
  West's, 205, 215
Hydegy (Hey de Guize), 151, 265

Jig (Dramatic):
  Auld Glenae (Kirk wad let me be *or* Ye Owld Man), a Scots Jig, 197–98
  Blythesome Bridal, 197
  Cailleach (Old Wife), 231
  Cailleach a'Stopan-Falaimh (Old Woman of the Empty Choppan), 231, 232
  Cailleach an Dordon, 231n.
  Cailleach an Dudain (Carlin of the Mill Dust), 142, 187, 225, 231, 233, 234, 238
  Cath nan Coileach (The Combat of the Cocks), 225, 226
  Cath nan Curaidh (Contest of the Warriors), 225
  Chuthaich Chaol Dubh (The thin, black, little woman), 236
  Coille Bharrach (The Barra Wood), 226, 227
  Croit am Droighan (Thorny Croft), 142, 235
  Croit an Dreathan (The Wren's Croft), 236, 237
  Dance of Death (Deid Dance), 39, 234
  Dannsadh an Chleoca (The Cloak Dance), 236
  Dannsadh Chriosgaidh, 236
  Dannsadh an Dubh Luidnaich, 236
  Dannsadh Fear Druim o'Chairidh, 236
  Dannsadh na Goraig (Crazy Woman's Dance), 235
  Dannsadh o'Chroig Leith, 235
  Dubh-Luidneath (Black Sluggard), 142
  Egiptiane Dance (Gypsy Dance), 26
  Fidh an Gunn (Weave the Gown), 142, 227, 235
  Fisherwives' Creel Dance, 236
  Flail Dance (Tiree), 39, 236
  Flaughter Spade Dance, 39, 236
  Frog Dance (Isle of Man), 38
  Goat Dance, 142, 235

Gossips Dance, 39

Irish Washerwoman (Irish "Jig"), 178, 199

Marabh na Beiste Dubh (Death of The Otter), 235

Quaker's Wife, 197

Roke and the Wee Pickle Tow, 198–99

Rungmor (Sean Rong Mhor), 232

Ruileadh Cailleach Sheatadh Cailleach, 232

Salmon Dance (Schamous or Salmon's), 22, 36

Selkie's (Seal's) Dance, 228

Shane Dance, 236

Sior Bhuain Culaig, 236

Speyde, 39, 236

Wooing of the Maiden, 198

Jig, 45, 139, 151, 152, 180, 184, 194, 199–203, 211, 219, 221, 225; earliest use of word, 40; Country Dance, 123; origin of word, 193; Scotch (Scottish) Jig, 156, 163, 175, 184, 194–97

Joan Sanderson. *See* Cushion Dance

Lancers, 147, 271, 283, 284

La Tempête, 148

Licht Dances, 138, 149, 265–66, 292

Lochaber Axe (or lance), 187

Lochaber Broadswords, 192

Louvre, 65, 115, 150, 209

MacCombish's Dirk. *See* Dirk Dance

Mc an Fhorsair. *See* Broadsword Exercise

Maiden Trace, 70

Mazurkas, 147

Measure, 45, 59, 149, 202

Medley, 167

Merrily Danced the Quaker's Wife, 260

Minuet; 55, 65, 87, 90, 99, 101, 115, 120, 123, 148, 150, 156, 160, 197, 209, 255, 257, 258, 271, 287, 292; Spanish Minuet, 55; Minuet de la Cour, 114; its virtues, 145. *See also* Strathspey Minuet

Morris Dance, 14, 20, 22, 28, 37, 151, 173; ancient derivation, 17; and guizers at court, 23; theories of origin, 29; Morris Jig, 202; Cotswold Morris, 229

Nizzarda, 44

Orleans: (Basse Dance); 35, 36

Pantomimic Reels:

    Coillie Bharrach (The Barra Wood), 226–27

    Dannsadh nam Boc (Dance of the Bucks), 226

    An Dannsa Mor, 224, 227

    Hebridean Weaving Lilt, 225

    Long Bharrach, 224

    Reel of the Black Cocks (Ruidhleadh nan Coileach Dubha), 151, 177, 225, 226

    Strip the Willow, 143, 213, 224, 225, 266, 273, 284, 294

    Tri-Croidhan Caorach (Three Sheep's Trotters), 236

    Trow Dance, 228

    Turraban nan Tunnag (Waddling of the Ducks), 225, 226

    Weaving Dances, 225

Pas de Quatre, 144, 148

Passameze, 150

Passecaille, 46

Passepied, 46, 65

Pavane (Paven, Pavion): Arbeau's description of, 34, 38, 45, 53; Spanish Pavane, 55, 58, 59, 150, 208

Phadric MacCombish. *See* Dirk Dance

Piva, 34

Polka, 143, 144, 146, 147, 223, 271, 283, 284

Processional Dance, 31

Purpose, 41, 55

Pyrrhic, 7–9, 187; The Battle, 161, 245; Cudgel Play, 228, 229; Rungmor, 232; Weapon Dance or Play, 8–9. *See* Broadsword Exercise *and* Lochaber Axe

Quadrille, 55, 119, 143, 144, 145–48, 154, 166, 258, 270, 271, 282, 283, 284, 288, 292

Reel: 2, 10, 35, 70, 100, 102, 114, 150, 152, 154, 163, 182, 197, 247, 250–1, 257, 260; arm, fingers and hands, 172; footwear in, 170; Highlanders excel in, 174; "hooch," 172–73; use of skirt in, 172; distinguished from "dances," 238; preferred to Country Dance, 280; and witches, 58; "Reiling," 21, 265; various early use of word, 40, 151, 152

America Reel; 223
    Auld Reel from Whalsay, 228. *See also* Whalsay Reel
    Auld (or Muckle) Reel o'Finnigarth, 228
    Axum Reel, 228
    Big Reel (Ruidhleadh Mor), 176
    Breadalbane Ball Reel, 246. *See also* Reel of Tulloch
    Cape Breton: Eight-Handed Reel, 176; Four-Handed Reel, 176, 226
    Donald Couper, Reel or Country Dance, 153
    Duchess of Sutherland's New Highland Reel, 177. *See also* Reel of Tulloch
    Eight Men of Moidart, 224
    Eightsome Reel, 143, 148, 158, 178, 179, 180, 227, 228, 282, 284, 299; Buchan Eightsome, 180; Double Eightsome, 180; Quadruple Eightsome, 180; RSCDS, 179, 180
    Foula Reel, 224, 225
    Foursome Reel (Ruidhleadh Cheathrar), 29, 148, 158, 167, 176, 228, 283, 284; of Hebrides, 176
    Great Reel of the Bride, 136. *See also* Babbity Bowster
    Hebridean Reel, 167, 176
    Highland Reel (Scotch Reel), 45, 126, 128, 148, 149, 152, 154, 165, 207, 244, 247, 282
    Hullochan, 143, 177–78, 184. *See* Reel of Tulloch
    Kissing Reel (Ruidhleadh nam Pog): 133, 136; 190. *See also* Babbity Bowster
    Lang Reel, 136
    Merry Man's Reel, 228
    Muckle Reel o'Finnigarth, 228
    Ninesome Reel, 134, 178, 270. *See also* Bumpkin
    Orkney Reels, 179, 228
    Penny Reels, 138
    Pin Reel, 226, 227
    Ram Reel, 167
    Reel of Aves, 152
    Reel of Bogie, 151, 175
Reel of Tulloch (Ruidhleadh Thulachain), 143, 148, 151, 177, 178, 245, 247, 248, 283, 284
    Round Reels, 176

    Ruidhleadh na Banais (Wedding Reel), 132
    Ruidhleadh Beag (Small Reel), 176
    Ruidhleadh Cheathrar. *See* Foursome Reel
    Ruidhleadh Ghoid, 132
    Ruidhleadh Mor, 176
    Ruidhleadh nam Pog (Kissing Reel), 133, 136, 190. *See also* Babbity Bowster
    Ruidhleadh Thulachain. *See* Reel of Tulloch
    Scotch Reel (Highland Reel), 147, 149, 151, 152, 165–67, 169, 174, 263, 290, at Almack's 119, 122; style, 155
    Shemit Reel; 132, 179
    Shepherd's Crook, 166
    Shetland Reels, 179, 228
    Sixsome Reel, 178, 179
    Small Reel (Ruidhleadh Beag), 176
    Stealing Reel (Ruidhleadh Ghoid), 132
    Strathspey and Reel, 167
    Strathspey Reel, 154. *See also* Strathspey
    Swine's Reel, 136
    Thirty-twosome Reel, 180
    Threesome Reel, 128, 166, 228
    Wedding Reel (Ruidhleadh na Banais); 132
    West Highland Reels, 159
    Whalsay Reel, 151
    Wilson's Reels, 178-79
Rigadon (Rigadoon): 46, 65, 150
Ring Dance. *See* Festival Dance
Rinnce Fada. *See* Festival Dance
Robinette, 150
Rounds. *See* Festival Dance
Rungmor (Rong Mhor), 232

Saltarello, 34
Saraband, 46, 150
Schottische, 35, 284
Scottish Dance, 155–56, 160–64, 170; in 18th c. London Theatres, 127, 128; in 18th c. American Theatres, 129
Scottish Lilt, 162
Scottish *or* Scotch Measure (Hornpipe), 161, 163, 175, 207, 208, 293; on London stage, 128; origin of, 163; characteristic Scottish tune, 196, 207
Seann Triubhas (Shean Trews, Shawin-trews, etc.), 2, 144, 157, 158, 163, 182, 183, 184, 186, 188, 238, 247, 250, 251,

252; Seann Triubhas Willichan; 165, 185n.8. 186, 238, *See* Steps.

Sobria, 34

Spanish Country Dance, 147

Spanish Dances, 282

Spring, 184, 194

Square Dance, 147

Stage Dances (18th c.), Hornpipe and Scottish. *See* Scottish Measure

  Auld Robin Grey (Ballet), 129

  Baker in a Highland Character, 190

  The Dance of the Bonny Highlander, 127

  The Dutch Skipper, 209

  Fingalian Dance, 128

  Fisherman and His Wife, 209

  French Sailor and His Wife, 209

  French Sailor's Dance, 209

  The Highland, 127, 257

  The Highland Laird and His Attendants, 127

  Highland Lilt, 127, 128, 160

  Hornpipe, 209, 214, 215

  La Fricasse, 216

  Mad Man's Dance, 209

  New Hornpipe, composed by Mrs. Vernon, 208

  New Hornpipe by Miss Snow, 215

  New Scotch Dance, 127, 207

  Peasant's Dance, 216

  Rustic Dance, 127

  Sailor and His Lass, 209

  Sailors' Dance from Dido & Aeneas (Purcell), 219

  The Sailor's Song by Champnes and a Dance in Character by the Sailor, 127

  Scotch Dance, 127, 209

  Scotch Highlander, 127

  Scotch (Scottish) Lilt, 128, 162

  Scotch Medley, 163

  Scotch Whim, 127, 160

  Scots Pastoral Dance: The Caledonian Frolic, 217

  Seaman's Dance, 219

  Wapping Landlady, 216

  The Whip of Dunboyne, 127

Steps (see Quadrille, Galliard, Branle), 155, 158; Country Dance Steps, 286–90, 292–94; Hornpipe stepping, 177, 217–18; Reel Steps, 147, 158, 167–71, 182, 188, 293–94, Appendix B

Step Dances (*See also* Highland Fling, Hornpipe, Jig, Seann Triubhas, Stage Dances): Belile's Marches, 158; Earl of Erroll, 161, 162; Flora Macdonald's Fancy, 161, 162, 247, 252; Irish Lilt, 209; Irish Trot, 127; King of Sweden, 161, 162; Merrily Danced the Quaker's Wife, 196; Miss Forbes, 160, 162; O'er the Water to Charlie, 162; Over the Hills and Far Away, 163, 246; The Graces, 160, 163; Tullochgorm, 162; Wiltu Gang tae the Barracks Johnnie?, 252.

Strathspey, 129, 143, 145, 150, 152, 182, 196, 197, 244, 246, 257; Reel gains favour, 166; Steps, 168–69; origin, 173–74; Strathspey Minuet, 128, 129, 175, 207, 294; Strathspey Twosome (Minuet), 245

Swedish Dances, 282

Sword Dance (Hilt-and-Point Ritual), 20, 22, 58, 155, 283; Tacitus and Germans, 7; and Yule, 14; ancient derivation, 17; at Elgin, 19; contrasted with Morris, 23; Scandinavian influence, 29; in Scotland, 186; Baccu-Ber, 192; Vikings and, 229

  Papa Stour: text of, Appendix A; 30, 31, 192

  Perth Glovers (Skinners), 23, 26, 28, 30, 31, 58, 77

Tordion (Turdian, Turgion), 34, 38, 53, 58

Trenchmore, 203, 265, 266, 270

Trixie, 70

Trotto, 34, 35. *See also* Allemande

Turkeyloney, 266

Twasome, 146, 174, 197, 207, 245, 260, 284

Varsovienne (Varsovianna, La Va), 144, 271

Volta (Lavolta), 44, 45, 59, 60

Waltz, 119, 143, 146, 147, 148, 223, 271, 284, 290

Wedding Dance (Grand), 209. *See* Babbity Bowster.